ɔeating England at The Oval, a 'tragedy' that prompted
ıial conquerors are: S. P. Jones, A. C. Bannerman,
ɔch, G. E. Palmer, G. Giffen, H. F. Boyle, T. W. Garrett,

ENGLAND
VERSUS
AUSTRALIA

VIKING

ENGLAND VERSUS AUSTRALIA

An illustrated history of every Test Match since 1877

DAVID FRITH

FOREWORDS BY MICHAEL ATHERTON
AND JUSTIN LANGER

VIKING
an imprint of
PENGUIN BOOKS

VIKING

Published by the Penguin Group
Penguin Books Ltd
80 Strand, London WC2R 0RL, England
Penguin Group (USA) Inc.
375 Hudson Street, New York, New York 10014, USA
Penguin Group (Canada)
90 Eglinton Avenue East, Suite 700, Toronto, Canada ON M4P 2Y3
(a division of Pearson Penguin Canada Inc.)
Penguin Ireland
25 St Stephen's Green, Dublin 2, Ireland
(a division of Penguin Books Ltd)
Penguin Group (Australia)
250 Camberwell Road, Camberwell, Victoria 3124, Australia
(a division of Pearson Australia Group Pty Ltd)
Penguin Books India Pvt Ltd
11 Community Centre, Panchsheel Park, New Delhi – 110 017, India
Penguin Group (NZ)
67 Apollo Drive, Mairangi Bay, Auckland 1310, New Zealand
(a division of Pearson New Zealand Ltd)

Penguin Books (South Africa) (Pty) Ltd
24 Sturdee Avenue, Rosebank, Johannesburg 2196, South Africa

Penguin Books Ltd, Registered Offices: 80 Strand, London, WC2R 0RL, England

www.penguin.com

First published by Richard Smart Publishing 1977
This 12th edition published 2007 by Penguin Books, by arrangement with Richard Smart Publishing

1

Cover design by Karen Trump
Cover photograph by Robert Cianflone/Getty Images
Cover photograph of the author by John Frith
Typeset by Midland Typesetters, Maryborough, Victoria, Australia
Printed in Singapore by Kyodo Printing

PRODUCED BY RICHARD SMART PUBLISHING, SYDNEY

ISBN: 978-0-67007-073-2

Picture sources
MCC Collection: page 1; illustrations 29, 111, 135, 153.
Radio Times Hulton Picture Library: 11, 313, 314, 476.
Illustrated London News: 27.
Ron Yeomans: 32.
New South Wales Government Printing Office: 110, 201.
David Wells: 132.
Punch: 142.
EP Ellison: 266.
Central Press Photos Ltd: 398, 418, 473, 475, 485, 487–9, 491–2, 494, 532, 534, 537, 540, 547–9, 554, 556–9, 588, 590–2, 614, 638–9, 642, 651–2, 657, 674, 676, 681, 683–4, 697–9, 723–4, 726, 732, 734, 739, 741–4, 746, 766–7, 786, 788, 810, 812, 821–3, 826–7, 829, 830, 848, 851, 854, 863–4, 866–71, 874–5, 877, 882, 884–5, 892, 895–8, 903–6, 911–13, 915–17, 922–3, 925, 929, 930, 932, 937, 950, 958, 963–5, 970–2, 981, 983, 985, 991, 1004.
Press Association-Reuter: 405–6, 421, 423, 688, 752, 838, 845, 949, 954–5, 959, 986, 1049, 1059.
Sport & General Press Agency Ltd: 413, 463–72, 474, 477–81, 484, 486, 519, 521, 533, 536, 539, 541–2, 544, 546, 550–1, 553, 555, 564, 570–1, 573, 575–8, 581, 593, 597–9, 606, 645, 647, 689, 690, 694, 715, 736–8, 748, 750, 754–5, 758, 760, 769, 770, 775, 778–82, 785, 813–14, 816–17, 819, 855–7, 859–62, 872, 876, 889, 893, 899, 901–2, 907, 910.
Australian News & Information Bureau: 879, 880, 887, 890–1, 894, 962, 980, 1002.
Keystone Press Agency Ltd: 886, 938, 978, 982, 984.
Times Newspapers Ltd: 900.
Australian Cricket: 918, 920–1, 924, 931, 940.
Patrick Eagar: 941, 943–6, 948, 953, 966–9, 973–7, 987–8, 992–6, 998–9, 1001, 1003, 1005–21, 1025–6, 1029–32, 1042–8, 1050–6, 1058, 1060, 1062–6, 1071, 1074, 1077–93, 1096–8, 1101, 1103–5, 1107–12, 1114, 1116–8, 1120–1, 1125–41, 1143, 1145–55, 1157–63, 1167–72, 1174, 1177, 1179–82, 1184, 1186–91, 1193, 1195, 1197–8, 1200, 1205–6, 1210, 1218–36, 1241–71.
Sporting Pictures (UK) Ltd: 989, 990, 1000, 1067.
Marshall's Sports Service: 997.
News Ltd: 1022–4, 1028, 1033–41.
West Australian: 1027.
Bob Thomas: 1057, 1061, 1068–70, 1072–3, 1075–6, 1156.
Varley Picture Agency: 1102.
Brendan Monks: 1106.
Ken Kelly: 1113, 1115, 1119.
Graham Morris: 1122–4, 1164–5.
David Munden: 1144, 1173, 1175–6, 1178, 1183, 1185, 1196, 1199, 1201, 1214, 1237–40, 1272–5, 1288.
AllSport UK Ltd: 1166, 1212–3.
PA News Ltd: 1192, 1194, 1203, 1207–9, 1211, 1215–7.
Empics Ltd: 1202.
EPA-Agence, France: 1204.
Philip Brown: 1276–87, 1289–91, 1293, 1295–6, 1298–1302, 1304–33.
David Ashdown: 1292, 1294, 1297, 1303.

All other illustrations are from the author's private collection of photographs, scrapbooks, postcards, cigarette-cards, prints, books and relics.

CONTENTS

FOREWORD BY MICHAEL ATHERTON OBE

It is inconceivable that any English or Australian cricketer could tell you of a time when he was not aware of the Ashes. It is simply the greatest prize that cricket has to offer.

How odd then that it should be just about the smallest prize in cricket – or in world sport for that matter. How could the Honourable Ivo Bligh have known that a precarious ocean voyage more than a century ago to regain lost honour, combined with a love affair with an Aussie girl that resulted in the gift of a tiny terracotta urn, would ever after inspire such feelings of passion?

The only days of Test cricket I saw 'live' before I played in a Test match happened to be one of the most famous Ashes encounters of them all: the 'Botham Test' at Headingley in 1981, when England miraculously rose from the dead to reignite the series. I didn't choose luckily. I watched John Dyson grind out a century on the first day – although I did catch the thrilling sight at the end of the second day of Dennis Lillee running in from the football stand end. He must have had some hair then because I clearly remember a bright yellow headband illuminating the Northern gloom.

But I wasn't put off. My next memory is from a year later, as a fourteen-year-old, huddled under my duvet in the middle of the night, radio held fast to my ear. It is hard to remember a time when you couldn't watch live televised sport at will. Young cricket tragics today have never had it so good. But for England's tour of 1982–83, apart from the Richie Benaud-fronted half-hour highlights (that Channel 9 music at the start of the show has never left my mind), radio was the only source of instantaneous cricket description.

So there I was, ready to suffer red eyes and next-morning scowls from teachers, listening as Allan Border and Jeff Thomson, Australia's last pair, nearly did what Botham had done the year before: the unthinkable. Thrillingly the edge came: a parried attempt at slip, then the commentator's wonderful words: 'England have won!'

Then came – for me – the real thing: an Ashes Test when I was twenty-one years old, only a couple of months out of university and as green as grass. Did it live up to expectations? Well, not entirely. At the end of my first day Australia were 301 without loss; Mark Taylor and Geoff Marsh were gorging themselves on an England bowling attack shorn of experience because of recruitment to a rebel tour of South Africa.

More damaging, for me personally, was the comment from an old England hand who told me during the match: 'you play your first [Test] for love and the rest for money'. No matter how well – or more often how badly – my Ashes experiences went, I always remembered that comment and was determined to eradicate the attitude as best I could through deed and example.

That first day in Ashes cricket was a signal for what was to follow. I played in seven Ashes series, winning none. It was, in truth, a poor era for English cricket, stymied as we were by an appalling feeder system. And it was a golden era for Australian cricket, blessed with a couple of players who will go down as all-time greats. The combination ensured a more one-sided contest than I or anyone else would have hoped for. Still, to have played against the great Shane Warne, among others, and to have tried, fallen short, mired in dust and sweat, and kept coming back for more, to try again (as Theodore Roosevelt might have said), was a thrill in itself. Looking back now, I don't regard it as being of any importance at all in my life that I didn't win an Ashes series.

But of course I'm glad, as I write, that England hold the Ashes. Who could ever forget that five-act drama of 2005, the greatest series that I have ever seen? Only an *Ashes* series, I believe, could have inspired such emotion, such passion, and such theatre. It will be so again. Ivo Bligh has a lot to answer for.

FOREWORD BY JUSTIN LANGER

Hanging on one of the walls in my home in Perth, Western Australia, are three wonderful pieces of memorabilia. One is a bat autographed in 1938 by the Australian touring team and their rivals England. Among the ink-penned names are legends of the game, including Denis Compton, Len Hutton, Don Bradman, Wally Hammond, Bill O'Reilly, Bill Brown, Jack Fingleton, Lindsay Hassett and Leslie Fleetwood-Smith.

Alongside the bat is an old photograph and another bat signed by the 1930 Australian team. This is brilliant because the photo lends life to the signatures of players such as a young Bradman, Bert Oldfield, Alan Kippax, Archie Jackson and Clarrie Grimmett. Sitting on top of that jarrah-framed jewel is a wooden boomerang presented to Herbert Sutcliffe after the 1924–25 series in Australia. After scoring 735 runs at 81.55 in a losing team, the majestic Yorkshireman was given this iconic symbol as a reminder of his peerless performance.

Thankfully, these invaluable possessions have been given greater meaning by this pictorial history. Names and statistics are one thing, but stories and photographs bring objects like autographed bats and trophies to life: David Frith's writing puts a heartbeat into my treasures.

Cricket is quite simply an integral part of Australian society, and nothing brings a summer alight like an Ashes series. There weren't many summers as a young lad when an Ashes battle didn't dominate our backyard 'Test matches'. Fortunately my younger brother Adam would always wear the navy-blue cap of England while I fought hard for the pride of the imaginary baggy green. The only time I considered changing teams was when, as a six-year-old, I marvelled at that joker Derek Randall who scored 174 against D.K.Lillee in the Centenary Test at the MCG. For a few days I thought Randall was a hero and tried to imitate his antics. But it didn't really feel right batting against my other new heroes Dennis Lillee and Maxie Walker. It wasn't long before I changed back to being Kim Hughes, Allan Border or Graeme Wood, and bowling like Rodney Hogg or Jeff Thomson.

The history of the Ashes is the stuff of legend, and I feel privileged and proud to have progressed from a daydreaming lad to a participant in the real-life drama of Ashes Tests. On Thursday, July 21, 2005 I had the rare opportunity of facing the first ball of the eagerly awaited Ashes series at the Home of Cricket, Lord's. After making my way down the polished staircase and through the unforgettable Long Room, I stepped onto the hallowed turf, which was like a manicured carpet fit for a king. Within a few minutes Steve Harmison was roaring in from the members' end to deliver a thunderbolt that thudded into the gloves of Geraint Jones. He finished his followthrough just a few metres from my face, and it was at that moment I knew England really meant business. The first hour was played with cut-throat intensity and saw Matty Hayden and Ricky Ponting take blows to their helmeted heads. The battle was on and the scene set for what became the toughest Test series I have ever been involved in. By the time it was over, and England had regained the Ashes for the first time in 16 years, although we were disappointed to have lost the series we were proud to have been part of an historic encounter. There is an old saying: 'the best thing in the world is to play and win, the second-best is to play and lose; as long as you're still playing.'

Despite the outcome of that 2005 series, the contest made us feel we were alive. The fight was rough on the field, but the spirit between the two teams was extraordinary. Not only did the series reach unforgettable heights in terms of skill and commitment but, more importantly, it left an important legacy of unbridled interest in the great game.

Throughout history the Ashes competition has produced many heroes, and heroes inspire the future. While England and Australia continue to play with such passion then cricket will prosper for at least another 130 years.

INTRODUCTION BY DAVID FRITH

Although patriotic zealots might be reluctant to agree, in an ideal world the Ashes would change hands after every England v Australia Test series. Take the last three encounters: four-one to Australia in 2002–03; two-one to England in 2005; five-nil to Australia in 2006–07. And many a forecast for the 2009 series seems to favour England to recover the urn again now that so many of Australia's turn-of-the-century champions have retired.

Australia's crushing dominance from 1989 to 2005 was a long-term source of pride for one country and of depression for the other. For objective cricket-lovers (if there be such a species) it was a relief when the triumphant spell ended. It so happens that the turnaround came in the shape of the most thrilling Test series ever between any countries, let alone the two senior ones. Then came the extraordinary '06-07 series in which Ricky Ponting's troupe smothered England with a 'whitewash', a humiliation inflicted only once before in the long history of Anglo-Australian combat. So-called 'Ashes cricket', the Test competition with the greatest archive of folklore, statistical marvels, and pictorial fascination, was alive with possibilities once again.

Dave Gregory and Jim Lillywhite can't have had any real notion of what they were starting when they tossed for choice of innings at the semi-rural Melbourne Cricket Ground in March 1877. Nowadays it seems as if half the world stands still whenever England and Australia go to war on the cricket field.

The symbol of supremacy, almost from the start, has been the little glazed terracotta pot with its mysterious contents: the Ashes urn, presented to the Honourable Ivo Bligh by some Melbourne ladies during the 1882-83 series. Bligh married one of them, and the wedding ring that he placed on Florence's finger seems like a symbol of an everlasting bond which cricket competition between the two countries represents. Upon Ivo's death in 1927 his widow presented the urn to Marylebone Cricket Club. Together with its velvet bag, it was in due course put on display in the museum at Lord's.

While the fragile symbol has twice been shown around Australia's State capitals, persistent calls to allow Australia to take delivery of the urn after series victories have been resisted. Instead, a large crystal replica was created by Marylebone Cricket Club in 1998-99 in an endeavour to soothe the agitators. Not all Australians were satisfied. Test captain Mark Taylor expressed the hope that the replica might topple and disintegrate. Through those sixteen years of Australian supremacy it sometimes seemed that, while England were constant losers in the field of play, the stubborn retention of the tiny Ashes urn itself was their sole means of irritating the old enemy.

These battles, which have been going on for so long now, have been a very important part of the lives of many millions. It began when the pioneer players braved the seas in vulnerable ships driven by sail and steam. Then came the more comfortable liners, and then in the 1960s Jumbo jets began lifting the cricketers into the enemy's stronghold in a mere twenty-four hours, with womenfolk and families now often joining them.

In Victorian times, delayed but lengthy reports of the matches in the broadsheets reached the breakfast tables, devoid of illustrations and with match details often flawed. Compare this with the luxury enjoyed today by cricket-lovers in their armchairs in the middle of the night, gazing at a colour television picture which displays even more fine detail than is available to the spectator at the ground.

So much has changed as the world has rushed to embrace scientific advances. And yet there is still a vital thread of continuity here, ensuring that even the oldest of men cherish their earliest memories of Ashes cricket. One thing is certain: the urgent sense of immediacy which grips the mind of young people today will in time give way to an overpowering sense of nostalgia. If the innocent lament 'Ah, you should have seen Lindwall . . . and Hutton' meets with impatience today, that impatient listener, to whom Jessop's name is probably unknown, will one day assuredly be heard insisting that 'there'll never be a hitter to match Gilchrist . . . or such an inventive batsman as Pietersen'.

Alfred Shaw started it all. A plump, bearded, cunning Nottinghamshire slow-medium bowler, he sent down the first-ever ball in Test cricket just after one o'clock on Thursday, March 15, 1877 from the eastern end of the MCG. It was a fine day, but there were only about 1500 spectators present. As word spread around town the attendance trebled. (Sixty years later just over a quarter of a million people passed through the turnstiles of the expanded MCG over the five days of the deciding Test match.)

Charlie Bannerman cut the second ball past point for the first Test run. Nat Thomson was the first batsman dismissed, bowled by a shooter from Allen Hill. The first boundary came from the bat of Irish-born Tom Horan, an edge off Hill. Hill was soon registering another first when he caught Horan. Bearded like Ned Kelly, the bushranger who was currently developing his iniquitous career in the north-eastern reaches of Victoria, the Australian captain Dave Gregory became the first run-out victim (Harry Jupp the fieldsman). Dave's brother Ned registered the first duck. Then at 4.15pm on that inaugural afternoon Bannerman drove the veteran Jim Southerton and ran a single to reach 100. When Adam Gilchrist reached his swashbuckling hundred at Edgbaston in 2001 it was Australia's 250th against England. Just try to evaluate all the endeavour and sweat expended in between.

Bannerman's was a truly marvellous innings in an era when centuries were much rarer than today. He had to cope with Tom Armitage's grotesque full-tosses and grubbers as well as George Ulyett's vicious kickers, one of which eventually split his middle finger. The closest score to Bannerman's 165 in that first of all Test innings was Tom Garrett's 18 (a run for every year of his life). Bannerman's personal contribution of 67.35 percent of Australia's total – and here's continuity for you – is still a record, though Michael Slater came very close at Sydney in 1999.

Of all the players in that inaugural Test match, the recorded voice of Garrett (the last to die, in 1943) alone survives. In a fine, steady voice he recalled that 'with the wickets pitched east and west . . . at one end the sun was in your eyes and on the other end you were playing a ball out of the shadow of your own figure'.

Bannerman, Garrett, Gregory, Horan, Blackham . . . even though Australia still had some way to go before securing nationhood, these names somehow seem to be Australian cricket's equivalent of the signatories to America's Declaration of Independence.

From Bannerman's first run to the 100,000th for Australia, stroked by Doug Walters in 1975, and beyond that, the parade of skill and character in both teams has been awesome. It is fortunate that before the advent of sharply defined television pictures and the facility of personal video/DVD libraries, and even before the synthetised wireless commentaries of the 1930s, Ashes Test cricket was copiously recorded in newspapers, books and magazines. It is a further precious bounty that cameras were clicking as long ago as 1882, though with nothing of the close-up capability of forty years later. We even have in this book a photograph of the first touring Test team, England's in 1877.

It is a book which concentrates on pictorial images, each one of which, by tradition, is said to 'paint a thousand words'. For all his lyrical prose, even Neville Cardus sometimes described an incident without embellishment – or even not at all. In *Good Days*, his book on the 1934 Ashes series, he does not even mention Bill Brown's dismissal in the Oval Test. But the picture shows the batsman's backward step, his angled bat, the inside-edge that caused his downfall, and the half-raised arms of bowler Nobby Clark.

Words may capture the movement, the context, the spirit and the mood, but the photograph usually preserves a perfect outline of reality, the moment of truth, nothing added, nothing deleted. Time's cruel and relentless passage is defied, cheated, resisted for all time, if only to the extent of a hundredth of a second.

My own enslavement to the passion that is cricket began during a boyhood in north-west London, where the carefree and capless hero Denis Compton was imitated by youngsters with makeshift bats on most of the car-less streets. Crackly wireless reports from Australia during the first post-war Ashes series were followed by sightings of Bradman's 1948 team at play, courtesy of a tiny, grainy, monochrome television picture in the living-room of a schoolpal who had wealthier parents than mine.

Transported to the other side of the globe (proud, too, to sail in SS *Orion*, the vessel which had taken the 1936-37 MCC team to Australia), in my early youth, in a quiet suburb of Sydney, I transformed myself into a combination of Len Hutton and Ray Lindwall in street and school cricket. This confused my Dad: a Yorkshire and England batsman and a St George and Australia fast bowler within the same mind and body?

The fateful hour came with the arrival on the front porch of old Mr Sullings, grandfather of Keith across the road. Would I like to go to the Test match next day? I would be in excellent company for the old boy and his white-haired neighbour were always talking about Bardsley and Trumper and Jack Gregory, Oldfield and Kippax, Mailey, Macartney and Bradman, and the token Victorian Armstrong.

Keith scratched in the dust an outline of the Sydney Cricket Ground: the M.A.Noble Stand is here, the Sheridan Stand there, the pavilion there;

this is the Hill, this is the Brewongle Stand. These areas and edifices soon became every bit as familiar to me as my parents' facial features, and although I have never met anybody who was born nearer than I was to Lord's, the SCG became my spiritual home from January 8, 1951. And so it remains to this day, despite its transformation from the most charming and evocative of cricket grounds, a strong Victorian feel about its every feature and surround, into one of the world's concrete super-stadiums.

We set out on that shimmering morning in the 1930s canvas-hooded motor car, Keith and I rocking and bouncing on the leather back seat as it groaned up Princes Highway and clattered over the tramlines of Newtown. Through old South Sydney we nosed – drab little factories all around, stray Europeans, neat little English-style terraces – then out through the broad expanse of Moore Park. Curiosity bursting, I followed my party through the clacking turnstiles and into a great new world.

Passing beneath the Victor Trumper memorial plaque, we made our way along the sunlit pathway across the base of the jam-packed Hill, which was abuzz. We found a space on the brown timber seating in the old covered 'Bob' Stand, side-on to the pitch. The scoreboard, a solid architectural marvel, was away to our left. The divine, green, ornate members' pavilion stood beyond to the right. If somebody had whispered that one day I would bat out on that pitch, albeit only in a first-grade match, I would have swooned.

The first player I set eyes on was a square-shouldered fieldsman by the fence in front of us. This was young David Sheppard, the future Bishop of Liverpool. He was on the field as a substitute. Bowlers Trevor Bailey and Doug Wright had both been injured, and England's depleted bowling line-up consisted of the tireless giant Alec Bedser, red-faced skipper Freddie Brown in his white neckerchief, and the ineffective John Warr, with back-up from the left-arm twiddlers of the glamorous Compton. So there he was at last, in the flesh, as was Len Hutton.

Sam Loxton's clout to midwicket and the smack of the ball into Bedser's great hands are still with me over half-a-century later, and so too are visions of Keith Miller's driving and cutting and the dapper movements of left-hander Neil Harvey, before Ian Johnson came in to whack a few late runs. They were all bare-headed, which made it easier to identify them from the portraits in the programme and for when autographs were sought.

The devotion of one more boy was thus sealed. Soon there were pilgrimages to the sports shops of Alan Kippax and Stan McCabe and the dapper Bert Oldfield, who gave me his 1930 Australian tour blazer. A mesmerising lifesize cut-out of the Hammond cover-drive dominated the Hunter Street shop window, and another of Tibby Cotter stood by the staircase. Upstairs was the real-life legendary Charlie Macartney, short, chunky and reclusive. He seldom came down to the shop.

A matriculation was achieved despite the night-time distraction of the memorable 1953 Ashes series over in England. A bulky radio became a furtive lifeline in 1954-55 for a young cricket addict at work in the bank, one of whose clients was none other than Arthur Mailey, who would talk if pressed, which he was. Tactical sore throats secured time off work whenever the English cricketers played in Sydney. There was no television then, so there was no risk that the bank manager might have spotted my face in the crowd.

Later in life a bemused family waved farewell as I went off in search of old players in both countries. What a privilege it was, and what a roll-call: Jack Gregory, the recluse; Harold Larwood, who warned my son not to become a fast bowler; S.F.Barnes, describing in detail his 5 for 6 at Melbourne in 1911; Frank Woolley, horrified still by Armstrong's cheating in 1920-21; Jack Fingleton sensitively on the Bodyline goings-on; the blind Wilfred Rhodes with his vivid visions of bowling to Grace and Trumper; Arthur Chipperfield on getting out for 99 on Ashes debut; 'Tiger' Smith on keeping wicket in '11-12 to Barnes and Foster; Ernie McCormick laughing at everything; Bob Wyatt frowning; Ian Peebles on bowling to Bradman; Percy Fender smouldering still over Johnny Douglas's dim opinion of his skills in 1920; Les Ames gasping at film of Larwood, he himself reaching high to gather the thunderbolts; Bill O'Reilly, still belligerent in his eighties; little Herbert Strudwick on keeping as an apprentice to Tom Richardson's wicked bumpers; Cyril Walters on the curious personality of Bodyline architect Jardine; Bill Bowes and the polished Herbert Sutcliffe united on Verity's genius; Arthur Gilligan on the pleasures of Anglo-Australian relations in the 1920s; Leo O'Brien on facing Larwood without a helmet; Gubby Allen trying to kid that Bodyline didn't start until the third Test; George Geary on bowling 101 overs in an eight-day Melbourne Test; Eddie Paynter still miffed at that 99 at Lord's when he edged into his pad; Sir Don Bradman fascinating on anything and everything over a precious 30-year friendship.

Going, in a sense, beyond the grave, there were pilgrimages to cricketers' final resting places, starting with Trumper's in 1952. And I even found myself tentatively claiming the abandoned ashes of 1880s champion bowler Charlie Turner, which had reposed since 1944 in a blue box on a shelf in Hanson Carter's funeral parlour in Sydney. After enquiries, they were properly removed to Bathurst, his native town.

Add countless conversations with the Huttons, Comptons, Bedsers, Lakers, Truemans, Lindwalls, Harveys, Johnstons, Benauds and Millers and with a cavalcade of the more modern Ashes warriors – sometimes even players' descendants have made for good interviews – and there would have been quite enough cultural material on Ashes Test cricket to fill this volume with words alone. But that's not the idea.

Continuity remains the powerful underlying influence. Norm O'Neill, who emerged from our St George youth ranks, took up the No.3 position in the Australian XI batting order which had once been tenanted by Harvey, who had followed Bradman, Macartney, Hill, Giffen, right back to Murdoch. It was thrilling to witness O'Neill's ascent and the clean power of his strokeplay. But I now contemplate with mixed feelings the fact that a grade cricket team-mate of mine from the early 1960s has a son, then unborn, who in 2001 scored a century on Ashes debut and later made the fastest hundred in Ashes history: Adam Gilchrist. Tempus sure does fugit, as old George Geary once murmured.

In the corporate entity which is the England XI, the lovable Godfrey Evans crouched behind the stumps in succession to the likes of Lyttelton, MacGregor, Lilley, Strudwick, Duckworth and Ames, and then passed the gloveman's job to others until the immaculate Alan Knott, another Kent man, wore them. Cricket's proneness to stretch credibility showed again when Alec Stewart entered Ashes Tests with the *triple* responsibilities of top-order batsman, wicketkeeper and captain. And we have had Australian twins, Steve and Mark Waugh, bestowing an unreal appearance on many a scorecard as they stacked up their runs and held their catches and set all kinds of fraternal Test records.

Duels between the slender, solemn Hutton and the fearsome, kindly Lindwall have given way to confrontations between John Edrich and Graham McKenzie and then the arrival of Dennis Lillee and Jeff Thomson, new names in the electrifying breed of blitz bowlers which had been given lift-off in the 19th century by Fred Spofforth, Tom Richardson and Ernie Jones. They were succeeded by Tibby Cotter, Jack Gregory and Ted McDonald, Harold Larwood and Bill Voce, Fred Trueman, Brian Statham, Frank Tyson, John Snow, Bob Willis, Merv Hughes, Geoff Lawson, Craig McDermott, through to Darren Gough, Steve Harmison, and the intimidating trio of Glenn McGrath, Jason Gillespie and Brett Lee, who have done so much to ensure Australia's sure grip on the Ashes through series after series. And yet two bowlers who relied less on sheer pace – Rodney Hogg and Terry Alderman – hold series wicket-taking records.

Jack Hobbs, Herbert Sutcliffe, Frank Woolley, Patsy Hendren, Wally Hammond, Maurice Leyland, Denis Compton, Len Hutton, the cousins Edrich, Peter May, Colin Cowdrey, Ken Barrington, Ted Dexter, Geoff Boycott, Derek Randall, Ian Botham, Graham Gooch, David Gower, Mike Gatting, Chris Broad, Graham Thorpe, Nasser Hussain, and most recently Michael Vaughan, Freddie Flintoff, Paul Collingwood and Kevin Pietersen: these and many others conjure up visions of English glory and endeavour. There is poignancy too in such careers as Mike Atherton's. He was never, in twelve years, a member of an Ashes-winning side.

There has also been isolated glory. Mark Butcher made a stirring century in 2001 at Headingley, stroked after a lunch break spent in the shower-room with coffee and cigarettes. Another fleeting career was that of Greg Blewett for Australia, who has the glorious distinction of being the only batsman to score a century in each of his first three Ashes Tests.

It's important to remind ourselves that during the twenty years of Don Bradman's astounding achievements there were many other Australian batsmen of very high quality who were destined to be overshadowed: Alan Kippax, Bill Ponsford, Bill Woodfull, Stan McCabe, Archie Jackson, Bill Brown, Jack Fingleton, Sid Barnes, Lindsay Hassett, Arthur Morris. Their successors as batting pillars have included Peter Burge, Bob Simpson, Norm O'Neill, Bob Cowper, Bill Lawry, the Chappells and the Waughs, Kim Hughes, Dean Jones, David Boon, the tough-as-teak Allan Border (only Bradman and Hobbs have scored more Ashes runs), tearaway Michael Slater, the solid opening pair of Mark Taylor and Geoff Marsh, burly Matt Hayden, the fiercely devoted Justin Langer, and Ricky Ponting, whose recent record has elevated him in public perception to a kind of Bradman understudy.

The very mention of a name – such as Keith Miller – will flood the mind with pictures if he was part of your spectatorship and acquaintance. Same with Shane Warne, whose 195 Ashes wickets, beginning with that Gatting ball, will take some beating. The quantity of star names reinforces the certainty that Ashes cricket has been the supreme stage, the Sydney Opera House and the London Palladium superimposed over the colossal MCG and ancient Lord's.

There have now been almost 1400 days of Test cricket between Australia and England (including partial days and a few rained off), and in this book we have over 1350 frozen particles of action, arranged for the reader to choose a time and a place and visit it. While the deep emotional links binding Britain and Australia may have become slightly frayed in recent years, it says much for Ashes competition that it has continued to render each country important unto the other. Engineered by political machination, adverse economic forces have affected the old bond, but every time Australia and England face up to each other, with their hordes of vocal but mainly good-humoured supporters forming the ring, the need for each other is reasserted.

Long may these two wonderful countries, with their special historic ties, continue to beat each other up on the cricket pitch – within the sad necessity of the ICC Code of Conduct – and share a few beers afterwards, raising a respectful glass from time to time to the broad ranks of their illustrious predecessors.

1876–77 FIRST TEST

Melbourne, March 15, 16, 17, 19

Australia *245 (C. Bannerman 165 ret.ht) and 104 (A. Shaw 5 for 38, G. Ulyett 4 for 39);* England *196 (H. Jupp 63, W.E. Midwinter 5 for 78) and 108 (T. Kendall 7 for 55).* Australia won by 45 runs.

The first of some 800 Test matches during Test cricket's first hundred years was played between sides that were hardly fully representative. The term 'Test' was as yet unknown, and few of the participants or onlookers could have had any idea of the vast importance that England-Australia matches – let alone cricket contests between other countries – would assume in years to follow. It was sunny and warm as, at one o'clock on Thursday, March 15, Charles Bannerman received the first ball from Alfred Shaw. By the end of play, at five o'clock, Australia were 166 for 6, Bannerman 126 not out; he played with great freedom, and punished Armitage's lobs so mercilessly that the bowler began trying to drop the ball on the full over the batsman's head onto the bails before resorting to 'grubbers' along the ground. Bannerman's historic innings was ended when a fast ball from Yorkshireman Ulyett split a finger, causing his retirement. Next-highest score came from Garrett, 18 not out, a run for every year of his age. Southerton, then aged 49, and Shaw were England's best bowlers, taking three wickets each. England replied with 196 – a deficit of 49 – but Australia's second-innings collapse left the touring team with only 154 for victory. The task would have been simpler without the last-wicket stand of 29 by Kendall and Hodges. England's first wicket fell without a run on the board, and a steady procession of batsmen followed as left-arm slow bowler Kendall broke through time and again. The crowd, which had built up to around 3000, gave both teams a hearty reception at the end. For years Australia's cricket had been developing fast. The three earlier English touring sides – Stephenson's in 1861-62, Parr's in 1863-64, and Grace's in 1873-74 – had played only against odds. Now Dave Gregory's side had won on even terms over Lillywhite's professionals, and a great sporting tradition had begun.

1, above: *The newly-built grandstand at Melbourne, from which the more privileged had a comfortable view of play.* 2, below, left: *Alfred Shaw, who bowled the first ball for England.* 3, right: *Charles Bannerman, who faced it – and many more before being compelled by injury to retire*

4: *The 1876–77 English touring team: back — H. Jupp, T. Emmett, A. Hobgen (tour financier), A. Hill, T. Armitage; seated — E. Pooley, J. Southerton, James Lillywhite (captain), A. Shaw, G. Ulyett, A. Greenwood; in front — H.R.J. Charlwood, J. Selby*

1876–77 — SECOND TEST

Melbourne, March 31, April 2, 3, 4

Australia *122 (A. Hill 4 for 27) and 259 (D.W. Gregory 43, N.F.D. Thomson 41, J. Southerton 4 for 46, J. Lillywhite 4 for 70);* England *261 (G. Ulyett 52, A. Greenwood 49, A. Hill 49, T. Emmett 48, T. Kendall 4 for 82) and 122 for 6 (G. Ulyett 63).* England won by 4 wickets.

English pride was restored in a return fixture in which they fielded the only eleven players fit and available. Pooley, the first-choice wicketkeeper, did not rejoin the team after being caught up in some off-the-field trouble in New Zealand. For Australia, Spofforth, who refused to play in the earlier match because Murdoch was not to keep wicket, announced himself with some decidedly quick bowling, but Blackham, Australia's craftsman wicketkeeper, stood up at the stumps and even effected a stumping off Spofforth. Australia lost their first four wickets to Hill and finished dismally with 122, with Midwinter (31) top-scorer. Five Yorkshiremen contributed 219 of England's 243 from the bat, but an opening stand of 88 by Gregory and Thomson bit into the arrears, and though wickets fell steadily, Australia eventually led by 120. England began disastrously. Three wickets fell for nine runs, and even at 76 for 5 the match was anyone's. Then Ulyett, top-scorer in the first innings, hammered his side to the brink of victory and Hill did the rest. Lillywhite's team failed to generate high regard in Australia, where in many quarters it was being suggested that only the strongest side available visit the colony in future.

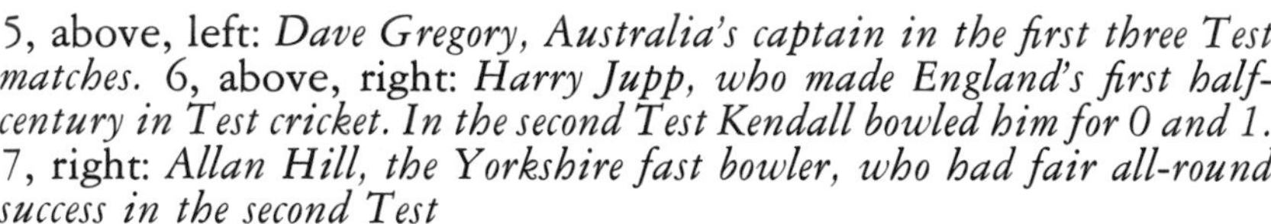

5, above, left: *Dave Gregory, Australia's captain in the first three Test matches.* 6, above, right: *Harry Jupp, who made England's first half-century in Test cricket. In the second Test Kendall bowled him for 0 and 1.* 7, right: *Allan Hill, the Yorkshire fast bowler, who had fair all-round success in the second Test*

1878–79 ONLY TEST

Melbourne, January 2, 3, 4

England *113 (C.A. Absolom 52, F.R. Spofforth 6 for 48) and 160 (F.R. Spofforth 7 for 62);* Australia *256 (A.C. Bannerman 73, T. Emmett 7 for 68) and 19 for 0.* Australia won by 10 wickets.

Australia had shown during the 1878 tour of England (when no Tests were played) that they had an enviable array of bowlers. Lord Harris's side, which was all-amateur except for Ulyett and Emmett, was rich in batting. Thus the confrontation between the tourists and a team which with one exception had toured England only months earlier (shocking MCC by bowling them out for 33 and 19 and winning in a day) was anticipated with some fervour. A morning thunderstorm failed to dissuade Lord Harris from batting after winning the toss, and before lunch England were 26 for 7. Spofforth, in dismissing Royle, Mackinnon and Emmett, performed the first Test hat-trick. The captain (33) and Absolom managed to lift the total out of the depths of humiliation, but Australia were 95 for 3 at the close. Alec, small younger brother of Charles Bannerman of first-Test immortality, led Australia to a handsome lead with a slow but chanceless 73. England only just avoided an innings defeat, Lord Harris top-scoring with 36. Spofforth's match figures of 13 for 110 confirmed him as the world's most penetrative bowler. A return match was cancelled after the touring team's match against New South Wales was interrupted by larrikins who invaded the pitch and assaulted some of the players and an umpire.

8, above, left: *The amateurs, who formed the bulk of Lord Harris's side: standing – R.D. Walker, F. Penn, Lord Harris, L. Hone, F.A. Mackinnon; centre row – A.P. Lucas, S.S. Schultz, Mrs Hornby, Lady Harris, H.D. Maul, C.A. Absolom; front – A.N. Hornby, Miss Ingram, V.P.F.A. Royle, A.J. Webbe.* 9, right: *Tom Emmett, the bluff Yorkshireman, whose 7 for 68 was not supported by very distinguished England batting.* 10, left: *'Demon' Spofforth, who took the first Test hat-trick among his 13 wickets at Melbourne*

1880 ONLY TEST

The Oval, September 6, 7, 8

England *420 (W.G. Grace 152, A.P. Lucas 55, Lord Harris 52, A.G. Steel 42) and 57 for 5;* Australia *149 (F. Morley 5 for 56) and 327 (W.L. Murdoch 153*, P.S. McDonnell 43).* England won by 5 wickets.

The first Test match ever played in England was dominated by Dr W.G. Grace, who made 152 upon his debut, and W.L. Murdoch, who passed the new individual batting record when Australia followed on. Following upon the Sydney riot of 1879, the 1880 Australians had certain difficulties in obtaining fixtures in England, and it was only because of the efforts of the Surrey authorities that the first Test in England was not postponed still further. Apart from Spofforth's absence through injury, both sides were at near-full strength. At the close of the first day England were 410 for 8, Grace having put on 91 for the first wicket with his elder brother EM, and 120 for the second with Lucas. By lunch on the second day Australia were 126 for 9, light rain the previous evening probably having changed the nature of the pitch. All seemed lost when three wickets fell for 14 in the follow-on, but McDonnell and others stayed with the gallant Murdoch, who went in at the fall of the first wicket, and England were eventually set 57 to win. After some frights, the runs were made, though the third Grace brother – GF (Fred) – made his second nought in his only Test appearance, having made one of history's most famous catches off a monster hit by the giant Bonnor – the batsmen were on their third run as the ball was safely caught. G.F. Grace, aged 29, died a fortnight later from a chill and lung congestion.

11: *Lord Harris, England's captain in the first home Test, runs to save a boundary*

TELEPHONE, EASTLING 11.

6·9·30

BELMONT,
FAVERSHAM.

Dear Sir

I am greatly obliged for your very flattering letter & for the notes on the 1880 match. I remember some of the incidents but not many. It was a very interesting & exciting game: but the absence of Spofforth made a great difference.

Yrs faithfully

Harris

12, above, left: *A commemorative belt buckle.* 13, above, right: *Lord Harris concedes the importance of Spofforth's absence even 50 years later.* 14, right: *General view of the match*

1881–82 FIRST TEST

Melbourne, December 31, January 2, 3, 4

England *294 (G. Ulyett 87, W. Bates 58, J. Selby 55) and 308 (J. Selby 70, W.H. Scotton 50*, W. Bates 47, A. Shaw 40, W.H. Cooper 6 for 120);* Australia *320 (T.P. Horan 124) and 127 for 3.* Match drawn.

Four Tests were played during the 1881–82 tour, the first of several enterprises embarked upon by the partnership of Shaw, Shrewsbury and Lillywhite, with the first-named as captain, and the team composed entirely of professionals, including W.E. Midwinter, who became the only man ever to play for Australia against England and *vice versa.* England's innings owed most to a second-wicket stand of 137 between the hard-hitting Ulyett and little Selby. Medium-pacer Edwin Evans took 3 for 81 off 71 four-ball overs, of which 35 were maidens. In reply, Australia owed much to Irish-born Horan, whose century was founded on the straight-drive. He added 107 for the fifth wicket with Giffen, who was to become a major all-rounder, and now made 30 on his debut. England soon wiped off the deficit, but Cooper, an ancestor of A.P. Sheahan, who played against England from 1968 to 1972, created some havoc with his leg-breaks, and only an obdurate innings by Scotton, supported by Shaw, saw to it that, on a still blameless pitch, Australia would not have time to bat their way to victory.

15: *Tom Horan, who featured with Giffen in the first century partnership in Tests for Australia*

16: *John Selby, of Notts, who played two staunch innings for England*

17: *William Cooper, whose leg-breaks embarrassed England*

1881–82 SECOND TEST

Sydney, February 17, 18, 20, 21

England *133 (G.E. Palmer 7 for 68) and 232 (G. Ulyett 67, R.G. Barlow 62, T.W. Garrett 4 for 62, G.E. Palmer 4 for 97);* Australia *197 (H.H. Massie 49, J.McC. Blackham 40, W. Bates 4 for 52) and 169 for 5 (W.L. Murdoch 49).* Australia won by 5 wickets.

Sydney's first Test match fluctuated between Australian ascendancy and an even balance: England were never quite in command after back-pedalling all the first day. Palmer and Evans bowled unchanged for over three hours throughout England's modest first innings, and by the second evening the tourists were in again, facing arrears of 64. Yet Ulyett and Barlow, in their contrasting styles, built an opening of 122, and a sizable task seemed in prospect for Australia. The batting then collapsed before the bowling of Palmer and Garrett, and Murdoch, with care and supported by several determined partners, took Australia to the point of victory. During the match Murdoch and Blackham shared the wicketkeeping duties. Between this and the previous Test, the English party played seven matches in New Zealand.

18: *Hugh Massie, bank officer, strong driver, lethal cutter*

19: *G.E. 'Joey' Palmer, young bowler with a touch of genius*

20: *Edwin Evans, a supreme all-rounder from New South Wales*

1881–82 THIRD TEST
Sydney, March 3, 4, 6, 7

England *188 (A. Shrewsbury 82, G.E. Palmer 5 for 46) and 134 (A. Shrewsbury 47, T.W. Garrett 6 for 78, G.E. Palmer 4 for 44);* Australia 262 *(P.S. McDonnell 147, A.C. Bannerman 70, E. Peate 5 for 43) and 64 for 4.* Australia won by 6 wickets.

England's first five wickets fell for 56 on a difficult pitch, and only the great skill of Shrewsbury enabled them to approach 200. Australia were allowed to prepare a fresh pitch for their innings, and were themselves 24 for 3 at the end of the first day, a score taken to 146 for 3 when heavy rain cut short the second day. Young McDonnell, London-born, displayed his great hitting powers, once putting Bates over the pavilion. His stand with Bannerman realised 199, but once it was broken, Peate ran through the side. The next-highest scorer after McDonnell and Bannerman was S.P. Jones with seven not out. Shrewsbury again stood almost alone when England batted, and Australia gathered in the necessary runs by the 50th over to go two-up in the series.

21, left: *Percy McDonnell, another of Australia's mighty hitters.* 22, right: *Tom Garrett, still the youngest player to appear in these Test matches*

1881–82 FOURTH TEST

Melbourne, March 10, 11, 13, 14

England 309 *(G. Ulyett 149, T.W. Garrett 5 for 80) and 234 for 2 (G. Ulyett 64, R.G. Barlow 56, W. Bates 52*, J. Selby 48*);* Australia 300 *(W.L. Murdoch 85, P.S. McDonnell 52, W.E. Midwinter 4 for 81).* Match drawn.

'Happy Jack' Ulyett started his big innings unusually cautiously, but accelerated later. Its value may be assessed against the next-highest score – Emmett's 27. Ulyett was ninth out. In continuing great heat, Australia led off with 110 for the first wicket by A.C. Bannerman (suffering from sunstroke) and Murdoch, but this was easily the highest stand of the innings, and when England progressed to an overall lead of 243 with eight wickets standing they seemed to be headed for a morale-boosting victory at last. Then the weather broke, and the fourth day was washed out. With the Australians due to sail for England, there was no chance of extending the match, which was the last to be drawn in Australia until 1946–47.

23, left: *George Ulyett, the strong Yorkshire all-rounder.* 24, above: *William Midwinter, the only man to play for Australia against England and vice versa*

1882 ONLY TEST

The Oval, August 28, 29

Australia 63 *(R.G. Barlow 5 for 19, E. Peate 4 for 31) and 122 (H.H. Massie 55, E. Peate 4 for 40);* England *101 (F.R. Spofforth 7 for 46) and 77 (F.R. Spofforth 7 for 44).* Australia won by 7 runs.

One of the most famous of all cricket matches, this extraordinary contest led to the creation of the Ashes. After the 'Colonials', from a dreadful beginning, had fought back to defeat the full might of England in two days, the *Sporting Times* published a mock obituary of English cricket. It concluded: 'The body will be cremated and the ashes taken to Australia.' The man chiefly responsible for the upset was Fred Spofforth, 'The Demon'. Only Bob Massie in 1972 has surpassed his figures of 14 for 90 for Australia in a Test against England. Australia were first bowled out in 2¼ hours by the left-handers Barlow and Peate on a pitch which had absorbed two days' rain. Spofforth bowled Grace for four, and six England wickets fell before a lead was obtained. The 'Demon' bowled with fire and with guile, stirred, it is said, by some derogatory remarks overheard in the pavilion. On the second day, with the ground wet after further downpours, Massie went after the bowling and made 55 in three-quarters of an hour. Missed at 38, he made possible by his strength and audacity a victory that was to be celebrated in prose and verse for decades to come. A.C. Bannerman, his fellow opener, made 13 and Murdoch 29, but no-one else reached double-figures, and Australia's total of 122 left England a mere 85 to win. Grace's running out of Sammy Jones when the youngster left his crease to attend to a divot in the pitch did nothing to reduce the grim if seemingly farfetched determination of the Australians. At 3.45 pm Grace and Hornby walked out to begin the job. With 15 on the board, England lost Hornby, bowled by Spofforth. Barlow went the same way next ball. Ulyett came in, and the runs began to flow. The fifty came up, and the match seemed over. Then Ulyett was caught at the wicket. Lucas joined Grace, but the Champion himself, having made 32, was caught at mid-off off Boyle. 53 for 4. Lyttelton, the wicket-keeper, joined Lucas, and soon, in almost total silence, the match fell into an eerie stalemate. Twelve successive maiden overs: then a deliberate misfield got Lyttelton opposite Spofforth. Having made 12, the 'keeper was bowled by Australia's master fast bowler. A.G. Steel, the talented amateur all-rounder, came in. Lucas hit a four – loudly cheered by the nervy twenty thousand – then Steel was caught-and-bowled Spofforth. 70 for 6. Maurice Read was then bowled second ball. Barnes hit a two, Blackham allowed three byes, then Lucas played on to Spofforth after a patient five runs. 75 for 8. Barnes was caught off his glove off Boyle's bowling. 75 for 9. Last man Peate joined C.T. Studd, who had oddly been kept back by Hornby to number 10 and had been observed shivering with a blanket around him in the dressing-room. Peate struck a two, then was bowled after heaving at a ball from Boyle. 'Ah couldn't troost Maister Stood,' he said later. Studd had made two centuries already that summer against the Australians. One spectator died of heart failure during the tense closing stages, and another had bitten through his umbrella handle. Henceforth Englishmen knew, if they had not known by now, that Australia offered the sternest of challenges to their national cricket eleven – and their pride.

25, above: *A precious photograph of The Oval during the 'Ashes match'. The players were moving rather too fast for the shutter speed of the camera.* 26, below: *As the artist from* The Illustrated Sporting and Dramatic News *saw play. The batsman is Grace, the bowler Spofforth, and the umpire Bob Thoms*

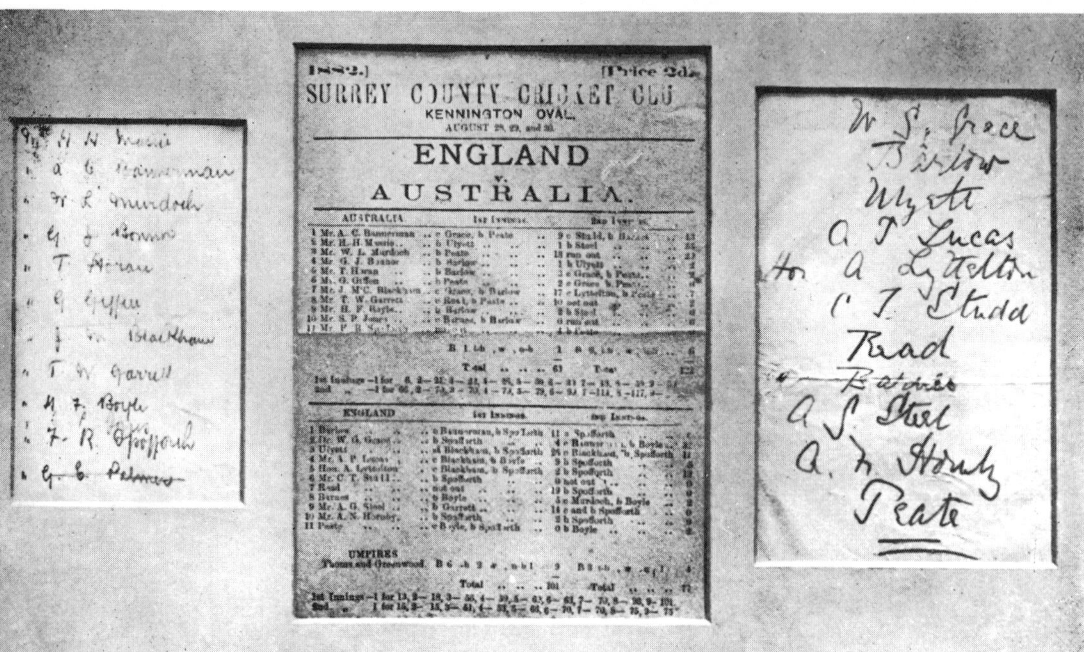

1882.] [Price 2d.

SURREY COUNTY CRICKET CLUB

KENNINGTON OVAL,

AUGUST 28, 29, and 30.

ENGLAND

v.

AUSTRALIA.

W. G. Grace
Barlow
Ulyett
A. P. Lucas
Hon. A. Lyttelton
C. T. Studd
Read
~~Barnes~~
A. G. Steel
A. N. Hornby
Peate

27, top: *An impression of the famous Oval match from* The Illustrated London News. 28, centre: *The scorecard and the captains' batting lists: Hornby's for England could be said to reflect the tension of the hour.* 29, left: *The urn containing the Ashes, with embroidered velvet bag.* 30, below: *The mock obituary notice in* The Sporting Times *which was to have unforeseen widespread effect*

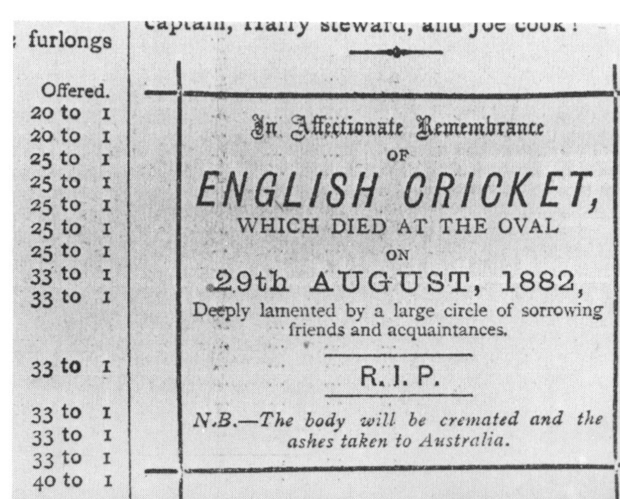

In Affectionate Remembrance

OF

ENGLISH CRICKET,

WHICH DIED AT THE OVAL

ON

29th AUGUST, 1882,

Deeply lamented by a large circle of sorrowing friends and acquaintances.

R. I. P.

N.B.—The body will be cremated and the ashes taken to Australia.

1882–83 FIRST TEST
Melbourne, December 30, January 1, 2

Australia *291 (G.J. Bonnor 85, W.L. Murdoch 48, P.S. McDonnell 43) and 58 for 1;* England *177 (G.E. Palmer 7 for 65) and 169 (G. Giffen 4 for 38).* Australia won by 9 wickets.

The Hon. Ivo Bligh took a fairly strong side to Australia in a crusade to recover the Ashes, but had to withstand a setback precipitated by the weather in the first Test. Australia's sound 291 owed much to the huge, muscular Bonnor, who lofted a number of balls towards – and over – the boundary. After rain on the Sunday, the pitch was slower. Australia's last three wickets fell for 33 and England's first three for eight. Wicketkeeper Tylecote top-scored with 33, and repeated the feat with 38 in the follow-on, when, despite a more agreeable pitch, England managed only 169. 'Joey' Palmer, a talented young medium-pace spinner (and married to Blackham's sister), took 10 for 126 in the match.

31, above, left: *The team that brought back the Ashes: standing – W. Barnes, F. Morley, C.T. Studd, G.F. Vernon, C.F.H. Leslie; seated – G.B. Studd, E.F.S. Tylecote, Hon. Ivo Bligh (captain), A.G. Steel, W.W. Read; in front – R.G. Barlow, W. Bates.* 32, above, right: *The 1773 George III penny used by Bligh to toss in these Tests.* 33, left: *George Giffen, 'the Australian WG'.* 34, right: *George Bonnor, one of the heftiest hitters of them all*

1882–83 SECOND TEST

Melbourne, January 19, 20, 22

England *294 (W.W. Read 75, W. Bates 55, C.F.H. Leslie 54, G.E. Palmer 5 for 103, G. Giffen 4 for 89);* Australia *114 (H.H. Massie 43, W. Bates 7 for 28) and 153 (W. Bates 7 for 74).* England won by an innings and 27 runs.

Fred Morley, who was seriously injured during the voyage out when the ship collided with another, was brought into England's team, but his fast, left-arm, roundarm deliveries lost their effect with his disability, and he was to die the following year. This was 'Billy Bates's match'. The Yorkshireman, coming in at the fall of the seventh wicket at 199, dominated a stand of 88 with Read. Then, coming on as England's fifth bowler, he found a spot at the northern end which Giffen had used to perplex some of England's batsmen, and proceeded to decimate Australia. Massie and Bannerman had posted 56 for the first wicket – the former making 43 of them – and this was all but half the final total. The crescendo of Bates's success came as he bowled McDonnell, caught-and-bowled Giffen next ball, then bluffed Bonnor out for the hat-trick. By placing a short mid-on he persuaded the big hitter to poke timidly at his first ball, jabbing it for a catch to Read. Murdoch's unbeaten 19 occupied 2½ hours. In the follow-on only Bonnor showed any real resistance. His 34 contained three hits over the boundary, which then counted as only five runs. Bates's slow-medium roundarm bowling, breaking appreciably from the off, was again too much for the home batsmen. His 14 wickets linked with a half-century is a unique distinction in a Test match against Australia. For his hat-trick, admirers presented him with £31 and a tall hat made of silver.

35, below: *How a cartoonist saw Australia's pathetic batting procession.* 36, bottom, left: *Walter Read, the splendid Surrey amateur.* 37, right: *Billy Bates – a fifty, a hat-trick, and 14 wickets in the match*

1882–83 THIRD TEST
Sydney, January 26, 27, 29, 30

England *247 (W.W. Read 66, E.F.S. Tylecote 66, F.R. Spofforth 4 for 73) and 123 (F.R. Spofforth 7 for 44);* Australia *218 (A.C. Bannerman 94, G. Giffen 41, F. Morley 4 for 47) and 83 (R.G. Barlow 7 for 40).* England won by 69 runs.

A stand of 116 between Read and Tylecote saved the England innings when it stood at 75 for 5. By the end of the first day, which had attracted over 20,000 spectators, Australia, batting on a fresh pitch, by arrangement, to offset the advantage of the toss, were eight without loss. There was rain about during the night and on the second day, but Bannerman and Giffen raised 76 for the first wicket, and Australia were strongly set at 133 for one on Saturday evening. More rain on Sunday left the pitch treacherous, and but for poor English fielding Australia would not have made as many as 218. Resuming on the pitch they had used in their first innings, England did not expect– and did not make– many runs to add to their early advantage of 29. There was an inevitability about the play as Spofforth used the conditions as he pleased. Australia's target of 153 was distant in the circumstances, and receded from sight altogether as Barlow, the slow-medium left-arm bowler from Lancashire, keeping a full length, confounded the opposition, for whom Blackham top-scored with 26. Following England's triumph, some Melbourne ladies (one of whom became Bligh's bride) burnt a bail, sealed it in an urn, and presented it to the England captain. Lord Darnley (as he became), who died in 1927, bequeathed the Ashes to Lord's, where they now remain as an eternal symbol of England v Australia competition.

38, left: *The ill-fated Fred Morley, an early commuter casualty.* 39, above: *Edmund Fernando Sutton Tylecote, England wicketkeeper and joint saviour of the first innings*

1882–83 FOURTH TEST
Sydney, February 17, 19, 20, 21

England *263 (A.G. Steel 135*, C.T. Studd 48) and 197 (W. Bates 48*);* Australia *262 (G.J. Bonnor 87, J.McC. Blackham 57) and 199 for 6 (A.C. Bannerman 63, J.McC. Blackham 58*).* Australia won by 4 wickets.

Australia levelled the series in this additional match, though it was accepted that Bligh had already restored England's honour in the decisive third Test. Here, in a match where a fresh pitch was prepared *for each innings,* an evenly-contested game was won at the crucial stage by Bannerman's uncharacteristic flair and Blackham's determination. Steel's innings on the first day was in two distinct parts. Missed by Murdoch before he had scored, the Lancashire amateur moved unimpressively to his fifty, then revealed the polished batsmanship that had made his name. Bonnor's innings was hardly typical: he was unwell. But the runs were invaluable, as were Blackham's– this is a rare instance of two half-centuries in a match by a wicketkeeper.

40, left: *A.G. Steel – a 'curate's egg' of a century at Sydney.* 41, centre: *C.T. Studd – 48 here; a missed opportunity at The Oval six months earlier.* 42, right: *Jack Blackham – two half-centuries for Australia*

1884 FIRST TEST
Old Trafford, July 10, 11, 12

England 95 *(A. Shrewsbury 43, H.F. Boyle 6 for 42, F.R. Spofforth 4 for 42) and 180 for 9 (G.E. Palmer 4 for 47);* Australia *182.* Match drawn.

Manchester's first scheduled day of Test cricket was washed out, and in muddy conditions batsmen struggled thereafter. Shrewsbury gave a wonderful display of wet-wicket batsmanship against the feared partnership of Spofforth and bearded medium-pace spinner Boyle. Seven Australians made double-figures, with Midwinter, now playing against England once more, heading the innings with 37. On a drier pitch England had to exercise care in regaining the lead, and again the stylish Lucas batted with patience and fine judgment. Grace's 31 was of great value, but it was well into the final day before England were out of danger.

43, left: *Harry Boyle, excellent foil for Spofforth, and pioneer of the silly mid-on position.* 44, right: *A.P. Lucas, correct, elegant batsman, sometime opener, sometime in the middle order*

1884 SECOND TEST
Lord's, July 21, 22, 23

Australia *229 (H.J.H. Scott 75, G. Giffen 63, E. Peate 6 for 85) and 145 (G. Ulyett 7 for 36);* England *379 (A.G. Steel 148, G.E. Palmer 6 for 111).* England won by an innings and 5 runs.

Steel's century, made out of 261 while he batted, was a splendid innings, surpassing in quality of strokeplay his hundred at Sydney the previous year. When he went in, England were 90 for 3, and a long way from their eventual triumph. Spofforth bowled unluckily, and unwittingly aided England in cutting up the pitch with his spikes. Ulyett brought the ball back sharply off the rough area, and sank Australia in their second innings. His dismissal of Bonnor was notable: he clung to a ferocious straight drive in his followthrough. Australia's first innings owed much to a last-wicket stand of 69 between Scott and Boyle. The former was caught by his own captain, Murdoch, fielding as substitute for Grace, whose finger was injured.

45, left: *Dr H.J.H. 'Tup' Scott, who was to lead Australia in England in 1886.* 46, right: *Ted Peate, one of the long line of clever slow left-arm bowlers from Yorkshire*

1884 THIRD TEST
The Oval, August 11, 12, 13

Australia *551 (W.L. Murdoch 211, P.S. McDonnell 103, H.J.H. Scott 102, A. Lyttelton 4 for 19);* England *346 (W.W. Read 117, W.H. Scotton 90, G.E. Palmer 4 for 90) and 85 for 2.* Match drawn.

Australia's innings, in hot conditions and with a fast pitch and outfield, was spread over 9½ hours, and Murdoch was in for over eight hours for the first double-century in Test cricket. McDonnell, in contrast, having opened the innings, was out with the total 158, a stand of 143 for the second wicket. Murdoch added 207 for the third with Scott in even time, Australia ending the first day at 363 for 2. By the end of the mammoth innings all eleven England players had bowled, the Hon. Alfred Lyttelton, the wicket-keeper, taking four cheap wickets with underarm lobs. By mid-afternoon on the final day England were 181 for 8, but Read, seething at having to bat at number 10, struck a furious century in just under two hours and added 151 with the somnolent left-hander Scotton, who had opened the innings. This is now the oldest partnership record in England-Australia Tests. Scotton's 90 took 340 minutes and inspired some satirical verse in *Punch.* The follow-on was enforced as a matter of routine. The Ashes remained in England's custody.

47, below, left: *Hon. Alfred Lyttelton, 'keeper-bowler.* 48, centre: *William Scotton, dour left-hander.* 49, right: *Billy Murdoch, first double-centurion*

1884–85 FIRST TEST

Adelaide, December 12, 13, 15, 16

Australia *243 (P.S. McDonnell 124, J. McC. Blackham 66, W. Bates 5 for 31) and 191 (P.S. McDonnell 83, G. Giffen 47, R. Peel 5 for 51);* England *369 (W. Barnes 134, W.H. Scotton 82, G. Ulyett 68, G.E. Palmer 5 for 81) and 67 for 2.* England won by 8 wickets.

The first five-Test series was closely fought, though Australia, rent by internal disputes, were under full strength. McDonnell's second Test century in succession was made in typically robust manner, and he might have repeated the performance in the second innings but for Giffen's refusal to respond to his call for a single. Australia were 190 for 3 at one point, but fell away before Bates's bowling. England were 232 for 2 at the close of the second day – a day of dust-storms. Barnes's innings lasted five hours, and Scotton's 5¾. Peel's slow-medium left-arm bowling tore the heart out of Australia's second innings – from which Alec Bannerman was missing because of a hand injury sustained in fielding a lusty hit by Ulyett.

50, left: *Bobby Peel, in the first of his 20 Tests against Australia, took eight wickets.* 51, right: *Billy Barnes, the Notts all-rounder*

1884–85 SECOND TEST

Melbourne, January 1, 2, 3, 5

England *401 (J. Briggs 121, A. Shrewsbury 72, W. Barnes 58, S.P. Jones 4 for 47) and 7 for 0;* Australia *279 (A.H. Jarvis 82, T.P. Horan 63, J.W. Trumble 59) and 126 (W. Bruce 45, W. Barnes 6 for 31).* England won by 10 wickets.

Australia, with nine new caps pressed into service, contained England reasonably well – apart from Shrewsbury's virile innings – until the later stages of the innings, when Briggs batted with increasing confidence. His 121 took only 2½ hours and included 15 fours: he was missed twice towards the end. His stand of 98 with wicketkeeper Joe Hunter (39 not out) disheartened the home side. The efforts of Horan, Trumble and Jarvis almost saved the follow-on, but a fine catch at mid-on by Briggs at a crucial time helped end the innings. Bruce, who went in second-last, opened the second innings and was the only Australian to withstand Peel and the fast-medium Barnes for any length of time.

52, left: *Johnny Briggs, the little Lancashire left-hander, who excelled himself with the bat at Melbourne.* 53, right: *'Affie' Jarvis, from South Australia: 82 in his first Test innings*

1884–85 THIRD TEST

Sydney, February 20, 21, 23, 24

Australia *181 (T.W. Garrett 51*, W. Flowers 5 for 46, W. Attewell 4 for 53) and 165 (W. Bates 5 for 24);* England *133 (T.P. Horan 6 for 40, F.R. Spofforth 4 for 54) and 207 (W. Flowers 56, J.M. Read 56, F.R. Spofforth 6 for 90).* Australia won by 6 runs.

A brilliant catch by Edwin Evans at point, to dismiss England's most successful batsman in the match, Wilfred Flowers, off Spofforth, gave Australia a thrilling victory and brought them back into the series. Flowers and Read had taken England to the brink of victory with a seventh-wicket stand of 102, but the last four wickets fell for 13 runs. Australia's opening innings had been saved by a last-wicket stand of 80 by Garrett and Evans after a lunchtime hailstorm had turned the ground into a great white expanse. England, batting on a fresh pitch, found Horan too difficult as he exploited a responsive patch where Spofforth's foot had come down. Smart fielding and catching kept England in contention, but in their quest for the required 214 runs, the turning point came with the glorious ball with which Spofforth bowled Shrewsbury, England's captain.

54, above, left: *William Attewell, steadiest of fast-medium bowlers.* 55, centre: *J.M.(Maurice) Read, all-rounder from Surrey.* 56, right: *Wilfred Flowers – wickets, runs, and in at the death at Sydney*

1884–85 FOURTH TEST

Sydney, March 14, 16, 17

England *269 (W. Bates 64, W. Barnes 50, J.M. Read 47, A. Shrewsbury 40, G. Giffen 7 for 117) and 77 (F.R. Spofforth 5 for 30, G.E. Palmer 4 for 32);* Australia *309 (G.J. Bonnor 128, A.C. Bannerman 51, S.P. Jones 40, W. Barnes 4 for 61) and 40 for 2.* Australia won by 8 wickets.

Bonnor's innings was magnificent. Starting uncertainly, he then began to employ his peerless power, sometimes trusting to luck, and in just under two hours he made 128 out of 169. When he entered, Australia were 119 for 6 – still 150 behind. He was missed at slip from the stroke that brought him his century – his only one in Tests – but in conditions which favoured the bowlers, his was an extraordinary innings. England batted a second time on the pitch used by Australia, but it broke up, and they were helpless against Palmer and Spofforth, who bowled unchanged. The home side then decided to use England's first-innings pitch, and squared the series.

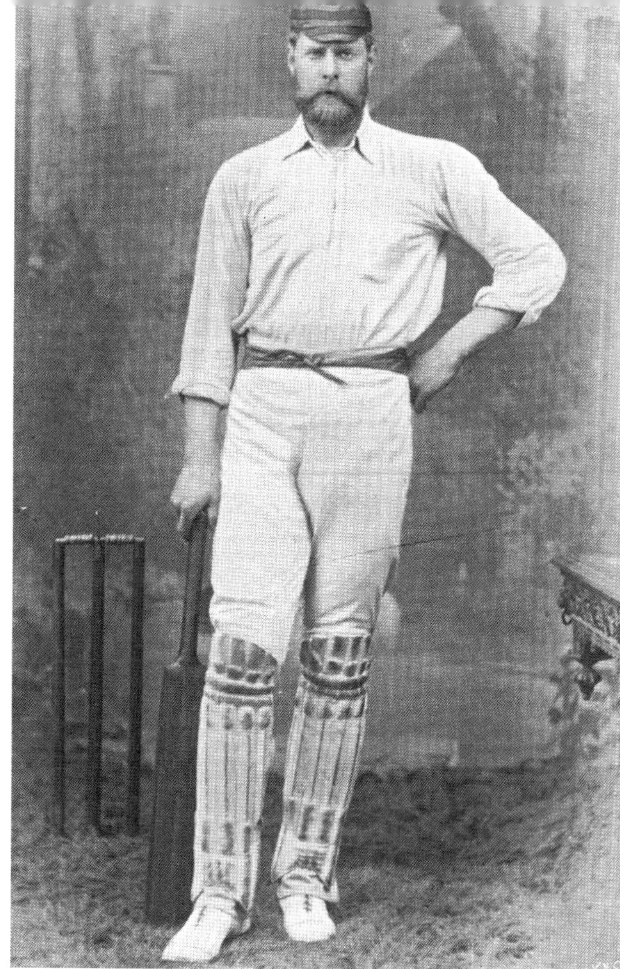

57, left: *Bonnor, the giant, whose only Test century was made in better than even-time.* 58, above: *Sammy Jones, who stayed with him while 154 runs were added*

1884–85 FIFTH TEST
Melbourne, March 21, 23, 24, 25

Australia *163 (F.R. Spofforth 50, G. Ulyett 4 for 52) and 125;* England *386 (A. Shrewsbury 105*, W. Barnes 74, W. Bates 61, J. Briggs 43).* England won by an innings and 98 runs.

The pitch was still damp from heavy watering, and Peel, Ulyett and Barnes took the first nine Australian wickets for 99. Then last man Spofforth, with some exotic strokes, put on 64 with J.W. Trumble (34 not out). Nevertheless, England were 44 without loss that evening, and progressed steadily to a commanding lead. Shrewsbury's century, the first by an England captain, was scored at the rate of 19 an hour, but contained many sweet pulls to rising off-side balls. Bates's contribution was valuable, though he was dropped several times, and retired unwell at one stage. Again Australia began disastrously, and never recovered, Ulyett, Flowers and Attewell taking three wickets apiece as England went on to retain the Ashes. One of the home players, Garrett, took the place of umpire Hodges when he refused to continue after tea on the third day. Hodges was protesting at the complaints by some of the Englishmen at some of his decisions.

59, left: *Arthur Shrewsbury, the premier professional batsman in England in the 1880s.* 60, right: *Billy Bruce, who top-scored with 35 in Australia's second innings*

1886
Old Trafford, July 5, 6, 7

Australia 205 *(S.P. Jones 87, A.H. Jarvis 45, G. Ulyett 4 for 46) and 123 (H.J.H. Scott 47, R.G. Barlow 7 for 44);* England 223 *(W.W. Read 51, F.R. Spofforth 4 for 82) and 107 for* 6. England won by 4 wickets.

Australia, again under strength – without Murdoch, Horan, McDonnell, Bannerman and Massie – and unsettled by camp squabbles, had a disastrous series. With Jones and Jarvis at the wicket, the score had reached 134 for 2, but the innings then fell away. England, with Spofforth bowling almost at his fastest, were made to fight for the lead, but Australia went to pieces again in the second innings. They saw a glimmer of hope when Grace, Shrewsbury and Read were dismissed cheaply, but Barlow's dourness made sure that his bowling success was not wasted.

GRAND CRICKET MATCH
ENGLAND-V-AUSTRALIA

Played on the County Ground, Old Trafford, July 5th, 6th, and 7th, 1886.

	AUSTRALIANS.	1st Innings.		2nd Innings	
1	Mr. S. P. Jones	lbw b Grace	87	c Ulyett b Steel	12
2	Mr. H. J. H. Scott	c Barlow b Ulyett	21	b Barlow	47
3	Mr. G. Giffen	b Steel	3	c Shrewsbury b Barlow	1
4	Mr. A. H. Jarvis	c Scotton b Ulyett	45	c Lohmann b Barlow	2
5	Mr. G. J. Bonnor	c Lohmann b Barlow	4	c Barlow b Peate	2
6	Mr. J. W. Trumble	c Scotton b Steel	24	c Ulyett b Barlow	4
8	Mr. W. Bruce	run out	2	c Grace b Barlow	0
9	Mr. T. W. Garrett	c Pilling b Lohmann	5	c Grace b Ulyett	22
7	Mr. J. McC. Blackham	not out	7	lbw b Barlow	2
10	Mr. G. E. Palmer	c Lohmann b Ulyett	4	c Pilling b Barlow	8
11	Mr. F. R. Spofforth	c Barlow b Ulyett	2	not out	20
		Wds 1 bys lb nb	1	Wds. bys 3 lb nb	3
	Fall of the Wickets.	Total	205	Total	123

1	2	3	4	5	6	7	8	9	10	1	2	3	4	5	6	7	8	9	10
58	71	134	141	181	187	188	192	201	205	37	42	44	55	68	70	70	73	103	123

ANALYSIS of the BOWLING. 1st Innings. 2nd Innings.

	Overs.	Mdns.	Runs.	Wkts.	Wd.	Overs.	Mdns.	Runs.	Wkts.
Peate	19	7	30	0	..	46	25	45	1
Lohmann	23	9	41	1	..	5	3	14	0
Steel	27	5	47	2	..	8	3	9	1
Ulyett	36·1	20	46	4	1	6·3	5	7	1
Barlow	23	15	19	1	..	52	34	44	7
Grace	9	3	21	1	.	1	0	1	0

	ENGLAND.	1st Innings.		2nd Innings.	
1	Mr. W. G. Grace	c Bonnor b Spofforth	8	c Palmer b Giffen	4
2	W. Scotton	c Trumble b Garrett	21	b Palmer	20
3	A. Shrewsbury	b Spofforth	31	c and b Giffen	4
4	Mr. W. W. Read	c Scott b Garrett	51	c Jones b Spofforth	9
6	Mr. A. G. Steel	c Jarvis b Palmer	12	not out	19
5	R. G. Barlow	not out	38	c Palmer b Spofforth	30
7	G. Ulyett	b Spofforth	17	c Scott b Spofforth	8
8	J. Briggs	c Garrett b Spofforth	1	not out	2
9	G. Lohmann	b Giffen	32		
10	E. Peate	st Jarvis b Palmer	6		
11	R. Pilling	c Bruce b Palmer	2		
		Wds bys 2 lb 2 nb	4	Wds bys 10 lb 1 nb	11
	Fall of the Wickets.	Total	223	Total	107

1	2	3	4	5	6	7	8	9	10	1	2	3	4	5	6	7	8	9	10
9	51	80	109	131	156	160	206	219	223	7	15	24	65	90	105	..	..	..	..

ANALYSIS of the BOWLING. 1st Innings. 2nd Innings.

	Overs	Mdns	Runs	Wkts	Overs	Mdns	Runs	Wkts.	Wd
Spofforth	53	22	82	4	29·2	13	40	2	..
Giffen	32	15	44	1	24	9	31	2	..
Garrett	45	23	43	2	17	9	14	1	..
Bruce	10	7	9	0	..	..	..	..	..
Palmer	17·2	4	41	3	7	3	11	1	..

Umpires:—Messrs. West and Pullen

Test Match
England-v-Australia 1886
Presented to RGBarlow for his very fine Batting & Bowling

61, above, left: *Dick Barlow, the Lancashire all-rounder, who made 38 not out and 30 and took 7 for 44.* 62, above, right: *A silk scorecard of the match, presented to Barlow.* 63, right: *Dick Pilling, also of Lancashire, who kept wicket for England on his home ground*

1886 SECOND TEST

Lord's, July 19, 20, 21

England *353 (A. Shrewsbury 164, W. Barnes 58, F.R. Spofforth 4 for 73);* Australia *121 (J. Briggs 5 for 29) and 126 (G.E. Palmer 48, J. Briggs 6 for 45).* England won by an innings and 106 runs.

Shrewsbury's was one of the most praiseworthy innings in the history of the game. Rain soon after the start left the pitch ideal for bowling, and Shrewsbury's skill against the skidding ball, the kicking ball, the sharp turner, and the one that stops was put to the ultimate test, and with the aid of three difficult chances he survived for almost seven hours. At the end of the first day he was 91 and England miraculously had made 202 for the loss of Grace, Scotton, W.W. Read and Steel. The Shrewsbury-Barnes stand eventually realised 161. That evening Australia were 12 for one in the follow-on – still 220 behind – after Briggs had demolished them with his slow-medium left-arm bowling. He was even more successful on the last day, bowling from the pavilion end. Palmer, who opened, stayed 2½ hours, shaming some of his team-mates.

64, above: *An interpretation of the match, with Lord's still looking more rural than metropolitan.* 65, left: *Shrewsbury, an exceptionally skilful defensive player.* 66, right: *Briggs – his bowling and Shrewsbury's batting gave England a handsome victory at Lord's*

1886 THIRD TEST
The Oval, August 12, 13, 14

England *434 (W.G. Grace 170, W.W. Read 94, J. Briggs 53, A. Shrewsbury 44, F.R. Spofforth 4 for 65)*; Australia *68 (G.A. Lohmann 7 for 36) and 149 (G. Giffen 47, G.A. Lohmann 5 for 68)*. England won by an innings and 217 runs.

The weather dealt cruelly with the disappointed and disappointing Australians. After England's heavy innings, rain fell and assisted England's clever pair, Lohmann and Briggs, who bowled unchanged through Australia's first innings. Giffen, making runs at last after a poor series, saved his side from complete humiliation. Grace's 170 was made out of only 216 scored while he was in. His opening partner Scotton had taken 3¾ hours for 34, and the 19 posted in the first hour's play might have been less unexpected in a modern Test match. The first-wicket stand – 170 – was the highest so far for any England wicket, and Grace's was the best individual score for England to date. It took him 4½ hours and included 22 boundaries, one a huge drive off Spofforth into the crowd.

67, above: *Another of the earliest 'location' photographs – the Oval Test 1886. The batsman appears to be marking his guard.* 68, left: *Dr W.G. Grace, whose 170 added just one more to his numerous records.* 69, right: *George Lohmann, taker of 77 wickets in only 15 Tests against Australia*

1886–87 FIRST TEST
Sydney, January 28, 29, 31

England *45 (C.T.B. Turner 6 for 15, J.J. Ferris 4 for 27) and 184 (J.J. Ferris 5 for 76);* Australia *119 and 97 (W. Barnes 6 for 28).* England won by 13 runs.

McDonnell put England in and had the pleasure of seeing them humbled by a pair of new bowlers, 'Terror' Turner, right-arm, fast-medium off-break, and Ferris, left-arm fast-medium. Often taking advantage of each others' 'footprints' at the other end, they became a feared and almost incredibly successful partnership. Bowling unchanged, and with the help of some superb catches – two by Spofforth – they reduced the tourists to a score which is still England's lowest in Test cricket. Lohmann (17) alone reached double-figures. Australia were ahead with only two men out, but wickets fell steadily and the lead was confined to 74. This was absorbed before England's second wicket fell, but there was a mid-innings collapse, and England owed much to the last three wickets, which added 81. Well controlled by Shrewsbury, England somehow prevented Australia from reaching their target of 111 (which took on an ominous ring in the 1950s). Barnes bowled 46 four-ball overs, of which 29 were maidens. This match and the next were poorly promoted and attended.

70, left: *The only known action picture of Charlie 'Terror' Turner.* 71, centre: *Turner in Australian cap.* 72, right: *Jack Ferris, his partner in destruction*

1886–87 SECOND TEST
Sydney, February 25, 26, 28, March 1

England *151 (C.T.B. Turner 5 for 41, J.J. Ferris 5 for 71) and 154 (R.G. Barlow 42*, C.T.B. Turner 4 for 52, J.J. Ferris 4 for 69);* Australia *84 (G.A. Lohmann 8 for 35) and 150 (W. Bates 4 for 26).* England won by 71 runs.

Several names were missing, including that of Spofforth, who had thus played his final Test, and Barnes, the Notts all-rounder, who had damaged his hand in throwing a punch at McDonnell; he hit a wall instead. The best stand of England's first innings was 57 by Barlow and Flowers for the eighth wicket, Turner and Ferris again carrying all before them. The genius of Lohmann, of Surrey, overcame Australia, for whom Moses top-scored with 28, and Barlow set about stretching England's lead: coming in at number three, he stayed over three hours. Bates made a robust 30. McDonnell, Allen and Moses (who once hit Lohmann over the fence) all reached the thirties, but it would have been expecting too much for Australia to have attained what would have been by some way the highest score of the match. This was England's sixth victory in as many Tests.

73, above: *Harry Moses, a fine left-hander who favoured the leg glance, top-scored with 28 in the first innings, and only McDonnell exceeded his 33 in the second.* 74, right: *Mordecai Sherwin, the massive wicketkeeper, who made four dismissals in Australia's second innings*

1887–88 ONLY TEST

Sydney, February 10, 11, 13, 14, 15

England *113 (A. Shrewsbury 44, C.T.B. Turner 5 for 44, J.J. Ferris 4 for 60) and 137 (C.T.B. Turner 7 for 43);* Australia *42 (G.A. Lohmann 5 for 17, R. Peel 5 for 18) and 82 (R. Peel 4 for 40, G.A. Lohmann 4 for 35).* England won by 126 runs.

Lillywhite, Shaw and Shrewsbury's third touring team joined forces with another English side taken to Australia by Lord Hawke to play what can only be considered in somewhat loose terms as a Test match. At least one other contest during the season was played between respective sides of greater strength. On a rain-ruined wicket only Shrewsbury could cope with Turner and Ferris: the latter often spun the ball across to slip, and Blackham's task behind the stumps often bordered upon the impossible. In an hour before the close of the first day Australia lost eight for 35. Their final 42 remains their second-lowest ever in Tests. J.M. Read enjoyed the greatest luck in England's second innings on a pitch still extremely difficult. Hitting boldly, he made 39 on the fourth day after the second and third were washed out. That evening, Australia, needing 209, were 47 for 5.

75: *In 1887–88 two English teams toured Australia. This is Lillywhite's party: standing – G. Brann, L.C. Docker, James Lillywhite, J.M. Read, A.D. Pougher; seated – G. Ulyett, R. Pilling, C.A. Smith (captain), A. Shrewsbury, G.A. Lohmann; in front – J.M. Preston, J. Briggs, W. Newham*

76: *The other English team in Australia in 1887–88: standing – G.F. Vernon, J.T. Rawlin, T.C. O'Brien, J. Beaumont; seated – A.E. Newton, R. Peel, Lord Hawke (captain), W. Bates, W.W. Read; in front – R. Abel, W. Attewell, A.E. Stoddart. Four of this side joined with seven of the other to play in the Test match, with Walter Read as captain.*

1888 FIRST TEST

Lord's, July 16, 17

Australia *116 (R. Peel 4 for 36) and 60 (R. Peel 4 for 14, G.A. Lohmann 4 for 33);* England *53 (C.T.B. Turner 5 for 27) and 62 (J.J. Ferris 5 for 26, C.T.B. Turner 5 for 36).* Australia won by 61 runs.

Of the ten innings in this three-Test series, seven were completed for 100 or less. Australia began with a long-awaited victory, but their satisfaction was short-lived. The pitch at Lord's was muddy, and despite a dropped catch or two England soon had the visitors on their knees. The biggest stand was for the last wicket – 34 by Edwards and Ferris. The pitch grew even worse, and England actually came close to following on (the margin was then only 80 runs), being 26 for 7. Briggs's 17 and Grace's 10 were the highest scores. Australia, with a lead of 63, then collapsed to 18 for 7 before Ferris heaved 20 not out. England's target of 124 was always distant, and ostensibly disappeared with the dismissal of Grace, who made an admirable 24. More licence in the batting might just have brought off an odds-against victory.

77, below, left: *The 1888 Australians: standing – J.J. Ferris, A.H. Jarvis, J. Worrall, C.W. Beal (manager), J.McC. Blackham, H.F. Boyle, J.D. Edwards; seated – G.J. Bonnor, C.T.B. Turner, P.S. McDonnell (captain), G.H.S. Trott, A.C. Bannerman. S.M.J. Woods played instead of Boyle at Lord's and The Oval.*
78, right: *Blackham, the great wicketkeeper*

79: *Returning batsman's view of the Lord's pavilion assembly. An 1888 impression*

1888 — SECOND TEST

The Oval, August 13, 14

Australia *80 (J. Briggs 5 for 25) and 100 (W. Barnes 5 for 32, R. Peel 4 for 49);* England *317 (R. Abel 70, W. Barnes 62, G.A. Lohmann 62*, C.T.B. Turner 6 for 112).* England won by an innings and 137 runs.

There was little wrong with the wicket as Australia plunged to 50 for 7 by lunch. Bannerman's 13 lasted 100 minutes, and ended with an amazing full-stretch slip catch by Lohmann, who had already caught McDonnell at the start with a low, left-handed catch. Abel and Barnes arrested an early England slide by adding 112 for the fifth wicket, and Lohmann, at number 10, hit hard and cleanly. McDonnell made 32 of Australia's first 34, and Alec Bannerman dropped anchor this time for 75 minutes for five runs. Australia's performance was a great disappointment since the pitch presented no problems. Five Surrey men represented England.

80, left: *Bobby Abel, England's small, tenacious opener.* 81, right: *His 'opposite number', Alec Bannerman, from Sydney*

1888 — THIRD TEST

Old Trafford, August 30, 31

England *172 (C.T.B. Turner 5 for 86);* Australia *81 (R. Peel 7 for 31) and 70 (R. Peel 4 for 37).* England won by an innings and 21 runs.

Grace top-scored for England with a freely-struck 38, which included a hit off Turner over the sightscreen and ended with an astonishing catch by Bonnor at long-on: the fieldsman, when seemingly unable to reach the ball, thrust out a hand and the catch stuck. The pitch was dead after recent rains, and was kept so with occasional showers. 32 for 2 overnight, Australia had the misfortune to bat on a pitch now sticky under a hot sun. Lyons top-scored with 22, and seemed certain to save the follow-on, but he became one of Peel's 11 victims in the match, and Australia had to go in again. Their start was appalling: 0 for 1, 0 for 2, 1 for 3, 7 for 4, 7 for 5, 7 for 6. Turner (26) and Lyons (32) then added 48, but Peel, Lohmann and Briggs bowled England to an innings victory shortly before lunch on the second day, making this the shortest Test match of all time.

82, left: *Jack Lyons, the strong and willing South Australian opener.* 83, right: *Sammy Woods, Australian-born, residing in England, was called up by the 1888 touring team*

1890 — FIRST TEST
Lord's, July 21, 22, 23

Australia *132 (J.J. Lyons 55, W. Attewell 4 for 42) and 176 (J.E. Barrett 67*);* England *173 (G. Ulyett 74, J.J. Lyons 5 for 30) and 137 for 3 (W.G. Grace 75*).* England won by 7 wickets.

Lyons gave the match a frantic start with 55 in 45 minutes, but Australia failed to capitalise. The last seven wickets fell for 23 runs. England's innings also began sensationally: Grace was caught-and-bowled by Turner second ball for a duck. At 20 for 4, they were saved by J.M. Read and Ulyett, who added 72. Lyons, medium-pace, got them both out, and restricted England to a narrow lead. Australia's second innings was built around Barrett, a left-hander, who carried his bat through the innings in his first Test. Lyons continued to imprint his personality on the match with a swift 33, but Grace steered England to victory in favourable conditions, though dropped at 44. No byes were conceded throughout the match, which marked the return of Murdoch as Australia's leader.

84: *Quick sketches of events during the final day's play. The new Lord's pavilion had recently been opened*

85, left: *Dr John Barrett, who carried his bat through the Australian innings.* 86, right: *'WG' – his very presence in the England XI was worth two men*

1890 — SECOND TEST

The Oval, August 11, 12

Australia *92 (F. Martin 6 for 50) and 102 (F. Martin 6 for 52);* England *100 (J.J. Ferris 4 for 25) and 95 for 8 (J.J. Ferris 5 for 49).* England won by 2 wickets.

Three players – Stoddart, Peel and Ulyett – chose to play for their counties rather than for England. The other oddity was that 'Nutty' Martin, Kent left-arm fast bowler, was brought in for what was to be his only Test, apart from an appearance in South Africa a year later. His 12 for 102 was a remarkable debut performance. On the opening day 22 wickets fell for 197 runs. Preceding rain was the underlying cause. Harry Trott's 39 was easily Australia's top score, and William Gunn made 32 for England in 1¾ hours. Australia were 54 for 7 after Lyons had made a forceful 21; then Trott and Charlton put on 36, and England were left with the exciting prospect of making 95 for victory on a still-difficult pitch. Grace almost suffered a 'king pair', Trott putting him down at point. Even so, England were soon floundering at 32 for 4. J.M. Read (35) and Cranston (15) then added 51 in even time, but Turner trapped them with successive balls. Lohmann went at 86, Barnes at 93. Sharpe played at Ferris for an entire over without connecting; a single was run; three maidens passed; then Sharpe and MacGregor were stranded in mid-pitch attempting a run, but Barrett threw wide and the winning run was scampered.

A third Test, scheduled at Old Trafford for August 25, 26, 27, was completely washed out.

87, below, left: *Gregor MacGregor, England's Scots-born wicketkeeper, whose gloves offered little by way of protection.* 88, centre: *Frank Martin – 12 for 102 in his only Test against Australia.* 89, right: *Harry Trott, top-scorer in both Australian innings with 39 and 25*

1891–92 FIRST TEST

Melbourne, January 1, 2, 4, 5, 6

Australia 240 *(W. Bruce 57, A.C. Bannerman 45, J.W. Sharpe 6 for 84) and 236 (J.J. Lyons 51, A.C. Bannerman 41, W. Bruce 40)*; England 264 *(W.G. Grace 50, G. Bean 50, J. Briggs 41, R.W. McLeod 5 for 53) and 158 (C.T.B. Turner 5 for 51)*. Australia won by 54 runs.

The English side, which went to Australia under Lord Sheffield's auspices, was led by W.G. Grace, whose only other tour of Australia was 18 years before. Bruce and Bannerman put on an important 87 for Australia's third wicket, but the innings was kept in check by Sharpe and Peel, who bore the brunt of the bowling duties. Grace and Abel began with 84 in reply, but McLeod then got them both and Stoddart in 12 balls. Bean, J.M. Read and Briggs fought England into a narrow lead which Lyons soon wiped away with characteristic power. Grace and Stoddart began with 60, but Australia's varied bowling, following some very determined batting, won a welcome victory.

90, left: *Billy Bruce, Victorian left-hander.* 91, centre: *George Bean, Sussex all-rounder, formerly with Notts.* 92, right: *Bob McLeod, one of a talented Melbourne brotherhood.* 93, below: *Lord Sheffield's team pictured upon their return to England: standing – R. Carpenter (umpire), W. Attewell, G.A. Lohmann, J.M. Read, G. Bean, J.W. Sharpe, R.A. Thoms (umpire); seated – J. Briggs, G. MacGregor, W.G. Grace, R. Peel, A.E. Stoddart, R. Abel*

1891–92 SECOND TEST

Sydney, January 29, 30, February 1, 2, 3

Australia *144 (J.J. Lyons 41, G.A. Lohmann 8 for 58) and 391 (J.J. Lyons 134, A.C. Bannerman 91, W. Bruce 72, G. Giffen 49, J. Briggs 4 for 69);* England *307 (R. Abel 132*, G. Giffen 4 for 88) and 156 (A.E. Stoddart 69, G. Giffen 6 for 72, C.T.B. Turner 4 for 46).* Australia won by 72 runs.

By the end of the second day Australia seemed in a hopeless position. They had failed miserably after Lyons's robust opening, and England, in the small figure of Abel, had piled up a lead of 163. That evening Trott was lost, and it was known that Moses' leg injury would prevent him from batting. Grace fell out of favour with the crowd for refusing Moses either a runner in the first innings or a substitute in the field (until late in the match) because Blackham knew of the injury before the start. The match was turned in a stand of 174 by the contrasting Lyons and Bannerman, the former batting for 2¾ hours, the latter for 7½ (12 runs per hour) during which he was at the crease on three separate days and hit a mere three boundaries. Lyons was missed twice at slip by Abel when 49. Briggs finished the innings with a hat-trick, and England needed 229. That night they were 11 for 3. Rain had fallen, but the pitch rolled out well, and Grace was condemned for not sending in nightwatchmen. Stoddart alone batted with assurance, hitting Turner for a second time into the crowd. Australia thus deservedly won the series, and Lohmann's grand effort and Abel's feat of carrying his bat through the innings were to no avail.

94, left: *George Giffen with G.E. Palmer.* 95, above: *Bobby Abel – carried his bat.* 96, below: *George Lohmann – 8 for 58.* 97, right: *Murdoch, Spofforth, Boyle, and A.C. Bannerman*

1891–92 THIRD TEST

Adelaide, March 24, 25, 26, 28

England *499 (A.E. Stoddart 134, R. Peel 83, W.G. Grace 58, J.M. Read 57, W. Attewell 43*);* Australia *100 (J. Briggs 6 for 49) and 169 (J. Briggs 6 for 87).* England won by an innings and 230 runs.

A classic case of victory going with the winning of the toss. England made the most of a good pitch, but rain on the second day turned it into a juicy strip full of good things for bowlers. Briggs often bowled the unplayable ball, and ran through Australia the first time unchanged with Lohmann. Attewell took three wickets in the follow-on. Grace again did little for his popularity by insisting on quarter-hourly inspections of the pitch during the rain interruptions. Stoddart's century was punctuated by several misses, and also some mighty hits. He batted just under four hours.

98, left: *A.E. 'Drewy' Stoddart, whose century set up England's victory at Adelaide.* 99, right: *Bobby Peel, who excelled with the bat this time*

1893 FIRST TEST

Lord's, July 17, 18, 19

England *334 (A. Shrewsbury 106, F.S. Jackson 91, C.T.B. Turner 6 for 67) and 234 for 8 dec (A. Shrewsbury 81, W. Gunn 77, G. Giffen 5 for 43);* Australia *269 (H. Graham 107, S.E. Gregory 57, W.H. Lockwood 6 for 101).* Match drawn.

Shrewsbury, beginning cautiously on a rain-affected pitch, and Jackson, who batted gloriously on his debut, added 137 for the third wicket, and England's 334 was achieved before close of play. Jackson drove and pulled with masterful ease. Shrewsbury became the first batsman to reach 1000 Test runs. That evening Lockwood bowled Lyons and Giffen, and went on to take the next three wickets the following day before being rested after a stoical spell of almost two hours. Soon he was called up again, and eventually broke the saving partnership of Gregory and Graham, which realised 142 in only 100 minutes. This was 'Tich' Gregory's first substantial innings in a Test career which was to span 22 years. Graham, missed three times, batted for 140 minutes in his maiden Test innings – the first century for Australia at Lord's. Shrewsbury and Gunn scored 152 for England's second wicket, and though wickets tumbled thereafter, the lead was formidable when rain came. In mid-afternoon, Stoddart (captaining England this match in Grace's absence) made the first declaration in Test matches, but the drizzle returned.

100, below, left: *The Hon. F.S. Jackson, immaculate all-rounder for Cambridge, Yorkshire, and England.* 101, centre: *William Gunn, partner to Shrewsbury for county and country.* 102, right: *Harry Graham – century on Test debut*

103: *Lord Sheffield's greeting in fireworks at Sheffield Park to Blackham's 1893 Australians*

1893 SECOND TEST
The Oval, August 14, 15, 16

England *483 (F.S. Jackson 103, A.E. Stoddart 83, W.G. Grace 68, A. Shrewsbury 66, A. Ward 55, W.W. Read 52, G. Giffen 7 for 128);* Australia *91 (J. Briggs 5 for 34, W.H. Lockwood 4 for 37) and 349 (G.H.S. Trott 92, A.C. Bannerman 55, G. Giffen 53, H. Graham 42, J. Briggs 5 for 114, W.H. Lockwood 4 for 96).* England won by an innings and 43 runs.

England's strong XI took command from the start, though Stoddart had much luck in his opening stand of 151 with Grace. The score at the end of the first, hot day was 378 for 5. Jackson batted on next day with power and poise to be 98 when last man Mold joined him. Run-outs were narrowly avoided, Jackson drove Giffen high onto the pavilion stand to reach his century, and soon his reckless partner did run him out. The tired Australians were without an answer to Lockwood and Briggs, and followed on 392 behind. Bannerman and Bruce began with 54, and Trott and Graham added 106 for the fifth wicket, raising their side's hopes of escape. But with Trott caught at mid-on Australia's tail offered little resistance, though Lyons made a few thunderous hits. England had had to work for the victory which was to regain them the Ashes.

104, below, left: *Bill Lockwood, a top-class all-rounder, whose fast bowling had much to do with England's supremacy in the 1893 series.* 105, right: *The Vauxhall end at The Oval as seen from the Press box during the Test match of 1893*

1893 THIRD TEST
Old Trafford, August 24, 25, 26

Australia *204 (W. Bruce 68, T. Richardson 5 for 49, J. Briggs 4 for 81) and 236 (A.C. Bannerman 60, T. Richardson 5 for 107);* England *243 (W. Gunn 102*, W.G. Grace 40, G. Giffen 4 for 113) and 118 for 4 (W.G. Grace 45, A.E. Stoddart 42).* Match drawn.

Jackson and Peel were absent – playing instead for Yorkshire – and Lockwood, with a strained side, was replaced by Surrey team-mate Richardson, who took ten wickets upon debut. Bruce, hitting well to leg, made his 68 in 100 minutes, but the next-highest score was only 35, from Trumble. As Gunn began to run out of partners, he went after the bowling – with some elegance. His century took just over four hours, and his second 50 was twice as fast as the first. Bannerman was, as so often, the anchor-man as Australia fought for a sizable lead. His 60 – his final Test innings – took 205 minutes. Turner and Blackham, in a last-wicket stand of 36, cheated England of a run-a-minute chase, and after Grace and Stoddart had 70 up in 78 minutes, England were content to play out time for their fifth home series victory running.

106, below, left: *Moments and musings during the Manchester Test.* 107, right: *Tom Richardson, the lion-hearted Surrey fast bowler, who took 10 wickets in his first Test.* 108, bottom, right: *Albert Ward, whose modest start in 1893 preceded greater deeds*

Grace after a four
Umpires on duty
Giffen hits out at Briggs
Bails off again
Grace & Briggs argue a point
Briggs at coverpoint
Australians in – sketch from the Press Box
How's that?
Bannerman out.
Read catches Bruce
Bruce batting
Trott caught by Grace

1894–95 FIRST TEST

Sydney, December 14, 15, 17, 18, 19, 20

Australia *586 (S.E. Gregory 201, G. Giffen 161, F.A. Iredale 81, J.McC. Blackham 74, T. Richardson 5 for 181) and 166 (J. Darling 53, G. Giffen 41, R. Peel 6 for 67)*; England *325 (A. Ward 75, J. Briggs 57, W. Brockwell 49, G. Giffen 4 for 75) and 437 (A. Ward 117, J.T. Brown 53, F.G.J. Ford 48, J. Briggs 42, G. Giffen 4 for 164).* England won by 10 runs.

An enthralling series began with one of the strangest turnabouts of all time. Following on, England made enough a second time to place unanticipated pressure on Australia in the fourth innings after overnight rain had converted the pitch into a quagmire. Australia had started the match badly, three men being bowled by fast bowler Richardson while 21 runs were scored. Giffen added 171 with Iredale and 139 with Gregory, who registered Test cricket's second double-century in only 244 minutes. The run quest reached a peak with Gregory and Blackham together: 154 were added in an hour and a quarter. The stamina of Peel and of Richardson in particular were marvelled at. There were few complete failures in England's innings, and Ward batted stoutheartedly. Batting seemed even a trifle easier in the follow-on, Ward and Brown hitting 102 for the third wicket and Ford and Briggs a crucial 89 for the seventh, when England were just ahead. Only wicketkeeper Gay failed to obtain double-figures, and with several dropped catches, Australia had placed themselves in need of 177 to win. On the fifth evening, with dark clouds banking up, they had made 113 for 2, Darling having hit a brisk 44 in contrast to Giffen's cautious 30. Some English players 'relaxed' that night, thinking the game lost. Peel was one, but Stoddart ordered him under a cold shower, and on a pitch saturated by heavy overnight rain the Yorkshireman proceeded to run through Australia. Briggs (3 for 25) took the other end, and after some nerve-shattering cricket England stole a narrow victory. Blackham, in his final Test, batted with a painful hand injury and was last out.

109, above: *Stoddart's team line the ship's rail as the great journey begins.* 110, below: *The contented Sydney crowd during the Gregory-Blackham partnership. The Hill now rises from this area, and the flimsy scoreboard has long since been replaced*

The Australia **~~Cricket Club~~ v. the** England **Cricket Club**

Match Played at Sydney on 14. 15. 17. 18 December 18[illegible]

1st Innings of Australia Result

Time 12.12		BATSMAN.	RUNS SCORED.	HOW OUT.	BOWLER.	TOTAL
12.12 / 12.20	1.1	Lyons J	1	Bowled	Richardson	1
12.12 / 12.34	2.2	Trott H	2114121	Bowled	Richardson	12
12.22 / 5.47	5.3 3	Giffen G	1442224411114114421442111124 / 124444111422111141114224415212142314411111211124	caught Ford	Brockwell	161
12.36 / 12.37	3.4	Darling J		Bowled	Richardson	0
12.39 / 3.57	4.5	Iredale F	4224114111444411111114112332413444 1	caught Stoddart	Ford	81
3.18 / 3.16	9.6	Gregory S	21414434211414324114442411142434 3 / 331434234224244414411112222422442142142132241111	caught Peel	Stoddart	201
5.49 / 12.30	6.7	Reedman J	4121153	caught Ford	Peel	17
12.32 / 12.55	7.8	McLeod C	2112321111	Bowled	Richardson	15
12.57 / 1.10	8.9	Turner CB	1	caught Gay	Peel	1
1.12 / 3.26	10.10	Blackham J	111412211221244231412412134224111 41	Bowled	Richardson	74
3.18	11	Jones E	443	Not out		11
UMPIRE			Byes 44			8
			Leg Byes 111			3
			Wide Balls 1			1
			No Balls			

Runs at the fall of each Wicket	1	2	3	4	5	6	7	8	9	10	Total of Innings.
Time	12.20	12.34	12.37	3.57	5.43	12.30	12.55	1.10	3.16	3.26	
Runs	10	21	21	192	331	379	400	409	563	586	586

BOWLING ANALYSIS.

Total time at wkt 7 hours 11 m

BOWLER.	RUNS FROM EACH OVER.	Overs	Maidens.	Wides	No Balls.	Runs.	Wickets.
Richardson	[illegible]	55.3	13	.	.	181	5
Peel	[illegible]	53	14			140	2
Briggs	[illegible]	25	4			96	–
Brockwell	[illegible]	22	7			78	1
Ford	[illegible]	11	2	1		47	1
Stoddart	[illegible]	3	.			31	1
Lockwood		3	2			1	

Published by ALFRED SHAW & ARTHUR SHREWSBURY, Football and General Athletic Sports Warehouse, Carrington St. Bridge, Nottingham.

111, above: *The scorebook records some relentless batting and gallant bowling.* 112, left: *Syd Gregory, Australia's little double-century hero.* 113, below: *Stoddart and the Kangaroo – the Ashes war is on again*

Geo. Ashton
I say "Old Man"
"Who's got those Ashes?"

114: *View of play from the Randwick end at Sydney. In 1936 the Noble Stand was built on the far side*

1894–95 SECOND TEST

Melbourne, December 29, 31, January 1, 2, 3

England 75 *(C.T.B. Turner 5 for 32) and 475 (A.E. Stoddart 173, R. Peel 53, A. Ward 41, G. Giffen 6 for 155);* Australia *123 (T. Richardson 5 for 57) and 333 (G.H.S. Trott 95, F.A. Iredale 68, W. Bruce 54, G. Giffen 43, R. Peel 4 for 77).* England won by 94 runs.

Giffen was elected Australia's new captain just before the start, and he put England in to bat. Two hours later they were all out on a pitch that still presented difficulties to batsmen. Coningham, in his only Test, had removed MacLaren with the first ball of the match. Only Ward (30) prospered for any length of time. Australia were ahead with six wickets in hand, but Richardson held their first-innings advantage to 48, and on the Monday, the pitch having had 15 minutes' rolling, heavy scoring was expected. That evening England were 287 for 4, Stoddart 150 made coolly and authoritatively. He went on to pass Grace's England record of 170, and his 173 (in 320 minutes) was to be the highest by an England captain in Australia for 80 years. Last man Richardson's 11 was the lowest score of the innings, and England's courage and concentration presented Australia with a weighty task. They were 98 for one on the fourth evening: 330 still required. Giffen went at 191, Trott, to a boot-high caught-and-bowled by Brockwell, soon afterwards. Iredale defended with scarce support until Turner shared 65 with him for the last wicket. England, hardly clear-cut superiors, were two-up.

115, left: *Andrew Stoddart, whose 173 led England to a big second innings.* 116, below: *Arthur Coningham – a wicket with his first ball.* 117, right: *Billy Brockwell – three vital wickets in the last innings*

118: *All eyes on the middle as the second Test match runs its enthralling course at Melbourne*

1894–95 THIRD TEST
Adelaide, January 11, 12, 14, 15

Australia *238 (G. Giffen 58, G.H.S. Trott 48, S.T. Callaway 41, T. Richardson 5 for 75) and 411 (F.A. Iredale 140, W. Bruce 80, A.E. Trott 72*, R. Peel 4 for 96);* England *124 (S.T. Callaway 5 for 37, G. Giffen 5 for 76) and 143 (A.E. Trott 8 for 43).* Australia won by 382 runs.

England were beaten as much as anything by the intense heat and Albert Trott, who, in his first Test, made 110 runs without losing his wicket, then hounded England to abject defeat with varied fast-medium bowling on a pitch which the tourists never quite trusted. Richardson won universal admiration for his courageous bowling effort, but even he wilted in temperatures which touched 155°F in the open. Australia enjoyed two big last-wicket stands by Trott and Callaway – 81 and 64 – but the damage to England was done in their first innings. Only J.T. Brown, with a stylish 39 not out, maintained any English pride. Iredale's century was polished, and ended only through fatigue, and Bruce batted with charm. As young Trott ran amok, only the majestic MacLaren and Stoddart held fast long enough to pass 30. Albert Trott was a national hero overnight.

119, left: *Albert Trott, fit for canonisation after his startling debut.* 120, right: *'The Cause of Defeat' – a cynical view of the Englishmen's alleged drinking excesses*

121, left: *Frank Iredale – a monumental 140 at Adelaide in stifling heat.* 122, right: *Syd Callaway, who had a good all-round match*

1894–95 FOURTH TEST

Sydney, February 1, 2, 4

Australia *284 (H. Graham 105, A.E. Trott 85*, J. Briggs 4 for 65);* England *65 and 72 (G. Giffen 5 for 26, C.T.B. Turner 4 for 33).* Australia won by an innings and 147 runs.

With this troucing, Australia drew level two-all and set up a highly exciting prospect for the decider in Melbourne. Stoddart won his only toss of the series and put Australia in on a dubious pitch. Six wickets fell for 51, but Giffen had rearranged the batting order, and Graham added 68 with Darling (who once hit Briggs into the tennis courts) and 112 with Albert Trott (who now had 195 Test runs without a dismissal). Graham, who batted gamely and enterprisingly against the fierce bounce of Richardson, achieved the unique double of a century in his first Test innings in both England and Australia. England lost MacLaren that evening, and Saturday's play was washed out. More rain Sunday night left the pitch in a dreadful condition when play resumed, and Stoddart expressed doubts that England would last out the day. He was right. Strangely, A.E. Trott, the destroyer at Adelaide, was not called upon to bowl a ball. Charlie 'Terror' Turner was dropped after this match, having taken 101 wickets at 16.53 in 17 Tests – an illustrious career ended in controversy.

123, left: *Harry Graham, 'The Little Dasher', who completed a unique double when he made a century at Sydney.* 124, top, right: *Spectators examine the pitch on which England were all but bowled out twice in a day.* 125, right: *The England players prepare to take the field at Sydney*

1894–95 FIFTH TEST

Melbourne, March 1, 2, 4, 5, 6

Australia 414 *(J. Darling 74, S.E. Gregory 70, G. Giffen 57, J.J. Lyons 55, G.H.S. Trott 42, R. Peel 4 for 114) and 267 (G. Giffen 51, J. Darling 50, G.H.S. Trott 42, T. Richardson 6 for 104);* England 385 *(A.C. MacLaren 120, R. Peel 73, A.E. Stoddart 68, G.H.S. Trott 4 for 71, G. Giffen 4 for 130) and 298 for 4 (J.T. Brown 140, A. Ward 93).* England won by 6 wickets.

Thousands converged on Melbourne by all manner of means for 'the match of the century'. It was said that even Queen Victoria took a close interest in reports of the contest. Those in attendance on the final day saw one of the greatest attacking innings as well as one of the finest supporting roles. Australia's 414 after winning the toss seemed an insurance against defeat, even though England came within 29. Gregory and Darling put on 142 for the fifth wicket, and runs came from most of the side. MacLaren's century, the first of his five against Australia, ended when he trod on his stumps in pulling at a short ball from Harry Trott. His important stand with Peel (who had made a 'pair' in each of the previous Tests) amounted to 162. This together with Ward and Stoddart's second-wicket stand of 104 kept England in the fight. Another heroic effort by Richardson, supported by Peel, confined Australia to an overall lead of 296, and though Brockwell was out that evening, the fifth day began with England hopeful. Immediately, however, Stoddart was lbw, and under an overcast sky, Brown of Yorkshire came in. He square-drove his first ball to the boundary and hooked the next for four. In less than half an hour he had his fifty – the fastest ever in Tests – and with rain still threatening, he raced to his century in 95 minutes. The stand reached 210, then the highest in Test cricket, before Brown was caught at slip. Ward, his partner, missed his century, but had taken England to the threshold of a famous victory.

126: *The Englishmen practise before the deciding Test at Melbourne*

127, above, left: *The* Melbourne Argus *office displays progress scores for those who cannot get to the ground.* 128, above, right: *The bat with which Brown made his historic 140.* 129, right: *The crowded stands and (inset) players leaving the field.* 130, below, left: *Scoreboard during the vital first-innings MacLaren-Peel partnership.* 131, below, right: *J.T. Brown, pride of Yorkshire and England*

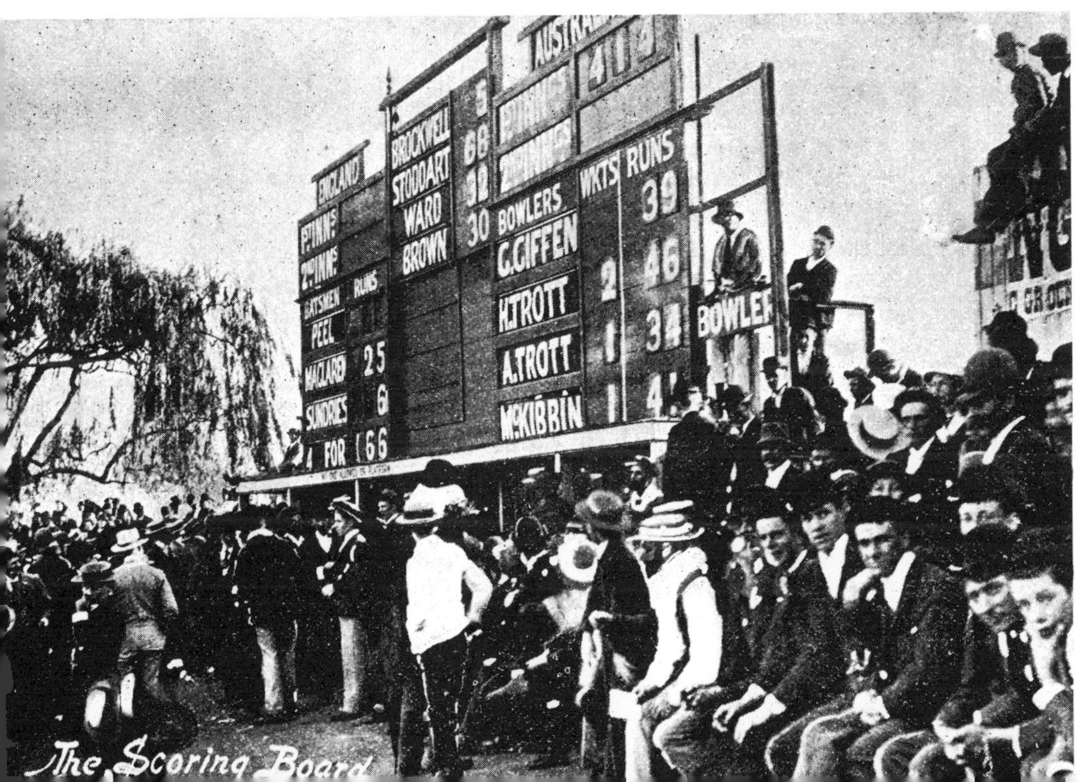

1

LAUNCESTON HOTEL
MRS HUSTON
LAUNCESTON
TASMANIA.

Brisbane Street
Launceston March 10th 1895

Dear Father and Mother, Brother and Sister

It gives me pleasure to write you a few lines and let you know how we are going on. As you can imagine we are all very happy now that we have won the final test match and what a match it was. The greatest match on record. The excitement was intense. We outplayed them at every point. When we had 297 to get to win and Brockwell was out at 6 and then Stoddart at 28 the betting men offered 5 to 1 against us. If I ever felt determined to do well I did when I heard the people say 'Its all over now'. I got 51 in 27 minutes and then the people

2

began to think that it was not all over yet and it was not for Albert Ward and myself took the score to 238 before I was out. Of course you will have read all about the match before you recieve this letter but I am glad to say that everybody gave us great credit for winning. It was a glorious win one that we shall never forget. The gate reciepts were 4003£ so you me guess what a lot of people saw the match. The cricketers out here are very good players indeed and take a lot of beating. We left Melbourne on Thursday night at 6-30 and arrive here that is Launceston in Tasmania at 2 in the afternoon on Friday after a very rough voyage. It was a terrible night the ship rolled awfully and nearly everybody was bad, but I

132, above: *Jack Brown's letter, written four days after the great Melbourne match, tells of his fast fifty and of the tremendous interest and excitement generated by this decider.* 133, below: *It is all over, and the Australians, with MacLaren and Peel, leave the field*

1896 FIRST TEST
Lord's, June 22, 23, 24

Australia 53 *(T. Richardson 6 for 39) and 347 (G.H.S. Trott 143, S.E. Gregory 103, J.T. Hearne 5 for 76, T. Richardson 5 for 134);* England 292 *(R. Abel 94, W.G. Grace 66, F.S. Jackson 44) and 111 for 4.* England won by 6 wickets.

The mighty Richardson, bowling from the pavilion end, bowled six Australians before lunch, by which time England were already setting about their reply. The pitch was fast, and Richardson's success was based on sheer speed. Only Darling (22) stayed for any length of time. That evening England were 233 ahead with two wickets left. About 30,000 had crammed into Lord's that day, and there was much rowdyism in some quarters. Those with an uninterrupted view of play saw Grace notch his 1000th Test run and Abel bat studiously. Australia were 62 for 3 on the second day, and apparently well on the way to defeat, when Trott, the captain, who failed to score in the first innings, was joined by Gregory, and bravely they added 221 – a new all-wicket Test record – in only 160 minutes. Even Richardson was driven to the boundary. Australia fell away after this breathtaking stand, but after rain on the second night England had to fight for victory, and Brown considered his 36 against Jones at his most aggressive and in failing light to have been quite as satisfying as his magnificent century at Melbourne.

134, above: *Photograph of Lord's during England's first innings.* 135, below: *W.B. Wollen's painting of the match, probably set during the Trott-Gregory partnership. Lohmann chases the ball; WG at point*

136, above: *England batting at Lord's, 1896, with the bowler coming in from the Nursery end.* 137, right: *The four South Australians in the tourists' side: Joe Darling, George Giffen, Ernest Jones, and (in front) Clem Hill*

1896 SECOND TEST
Old Trafford, July 16, 17, 18

Australia *412 (F.A. Iredale 108, G. Giffen 80, G.H.S. Trott 53, T. Richardson 7 for 168) and 125 for 7 (T. Richardson 6 for 76);* England *231 (A.F.A. Lilley 65*, K.S. Ranjitsinhji 62) and 305 (K.S. Ranjitsinhji 154*, A.E. Stoddart 41).* Australia won by 3 wickets.

Richardson and Ranjitsinhji were the heroes who caught the imagination, but the victory was Australia's – though Richardson's relentless attack on the last day almost reversed the match. Lilley's spilling of Kelly, his opposite number, as his arm hit the ground gave the visitors the respite they needed in the closing stages. The first day ended with Australia in command: 366 for 8. Iredale's was a pleasant innings, and with Giffen he added 131. Trott was dismissed by Lilley, England's wicketkeeper, whom Grace gambled upon to break a threatening partnership. Richardson bowled 68 five-ball overs, and was to manage another 42.3 in the second innings. Trott had Grace and Stoddart stumped off his leg-breaks at the start of England's innings, and only 'Ranji' and Lilley saved complete embarrassment. The Indian prince was making his Test debut at last, the Lord's authorities having considered him ineligible. In the follow-on he played an enchanting innings, all ease and fluidity, hooking Jones's thunderbolts, cutting wristily, glancing with sweet precision. He batted for 185 minutes, and made 113 runs before lunch on the third morning. He showed no sign of fallibility, but the others did, and he was left undefeated. Richardson then took over to make Australia's task more difficult than could ever have been foreseen 24 hours earlier.

138, above, left: *Tom Richardson, who bowled his heart out in the second Test.* 139, right: *Ernie Jones bowls at practice on Mitcham Green.* 140, below, left: *'Dick' Lilley, England's wicketkeeper, whose unfortunate error probably cost his side victory.* 141, right: *'Ranji', maker of a brilliant century in his first Test*

1896 — THIRD TEST

The Oval, August 10, 11, 12

England *145 (F.S. Jackson 45, H. Trumble 6 for 59) and 84 (H. Trumble 6 for 30);* Australia *119 (J. Darling 47, J.T. Hearne 6 for 41) and 44 (R. Peel 6 for 23, J.T. Hearne 4 for 19).* England won by 66 runs.

England retained the Ashes, though when five players threatened strike action over match fees before the start it seemed the home team would be appreciably weakened. Three – Abel, Richardson and Hayward – relented, but Gunn and Lohmann withdrew their services. England made 69 for one in the 95 minutes' play allowed by the weather on the first day, but subsided before the medium-pace of tall Trumble, who got among the wickets in a Test for the first time. He was to finish, in 1904, with a record 141 wickets in England-Australia Tests. Darling and Iredale made 75 in 45 minutes for Australia's first wicket, the latter being run out on a fifth run by a prodigious throw from Ranji. Medium-pacer Hearne forced a collapse, and England made a painful 60 for 5 that evening. Abel top-scored with a fine defensive 21, and Australia, set 111 on a worsening pitch, were devastated. Last man McKibbin made 16 of the total of 44.

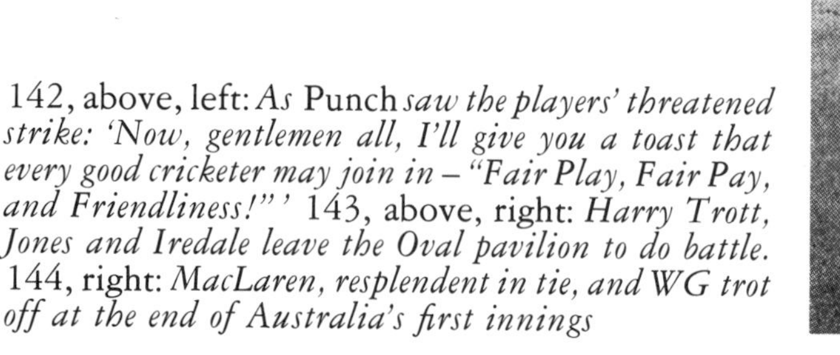

142, above, left: *As* Punch *saw the players' threatened strike: 'Now, gentlemen all, I'll give you a toast that every good cricketer may join in – "Fair Play, Fair Pay, and Friendliness!"'* 143, above, right: *Harry Trott, Jones and Iredale leave the Oval pavilion to do battle.* 144, right: *MacLaren, resplendent in tie, and WG trot off at the end of Australia's first innings*

145, above: *Clem Hill about to be run out by Wynyard for one after turning a ball to leg – part of the Australian first-innings collapse.* 146, left: *The vast crowd stays to cheer England after their Oval victory*

1897–98 FIRST TEST

Sydney, December 13, 14, 15, 16, 17

England 551 *(K.S. Ranjitsinhji 175, A.C. MacLaren 109, T.W. Hayward 72, G.H. Hirst 62, W. Storer 43) and 96 for 1 (A.C. MacLaren 50*)*; Australia 237 *(H. Trumble 70, C.E. McLeod 50*, S.E. Gregory 46, J.T. Hearne 5 for 42) and 408 (J. Darling 101, C. Hill 96, J.J. Kelly 46*, J.T. Hearne 4 for 99)*. England won by 9 wickets.

Stoddart's second team flattered to deceive in the first Test. The captain himself withdrew, grief-stricken, after news of his mother's death a few days before the start – which was postponed because of rain, allowing Ranji to regain some sort of fitness after a bout of quinsy. George Giffen's grand Test career came to an end when, after speculation and many 'quotes', he announced his retirement to pursue his career in the Post Office. MacLaren, captaining England, made a chanceless century on his favourite ground, adding 136 with Hayward. Ranji, still unwell, took his 39 overnight to 175, also chanceless, and was last man out, having dealt wonderfully well with Jones's fast and often short-pitched attack. Richardson, having helped in a final stand of 74, made his usual wholehearted effort with the ball, but was carrying surplus weight. Trumble surprisingly top-scored for Australia, but in the follow-on Darling displayed his skill and Hill batted with dash and flair. McLeod, who was deaf, left his ground after being bowled, but it was a no-ball; he had not heard the umpire's call, and Storer ran him out.

147, above, left: *The captain goes aboard – Stoddart sets out on his second tour as skipper.* 148, right: *The 'Pro-Test' match: a frustrating situation for everyone involved.* 149, below: *Sydney, first Test, 1897*

150, above, left: *Ranji runs in at the end of his great innings.* 151, above, right: *England take the field, wearing mourning bands out of respect for Stoddart's mother, who died before the match.* 152, left: *Painting by A. Henry Fullwood from the popular side during the first Test.* 153, below: *The scorebook records Ranjitsinhji's 175 and MacLaren's cultured century*

First Test at Sydney

A CRICKET MATCH between Australia **and** England

FIRST INNINGS OF England 13·14th December 97

	STRIKER.	SCORE.	TOTAL	HOW OUT.	BOWLER.	REMARKS.
1	Mason	24	6	Bowled	Jones	
2	McLaren	[illegible]	109	Caught Kelly	McLeod	
3	Hayward	[illegible]	72	Caught Trott	Trumble	
4	Storer	[illegible]	43	Caught & bowled	Trott	
5	Druce	[illegible]	20	Caught Gregory	McLeod	
6	Hirst	[illegible]	62	bowled	Jones	
7	Ranjitsinhji	[illegible]	175	Caught Gregory	McKibbin	
8	Wainwright	1441	10	bowled	Jones	
9	Hearne	11412122111	17	Caught & bowled	McLeod	
10	Briggs	1	1	run out		
11	Richardson	341411112411	24	Not out		
	Byes - -					
	Leg Byes -	212411	11			
	Wide Balls -	1	1			
	No Balls - -					
		TOTAL	551			

RUNS AT THE FALL OF EACH WICKET	For 1	For 2	For 3	For 4	For 5	For 6	For 7	For 8	For 9	For 10
	26	162	224	256	258	382	422	471	477	

ANALYSIS OF THE BOWLING OF THE FIRST INNINGS.

	BOWLER.	RUNS FROM EACH OVER.	WIDE BALLS.	NO BALLS.	RUNS.	WICKETS.	MAIDEN OVERS.
1							
2	McKibbin		-	-	113	1	5
3	Jones		-		130	3	8
4	McLeod				80	3	12
5	Trumble		.	.	138	1	7
6	Trott		1	-	78	1	[illegible]

154: *McLeod and Trumble go forth after lunch on the third day*

1897–98 SECOND TEST

Melbourne, January 1, 3, 4, 5

Australia *520 (C.E. McLeod 112, F.A. Iredale 89, G.H.S. Trott 79, S.E. Gregory 71, C. Hill 58);* England *315 (K.S. Ranjitsinhji 71, W. Storer 51, J. Briggs 46*, N.F. Druce 44, H. Trumble 4 for 54) and 150 (M.A. Noble 6 for 49, H. Trumble 4 for 53).* Australia won by an innings and 55 runs.

In uncomfortable heat Australia piled up 283 for 3 on the first day, with McLeod compiling a careful century. England's bowling inadequacy was completely exposed, and the seven who tried (Wainwright was ignored by MacLaren) were defeated by broad bats and fatigue. Australia's impressive resurgence hiccoughed when Ernie Jones was no-balled for throwing by Anglo-Australian umpire Jim Phillips, but the incident seemed soon forgotten. England passed 200 with only four men out, but Ranji's, the key wicket, was taken by Trumble and only a ninth-wicket stand of 87 by Briggs and Druce saved a total collapse. The pitch by now was cracked all over, and in the follow-on Noble (in his first Test) and Trumble proved insuperable.

We are given to understand that the
English Cricketers, on seeing the
ladies piled up behind those iron
railings at the M.C.C. ground, imagi
the officials had taken this preca
to prevent the Australian girls ge
at Prince Ranji. and eloping wi
him in a mass.

155, left: *The England fielders come off for lunch at Melbourne.* 156, centre: *Charlie McLeod, century-maker: sweet revenge for the controversial run-out in the preceding Test.* 157, right: *Ranji, the Indian prince, was a 'pop idol' in Australia*

158, left: *Norman Druce, who made runs at Melbourne.* 159, above: *The cracked pitch after England's second innings – a snapshot by Jim Phillips*

1897–98 THIRD TEST

Adelaide, January 14, 15, 17, 18, 19

Australia *573 (J. Darling 178, F.A. Iredale 84, C. Hill 81, S.E. Gregory 52, T. Richardson 4 for 164);* England *278 (G.H. Hirst 85, T.W. Hayward 70, W.P. Howell 4 for 70) and 282 (A.C. MacLaren 124, K.S. Ranjitsinhji 77, C.E. McLeod 5 for 65, M.A. Noble 5 for 84).* Australia won by an innings and 13 runs.

Australia batted into the third day to reach 573, a new second-highest total in Test cricket, having ended the first day at 310 for 2. The left-handers, Darling and 20-year-old Hill, struck 148 for the second wicket after McLeod had raised 97 with Darling for the first. The latter reached his century in grand style, hoisting Briggs out of the ground. England's misfortunes continued to pile up: Richardson was unwell, Hirst and Ranji were injured, and catches were spilt. Howell, an off-spinner, Jones and Noble cut swathes through the England batting a first time, and in the follow-on, after a promising second-wicket resistance of 142 by MacLaren and Ranji, McLeod broke through the middle order and Noble, using a wind that earlier created a dust-storm, did the rest. Stoddart, having resumed the England captaincy, batted low down and made only 15 and 24.

160: *Again a pitch is the focus of attention: Hayward, Board, and MacLaren study the Adelaide strip*

161, left: *Joe Darling – three centuries in the series, including one on his home ground, Adelaide.* 162, right: *Archie MacLaren – two centuries in the series for England*

1897–98 FOURTH TEST

Melbourne, January 29, 31, February 1, 2

Australia *323 (C. Hill 188, H. Trumble 46, J.T. Hearne 6 for 98) and 115 for 2 (C.E. McLeod 64*);* England *174 (E. Jones 4 for 56) and 263 (K.S. Ranjitsinhji 55, A.C. MacLaren 45).* Australia won by 8 wickets.

The 50th England-Australia Test match further established the renascence of the home side, though when, on the first day, Australia were 58 for 6 it seemed England were at last about to come back into the series. Hearne and Richardson made the breakthrough, but without the support of Hirst they wilted in the heat and young Hill mounted his rescue act, chiefly with Trumble. Their 165 remains a record for the seventh wicket in these matches. Hill drove beautifully and treated anything outside leg stump with vicious contempt; he batted for 294 minutes and gave only one chance. With bushfires filling the air with smoke, England gave their feeblest display yet, and did little better in the follow-on. MacLaren claimed a fly in his eye caused his dismissal, and this – with several English players' protests at crowd behaviour – reduced the popularity of the touring team and increased its misery.

163, below: *Clem Hill, only 20, made 188 at Melbourne (wicketkeeper in picture is Jim Kelly).* 164, right: *The coin drops, and Trott (left) beats Stoddart for choice of innings*

What a tail our Kangaroo has got.
Stoddart.—"They said we could do as we liked with you, old man. Alas! not with a tail like that."
Re the fly which, according to Prince Ranjit., got into Maclaren's eye and won the last test for Australia, there is now no doubt but that the fly was but an instrument in the hands of a designing Australian. We hasten to expose the horrid plot.
1 'Twas thus he trained the wicked fly
To dart and fill Maclaren's eye.
2. And when the fatal moment came—
"Now go," he said, "and spoil his game."
3 The insect went—result, a catch!
That's how Australia won the match!
John Bull.—What must I do to beat you, my boy?"
Australia.—"Take Tennyson's advice, dad. 'Break, break, break.'"
J. BULL
"He (Captain Stoddart) felt that the Australian victory in these test matches would help cricket in this country,—(hear, hear)—and it would do English cricket a lot of good."
AUSTRALIA
"When I say that we had no luck I would instance Briggs' downfall to a very poor ball, while it was ill-fortune for him that a man should have been standing in the precise spot where it fell."—Ranji.
Ranji.—"Just my beastly luck that the wicket should be in the precise spot where the blessed ball fell!"
Anti-Australian.—"Pooh! I dont think much of the Australian team. Take away Hill, and Trumble, and M'Leod, and Jones, and Darling, and Trott, and Noble and a few more and where are you?"
"Yes, you have won it; but really, you know, the victory is absolutely due to Hill."—Ranji.
HILL
In this sketch we have striven to give Ranji's view of the Australian Eleven.

165, opposite: *A satirical account of the fly that got in MacLaren's eye, and some of Ranji's published remarks.* 166, above: *Hill cuts Richardson during his 188 at Melbourne. Trumble non-striker, Storer wicketkeeper*

1897–98 FIFTH TEST

Sydney, February 26, 28, March 1, 2

England *335 (A.C. MacLaren 65, N.F. Druce 64, E. Wainwright 49, T.W. Hayward 47, W. Storer 44, G.H. Hirst 44, E. Jones 6 for 82) and 178 (T.W. Hayward 43, H. Trumble 4 for 37);* Australia *239 (C.E. McLeod 64, T. Richardson 8 for 94) and 276 for 4 (J. Darling 160, J. Worrall 62).* Australia won by 6 wickets.

A large total seemed probable when England finished the first day at 301 for 5, but Jones wiped out the tail. MacLaren and Wainwright began with a stand of 111, and several previous failures found form rather too late in the series. Richardson, free of rheumatism at last, and playing in what transpired to be his final Test, bowled his fastest and got most of the wickets bowled or caught behind the wicket. Trumble and Jones bowled well enough to keep England's overall lead down to 274, but, setting out on the chase for their fourth straight victory, Australia lost two wickets for 40. Worrall then helped Darling add 193, which effectively decided the match. Darling's superb innings lasted only 175 minutes and contained 30 fours and only 18 singles. He drove Richardson furiously in a concerted attempt to hit him from the firing line, and reached his hundred – his third of the series – in a mere 91 minutes (20 fours) – an Australian speed record against England. It was said that Australia's overwhelming success in the Test matches had done more to promote the idea of Federation than any number of conferences.

167, left: *John Bull: 'Now, Stoddart, what was it?' It was a long story.* 168, below: *The ball with which Richardson took 8 for 94.* 169, right: *Ernie Jones – nine wickets at Sydney*

1899 FIRST TEST

Trent Bridge, June 1, 2, 3

Australia *252 (C. Hill 52, S.E. Gregory 48, J. Darling 47, M.A. Noble 41, W. Rhodes 4 for 58, J.T. Hearne 4 for 71) and 230 for 8 dec (C. Hill 80, M.A. Noble 45);* England *193 (C.B. Fry 50, K.S. Ranjitsinhji 42, E. Jones 5 for 88) and 155 for 7 (K.S. Ranjitsinhji 93*).* Match drawn.

The first Test of the first five-match series played in England was the last of W.G. Grace's 22 Test appearances and the first of Wilfred Rhodes's 58. The Test careers of the two spanned 50 years all but a few months. After Australia had fought every inch of the way for their 252, Grace – now almost 51, and often uncomfortable against the pace of Jones – put on 75 with Fry for the first wicket. The only other real stand was 55 by Ranji and Tyldesley. Australia then went after a largish lead while leaving time to bowl England out. The challenge was 290 in four hours, and when four wickets fell for 19, defeat for England loomed large. However, Ranji played with genius and Hayward, dropped once, stayed with him while 58 were added and the crisis was overcome.

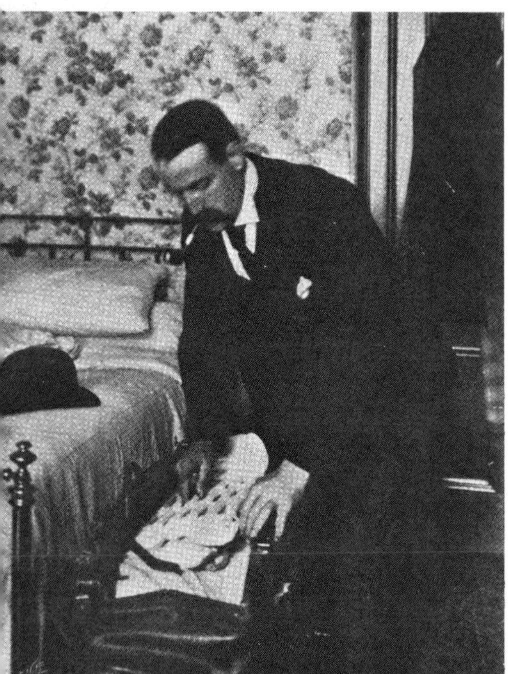

170, above, left: *The Australians at breakfast at the Inns of Court Hotel, Holborn – from left: Trumper, Iredale, Worrall, Gregory, Howell.* 171, right: *Hill packs his bag for the match.* 172, left: *Jones, relaxed with pipe, packs his cane-ribbed pads.* 173, below, left: *W.G. Grace c Kelly b Noble 28 – his penultimate Test innings.* 174, right: *WG and Fry open for England at Trent Bridge*

175: *Darling and Iredale open Australia's innings*

176: *Hill celebrates his fifty with a drink . . .*

177: *and comes in soon afterwards, run out 52*

178: *England come in on the first evening*

179: *WG, Laver, Jackson, and Ranji leave the field at Trent Bridge*

180: *Fry hurries in after making 50*

1899 — SECOND TEST
Lord's, June 15, 16, 17

England 206 *(F.S. Jackson 73, G.L. Jessop 51, E. Jones 7 for 88) and* 240 *(A.C. MacLaren 88*, T.W. Hayward 77)*; Australia 421 *(C. Hill 135, V.T. Trumper 135*, M.A. Noble 54) and 28 for 0.* Australia won by 10 wickets.

This proved to be the decisive Test of the series, and Jones's fast-bowling onslaught on the first day did much to bring ultimate victory to Australia. He dismissed Fry, MacLaren, Ranji and Tyldesley as England slumped to 66 for 6. Jessop and Jackson hit 95 in little more than an hour, but the total soon faded into insignificance as Hill and Noble added 130 for Australia's fourth wicket and Trumper, a fresh-faced 21-year-old in his second Test, 82 with Hill for the fifth. Fry, Ranji and Townsend again went early, but Jackson stayed with Hayward, who resisted further on the last day with MacLaren. Laver's three good wickets then settled the outcome.

POET CRAIG ANNOUNCING THE RESULT OF THE TOSS

ARCHIE MACLAREN

STARTS WITH A BOUNDARY THROUGH THE SLIPS

DR GRACE LOOKS GLUM

BY LILLEY GETS RID OF NOBLE

VICTOR TRUMPER, AUSTRALIA'S PRETTIEST BAT, GLANCING ONE TO LEG

HILL'S NARROW ESCAPE.

LASHING OUT AT MEAD

FRANK GILLETT

A GOOD CATCH BY JONES DISMISSES RANJITSINHJI

TRUMBLE CATCHES FRY

GILBERT JESSOP

POSITION I

POSITION II

STANLEY JACKSON DARES TO DRIVE JONES

FRANK GILLETT

181, 182, 183: *Frank Gillett's views in* The Daily Graphic *of the three days' play at Lord's*

A.C. MACLAREN WHOSE GRAND 88 NOT OUT SAVED ENGLAND FROM A SINGLE INNINGS DEFEAT

LATE CUTTING JONES

DRIVING HOWELL

GLANCING TRUMBLE AWAY TO LEG

A LONG HEADED SCOT IS ARCHIE

A NEAR THING FOR HAYWARD

LILLEY DRIVING LAVER

MAJOR WARDILL BEAMS

WORRALL AND KELLY MAKE A DASH FOR THE BALL AT THE END OF ENGLAND'S INNINGS

WEST TO MYCROFT 'THEY'D BETTER PLAY YOU AND ME NEXT MATCH, TOM.

DARLING MAKES THE WINNING HIT

DARLING ACKNOWLEDGES THE CHEERS OF THE CROWD

FRANK GILLETT

184: *Victor Trumper, whose peerless beauty of style showed in his first Lord's Test appearance*

1899
Headingley, June 29, 30, July 1

Australia *172 (J. Worrall 76, H.I. Young 4 for 30) and 224 (H. Trumble 56, F.J. Laver 45, J.T. Hearne 4 for 50);* England *220 (A.F.A. Lilley 55, T.W. Hayward 40*, H. Trumble 5 for 60) and 19 for 0.* Match drawn.

Rain before the start of this first-ever Test at Leeds caused widespread conjecture over the state of the pitch. Darling decided to bat, expecting conditions to worsen. His first three men were dismissed without a run between them. Worrall, who opened, made the first 24 runs, and his 76 came out of 95 in 90 minutes before he was run out. 'Sailor' Young, fast left-arm, had Hill and Trumper among his victims. That evening England were already 119 for 4, the tiny W.G. Quaife's 20 taking 1¾ hours. That night real-life tragedy struck when Johnny Briggs had a violent fit while watching a performance at the Empire Theatre. He was to spend most of the few months left to him in Cheadle Asylum. Hayward and Lilley took England into the lead with a stand of 93, and Australia were in grave danger after their first four wickets fell at 34, Hearne doing the hat-trick with the distinguished wickets of Hill, Gregory and Noble (the last two registering 'pairs'). Five runs later Darling was out, but Trumper, Trumble and Laver in turn held on resolutely, and England were set 177. When all was poised for a fascinating final day the rain returned, causing abandonment.

185: *The third Test, at Leeds – an eventful first day*

A Great Crowd of Spectators.

Exceedingly pleasant weather prevailed during the greater part of the afternoon, although there were times when some heavy clouds threatened rain, but a slight breeze carried them away, and the first stage of the encounter was concluded in brilliant sunshine. The match proved a huge attraction, and before lunch time there were nearly 20,000 people on the ground, and this number was largely increased as the afternoon advanced. To keep the crowd in order there were over a hundred police present, and though they had no great disorder to deal with, several thousand people forced their way right up to the boundary after lunch, obstructing the view of those who occupied the proper seats, and for the rest of the day the cricket went on to a ceaseless accompaniment of shouting and cries of "Sit down." Except for this nuisance the first stage of the match passed off quite satisfactorily.

Brockwell Unable to Play.

Not until within a few minutes of the start was it definitely settled to play Hayward instead of Brockwell, who had hurt his hand. Brockwell must have been greatly disappointed, for it will be remembered that he was twelfth man both at Nottingham and at Lord's. The Australians left out Iredale—now recovered from his recent illness—McLeod and Johns, the Colonial team being exactly the same as that

(Continued on page 3.)

C. B. Fry's fine one-handed catch which dismissed Kelly.

Johnny Briggs in the team again.

CRICKET FEVER IN THE CITY: TEST MATCH RESULTS IN QUEEN VICTORIA STREET.

Worrall takes the first ball.

Noble fools away his wicket.

Lilley plays delightful cricket.
Willis Quaife stands up pluckily to Jones.
An uncomfortable way of watching a cricket match.
Brown does some vigorous boundary cutting.
A good catch by Worrall dismisses Ranjitsinhji.
Jones never bowled faster.
F. Gillett

186, above (inset): *Jack Hearne, who performed a high-quality hat-trick at Headingley.* 187: *Frank Gillett chose to record other incidents*

1899 FOURTH TEST
Old Trafford, July 17, 18, 19

England *372 (T.W. Hayward 130, A.F.A. Lilley 58, F.S. Jackson 44, H.I. Young 43) and 94 for 3 (K.S. Ranjitsinhji 49*);* Australia *196 (M.A. Noble 60*, H. Trumble 44, W.M. Bradley 5 for 67, H.I. Young 4 for 79) and 346 for 7 dec (M.A. Noble 89, V.T. Trumper 63, J. Worrall 53).* Match drawn.

A fine innings by Hayward, who went in at 47 for 4 and was 20 at lunch after 1½ hours, put England in command of the match on a pitch which interested bowlers throughout. Lilley added 113 with him for the seventh wicket. Australia reeled before Young and Bradley, and were only 57 when the seventh wicket fell. Trumble then stayed with Noble, who batted altogether for 8½ hours in the match in one of the most remarkable defensive fights ever. MacLaren drained Bradley so that in the follow-on Australia were not so severely tested. There were moments when England glimpsed victory, but Darling and Iredale saw to it that Noble's grim efforts were not wasted. The compulsory follow-on rule was dispensed with as a result of this contest.

188, above, left: *Bill Bradley, Kent fast bowler.* 189, centre: *'Sailor' Young – 12 top wickets in his only two Tests.* 190, right: *Tom Hayward – first century against Australia. Another followed next Test.* 191, below: *The first day's play at Old Trafford depicted in not the most fluid of illustrations.*

Quaife gets considerably knocked about.

Darling leads out his men.

Fry opens England's account with a single.

M. A. Noble.

Darling catches Quaife.

Exit W. P. Howell.

John Worrall retires sadly.

W. M. Bradley ("good laad!") in the middle of his run.

Lilley taking Bradley on the leg side—(no child's play this).

Tom Hayward's favourite stroke—rather high and rather late.

Station end.

Young about to deliver the ball.

Quaife shines at cover point.

Montague Noble, the saviour of his side.

Beautiful catch by Ranjitsinhji.

Brockwell catches Worrall.

192, 193: *Failures and triumphs on the second and final days at Old Trafford*

1899 FIFTH TEST

The Oval, August 14, 15, 16

England 576 (*T.W. Hayward 137, F.S. Jackson 118, C.B. Fry 60, K.S. Ranjitsinhji 54, A.C. MacLaren 49, E. Jones 4 for 164*); Australia 352 (*S.E. Gregory 117, J. Darling 71, J. Worrall 55, W.H. Lockwood 7 for 71*) *and 254 for 5* (*C.E. McLeod 77, J. Worrall 75, M.A. Noble 69**). Match drawn.

An orgy of runs – 435 for 4 – on the first day led to the second-highest total in Tests so far, and left England over 10 hours to bowl Australia out twice. On a still-perfect pitch the task proved too much for England's varied array of bowlers. Jackson and Hayward put up a record 185 for the first wicket in better than even-time after making only two runs off the first 10 overs. The score was 316 before the second wicket – Ranji's – fell. A further century stand took place between MacLaren and Fry, who made 110 for the fourth wicket in only 65 minutes. Ernie Jones toiled through 53 five-ball overs. Lockwood was England's hero, Gregory, with Darling, Australia's. Hill was missed, as in the previous Test. It was two hours into the last day when Australia went to the wicket a second time, and after Worrall and McLeod opened with 116 and Lockwood left the field with a strain it was never seriously supposed that Australia would let England in to level the series.

194, above, left: *England's successful first day.* 195, right: *Australia's resistance on the second day.* 196, below: *Ranjitsinhji batting in the fifth Test – just the man to come in after an opening stand of 185*

1901–02 FIRST TEST

Sydney, December 13, 14, 16

England 464 *(A.C. MacLaren 116, A.F.A. Lilley 84, T.W. Hayward 69, L.C. Braund 58, C.E. McLeod 4 for 84)*; Australia *168 (S.E. Gregory 48, C. Hill 46, S.F. Barnes 5 for 65) and 172 (S.E. Gregory 43, L.C. Braund 5 for 61, C. Blythe 4 for 30)*. England won by an innings and 124 runs.

As happened four years earlier, England blazed away to an opening victory only to finish second-best in the remaining matches. Ranji, Fry, Jackson, Hirst and Rhodes were all unavailable for the tour, but it hardly seemed to matter here at Sydney. MacLaren and Hayward started with a brisk 154, and Lilley and Braund added 124 for the seventh wicket. Australia bowled around 25 six-ball overs an hour throughout. S.F. Barnes, an 'unknown' whose great ability MacLaren had perceived, gave Australia an immediate taste of the bowling skills that were to bring him 106 wickets in 20 Tests. Braund (leg-breaks) and Blythe (slow left-arm) had Australia out a second time in under three hours.

197, left: *Fred Leist's impressions of the first day's play at Sydney.* 198, above: *'Charlie' Blythe – seven wickets with slow left-arm.* 199, right: *Len Braund – seven wickets with leg-breaks.* 200, below: *View towards Randwick end; Jones bowling for Australia*

201: *View from Sydney's Hill end during the first Test; Trumble about to bowl*

1901–02 SECOND TEST

Melbourne, January 1, 2, 3, 4

Australia *112 (S.F. Barnes 6 for 42, C. Blythe 4 for 64) and 353 (R.A. Duff 104, C. Hill 99, W.W. Armstrong 45*, S.F. Barnes 7 for 121);* England *61 (M.A. Noble 7 for 17) and 175 (J.T. Tyldesley 66, M.A. Noble 6 for 60, H. Trumble 4 for 49).* Australia won by 229 runs.

Barnes took Trumper's wicket with the second ball of the match, and on a rain-affected pitch runs were only ever likely to come from bold batsmanship. Barnes and Blythe bowled unchanged, and Duff, in his initial Test, top-scored with 32. England in turn were bundled out, lasting a mere 68 minutes, with Jessop coming out best with 27 in 20 minutes. Noble and Trumble (3 for 38) also bowled throughout the innings. Darling almost reversed his batting order and at the close of the opening day Australia were 48 for 5. Hill was dropped – a vital miss – on the second day, but Australia took hold of the match in an unusual last-wicket stand of 120, Duff coming in at No. 10 and Armstrong at 11. Barnes bowled 42 overs unchanged and 64 in all. Set 405 for victory on a reformed pitch, England slid to 147 for 5 by the third evening. Heavy rain then rendered the pitch spiteful again, and Trumble cleaned up with a hat-trick: A.O. Jones, John Gunn and Barnes.

202, left: *Reg Duff – century for Australia on debut – batting No. 10.*
203, right: *Johnny Tyldesley – a brilliant cutter*

204, left: *S.F. Barnes, MacLaren's momentous discovery.* 205, above: *M.A. Noble, master swerve bowler – 13 for 77 at Melbourne*

206: *No room in the grandstand during the second Test*

1901–02 THIRD TEST
Adelaide, January 17, 18, 20, 21, 22, 23

England *388 (L.C. Braund 103*, T.W. Hayward 90, W.G. Quaife 68, A.C. MacLaren 67) and 247 (T.W. Hayward 47, A.C. MacLaren 44, W.G. Quaife 44, H. Trumble 6 for 74);* Australia *321 (C. Hill 98, V.T. Trumper 65, S.E. Gregory 55, R.A. Duff 43, J. Gunn 5 for 76) and 315 for 6 (C.Hill 97, J. Darling 69, H. Trumble 62*).* Australia won by 4 wickets.

The loss of Barnes with a twisted knee after only seven overs was critical to the balance of the match – and the series, for he was unable to resume his place at the head of England's attack. MacLaren and Hayward got England off to a strong start: 149; but the innings was slipping away when Quaife and Braund added 108 for the sixth wicket. Led by Hill's 98, Australia responded well until Gunn ran through the second half of the order. England extended their lead, with rain falling on the third evening and a dust-storm cutting play on the fourth. Set 315, Australia were 201 for 4 by the fifth evening, Hill having been bowled by Jessop towards the end to complete a bizarre sequence of 99, 98 and 97. Despite one worn end, the pitch remained fairly sound, and Australia went 2–1 up on the sixth day.

207: *Jessop at cover throws to 'keeper Lilley with Trumble, having crossed with Darling, still well out of his crease. The batsman survived*

208, above: *Trumble catches A.O. Jones off his own bowling.* 209, left: *John Gunn – eight wickets at Adelaide.* 210, right: *W. G. Quaife – a valuable double of 68 and 44, but in a losing cause*

1901–02 FOURTH TEST

Sydney, February 14, 15, 17, 18

England *317 (A.C. MacLaren 92, J.T. Tyldesley 79, T.W. Hayward 41, A.F.A. Lilley 40, J.V. Saunders 4 for 119) and 99 (J.V. Saunders 5 for 43, M.A. Noble 5 for 54);* Australia *299 (M.A. Noble 56, W.W. Armstrong 55, A.J.Y. Hopkins 43, G.L. Jessop 4 for 68, L.C. Braund 4 for 118) and 121 for 3 (R.A. Duff 51*).* Australia won by 7 wickets.

England scored 179 before their second wicket fell, but persistent outcricket by Australia under their new captain, Trumble, prevented a mammoth score. Jessop's fast bowling cut down the first four Australian wickets for only 48, but the middle batsmen resisted stoutly, and the first-innings margin was kept to insignificance after all. Then England collapsed unaccountably against Noble and Saunders, who bowled unchanged through the innings, supported by smart fielding and catching. Saunders, fast-medium left-arm, had match figures of 9 for 162 but was omitted from the following Test.

211, left: *Montague Alfred Noble – a superb all-round match: 56 and eight wickets.* 212, right: *Jack Saunders, the Victorian left-hander*

1901–02 FIFTH TEST

Melbourne, February 28, March 1, 3, 4

Australia *144 (T.W. Hayward 4 for 22, J. Gunn 4 for 38) and 255 (C. Hill 87, S.E. Gregory 41, L.C. Braund 5 for 95);* England *189 (A.F.A. Lilley 41, H. Trumble 5 for 62) and 178 (A.C. MacLaren 49, M.A. Noble 6 for 98).* Australia won by 32 runs.

Australia, winning the toss for the first time in the series, failed on a pitch which several times changed character as showers occurred during the four days. Jessop (35) and MacLaren had 50 up for England in a mere 20 minutes, but Australia restored a balance and set about building up a new lead, and were ahead by 181 with four wickets left on the second evening. Hill was missed twice during his stylish innings. Eventually set 211 to win, England finished the day 87 for 3. Jessop went first ball next morning and against Noble and Trumble on a lifting pitch the going was difficult. Tyldesley, a master in such circumstances, held one end secure, but lost partners steadily and was last out.

213, left: *A.O. Jones leads out some of his men – from left: Tyldesley, Braund, Blythe, Jessop (in sunhat), and McGahey.* 214, below, left: *Hugh Trumble, whose total of 141 wickets in these Tests remained a record until Lillee passed it in 1981.* 215, below, right: *Darling and his second side embark for England in Coronation Year*

HERE WE ARE AGAIN!

1902
Edgbaston, May 29, 30, 31

England *376 for 9 dec (J.T. Tyldesley 138, F.S. Jackson 53, W.H. Lockwood 52*, G.H. Hirst 48);* Australia *36 (W. Rhodes 7 for 17) and 46 for 2.* Match drawn.

One of the most fascinating of Test series began with Birmingham's first Test and Australia's lowest-ever score. An England XI perhaps without equal across the hundred years of Test cricket recovered from a shaky start primarily through Tyldesley's artistry, with support from Jackson and Hirst and an unfinished tenth-wicket stand of 81 by Lockwood and Rhodes. Tyldesley played supremely well through the off side, and was missed just twice – when 43. After a delay for rain, MacLaren allowed the innings to continue awhile before declaring. The pitch was now drying but never beastly, and Hirst (who finished with 3 for 15) bowled so well that Rhodes, appearing less lethal to the batsmen, reaped the greater harvest. Trumper's 18 was half the final pathetic total, which was reached in 85 minutes. The two Yorkshiremen bowled through the innings except for one over by Braund to enable them to change ends. Further rain on the second night meant a late start on the last day, and though the crowd burst into the ground with great excitement – several people were injured – the pitch was dead and Australia had no trouble in playing out time. Three days later, in their match with Yorkshire, the Australians were dismissed by Hirst and Jackson for 23.

216: *Glimpses of the first day's play, with hardly a hint of the sensations to follow*

217, 218, above: *Rain, sawdust, thrills galore – the story of the second and third days at Edgbaston*

219, above, left: *The Australians set off from their Birmingham hotel.* 220, above: *Wilfred Rhodes, 7 for 17, was – with Hirst – irresistible on the damp pitch.* 221, left: *How Tom Webster remembered the wonderful England XI*

1902
Lord's, June 12, 13, 14

England *102 for 2 (F.S. Jackson 55*, A.C. MacLaren 47*).* Match drawn.

Australia, without Trumble (still injured) and Howell, and with a few other players off-colour, were not too disconsolate at the abandonment of this rain-ruined match, although the opening overs midway through the first day were not without sensation. Hopkins had Fry caught at short leg in his first over and bowled Ranji off his pads in his second to render England 0 for 2. Jackson made a run then gave a sharp chance to slip. That would have made it three down for one run. However, the crisis was overcome, and was soon seen in perspective as rain and more rain washed out the remaining two days.

222: *The first day – and Hopkins' moments of glory. There was to be no second or third day*

JONES LEADS OFF WITH A MAIDEN OVER
RANJITSINHJI ALL AT SEA WITH ONE OF HOPKINS' BREAK BACKS
(2 WICKETS FOR 0)
FRY FALLS INTO AN OBVIOUS TRAP
(1 WICKET FOR 0)
ARMSTRONG GIVES JACKSON A LIFE AT SLIP
JACKSON SCORES THE FIRST RUN OF THE MATCH IN THE SIXTH OVER
A WEIRD CHOP OF JACKSON'S BOUNCES OVER KELLY'S HEAD
A. J. HOPKINS WHO DISPOSED OF FRY AND RANJITSINHJI
HIRST AND RHODES CHUCKLE
FRANK GILLETT

1902 THIRD TEST

Bramall Lane, July 3, 4, 5

Australia *194 (M.A. Noble 47, S.F. Barnes 6 for 49) and 289 (C. Hill 119, V.T. Trumper 62, A.J.Y. Hopkins 40*, W. Rhodes 5 for 63);* England *145 (J.V. Saunders 5 for 50, M.A. Noble 5 for 51) and 195 (A.C. MacLaren 63, G.L. Jessop 55, M.A. Noble 6 for 52, H. Trumble 4 for 49).* Australia won by 143 runs.

Sheffield's only Test match saw a full-strength Australia move into a series lead, though their start was unsteady. MacLaren gave the new ball to Hirst and leg-spinner Braund, and the latter bowled Trumper in his first over. When Barnes came into the attack he took 3 for 3, but from 73 for 5 Australia managed a reasonable total. MacLaren and Abel raised 61 for England's first wicket, but the innings became a procession, some of the batsmen's downfalls doubtless attributable in part to dreadful light due in no small part to the smoke from factory chimneys. Australia grasped the initiative when Trumper began their second innings with 62 out of 80 in only 50 minutes. Darling made a 'pair' (c Braund b Barnes both times), but Hill tore into the bowling, adding 107 with Gregory in 67 minutes, and batting in all for only 145 minutes. England's target of 339 was plainly beyond them in the conditions, yet Jessop opened with 55 at his customary tearaway rate, and MacLaren commanded for a time. Noble cut the ball back briskly and used the wearing pitch cleverly to finish with 11 wickets in the match.

223, left: *Australia's grim start at Sheffield as seen by* The Daily Graphic. 224, below: *England do even less well in their first innings*

225: *The demise of Jessop and of Jackson in England's second innings*

1902 — FOURTH TEST

Old Trafford, July 24, 25, 26

Australia *299 (V.T. Trumper 104, C. Hill 65, R.A. Duff 54, J. Darling 51, W.H. Lockwood 6 for 48, W. Rhodes 4 for 104) and 86 (W.H. Lockwood 5 for 28);* England *262 (F.S. Jackson 128, L.C. Braund 65, H. Trumble 4 for 75) and 120 (H. Trumble 6 for 53, J.V. Saunders 4 for 52).* Australia won by 3 runs.

One of the most famous cricket matches began with a pyrotechnic innings from Victor Trumper, who reached his century before lunch, when Australia were 173 for one. Trumper and Duff posted 135 for the first wicket – a record for Australia – in 78 minutes. Lockwood got Duff in his first over, much delayed because of slippery footholds, and continued to present the batsmen with problems, especially in his third spell, when he wrapped up the innings with five wickets for eight. Meanwhile, Rhodes had trapped Trumper (who batted only 115 minutes), Noble and Gregory in four overs after lunch, only to be hit right out of the ground twice by Darling. Hill and his captain, apart from the two openers, were the only ones to make more than five runs. England suffered early shocks and were 44 for 5 before Jackson and Braund stayed together in an admirable stand of 141. Jackson was last out, having withstood a high-class attack on a dubious pitch for 4¼ hours. Australia, 37 ahead, lost three for 10, and Fred Tate, on the square-leg boundary, made a fateful miss when he dropped Darling – the eventual top-scorer with 37 – when the total was still only 16. The next wicket did not fall until 64, and after that Australian wickets cascaded. England needed 124, and MacLaren and Palairet saw them to 44 before the first wicket fell. Trumble and Saunders steadily gathered wickets thereafter, and with the last pair at the wicket and eight runs needed, a shower forced a dramatic pause. It was 45 minutes before Rhodes and Tate were able to resume, and the latter then jabbed Saunders for four. Four needed. Saunders bowled a faster ball, Tate played helplessly at it and was bowled. It bears the macabre label 'Tate's match', but the batting of Trumper and Jackson, the bowling of Lockwood, and Hill's diving one-handed boundary catch to dismiss Lilley should never be forgotten.

226, left: *Fred Tate, a fine bowler, who will be remembered for his fielding and batting lapses at Manchester.* 227, below: *A premature memorial card, printed when England were 'certain' of victory.* 228, right: *Trumper's 1902 bat, signed by dozens of Test players*

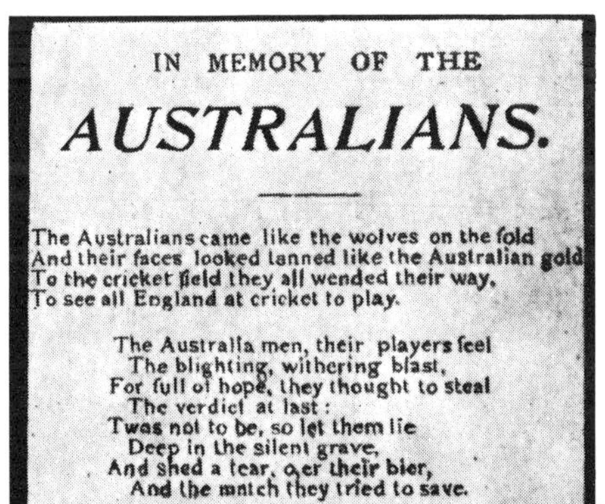

IN MEMORY OF THE

AUSTRALIANS.

The Australians came like the wolves on the fold
And their faces looked tanned like the Australian gold
To the cricket field they all wended their way,
To see all England at cricket to play.

The Australia men, their players feel
The blighting, withering blast,
For full of hope, they thought to steal
The verdict at last:
Twas not to be, so let them lie
Deep in the silent grave,
And shed a tear, o'er their bier,
And the match they tried to save.

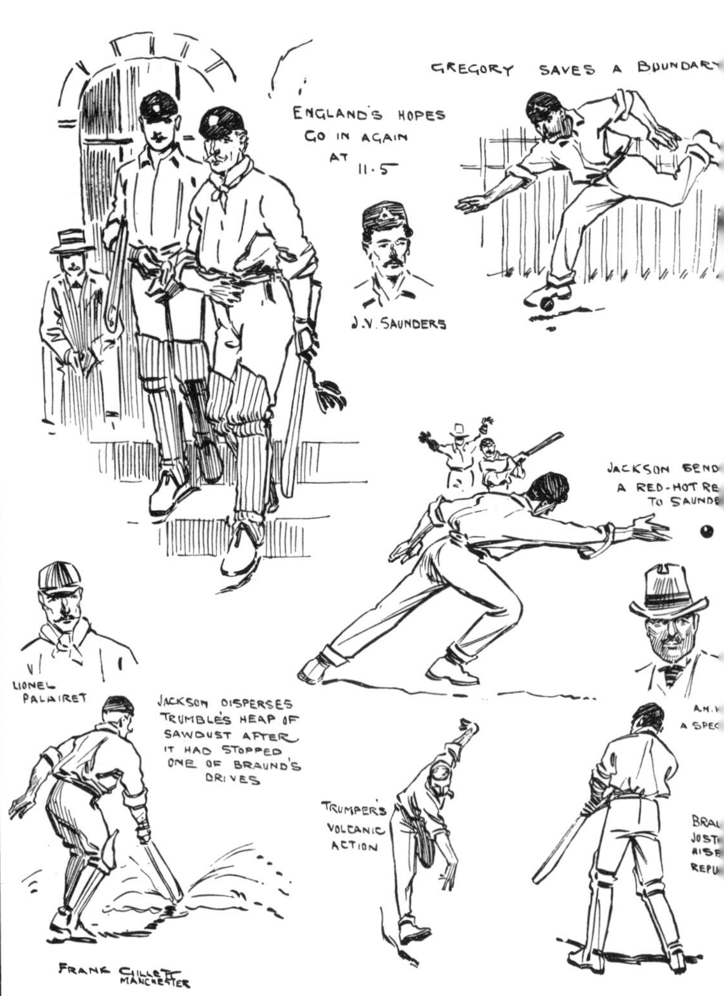

229, above, left: *Trumper and Duff put on 135 in only 78 minutes before lunch on the first day at Old Trafford.* 230, right: *Braund and Jackson resumed for England on the second day with the score 70 for 5 in reply to Australia's 299. England were 185 before Braund was bowled by Noble.* 231, left: *Chasing 124 for victory, England saw only four batsmen reach double-figures – Palairet 17, Abel 21, MacLaren 35, and Tyldesley 16. Tate was last out, bowled by Saunders four runs from England's target*

1902
The Oval, August 11, 12, 13

Australia *324 (H. Trumble 64*, M.A. Noble 52, V.T. Trumper 42, A.J.Y. Hopkins 40, G.H. Hirst 5 for 77) and 121 (W.H. Lockwood 5 for 45);* England *183 (G.H. Hirst 43, H. Trumble 8 for 65) and 263 for 9 (G.L. Jessop 104, G.H. Hirst 58*, F.S. Jackson 49, J.V. Saunders 4 for 105, H. Trumble 4 for 108).* England won by one wicket.

'Jessop's match' reached its climax when Rhodes joined Hirst for England's last wicket with 15 needed for victory. The runs were not obtained in singles, as legend has it; not did the two realistic Yorkshiremen plan to get them necessarily in that way. England's chance came only by virtue of Jessop's historic century. He went in when England, needing 263 in the fourth innings, were 48 for 5, and, with lunch intervening, he was 50 in 43 minutes. Jackson continued to bat gracefully as the rugged Jessop charged Trumble and Saunders – especially the latter – on an improving pitch. In only 75 minutes he had his century, and his 104 took 77 minutes and included 17 fours and an all-run five. Three times he drove the ball into the pavilion. He was missed twice. Jackson, who made only 18 of a sixth-wicket stand of 109, was succeeded by Hirst, who added 30 in eight minutes with 'The Croucher'. With Jessop's departure, caught at short leg off Armstrong, much responsibility fell on Hirst. Lockwood made two in a stand of 27 and Lilley 16 in a ninth-wicket stand of 34. Hirst and Rhodes (6 not out) did the rest. The course of this magnificent match was altered by England's success in averting a follow-on on a wet pitch which was worsening under a warm sun, and by Hill's dropping of Lockwood when the follow-on still seemed inevitable. Trumble bowled unchanged throughout both England innings, often spinning sharply from the off, but Saunders was the bowler to wilt most noticeably before the Jessop barrage. Against Trumble Jessop disciplined himself not to sweep hard across the line: he cracked him straight and through the off field. He faced only 80 balls and, after a number of failures, he had shown doubting opponents in that brief time that he was an attacking batsman without equal anywhere.

232, below, left: *A memorable innings begins.* 233, right: *Gilbert Jessop, whose 104 was perhaps the most famous innings in history*

hurt by the ball that bowled Palairet.
S.T. DADD
Jessop receiving his first ball.

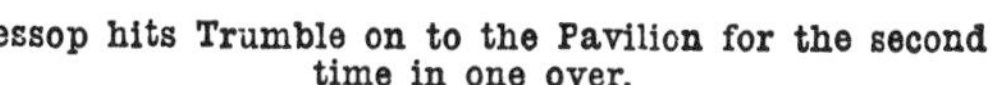

Jessop hits Trumble on to the Pavilion for the second time in one over.

234, above, left: *Lockwood bowls to Trumper in the fifth Test at The Oval.* 235, right: *Australia batting, Lilley keeping wicket, Braund at slip, MacLaren at gully.* 236, below: *Trumper cuts at Lockwood and misses; Lilley takes*

237, above, left: *Jessop pulls Saunders during his matchwinning century.* 238, right: *An extraordinary match ends: Rhodes has hit the winning single, and the players race off to escape the eager clutches of the frenzied spectators*

1903–04 FIRST TEST

Sydney, December 11, 12, 14, 15, 16, 17

Australia *285 (M.A. Noble 133, W.W. Armstrong 48, E.G. Arnold 4 for 76) and 485 (V.T. Trumper 185*, R.A. Duff 84, C. Hill 51, S.E. Gregory 43, W. Rhodes 5 for 94)*; England *577 (R.E. Foster 287, L.C. Braund 102, J.T. Tyldesley 53, W. Rhodes 40*) and 194 for 5 (T.W. Hayward 91, G.H. Hirst 60*)*. England won by 5 wickets.

The third truly enthralling Test in succession marked this as a halcyon period. For the first time MCC chose and managed the English touring team, and though Fry, Jackson and MacLaren were unavailable, it was a strong all-round combination. Arnold took Trumper's wicket with his first ball in Test cricket, and Australia were soon 12 for 3. Noble, with his only Test century, saved the innings in a 280-minute devotion on his debut as captain. A thunderstorm made batting anything but easy, and England were 117 for 4 before Braund and a hesitant Foster took the score to 243 that evening. In better conditions on the third day England took control. Foster, much more impressive now, in his first Test innings, reached his hundred and Braund did likewise next over and was then out. Their stand was worth 192 and England were 24 ahead. Three wickets fell, then Relf stayed while 115 were added, Foster off-driving and cutting with ease and charm and forcing through the leg side with powerful wristwork. His footwork, too, was attractive. He was 203 when Relf was out just before tea, but Australia had to wait a further record 130 runs before Foster was caught at mid-off after a seven-hour innings that included 37 fours. He and Rhodes were together only 66 minutes. England's record Test innings was surpassed and Foster's new individual Test record was to stand for 26 years. Australia, 292 behind, retrieved their honour through Trumper, who played probably his greatest innings, treating all the bowlers except Rhodes as if they were schoolboys, and being particularly severe on Braund. His 94-minute hundred is the third-fastest in these Tests, and in all he scored 26 fours. The crowd demonstrated when Hill was given 'run out', and Warner came close to calling his team off the field. Trumper ran out of partners, but England were still left a tallish task on a wearing pitch. Hayward and Hirst made sure of victory with a stand of 99 for the fifth wicket.

239, left: *Warner (left) and Noble toss at Sydney.* 240, above, right: *The scoreboard proclaims England's 577 and Foster's 287.* 241, below, left: *England enter the field – across the cycle track.* 242, right: *Bosanquet – revolutionary among bowlers*

243, left: *R.E. 'Tip' Foster, whose 287 is still the highest innings by any player in his first Test.* 244, right: *Victor Trumper, whose century at Sydney was probably his finest*

245, above: *Cartoonist's view of the unsavoury crowd behaviour during the first Test.* 246, left: *Ted Arnold – a wicket with his first ball in Tests.* 247, right: *Wilfred Rhodes, 54 years later, holds the emu egg trophy presented to him to mark his 7 for 135 in the match*

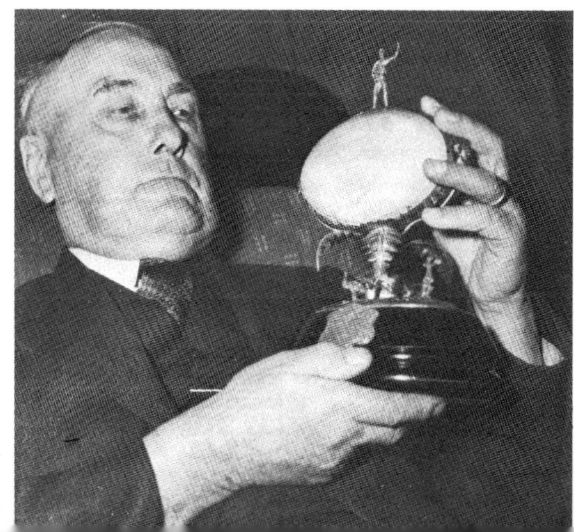

1903–04 SECOND TEST

Melbourne, January 1, 2, 4, 5

England *315 (J.T. Tyldesley 97, P.F. Warner 68, T.W. Hayward 58, R.E. Foster 49 ret.ill, W.P. Howell 4 for 43, H. Trumble 4 for 107) and 103 (J.T. Tyldesley 62, H. Trumble 5 for 34);* Australia *122 (V.T. Trumper 74, W. Rhodes 7 for 56) and 111 (W. Rhodes 8 for 68).* England won by 185 runs.

England progressed slowly, making 221 for 2 on the first day. Warner and Hayward scored 122 for the first wicket. Rain cut the second day short, and the pitch on the third day was very difficult. Yet Trumper stroked 74 in 112 minutes, peerless as ever while bowlers had everything to suit them. Wilfred Rhodes, slow left-arm, exploited the pitch and took more wickets than had ever been taken in an England-Australia Test. Tyldesley saved England's second innings, making his 62 out of 85; Relf, 10 not out, was the next-highest scorer. Three Australians reached double-figures: Trumper 35, Hill 20, and Noble a fine, back-to-the-wall 31 not out. Eighteen Australian wickets fell to catches.

248, above: *Bill Howell, the Penrith beekeeper, who made his off-breaks buzz.* 249, top, right: *Warner and Hayward open for England in the second Test.* 250, centre: *Hayward has cut Howell to the boundary.* 251, right: *Noble forces Hayward to play back*

1903–04 THIRD TEST

Adelaide, January 15, 16, 18, 19, 20

Australia *388 (V.T. Trumper 113, C. Hill 88, R.A. Duff 79, M.A. Noble 59) and 351 (S.E. Gregory 112, M.A. Noble 65, V.T. Trumper 59, B.J.T. Bosanquet 4 for 73);* England *245 (G.H. Hirst 58, P.F. Warner 48) and 278 (P.F. Warner 79, T.W. Hayward 67, G.H. Hirst 44, A.J.Y. Hopkins 4 for 81).* Australia won by 216 runs.

Australia were 355 for 6 by the first night, Duff having dominated an opening stand of 129 with Trumper, whose century was his third in five Tests. Hill and Trumper took the score to 272 before the second wicket fell. Bosanquet's then-novel googlies were confusing at times, even to his own wicket-keeper, Lilley. England, with only four specialist batsmen, were bowled out comparatively cheaply on a good pitch, and when Australia – for whom Noble and Gregory put on 162 for the fourth wicket – were all out a second time, England needed 495. Warner and Hayward started with 148, but there was no further prolonged resistance.

252, top, left: *The toss at Adelaide, and this time Noble wins it.* 253, right: *Duff pulls Fielder for four to start a magnificent opening stand with Trumper.* 254, centre, left: *Duff (left) and Trumper, one of the truly great opening pairs, enter at Adelaide, where the former for once outshone the latter.* 255, right: *Hill pulls Braund with all his considerable strength.* 256, left: *Warner, England's captain, falls to a grand catch by McLeod (out of picture) at mid-on off Trumble for 48*

257, above, left: *George Hirst lofts Trumble to long-off, to be caught by Trumper for 58.* 258, right: *England come off for a welcome respite.* 259, below, left: *Hayward is lbw to Hopkins, and England's opening stand of 148 is ended.* 260, right: *Rhodes is run out, and Australia have won the Adelaide Test by 216 runs*

1903–04 FOURTH TEST

Sydney, February 26, 27, 29, March 1, 2, 3

England *249 (A.E. Knight 70*, M.A. Noble 7 for 100) and 210 (T.W. Hayward 52);* Australia *131 (R.A. Duff 47, E.G. Arnold 4 for 28, W. Rhodes 4 for 33) and 171 (M.A. Noble 53*, B.J.T. Bosanquet 6 for 51).* England won by 157 runs.

Knight, batting for 260 minutes, held England's innings together, with main support from Braund, and with occasional delays for rain-showers Australia's reply stuttered before Rhodes and Arnold, with Braund getting the key wicket of Trumper for only seven. Again there were crowd demonstrations, provoked this time by the stoppages. Monday's play was lost, with the pitch aflood, and Australia's last five wickets fell for the addition of 17. Foster and Hayward began well for England, but the best stand was 55 by Warner and Rhodes for the last wicket. On a well-behaved pitch Australia then needed 329, but Bosanquet struck with a 'startling' spell of googlies, taking 5 for 12 at one point. Warner's XI thus regained the Ashes.

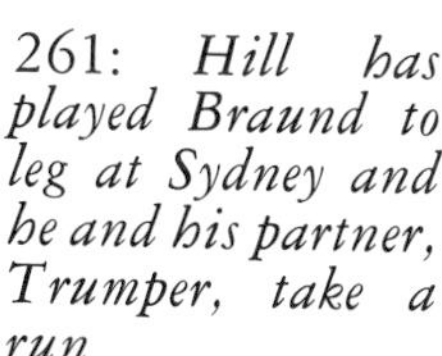

261: *Hill has played Braund to leg at Sydney and he and his partner, Trumper, take a run*

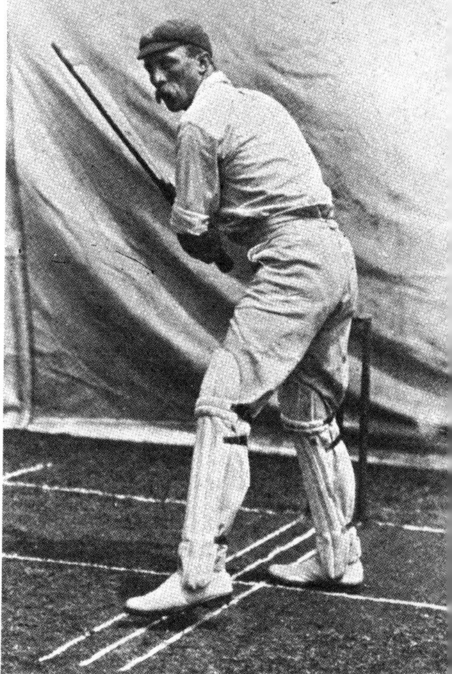

262, above: *Warner hits a four through the off side during his last-wicket stand of 55 with Rhodes in England's second innings.* 263, right: *Albert Knight, whose 70 not out saved England's first innings at Sydney*

1903–04 FIFTH TEST
Melbourne, March 5, 7, 8

Australia *247 (V.T. Trumper 88, L.C. Braund 8 for 81) and 133 (G.H. Hirst 5 for 48);* England *61 (A. Cotter 6 for 40, M.A. Noble 4 for 19) and 101 (H. Trumble 7 for 28).* Australia won by 218 runs.

Trumper led off with 88 in 110 minutes, but Braund, bowling his leg-breaks slightly faster than usual, proved too much for him and seven others. England lost Hayward and nightwatchman Arnold that evening without a run, and rain delayed the start of the second day's play until 4 pm, when the ball was lifting dangerously. Four were down for five runs before Tyldesley (10) and Foster (18) added 18, the highest stand of the innings. Fast bowler 'Tibby' Cotter, in his second Test, had batsmen retreating. He had the rare ability to keep steady balance even on wet footholds. Hirst was the principal agent in Australia's second-innings destruction; he bowled Trumper for nought. Hayward was absent, stricken with tonsilitis, but England's target was purely academic. Trumble bade farewell to Test cricket with glorious figures, including his second hat-trick: Bosanquet, Warner and Lilley. Foster (30) was caught off him by Trumper, one-handed running back to the long-on boundary.

264, left: *Hill, caught by Braund at slip off Rhodes for 16.* 265, below: *Hopkins hits Braund to square leg*

266, below: *Joy was unbridled at England's success in the 1903–04 series. Medallions were struck by MCC for each player. This is Ted Arnold's.* 267, right: *G. Hillyard Swinstead's drawing from the menu card of the dinner to welcome the team home*

1905 FIRST TEST

Trent Bridge, May 29, 30, 31

England *196 (J.T. Tyldesley 56, F.J. Laver 7 for 64) and 426 for 5 dec (A.C. MacLaren 140, F.S. Jackson 82*, J.T. Tyldesley 61, T.W. Hayward 47)*; Australia *221 (C. Hill 54, M.A. Noble 50, A. Cotter 45, F.S. Jackson 5 for 52) and 188 (S.E. Gregory 51, J. Darling 40, B.J.T. Bosanquet 8 for 107)*. England won by 213 runs.

Cotter, bowling fierily, and Laver, varying his medium-pace, bundled England out on a fair wicket. England then returned the compliment, Jackson cutting the heart of the innings out with the wickets of Noble, Hill and Darling in one over, after Trumper had retired with a back strain sustained earlier while attempting a slip catch. He did not bat in the second innings. MacLaren and Hayward set England off with 145, the former giving delight with his hooking of Cotter. Jackson and Rhodes added 113 unbroken, and Australia, having bowled defensively, now tried to bat out the 4½ hours remaining. Bosanquet, often erratic, was kept on and reaped his reward.

286, left: *Deft penwork shows some of the second-day action at Trent Bridge. A.O. Jones's catching of Gregory was the highlight.* 269, below: *Fast bowler Cotter hurls one down to Hayward*

Price 1d.

NOTTS. COUNTY CRICKET CLUB

Trent Bridge Ground, Monday, May 29, 30, 31, 1905.

ENGLAND v. AUSTRALIA.

Bowler's No.	ENGLAND.	1st Innings		2nd Inn.	
1	Mr. A. C. MacLaren (Lc)	c Kelly, b Laver	2	c Duff, b Laver	140
2	T. Hayward (Surrey)	b Cotter	5	c Darling, b Armstrong	47
3	J. T. Tyldesley (Lanc.)	c Duff, b Laver	56	c and b Duff	61
4	Mr. A. O. Jones (Notts)	b Laver	4	b Duff	30
5	Hon. F. S. Jackson (Cpt)	b Cotter	0	not out	82
6	Mr B. J. Bosanquet (Mx)	b Laver	27	b Cotter	6
7	W. Rhodes (Yorks.)	c Noble, b Laver	29	not out	39
8	A. A. Lilley (Wrk.)	c and b Laver	37	...	...
9	Mr. G. L. Jessop (Glo')	b Laver	0	...	...
10	J. Gunn (Notts.)	b Cotter	8	...	...
11	E. Arnold (Worc.)	not out	2	...	...
		Byes 21, leg-byes 5, wides 0, no-balls 0	26	B 11, l-b 9, w 1, n-b 0	21
		Total	196	Innings Closed	426

Wkts fell	1	2	3	4	5	6	7	8	9	10
1st Inn.	6	24	40	49	98	119	119	139	187	196
2nd Inn	145	222	276	301	313	...	...	...	...	...

Batsman's No.	AUSTRALIA.	1st Innings		2nd Inn.	
1	Mr. J. Darling (Capt.)	c Bosanquet, b Jackson	0	b Bosanquet	40
2	Mr. R. A. Duff	c Hayward, b Gunn	1	c and b Bosanquet	25
3	Mr. C. Hill	b Jackson	54	c and b Bosanquet	8
4	Mr. M. A. Noble	c Lilley, b Jackson	50	st Lilley, b Bosanquet	7
5	Mr. W. W. Armstrong	st Lilley, b Rhodes	27	c Jackson, b Bosanquet	6
6	Mr. S. E. Gregory	c Jones, b Jackson	2	c Arnold, b Bosanquet	51
7	Mr. C. E. McLeod	b Arnold	4	l b w, Bosanquet	13
8	Mr. F. Laver	c Jones, b Jackson	5	st Lilley, b Bosanquet	5
9	Mr. J. J. Kelly	not out	1	not out	6
10	Mr. A. Cotter	c and b Jessop	45	b Rhodes	18
11	Mr. V. Trumper	retired hurt	13	absent	0
		Byes 16, leg-byes 2, wides 1, no-balls 0	19	B 4, l-b 3, w 2, n-b 0	9
		Total	221	Total	188

Wkts fell	1	2	3	4	5	6	7	8	9	10
1st Inn.	1	129	130	130	200	204	209	216	216	221
2nd Inn.	62	75	82	93	100	139	144	175	188	...

ANALYSIS

Australia Bowling.	overs	mdns.	runs	wkts.	overs	mdns.	runs	wkts
Cotter	23	2	64	3	17	1	59	1
Laver	31 3	14	64	7	34	7	121	1
Noble	3	0	19	0	7	1	31	0
McLeod	8	2	19	0	28	9	84	0
Armstrong	6	3	4	0	52	24	67	0
Duff	...	...	...	...	15	2	43	2
England Bowling								
Arnold	11	2	39	1	4	2	7	0
Gunn	6	2	27	1		...	...	...
Jessop	7	2	18	1	1	0	1	0
Bosanquet	7	0	29	0	32 4	2	107	8
Rhodes	18	6	39	1	30	8	58	1
Jackson	14 5	2	52	5	5	3	6	0

Umpires, Jas. Phillips and John Carlin. Stumps drawn at 6.30

Charles H. Richards, Printer. Lower Parliament Street, Nottingham.

270, above, left: *Gregory and Darling lead the Australians off for lunch on the opening day at Trent Bridge, England 98 for 5, Tyldesley and Bosanquet the not-out batsmen.* 271, right: *The scorecard perpetuates MacLaren's fifth century against Australia and Bosanquet's remarkable analysis.* 272, left: *England build up a winning lead, though Trumper, unable to bat because of injury, was missed when Australia tried to play out time*

1905 SECOND TEST
Lord's, June 15, 16, 17

England *282 (C.B. Fry 73, A.C. MacLaren 56, J.T. Tyldesley 43) and 151 for 5 (A.C. MacLaren 79);* Australia *181 (J. Darling 41, F.S. Jackson 4 for 50).* Match drawn.

Only MacLaren and Tyldesley played with anything approaching freedom after ten days of wet weather had left the pitch helpful to bowlers. Thunderstorms occurred each night of the match. Fry spent 3½ hours over his 73, Darling's field having been placed tightly and Armstrong bowling many overs down the leg side. Trumper and Duff hit a swift 57 before the pitch dried to an awkward state, and a collapse was arrested by Darling and Armstrong, who saved the follow-on. MacLaren attacked on the second afternoon, and Fry held an end (36 not out in 90 minutes), leaving England 252 ahead, but the final day was washed out.

273, above, left: *Charlie McLeod bowls to MacLaren around the wicket with a strong offside field.* 274, right: *Stanley Jackson leads out the amateurs in the England XI at Lord's: MacLaren, Fry, and Jones.* 275, below, left: *Rhodes to Darling – with typically high backlift.* 276, right: *MacLaren majestically places Australian opening bowler McLeod to the legside boundary*

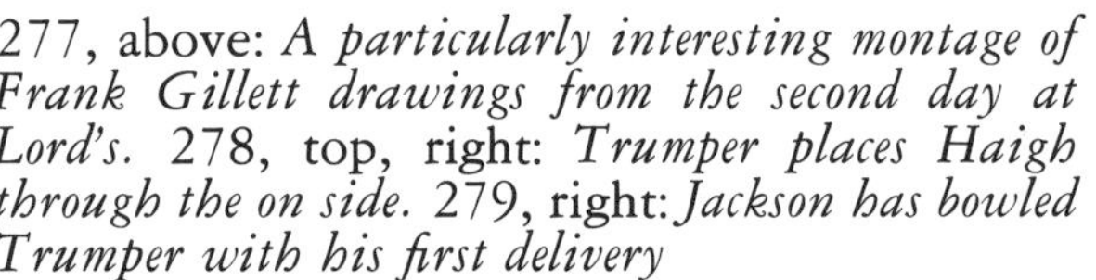

277, above: *A particularly interesting montage of Frank Gillett drawings from the second day at Lord's.* 278, top, right: *Trumper places Haigh through the on side.* 279, right: *Jackson has bowled Trumper with his first delivery*

1905 THIRD TEST

Headingley, July 3, 4, 5

England *301 (F.S. Jackson 144*) and 295 for 5 dec (J.T. Tyldesley 100, T.W. Hayward 60, G.H. Hirst 40*, W.W. Armstrong 5 for 122);* Australia *195 (W.W. Armstrong 66, R.A. Duff 48, A. Warren 5 for 57) and 224 for 7 (M.A. Noble 62).* Match drawn.

England's captain, going in at 57 for 3, lost Hayward at 64, but found support in Hirst, and went on to make Leeds' first Test century. He batted 268 minutes, hit 18 fours, and was missed just once, at 130. Warren, in his only Test, took Trumper's wicket twice (8 and 0), and bowled with plenty of life. Australia, so far behind, could only play a containing game, and Armstrong bowled 51 overs, mostly down the leg side, with an appropriate field-setting. Tyldesley batted beautifully and sometimes overcame the negative bowling by stepping to leg and hitting through the off side. Many critics felt England should have declared sooner, but Blythe took three early wickets, and only his dropping of a return catch from Noble interfered with England's drive to victory. Noble and Gregory hung on defiantly.

280: *An assortment of straw boaters, panamas, and other hats shelter the heads of the crowd at the Leeds Test match*

DARLING AGAIN LOSES THE TOSS MUCH TO HILL'S ANNOYANCE
FRY OPENS ENGLAND'S ACCOUNT WITH A CUT(!)

281, top, left: *Darling's third lost toss annoys Hill.* 282, above: *Arnold Warren, the Derbyshire fast bowler, who was highly successful in his only Test.* 283, centre: *Trumper drives.* 284, below, left: *Some of Australia's uncomfortable moments captured . . .* 285, right: *as is some of England's happiness on the final day*

INTERLUDE
TOOK HIS CAPTAIN OUT A GLASS OF SOMETHING
THREE OF THE AUSTRALIANS ALSO REFRESHED
FROM THE CLASS. ON RETURNING TO THE
A SMALL VOICE, WHICH CAUSED HIRST TO
A SERAPHIC SMILE, ENQUIRED
WHAT WUR IN IT, GEORGE HERBERT?"
A.R. WARREN, WHO, BY CLEAN BOWLING TRUMPER, FULLY JUSTIFIED HIS CHOICE
"GEORGE HERBERT" CATCHES HILL FROM HIS OWN BOWLING
TRUMPER CHOPS DOWN TOO LATE ON AN EXTRA FAST ONE FROM WARREN
A MISTAKE ONE HARDLY EXPECTED NOBLE TO MAKE
A GENTLE TAP TO TOM HAYWARD AT SLIP

A WELL-JUDGED CATCH BY HILL AT DEEP SQUARE LEG GETS RID OF DENTON
JACKSON IS LEARNING HOW TO HIT ARMSTRONG
"EVERYBODY LAUGHS" – EXCEPT KELLY!
IN SOLITARY GRANDEUR ON THE CYCLE TRACK
A GREAT BEGINNING – FROM ENGLAND'S POINT OF VIEW
HIRST CATCHES TRUMPER
JACKSON DECLARES AT 295

1905 FOURTH TEST

Old Trafford, July 24, 25, 26

England 446 *(F.S. Jackson 113, T.W. Hayward 82, R.H. Spooner 52, C.E. McLeod 5 for 125);* Australia 197 *(J. Darling 73, W. Brearley 4 for 72) and 169 (R.A. Duff 60, W. Brearley 4 for 54).* England won by an innings and 80 runs.

On a deadened pitch England went methodically about building a secure score. Hayward was his usual sound self and Spooner batted charmingly. But Jackson, who could do no wrong, was the century-maker, batting 3¾ hours altogether. By lunch on the second day Australia were reduced to 27 for 3, Brearley having bowled with exceptional speed. Throughout the remainder of the innings and in the follow-on the Australians, after the example of their leader, went after the bowling as if victory were imminent. Darling's 73 took only 85 minutes and included five hits clean into the crowd – then worth only four. (One of these blows scattered the inhabitants of the Press box). Following on, Australia were 118 for one that evening, and incredibly wickets were lost with such abandon that the match was all over by lunch on the last day. The pitch was now tricky, but no batsman attempted to 'book in' carefully. When rain began to fall later it was wondered why Australia had not fought harder for a draw, with an eye on the fifth Test.

286, left: *Brearley storms in to bowl to Trumper in the Manchester Test.* 287, below, left: *England stretch their score on the second day.* 288, right: *England press on to victory on the last day*

289, left: *Walter Brearley, the tear-away Lancashire amateur fast bowler.* 290, right: *Reggie Spooner, one of the Golden Age's premier stylists. Both played with credit on their home ground in the 1905 series*

1905 — FIFTH TEST

The Oval, August 14, 15, 16

England *430 (C.B. Fry 144, F.S. Jackson 76, T.W. Hayward 59, E.G. Arnold 40, A. Cotter 7 for 148) and 261 for 6 dec (J.T. Tyldesley 112*, R.H. Spooner 79);* Australia *363 (R.A. Duff 146, J. Darling 57, J.J. Kelly 42, W. Brearley 5 for 110) and 124 for 4.* Match drawn.

The Hon. F. Stanley Jackson, born the same day as Darling, the opposing captain, won his fifth successive toss, and for the fifth time in the series England took first innings. The draw gave England a 2–0 victory, and Jackson himself topped the batting aggregates and averages and the bowling averages for both sides. Fry at last showed the Australians how he won his great reputation, driving magnificently as he put on 151 for the fourth wicket with Jackson. Cotter bowled heroically on an immaculate pitch, though his field gave him scant support at times. Duff, who began his Test career with a century, ended it with another, attained in barely more than two hours. He was missed three times, once at slip off a high skyer, but his brilliance atoned in some way for the repeated failure of his illustrious partner, Trumper. Darling, also in his last Test match, batted with vigour. England's second innings began shakily but, after a couple of umpiring controversies, Tyldesley and Spooner added 158 in a display of the finest Edwardian batsmanship. The closure, with three England players indisposed, was delayed, and Australia played out time without much trouble.

291: *Jackson and Fry return after tea on the first day to extend their fourth-wicket stand to 151. Hill is the fieldsman deep in conversation*

on what was, perhaps, the best wicket they batted on since the match at Nottingham. aren and Hayward went in, and the old Engaptain began with his characteristic cut for le had only made 2 more wher he was caught he slips. Similarly with Tyldesley, who 16 in a style to suggest that he was about ock off the fast bowler, but was suddenly clean d by his adversary. That brought together rard and Fry, and these two steady men soon ned the flowing tide. They have both been ed for playing too slow a game—especially . Fry—but England had cause to be grateful em yesterday. They came together when the was 32; and they put on 100 runs before ward most unluckily set his heel in his wicket stepped back to pull Hopkins round to leg. batsmen were still running when the umpire up his hand. Hayward's had been an innings s usual style, which is to say that it was the which during yesterday morning was exactly England wanted and expected of him. Fry's gs was equally grateful. He was as steady rer; but on this occasion the Australians did succeed in tying up his strokes as on some ous occasions, and he hit with such vigour his fifty was put together in ten minutes over hour. This partnership was the thing which established England's position.

e new batsman was Jackson, and he and Fry ised another thorough mastery over the bowl- Their stand, indeed, provided by far the finest re of a memorable day's play. The Yorkshire- was a trifle unsteady to begin with, a lucky t of his going over slip's head, and later, when 7, he gave a palpable chance of stumping off strong which Kelly fumbled. These chances t, he batted in the same watchful style as at hester, Leeds, and Nottingham, quite content

292, above, left: *At The Oval, Fry caught in some stiff attitudes; and Hayward's is positively fatal.* 293, right: *Some of Duff's glorious farewell to Test cricket.* 294, below, left: *The crowd treads the hallowed turf between innings, though rain seems to be threatening.* 295, right: *Tyldesley makes the seventh and last century of the series; Gehrs and Spooner attract attention as substitutes*

1907–08 FIRST TEST

Sydney, December 13, 14, 16, 17, 18, 19

England 273 *(G. Gunn 119, K.L. Hutchings 42, A. Cotter 6 for 101) and 300 (G. Gunn 74, J. Hardstaff 63, J.V. Saunders 4 for 68);* Australia 300 *(C. Hill 87, V.T. Trumper 43, A. Fielder 6 for 82) and 275 for 8 (H. Carter 61, W.W. Armstrong 44, P.A. McAlister 41).* Australia won by 2 wickets.

A fascinating match had as its first-day highlight a robust century by Gunn, who was in Australia for his health, and called into the side when the captain, A.O. Jones, was unable to play because of a breakdown in his own health. It was Gunn's first Test. He moved from 78 to 102 with boundaries, and added 117 for the fourth wicket with Braund. Gunn put on 113 for the same wicket with Hardstaff in the second innings. The contest embraced some aggressive fast bowling, Cotter, Fielder and Barnes all inflicting hardships on the batsmen. Rain came on occasionally, and indeed the fifth day was washed out. On the last day Australia began at 63 for 3, and soon slipped to 124 for 6, still needing 150. Wicketkeeper Carter, in his first Test, hit about him for 61 in 67 minutes, and Cotter, more cautious than usual, and 19-year-old Hazlitt had a rapid, undefeated ninth-wicket stand of 56 to grasp victory. Young, England's reserve, bespectacled wicketkeeper, had an unfortunate match, and Fane, the stand-in captain, underbowled Crawford and Rhodes.

296, left: *Albert 'Tibby' Cotter, a wholehearted fast bowler with a slinging action.* 297, right: *George Gunn – in Australia for his health – a lively century in his first Test innings*

1907–08 SECOND TEST

Melbourne, January 1, 2, 3, 4, 6, 7

Australia 266 *(M.A. Noble 61, V.T. Trumper 49, J.N. Crawford 5 for 79) and 397 (W.W. Armstrong 77, M.A. Noble 64, V.T. Trumper 63, C.G. Macartney 54, H. Carter 53, S.F. Barnes 5 for 72);* England 382 *(K.L. Hutchings 126, J.B. Hobbs 83, L.C. Braund 49, A. Cotter 5 for 142) and 282 for 9 (F.L. Fane 50).* England won by one wicket.

Jack Hobbs's first Test match was a thriller. Australia were kept down to a modest first-innings total which England passed with only three men out. Hobbs batted for 195 minutes, and added 99 with Hutchings, who went on to his century in 125 minutes and put on 108 with Braund. Cotter and Saunders then had some success, and the deficit was only 116 when Australia went in again. Trumper and Noble wiped this off before being separated, and Armstrong and Macartney made 106 for the fifth wicket. The tail provided runs too, and England began the task of making 282 early on the fifth afternoon. Hobbs and Gunn fell at 54, and the classical Hutchings was restrained this time. The score reached 159 for 4 that evening. It slumped to 209 for 8, whereupon Humphries, the wicketkeeper, and Barnes managed 34 together. Armstrong had Humphries lbw, and Fielder took his place with 39 still needed. By correct and nerveless batting, against keen fielding and threatening bowling changes, the batsmen brought the scores level. Armstrong, with seven men on the leg side, bowled at Barnes's pads: he drew back and pushed the ball to cover: he ran, but saw his partner motionless: he shouted to Fielder, who started off: Hazlitt gathered the ball and had only to toss it to Carter to make the match a tie: instead, he hurled it at the stumps, missed, and Fielder was home.

298, above, left: *Kenneth Hutchings – 'the English Trumper' – 126 at Melbourne.* 299, above, right: *Frederick Fane, Irish-born, who led England in the first three Tests when illness forced Jones out.* 300, left: *Joe Hardstaff, third in the England batting averages for the series. His son played for England a generation later.* 301, right: *'Rip's' tribute to Barnes and Fielder, the last-wicket heroes*

1907–08

Adelaide, January 10, 11, 13, 14, 15, 16

Australia *285 (C.G. Macartney 75, R.J. Hartigan 48, V.S. Ransford 44, A. Fielder 4 for 80) and 506 (C. Hill 160, R.J. Hartigan 116, M.A. Noble 65)*; England *363 (G. Gunn 65, J.N. Crawford 62, J. Hardstaff 61, F.L. Fane 48) and 183 (J. Hardstaff 72, L.C. Braund 47, J.A. O'Connor 5 for 40, J.V. Saunders 5 for 65)*. Australia won by 245 runs.

Roger Hartigan made a conspicuous debut, batting at No. 8 in each innings. In the second, when Australia were 180 for 7 (only 102 runs on), he was joined by Hill, who came in late after an attack of influenza, and in tremendous heat they made a century apiece by stumps, when the Englishmen contemplated an Australian score of 397 for 7. Hill was exhausted, but the next day, after losing Hartigan after an all-wicket Test record partnership of 243 in even-time, he continued again in heat touching 106°F, until he had batted for 319 minutes, with only one chance. Hartigan was missed several times, once from a simple catch to Barnes at mid-off. England thus faced an unexpected and improbable score of 429 for victory, and apart from a stand by Hardstaff and Braund, which took the total from 15 for 3 to 128 for 4, the side faded out, with Hobbs retiring with a side strain. Medium-pacer O'Connor, like Hartigan, entered Test cricket with a fanfare: eight wickets for 150.

302, above, left: *Jack Crawford, who took 30 wickets in the series with medium-pace spin bowling.* 303, above, right: *Roger Hartigan, the fourth Australian to make a century in his first Test against England.* 304, right: *'The Invalid: Do I look very seedy, boys?' A jibe at Clem Hill, whose indisposition did not prevent him from batting over five hours at Adelaide*

1907–08 FOURTH TEST

Melbourne, February 7, 8, 10, 11

Australia *214 (V.S. Ransford 51, M.A. Noble 48, J.N. Crawford 5 for 48, A. Fielder 4 for 54) and 385 (W.W. Armstrong 133*, H. Carter 66, V.S. Ransford 54, A. Fielder 4 for 91);* England *105 (J.B. Hobbs 57, J.V. Saunders 5 for 28) and 186 (G. Gunn 43, J.V. Saunders 4 for 76).* Australia won by 308 runs.

For the third time running (and they were to do it again in the final Test) Australia returned a formidable second-innings total. Their first innings owed much to Ransford, a hard-cutting left-hander, and Armstrong, who put on 91 for the sixth wicket. Hobbs hit out for England before the pitch livened after rain, scoring ten boundaries in his 57, but the last eight wickets fell for 15 runs. Trumper failed to score in either innings, but from 77 for 5 the innings was rescued by Armstrong, first with Ransford then with Macartney, and Carter, with whom he added 112. The powerful Armstrong took over four hours for his hundred, but then struck Braund for two sixes. England, demoralised, were faced with another astronomical target, and fell dismally short, relinquishing the Ashes to Noble's confident XI.

305, above, left: *Arthur Fielder, the Kent fast bowler, who took 25 wickets in four Tests in the 1907–08 series.* 306, right: *Warwick Armstrong, immovable, ever-growing, uncompromising opponent.* 307, left: *Vernon Ransford, the Victorian left-hander, who contributed fifties in both innings at Melbourne*

1907–08 FIFTH TEST
Sydney, February 21, 22, 24, 25, 26, 27

Australia *137 (S.E. Gregory 44, S.F. Barnes 7 for 60) and 422 (V.T. Trumper 166, S.E. Gregory 56, C. Hill 44, J.N. Crawford 5 for 141, W. Rhodes 4 for 102);* England *281 (G. Gunn 122*, J.B. Hobbs 72) and 229 (W. Rhodes 69, F.L. Fane 46, J.V. Saunders 5 for 82).* Australia won by 49 runs.

A.O. Jones put Australia in to bat, and when England finished the first day at 116 for one the move could be said to have been successful. Barnes ran through the Australians, rendering the change in batting order of no account. Hobbs and Gunn put on 134 for England's second wicket, but rain interruptions on the second and third days lent frustration to the batting. Gunn batted for 4¾ hours, hitting a six and only seven fours. Australia went into the lead during a third-wicket stand of 114 between Trumper and Gregory, but Rhodes's dropping of Trumper off a ball from Barnes that kicked had a profound effect on the match; the batsman was only one at the time. He proceeded to bat in his most delightful manner, making 117 of his runs on the on side, batting four hours in all, and ending his sequence of failures in the most positive way. England needed 279, but more rain damaged the pitch, and the first six men went for 87.

308, left: *Victor Trumper, who, with luck, ended a depressing run of failures.* 309, above: *The Sydney scoreboard tells a tense tale*

310, below: *Jones and Noble, the captains, bid each other farewell.* 311, right: *Jack Hobbs (with veteran Tom Hayward) – a successful first series*

1909 FIRST TEST

Edgbaston, May 27, 28, 29

Australia *74 (C. Blythe 6 for 44, G.H. Hirst 4 for 28) and 151 (S.E. Gregory 43, V.S. Ransford 43, G.H. Hirst 5 for 58, C. Blythe 5 for 58);* England *121 (W.W. Armstrong 5 for 27) and 105 for 0 (J.B. Hobbs 62*).* England won by 10 wickets.

As the scores reflect, rain beforehand dictated the course of the match. Australia found the swerve of Hirst and the spin of Blythe, also left-arm, too much. They bowled unchanged through the innings. The fourth-wicket 48 by Tyldesley and A.O. Jones was the major stand of England's innings, though Jessop slammed 22 in 20 minutes. The pitch was far from 'impossible' when Australia batted again, and Gregory and Ransford added 81 for the third wicket; but the two left-arm bowlers had their way again, helped this time by some brilliant catching: Jones caught a hard hit by Noble left-handed at short leg, and Tyldesley, back against the pavilion rails, held a drive by Cotter. Hobbs and Fry, both dismissed first ball by Macartney, opened the final innings and gained for England a surprisingly resounding victory. Hobbs showed extraordinary class.

312, left: *George Hirst: he and Blythe took all 20 Australian wickets.* 313, left, below: *Hobbs and captain MacLaren open England's innings. Macartney dismissed them and Fry for five runs between them.* 314, below: *Hirst bowls to Armstrong; Bardsley is non-striker.* 315, bottom, right: *The Birmingham crowd relish England's victory*

1909 SECOND TEST

Lord's, June 14, 15, 16

England *269 (J.H. King 60, A.F.A. Lilley 47, J.T. Tyldesley 46, A. Cotter 4 for 80) and 121 (W.W. Armstrong 6 for 35);* Australia *350 (V.S. Ransford 143*, W. Bardsley 46, A.E. Relf 5 for 85) and 41 for 1.* Australia won by 9 wickets.

Noble put England – a much-altered side – in to bat, and the move would have been even more efficacious but for the unanticipated success of King, a 38-year-old left-hander playing in his only Test. England had no really fast bowler, and on a quicker pitch Australia took a useful lead on the second day. Ransford's century, his only one in Tests, lasted four hours, and he was missed three times, twice off King, who finished with one for 99. Relf bowled 45 overs. Armstrong took six good wickets, operating from the Nursery end, with the slope helping his leg-breaks. This victory marked the end of the touring team's poor performances. They lost only once again – at Scarborough towards the end of the season.

316, left: *Armstrong, whose 6 for 35 was the best return of his Test career.* 317, right: *John King – top-scorer for England in his only Test.* 318, below, left: *Albert Relf – Sussex all-rounder who carried the main burden of England's bowling at Lord's.* 319, below, right: *Fashion parade during an interval. The old Tavern is quiet*

1909 — THIRD TEST

Headingley, July 1, 2, 3

Australia *188 (S.E. Gregory 46, V.S. Ransford 45, W. Rhodes 4 for 38) and 207 (W.W. Armstrong 45, S.F. Barnes 6 for 63);* England *182 (J. Sharp 61, J.T. Tyldesley 55, C.G. Macartney 7 for 58) and 87 (A. Cotter 5 for 38, C.G. Macartney 4 for 27).* Australia won by 126 runs.

Gregory (46 in 130 minutes) and Ransford made 80 for Australia's second wicket, and Tyldesley and Sharp 106 for England's third. Otherwise, the bowlers had things much as they wished. Macartney, slow left-arm, spun the ball and used the 'arm ball' to good effect. The major setback for England, however, came on the first day, when Jessop strained his back. He was unable to bat in the match. Resolute batting by Australia, especially from Armstrong (45 in 2½ hours) and Macartney (18 out of 80 scored for the last three wickets) meant England needed 214, a task seemingly manageable at 60 for 2. But Macartney, this time with Cotter's speed from the other end, overthrew all batting endeavour. Hobbs top-scored with 30.

320, above, left: *MacLaren and Noble toss at Leeds. Australia won all five tosses in the series.* 321, right: *England take the field: Brearley, Fry, Jessop (probably), and MacLaren, followed by Hirst and Lilley.* 322, below: *Barnes bowls to McAlister*

323, above, left: *Peter McAlister and Syd Gregory, Australia's openers.* 324, top, right: *Lilley and MacLaren appeal against Gregory for lbw.* 325, above, right: *Tyldesley and Sharp, England's not-out pair on the first evening.* 326, below, left: *Tyldesley drives Armstrong for four.* 327, below, right: *Sharp st Carter b Macartney 61*

328: *Rhodes caught behind by Carter off Laver for 12*

1909 FOURTH TEST
Old Trafford, July 26, 27, 28

Australia *147 (S.F. Barnes 5 for 56, C. Blythe 5 for 63) and 279 for 9 dec (V.S. Ransford 54*, C.G. Macartney 51, V.T. Trumper 48, W. Rhodes 5 for 83);* England *119 (F.J. Laver 8 for 31) and 108 for 3 (R.H. Spooner 58).* Match drawn.

Armstrong (32 not out), going in at 48 for 4, saw Australia clear of humiliation on a damp pitch on which Barnes operated throughout the innings. Cotter once hit Blythe straight out of the ground, and was eventually caught trying to do it again. England were routed by Laver, who used the breeze from leg and sometimes brought the ball back off the pitch. His flight was often puzzling. Rain cut the second day with Australia 77 for 2, and on an easy third-day pitch Noble allowed the innings to continue until England were left with only 2½ hours.

329, above: *Noble plays Blythe to leg.* 330, left: *Frank Laver, whose skilful work on the ball brought him 8 for 31 at Old Trafford.* 331, right: *Opponents Armstrong and Hutchings come in from net practice.* 332, below: *Trumper, now batting in the middle order, is beaten down the leg side*

333, top: *MacLaren turns an eye to the weather as he leads England out; Warner, Tyldesley, Hutchings, and Sharp follow.* 334, above, left: *Blythe bowls, left-arm round-the-wicket.* 335, right: *Bardsley tries to sweep him*

336, left: *Sydney Barnes photographed at Old Trafford, where he took 5 for 56.* 337, top: *Gregory plays back to Barnes.* 338, above: *Bardsley defends with an upright bat. Lilley is England's wicketkeeper*

1909 FIFTH TEST

The Oval, August 9, 10, 11

Australia *325 (W. Bardsley 136, V.T. Trumper 73, C.G. Macartney 50, D.W. Carr 5 for 146) and 339 for 5 dec (W. Bardsley 130, S.E. Gregory 74, M.A. Noble 55);* England *352 (J. Sharp 105, W. Rhodes 66, C.B. Fry 62, K.L. Hutchings 59, A. Cotter 6 for 95) and 104 for 3 (W. Rhodes 54).* Match drawn.

Carr, 37 years old and in his first season of county cricket, was given the new ball by MacLaren after Noble had won his fifth toss of the series, and in his first seven overs, from the Vauxhall end, he obtained the wickets of Gregory, Noble and Armstrong with his googlies. Ransford fell to Barnes at 58, but Trumper, who batted in the middle order throughout the series with little success, regained the initiative with Bardsley, who went on to become the first batsman ever to make two centuries in a Test match. These two, with Macartney, hit Carr hard and often, and – grossly overbowled – he finished the match with 7 for 280 off 69 overs. Fry and Rhodes put on 104 for England's third wicket, Sharp and Hutchings 142 for the seventh, taking their side ahead. Sharp, missed by Carter off the speedy Cotter at 93, batted for 170 minutes. On a final day lacking in urgency, Australia batted until hardly more than two hours' play remained, Bardsley and Gregory posting 180 for the first wicket – a record for Australia against England until 1964. Left-hander Bardsley batted for 3¾ hours in each innings.

339, opposite: *Warren Bardsley reaches his first century at The Oval with a single off Rhodes. Macartney is his partner.* 340, above: *C.B. Fry is run out after being sent back by Rhodes, who played the ball to cover. Gregory threw to Noble at the stumps.* 341, below, left: *The end of Woolley's first Test innings: b Cotter 8.* 342, right: *Trumper faces the bowling during his stand of 118 with Bardsley for the fifth wicket*

343, left: *Fry hits out at Noble.* 344, below: *The twelfth man, in straw boater, brings welcome drinks.* 345, right: *Sharp cover-drives during his century*

1911–12 FIRST TEST

Sydney, December 15, 16, 18, 19, 20, 21

Australia 447 *(V.T. Trumper 113, R.B. Minnett 90, W.W. Armstrong 60, C. Hill 46) and 308 (C. Kelleway 70, C. Hill 65, F.R. Foster 5 for 92, J.W.H.T. Douglas 4 for 50);* England 318 *(J.W. Hearne 76, J.B. Hobbs 63, F.R. Foster 56, W. Rhodes 41, H.V. Hordern 5 for 85) and 291 (G. Gunn 62, J.W. Hearne 43, H.V. Hordern 7 for 90).* Australia won by 146 runs.

There was barely a clue here that England were to run away with the series. Australia made 317 for 5 on the first day, Trumper 95 not out. He and Minnett (in his first Test) added 109 for the sixth wicket. Dr Hordern, in his first Test against England, beset the batsmen with a flow of problems with his googly bowling, only 20-year-old Hearne – himself a leg-break/googly bowler and also on debut – playing him with confidence. Barnes and the left-arm swing bowler Foster foreshadowed their great successes by keeping Australia in check, Kelleway and Hill making the only lengthy stand of the innings. The first-innings advantage, however, gave Australia a long lead, and though several England players applied themselves, the home side had a matchwinner in Hordern, who bowled with uncanny accuracy for one of his kind: Trumper fielded close at short leg for him, and his dipping flight and tantalising pace induced constant doubt. P.F. Warner, who took this MCC side to Australia, fell ill after the opening match, and Johnny Douglas led England in all five Tests.

346, above, left: *Australia's captain Hill run out by Strudwick after smart fielding by Rhodes at backward square leg. Armstrong is non-striker.* 347, right: *Dr H.V. 'Ranji' Hordern, who had conspicuous success on his debut against England.* 348, below, left: *Frank Foster, the young Warwickshire left-arm fast-medium bowler, who took 32 wickets in the series.* 349, right: *Roy Minnett – unlucky to miss a century in his first Test innings*

1911–12 SECOND TEST

Melbourne, December 30, January 1, 2, 3

Australia *184 (H.V. Hordern 49*, V.S. Ransford 43, S.F. Barnes 5 for 44) and 299 (W.W. Armstrong 90, A. Cotter 41, F.R. Foster 6 for 91);* England *265 (J.W. Hearne 114, W. Rhodes 61, H.V. Hordern 4 for 66, A. Cotter 4 for 73) and 219 for 2 (J.B. Hobbs 126*, G. Gunn 43).* England won by 8 wickets.

A famous opening spell by the 38-year-old Barnes gave England a grip on the match which they never relinquished. Unwell before the match and forced to rest after nine overs, Barnes used the new ball with Foster, Douglas conceding that it was not in the side's best interests to take it himself as he did in the first Test. Barnes bowled Bardsley off his heel with his opening delivery; had Kelleway lbw; beat Hill three times before bowling him; had Armstrong caught behind. He now had 4 for one, and at lunch, after a brief rain stoppage, his figures were 9-6-3-4 after 70 minutes' bowling. When Foster bowled Trumper Australia were 33 for 5, and Barnes's dismissal of Minnett made it 38 for 6 – his figures now 11-7-6-5. There was a recovery, during which Barnes was booed for taking time in placing his field, and for a time he refused to bowl. Young Hearne again was the only batsman to play Hordern with assurance. His 114 lasted 3¾ hours, and his second-wicket stand with Rhodes realised 127. Armstrong drove forcefully and saved Australia's innings with a stand of 97 with Ransford, but Hobbs, making the first of his 12 centuries against Australia, spent 3¾ hours seeing his side home. He and Gunn put on 112 for the second wicket.

350, above, left: *Rhodes off-drives during his long stand with Hearne.* 351, right: *Hobbs stands up to play Australian express bowler Cotter.* 352, below, left: *The scoreboard at the end, showing the century by Hobbs (who took the photograph).* 353, right: *Hordern, who rescued Australia's first innings, hits Douglas into the covers*

1911–12 THIRD TEST

Adelaide, January 12, 13, 15, 16, 17

Australia *133 (F.R. Foster 5 for 36) and 476 (C. Hill 98, H. Carter 72, W. Bardsley 63, T.J. Matthews 53, S.F. Barnes 5 for 105)*; England *501 (J.B. Hobbs 187, F.R. Foster 71, W. Rhodes 59, C.P. Mead 46, A. Cotter 4 for 125) and 112 for 3 (W. Rhodes 57*, G. Gunn 45).* England won by 7 wickets.

England were ahead on first innings before losing a wicket. Foster and Barnes (3 for 71) had bowled Australia out on a fast pitch, Armstrong (33) heading the individual scores. Hobbs batted 334 minutes–flawlessly until he was 116, after which he was missed five times. It was the highest of his centuries against Australia and included many stirring drives, especially off Hordern. Carter went in as night-watchman for Australia on the third evening, and put on 157 with Hill on another very hot day. Further resistance left England with runs to make, but their task might have been more demanding if Trumper had not been reduced to coming in at No. 11 after taking a fierce drive by Woolley on a vein in the leg.

354, above, left: *Kelleway about to bowl to Mead. Hobbs is non-striker.* 355, right: *Another Hobbs century shows on the board.* 356, below: *The Australian Board of Control, for whom serious problems were developing, sits at Sydney, February 1912. Clockwise around table, from C.A. Sinclair (NSW) (in bow tie, extreme left): H.R. Rush (Vic), E.E. Bean (Vic), unidentified, Sydney Smith jnr (secretary), W.P. McElhone (chairman, NSW), unidentified, Col. J.F.G. Foxton (Qld), unidentified, C. Hill (SA) (a central figure in the Board/players dispute), Dr Ramsey Mailer (Vic), and H. Blinman (SA)*

1911–12 FOURTH TEST
Melbourne, February 9, 10, 12, 13

Australia *191 (R.B. Minnett 56, S.F. Barnes 5 for 74, F.R. Foster 4 for 77) and 173 (J.W.H.T. Douglas 5 for 46);* England *589 (W. Rhodes 179, J.B. Hobbs 178, G. Gunn 75, F.E. Woolley 56, F.R. Foster 50).* England won by an innings and 225 runs.

Douglas put Australia in, and the Foster-Barnes combination had done its work by late afternoon. England were 54 without loss that night. Hobbs and Rhodes carried their partnership to 323 in 268 minutes, when Hobbs was caught behind off Hordern. The stand – not chanceless – remains an England-Australia first-wicket record, and was followed immediately by 102 by Rhodes and Gunn. Rhodes, who batted No. 11 in his first series 12 years earlier, batted just short of seven hours – while 425 runs were scored – for his only century against Australia. Rain during the third night freshened the wicket, and Douglas rammed home his decision to field first by taking half the wickets, the final one bringing the Ashes back to England.

357, left: *Trumper, in sunhat, cuts Foster for four at Melbourne.* 358, above: *Hill plays Foster through the off*

359, above: *Umpires Young and Crockett.* 360, above, right: *Armstrong walks away, having been bowled for seven by a ball from Barnes which started on the line of leg stump and hit the off.* 361, right: *Hill (22) is caught by Hearne at long-on off Barnes*

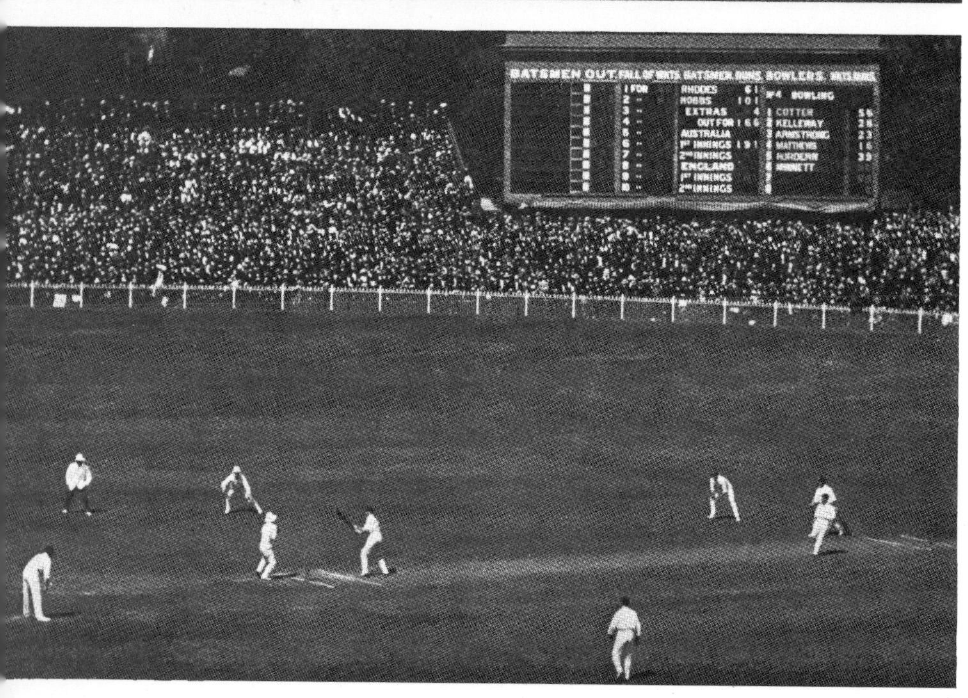

362, top left: *Minnett cuts Barnes to the boundary.* 363, right: *Hobbs and Rhodes, complete with neckerchiefs, resume their record stand at Melbourne. Hobbs's century was his third in successive Tests.* 364, left, centre: *Rhodes plays Minnett, the sixth bowler used, to short leg.* 365, left, below: *Hobbs, on 101 and with the opening stand worth 166, gives a difficult stumping chance to Carter off Jimmy Matthews. The partnership was almost doubled before Carter caught Hobbs off Hordern*

1911–12 FIFTH TEST

Sydney, February 23, 24, 26, 27, 28, 29, March 1

England *324 (F.E. Woolley 133*, G. Gunn 52, H.V. Hordern 5 for 95) and 214 (G. Gunn 61, J.B. Hobbs 45, H.V. Hordern 5 for 66);* Australia *176 and 292 (R.B. Minnett 61, V.T. Trumper 50, S.E. Gregory 40, F.R. Foster 4 for 43, S.F. Barnes 4 for 106).* England won by 70 runs.

After a blank third and sixth days because of rain, Australia came commendably close to their victory target of 363, for the seventh-day pitch, with the sun upon it, was anything but docile. Woolley's catch – one of his six in the match – to dismiss Minnett was a brilliant diving effort, and Hobbs's running out of Hordern was his 15th of the tour. Trumper ended his Test career (though this was not realised at the time) with 50 in his 40th consecutive appearance against England. Woolley, from No. 7 in the order, saved England's first innings, adding a seventh-wicket record 143 with Vine. His century was the first by an England left-hander against Australia. Barnes finished the series with 34 wickets, Foster with 32.

366, above: *Trumper, in his final Test, has been caught at slip by Woolley. England's wicketkeeper is 'Tiger' Smith.*
367, right: *Frank Woolley, a considerable left-arm slow bowler, excellent slip fieldsman, and scorer at Sydney of the first century by an England left-hander against Australia*

1912 FIRST TEST

Lord's, June 24, 25, 26

England *310 for 7 dec (J.B. Hobbs 107, W. Rhodes 59, C.B. Fry 42);* Australia *282 for 7 (C.G. Macartney 99, C. Kelleway 61).* Match drawn.

The Triangular Tournament of 1912 was a failure chiefly because of the ineffectiveness of the South African team and the wet summer. Australia, too, brought a side well below full strength after Hill, Armstrong, Trumper, Carter, Ransford and Cotter had withdrawn following disagreements with the Australian Board of Control, founded in 1905. The pitch at Lord's was saturated, and was becoming difficult as Hobbs entered the later stages of his century. He put on 112 with Rhodes for the first wicket. Only 20 minutes' play was possible on the second day, and when England declared on the Wednesday with 345 minutes remaining, Kelleway's obduracy (275 minutes) and Macartney's brilliance ensured that Australia were never in jeopardy. Macartney, who once pulled Barnes for six, batted only 140 minutes, and fell, caught by wicketkeeper Smith, to one of many leg-side deliveries from Foster.

368, above, left: *Charlie Kelleway, unsurpassed in Australian ranks for patience at the crease. His 61 at Lord's took 4½ hours.* 369, right: *The mercurial Charlie Macartney, a dashing contrast: his 99 took only 140 minutes*

1912 — SECOND TEST

Old Trafford, July 29, 30, 31

England *203 (W. Rhodes 92, W.J. Whitty 4 for 43, G.R. Hazlitt 4 for 77)*; Australia *14 for 0.* Match drawn.

After a delayed start, England finished the first day 185 for 6, Rhodes having given a fine display, 'digging his runs out of the slush', dealing selectively with the bad balls. He was 92 not out at the close, but played on second ball next day, when play began at 5 pm. The third day was washed out.

370: *The saddest sight of all. Old Trafford awash – a fairly symbolic picture of the summer of 1912*

1912 THIRD TEST

The Oval, August 19, 20, 21, 22

England 245 *(J.B. Hobbs 66, F.E. Woolley 62, W. Rhodes 49, R.B. Minnett 4 for 34, W.J. Whitty 4 for 69) and 175 (C.B. Fry 79, G.R. Hazlitt 7 for 25);* Australia *111 (C. Kelleway 43, F.E. Woolley 5 for 29, S.F. Barnes 5 for 30) and 65 (F.E. Woolley 5 for 20, H. Dean 4 for 19).* England won by 244 runs.

England, in this play-to-a-finish Test, ended the opening day 223 for 8 after Hobbs and Rhodes had begun with 107, the former continually finding runs on a soft, slow pitch, the latter content to hold his end. Yet more rain curtailed the second day, which saw Australia 51 for 2, and on the third day, as the pitch dried, Woolley from the pavilion end and Barnes overthrew the last eight wickets for 21 runs. Rain pacified the pitch for England for a time, and Fry played some exquisite strokes – though once he appeared to have trodden on his stumps. Gervys Hazlitt, with medium-pace bowling, had a field day as the pitch dried again, mopping up the last five wickets for one run. Woolley and Dean, both left-arm, then used the conditions well to dispose of Australia. Woolley returning 10 for 49 in the match after his powerful innings of 62 (11 fours). This was Australian captain Syd Gregory's last Test appearance – his 52nd, an England-Australia record still.

371, above, left: *A large crowd gathers at the Vauxhall end to watch the players at pre-match practice.* 372, right: *Bill Whitty, who took seven wickets with fast left-arm bowling*

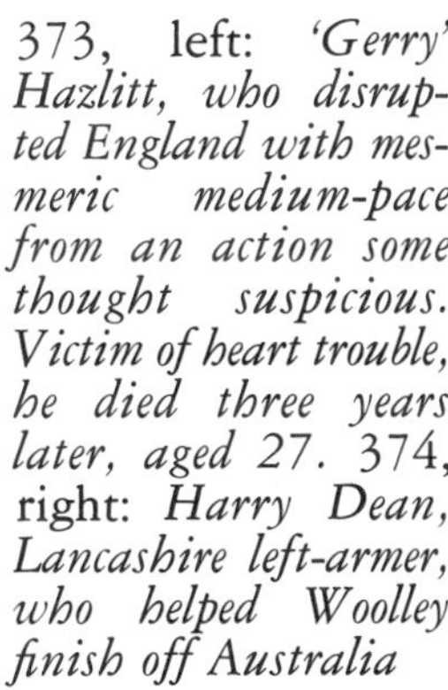

373, left: *'Gerry' Hazlitt, who disrupted England with mesmeric medium-pace from an action some thought suspicious. Victim of heart trouble, he died three years later, aged 27.* 374, right: *Harry Dean, Lancashire left-armer, who helped Woolley finish off Australia*

375, left: *Charles Fry, England's captain in the Triangular Tournament. He was undefeated, with one victory over Australia and three over South Africa.* 376, above: *Hearne is caught at short leg by Matthews off Hazlitt. Australia's wicketkeeper is Carkeek; Jennings is at slip.* 377, below, left: *Fry plays and misses during his innings of 79*

1920–21 FIRST TEST

Sydney, December 17, 18, 20, 21, 22

Australia *267 (H.L. Collins 70) and 581 (W.W. Armstrong 158, H.L. Collins 104, C. Kelleway 78, C.G. Macartney 69, W. Bardsley 57, J.M. Taylor 51);* England *190 (F.E. Woolley 52, J.B. Hobbs 49) and 281 (J.B. Hobbs 59, J.W. Hearne 57, E.H. Hendren 56, W. Rhodes 45).* Australia won by 377 runs.

Australia, led by the huge Victorian, Warwick Armstrong, recorded eight successive victories over England upon resumption of Test cricket after the First World War, with a unique (in England-Australia matches) 5–0 ascendancy in the 1920–21 series. Their first six wickets fell for 176, and there were three run-outs in the innings, but 'Jack' Russell played on to the first ball of England's innings and despite a fourth-wicket stand of 74 by Woolley and Hendren England conceded a lead. Australia built massively on this, Collins – a century in his first Test – and Bardsley starting with 123, Collins and Macartney making 111 for the second wicket, and Armstrong making two-thirds of a sixth-wicket stand of 187 with Kelleway to ram the advantage home. Catches were dropped, but Armstrong's 3½-hour assault was chanceless. England, set 659 for victory, were never in a position to feel optimistic. Jack Gregory and Arthur Mailey both took six wickets in their first Test.

378, above: *A passing threat to the resumption of Test cricket after the First War – the MCC side are in quarantine because of an infection aboard ship. Johnny Douglas, the team's captain, has his temperature read.* 379, right: *Hobbs b Gregory 49 – a straight ball, round his legs.* 380, below: *Bardsley c Strudwick b Hearne 22*

Johnny Douglas tore
his glove off in anger when
Armstrong 'fluked' him off my bowling

381, above: *Rhodes survives a chance to Gregory, who rarely missed slip catches.* 382, left: *Mailey's view of Douglas's demise*

383, top: *A view of the Sydney Cricket Ground on the first day of the first Test of the 1920–21 series. Collins and Kelleway are batting, and a ball from Woolley has just been taken by England wicketkeeper Strudwick.* 384, above: *The Australian XI at Sydney: standing – Bert Oldfield, Edgar Mayne (12th man), Charles Kelleway, Jack Gregory, Jack Ryder, Arthur Mailey, Johnny Taylor; seated – Herbie Collins, Warren Bardsley, Warwick Armstrong (captain), Charles Macartney, Clarrie 'Nip' Pellew*

1920–21 SECOND TEST

Melbourne, December 31, January 1, 3, 4

Australia 499 *(C.E. Pellew 116, J.M. Gregory 100, J.M. Taylor 68, H.L. Collins 64, W. Bardsley 51);* England 251 *(J.B. Hobbs 122, E.H. Hendren 67, J.M. Gregory 7 for 69) and 157 (F.E. Woolley 50, W.W. Armstrong 4 for 26).* Australia won by an innings and 91 runs.

A seemingly modest Australian score was inflated by an eighth-wicket stand of 173 on the second day by Pellew, batting No. 7, and Gregory, No. 9. Left-hander Gregory's innings lasted only 137 minutes. Roy Park, batting first-wicket-down, was beaten by the speed of Howell and bowled by the only ball he faced in Test cricket, after Bardsley and Collins had led off with 116; but England's catching let them down, Howell being a key sufferer. After heavy rain on the Sunday, the sun turned the pitch into a gluepot. Hugh Trumble said he would not have backed Australia to make 100 on it. Yet Hobbs (3½ hours) and Hendren stretched their third-wicket stand to 142 before the collapse took place. Hearne was ill and unable to bat in either innings, and in the follow-on had Australia held all their catches England's defeat would have been much more pronounced. Jack Gregory's success with bat and ball has few parallels.

385, above: *Taylor falls forward as he plays at Douglas.* 386, right: *Makepeace is lbw to Armstrong, and England are 32 for 2*

387, left: *Pellew (left) and Gregory, Australia's two centurions, resume their large eighth-wicket stand on New Year's Day 1921.* 388, above: *Hobbs, in trilby hat, comes in to a glad reception after his Melbourne century*

1920–21 THIRD TEST

Adelaide, January 14, 15, 17, 18, 19, 20

Australia *354 (H.L. Collins 162, W.A.S. Oldfield 50, J. Ryder 44, C.H. Parkin 5 for 60) and 582 (C. Kelleway 147, W.W. Armstrong 121, C.E. Pellew 104, J.M. Gregory 78*, H. Howell 4 for 115);* England *447 (A.C. Russell 135*, F.E. Woolley 79, J.W.H. Makepeace 60, J.W.H.T. Douglas 60, A.A. Mailey 5 for 160) and 370 (J.B. Hobbs 123, A.C. Russell 59, E.H. Hendren 51, P.G.H. Fender 42, A.A. Mailey 5 for 142).* Australia won by 119 runs.

A classic batsman's match, and England were well in it for three days. Howell again bowled with wretched luck; one of several chances off him – Collins to Rhodes at square leg – would have reduced Australia to 96 for 5, but they climbed to 313 for 7 by the first night, Collins's innings lasting 258 minutes. Woolley and Russell steadied England on the second evening, and Douglas added 124 with Russell next day, taking England into the lead. By the close, Australia were 71 for 3 and England felt they were back in the series. Armstrong (whose century was the 100th in these Tests) and the limpet-like Kelleway, however, were not separated until after tea on the third day, having put on 194. Kelleway, dropped before scoring, scored 24 between lunch and tea, and 96 in the day's play of 4¾ hours. When dismissed next day he had batted a shade under seven hours, and Pellew, with whom he added 126, made 84 of their stand. 'Nip' Pellew raced to his century with 16 off an over from Howell, and Gregory's aggression took Australia 489 ahead, a margin clearly beyond England once Hobbs's 2½-hour innings had ended and the middle order was cut away by Gregory, McDonald and Mailey.

389: *Two of the most popular Australian cricketers of the 1920s – Bert Oldfield (in hat) and Arthur Mailey. A tireless and adventurous spin bowler, Mailey was kept on long enough to concede 100 runs or thereabouts in eight innings during the series*

390, left: *A.C. 'Jack' Russell, of Essex – England century-maker at Adelaide.* 391, above: *Time for sandwiches: the crowded grandstand during the third Test.* 392, below: *A crucial miss: Fender at slip drops Kelleway before he had scored. He stayed nearly seven hours to make 147*

1920–21 FOURTH TEST

Melbourne, February 11, 12, 14, 15, 16

England *284 (J.W.H. Makepeace 117, J.W.H.T. Douglas 50, A.A. Mailey 4 for 115) and 315 (W. Rhodes 73, J.W.H.T. Douglas 60, P.G.H. Fender 59, J.W.H. Makepeace 54, A.A. Mailey 9 for 121);* Australia *389 (W.W. Armstrong 123*, J.M. Gregory 77, H.L. Collins 59, W. Bardsley 56, P.G.H. Fender 5 for 122) and 211 for 2 (J.M. Gregory 76*, J. Ryder 52*).* Australia won by 8 wickets.

The diminutive Makepeace, in his 39th year, spent 260 minutes over his innings-saving century, adding 106 for the fifth wicket with Douglas, who had won his first toss of the series. There was life in the pitch before lunch, and the batsmen had to withstand some hostile bowling from McDonald and Gregory. Makepeace hit only four boundaries. Australia were in trouble after Collins and Bardsley had started with 117, but Armstrong, though suffering from malaria, put on 145 with Gregory for the sixth wicket. The captain, who went on to his third century of the series, was given a grand reception for having won the Ashes in the previous Test. After Hobbs was lbw to Mailey, Rhodes and Makepeace cleared the arrears of 105, and Douglas again postponed his seemingly inevitable overthrow by Mailey. Fender batted aggressively, and England were 305 for 5 at one point; but the tail was confounded by Mailey. The wry and prodigal little wrist-spinner is still the only Australian to take nine wickets in a Test innings.

393, left: *A famous catch – Hobbs caught by wicketkeeper Carter off McDonald at Melbourne. Gregory at slip takes an anticipatory tumble.* 394, above: *Jack Gregory, Australia's beau ideal of an all-round cricketer*

395, above: *Harry Makepeace, a veteran when he scored 117.* 396, right: *Mailey almost catches Fender.* 397, inset: *Douglas somehow avoids being stumped*

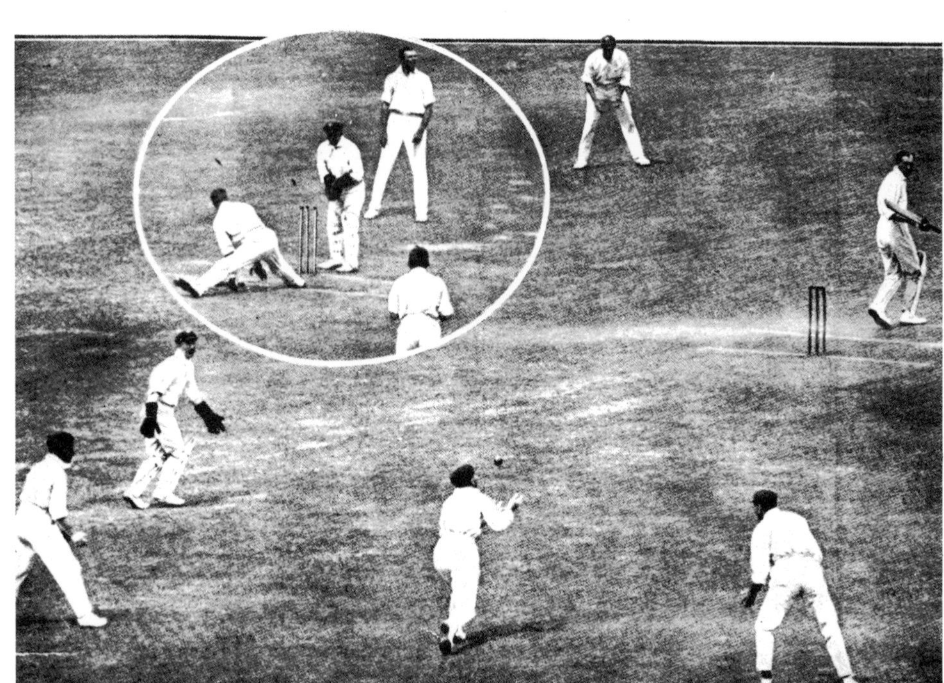

1920–21 FIFTH TEST

Sydney, February 25, 26, 28, March 1

England *204 (F.E. Woolley 53, J.B. Hobbs 40, C. Kelleway 4 for 27) and 280 (J.W.H.T. Douglas 68, P.G.H. Fender 40, A.A. Mailey 5 for 119);* Australia *392 (C.G. Macartney 170, J.M. Gregory 93, P.G.H. Fender 5 for 90) and 93 for 1 (W. Bardsley 50*).* Australia won by 9 wickets.

England, hampered by injuries (Hobbs played despite a strained thigh), again disappointed after a solid start, though Woolley's 53 came in almost even time. Australia were 22 for 3 and 89 for 3, but then Macartney, who missed the preceding three Tests through illness, put on 198 in only 133 minutes with Gregory (who averaged 73.66 in the series, took 23 wickets and held 15 catches). Macartney, the squat, pugnacious 'Governor General', batted only 244 minutes, struck 20 fours, and offered no chances. His footwork was universally admired. Hobbs, obviously lame in the field, was barracked by some of the crowd, who were criticised by Fender and E.R. Wilson in British newspapers. They in turn were shouted at on the third day. England were reduced to 91 for 6 at their second attempt before 'Johnny Won't Hit Today' Douglas resisted for 68 runs as his ship sank for the fifth time. Mailey finished with an Australian record of 36 wickets in the series.

398, above, left: *Percy Fender – 'PGH' – at times for him a troublesome tour, but in spite of restricted opportunities he finished at the head of England's bowling with 12 wickets at 34.* 399, right: *Before a sparsely-populated Hill, Gregory bowls to Hobbs at the start of the fifth Test – a photograph taken by Fender*

400, above: *Makepeace nicely taken by Gregory at slip.* 401, below: *The same fielder holds a more straightforward catch from Russell. Wicketkeeper is 'Sammy' Carter*

1921 FIRST TEST

Trent Bridge, May 28, 30

England *112 (J.M. Gregory 6 for 58) and 147 (E.A. McDonald 5 for 32)*; Australia *232 (W. Bardsley 66) and 30 for 0.* Australia won by 10 wickets.

England's traumas persisted. Indispositions kept Hobbs from the entire series except the third Test, where acute appendicitis prevented him from batting, and in the five contests England called upon as many as 30 players. The teams, who travelled to England together aboard *Osterley,* faced each other at Nottingham in the 100th England-Australia Test, a match settled in two days after a shocking start by England against the silken speed of McDonald and the violence of Gregory. Percy Holmes, in his only Test against Australia, top-scored with 30. Australia's 232 was almost enough for an innings win, their fast bowlers following up with another vigorous display – to which the crowd sometimes took exception. Ernest Tyldesley was hit in the face by a Gregory bouncer, the ball then falling on his stumps.

402, left: *Arthur Mailey, who was omitted from the first Test was able to apply himself to his sketches from the pavilion.* 403, above: *The captains, Armstrong and Douglas, go to inspect the Nottingham pitch.* 404, below: *Ted McDonald, whose speed brought him eight England wickets*

405: *Bardsley swings to leg in the first Test. Woolley at slip, Strudwick keeping wicket*

1921 SECOND TEST
Lord's, June 11, 13, 14

England *187 (F.E. Woolley 95, A.A. Mailey 4 for 55, E.A. McDonald 4 for 58) and 283 (F.E. Woolley 93, L.H. Tennyson 74*, A.E. Dipper 40, J.M. Gregory 4 for 76, E.A. McDonald 4 for 89);* Australia *342 (W. Bardsley 88, J.M. Gregory 52, H. Carter 46, C.E. Pellew 43, F.J. Durston 4 for 102) and 131 for 2 (W. Bardsley 63*, T.J.E. Andrews 49).* Australia won by 8 wickets.

Mailey came in for Collins, whose thumb was broken in the first Test, but England made six changes. C.B. Fry, at 49, was also invited to play, but declined. Woolley's two innings shone with fine drives and cuts, his courage in a losing cause being most conspicuous. He had support only from Douglas (34) in the first innings and Dipper (a stand of 94) in the second before Tennyson, at No. 7, came in and let loose a stream of hearty drives off the fast bowlers. Australia's 342 was made in only 84.1 overs, England having no bowler to match the containing Armstrong, whose 18 overs in England's first innings included 12 maidens. Bardsley topped both Australian innings, cutting soundly and hitting strongly to leg.

406: *Frank Woolley, the favourite of Kent, who scored two memorable nineties at Lord's off the fearsome Australian attack*

407: *Lord's almost full again as Australia forge ahead to their seventh straight victory over England since the post-war resumption*

408, left: *Curiosity at England's new fast bowler, Durston.* 409, centre: *Armstrong and his men meet King George V.* 410, right: *Lionel Tennyson's late selection and swift dismissal.* 411, below: *Mailey busy with sketchpad again*

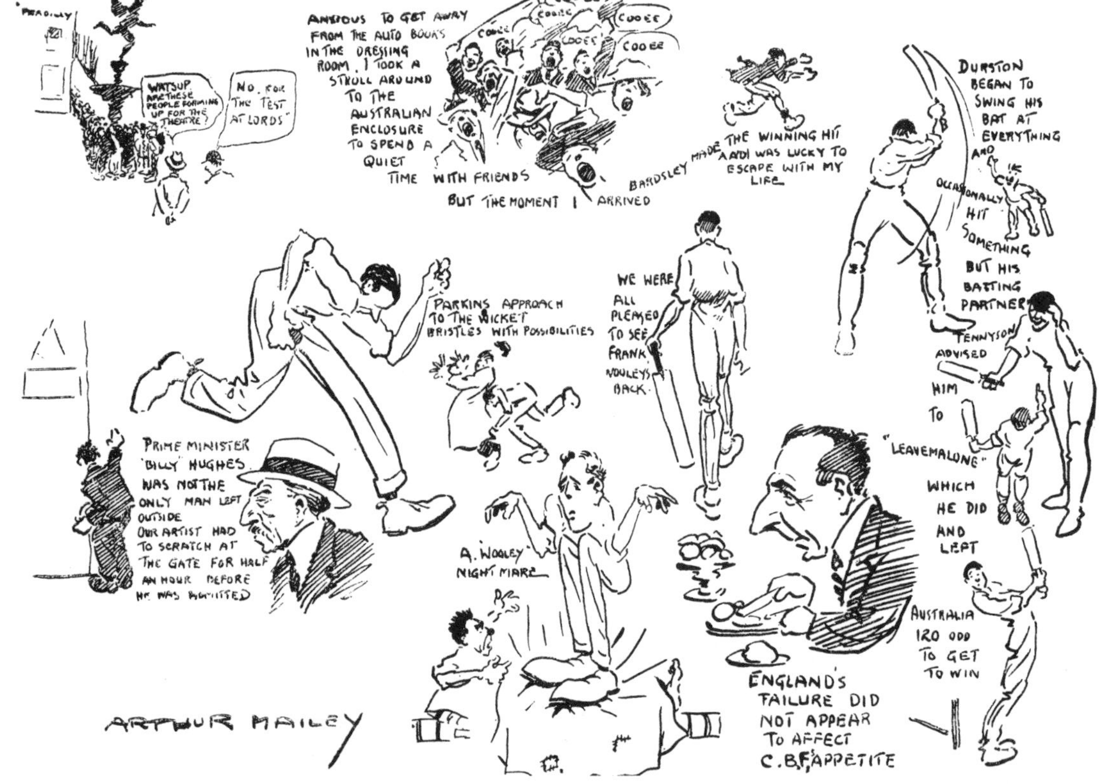

1921 THIRD TEST

Headingley, July 2, 4, 5

Australia 407 *(C.G. Macartney 115, W.W. Armstrong 77, C.E. Pellew 52, J.M. Taylor 50, C.H. Parkin 4 for 106) and 273 for 7 dec (T.J.E. Andrews 92, H. Carter 47);* England 259 *(J.W.H.T. Douglas 75, L.H. Tennyson 63, G. Brown 57, E.A. McDonald 4 for 105) and 202 (G. Brown 46).* Australia won by 219 runs.

England this time made seven changes, as well as transferring the captaincy to the Hon. Lionel Tennyson. Macartney, having just made 345 against Notts, batted 186 minutes for – oddly – Australia's only century of the series. He was not as his best, but dominant nevertheless. One of his drives split Tennyson's hand, and Douglas resumed the leadership for a time. Hobbs then went down with appendicitis, and another backs-to-the-wall situation for England developed. Armstrong hammered home Australia's ascendancy yet again – their 407 took only 296 minutes – and on a cloudy Monday England collapsed to 67 for 5. Here, left-hander Brown, brought in as wicketkeeper in preference to Strudwick to strengthen the batting, helped Douglas add 97, and Tennyson, his lacerated hand protected, but batting virtually one-handed, put on 88 with his deputy in an heroic display that saved the follow-on. Andrews and Carter – one a monumental mason, the other an undertaker – led the way as Australia built a lead, and England were eventually left 4½ hours. It was ample time for the tourists to go three-up.

412: *First wicket at Leeds – Bardsley caught by Woolley at slip off Douglas; but England had a great depth of Australian batting still to overthrow*

413, above: *Tennyson, England's new captain, gallantly drives Mailey with his one good hand; Gregory and Carter watch.* 414, right: *Headingley, well attended, as usual*

415, left: *Woolley plays on to Mailey for 37, second innings.* 416, above: *Mailey at slip fields a shot from Douglas.* 417, below: *Gregory bowled by Parkin for one in Australia's first innings*

1921 FOURTH TEST
Old Trafford, July 23, 25, 26

England *362 for 4 dec (A.C. Russell 101, E. Tyldesley 78*, C.P. Mead 47, P.G.H. Fender 44*, F.E. Woolley 41) and 44 for 1;* Australia *175 (H.L. Collins 40, C.H. Parkin 5 for 38).* Match drawn.

The succession of England defeats was finally stemmed in a match remembered for Tennyson's illegal declaration, which was nullified after Carter, Armstrong's wicketkeeper, pointed out that after loss of the first day it was a two-day match; no declaration could be made in such circumstances within 100 minutes of the end of play. Some of the crowd became unruly, and Tennyson and the umpires had to explain matters to them – by which time 25 minutes were lost. Armstrong then proceeded to bowl the first over, having bowled the last before the break. Russell, batting four hours for his hundred, made 81 of his runs on the leg side, and was missed twice off Gregory at slip. Tyldesley and Fender had added 102 in only 39 minutes before the overnight declaration, but England's overall progress on an easy pitch had never been rapid enough. Even so, Collins dropped anchor for 289 minutes for his 40, ensuring that Australia, though outplayed at last, would not seriously be threatened. At 78 for 5 there were tremors, but Collins continued to kill ball after ball from Parkin, Fender, Parker and Woolley. The innings time of 318 minutes was in stark contrast to some of Australia's performances of the past seven months.

418, left: *Once more to the toss: Tennyson and Armstrong, two pipe-smoking civilians.* 419, below, left: *Cecil Parkin (left), a rebellious player and inventive bowler, who shattered Australia on his home ground, shakes hands with Golden Age champion J.T. Tyldesley. Ted McDonald, who joined Lancashire, looks on.* 420, right: *The easy style of Ernest Tyldesley, JT's younger brother. He was floored at Trent Bridge, rehabilitated at Old Trafford*

1921 FIFTH TEST

The Oval, August 13, 15, 16

England *403 for 8 dec (C.P. Mead 182*, L.H. Tennyson 51, E.A. McDonald 5 for 143) and 244 for 2 (A.C. Russell 102*, G. Brown 84, J.W. Hitch 51*);* Australia *389 (T.J.E. Andrews 94, J.M. Taylor 75, C.G. Macartney 61).* Match drawn.

England's prospects were dim at the end of a rain-interrupted first day (129 for 4), but Phil Mead, having made 19 in 70 minutes, scored 109 in 2½ hours before lunch on the Monday. Missed twice, he batted altogether for 309 minutes, and added 121 with Tennyson. His score was the highest for England against Australia in England, and gave him the freak average for the series of 229. Australia used only four bowlers, McDonald sending down 47 overs and Gregory 38. Hitch removed Collins and Bardsley early and had catches dropped, but Macartney and Andrews consolidated without resorting to undue defence. When England batted again there was no prospect of a result, and Armstrong drifted out to the boundary and left his bowlers and fielders to organise themselves, once picking up a stray newspaper 'to see who we're playing'. It was the 'Big Ship's' way of protesting at Tests limited to three days. Russell and Brown's first-wicket partnership of 158 should therefore be seen in perspective. Hitch's half-century was reached in 35 minutes, second in speed only to J.T. Brown's in these Tests.

421, left: *Armstrong at The Oval, making the bowling seem like 'weak tea' again, his bat 'a teaspoon'.* 422, above, centre: *George Brown, of Hampshire, a rugged all-round player.* 423, above, right: *The skippers toss for the last time: Armstrong soon had to get his flannels on.* 424, below: *The England team in the fifth Test: standing – Andrew Sandham, Phil Mead, Charlie Hallows (12th man), Ernest Tyldesley, George Brown, Jack Russell, Cecil Parkin; seated – Bill Hitch, Johnny Douglas, Hon. Lionel Tennyson (captain), Percy Fender, Frank Woolley*

1924–25 FIRST TEST

Sydney, December 19, 20, 22, 23, 24, 26, 27

Australia *450 (H.L. Collins 114, W.H. Ponsford 110, J.M. Taylor 43, V.Y. Richardson 42, M.W. Tate 6 for 130) and 452 (J.M. Taylor 108, A.J. Richardson 98, H.L. Collins 60, A.A. Mailey 46*, M.W. Tate 5 for 98);* England *298 (J.B. Hobbs 115, E.H. Hendren 74*, H. Sutcliffe 59, J.M. Gregory 5 for 111, A.A. Mailey 4 for 129) and 411 (F.E. Woolley 123, H. Sutcliffe 115, J.B. Hobbs 57, A.P. Freeman 50*, A.P.F. Chapman 44).* Australia won by 193 runs.

Australia's 4–1 victory in this series was not a faithful reflection of the balance between the sides, though the home side's batting was on the whole more reliable. The series was the first to be played with eight-ball overs, and auspicious debuts were made by Ponsford (who was shielded by Collins from the menace of Tate in the early part of his innings), Arthur Richardson, Sutcliffe (whose opening stands with Hobbs were worth 157 and 110), and Maurice Tate, who took a record 38 wickets in the series. Collins and Ponsford put on 190 for Australia's second wicket, and but for a spell of 4 for 9 on the second day by fast-medium bowler Tate, Australia might have made a mammoth total. As it was, England trailed by a long way after their fine beginning, only Hendren of the remaining batsmen exceeding 13. Australia extended their lead by solid batting all down the order, and England's agony was added to by a last-wicket stand of 127 between Taylor (batting No. 8 because of a boil behind the knee) and Mailey, a record for Australia which still stands. Taylor's second 50 came in a mere 32 minutes. Mailey and Oldfield had added 62 for the tenth wicket in the first innings. Set 605, England began well, but Gregory, Kelleway, Mailey and Hendry whittled away at the order, and it was something of a surprise when Freeman stayed with Woolley while the tall left-hander went past his second century against Australia – the first having been made 13 years previously, also at Sydney.

425, left: *Australia's opening pair, Collins (left) and Bardsley, prepare to do battle at Sydney.* 426, above: *Kelleway and wicketkeeper Strudwick anxiously watch a catch go to slip, where Woolley held it.* 427, below: *Collins reaches his century; Tate at square leg, Woolley, Hearne and Freeman in slips*

428, top, left: *Herbert Sutcliffe, in his first innings against Australia, sweeps Mailey at Sydney.* 429, right: *A gloveless Collins, when 37, missed by Woolley off Hearne.* 430, above: *Tate bowls, trying to break the last-wicket stand of Oldfield and Mailey which stretched Australia's first innings by 62.* 431, left: *Taylor runs a ball through gully during his 108.* 432, below: *Mailey releases a googly, which Sandham tried to cut. He was bowled by it for seven*

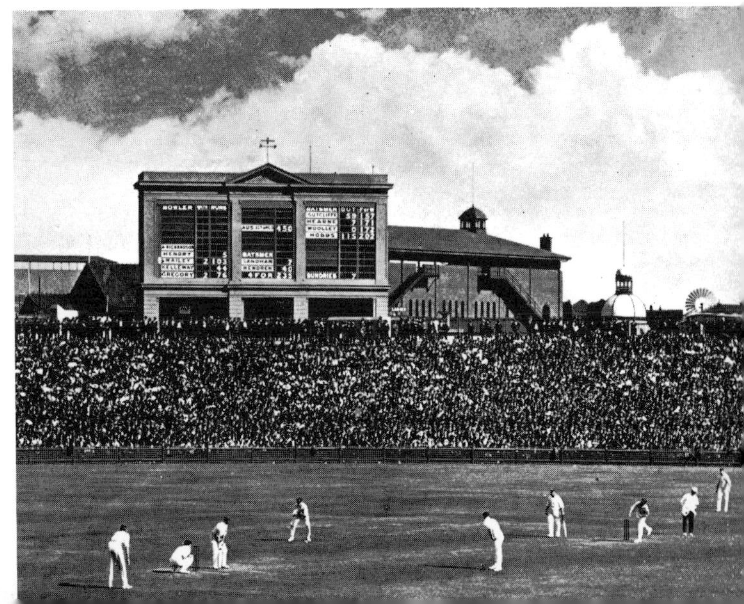

1924–25 SECOND TEST
Melbourne, January 1, 2, 3, 5, 6, 7, 8

Australia *600 (V.Y. Richardson 138, W.H. Ponsford 128, A.E.V. Hartkopf 80, J.M. Taylor 72, J.M. Gregory 44) and 250 (J.M. Taylor 90, M.W. Tate 6 for 99, J.W. Hearne 4 for 84)*; England *479 (H. Sutcliffe 176, J.B. Hobbs 154) and 290 (H. Sutcliffe 127, F.E. Woolley 50, A.A. Mailey 5 for 92, J.M. Gregory 4 for 87).* Australia won by 81 runs.

Collins again beat Gilligan at the toss, and after a quivering start (47 for 3) Australia settled down for two whole days. Ponsford and Taylor added 161, Richardson and Kelleway 123 (of which the latter contributed only 20), and Hartkopf (on debut) and Oldfield 100 for the ninth wicket during which the Test innings record was passed. Richardson moved from 109 to 130 with 4 4 4 4 2 3 off an over by Douglas. Ponsford's century followed his 110 on debut, but Herbert Sutcliffe went one better with two centuries in this match, giving him three in his first two Tests against Australia. Hobbs and Sutcliffe batted throughout the third day of 288 minutes for an opening stand of 283, without giving a chance, the senior man 154, Sutcliffe 123. It was batting of the highest class, unruffled and perfect in judgment. The stand ended next morning when Mailey began with a full-toss to Hobbs and then another, which hit the stumps almost on the full. Woolley and Hearne quickly followed, and England made not 200 more. Tate struck three times early in Australia's second innings, but Taylor with a pleasant innings and Gregory and Oldfield with vital late resistance saw to it that England's target was a big one. Sutcliffe for the second time in the match batted through a day's play, but apart from Woolley's 50, which started enterprisingly but lost its impetus when he replaced his broken bat at 40 just before the tea interval, the Yorkshireman lacked support.

433, above, left: *A gracious gesture: Sutcliffe (left) and Hobbs receive a silver tea and coffee service from the people of Melbourne in recognition of their splendid batting there.* 434, above, right: *Vic Richardson and Bill Ponsford, centurions both, resume their partnership.* 435, right: *Sutcliffe drives spinner Hartkopf during England's first-wicket stand of 283*

436, top, left: *Strudwick, sent in as night-watchman on the sixth evening at Melbourne, parries a short ball from Gregory.* 437, above: *Turning point on the final day – Hendren b Gregory 18.* 438, left: *Sutcliffe out at last, c Gregory b Mailey 127.* 439, below, left: *Gilligan c & b Mailey first ball.* 440, below: *Tate bowled by Gregory, and the Test is over; Chapman the non-striker*

1924–25 THIRD TEST

Adelaide, January 16, 17, 19, 20, 21, 22, 23

Australia 489 *(J. Ryder 201*, T.J.E. Andrews 72, A.J. Richardson 69, W.A.S. Oldfield 47, R. Kilner 4 for 127) and 250 (J. Ryder 88, W.H. Ponsford 43, R. Kilner 4 for 51, F.E. Woolley 4 for 77);* England 365 *(J.B. Hobbs 119, E.H. Hendren 92) and 363 (W.W. Whysall 75, H. Sutcliffe 59, A.P.F. Chapman 58).* Australia won by 11 runs.

The third successive match to enter a seventh day ended thrillingly when Freeman (24) was caught by 'keeper Oldfield off Mailey, but the margin of runs had yet again diminished, and England, unlucky enough with their third loss of toss, were cruelly reduced by injury during Australia's first innings. They had the home side 119 for 6, but with Tate forced out of action with a raw big toe, Gilligan with a groin strain, and Freeman with a damaged wrist from a fierce Ryder drive, the bulk of the bowling fell to Woolley and Kilner. Australia's last four wickets put on 370 runs, Ryder batting 395 minutes and adding 134 with Andrews and 108 with Oldfield. He hit a six, a five and 12 fours. Gilligan rearranged his batting order, and Hobbs and Sutcliffe were united at 69 for 4, adding 90. Hendren then stayed with Hobbs while 117 were put on. By the end of the fourth day Australia were 211 for 3 – 335 ahead, Ryder 86 – but rain on the fifth morning made the wicket tricky, and the left-arm bowlers Kilner and Woolley soon wrapped up the innings. Hobbs and Sutcliffe gave England a start of 63, but at 133 for 3 that evening, they were still 242 from victory. Whysall, aged 37, in his first Test, batted judiciously, but when rain cut the sixth day short England still needed 27 with two wickets left. With the gates open, 25,000 came to see the last overs, and Mailey, who had been up all night, resumed the bowling with Gregory to Freeman and Gilligan, who had also had a sleepless night. Gregory caught-and-bowled the England captain (31) with an accidental slower ball, and six runs later Mailey induced a fatal snick from Freeman.

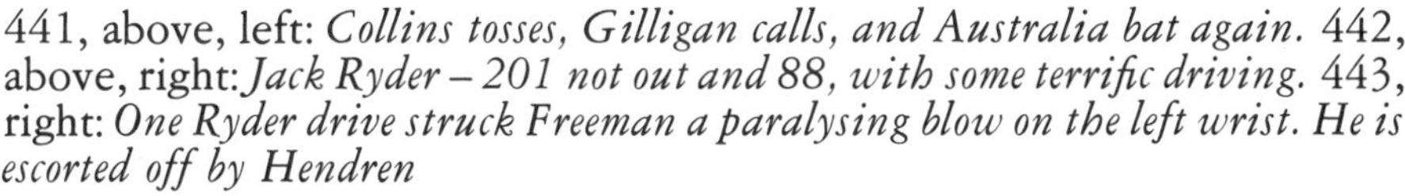

441, above, left: *Collins tosses, Gilligan calls, and Australia bat again.* 442, above, right: *Jack Ryder – 201 not out and 88, with some terrific driving.* 443, right: *One Ryder drive struck Freeman a paralysing blow on the left wrist. He is escorted off by Hendren*

444, top: *Another Hobbs century comes to an end. Gregory tosses the ball up after taking a low slip catch off Mailey's bowling in the Adelaide Test.* 445, centre: *The ball is a blur as Andrews prepares to catch Woolley (16) at cover in England's first innings.* 446, left: *A dozen runs from victory, England's last wicket falls: Freeman is caught behind by Oldfield off Mailey, and Australia keep the Ashes*

1924–25 FOURTH TEST

Melbourne, February 13, 14, 16, 17, 18

England 548 *(H. Sutcliffe 143, W.W. Whysall 76, R. Kilner 74, J.B. Hobbs 66, E.H. Hendren 65, J.W. Hearne 44, F.E. Woolley 40, A.A. Mailey 4 for 186)*; Australia *269 (J.M. Taylor 86) and 250 (J.M. Taylor 68, J.M. Gregory 45, C. Kelleway 42, M.W. Tate 5 for 75).* England won by an innings and 29 runs.

England at last secured a victory – their first over Australia since 1912. The weather played a part, but the general view was that this popular team deserved its luck. For two days England occupied the crease. Hobbs and Sutcliffe put up another century opening stand, their fourth, and Sutcliffe batted through a day for the third time in the series for his fourth century. Other big stands were 106 by Sutcliffe and Hearne, and 133 by Whysall and Kilner. Several light showers thereafter put some life in the pitch, and Tate was back at his best. Taylor batted twice commandingly and stylishly, but the strong rearguard which the public (and England bowlers) had come to expect did not eventuate in either innings.

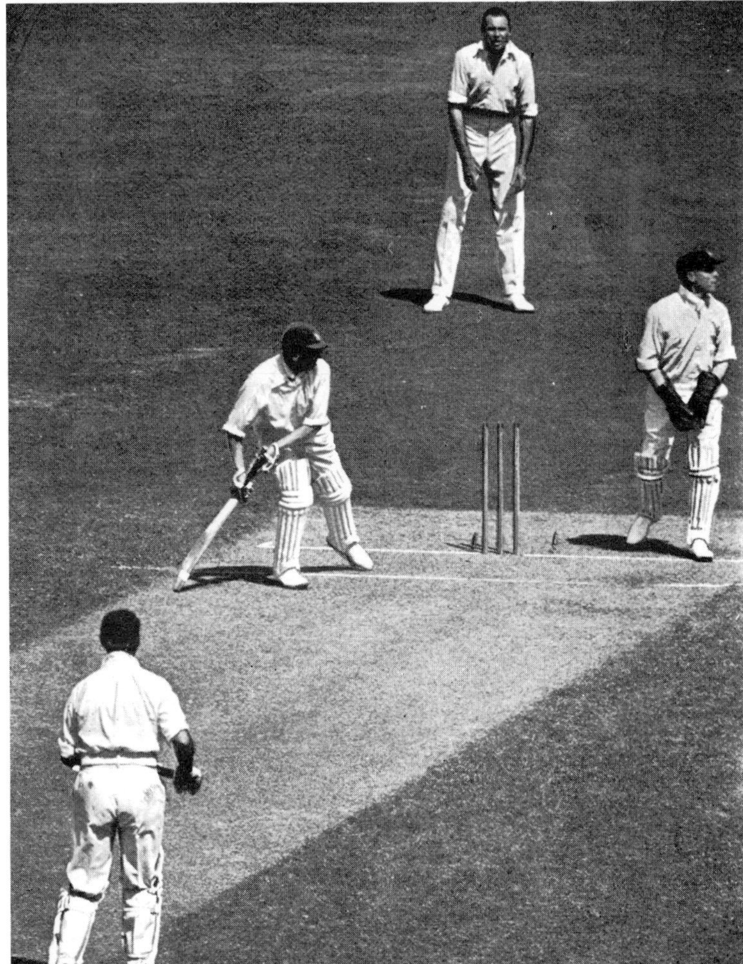

447, above: *Hobbs on 19 edges Gregory over gully, Kelleway, who gets his fingertips to the ball. Hobbs and Sutcliffe went on to score 126 for the first wicket.*
448, right: *The stand was broken when Oldfield stumped Hobbs down the leg side off Ryder, a medium-pacer. The wicket-keeper, who made four stumpings in the innings, regarded this one as the best of his career*

449, above, left: *Woolley, toe on line, is stumped by Oldfield off Mailey for 40.* 450, right: *Yet another Oldfield stumping – Chapman in disarray after stepping out to Mailey.* 451, below: *Whysall, in the course of another valuable seventy, misses a Mailey googly. Gregory at slip has evidently seen the 'wrong 'un' from the bowler's hand.* 452, bottom: *Kilner, with a helpful pitch at his disposal, bowls to Kelleway. Taylor is the non-striker, Hendren at silly point*

1924–25 FIFTH TEST

Sydney, February 27, 28, March 2, 3, 4

Australia *295 (W.H. Ponsford 80, A.F. Kippax 42, M.W. Tate 4 for 92, R. Kilner 4 for 97) and 325 (T.J.E. Andrews 80, C. Kelleway 73, W.A.S. Oldfield 65*, M.W. Tate 5 for 115);* England *167 (F.E. Woolley 47, C.V. Grimmett 5 for 45) and 146 (C.V. Grimmett 6 for 37).* Australia won by 307 runs.

England were confounded in both innings by 33-year-old New Zealand-born leg-spinner Clarrie Grimmett, who swept through the side after Woolley and Hearne had taken the score to 96 for 4. In the final innings he had Hobbs stumped and went on to decimate England, Gregory taking the vital wicket of Sutcliffe – said to be looking stale after his 734 runs in the series – by bowling him for a duck with a sharp breakback. Hobbs had failed to score in the first innings, memorably caught by Oldfield down the leg side off Gregory. Within minutes Sandham was run out, Gregory dislocating a finger as he dived for the stumps. Australia's first innings had slumped to 103 for 5, but the elegant newcomer Kippax then added 105 with Ponsford. Andrews stroked cleanly and placed the ball well in his 80, but the crucial second-innings stand for Australia was that between Kelleway and Collins, who had injured his hand in practice. They saw Australia through the third evening, and Oldfield next day put on an invaluable 116 with Kelleway – the highest stand of the match. Grimmett's accuracy and variation then put a seal on the game.

453, above: *Taylor about to be caught by Whysall off Tate for 15.* 454, centre: *Alan Kippax, in the second innings, chops Woolley wide of Tate at slip.* 455, right: *Hobbs makes a famous 'duck', glancing Gregory, with Oldfield, having sensed the stroke, moving across for the catch. A second later the Hill was in tumult*

456, top, left: *Mailey takes a competent two-handed catch off Kelleway's bowling to dismiss Sutcliffe for 22, his lowest score in eight innings so far.* 457, above: *Grimmett takes his first Test wicket, bowling Woolley.* 458, above, left: *Kilner, who played Grimmett with least discomfort, swings him for four. He was stumped off Grimmett for 24.* 459, left: *Tate thrashes at Ryder, with fatal results.* 460, below: *Hobbs st Oldfield b Grimmett 13 – a hotly-debated decision at Sydney*

1926
Trent Bridge, June 12, 14, 15

England *32 for 0.* Match drawn.

Herbie 'Lucky' Collins's side arrived in England with no fast attack to compare with that of Armstrong's 1921 side. Gregory, carrying a knee injury, was not quite the same force, and McDonald had settled in Lancashire. This lack of penetration was to show during the series. The opening contest, however, was blighted by the weather, only 50 minutes' batting by Hobbs and Sutcliffe on the first day being possible.

461, top: *Hobbs plays Gregory to leg and takes the first run in the truncated Trent Bridge Test.* 462, left: *The umpires, R.D. Burrows and Frank Chester.* 463, above: *The waterlogged ground – Jupiter Pluvius wins at Nottingham*

1926 SECOND TEST

Lord's, June 26, 28, 29

Australia 383 (*W. Bardsley 193*, R. Kilner 4 for 70*) and 194 for 5 (*C.G. Macartney 133**); England 475 for 3 dec (*E.H. Hendren 127*, J.B. Hobbs 119, F.E. Woolley 87, H. Sutcliffe 82, A.P.F. Chapman 50**). Match drawn.

A striking illustration of the difference between timeless Australian and three-day-limit English Tests, this match began with Root, an inswing, leg-trap bowler, removing one of Collins's stumps, and ended with the same batsman existing almost 2½ hours for 24, with Macartney, two days after his 40th birthday, hitting a magical century with deft and sometimes brutal strokeplay. In between, Bardsley, aged 42, had carried his bat through Australia's first innings, which lasted 398 minutes. He hit 14 fours, mostly with nudges off his pads and with cuts, and he was missed three times – all after he had passed 100. Larwood took his first Test wicket when he had Macartney caught. Hobbs and Sutcliffe yet again saw England into three figures: 182; and Woolley and Hendren hit a swift 140 for the third wicket before Chapman joined the latter and put on an unbeaten 116. This was Hendren's first century against Australia, and he was the youngest of the four centurions in the match at 37.

464, above: *England, led by Arthur Carr, take the field.* 465, right: *Collins (1) loses his leg stump to a Root inswinger.* 466, below, left: *Carr at short leg nimbly cuts off a shot from Bardsley. The umpire is Len Braund.* 467, right: *Hendren hits out at Macartney on the second day; Arthur Richardson is at backward point*

468, right: *Macartney clips a ball from Root, and it is stopped by short leg.* 469, below: *Sutcliffe drives. The sawdust absorbs water from a mains tap inadvertently left running overnight*

470, above, left: *Hobbs, after taking an hour for his last 12 runs, reaches his century.* 471, above, right: *Woolley deals powerfully with a ball from Macartney.* 472, right: *Macartney on-drives Kilner to reach his century*

1926 THIRD TEST

Headingley, July 10, 12, 13

Australia *494 (C.G. Macartney 151, W.M. Woodfull 141, A.J. Richardson 100, J. Ryder 42, M.W. Tate 4 for 99);* England *294 (G.G. Macaulay 76, J.B. Hobbs 49, C.V. Grimmett 5 for 88) and 254 for 3 (H. Sutcliffe 94, J.B. Hobbs 88, A.P.F. Chapman 42*).* Match drawn.

A.W. Carr asked Australia to take first innings: a fateful decision. Tate's first ball found the edge of Bardsley's bat and Sutcliffe took a neat catch at slip. Macartney came in, cut for two, played the next two with ease, then edged to Carr himself at third slip. The England captain got both hands to the ball but dropped it. Australia's second wicket did not fall until 235 was on the board. Macartney struck boldly in all directions to reach his century (out of 131) in 103 minutes, and to be 112 at lunch – the highest on the first morning of an England-Australia match. When he was caught at mid-on he had hit 21 fours and batted only 172 minutes. There had seemed no likely way of curbing his onslaught, much less dismissing him. Woodfull plodded on for almost five hours, Richardson (aged almost 38) dominating a fourth-wicket stand of 129 and going on to the third century of the innings before Macaulay, the bowler, ran him out as he followed through after driving. England's innings was saved from rout by Geary (35 not out) and Macaulay (No. 10), who added 108 for the ninth wicket. Hobbs and Sutcliffe put on 156 for the first wicket in the follow-on, seeing England to safety while Bardsley, deputising for Collins, who had neuritis, tried seven bowlers.

473, above: *One of the most famous of dropped catches – Carr fails to hold an edge from Macartney (2). Geary (in cap) watches in dismay.* 474, below: *Macartney, on nimble feet, drives during his glorious innings of 151, which started with a century before lunch*

475, above, left: *Macartney lofts Macaulay (bowling round the wicket), to be caught by Hendren (out of picture).* 476, right: *A great innings behind him, Charlie Macartney doffs his cap.* 477, below: *George Macaulay, England's first-innings top-scorer, is let off by Gregory after wicketkeeper Oldfield had touched the catch on its way*

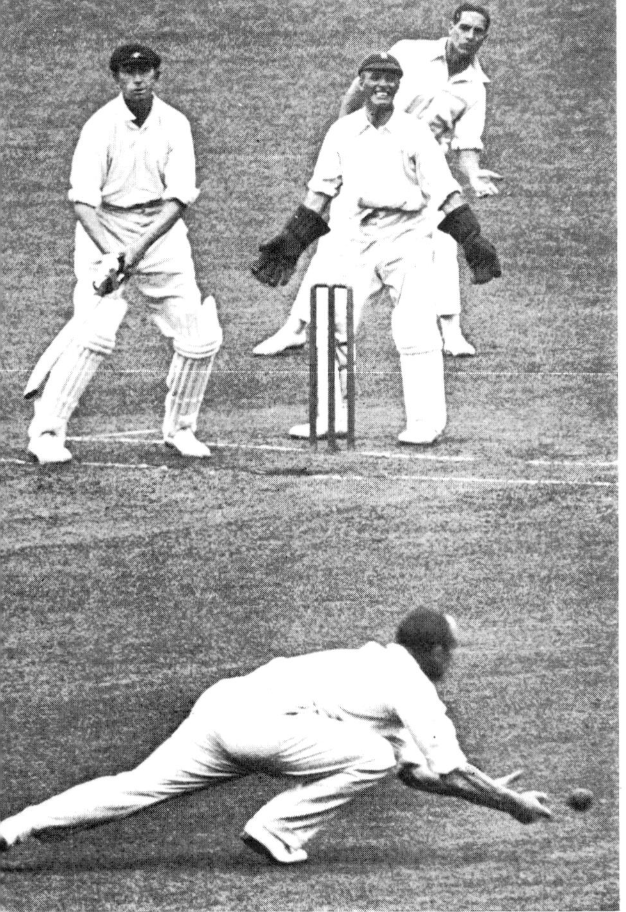

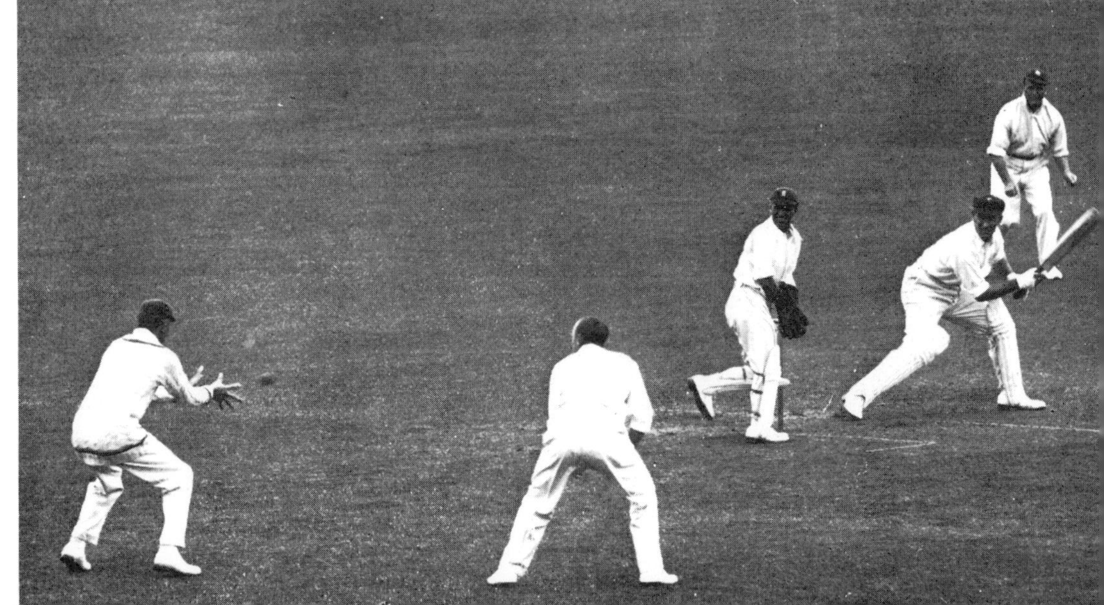

478, above: *Ryder dropped by Carr off Kilner. Strudwick and Sutcliffe show anguish.* 479, right: *Yet another error at Leeds – Geary about to miss Richardson off Macaulay. The batsman was then only 23*

1926 FOURTH TEST
Old Trafford, July 24, 26, 27

Australia *335 (W.M. Woodfull 117, C.G. Macartney 109, C.F. Root 4 for 84);* England *305 for 5 (E. Tyldesley 81, J.B. Hobbs 74, F.E. Woolley 58).* Match drawn.

Only ten balls were possible on the first day owing to rain, and on the Monday, as Carr was down with tonsilitis, Hobbs took over the captaincy – the first professional to lead England since the 1880s. Bardsley again led Australia in Collins's absence. Once more Macartney (making his third consecutive Test century) and Woodfull (his second) made a large second-wicket stand: 192. Macartney was almost as brilliant as at Leeds, but Woodfull this time was more forceful than during his maiden century. Wickets fell steadily thereafter to Root's leg-theory (52 overs) and G.T.S. Stevens's leg-spin. England went in at 11.45 am on the last day, and Hobbs batted splendidly. Tyldesley's was a chancy but attractive innings, and Woolley drove beautifully, putting Grimmett over the sightscreen and also hitting Mailey for six. Gregory had still to take a wicket in the series after five England innings.

480, above: *Jack Hobbs becomes England's first professional captain this century after Carr is taken ill. Immediately following Hobbs are (from left) Root, Chapman (12th man), Stevens, and Tate.* 481, below: *Woodfull drives Root through mid-on, once more depriving the short legs of a touch of the ball*

482, above, left: *Strudwick and Woolley admire a pull by Macartney at Old Trafford – a stroke based on clean footwork, keen eye, and confidence.* 483, above, right: *Macartney b Root 109.* 484, right: *Hobbs deals effortlessly with a full-toss from Mailey*

1926 FIFTH TEST
The Oval, August 14, 16, 17, 18

England *280 (H. Sutcliffe 76, A.P.F. Chapman 49, A.A. Mailey 6 for 138) and 436 (H. Sutcliffe 161, J.B. Hobbs 100);* Australia *302 (J.M. Gregory 73, H.L. Collins 61) and 125 (W. Rhodes 4 for 44).* England won by 289 runs.

England won back the Ashes five years after losing them, and won a series against Australia for the first time since 1912. This match was to be played to a finish, and England recalled Wilfred Rhodes – then in his 49th year and leading the national bowling averages – and replaced Root with the 21-year-old Notts fast bowler Harold Larwood. Collins returned to the Australian captaincy, Ryder being left out. England were all out on the first day, Mailey, on a pitch that offered a small something to the bowlers, getting rid of six of the first seven batsmen, Hobbs to a full-toss. Australia were 60 for 4 that evening, and not until Collins and Gregory made 107 for the seventh wicket did an Australian lead seem likely. Hobbs and Sutcliffe then made 49 without loss on the second evening, a stand which was to grow to 172, most of it in awkward conditions after heavy overnight rain and morning sun. Arthur Richardson bowled off-breaks round the wicket from the Vauxhall end, and it was felt by many that his figures of 41-21-81-2 ought to have been much better. This was to overlook the great skill shown by England's opening pair, who may just have encouraged – with a high degree of subtlety – the retention of Richardson. Hobbs was bowled by Gregory and Sutcliffe by Mailey (in the day's last over); of the rest, the highest score came from Tate (33 not out). A shower on the fourth morning enlivened the pitch, though it was still far from bad, having a worn patch only at the Vauxhall end. Australia, set 415, lost Woodfull for nought to Larwood – whose six wickets in the match were all top batsmen – and Macartney (16) fell to the same bowler, also caught well by Geary at slip. Rhodes spun the ball off the worn area, and midst noisy jubilation the innings fell apart. Geary bowled last-man Mailey at five past six, and of England's several heroes none was more popular than the drought-breaking, 25-year-old, new skipper, A.P.F. 'Percy' Chapman.

485, above, left: *England's new captain, Chapman, beats Collins at the toss at The Oval.* 486, right: *Woodfull bowled for 35 by the old fox, Rhodes*

487, above, left: *Macartney is bowled by leg-spinner Stevens for 25 in Australia's first innings.* 488, centre: *The action absorbs the Prince of Wales (leaning forward).* 489, above: *Grimmett bowls, Sutcliffe places the ball to extra cover with just the right touch, and without hesitation he and Hobbs steal another single during their classic stand in England's second innings.* 490, left: *Sutcliffe is hit in the mouth during the century partnership with Hobbs – their seventh against Australia*

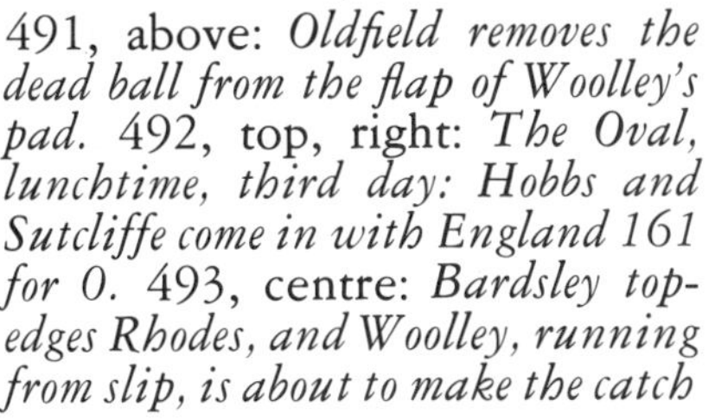

491, above: *Oldfield removes the dead ball from the flap of Woolley's pad.* 492, top, right: *The Oval, lunchtime, third day: Hobbs and Sutcliffe come in with England 161 for 0.* 493, centre: *Bardsley top-edges Rhodes, and Woolley, running from slip, is about to make the catch*

494, above: *Ponsford neatly caught by Larwood off Rhodes for 12.* 495, left: *The human floodtide washes over the ground as England's victory becomes an exciting reality*

1928–29 FIRST TEST

Brisbane (Exhibition Ground), November 30, December 1, 3, 4, 5

England *521 (E.H. Hendren 169, H. Larwood 70, A.P.F. Chapman 50, J.B. Hobbs 49, W.R. Hammond 44) and 342 for 8 dec (C.P. Mead 73, D.R. Jardine 65*, E.H. Hendren 45, C.V. Grimmett 6 for 131);* Australia *122 (H. Larwood 6 for 32) and 66 (J.C. White 4 for 7).* England won by 675 runs.

England's strong all-round side began a successful series with an overwhelming victory, made so by the advisability of not enforcing a follow-on in a 'timeless' Test. In such a large total there was but one century partnership, the record 124 of Hendren and Larwood for the eighth wicket. Hobbs was run out by Bradman (playing his first Test, and scoring 18 and one), and Hammond and Jardine, also in their first Test, had a stand of 53. Australia's woes, begun when Jack Gregory's knee finally gave way – forcing his retirement from cricket – and Kelleway later went down with food poisoning, continued with Woodfull's dismissal without scoring as Chapman took a magnificent left-hand catch at gully. Larwood's figures, won on a blameless wicket, were the best of his entire Test career. With a lead of 399, Chapman batted again against a four-man attack, Ironmonger and Grimmett sharing 94 overs, until on the fourth afternoon he made the first declaration in a Test in Australia. Australia were 17 for one when bad light stopped play, and after rain that night Tate, Larwood and White (slow left-arm) had things all their own way, many of the batsmen, by their desperate hitting, acknowledging this. Woodfull carried his bat, though Gregory and Kelleway were absent.

496, above: *The palm-fringed Exhibition Ground, during Brisbane's first Test match. This vista was photographed on the second day of play.* 497, below: *Hobbs is run out for 49, attempting a third run for Mead and failing to beat Bradman's throw and Oldfield's dive. Gregory leaps in delight*

498, above, left: *Hammond, in his first Test innings against Australia, is stranded against Grimmett, but the ball is lodged in Oldfield's pad-flap, and the stumping chance is missed.* 499, above, right: *Mead (back in Australia 17 years after his first tour) is lbw to Grimmett*

500, right: *Hendren cover-drives during his 169 – his second century against Australia.* 501, below, left: *Chapman is caught off Grimmett, Oldfield taking the bails off for good measure.* 502, below, right: *Gregory just fails to achieve a caught-and-bowled against Larwood. (The ball broke a shoulder of the bat.) The Australian's career ended with a knee injury aggravated by this fall. Kelleway (foreground), Oldfield, and Ironmonger watch anxiously*

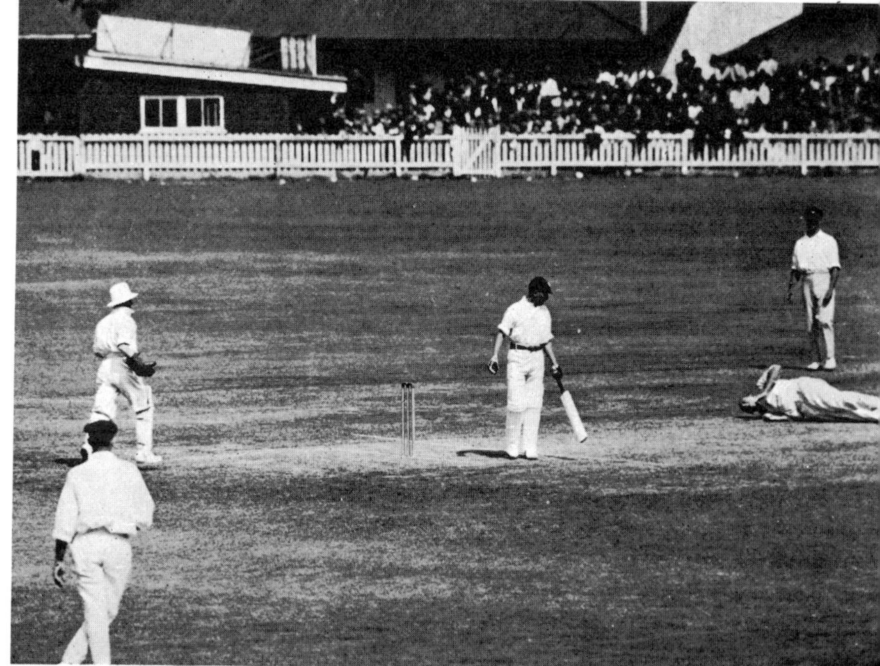

503, above, left: *Ryder, having tried to hook a short, fast ball from Larwood, has skyed a simple catch for Jardine in Australia's first innings.* 504, right: *Australia's batting misfortunes began with this amazing catch by Chapman to dismiss Woodfull (0)*

1928–29 SECOND TEST
Sydney, December 14, 15, 17, 18, 19, 20

Australia *253 (W.M. Woodfull 68, W.A.S. Oldfield 41*, G. Geary 5 for 35) and 397 (H.S.T.L. Hendry 112, W.M. Woodfull 111, J. Ryder 79, O.E. Nothling 44, M.W. Tate 4 for 99);* England *636 (W.R. Hammond 251, E.H. Hendren 74, G. Geary 66, H. Larwood 43, J.B. Hobbs 40, D.D. Blackie 4 for 148) and 16 for 2.* England won by 8 wickets.

Walter Hammond began an extraordinary run of scores with the second double-century ever made for England against Australia, an admirable innings lasting 461 minutes, with 30 boundaries – many from exquisite drives through the off – and with only one difficult chance. He put on 145 with Hendren. Australia's slow bowlers, Grimmett, Ironmonger and 46-year-old debutant off-spinner Blackie, sent down 191 six-ball overs for 481 runs and eight wickets. Geary, the Leicestershire medium-pacer, moved the ball cleverly and was chiefly responsible for Australia's disappointing first innings, but Tate took four good wickets in the second, during which Woodfull and Hendry put on 215 for the second wicket in a most adverse situation. Ponsford's left hand was broken by a flyer from Larwood on the first day, forcing him out of the match. His substitute in the field was Bradman, who had been dropped for the only time in what was to be a 20-year Test career. On the second afternoon, the eve of Jack Hobbs's 46th birthday, 'The Master' was presented out in the middle by M.A. Noble with a shilling-fund collection, the result of a newspaper appeal. He was then escorted around the outfield to the acclaim of a record crowd of 58,456.

505: *'The Kippax Incident': trying to sweep Geary, Kippax was apparently bowled off his pads, but the umpires had to confer before the batsman (left) was confirmed as 'out'*

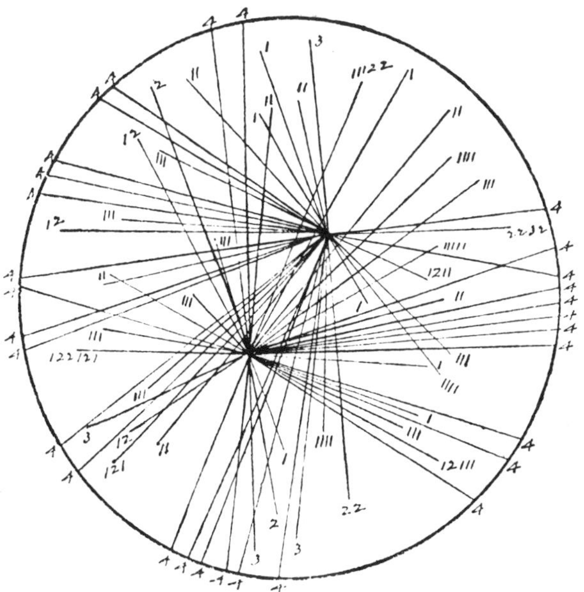

DIAGRAM OF HAMMOND'S FIRST INNINGS

Hammond's score of 251 runs, compiled in seven hours and thirty-one minutes, comprised thirty 4's, four 3's, eighteen 2's, and eighty-three singles.

506, above: *Don Blackie, the Bendigo-born off-spinner, who was well into his 47th year when he made his Test debut at Sydney.* 507, top, right: *Hendry (37) perplexed and bowled by a ball from Geary.* 508, centre: *The run-chart of Hammond's 251 shows the wide range of his scoring strokes.* 509, below: *Hammond drives Blackie and goes past 150*

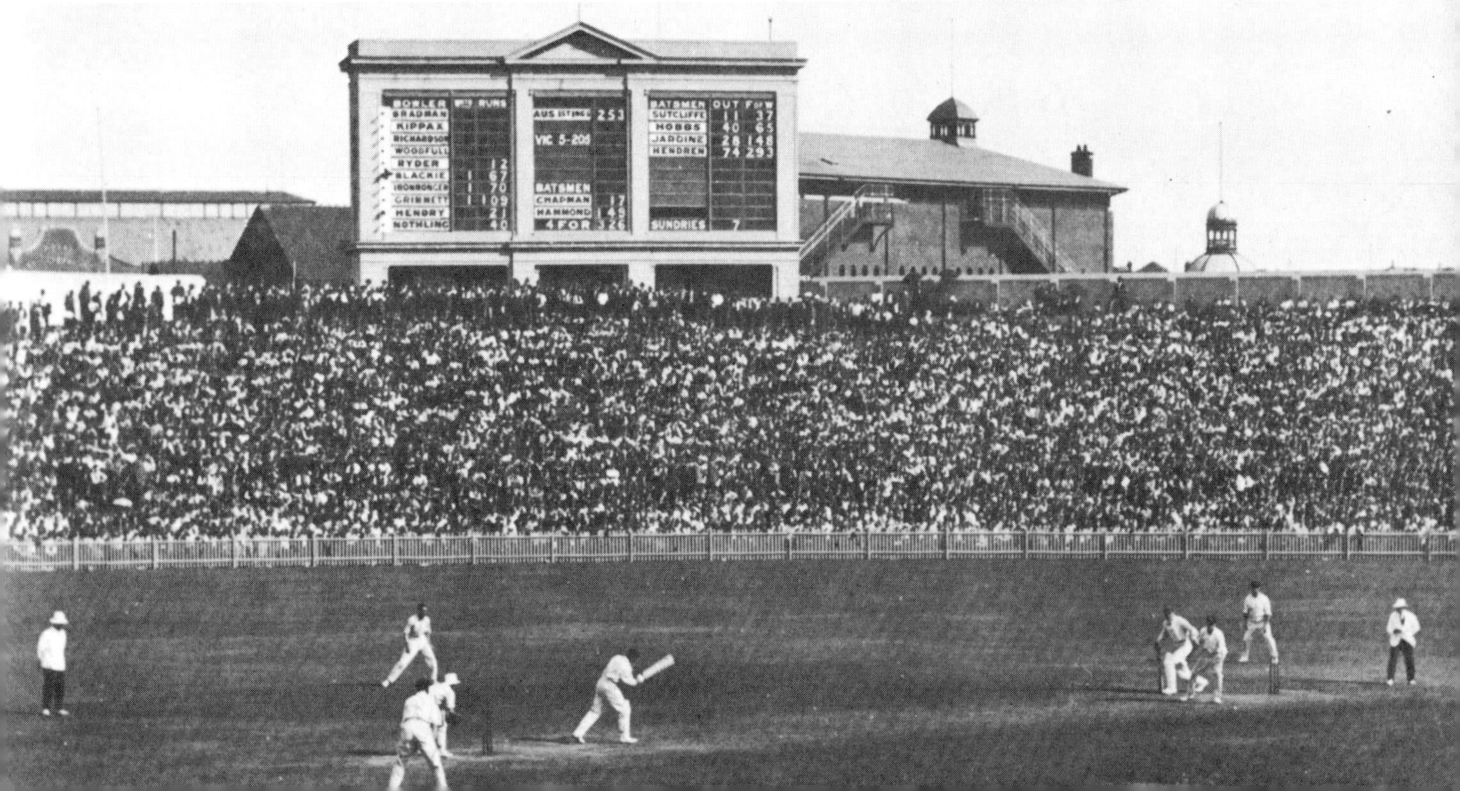

510, above, left: *Jack Hobbs is presented by M.A. Noble (representing a newspaper) with a boomerang and a wallet of notes to mark his 46th birthday.* 511, right: *A confident England take the field on the fifth day: from left – Hobbs, Chapman, Tate, White, Duckworth, Jardine, Larwood, Hammond.* 512, left: *Jack White makes the winning hit in the second Test, and England go two-up*

1928–29 THIRD TEST

Melbourne, December 29, 31, January 1, 2, 3, 4, 5

Australia 397 *(J. Ryder 112, A.F. Kippax 100, D.G. Bradman 79, E.L.a'Beckett 41) and 351 (D.G. Bradman 112, W.M. Woodfull 107, A.F. Kippax 41, J.C. White 5 for 107)*; England 417 *(W.R. Hammond 200, D.R. Jardine 62, H. Sutcliffe 58, D.D. Blackie 6 for 94) and 332 for 7 (H. Sutcliffe 135, J.B. Hobbs 49, E.H. Hendren 45).* England won by 3 wickets.

England's victories, like Australia's in 1924–25, were by ever-decreasing margins. Success here depended heavily on how Hobbs and Sutcliffe negotiated the sticky wicket on the sixth day. They posted 105 for the first wicket. Jardine (on Hobbs's suggestion) then came in, and the day was seen through. On the final day Sutcliffe steered England to the verge of their target. Australia were 57 for 3 on the opening day before Kippax, hooking well, and Ryder, making a multitude of singles, put on 161. The 20-year-old Bradman took 3¼ hours over his 79. Hammond made history with his second double-century running – batting 398 minutes, giving no chance, hitting only 17 boundaries, and drawing rich applause for his powerful drives, especially off the back foot. He had long stands with Sutcliffe and Jardine. Woodfull's innings lasted 4½ hours, and Bradman's – the first of his 19 centuries against England and 29 in all Tests – took just over four hours. Troubled early on by the accurate floaters of White, he later used swift footwork to advantage, and actually reached his hundred with an all-run four off the back foot through mid-on.

513, above, left: *Hammond has driven Blackie and reaches his 200. His partner, in multi-coloured cap, is Jardine.* 514, right: *In the second innings Hammond advances to Grimmett, jams down on the ball, and is stumped by Oldfield as it curls behind him.* 515, left: *Bradman goes down the pitch and drives White.* 516, below, left: *Disastrous start to Australia's second innings: Vic Richardson b Larwood 5.* 517, right: *Woodfull c Duckworth b Tate 107. Chapman at gully, Hendren short leg*

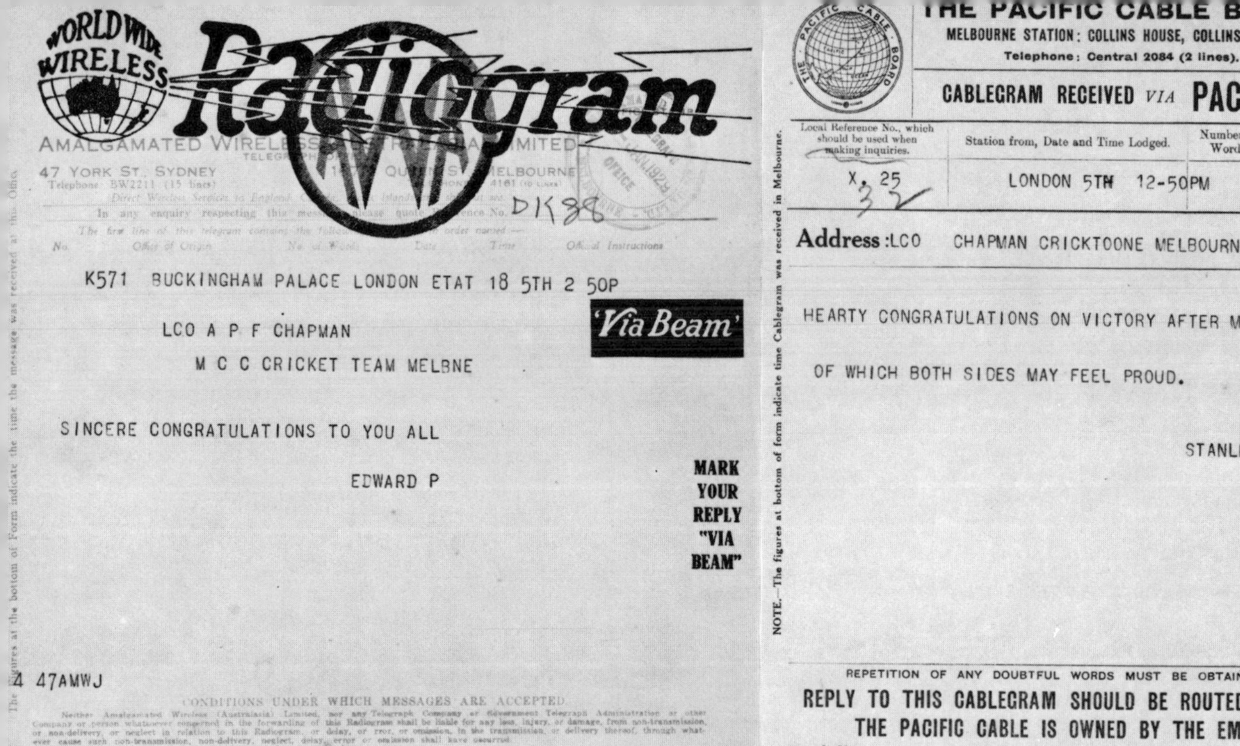

WORLD WIDE WIRELESS
Radiogram
AMALGAMATED WIRELESS (AUSTRALASIA) LIMITED
47 YORK ST., SYDNEY
QUEEN ST., MELBOURNE

K571 BUCKINGHAM PALACE LONDON ETAT 18 5TH 2 50P

LCO A P F CHAPMAN

M C C CRICKET TEAM MELBNE

SINCERE CONGRATULATIONS TO YOU ALL

EDWARD P

'Via Beam'

MARK YOUR REPLY "VIA BEAM"

4 47AMWJ

CONDITIONS UNDER WHICH MESSAGES ARE ACCEPTED.

THE PACIFIC CABLE BOARD
MELBOURNE STATION: COLLINS HOUSE, COLLINS STREET.
Telephone: Central 2084 (2 lines).

CABLEGRAM RECEIVED *VIA* PACIFIC.

Local Reference No., which should be used when making inquiries.	Station from, Date and Time Lodged.	Number of Words.	Official Instructions.
X 25	LONDON 5TH 12-50PM	22	LCO.

Address: LCO CHAPMAN CRICKTOONE MELBOURNE AUSTRALIA.

HEARTY CONGRATULATIONS ON VICTORY AFTER MOST GALLANT FIGHT OF WHICH BOTH SIDES MAY FEEL PROUD.

STANLEY BALDWIN

2-45A MT.

NOTE.—The figures at bottom of form indicate time Cablegram was received in Melbourne.

REPETITION OF ANY DOUBTFUL WORDS MUST BE OBTAINED THROUGH THIS OFFICE.

REPLY TO THIS CABLEGRAM SHOULD BE ROUTED "VIA PACIFIC.

THE PACIFIC CABLE IS OWNED BY THE EMPIRE GOVERNMENTS.

In Messages emanating America, date and time following station of origin indicates when passing Montreal or Vancouver.

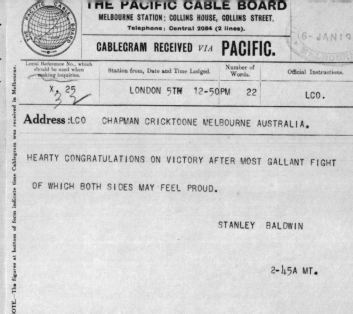

518: *Telegrams of congratulations from the Prince of Wales and Prime Minister Baldwin to Chapman and the team upon their Ashes triumph at Melbourne. Four years later cables of a less cordial nature were being sent back and forth by the administrators*

1928–29 FOURTH TEST

Adelaide, February 1, 2, 4, 5, 6, 7, 8

England *334 (W.R. Hammond 119*, J.B. Hobbs 74, H. Sutcliffe 64, C.V. Grimmett 5 for 102) and 383 (W.R. Hammond 177, D.R. Jardine 98, M.W. Tate 47, R.K. Oxenham 4 for 67);* Australia *369 (A.A. Jackson 164, J. Ryder 63, D.G. Bradman 40, J.C. White 5 for 130, M.W. Tate 4 for 77) and 336 (J. Ryder 87, D.G. Bradman 58, A.F. Kippax 51, J.C. White 8 for 126).* England won by 12 runs.

The seventh day dawned with Australia, 260 for 6, needing 89 for victory, and 48 runs were made before Chapman dived to catch Oxenham. The crucial wicket then followed, Bradman being tragically run out after Oldfield had played a ball to Hobbs at cover. The match was still poised at lunch, but White (124.5 overs in the match) took his seventh and eighth wickets, and England went four-up. Hammond and Jackson were the major figures, the former making 72 of the last 88 runs in England's first innings and batting masterfully in the second until exhaustion defeated him. He was on the field for over 26½ hours, and took his aggregate to 602 in four successive innings. His stand of 262 with Jardine is a third-wicket record for England against Australia. Archie Jackson, opening Australia's innings, saw three wickets fall for 19, but with sweet strokeplay the slightly-built 19-year-old reached his hundred in 250 minutes, adding 60 in a further hour. The Scottish-born Sydneysider, who died four years later of tuberculosis, became the youngest centurion in England-Australia matches in this his first Test.

519: *Wally Hammond, maker of two centuries at Adelaide, comes close to being stumped off Grimmett*

520, top: *Young Archie Jackson's poised and stirring debut innings ends as he is adjudged lbw to White for 164. Duckworth, Hammond, and Jardine are also shown.* 521, above, left: *Jackson reaches the boundary by timing rather than force with an off-drive off White.* 522, above, right: *Duckworth dives but fails to hold a ball from White popped up by Oxenham.* 523, right: *Kippax (51) about to be caught by Hendren (in cap), who took the rebound from second slip Geary*

524, above: *Left-handed Blackie, Australia's last man, has hit White to square leg, where Larwood makes a safe catch – and England have won by 12 runs at Adelaide.* 525, left: *Archie Jackson is congratulated on his maiden-Test success by the scorer of Australia's first century – 52 years earlier – Charles Bannerman, now 77*

1928–29 FIFTH TEST

Melbourne, March 8, 9, 11, 12, 13, 14, 15, 16

England *519 (J.B. Hobbs 142, M. Leyland 137, E.H. Hendren 95) and 257 (J.B. Hobbs 65, M.W. Tate 54, M. Leyland 53*, T.W. Wall 5 for 66);* Australia *491 (D.G. Bradman 123, W.M. Woodfull 102, A.G. Fairfax 65, G. Geary 5 for 105) and 287 for 5 (J. Ryder 57*, W.A.S. Oldfield 48, A.A. Jackson 46).* Australia won by 5 wickets.

Jack Ryder's side, altered to let in more young players (Wall, Fairfax and Hornibrook), triumphed at last – and worthily, though England lacked Sutcliffe and Chapman. Hobbs's century was the last of his 12 against Australia, and left-hander Leyland's was in his first innings against them. He reached 100 with the last man in, and added 141 with Hendren, whose 95 included an eight (four run and four overthrows). The core of Australia's determined reply was a stand of 183 for the fifth wicket between Bradman and Fairfax. The total of 491 was made at less than two runs an over, Geary bowling 81 overs (36 maidens), captain White 75.3 (22), and Tate 62 (26). Grimmett and Hornibrook managed 59 for the tenth wicket, and the latter, after England's second-innings decline, did a stout job in putting on 51 as nightwatchman opener with Oldfield, who himself stayed 2½ hours. The running-out of Kippax poised the match on the eighth morning, but Ryder and Bradman then saw their side home. Hammond's 54 runs in the match gave him a record series aggregate of 905.

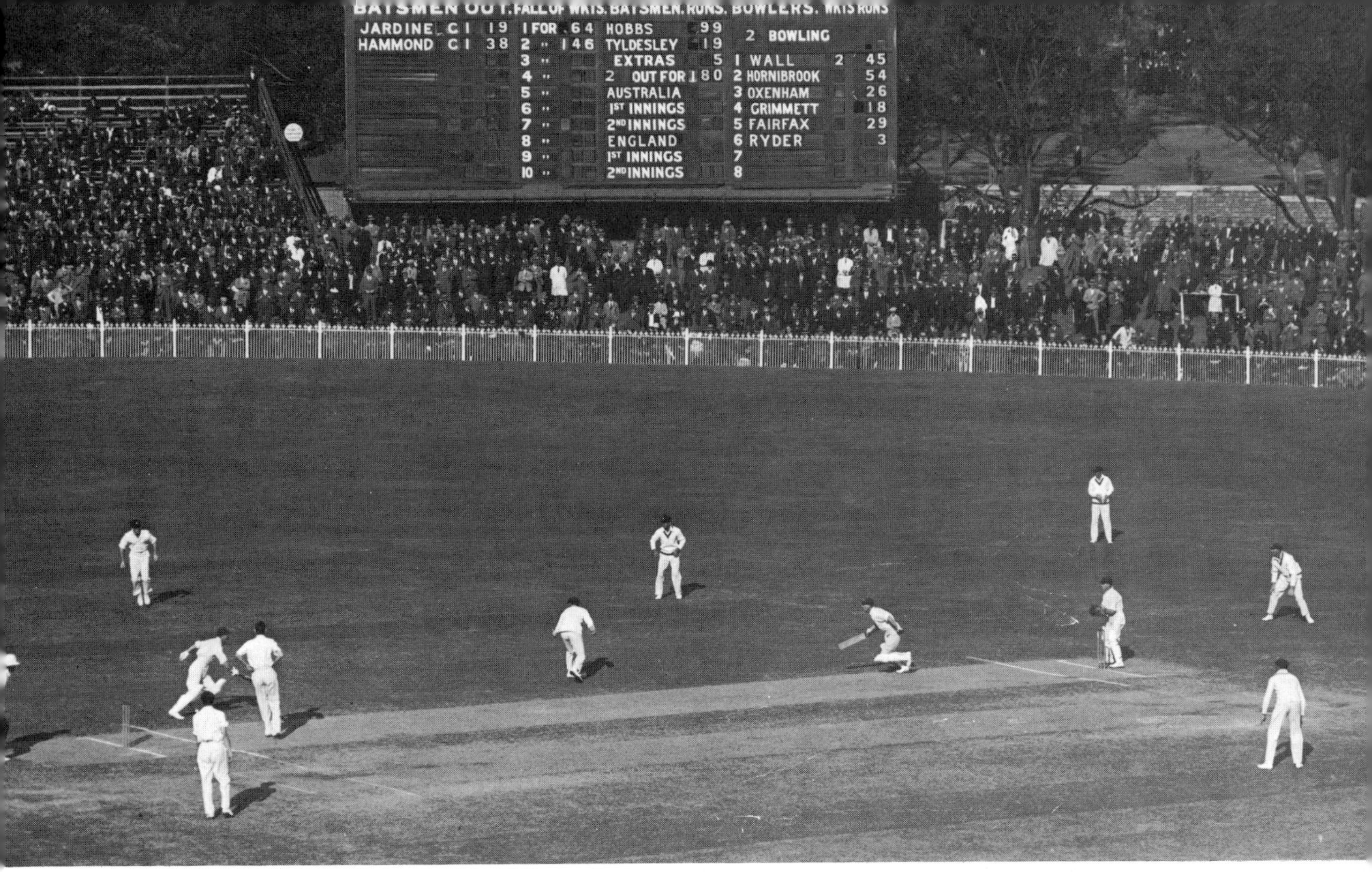

526: *Jack Hobbs sets off on his 100th run. It was 'The Master's' final century against Australia*

527, above: *Hammond well caught by Fairfax off Wall for 38, England first innings.* 528, right: *Hendren bowled by Grimmett for one, and England's second innings at Melbourne falls away still further*

529, above: *Oldfield's valuable 2½-hour innings of 48 ends as Hammond bowls him.* 530, below: *On the eighth day, Ryder swung, byes resulted, and Australia had victory at last*

531: *Some of the former Australian Test players who gathered at the match: from left – V.S. Ransford, C. Hill, M.A. Noble, H. Trumble, J.M. Gregory, J. Darling, J. Worrall, W.W. Armstrong, P.A. McAlister*

1930 FIRST TEST

Trent Bridge, June 13, 14, 16, 17

England *270 (J.B. Hobbs 78, A.P.F. Chapman 52, R.W.V. Robins 50*, C.V. Grimmett 5 for 107) and 302 (J.B. Hobbs 74, E.H. Hendren 72, H. Sutcliffe 58 ret.ht, C.V. Grimmett 5 for 94);* Australia *144 (A.F. Kippax 64*, R.W.V. Robins 4 for 51) and 335 (D.G. Bradman 131, S.J. McCabe 49).* England won by 93 runs.

A grand diving catch at mid-on by a comparatively unknown substitute fieldsman, Syd Copley of the Notts groundstaff, broke a threatening stand between Bradman and McCabe on the last day and opened the way for victory to a mature – perhaps over-mature – England side. The new, young Australian team owed much to their 38-year-old leg-spinner Grimmett, who took ten wickets in the match. Hobbs on the opening day batted over 3½ hours, and Chapman alone – with typical nonchalance – set about the bowling with any success. The tourists unluckily had to bat on a rain-affected pitch: their hero was Kippax, who showed great skill on a drying surface. Tate's opening burst of 3 for 7 reduced Australia to 16 for 3. Hobbs and Sutcliffe put on 125 for England's first wicket in the second innings – their tenth century stand against Australia. The former, at the age of 47, played gloriously. Sutcliffe retired after a blow on the right thumb, and it was left to 41-year-old Hendren, with nimble footwork, to sustain England's command. Set 429, Australia were 229 for 3 when Copley, fielding as 'thirteenth man' for Larwood (stomach upset) with Duleepsinhji already substituting for Sutcliffe, made his fateful catch down near his toes. The target was now 200 in 195 minutes, but when Robins deceived Bradman with a googly all real hope was lost. Some further fine catches were taken, and Chapman had now led England to nine consecutive victories, six against Australia. Bradman's century, in his first Test in England, was the first of 11 in that country.

532, above: *Don Bradman plays to leg during his first Test century in England. Chapman is at gully, Hendren slip, Duckworth wicketkeeper.* 533, below: *Alan Fairfax about to be caught by Hobbs at cover off Robins for 14*

534, above, left: *Sutcliffe sustains a split thumb in trying to hook Wall. Hammond is non-striker.* 535, right: *S. H. Copley, who usually features in England-Australia Test history as plain 'sub'. His catch swung the Trent Bridge match.* 536, left: *Bradman b Robins 131*

1930 SECOND TEST

Lord's, June 27, 28, 30, July 1

England *425 (K.S. Duleepsinhji 173, M.W. Tate 54, E.H. Hendren 48, F.E. Woolley 41, A.G. Fairfax 4 for 101) and 375 (A.P.F. Chapman 121, G.O.B. Allen 57, K.S. Duleepsinhji 48, C.V. Grimmett 6 for 167);* Australia *729 for 6 dec (D.G. Bradman 254, W.M. Woodfull 155, A.F. Kippax 83, W.H. Ponsford 81, S.J. McCabe 44, W.A.S. Oldfield 43*) and 72 for 3.* Australia won by 7 wickets.

This spectator's Test match began with a brilliant rescuing innings by Duleepsinhji, who emulated his illustrious uncle, Ranji, in scoring a century in his first Test. He drove and cut with great charm, adding 104 with Hendren for the fourth wicket, 98 with Tate for the seventh, and scoring 21 fours before holing out at long-off after 292 minutes. Woodfull (scoring his sixth and final hundred against England) and Ponsford made 162 for Australia's first wicket, and when Bradman joined his captain he was obviously seeing the ball well from the start. They put on 231 in only 154 minutes, and Bradman was 155 at the end of the second day, with Australia already 404 for 2. He passed Murdoch's Australian record of 211 while adding 192 with Kippax, and 585 was on the board before Bradman's, the third wicket, fell. He was in for 339 minutes (25 fours) with only one stroke that could have been considered imperfect before he hit White within the reach of Chapman, who made a thrilling right-hand catch at extra cover. Australia have only once exceeded 729 for 6: against West Indies in 1955, 758 for 8 at Kingston. England, 304 behind, were 93 for 2 at the start of the final day, and Grimmett took his fourth wicket before lunch. Chapman, hitting very hard, then put on 125 with Allen for the sixth wicket. The England captain, who hit three sixes off Grimmett into the Mound Stand and 12 fours, saw the innings defeat staved off before his dismissal. Australia, 22 for 3, still had time and little trouble in making the runs.

537, left: *Duleepsinhji – with a favourite bat, judged from its binding – pulls Grimmett.* 538, above: *'Duleep', dropped at 98, now cuts Wall to bring up his century, the first by an amateur for England against Australia since 1908 (Hutchings, Melbourne)*

539, above: *On the second day Bradman cuts Tate past Chapman at point. Allen is at short leg, Duckworth wicketkeeper.* 540, right: *Chapman blazes away, salvaging some late honour for England*

541, left: *The King greets the Australians at Lord's. Woodfull stands with the monarch, who is shaking hands with McCabe.* 542, above: *Hobbs b Grimmett 19. Woolley is non-striker*

543, above, left: *Bradman (1), in the second innings, back-cuts Tate into the prehensile hands of Chapman.* 544, right, centre: *Hammond dives in an unsuccessful attempt to catch Kippax after a ball from Robins had brushed his glove.* 545, above, right: *An eerie presence – the ill-fated R101 airship makes an appearance during the Lord's Test*

1930 THIRD TEST
Headingley, July 11, 12, 14, 15

Australia 566 *(D.G. Bradman 334, A.F. Kippax 77, W.M. Woodfull 50, M.W. Tate 5 for 124);* England *391 (W.R. Hammond 113, A.P.F. Chapman 45, M. Leyland 44, C.V. Grimmett 5 for 135) and 95 for 3.* Match drawn.

Bradman, the phenomenon, reached yet new heights with the highest score yet made in Test cricket. A few weeks from his 22nd birthday, he went in when Jackson was out in the second over, and against some testing new-ball bowling from Larwood and Tate he moved to 50 in 49 minutes and his century in only 99 minutes (out of 127 scored). He was 105 at lunch, 220 at tea, and 309 at the end of the day, having passed 1000 Test runs in only his seventh match. In all he batted 383 minutes and hit 46 fours, adding 192 with Woodfull and 229 with Kippax for the third wicket. His only chance was a difficult one to Duckworth (who eventually caught him off Tate) behind the stumps. Bradman's strokeplay, footwork and placement were marvelled at, and if overall his innings fell a trifle short of the perfection of his Lord's double-century, his skills were now comprehensively appreciated by players, Press and public. The pitch began to wear, and England were in difficulties, Hammond staying at the wicket for almost 5½ hours and reaching his 1000 Test runs in this his eighth Test. Rain and bad light came to England's salvation despite the follow-on, and though the series remained alive the prospects depended much upon whether Bradman could be held in check.

546, above, left: *Bradman has passed Foster's England-Australia record 287, and responds to the warm Yorkshire acclaim.* 547, above, right: *The great innings ends: Bradman c Duckworth b Tate 334.* 548, right: *He returns to the pavilion, the luckier spectators getting a touch as he passes*

549, left: *McCabe bowled leg stump by Larwood for 30 at Leeds.* 550, above: *England's champion, Hammond, is caught by Oldfield for 113*

1930 FOURTH TEST
Old Trafford, July 25, 26, 28, 29

Australia *345 (W.H. Ponsford 83, W.M. Woodfull 54, A.F. Kippax 51, C.V. Grimmett 50, A.G. Fairfax 49);* England *251 for 8 (H. Sutcliffe 74, K.S. Duleepsinhji 54, S.J. McCabe 4 for 41).* Match drawn.

On a slow pitch, after rain, Australia made heavy work of it, and crumpled after Woodfull and Ponsford's tedious 106 opening. Fairfax and Grimmett took them to a respectable total, but England's reorganised attack had had its say. Ian Peebles, bowling more googlies than leg-breaks, took 3 for 150, including Bradman (14), caught at slip. Sutcliffe dominated a first-wicket stand of 108 with Hobbs – their last of three-figures against Australia – before being caught breathtakingly by Bradman at long leg, and after Duleep's fine innings, during which he ran out to Grimmett, Leyland batted cautiously. During the brief period of play at 5.30 on the Monday the pitch was lively, but the fourth day was called off at 11 am, so wet were pitch and outfield.

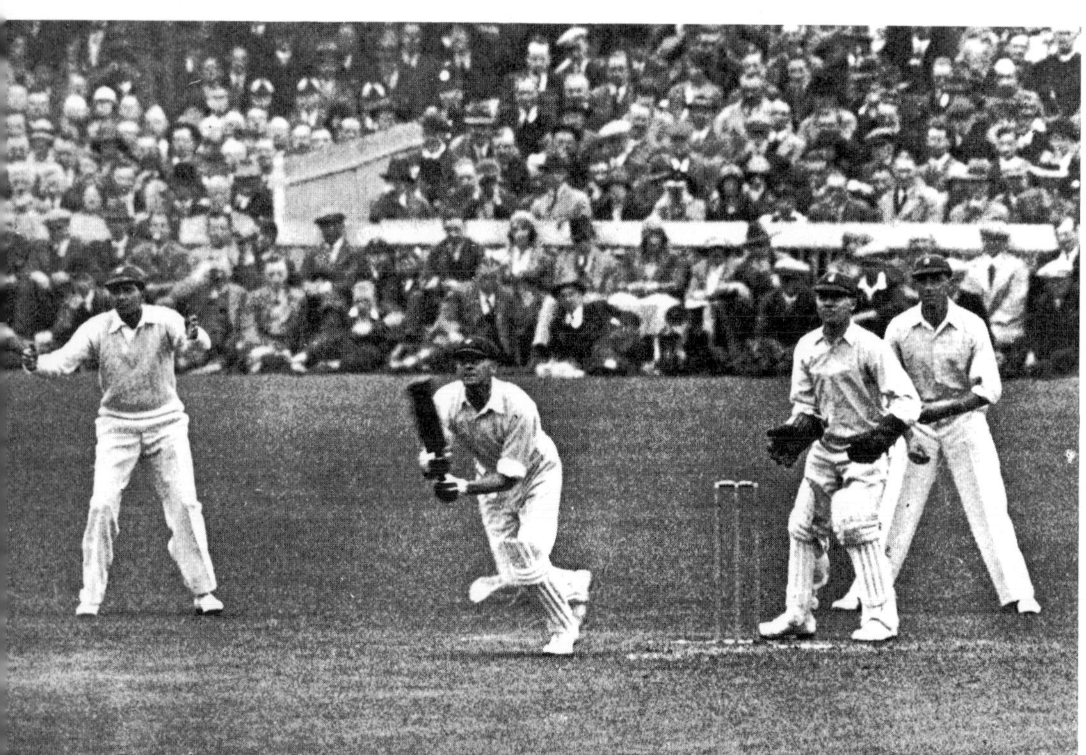

551: *Woodfull, Australia's captain, hits Peebles for four. Duleepsinhji, Duckworth, and Hammond watch*

COMING EVENTS CAST THEIR SHADOWS AT OLD TRAFFORD OR— – THE ENGLISH CAPTAIN SEES SOMETHING "FUNNY" ABOUT THE WICKET.

552, above: *Tom Webster's cartoon reflects England's neurosis over Bradman's domination of her bowlers. Australia's freshfaced champion for once did not trouble them in the Old Trafford Test – perhaps only because there was no second innings.* 553, right: *The 'old firm' – 'the two Bills' – 'Mutt and Jeff' – Woodfull (left) and Ponsford open in the fourth Test*

554, above: *Peebles bowls to Fairfax at Old Trafford.* 555, left: *Leyland is bowled by McCabe for 35, one of the medium-pacer's four wickets*

1930 FIFTH TEST

The Oval, August 16, 18, 19, 20, 21, 22

England 405 *(H. Sutcliffe 161, R.E.S. Wyatt 64, K.S. Duleepsinhji 50, J.B. Hobbs 47, C.V. Grimmett 4 for 135)* and 251 *(W.R. Hammond 60, H. Sutcliffe 54, K.S. Duleepsinhji 46, P.M. Hornibrook 7 for 92);* Australia 695 *(D.G. Bradman 232, W.H. Ponsford 110, A.A. Jackson 73, W.M. Woodfull 54, S.J. McCabe 54, A.G. Fairfax 53*, I.A.R. Peebles 6 for 204).* Australia won by an innings and 39 runs.

Bradman did it again, taking his aggregate for the series to a (still) record 974 (average 139.14) and setting up – with the vital and courageous support of Jackson – a winning position in a match to be played to a finish. The two young New South Welshmen added 243 for the fourth wicket at a time when the ball sometimes lifted dangerously and Australia might have been overcome. Chapman was dropped – not a popular decision – and Bob Wyatt led England on his first appearance against Australia. He came in at the crisis point of 197 for 5 and settled to add 170 with Sutcliffe. Woodfull and Ponsford gave Australia a start of 159, but the Bradman-Jackson stand turned the match, the former this time making many of his runs behind the wicket, and batting 578 minutes, with one chance at 82. Peebles bowled 71 overs, and Tate (one for 153) 65.1. Larwood, who once struck Bradman painfully on the chest, took one for 132. Hobbs, in his final Test match, was bowled for nine by Fairfax, and finished with a record 3636 runs against Australia, average 54.26, with 12 centuries. Hammond ended a disappointing series with 60, last man out, the seventh of left-arm bowler Hornibrook's wickets after a blank fifth day through rain. Australia thus regained the Ashes on their captain Woodfull's 33rd birthday.

556: *A tense moment for new England captain Wyatt – his first ball, from Grimmett*

557, top, right: *A rare Sutcliffe error: the ball flies between Hornibrook and a diving McCabe.* 558, above: *Wyatt takes a superb catch to end Kippax's innings. Peebles was the bowler; Larwood is the other short leg.* 559, below: *Bradman hooks during his Oval double-century*

560, above: *Jackson swings a loose ball from Peebles to the leg boundary on the fourth morning of the Oval Test.* 561, left: *That evening Jack Hobbs embarked on his final Test innings, and was accorded an affectionate reception by the Australians*

562: *The end: Hobbs b Fairfax 9*

1932–33
Sydney, December 2, 3, 5, 6, 7

Australia *360 (S.J. McCabe 187*, V.Y. Richardson 49, H. Larwood 5 for 96, W. Voce 4 for 110) and 164 (J.H.W. Fingleton 40, H. Larwood 5 for 28);* England *524 (H. Sutcliffe 194, W.R. Hammond 112, Nawab of Pataudi 102) and 1 for 0.* England won by 10 wickets.

The 'Bodyline' tour began with one of the most heroic innings in the game's history. With Larwood and Voce (fast left-arm) bowling short-pitched balls in the direction of the batsman, with a cluster of short legs and a man or two out for the hook or top-edge, England's attack, under the unrelenting direction of captain Douglas Jardine, created unparalleled discomfort for batsmen and controversy which spread from onlookers through the sports pages into editorials and even to the music halls. Stan McCabe (22) hooked boldly and with the necessary good fortune and used his feet nimbly to get into position to cut ferociously. He hit 51 of a last-wicket stand of 55 after putting on 129 with Richardson for the fifth wicket. He hit 25 fours in his four hours, and, if anything, gave the Englishmen an argument for continuing with their policy: 'leg theory' could be hit, or so some claimed. Sutcliffe's eighth, last and highest century against Australia spanned century stands for the first three wickets: 112 with Wyatt, 188 with Hammond, and 123 with Pataudi (whose first Test it was). Sutcliffe at 43 played a ball from O'Reilly into his stumps but the bails were not dislodged. Larwood, with a strained side strapped, bowled very fast and accurately, seldom pitching short, in Australia's second innings.

563, above: *Jack Fingleton is caught by Allen in the leg-trap off Larwood. Ames is wicketkeeper and the other fielders are Jardine, Wyatt, and Hammond.* 564, right: *The slow bowling of Verity came as a kind of relief from hostilities: McCabe hits him to leg*

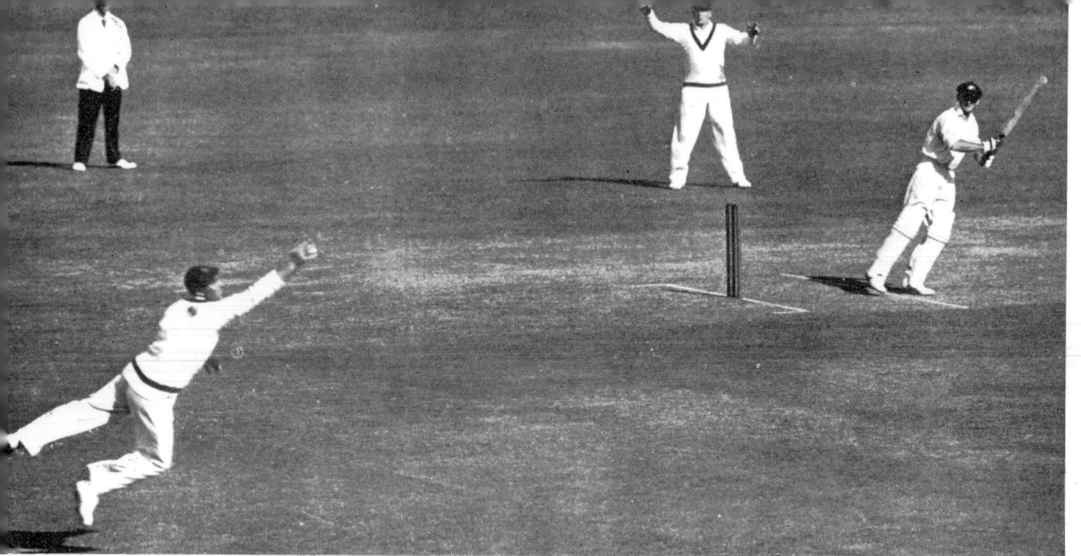

565, left: *Stan McCabe, thriving on audacity allied to quick reflexes, slashes the ball just wide of Voce at slip.* 566, below, left: *Sutcliffe plays a ball from O'Reilly into his stumps, to the mortification of McCabe and Oldfield, among others, but not himself. He went on to his highest Test score*

567, left: *The Hill usually accommodates more spectators than this, but little action was expected on the final morning.* 568, above: *Nawab of Pataudi b Nagel 102 at Sydney.*

1932–33 SECOND TEST

Melbourne, December 30, 31, January 2, 3

Australia *228 (J.H.W. Fingleton 83) and 191 (D.G. Bradman 103*);* England *169 (H. Sutcliffe 52, W.J. O'Reilly 5 for 63, T.W. Wall 4 for 52) and 139 (W.J. O'Reilly 5 for 66, H. Ironmonger 4 for 26).* Australia won by 111 runs.

Against the ominous portents, Australia drew level, with Bradman returning after a one-match absence to pull Bowes's first ball into his stumps, only to make a highly creditable century in the second innings, ducking and stepping across his wicket to Larwood, who sometimes had no off-side fielder in front of point. England erred in playing no slow bowler, Larwood, Voce, Allen, Hammond and Bowes carrying the attack. Fingleton's was a dour and courageous innings and McCabe and Richardson contributed valuably. Wall's pace and O'Reilly's fast-medium spinners were too much for England, who, after Bradman's grand knock (which sustained the nation's fervent faith in him), had no answer to O'Reilly again and the left-arm spin of Ironmonger. Over 200,000 watched the four days' play.

569, above: *Film sequence of Bradman's shock first-ball dismissal by Bowes; Fingleton is non-striker.* 570, below: *When the ball had to be changed soon after the start of the match, Woodfull patted the replacement back and forth with Jardine until enough shine had been taken off*

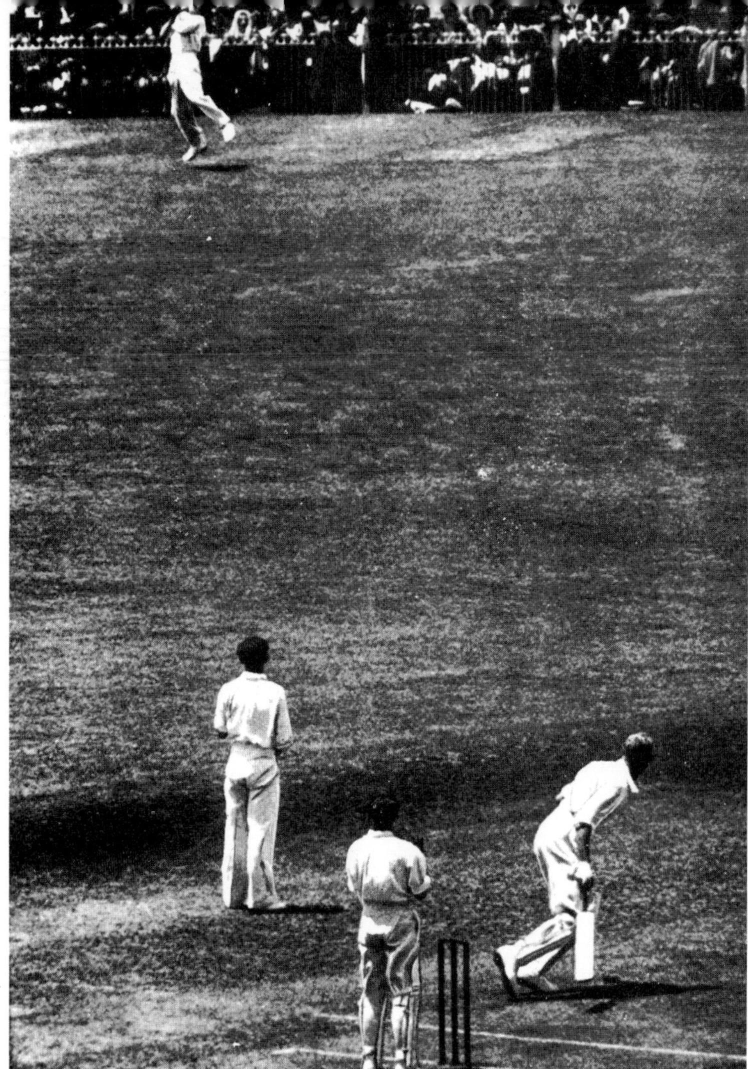

571: *Allen (out of picture) beautifully caught by Vic Richardson on the mid-wicket boundary off O'Reilly for 30 in England's first innings at Melbourne. Bowes is the not-out batsman*

1932–33 THIRD TEST

Adelaide, January 13, 14, 16, 17, 18, 19

England *341 (M. Leyland 83, R.E.S. Wyatt 78, E. Paynter 77, H. Verity 45, T.W. Wall 5 for 72) and 412 (W.R. Hammond 85, L.E.G. Ames 69, D.R. Jardine 56, R.E.S. Wyatt 49, M. Leyland 42, H. Verity 40, W.J. O'Reilly 4 for 79);* Australia *222 (W.H. Ponsford 85, W.A.S. Oldfield 41 ret.ht, G.O.B. Allen 4 for 71) and 193 (W.M. Woodfull 73*, D.G. Bradman 66, G.O.B. Allen 4 for 50, H. Larwood 4 for 71).* England won by 338 runs.

The series erupted at Adelaide, where Woodfull, hit sickeningly over the heart by Larwood, who then reverted to the leg-side attack, told P.F. Warner, the MCC manager, that only one of the sides was playing cricket. Oldfield, having survived two hours, then suffered a cracked skull as he mishooked at Larwood. Mounted police lined up in readiness as the crowd's fury reached white heat. The Australian Board, who had prepared a cable of protest, sent it to Lord's, where the response several days later stated that MCC had full confidence in their team management. If an amendment to the Laws was proposed, it said, then full consideration would be given to it. Meanwhile, if Australia thought fit to cancel the rest of the tour, MCC would consent 'with great reluctance'. A further despatch was sent by the Board, reasserting that Bodyline was 'opposed to the spirit of cricket' and 'dangerous to players', but saying that cancellation was not considered necessary; a committee (Noble, Woodfull, Richardson and Hartigan) was to be set up and a report would later be submitted. A Law was adopted in November 1934 which outlawed 'direct bowling attack'. The Battle of Adelaide began with an England collapse, but Leyland, Wyatt and Paynter shored up the innings. Larwood and Allen (who refused to bowl Bodyline– and as an amateur, Australian-born at that ,was still able to hold his place) then demolished Australia, Ponsford, reinstated, bravely taking much fast stuff on the back. England built a lead laboriously, and on the fifth afternoon, after an animated innings from Bradman, the back of Australia's innings was broken, Woodfull going on valiantly to carry his bat for the second time against England.

572, above: *A victim of 'leg theory' – Bradman is caught by Allen off Larwood for 8 at Adelaide*

573, below: *Ponsford glances Voce past Verity*

574, top: *Woodfull hit over the heart at Adelaide by a ball from Larwood. Allen is at short leg.* 575, centre: *Hammond becomes a casualty, if less serious, as a ball from spinner Ironmonger strikes his mouth. Vic Richardson is keeping wicket in place of the injured Oldfield.* 576, bottom: *Bradman hits Verity for six (but was caught-and-bowled by the spinner's next ball)*

1932–33 FOURTH TEST

Brisbane, February 10, 11, 13, 14, 15, 16

Australia *340 (V.Y. Richardson 83, D.G. Bradman 76, W.M. Woodfull 67, H. Larwood 4 for 101) and 175;* England *356 (H. Sutcliffe 86, E. Paynter 83, D.R. Jardine 46, W.J. O'Reilly 4 for 120) and 162 for 4 (M. Leyland 86).* England won by 6 wickets.

Woolloongabba's first Test was fought closely on the first innings in oppressive, sultry heat, but Larwood, Allen and Verity found ways of getting rid of the home batsmen in the second innings, and a rocklike 24 from Jardine aiding Leyland's effort at No. 3 saw England to victory and the Ashes, the winning hit being a six by Paynter. Richardson and Woodfull had begun the match with a stand of 133, but apart from Bradman, who was bowled leg stump by Larwood as he tried to cut, no-one else made an impression. Jardine and Sutcliffe too began with a century stand, but a minor collapse was stemmed only when Paynter, the small Lancashire left-hander, left hospital, where he had been confined with acute tonsillitis, to make 24 before returning for another night under observation. Next day he put on a crucial 92 with Verity for the ninth wicket.

577, above: *Richardson pulls Larwood during by far the best opening stand for Australia in the series.* 578, below: *Paynter, England's sick Brisbane hero, skies O'Reilly. The wicketkeeper is 'Hammy' Love*

579, above: *McCabe cleverly caught left-handed by Jardine off Allen for 20 at Brisbane.* 580, left: *Left-hander Ernie Bromley fails to keep down a kicker from Larwood and is caught by Verity*

1932–33 FIFTH TEST
Sydney, February 23, 24, 25, 27, 28

Australia *435 (L.S. Darling 85, S.J. McCabe 73, L.P.J. O'Brien 61, W.A.S. Oldfield 52, D.G. Bradman 48, P.K. Lee 42, H. Larwood 4 for 98) and 182 (D.G. Bradman 71, W.M. Woodfull 67, H. Verity 5 for 33);* England *454 (W.R. Hammond 101, H. Larwood 98, H. Sutcliffe 56, R.E.S. Wyatt 51, G.O.B. Allen 48, M. Leyland 42, P.K. Lee 4 for 111) and 168 for 2 (W.R. Hammond 75*, R.E.S. Wyatt 61*).* England won by 8 wickets.

Woodfull won his fourth toss of the series, but Vic Richardson was dismissed before a run was scored – as he was in the second innings, suffering the same fate as Fingleton at Adelaide. Bradman batted with a kind of abandon, and McCabe, standing up to hit the fast bowlers, added 99 with O'Brien and 81 with Darling, both left-handers. Australia's overnight 296 for 5 was extended to 435 thanks in part to a continuation of dropped catches and near misses, and England were 159 for 2 that night after Sutcliffe and Hammond had put on 122 for the second wicket. Hammond's century owed its accomplishment to several dropped catches, but the emotive innings was Larwood's. Sent in as nightwatchman, he surprised everyone in making 98 – caught by the cumbersome Ironmonger off off-spinner Lee. For once the crowd received Larwood joyously. Australia's second innings owed almost everything to a stand of 115 between the defiant Woodfull and again a seemingly desperate Bradman. Verity used worn patches well, but Ironmonger was not so devastating when England set about getting 164. Jardine was barracked loudly as he protested when 'Bull' Alexander, Australia's squarely-built fast bowler, ran through across the batsman's area. Hammond finished the series with a six off Lee to the right of the sightscreen. Oldfield returned to the Australian XI and showed no ill-effects. Larwood, slowed down at the end of this acrimonious series by a splintered bone in the foot, finished with 33 wickets at 19.51 in the five Tests.

581, top: *Hammond's distinctive cover-drive; he scored heavily again here at Sydney, his favourite ground.* 582, centre: *Richardson takes a sharp catch at slip to dismiss Jardine – probably the wicket Australia always wanted most of all – off Ironmonger.* 583, below: *Larwood falls two short of a century, caught at mid-on*

584, left: *An odd sight: Don Bradman as drinks waiter. After a blow on the arm while batting against Larwood, he was off the field for a while when Australia fielded, but made himself useful at refreshment time.* 585, below: *Hammond (left) and Wyatt leave the field at Sydney after seeing England to their fourth victory of the 1932–33 series. Wall follows.* 586, bottom: *As* The Australian Cricketer *saw it*

1934 FIRST TEST

Trent Bridge, June 8, 9, 11, 12

Australia *374 (A.G. Chipperfield 99, S.J. McCabe 65, W.H. Ponsford 53, K. Farnes 5 for 102) and 273 for 8 dec (S.J. McCabe 88, W.A. Brown 73, K. Farnes 5 for 77);* England *268 (E.H. Hendren 79, H. Sutcliffe 62, G. Geary 53, C.V. Grimmett 5 for 81, W.J. O'Reilly 4 for 75) and 141 (C.F. Walters 46, W.J. O'Reilly 7 for 54).* Australia won by 238 runs.

Left 4¾ hours to bat, 379 in arrears, England could not withstand the spin of O'Reilly and Grimmett (who took 19 of the wickets between them), and lost with ten minutes remaining. England were led by Walters in his maiden Test against Australia, Wyatt missing the match with a broken thumb. Chipperfield, batting No. 7 in his first Test, often hit uppishly through the off, but reached 99 by lunch on the second day. He fell, however, to Farnes's third ball after the interval, caught behind by Ames. A seventh-wicket stand of 101 by Hendren and Geary saved the follow-on, and although 106 behind, England fought back to get Woodfull, Ponsford and Bradman for 69. Brown and McCabe then added 112, the latter once more batting with great flair. When Ames missed stumping the dour Brown, however, it was thought he might have done England a favour. Sutcliffe and Walters began soundly, making 51 by half an hour after lunch, but O'Reilly – into the dusty end – and Grimmett – who had Hammond stumped when he fell forward – bowled their side to victory. The tall Essex fast bowler Farnes had an impressive debut, helping for the moment to soften the loss of Larwood and Voce, who, with Jardine – for various reasons – were not playing.

587, above: *Chipperfield kills a ball from Geary at Trent Bridge. His 99 on debut brought him an odd kind of notoriety.* 588, right: *A balloon obstructs the camera view of a rival company who set up position outside the ground*

589, left: *The new firm – Sutcliffe (left) and Walters open at Trent Bridge.* 590, above: *Woodfull goes too far across to Farnes and loses his leg stump*

591, left: *Hammond st Oldfield b Grimmett 16, in England's second innings.* 592, below: *O'Reilly's hammer-blow – he has Leyland caught behind and England are eight down with 20 minutes left on the last afternoon*

1934 SECOND TEST

Lord's, June 22, 23, 25

England 440 *(L.E.G. Ames 120, M. Leyland 109, C.F. Walters 82, T.W. Wall 4 for 108);* Australia 284 *(W.A.Brown 105, H. Verity 7 for 61) and 118 (W.M. Woodfull 43, H. Verity 8 for 43).* England won by an innings and 38 runs.

'Verity's match', the first to be won by England against Australia at Lord's since 1896 and the last to the time of writing, was a triumph for rain, though in the opinion of most the Australian batting was rather too desperate at times. England were none too soundly placed after Walters's elegant innings until Leyland and Ames (the only wicketkeeper to make a century in these Tests until 1974–75) added 129 for the sixth wicket. Ames was missed by Oldfield at 96. Australia were 192 for 2 over the weekend, Brown having made a handsome 103 not out; but heavy rain left the pitch a 'slow turner' and the Yorkshire slow-medium left-arm bowler Hedley Verity used it to wonderful advantage. Farnes, Geary and Hammond were all injured, but Verity spun Australia to a follow-on by a margin of only seven runs, and returned even better figures in the second innings, when the pitch did become more difficult and only Woodfull and Chipperfield coped for any time. Verity took 14 wickets in the day.

593, above, left: *Cyril Walters is caught by Bromley in O'Reilly's leg-trap for 82.* 594, above, right: *England captain Wyatt loses his aluminium finger-guard as he hooks O'Reilly.* 595, right: *A royal interest: King George V examines Wyatt's injured thumb*

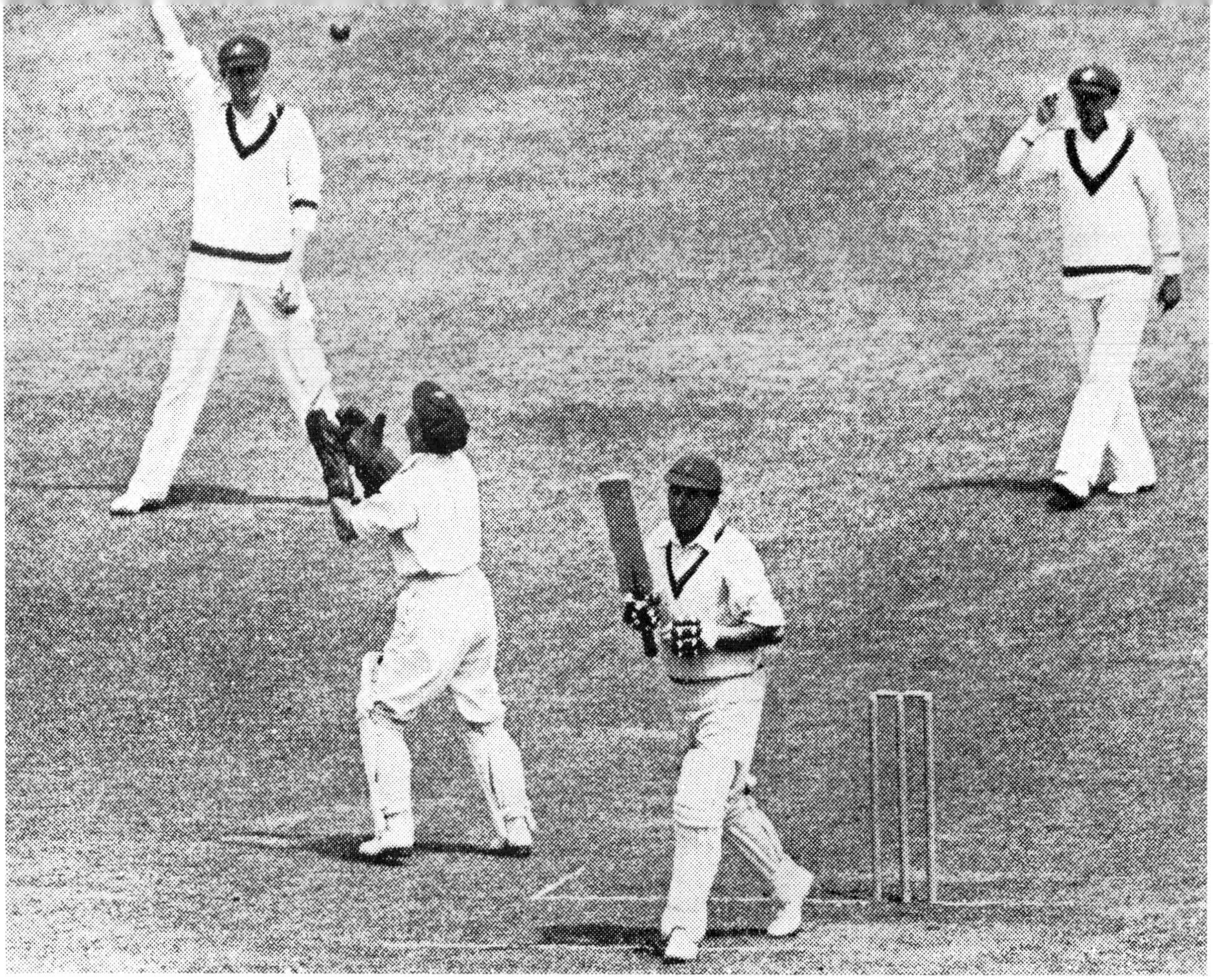

596, top: *Les Ames's fine innings at Lord's ends at 120 as his opposite number, Oldfield, catches him off McCabe.* 597, centre: *Hendren holds an outstanding catch to add Wall to Verity's heavy bag of wickets.* 598, left: *Bradman mis-hits Verity and is about to be caught by Ames in Australia's catastrophic second innings*

1934 THIRD TEST
Old Trafford, July 6, 7, 9, 10

England *627 for 9 dec (M. Leyland 153, E.H. Hendren 132, L.E.G. Ames 72, H. Sutcliffe 63, G.O.B. Allen 61, H. Verity 60*, C.F. Walters 52, W.J. O'Reilly 7 for 189) and 123 for 0 dec (H. Sutcliffe 69*, C.F. Walters 50*);* Australia *491 (S.J. McCabe 137, W.M. Woodfull 73, W.A. Brown 72, H. Verity 4 for 78) and 66 for 1.* Match drawn.

On a pluperfect wicket, the outcome after the first day revolved around whether Australia could avoid following on. Brown and McCabe went a long way to achieving that safety with a second-wicket stand of 196, McCabe making most of the strokes. The match is remembered as much as anything for O'Reilly's sensational spell on the first morning. With successive balls he had Walters caught at short leg, bowled Wyatt, elicited a not entirely voluntary leg glance for four by Hammond, and then bowled him. England were 72 for 3, the 'Tiger' having done the damage with a substitute ball. Hendren and Leyland added 191 for the fifth wicket, and Leyland and Ames 142 for the sixth. It was 4 pm on the second day before Wyatt declared. Australia found safe waters, but might have done so with greater comfort had not Bradman and Chipperfield been off-colour with throat infections. A talking point was Allen's first over, which contained three wides and four no-balls.

599, above: *Leyland's great rescue innings comes to an end as Ben Barnett (fielding substitute) catches him at mid-on off O'Reilly.* 600, below: *Hammond becomes O'Reilly's third victim in a sensational four balls*

601, above, left: *Allen sweeps during his innings of 61 at Old Trafford.* 602, right: *McCabe lays his bat aside for a few moments to gargle. Several of the Australians were stricken with throat infections*

1934 FOURTH TEST

Headingley, July 20, 21, 23, 24

England *200 (C.F. Walters 44, C.V. Grimmett 4 for 57) and 229 for 6 (M. Leyland 49*, C.F. Walters 45, R.E.S. Wyatt 44, E.H. Hendren 42);* Australia *584 (D.G. Bradman 304, W.H. Ponsford 181, W.E. Bowes 6 for 142).* Match drawn.

After an inept England batting performance against the spinners, the match was given over to a record-smashing fourth-wicket stand of 388 between a fully fit and resolute Bradman and a masterly Ponsford. On the first evening Bowes had dislodged Brown, Oldfield and Woodfull in a runless spell, but Australia's 39 for 3 at the start of the second day had become 494 for 4 by the close, Bradman 271. He and Ponsford dealt with Bowes, Hammond, Mitchell, Verity and Hopwood in an untroubled manner, only one sharp chance from each being missed before lunch. Ponsford, who hit 19 fours in 387 minutes, was out when he trod on his stumps in hitting Verity to long-on. Next day Bradman reached his second triple-century against England with a leg snick for four off Bowes, who five minutes later bowled him. He batted 430 minutes, and hit two sixes and 43 fours. There was a minor collapse after that, but England faced arrears of 384, and were 188 for 5 on the third evening. Rain then came as the saviour.

603: *Bradman, on the way to his second triple-century against England, hooks Lancashire left-arm bowler Hopwood*

604, top: *A stray paper bag was more of a nuisance to Bradman and Ponsford during their great stand than some of England's bowling. Bradman has evil intentions towards it.* 605, centre: *Leg-spinner Tommy Mitchell fields a Ponsford drive off his own bowling.* 606, right: *Bradman dislodged at last – b Bowes 304*

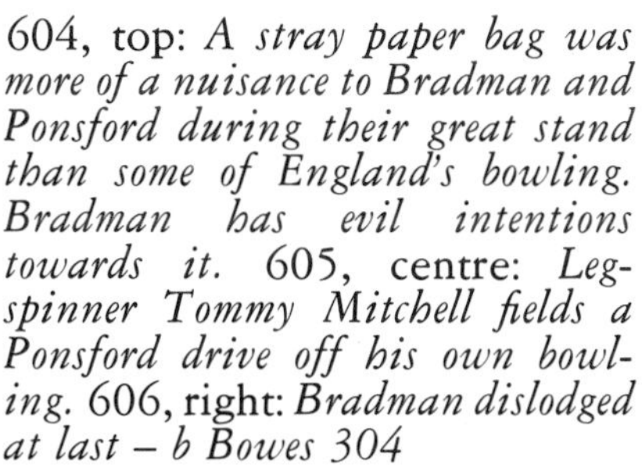

607: *That sinking feeling: Hammond is run out for 20 at Leeds from a throw from square leg to Grimmett. The other batsman is Walters; Chipperfield at slip, Oldfield the wicketkeeper*

1934 FIFTH TEST
The Oval, August 18, 20, 21, 22

Australia *701 (W.H. Ponsford 266, D.G. Bradman 244, W.M. Woodfull 49, W.A.S. Oldfield 42*, W.E. Bowes 4 for 164, G.O.B. Allen 4 for 170) and 327 (D.G. Bradman 77, S.J. McCabe 70, H.I. Ebeling 41, W.E. Bowes 5 for 55, E.W. Clark 5 for 98);* England *321 (M. Leyland 110, C.F. Walters 64) and 145 (W.R. Hammond 43, C.V. Grimmett 5 for 64).* Australia won by 562 runs.

The enormous stand by Bradman and Ponsford in the previous Test seemed but a rehearsal, for here on a fine pitch at The Oval they put on 451 for Australia's second wicket, stretching the world Test record partnership to a figure which was to stand for 63 years. Bradman was in marvellous form, making his runs in 316 minutes, with a six and 32 fours. He was caught behind hooking at a Bowes bouncer. Ponsford enjoyed six reprieves during his 460 minutes and hit a five and 27 fours. Again he was out hit-wicket, this time in ducking a short ball from Allen, having seen 574 runs on the board. This was Ponsford's last Test; he had also made a century in his first. England were in at 4.55 pm on the second day, and Sutcliffe and Walters began with 104. Wickets then clattered, until Leyland was supported by Ames (who had then to drop out of the match with severe lumbago) and Allen. The Yorkshire left-hander's third century in five Test innings took 2¾ hours. Woodfull batted again and England were eventually set 708. Australia's crushing victory—their biggest in runs against England—once more occurred on captain Woodfull's birthday. Australia were not to relinquish the Ashes for 19 years. Frank Woolley, now 47, was brought back for this Test, his last, and kept wicket in Ames's absence; but he made only 4 and 0.

608: *Even Bradman tired at times. He rests on his haunches as Leyland, England's seventh bowler, places his field in the Oval Test*

609, above, left: *Bradman and Ponsford aren't finished yet – resuming their mammoth second-wicket world-record stand.* 610, above, right: *Bill Brown is bowled by 'Nobby' Clark for 10 early on the first day. Australia's next wicket fell a few minutes before close of play.* 611, right: *Bradman pulls a ball from Allen in Australia's second innings, which built on a first-innings lead of 380*

612, left: *McCabe b Allen 10: Australia 488 for 3.* 613, below: *Ponsford's second innings at The Oval was much shorter. He is caught by Hammond in Clark's leg-trap. Woolley is keeping wicket*

614: *Hammond and Sutcliffe at slip watch veteran Woolley hold a catch from Chipperfield in Australia's second innings*

1936–37 FIRST TEST
Brisbane, December 4, 5, 7, 8, 9

England 358 *(M. Leyland 126, C.J. Barnett 69, J. Hardstaff 43, W.J. O'Reilly 5 for 102) and 256 (G.O.B. Allen 68, F.A. Ward 6 for 102)*; Australia 234 *(J.H.W. Fingleton 100, S.J. McCabe 51, W. Voce 6 for 41) and 58 (G.O.B. Allen 5 for 36, W. Voce 4 for 16)*. England won by 322 runs.

A cliffhanger series in which several attendance records were broken began with a grand spell of fast bowling from McCormick (3 for 17), who then bowled only three overs more before being forced out by acute lumbago. Barnett and the ever-reliable Leyland added 99, and Leyland and Hardstaff 90, but Hammond's dismal form of 1934 continued with 0 and 25. Australia were 151 for 2 by the second evening, but after Fingleton's careful century Australia fell away before Voce and the new ball. Leg-spinner Ward was England's second-innings problem until Allen, the captain, paired with Hardstaff (who, as one of Oldfield's three stumping victims in the innings, enabled the Australian 'keeper to pass Lilley's record 84 dismissals in these Tests). Australia, faced with scoring 381 for victory, lost Fingleton first ball of the innings in poor light, and after overnight rain found themselves 16 for 5, 20 for 6, and soon one-down in the series as Allen and Voce bounced the ball off a distinctly unpleasant pitch. Chipperfield finished 26 not out, but Ward's nose was broken as he attempted a hook. The hook had also cost Worthington his wicket to the first ball of the match.

615, above, left: *T.W. Garrett, 78, the sole survivor from the first Test match, meets the England captain, 'Gubby' Allen, at a Sydney reception. NSW Premier B.S.B. Stevens is in the centre.* 616, right: *Maurice Leyland swings during his Brisbane century.* 617, below, left: *Sievers caught by Voce off Allen in Australia's dismal second innings.* 618, right: *Lilley's record is passed as Oldfield stumps Hardstaff*

1936–37 SECOND TEST

Sydney, December 18, 19, 21, 22

England *426 for 6 dec (W.R. Hammond 231*, C.J. Barnett 57, M. Leyland 42);* Australia *80 (W. Voce 4 for 10) and 324 (S.J. McCabe 93, D.G. Bradman 82, J.H.W. Fingleton 73).* England won by an innings and 22 runs.

Bad weather was to render Bradman's second Test as captain even more unpropitious than the first. England were 279 for 3 at the end of the first day, Hammond 147; and with rain interruptions later on the second day he confirmed his return to his best, batting altogether for 458 minutes and hitting 27 fours. His sequence of Test scores at Sydney was now: 251, 112, 101, 75 not out, and 231 not out. A thunderstorm on the third morning left Australia with uneasy prospects, and Voce was soon bouncing wickedly off a length. The first three wickets fell with the score one, Bradman among them, for his second successive duck. O'Reilly (37 not out) swung at the slow bowlers later in the innings, but Allen soon had the decision whether or not to put Australia in again. He did, and that evening they were 145 for one. Fingleton and Bradman put on 124 before the former was bowled by a Sims googly next day. After Bradman's departure only McCabe offered resistance, batting enchantingly as ever until given out lbw. He may have touched the ball from Voce into his pads; but then he was within a whisker of lbw before he had scored.

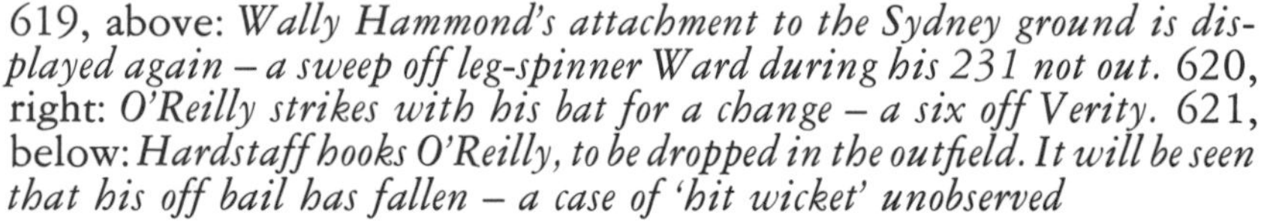

619, above: *Wally Hammond's attachment to the Sydney ground is displayed again – a sweep off leg-spinner Ward during his 231 not out.* 620, right: *O'Reilly strikes with his bat for a change – a six off Verity.* 621, below: *Hardstaff hooks O'Reilly, to be dropped in the outfield. It will be seen that his off bail has fallen – a case of 'hit wicket' unobserved*

1936–37 THIRD TEST

Melbourne, January 1, 2, 4, 5, 6, 7

Australia *200 for 9 dec (S.J. McCabe 63) and 564 (D.G. Bradman 270, J.H.W. Fingleton 136, K.E. Rigg 47)*; England *76 for 9 dec (M.W.S. Sievers 5 for 21) and 323 (M. Leyland 111*, R.W.V. Robins 61, W.R. Hammond 51, L.O'B. Fleetwood-Smith 5 for 124)*. Australia won by 365 runs.

At 130 for 6 the series seemed all but lost, but McCabe and Oldfield took the score to 183 before McCabe was caught at slip next day after rain had delayed the start. The pitch was obviously nasty, and Bradman declared for England to begin batting at 3 pm. The luck had turned. Worthington once again went without a run on the board, and apart from Hammond, whose 32 in 80 minutes was one of the finest innings of his life, only Barnett and Leyland reached double-figures as medium-pacer Sievers and O'Reilly made the ball leap. The art was in taking the bat from the ball much of the time. Darling made three catches, two of them superb. England batted on, when some thought an earlier declaration might have been worthwhile in putting Australia back in when the pitch was misbehaving. As it was, Bradman sent in O'Reilly (out for nought) and Fleetwood-Smith (who went early next day). After the fifth wicket fell at 97, Bradman joined Fingleton and saw the score to 194 that evening, and on a recovered pitch their stand climbed to a record 346 before Fingleton (386 minutes) was out. He hit only six fours. Bradman was 248 at the close, Australia 500 for 6. His innings, which was chanceless, finally closed with a catch to Allen off Verity after he had batted for 458 minutes, hitting 22 fours and as many as 110 singles. For much of his innings – which was then the highest by an Australian captain and for Australia in Australia – he was labouring under the effects of a chill. McCabe led Australia in the field for a while when England set about making 689. Their 323 was made at a happy rate, Hammond and Robins striking well as Leyland made a professional sixth century against Australia. The attendance of 350,534 over the six days is a record.

622, above, left: *Hammond's supremely skilful innings of 32 ends as Darling dives for a catch off Sievers's bowling. Sims is non-striker.* 623, right: *Leyland turns O'Reilly to leg only for Darling to pick up another lovely catch.* 624, below, left: *Walter Robins bowled by O'Reilly for 61.* 625, right: *Bradman is about to catch England's last man, Voce. Fleetwood-Smith waits to take stumps as souvenirs, while Ward runs in*

626: A section of the Melbourne Press box. In the fourth row former players Kippax, Ponsford and Woodfull have joined the ranks of the journalists (one of whom, Ray Robinson, is between Kippax and Ponsford)

1936–37 FOURTH TEST

Adelaide, January 29, 30, February 1, 2, 3, 4

Australia *288 (S.J. McCabe 88, A.G. Chipperfield 57*, W.A. Brown 42) and 433 (D.G. Bradman 212, S.J. McCabe 55, R.G. Gregory 50, W.R. Hammond 5 for 57);* England *330 (C.J. Barnett 129, L.E.G. Ames 52, M. Leyland 45, W.J. O'Reilly 4 for 51, L.O'B. Fleetwood-Smith 4 for 129) and 243 (R.E.S. Wyatt 50, J. Hardstaff 43, L.O'B. Fleetwood-Smith 6 for 110).* Australia won by 148 runs.

England bowled and fielded well to dismiss Australia for only 288 on a good pitch – McCabe batted with customary skill and sparkle. Then, when a push towards command seemed there for the taking, wickets fell to the left-arm spin of Fleetwood-Smith and to the domineering O'Reilly. Barnett was 92 on the second evening after four hours, and was unusually restrained next day until he hit McCormick for four boundaries in an over. If his innings was of great value, Bradman's saved the series. Starting with 26, he batted all through the fourth day, adding 109 with McCabe and 135 with 20-year-old Gregory. When he was caught-and-bowled by Hammond, Bradman had batted 441 minutes, hitting only 14 fours, and making 99 singles in a wonderful display of concentration and skill. England faced a target of 392, and were 148 for 3 on the fifth evening. But Fleetwood-Smith spun one in from the off to bowl Hammond first thing next morning, and the remaining wickets fell steadily as the Victorian tossed and teased his way to ten in the match.

627, left: *At Adelaide, Bradman (in hat) and Allen talk to a man captains always should take the trouble to consult – the head groundsman.* 628, above: *Bob Wyatt, mended ulna fracture still protected by a leather sheath, awaits his turn to bat*

629, above, left: *Intrusion: a man with a box camera ran on to the ground and attempted to photograph Bradman (top), who turned away.* 630, left: *Charles Barnett caught by Chipperfield off Fleetwood-Smith for 21.* 631, above: *Ross Gregory (left) and Bradman resume their stand*

1936–37 FIFTH TEST

Melbourne, February 26, 27, March 1, 2, 3

Australia *604 (D.G. Bradman 169, C.L. Badcock 118, S.J. McCabe 112, R.G. Gregory 80, K. Farnes 6 for 96);* England *239 (J. Hardstaff 83, T.S. Worthington 44, W.J. O'Reilly 5 for 51, L.J. Nash 4 for 70) and 165 (W.R. Hammond 56, C.J. Barnett 41).* Australia won by an innings and 200 runs.

Bradman won the vital toss and demonstrated his apparent infallibility once more with a faultless innings lasting 3¾ hours. His stand with McCabe – a new Australian third-wicket record in these Tests – after two wickets had fallen for 54 amounted to 249 in only 163 minutes. McCabe, missed at 11 and 86, claimed 16 fours, many from juicy cuts. The second big stand was between the youngsters Badcock and Gregory: 161 for the fifth wicket. Australia seemed safe at 604. For England's part, admiration went out to Farnes, who bowled fast for 28.5 eight-ball overs. On the Monday England began with 33 in 17 minutes, but Barnett was then out, and later, when the key wickets of Hammond and Leyland fell, and rain deadened the pitch before it became spiteful as it dried, the result was a foregone conclusion. The last five wickets fell for three runs, and in the follow-on Hammond and Barnett's 60 was the highest stand. O'Reilly and Fleetwood-Smith took three wickets each, and the Ashes were safe in Australia's keeping – a longish-odds prospect at Christmas.

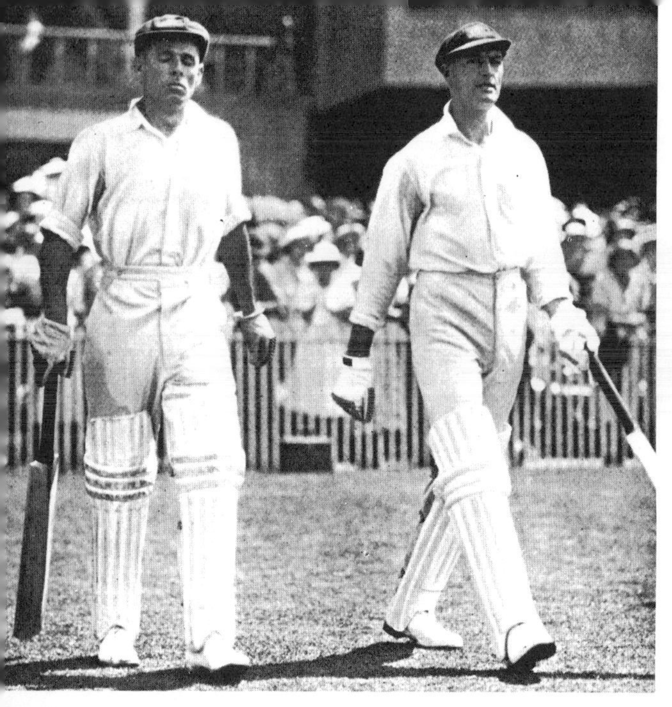

632, left: *Fingleton (left) and Keith Rigg open for Australia in the Melbourne 'decider'.* 633, above: *Bradman, at 101, almost perishes to a direct hit by Hardstaff. Bowler Farnes shouts expectantly*

634, above, left: *Rigg caught behind by Ames off Farnes.* 635, right: *Clayvel ('Musso') Badcock, one of three Australian centurymakers in the final Test.* 636, left: *Barnett c Oldfield b Nash 18, England first innings.* 637, below: *Stan Worthington out 'hit wicket' in pulling Fleetwood-Smith*

1938 FIRST TEST
Trent Bridge, June 10, 11, 13, 14

England *658 for 8 dec (E. Paynter 216*, C.J. Barnett 126, D.C.S. Compton 102, L. Hutton 100, L.E.G. Ames 46, L.O'B. Fleetwood-Smith 4 for 153);* Australia *411 (S.J. McCabe 232, D.G. Bradman 51, W.A. Brown 48, K. Farnes 4 for 106, D.V.P. Wright 4 for 153) and 427 for 6 dec (D.G. Bradman 144*, W.A. Brown 133, J.H.W. Fingleton 40).* Match drawn.

Hammond won the toss, and at lunch England were 169 without loss, Barnett 98, Hutton, a fortnight from his 22nd birthday, 61 in his first Test against Australia (having played a ball onto his stumps in the third over without disturbing a bail). Barnett reached his century with an off-driven boundary first ball after the interval, and the opening stand eventually ended at 219 (in only 172 minutes, and the first double-century stand for England at home against Australia). Hutton went on to his century in 200 minutes. The next big stand was for the fifth wicket, carried overnight to a record 206 by Paynter and 20-year-old Compton (another debutant against Australia), and lasting a mere 138 minutes. Paynter, aged 36, reached his 200 in 306 minutes, and the declaration came at 3.15 on the second day. Australia at stumps were 138 for 3. The third day belonged to McCabe. Adding 69 with wicketkeeper Barnett for the seventh wicket, at the fall of which he was 105, McCabe slaughtered the bowling while shielding his tailend partners. His second hundred took only 84 minutes – the second 50 of it just 24 minutes. He was particularly severe on medium-pace leg-spin/googly bowler Wright. With more than half England's fielders on the boundary, and with last-man Fleetwood-Smith in, McCabe drove, cut and hooked 72 of Australia's last 77. That day he made 213 of the 273 scored while he batted, and altogether he hit a six and 34 fours in his 235 minutes at the crease in one of cricket's truly outstanding innings. Verity, whom Hammond was saving for the follow-on, finally had him caught at cover. Australia survived the eight hours of their second innings with little difficulty on a still-perfect pitch. Brown and Fingleton launched the innings with 89, then Bradman (365 minutes, with only five fours) put on 170 with Brown (320 minutes), and during the final day, when Verity and Wright sometimes spun sharply off the dry wicket, the captain reached his 13th century in these Tests, passing Hobbs's record.

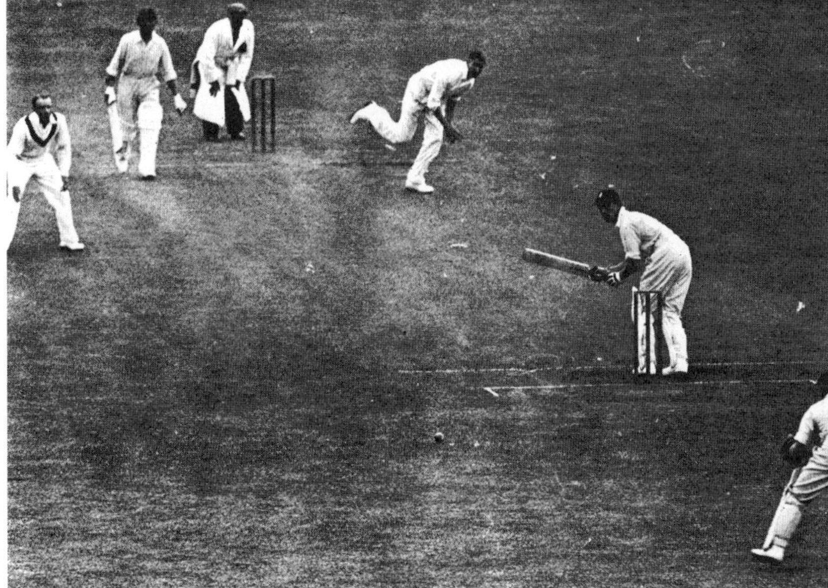

638, above, left: *Barnett and Hutton start their great opening stand at Trent Bridge.* 639, above, right: *Compton turns McCormick to long leg. Paynter is non-striker.* 640, right: *Hutton drives through mid-off*

641, left: *McCabe drives during his phenomenal innings at Trent Bridge.* 642, above: *Hassett caught by Hammond off Wright. Ames is the wicket-keeper, Hutton at short leg*

1938 — SECOND TEST

Lord's, June 24, 25, 27, 28

England *494 (W.R. Hammond 240, E. Paynter 99, L.E.G. Ames 83, W.J. O'Reilly 4 for 93, E.L. McCormick 4 for 101) and 242 for 8 dec (D.C.S. Compton 76*, E. Paynter 43);* Australia *422 (W.A. Brown 206*, A.L. Hassett 56, W.J. O'Reilly 42, H. Verity 4 for 103) and 204 for 6 (D.G. Bradman 102*, A.L. Hassett 42).* Match drawn.

England, reduced to 31 for 3 by McCormick on a lively pitch, ran to a creditable 409 for 5 by the end of the day, Hammond 210, Ames 50. Paynter, finding touch after lunch, added a record 222 with Hammond for the fourth wicket before O'Reilly trapped him leg-before. Hammond was at his most majestic, reaching his hundred in 146 minutes, adding 186 with Ames, and batting altogether 367 minutes for his fourth double-century (and the highest score by an England captain) against Australia. He gave no chances. Bill Brown held Australia's innings together, ensuring the follow-on was avoided. The best stand was a fast 124 between him and Hassett, and in carrying his bat Brown batted two minutes longer than Hammond, and registered the 100th century for Australia v England. When Compton dropped Fleetwood-Smith at slip he deprived Farnes of a hat-trick. McCormick was again a problem to England on a damp pitch, but on the fourth day Compton and Wellard (38) saw to it that Australia's target was too distant. Nevertheless, Bradman went with customary ease to a century, the 200th in these Tests (101 for Australia), passing Hobbs's record aggregate of 3636 in England-Australia Tests.

643, below, left: *Hammond reaches his 200 at Lord's.* 644, centre: *A standing ovation for him from the members.* 645, right: *Eddie Paynter hooks during his 99*

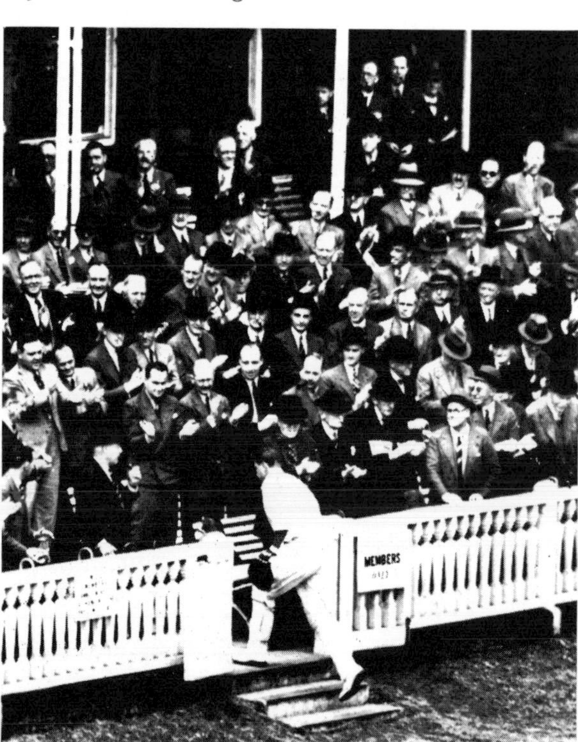

646, above, left: *Paynter lbw b O'Reilly 99, at Lord's.* 647, right: *Bradman b Verity 18*

1938 — THIRD TEST

Headingley, July 22, 23, 25

England *223 (W.R. Hammond 76, W.J. O'Reilly 5 for 66) and 123 (W.J. O'Reilly 5 for 56, L.O'B. Fleetwood-Smith 4 for 34);* Australia *242 (D.G. Bradman 103, B.A. Barnett 57, K. Farnes 4 for 77) and 107 for 5.* Australia won by 5 wickets.

The match set down for Old Trafford on July 8 having been abandoned because of rain without a ball being bowled, Australia seized the chance to retain the Ashes with magnificent performances by Bradman and O'Reilly. Only Hammond was unaffected for long by the pace of McCormick and the spin of O'Reilly and Fleetwood-Smith, and by the first evening Australia were 32 for one, Barnett the nightwatchman. The second day was Don Bradman's. In the gloom and on a moist pitch he manoeuvred the strike and dealt with varied bowling to put his side in the lead. In one of his finest innings he stayed three hours, striking nine boundaries. O'Reilly, attacking England's batsmen with fast-medium spinners to a packed leg-side field, then took over. He had Hammond, the key batsman, caught first ball at short leg. Left 105 for victory, Australia suffered early setbacks, and Wright, given a few more runs to bowl against, might have won it for England on his form that afternoon. The tiny Hassett, however, batted confidently for 33 after being missed at slip second ball, and the match was won before the rain came.

648, below, left: *Bradman and Hammond (in his Gloucestershire blazer) go to toss at Leeds.* 649, right: *Bill Edrich hurls his slight frame into a delivery to Bradman*

650: *Compton c Barnett (wicketkeeper) b O'Reilly 15 – England headed for defeat at Leeds*

1938 FOURTH TEST
The Oval, August 20, 22, 23, 24

England *903 for 7 dec (L. Hutton 364, M. Leyland 187, J. Hardstaff 169*, W.R. Hammond 59, A. Wood 53);* Australia *201 (W.A. Brown 69, A.L. Hassett 42, S.G. Barnes 41, W.E. Bowes 5 for 49) and 123 (B.A. Barnett 46, K. Farnes 4 for 63).* England won by an innings and 579 runs.

The course of a match whose details many an English schoolboy has been able to recite with greater ease than his multiplication tables was virtually predetermined when Hammond won the toss and batted on a grossly overprepared pitch. His instructions were for England's batsmen to conduct the innings as if no total was too high. Had Bradman and Fingleton not been injured during the innings, the match could have lasted many days more. England were 347 for one by Saturday evening, Hutton 160, Leyland 156. Hutton's century was the 100th for England against Australia. The Yorkshiremen continued their stand to 382, the highest for England in these Tests, and after Leyland was run out (having made a century in his last as well as his first Test), Hammond added 135 with Hutton, who reached 200 in 468 minutes. Paynter made nought and Compton one, but the 'collapse' was steadied by Hardstaff, who put on 215 with Hutton before the 22-year-old batsman was caught at extra-cover by Hassett off O'Reilly for 364, a score still only once exceeded in any Test. He gave only one chance – of stumping at 40 – during his 797 minutes at the wicket, having hit 35 fours and seen 770 runs recorded while he was in. 300 not out on the second evening, he took some time to overtake Bradman's record 334, but eventually square-cut Fleetwood-Smith for four to reach 336. Only Hanif Mohammad of Pakistan has batted longer in a Test innings. Hardstaff and Wood posted a fourth stand of three-figures. After the declaration at tea on the third day, Australia, having made 695 and 701 in their previous two Tests at The Oval, crumbled against the pace of Bowes and, second time round, of Farnes. Brown, first in and last out in the first innings, was on the field for the first 18½ hours of the match, as he had been in the previous Test. On a pitch perfect throughout the match O'Reilly (85-26-178-3), Fleetwood-Smith (87-11-298-1) and Waite (72-16-150-1) did a manful if unavailing job for Australia.

651, left: *With England's total around 800, Bradman put himself on to bowl – but soon fell and fractured a shinbone.* 652, right: *Hutton cuts. Wicketkeeper is Barnett, Fingleton short leg*

653, right: *A big drive by Leyland off Fleetwood-Smith during his long stand with Hutton.* 654, below: *A cut for four, and Hutton is 336.* 655, below, right: *Handshakes from Bradman and Hardstaff. (Inset: a remarkable scoreboard.)*

656, below, left: *Fellow-Yorkshiremen Verity, Bowes and Wood congratulate Hutton in the dressing-room.* 657, bottom: *England's massive victory is achieved, and Hutton leads umpire Chester, Wood, Edrich, umpire Walden, and Bowes from the field. That was it, until another world war had been started and ended*

1946–47 FIRST TEST
Brisbane, November 29, 30, December 2, 3, 4

Australia *645 (D.G. Bradman 187, A.L. Hassett 128, C.L. McCool 95, K.R. Miller 79, I.W. Johnson 47, D.V.P. Wright 5 for 167);* England *141 (K.R. Miller 7 for 60) and 172 (E.R.H. Toshack 6 for 82).* Australia won by an innings and 332 runs.

The last match before the Second World War having produced England's heaviest defeat ever of Australia (or any other country), the first match upon resumption produced Australia's heaviest victory over England. The home side emerged from the war with several bright prospects, whereas England, on the whole, depended on pre-war players. Only Bedser, Evans, Washbrook and Yardley, of those new to Tests against Australia, enjoyed any real success. Curiosity over the future of 38-year-old Bradman was soon settled when he overcame a nervy start and a debated 'not-out' decision to a ball caught by Ikin at slip to bat all told for 318 minutes. With Hassett, who batted over an hour longer, he added a third-wicket record of 276. Miller, a dynamic all-rounder, and McCool, both on Ashes debuts, each featured in further century partnerships, and by the time a demoralised England started to bat on the third day the light had deteriorated and rain interfered. England, 21 for one overnight, had a fearful day on a spiteful pitch after almost two inches of rain, and Miller was unplayable. Edrich made a courageous 16 in 1¾ hours, but after an even more torrential storm, accompanied by hail and 79 mph winds, during which the ground was submerged and the covers and stumps floated away, play was miraculously resumed on the fifth morning, and England were soon out a first time. Hutton fell to the first ball of the second innings, and left-arm medium-pacer Toshack finished off a match won almost as much by the elements.

658, above, left: *Hammond, in stormproof trilby, goes out with Bradman to inspect the pitch at Brisbane.* 659, right: *One of history's most famous disputed catches – Bradman to Ikin. It was given 'not out'.* 660, below, left: *Miller hits Wright for six. Wicketkeeper is Gibb.* 661, right: *The ground after the memorable downpour*

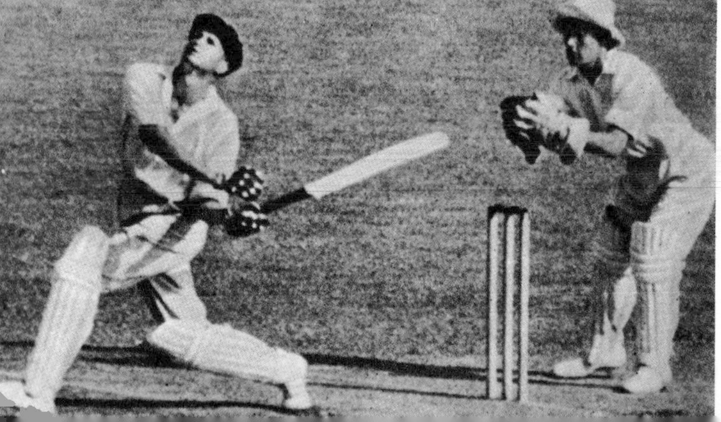

662: *Hammond holds his bat high to avoid one of many lifting balls on the Brisbane 'sticky'*

1946–47 SECOND TEST

Sydney, December, 13, 14, 16, 17, 18, 19

England *255 (W.J. Edrich 71, J.T. Ikin 60, I.W. Johnson 6 for 42) and 371 (W.J. Edrich 119, D.C.S. Compton 54, C. Washbrook 41, C.L. McCool 5 for 109);* Australia *659 for 8 dec (S.G. Barnes 234, D.G. Bradman 234, K.R. Miller 40).* Australia won by an innings and 33 runs.

Johnson's off-spin and McCool's leg-spin spelt England's batting downfall, the batsmen usually preferring to try to play the flighted ball from the crease. Barnes batted right through the third day for 88 runs, and stayed in all for 642 minutes, putting on a record 405 with Bradman, who came in No. 6 because of a leg strain and gastric trouble. They wore down the somewhat thin bowling attack for almost all the fourth day until Bradman's 6½-hour, chanceless innings ended as he was lbw to Yardley. He had now taken part in record stands for the second, third, fourth, fifth and sixth wickets. Australia batted into the fifth day before declaring, and in 24 minutes before lunch Hutton gave a sparkling display in making 37 before his bat slipped into his wicket as he played at Miller's last ball before lunch. By close of play England were 247 for 3, and slowly next morning Edrich attained his century, batting in all for 314 minutes, hitting only seven fours and as many as 63 singles. For a time it seemed England might hold out, but 43-year-old Hammond, a shadow of his former self, failed again, and Australia were victors once more by an innings by mid-afternoon. Godfrey Evans, in his first Test against Australia, allowed no byes in Australia's huge total.

663: *Bradman and Barnes, both already past 200, come in for an interval. Yardley, Evans and Compton follow*

664, above, left: *Ikin pulls McCool during his 60 at Sydney.* 665, right: *Edrich drives McCool for four. Tribe is at forward short leg.* 666, left: *Compton cuts to Johnson at slip, from where the ball bounced to wicketkeeper Tallon, who completed the catch*

1946–47 THIRD TEST
Melbourne, January 1, 2, 3, 4, 6, 7

Australia *365 (C.L. McCool 104*, D.G. Bradman 79, S.G. Barnes 45) and 536 (A.R. Morris 155, R.R. Lindwall 100, D. Tallon 92, D.G. Bradman 49, C.L. McCool 43);* England *351 (W.J. Edrich 89, C. Washbrook 62, N.W.D. Yardley 61, J.T. Ikin 48, B. Dooland 4 for 69) and 310 for 7 (C. Washbrook 112, N.W.D. Yardley 53*, L. Hutton 40).* Match drawn.

England, hampered by injuries to Voce and Edrich, did well to have Australia 192 for 6, but McCool, having narrowly missed a debut century, now reached a timely hundred, hitting powerfully off the back foot. England's innings owed everything to two stands: 147 by Washbrook and Edrich, and 113 for the sixth wicket by Ikin and Yardley. Thus, with little in it on first innings, England for the first time saw a glimmer of hope. But left-hander Arthur Morris, in his third Test, batted just over six hours, hitting only eight fours, and after his dismissal at 333 for 5, though two more wickets soon fell, Tallon and Lindwall drove vigorously and made 154 in a hectic 88 minutes. The wicketkeeper batted only 104 minutes, and Lindwall, who was already making an impression as a fast bowler, 113 minutes. Set an out-of-reach 551, England had a good start (138) from Washbrook and Hutton, but wickets fell steadily until Yardley and Bedser, with a delay for rain, saw the crisis through.

667: *Hassett c Hammond b Wright 12 – Hammond's 40th catch against Australia, eclipsing W.G. Grace's record*

668, left: *The England team presented at Melbourne to the Duke and Duchess of Gloucester. The Duke was then Governor-General.* 669, below, left: *Miller c Evans b Wright 33.* 670, centre: *Hutton caught for 40 by Bradman beyond the bowler's wicket.* 671, right: *Morris's 155 is ended as he is bowled by Bedser*

1946–47 FOURTH TEST
Adelaide, January 31, February 1, 3, 4, 5, 6

England *460 (D.C.S. Compton 147, L. Hutton 94, J. Hardstaff 67, C. Washbrook 65, R.R. Lindwall 4 for 52) and 340 for 8 dec (D.C.S. Compton 103*, L. Hutton 76, W.J. Edrich 46, E.R.H. Toshack 4 for 76);* Australia *487 (K.R. Miller 141*, A.R. Morris 122, A.L. Hassett 78, I.W. Johnson 52) and 215 for 1 (A.R. Morris 124*, D.G. Bradman 56*).* Match drawn.

Compton and Morris provided an unusual double in each making two hundreds in the match, though Compton's second was of greatest value, coming as it did when England needed time as well as runs. Hutton and Washbrook gave England starts of 137 in the first innings and 100 in the second, avoiding the short-pitched bowling of Lindwall and Miller and sometimes hooking it convincingly. Compton and Hardstaff added 118 in the first innings to make certain of a considerable total (Lindwall bowling the last three men in four balls) yet if England were disappointed that it was passed – especially after Bedser had bowled Bradman for nought – it was because of some dour batting by Hassett and Morris, and a brilliant fourth-morning innings by Miller. The climax came on the final morning, when Evans continued to defend for 95 minutes before making the first of his ten runs. Compton farmed the strike and handled all bowlers with relative ease. At the declaration they had added 85 in 2¼ hours. In the 3¼ hours remaining Morris made his third consecutive century against England. Hammond, in his last Test against Australia, made only 18 and 22.

672, above: *Bradman is bowled by a perfect ball from Bedser.* 673, below, left: *Compton beats the field and sets off for a run during his grand double effort at Adelaide.* 674, right: *Washbrook c Tallon b Dooland 65.* 675, bottom, left: *Arthur Morris, maker of two centuries for Australia.* 676, right: *Compton hooks*

1946–47 FIFTH TEST

Sydney, February 28, March 1, 3, 4, 5

England *280 (L. Hutton 122 ret.ill, W.J. Edrich 60, R.R. Lindwall 7 for 63) and 186 (D.C.S. Compton 76, C.L. McCool 5 for 44);* Australia *253 (S.G. Barnes 71, A.R. Morris 57, D.V.P. Wright 7 for 105) and 214 for 5 (D.G. Bradman 63, A.L. Hassett 47).* Australia won by 5 wickets.

Hutton and Edrich resisted some hostile early bowling on a moist pitch to add 150 for the second wicket, and England were 237 for 6 at the end of the first day. Hutton had hit only eight fours and batted five hours, but after Saturday was washed out he was stricken by tonsillitis and could not resume on Monday, when England's innings faded away. Barnes and Morris gave Australia a start of 126, but Bedser dismissed them both and in a grand piece of bowling – not as fast as usual, but with characteristic spin – Doug Wright took 7 for 105 off 29 eight-ball overs. But Lindwall had Fishlock lbw first ball of England's second innings, and McCool with leg-breaks and googlies troubled everyone but Compton. Hutton was unable to bat; Ikin made a 'pair'. Thus Australia were set only 214. Yet two wickets fell for 51, and Bradman was missed off Wright by Edrich at slip when only two. The captain and Hassett added 98, and Miller's bold strokeplay saw Australia home that evening. Yardley, having taken over from Hammond, had cause for pride in his team's fighting play.

677, left: *Leg-spin/googly bowler Wright in action at Sydney. Barnes is the non-striker.* 678, above: *McCool flights one to Yardley, who was bowled by this ball. Evans backs up*

679: *Edrich at slip misses Bradman when he was two*

1948 FIRST TEST
Trent Bridge, June 10, 11, 12, 14, 15

England *165 (J.C. Laker 63, W.A. Johnston 5 for 36) and 441 (D.C.S. Compton 184, L. Hutton 74, T.G. Evans 50, J. Hardstaff 43, K.R. Miller 4 for 125, W.A. Johnston 4 for 147);* Australia *509 (D.G. Bradman 138, A.L. Hassett 137, S.G. Barnes 62, R.R. Lindwall 42, J.C. Laker 4 for 138) and 98 for 2 (S.G. Barnes 64*).* Australia won by 8 wickets.

Australia, led by Bradman, were to go through Britain undefeated, batting impressively into the lower depths of the order and using the 55-overs new-ball regulation to advantage, with Lindwall, Miller and Johnston a formidable pace trio. England began catastrophically, being 74 for 8 when Bedser linked with Laker to add 89. Lindwall had to retire with a strained groin, or the match might not have reached its fifth day. Laker took the first three Australian wickets, but Bradman and Hassett carefully added 120 for the fifth, and Hassett and Lindwall 107 for the eighth. Facing an enormous deficit, England, 39 for 2, were steadied by an even-time partnership of 111 by Hutton and Compton, and, weathering bad light, occasional drizzle and a lot of short-pitched bowling, Denis Compton went on to play a gallant innings lasting almost seven hours during which he had to play himself in nine times. He was out hit-wicket on the last morning in avoiding a bouncer from Miller, his 84-run stand with Evans having taken England into a small lead. The Trent Bridge crowd, remembering their own Larwood and Voce, often shouted at Miller as he struck England's batsmen or forced them to duck. Bradman now failed to score for only the fifth time against England, being caught by Hutton at backward short leg as in the first innings.

680, left: *On the fourth day Hutton and Compton resume their stand.* 681, left, below: *Hutton evades a Miller bouncer.* 682, below: *Miller's tumbling catch to dismiss Hardstaff off Johnston for 0*

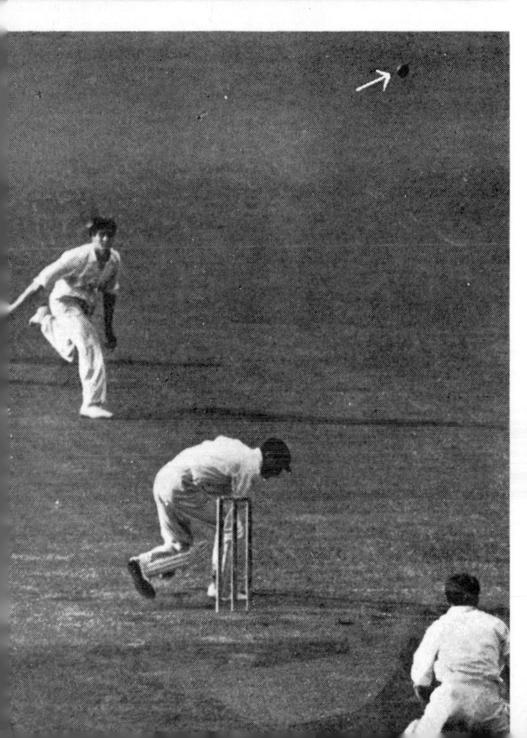

683, left: *Compton's 184 is brought to a violent end as he falls into his stumps.* 684, above: *Bradman pulls during his Trent Bridge century*

1948
Lord's, June 24, 25, 26, 28, 29

SECOND TEST

Australia *350 (A.R. Morris 105, D. Tallon 53, A.L. Hassett 47, A.V. Bedser 4 for 100) and 460 for 7 dec (S.G. Barnes 141, D.G. Bradman 89, K.R. Miller 74, A.R. Morris 62);* England *215 (D.C.S. Compton 53, N.W.D. Yardley 44, R.R. Lindwall 5 for 70) and 186 (E.R.H. Toshack 5 for 40).* Australia won by 409 runs.

The 150th Test match between England and Australia bore the hallmark of Australia's all-round competence. England did well to have them 258 for 7 the first evening, but the tail held on, and Lindwall then breached England's innings in a fiery spell, though Miller was injured and did not bowl in the match. Lindwall's work was supplemented this time by the left-arm swing and pace-change of Johnston and the off-spin of Johnson. Barnes and Morris extended Australia's lead with an opening of 122, and Barnes and Bradman than put on 174. After Miller's virile innings the declaration came and, ironically, rain. England, facing an absurd victory demand of 596 (hastened by many dropped catches), now began the task on an enlivened pitch. In the circumstances there was no resisting Lindwall, Toshack and Johnston, especially once Compton was superbly caught by Miller at slip on the final morning.

685: *Bedser has Bradman caught by Hutton at backward square leg (out of picture) for 38*

686, above, left: *Edrich bowled middle stump for five by Lindwall at Lord's.* 687, right: *Scramble for souvenir stumps and bails at the end of the match*

1948 THIRD TEST
Old Trafford, July 8, 9, 10, 12, 13

England *363 (D.C.S. Compton 145*, R.R. Lindwall 4 for 99) and 174 for 3 dec (C. Washbrook 85*, W.J. Edrich 53);* Australia *221 (A.R. Morris 51, A.V. Bedser 4 for 81) and 92 for 1 (A.R. Morris 54*).* Match drawn.

Compton was again the hero in a match which was as heartening to England as it was frustrating, as rain took the fourth day and restricted the last. England were 32 for 2 when Compton had to leave the field for repairs after edging a ball from Lindwall into his brow. Stitched and with a little internal fortification, he returned at 119 for 5 and was 64 that evening. His eighth-wicket stand with Bedser was worth 121 and he batted in all for 5½ hours, having been dropped three times by Tallon behind the stumps. Towards the end of England's innings Barnes at silly mid-on was seriously injured when hit by a pull-drive by Pollard, and Australia, disrupted by his absence at the start of the innings, began badly and for once never recovered, Bedser and Pollard doing the damage with the new ball and its later replacement on an overcast day. Hutton had been dropped from the side, but his substitute, Emmett, failed a second time, and it was left to Washbrook and Edrich to build on England's lead. At 174 for 3 England nurtured daring hopes. Then came the rain.

688, left: *Compton is hit in the face by a Lindwall bouncer, which forced him to retire for treatment. Miller goes to his aid.* 689, above: *George Emmett, Hutton's replacement, is caught by Barnes off Lindwall*

690, above: *Barnes, having been struck while fielding at close mid-on, is helped from the field by Toshack and Bradman.* 691, right: *The battered Compton raises his bat upon reaching his hundred. Tallon joins the applause*

1948 FOURTH TEST
Headingley, July 22, 23, 24, 26, 27

England 496 *(C. Washbrook 143, W.J. Edrich 111, L. Hutton 81, A.V. Bedser 79) and 365 for 8 dec (D.C.S. Compton 66, C. Washbrook 65, L. Hutton 57, W.J. Edrich 54, T.G. Evans 47*, W.A. Johnston 4 for 95);* Australia 458 *(R.N. Harvey 112, S.J.E. Loxton 93, R.R. Lindwall 77, K.R. Miller 58) and 404 for 3 (A.R. Morris 182, D.G. Bradman 173*).* Australia won by 7 wickets.

At one point 423 for 2, England had cause to feel disappointment at being all out for 496. Hutton, returning triumphantly, and Washbrook began with 168, following it with 129 in the second innings, and Bedser, sent in as nightwatchman, excelled himself in adding 155 with Edrich. Australia began shakily, but Harvey, aged 19 and in his first Test against England, put on 121 in 95 minutes with Miller in a whirl of contemptuous strokes and 105 with Loxton almost as quickly. Loxton hit five sixes, and Lindwall saw to it that Australia came close to England's considerable total. Yardley's team made steady progress towards a big lead, and he declared after five minutes on the last morning, hoping the roller would break up the surface of the pitch. Australia needed 404 in 344 minutes. Their victory has only once been emulated – by India, who made 406 for 4 to beat West Indies in Trinidad in 1976. Although the pitch took spin, England had to depend on Compton for the left-arm variety, and as stumping and catching chances were missed England became disheartened at the same rate as the batsmen raced to seize their unique prize. Morris and Bradman hit 301 for the second wicket in only 217 minutes, the left-hander having 33 boundaries in his 182 and Bradman 29 fours in his unbeaten 173 (which gave him 963 runs, average 192, in four Tests at Leeds). It was the Australian captain's 19th and final century against England, and took his aggregate to 5028 – still unapproached.

692, above, left: *Harvey swings a ball to leg during his debut century.* 693, right: *Bradman and Morris resume their matchwinning partnership.* 694, below, left: *Bradman doubles up after being hit by a ball from Bedser.* 695, right: *Crapp at slip misses Bradman – one of several English fielding lapses as Australia raced to an historic victory at Leeds*

1948 FIFTH TEST
The Oval, August 14, 16, 17, 18

England 52 *(R.R. Lindwall 6 for 20) and 188 (L. Hutton 64, W.A. Johnston 4 for 40);* Australia *389 (A.R. Morris 196, S.G. Barnes 61, W.E. Hollies 5 for 131).* Australia won by an innings and 149 runs.

Australia hammered home their superiority to finish victors 4–0 after a match remembered for England's batting humiliation and Bradman's final Test innings. Batting first on a sodden pitch, England were 29 for 4 at lunch and all out in under 2½ hours. Hutton stood firm among the wreckage and was last out, caught down the leg side by Tallon off the insatiable Lindwall for 30. That evening Australia were already 101 ahead for the loss of two wickets. Barnes and Morris opened with 117, then Bradman was bowled second ball for nought by a googly from Hollies. Hassett and Morris added 109, but it was left to the latter, who batted 6¾ hours, to carry his side to a truly decisive lead as he made his sixth century against England. Once more Len Hutton stood alone, batting 4¼ hours with a variety of partners, some of whom it was generally felt should never have been selected. Miller, bowling an exotic range of balls, got him in the end.

696: *Compton hooks Lindwall and is about to be caught by Morris (extreme right)*

697, left: *Hutton (30) is caught by Tallon down the leg side off Lindwall and England are all out for 52.* 698, above: *Bradman's Test batting career ends, bowled by Hollies for 0.* 699, right: *Miller prostrate after being stumped off Hollies for five*

1950–51 FIRST TEST

Brisbane, December 1, 2, 4, 5

Australia *228 (R.N. Harvey 74, R.R. Lindwall 41, A.V. Bedser 4 for 45) and 32 for 7 dec (T.E. Bailey 4 for 22)*; England *68 for 7 dec (W.A. Johnston 5 for 35) and 122 (L. Hutton 62*, J.B. Iverson 4 for 43)*. Australia won by 70 runs.

Hutton (8 not out and 62 not out) might have won this match for England had he not batted as low as No. 6 in the first innings and No. 8 in the second – on both occasions with the idea of utilising him when the rain-damaged pitch improved. On the last day it was heartbreakingly obvious to England that he needed only one worthwhile partner and victory would be theirs. Australia were bowled out on a good pitch on the first day, but heavy rain washed out the second and on the third batting became an evil joke as the ball leapt and turned. Twenty wickets fell that day for 130, England having no answer in the conditions to Johnston and Miller, and Australia also declaring after being overwhelmed by medium-pacers Bedser and Bailey. Moroney failed to score in either innings. By close of play England, set 193, were 30 for 6, with Hutton held back. The pitch had hardened on the fourth day, but Hutton, batting classically, was doomed to see his remaining partners all beaten. Freddie Brown, his captain, was the only other batsman to reach double-figures.

700, left: *Morris is well caught by Bailey and Australia are 0 for two wickets.* 701, above: *Hutton, England's lone batting hero, lofts Miller.* 702, below, left: *An extraordinary scoreline.* 703, below, right: *Evans catches and stumps Harvey off Bedser*

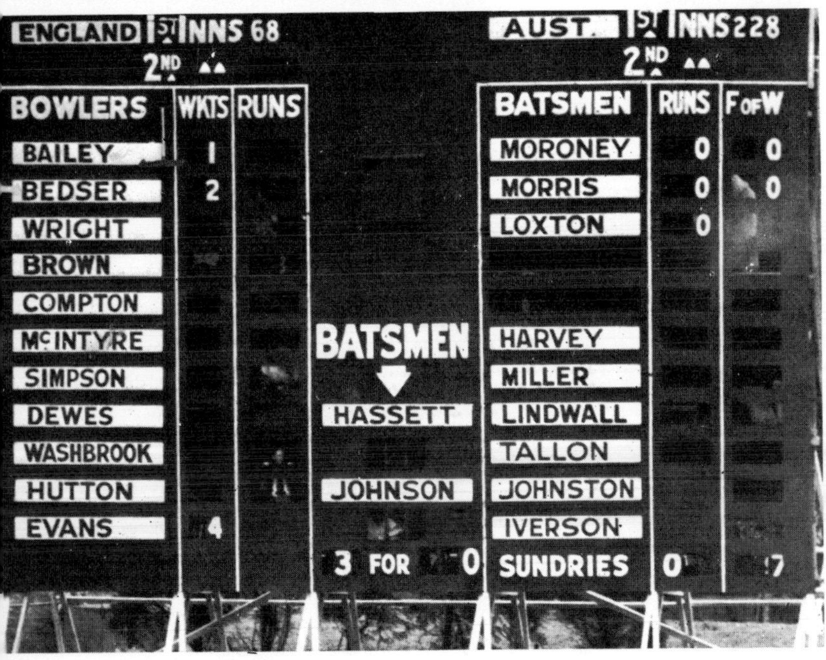

704: *Compton c Loxton b Johnston first ball – the start of a grim run of failures for him in the series*

1950–51 SECOND TEST
Melbourne, December 22, 23, 26, 27

Australia *194 (A.L. Hassett 52, R.N. Harvey 42, A.V. Bedser 4 for 37, T.E. Bailey 4 for 40) and 181 (K.A. Archer 46, F.R. Brown 4 for 26)*; England *197 (F.R. Brown 62, T.G. Evans 49, J.B. Iverson 4 for 37) and 150 (L. Hutton 40, W.A. Johnston 4 for 26).* Australia won by 28 runs.

England showed again, with a smaller margin of defeat, that there was not a great deal between the sides. The fast-medium bowlers dismissed Australia on the opening day, but England, without Compton, seemed to have lost their chance at 61 for 6, Brian Close, at 19 years 301 days the youngest ever to play for England against Australia, failing to score. Brown, with Bailey's help, then more than doubled the score, and Evans followed with a bright 49. Iverson, the large, 35-year-old 'mystery' finger-spinner, did most damage, including the removal of Hutton (now batting at No. 4), controversially given out caught off bat and pad. A two-day break for Sunday and Christmas Day was followed by England's fightback. Bedser and Bailey again bowled admirably and Brown took four middle-order wickets, leaving England in need of 179. They were 28 that evening for the loss of Washbrook and Bailey. Hutton, upon whom everything once more depended, batted with consummate skill, but the combination of Johnston, Lindwall and Iverson was too much for the tourists.

705: *Harvey is run out by a direct hit from Washbrook (out of picture)*

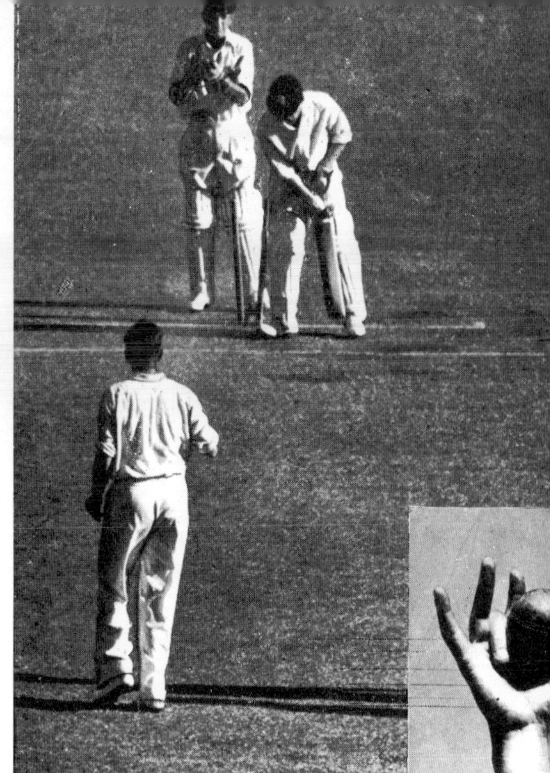

706, above, left: *Bailey's brilliant full-length catch to dismiss Hassett off Brown at Melbourne.* 707, above, right: *Washbrook deceived and bowled by Iverson, whose grip is shown (inset).* 708, left: *Evans prepares to catch Johnson from out of the sun – but he was to drop it.* 709, right: *Hassett b Bailey 52*

1950–51 — THIRD TEST
Sydney, January 5, 6, 8, 9

England *290 (F.R. Brown 79, L. Hutton 62, R.T. Simpson 49, K.R. Miller 4 for 37) and 123 (J.B. Iverson 6 for 27);* Australia *426 (K.R. Miller 145*, I.W. Johnson 77, A.L. Hassett 70, K.A. Archer 48, A.V. Bedser 4 for 107, F.R. Brown 4 for 153).* Australia won by an innings and 13 runs.

Injuries to Bailey (thumb broken by a ball from Lindwall) and Wright (torn tendon as he was run out) left England with three main bowlers, and Bedser, 40-year-old Brown and Warr toiled through 123 eight-ball overs to take 8 for 402 between them. Brown had saved England's first innings, driving bravely, though Hutton (restored to opening) and Simpson had put on a promising 94 for the second wicket. Keith Miller, unusually circumspect, made 96 not out in over 4½ hours on the third day, and batted almost six hours altogether, hitting only six fours and a six (an off-drive off Warr). Johnson helped him add 150 for the seventh wicket. Miller thus had exerted a huge influence on the match so far, having taken three key wickets and a dazzling slip catch to dismiss Washbrook. Now Iverson, the spinner, took over, bemusing most of England's batsmen and hitting the pads repeatedly. Australia found themselves winners of the rubber with an apparent ease that surprised many who recalled the close contests at Brisbane and Melbourne.

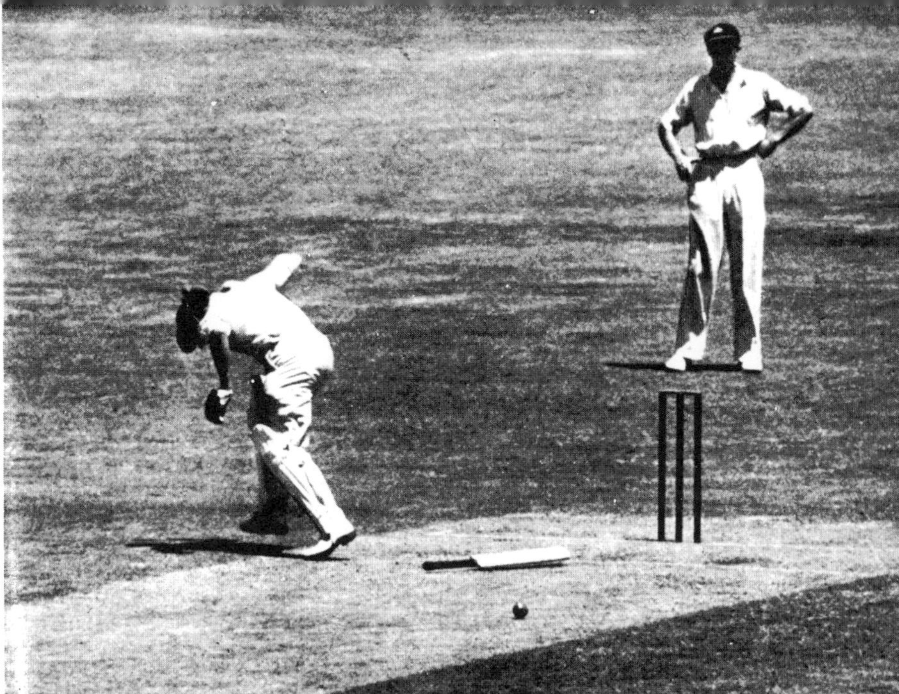

710, above: *Brown drives Johnson during his stand with Bailey.* 711, top, right: *Bailey's thumb is broken by a ball from Lindwall. Ken Archer at slip.* 712, right: *Miller dives instinctively to catch Washbrook off Johnson*

713, left: *Miller reaches his century with a cut off Warr.* 714, above: *Tallon makes a miraculous catch after the ball has rebounded from Johnson at slip, dismissing Hutton*

1950–51 FOURTH TEST

Adelaide, February 2, 3, 5, 6, 7, 8

Australia *371 (A.R. Morris 206, K.R. Miller 44, A.L. Hassett 43, R.N. Harvey 43, D.V.P. Wright 4 for 99) and 403 for 8 dec (J.W. Burke 101*, K.R. Miller 99, R.N. Harvey 68);* England *272 (L. Hutton 156*) and 228 (R.T. Simpson 61, L. Hutton 45, D.S. Sheppard 41, W.A. Johnston 4 for 73).* Australia won by 274 runs.

Morris, first in and last out, batted 7¾ hours for his highest Test score. He was shielded by Hassett from Bedser during the early stages after Archer had gone without a run posted, and fought his way back to form after five successive Test failures. He had stands of 95 with Hassett and 110 with Harvey, and was eventually bowled when swinging at Tattersall (who, with Statham, had been flown out to assist an injury-ridden MCC side). England's innings owed everything to Hutton. The next-highest score was Simpson's 29. Hutton became the second England player to carry his bat through the innings against Australia, and his exhibition was almost flawless. He was missed twice and stroked 11 fours in his 370 minutes. He was close to exhaustion at the end, and yet he had to field, being involved in play for the first 23¼ hours of play. Miller added 99 with Harvey for the fourth wicket and 87 with Burke before chopping his stumps with his bat just as a googly from Wright hit them when he was one short of his century. Burke, only 20 and playing his first Test, proceeded to his hundred before Hassett closed, leaving England 503 to make to win. Hutton and Washbrook started with 74, but Compton's wretched run of cheap dismissals persisted (he averaged 7.57 in eight innings), and after Simpson became Johnston's fourth victim on the last morning, Miller and Johnson took the last five wickets for seven runs, Brown not batting because of injuries sustained in a car crash.

715, above, left: *Morris out at last: b Tattersall 206.* 716, right: *Burke b Tattersall 12 – his first Test innings. He made a century in his second.* 717, below, left: *A tired Hutton leaves the field having carried his bat through the innings.* 718, right: *The Press box, Adelaide, during the fourth Test*

1950–51 FIFTH TEST

Melbourne, February 23, 24, 26, 27, 28

Australia *217 (A.L. Hassett 92, A.R. Morris 50, A.V. Bedser 5 for 46, F.R. Brown 5 for 49) and 197 (G.B. Hole 63, R.N. Harvey 52, A.L. Hassett 48, A.V. Bedser 5 for 59)*; England *320 (R.T. Simpson 156*, L. Hutton 79, K.R. Miller 4 for 76) and 95 for 2 (L. Hutton 60*)*. England won by 8 wickets.

After an interval of 12½ years and in their 15th Test since the war England at last knew what it felt like to beat Australia. Losing his fourth toss of the series, Brown must have had visions of emulating J.W.H.T. Douglas 30 years earlier in losing 5–0, for Australia were 111 for one 20 minutes before tea on the first day. Brown, bowling medium-pace, then put himself on again and took the wickets of Morris, Harvey and Miller while 12 runs were added. Hutton caught Hassett beautifully one-handed at slip, and Bedser used the second new ball to advantage, so that Australia were humbled as in the first two Tests. This time England followed up, though their lead was not as large as at one time seemed likely. Reg Simpson batted 338 minutes in a memorable display of footwork and strokeplay. He added 131 with Hutton for the second wicket, after which there was a collapse so resounding before Lindwall and Miller that at 246 for 9 Simpson was still eight short of his century. Tattersall then stayed with him while 74 precious runs were made. Simpson reached his hundred on his 31st birthday. Australia lost four wickets in erasing the deficit, Wright removing the dangerous Harvey and later bowling Hassett with a perfect leg-break. Hole, just 20, batted well in his first Test and helped set England a modest target, which was attained quite nervelessly. Alec Bedser took his haul of wickets for the series to 30, and Hutton averaged 88.83.

719, above, left: *Simpson elegantly on-drives Iverson during his century.* 720, right: *Hassett bowled by a perfect leg-break from Wright; and England glimpse victory*

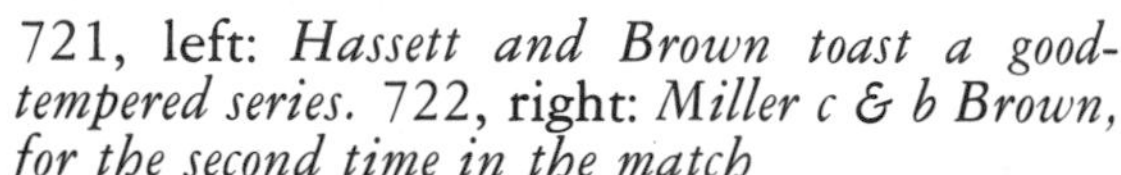

721, left: *Hassett and Brown toast a good-tempered series.* 722, right: *Miller c & b Brown, for the second time in the match*

1953 FIRST TEST

Trent Bridge, June 11, 12, 13, 15, 16

Australia *249 (A.L. Hassett 115, A.R. Morris 67, K.R. Miller 55, A.V. Bedser 7 for 55) and 123 (A.R. Morris 60, A.V. Bedser 7 for 44);* England *144 (L. Hutton 43, R.R. Lindwall 5 for 57) and 120 for 1 (L. Hutton 60*).* Match drawn.

Fine fast-medium bowling by Bedser and a staunch century by Hassett were the features of a grimly-contested match in generally poor light and in damp conditions. The only substantial partnerships until the anticlimactic final stages were the 122 put on by Hassett and Morris for the second wicket on the opening day and 109 for the fourth by Miller and his captain. Hassett needed 5¾ hours to reach his hundred. With the third new ball Bedser and Bailey took the last six wickets for five runs. Lindwall had England 17 for 3, but Hutton and Graveney then added 59. Wickets then fell steadily to Lindwall, top-spinner Hill and left-arm swinger Davidson. Bedser routed Australia on the third day, Morris making his 60 out of 81, but a washed-out fourth day and a delayed start on the last meant England could only play out time.

723, above, left: *Hassett is bowled by Bedser for 115. The fieldsmen's expressions give some idea of how much the ball deviated.* 724, right: *Harvey cracks Bedser to leg only to be caught by Graveney.* 725, below, left: *Davidson becomes another of Bedser's 14 wickets.* 726, right: *Bedser comes in, England's 7 for 55 first-innings hero. Even better was to follow*

1953 SECOND TEST

Lord's, June 25, 26, 27, 29, 30

Australia *346 (A.L. Hassett 104, A.K. Davidson 76, R.N. Harvey 59, A.V. Bedser 5 for 105, J.H. Wardle 4 for 77) and 368 (K.R. Miller 109, A.R. Morris 89, R.R. Lindwall 50, G.B. Hole 47, F.R. Brown 4 for 82);* England *372 (L. Hutton 145, T.W. Graveney 78, D.C.S. Compton 57, R.R. Lindwall 5 for 66) and 282 for 7 (W. Watson 109, T.E. Bailey 71).* Match drawn.

In one of the most celebrated of matchsaving stands, Watson and Bailey came together on the final day with England 73 for 4 – 270 runs from victory – and nearly five hours remaining. They withstood the whole range of Australian bowling until Watson, in his first Test against Australia, was caught at slip at 5.50 pm. He had batted 5¾ hours, and took 201 minutes over his second fifty. Bailey soon followed, having existed for 4¼ hours. A bonny 28 from Brown (chairman of selectors this year) averted any last-minute reversal after the sterling rescue. The captains, Hassett and Hutton, made worthy centuries, Hutton's especially so after he had missed several catches, and Davidson's attacking 76 saw Australia to a solid total. Graveney supported Hutton in a second-wicket stand of 168 but was bowled by Lindwall first thing on the third morning. Compton then put on 102 with Hutton, only their second (and last) century stand together against Australia. Morris and Miller set up Australia's second innings, adding 165 for the second wicket. Miller batted almost five hours. Lindwall made England's task appreciably more difficult with a rousing half-century – and by getting Hutton and Kenyon cheaply that evening. The final day was a story of patience and determination on one side and frustration on the other.

727, above, left: *Hutton, with an injured hand, going for runs.* 728, right: *Watson hits to leg.* 729, below, left: *Graveney c Langley b Johnston 2. England in dire second-innings trouble.* 730, right: *Bailey makes a rare attacking stroke*

1953 THIRD TEST

Old Trafford, July 9, 10, 11, 13, 14

Australia *318 (R.N. Harvey 122, G.B. Hole 66, J.H. de Courcy 41, A.V. Bedser 5 for 115) and 35 for 8 (J.H. Wardle 4 for 7)*; England *276 (L. Hutton 66, D.C.S. Compton 45, T.G. Evans 44*)*. Match drawn.

A little less rain could have made this match a thriller. As it was, too much time – including the whole of Monday – was lost, and the pitch, though sometimes spiteful, was usually too soggy to put batsmen in peril. Harvey's century took four hours, he and Hole, who added 173 for the fourth wicket, batting on each of three days. Harvey was dropped by Evans at four and eventually caught by the wicketkeeper on the leg side standing up to Bedser. England's main resistance came in a 94-run stand by Hutton and Compton, and it was left to Simpson and Bailey, in a seventh-wicket stand of 60, to avert the follow-on on the final day. Australia then, perhaps with less application than might have been expected, were somewhat humiliated by Wardle, Bedser and Laker.

731, above, left: *Hole and Harvey resume their large stand.* 732, right: *Harvey c Evans b Bedser 122.* 733, below, left: *Archer's hostile field to Wardle.* 734, right: *de Courcy stumped during Australia's last-day debacle*

1953 FOURTH TEST
Headingley, July 23, 24, 25, 27, 28

England *167 (T.W. Graveney 55, R.R. Lindwall 5 for 54) and 275 (W.J. Edrich 64, D.C.S. Compton 61, J.C. Laker 48, K.R. Miller 4 for 63);* Australia *266 (R.N. Harvey 71, G.B. Hole 53, A.V. Bedser 6 for 95) and 147 for 4.* Match drawn.

Australia were frustrated – by all manner of means – by Trevor Bailey, who held an end for 262 minutes for his 38 in England's second innings and then bowled, between time-consuming adjustments, down the leg side to a negative field when Australia looked like hitting their way to the 177 required for victory in 115 minutes. Once more time was lost for rain, and on an opening day cut by 25 minutes England reached a laboured 142 for 7, Hutton having been bowled second ball by Lindwall. Australia's main stand, 84, came from Harvey and Hole. Always struggling, England managed, after wiping off the arrears, to extend their lead against a shrunken timespan remaining. Laker's 48 at No. 9 was vital.

735, above, left: *A shock for the Yorkshire crowd – Hutton b Lindwall 0.* 736, right: *Graveney well caught by Benaud for 55.* 737, below, left: *Morris puts Bedser past Evans.* 738, right: *Langley, having moved the wrong way, misses Watson off Archer*

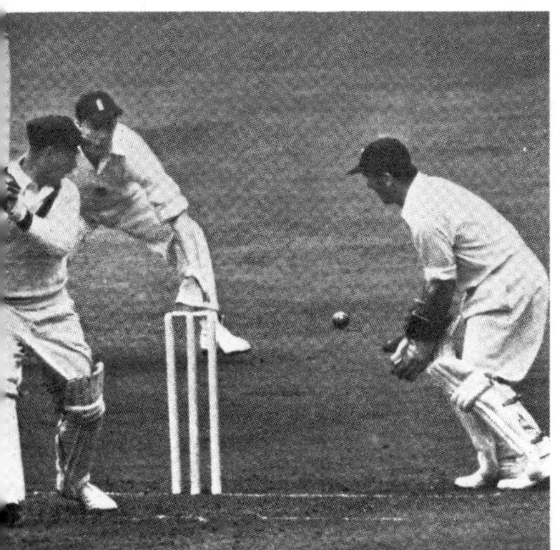

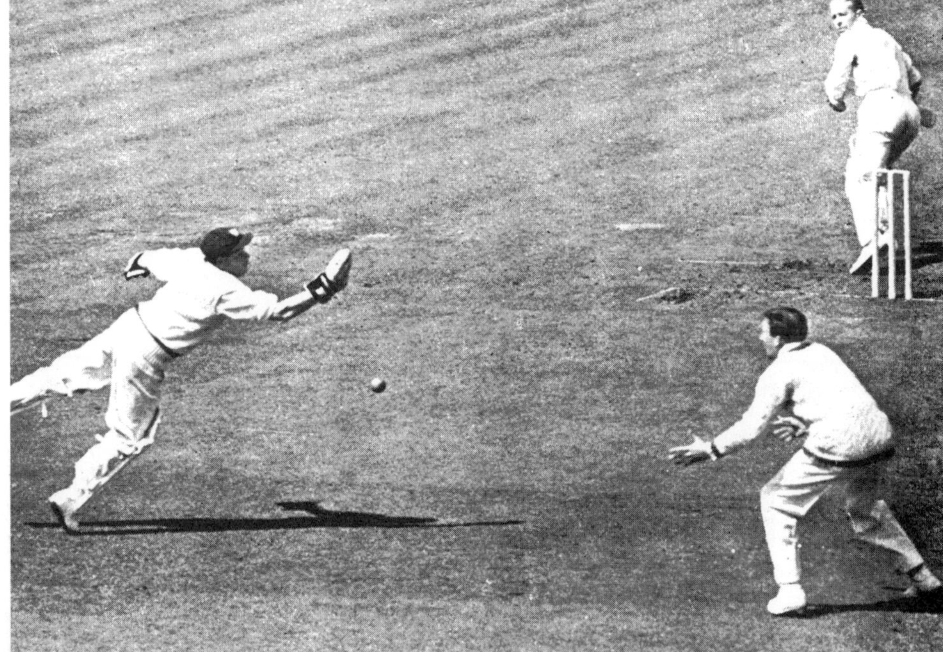

1953 FIFTH TEST

The Oval, August 15, 17, 18, 19

Australia *275 (R.R. Lindwall 62, A.L. Hassett 53, F.S. Trueman 4 for 86) and 162 (R.G. Archer 49, G.A.R. Lock 5 for 45, J.C. Laker 4 for 75);* England *306 (L. Hutton 82, T.E. Bailey 64, R.R. Lindwall 4 for 70) and 132 for 2 (W.J. Edrich 55*).* England won by 8 wickets.

England's cricket team, in the eventful year of achievement which accompanied the Coronation, won back the Ashes 19 years after Woodfull's 1934 Australians had appropriated them. Hassett beat Hutton at the toss for the fifth time, and though Morris soon fell to Bedser (for the 18th time in the 20 post-war Tests) and Miller scored only a single, a solid score seemed in prospect. Fred Trueman, in his initial Australian Test, finding life in a shower-freshened pitch, then had Harvey, de Courcy and Hole caught, and only a fine hard-driving innings from Lindwall saved Australia's face. Bedser finished with 39 wickets in the series – a record. Hutton, wearing his 1938 cap (which fell inches from the stumps as he avoided a short ball from Lindwall), put on 100 for the second wicket with Peter May (39), also in his first Australian Test, but the middle of the innings then fell away, and the ever-reliable and obdurate Bailey had to steer it up to, and – during a last-wicket stand of 44 with Bedser on the third morning – beyond Australia's total. A sensational afternoon ensued. On a responsive pitch Lock, left-arm spin, and Laker, off-breaks, had Australia reeling from 59 for one to 85 for 6. Archer and Davidson, one 19, the other 24, then endeavoured to hit their way out of trouble, and added 50; but Lock got them both, and soon England were faced with the task of making 132 for an emotional victory. Hutton, England's first appointed professional captain, was run out for 17 that evening, but May stayed for 64 runs with Edrich, and Compton, on the fourth afternoon, swung Morris for four to win the match and release a flood of jubilation.

739, above: *Trueman, England's fast bowling discovery, bowls to Hole with an aggressive field more typical of the Australians.* 740, left: *May, another new talent, edges past Miller*

741, above, left: *Hutton loses his composure and his cap as Lindwall digs one in.* 742, above, right: *Compton hits to the leg boundary and the Ashes are England's at last.* 743, right: *Bedser catches Ron Archer to pass Tate's record 38 wickets in an England-Australia series.* 744, below: *Len Hutton shares the pleasure of the crowd, whose enthusiasm recalled that at The Oval 27 years before*

1954–55

FIRST TEST

Brisbane, November 26, 27, 29, 30, December 1

Australia *601 for 8 dec (R.N. Harvey 162, A.R. Morris 153, R.R. Lindwall 64*, G.B. Hole 57, K.R. Miller 49);* England *190 (T.E. Bailey 88, M.C. Cowdrey 40) and 257 (W.J. Edrich 88, P.B.H. May 44).* Australia won by an innings and 154 runs.

Hutton put Australia in and soon had cause to regret it as his all-speed attack failed to make much impression on a lifeless pitch. Although chances were missed in the field, Australia always seemed certain to compile a massive total, and Morris and Harvey batted with more assurance the longer they were in. The two left-handers put on 202 for the third wicket, Morris, in his final hundred against England, batting seven hours, and Harvey, who went on to add 131 with Hole, batting 380 minutes. England's woes were complete when Compton broke a finger on the pickets, and had to bat last man and virtually ineffectively. Evans was missed behind the stumps. England began horrendously, losing four for 25. Cowdrey, in his first Test match, then batted steadily, and Bailey was characteristically defiant. Edrich and May, in a stand of 124, offered the only prolonged resistance in the follow-on, and the crushing Australian victory seemed to signal that their fast attack was still a force to be feared and that the side was capable of enough high scores to win the series. Few would have been prepared to believe that there would not be another century for Australia against England for four years and 11 Tests. This was to be the final appearance against Australia of Bedser, who was discarded under Hutton's plan to depend on pace and a sedate over rate.

745, above, left: *Miller picks up a rare half-volley from Bedser and lands it for six over long-on.* 746, right: *Lindwall traps May lbw.* 747, left: *A narrow escape for Harvey as he plays Tyson just wide of Andrew*

748: *Edrich bowled for 88 by a long-hop from Bill Johnston*

1954–55
Sydney, December 17, 18, 20, 21, 22

SECOND TEST

England *154 and 296 (P.B.H. May 104, M.C. Cowdrey 54)*; Australia *228 (R.G. Archer 49, J.W. Burke 44, F.H. Tyson 4 for 45, T.E. Bailey 4 for 59) and 184 (R.N. Harvey 92*, F.H. Tyson 6 for 85)*. England won by 38 runs.

Tyson, who cut down his run after Brisbane (where he took one for 160), bowled very fast for his ten wickets in the match, 'inspired' in the second innings after having been knocked out by a Lindwall bouncer that cracked him on the back of the head. Morris, deputising for injured Ian Johnson, put England in on a sultry morning, and Lindwall, Archer, Davidson and Johnston had them 111 for 9 before Wardle and Statham clouted 43 in the biggest stand of the innings. Bailey had early successes, and Tyson's yorkers and flyers did the rest, Statham supporting well. At 55 for 3 in their second innings England seemed doomed. Then May and Cowdrey batted very sensibly until 171. May, on the fourth morning, reached his first hundred against Australia, and batted five hours altogether. Once more there was a useful last-wicket stand, this time of 46 between Statham and Appleyard. Set 223, Australia were 72 for 2 that evening. On the final day, however, Tyson shocked his way through the batting line-up, only the masterful Harvey being able to cope. Johnston delayed the finish with a stand of 39, but the aching express bowler got him in the end.

749: *Tyson is helped from the field after being knocked cold by a Lindwall bouncer. He was never the same again – as Australia's batsmen soon discovered*

750, above, left: *Bailey b Lindwall 0 – the end of 35 minutes of concentration and torture at Sydney.* 751, right: *Favell caught low down at slip by Graveney for 26.* 752, centre: *May drives Johnston during his important stand with Cowdrey.* 753, bottom: *Evans catches Johnston off Tyson and the sides go one-all to Melbourne*

1954–55 THIRD TEST

Melbourne, December 31, January 1, 3, 4, 5

England *191 (M.C. Cowdrey 102, R.G. Archer 4 for 33) and 279 (P.B.H. May 91, L. Hutton 42, W.A. Johnston 5 for 25);* Australia *231 (L.V. Maddocks 47, J.B. Statham 5 for 60) and 111 (F.H. Tyson 7 for 27).* England won by 128 runs.

Australia faced the final day in a similar position to that at Sydney: 165 from victory with eight wickets in hand. Tyson then demolished the innings on a pitch of uneven bounce, taking 6 for 16 in 51 balls, bowling at devilish speed, with Statham probing from the other end. The collapse began when Evans made a grand diving leg-side catch from Harvey – the first of eight wickets to fall for 34 runs. England were in deep trouble on the opening day, when Miller used a damp pitch well in returning figures of 9-8-5-3 before lunch. Cowdrey, just 22, then put together an immaculate century in four hours. Though stuck on 56 for 40 minutes, he showed a fine temperament in a testing situation. England had their opponents 92 for 5 on an improved pitch (which was apparently illegally watered on the rest day), but the grip was relaxed, and Australia moved into the lead. May held the second innings together with an innings of some power, and Bailey excelled himself with 24 not out in 163 minutes.

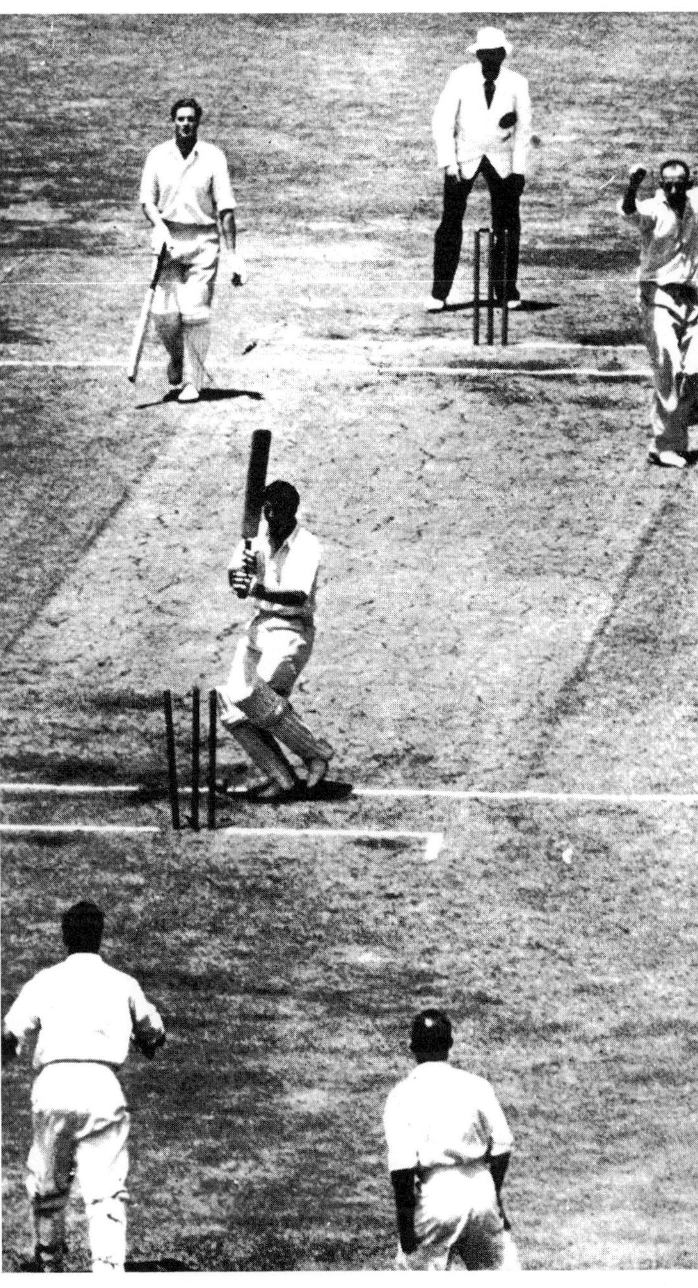

754, above, left: *Neil Harvey falls to a glorious leg-side catch by Evans, and the Australian collapse begins.*
755, right: *Benaud becomes the third of Tyson's seven victims*

756, above: *Cowdrey's admirable century innings ends as a ball from Johnson turns a great distance to bowl him.* 757, left: *The Australian fielders examine the Melbourne pitch, which mysteriously changed its nature overnight*

1954–55 FOURTH TEST

Adelaide, January 28, 29, 31, February 1, 2

Australia *323 (L.V. Maddocks 69, C.C. McDonald 48, K.R. Miller 44, I.W. Johnson 41) and 111;* England *341 (L. Hutton 80, M.C. Cowdrey 79, D.C.S. Compton 44, R. Benaud 4 for 120) and 97 for 5.* England won by 5 wickets.

Set only 94 to retain the Ashes, England were dazed by Miller, who had them 18 for 3 in a fiery spell of new-ball bowling. At 49 he tumbled and caught May at cover, and it took the resolution of Compton and Bailey to see their side to 90 before the latter was out. Australia were ailing at 229 for 8 on the second day when Maddocks, Langley's replacement as wicketkeeper, put on 92 with Johnson. Tyson, Bailey and Appleyard took three wickets apiece. Hutton and Cowdrey added 99 in high heat, and there was solid batting from the middle order, and when Morris, Burke and Harvey fell to Appleyard's medium-pace off-spin on the fourth evening it looked ominous for Australia. Yet it was Statham and Tyson who did the damage next day, and once more Australia could muster no more than the miserable, mystical 111.

758, above, left: *Maddocks sweeps Wardle during his valuable 69.* 759, right: *Archer snaps up a catch from May off Benaud.* 760, below, left: *Davidson at short leg holds a reflex catch to dismiss Hutton for 80.* 761, right: *After a fright or two England have held the Ashes – Compton and Evans the batsmen in at the kill*

1954–55 FIFTH TEST

Sydney, February 25, 26, 28, March 1, 2, 3

England *371 for 7 dec (T.W. Graveney 111, D.C.S. Compton 84, P.B.H. May 79, T.E. Bailey 72);* Australia *221 (C.C. McDonald 72, J.H. Wardle 5 for 79) and 118 for 6.* Match drawn.

Sydney was such a wet city that play was not possible until 2 pm on the fourth day, when England batted after losing the toss. Hutton's final Test innings against Australia ended with his fourth ball, Burge at leg slip touching the ball for the first time in a Test. Graveney and May then put on 182 in 161 minutes, both batsmen, tall and classical in their strokeplay, batting delightfully. Graveney reached his century with four fours off an over by Miller, and thus became the 100th player to score a hundred in these Tests (51 for England). Cowdrey, recently down with tonsillitis, was out first ball, but after May's dismissal Compton and Bailey – slowly at first – added 134. Bailey – voluntarily – became Lindwall's 100th wicket in these Tests, and the closure was immediately applied. Australia were 82 for 2 that evening, and the draw seemed certain. It became less of a certainty next day when Australia were bemused by Wardle's flighted wrist-spin, only McDonald enduring for long. With one run needed to avoid the follow-on, Johnson was run out, and in the two hours left Wardle spun out three more Australians, and Hutton bowled Benaud with the last ball.

762, above, left: *Jack Ryder, now 65 and an Australian selector, joins in the pre-match practice at Sydney.* 763, right: *Lindwall bowls Bailey – his 100th England wicket.* 764, below, left: *Johnson is run out, and for the sake of one run Australia are obliged to follow on.* 765, right: *An oddity: Graveney takes a wicket – the prized one of McDonald, caught behind by Evans for 37*

1956 FIRST TEST
Trent Bridge, June 7, 8, 9, 11, 12

England *217 for 8 dec (P.E. Richardson 81, P.B.H. May 73, K.R. Miller 4 for 69) and 188 for 3 dec (M.C. Cowdrey 81, P.E. Richardson 73);* Australia *148 (R.N. Harvey 64, J.C. Laker 4 for 58) and 120 for 3 (J.W. Burke 58*).* Match drawn.

Australia, having beaten only the Universities and lost to Surrey (the first defeat by a county since 1912), were handicapped in this match by injuries to Lindwall and Davidson. Yet England were missing Hutton (retired), Compton (knee trouble), and Tyson, Trueman and Statham (all injured). After a slow, shortened first day, and the second rained off, Richardson and May continued their partnership to 108, but Archer and Miller then cut away the middle. Australia were 19 for 2 that evening, and Laker, Lock and Appleyard had them out on a drying wicket by mid-afternoon of the fourth day. Richardson and Cowdrey made 129 that evening, and carried their opening stand to 151 on the last day, Richardson, a left-hander, completing a worthy double in his first Test. The declaration left Australia 258 to win in four hours– a prospect ruled out when three wickets fell for 41. Burke and Burge played out the last two hours.

766, right: *With the England total only six, Richardson falls after a call from Cowdrey and a run-out seems certain. The partners survived to put on 151.* 767, below, left: *Burke dropped by Watson off Lock.* 768, right: *May c Langley b Miller 73*

1956 SECOND TEST

Lord's, June 21, 22, 23, 25, 26

Australia *285 (C.C. McDonald 78, J.W. Burke 65) and 257 (R. Benaud 97, F.S. Trueman 5 for 90, T.E. Bailey 4 for 64)*; England *171 (P.B.H. May 63, K.R. Miller 5 for 72) and 186 (P.B.H. May 53, K.R. Miller 5 for 80, R.G. Archer 4 for 71)*. Australia won by 185 runs.

A good team performance by Australia brought well-earned victory. Miller, now 36, bowled 70.1 overs at a brisk speed to take ten wickets; Langley had a world Test record haul of nine dismissals (eight catches, one stumping); McDonald and Burke began with 137 in the solid, old-fashioned tradition; Benaud took a blinding catch at gully to dismiss Cowdrey, and put Australia in command with a hard-hit 97; Mackay (30), in his first Test, batted 160 minutes for 38 and 265 minutes for 31. May, though having missed several catches, showed himself to be as good a batsman as anyone in the world, Trueman as hostile a bowler, and Bailey still a brilliant close catcher. Evans made seven dismissals, so that 16 wickets fell to the wicketkeepers: indeed, Richardson's eight innings in the series were all terminated by Langley or his deputy Maddocks.

769, above, left: *Benaud's extraordinary left-hand 'self-preservation' catch in the gully to dismiss Cowdrey.* 770, right: *Benaud hooks during his 97.* 771, below, left: *May square-cuts powerfully during the Lord's Test; Langley wicketkeeper, Archer slip.* 772, right: *Miller, having taken a bail from umpire Lee's pocket, hurls it to some youngsters as he leaves the field, having taken 10 for 152 in the match*

1956
Headingley, July 12, 13, 14, 16, 17

England *325 (P.B.H. May 101, C. Washbrook 98, T.G. Evans 40);* Australia *143 (J.W. Burke 41, K.R. Miller 41, J.C. Laker 5 for 58, G.A.R. Lock 4 for 41) and 140 (R.N. Harvey 69, J.C. Laker 6 for 55).* England won by an innings and 42 runs.

Washbrook, now 41, was recalled by England, and, with his captain, turned the match – and the series – around. He and May took their side from the plight of 17 for 3, after Archer had used the seam alarmingly well, to 204 before May fell to a grand fine-leg catch by Lindwall. Washbrook was lbw to Benaud, but Bailey and Evans took the score past 300, and after Trueman had taken the valuable wicket of McDonald early in each innings, Laker and Lock, taking the other 18 wickets, dispatched Australia in highly professional manner, though Harvey (4½ hours) and Miller (26 in 2¼ hours) went down fighting. In depressing weather, and after having won a significant toss, England thus won against Australia for the first time at Leeds.

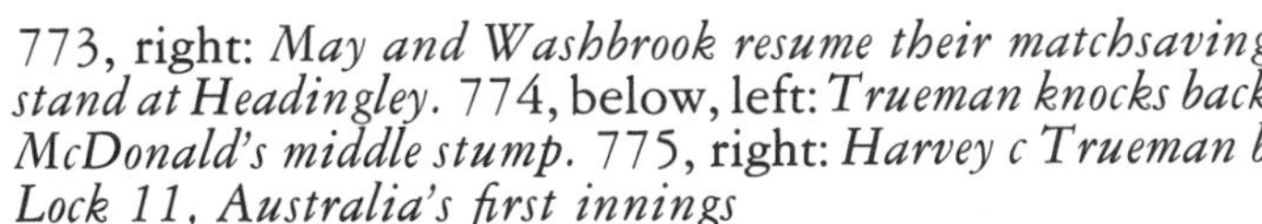

773, right: *May and Washbrook resume their matchsaving stand at Headingley.* 774, below, left: *Trueman knocks back McDonald's middle stump.* 775, right: *Harvey c Trueman b Lock 11, Australia's first innings*

1956 FOURTH TEST

Old Trafford, July 26, 27, 28, 30, 31

England 459 *(D.S. Sheppard 113, P.E. Richardson 104, M.C. Cowdrey 80, T.G. Evans 47, P.B.H. May 43, I.W. Johnson 4 for 151);* Australia 84 *(J.C. Laker 9 for 37) and 205 (C.C. McDonald 89, J.C. Laker 10 for 53).* England won by an innings and 170 runs.

Jim Laker, whose analyses were 16.4-4-37-9 and 51.2-23-53-10, performed the greatest bowling feat of all time in a match not without controversy. Pitch preparation was never easy in this wet summer, and patches were apparent during England's innings. The home side, all the same, proceeded steadily to their large total, Richardson and Cowdrey leading off with 174, and Sheppard, brought back to Test cricket after only four first-class innings that season, added 93 with May. England were healthily placed at 307 for 3 by the first evening, and Sheppard was out on the second afternoon after batting almost five hours – over an hour longer than Richardson. Evans made a breezy 47, and Johnson and Benaud shared 94 overs, taking 6 for 274. Laker and Lock were soon on when Australia batted, and, after changing ends, Laker struck at 48 with McDonald's wicket, caught at short leg. He bowled Harvey for nought, and at tea Australia were 62 for 2. First ball after the interval Lock took his one wicket in the match – Burke, caught at slip. The ball was turning sharply and the fieldsmen crowded in. Laker then had Craig and Mackay in one over, Miller and Benaud in another. Soon he had Archer as he tried to 'charge' him. Then Maddocks and Johnson went in one over. Australia all out 84; Laker 7 for 8 off 22 balls since tea – 9 for 16 after having begun with none for 21. The tourists had seemed to panic after the fall of the first few wickets. Following on, Australia were 53 for one that evening, McDonald retired hurt with a knee injury, and Harvey having hit his first ball, a full toss from Laker, to Cowdrey, thus 'bagging a pair'. Little play was possible on the Saturday, but Burke was lost, and Australia were now 59 for 2. Monday was wet – and windy enough for Evans's cap to be blown off – and in an hour the score advanced to 84, McDonald now returned. He and Craig batted to lunch on the final day, when Australia, 112 for 2, had just four hours to survive. Then the sun came out, and the pitch stirred. Bowling again from the Stretford end, from where he took all his wickets, Laker trapped Craig lbw: he had batted almost 4½ hours for 38. Mackay, a left-hander, then succumbed for his second duck, and Miller's scoreless innings was a quarter-hour of agony. Archer was out second ball, caught in the leg-trap, and then the sun disappeared and the pitch seemed easier. McDonald and Benaud were together at tea, but the former, after a 340-minute vigil, turned a lifter to Oakman, who held his fifth catch of the match. Benaud became Laker's 17th wicket – bowled playing, like several others, fatally back. Johnson appealed to the umpires at sawdust blowing in his eyes – a mark of Australia's despair. Laker bowled perfectly and relentlessly on. Lindwall, after making eight in 40 minutes, was caught by Lock at short leg. Then, with an hour to go, Maddocks was leg-before, and the incredible event was over. Lock, as aggressive a bowler as history has known, bowled 55 overs in the innings and finished with 0 for 69. That was almost as amazing as his Surrey partner's figures.

776, left: *the Rev. David Sheppard pulls Benaud for four during his 113.* 777, below, left: *The only wicket not taken by Laker: Burke c Cowdrey b Lock 22.* 778, right: *McDonald, caught by Lock for 32, another Laker leg-trap victim*

779, above, left: *Craig lbw b Laker 38.* 780, right: *Miller b Laker 0*

781, above, left: *Mackay c Oakman b Laker 0.* 782, right: *Archer c Oakman b Laker 0.* 783, centre: *Harvey, exasperated at having 'bagged a pair'.* 784, below, left: *Maddocks lbw b Laker 2 – the last wicket to fall (Laker's tenth in the innings and 19th of the match).* 785, right: *Laker leaves the scene of his unique triumph, enviably saddled for life with the task of discussing his 19 for 90 with eager fans*

1956 FIFTH TEST

The Oval, August 23, 24, 25, 27, 28

England 247 *(D.C.S. Compton 94, P.B.H. May 83*, R.G. Archer 5 for 53, K.R. Miller 4 for 91) and 182 for 3 dec (D.S. Sheppard 62)*; Australia 202 *(K.R. Miller 61, J.C. Laker 4 for 80) and 27 for 5.* Match drawn.

Denis Compton became the third inspired comeback selection for England in the series, making a lovely 94 despite the recent loss of his right kneecap. He went in at 66 for 3 and helped May take the score to 222. Three wickets then fell at that score, and the innings subsided next day. Rain made the pitch interesting, and Laker and Lock beset many problems, reducing Australia to 47 for 5 after a now-fit Tyson had removed McDonald. Harvey (39) and Miller saved the follow-on, and with Benaud's 32 there was little in it after all. England batted confidently either side of rain interruptions, and May left Australia only two hours. Far from being a chance to level the series, it was time enough for further humiliations, and Laker took his tally for the series to a record 46 wickets at 9.60. This was the last Test appearance in England of Miller and Lindwall.

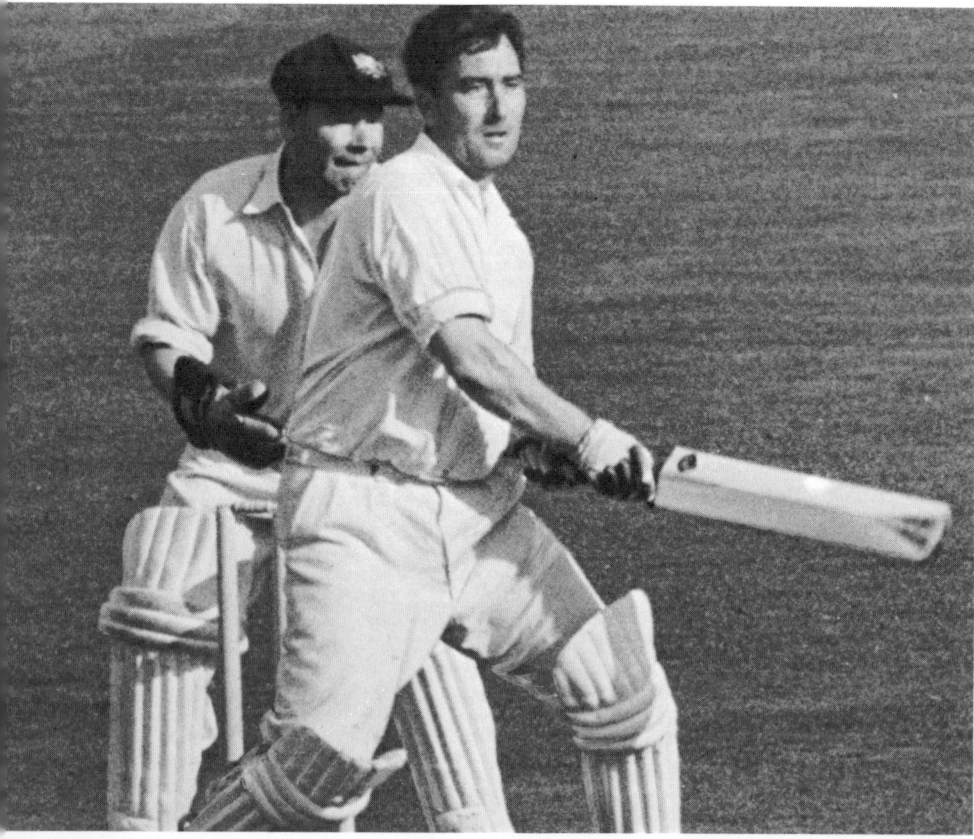

786, left: *A pull by Compton during his successful Oval comeback.* 787, below, left: *Richardson is caught behind for the seventh consecutive time in the series.* 788, right: *Australian wicketkeeper Langley, never renowned for a tidy appearance, bows to convention as Miller applies a safety pin to his split trousers*

1958–59 FIRST TEST
Brisbane, December 5, 6, 8, 9, 10

England *134 and 198 (T.E. Bailey 68, R. Benaud 4 for 66);* Australia *186 (C.C. McDonald 42, P.J. Loader 4 for 56) and 147 for 2 (N.C. O'Neill 71*).* Australia won by 8 wickets.

Australia, under Richie Benaud, came back with a vengeance after the defeats of the previous two series, though this opening contest featured some pitiful cricket. Slow over rates and negative batting evoked widespread protests. Bailey's was the most outrageous display: he batted 7½ hours for 68, going in when England were 28 for one in the second innings. The pitch, greenish on the first day, did not deteriorate as half-expected, and Burke matched Bailey in batting through 51.7 eight-ball overs for 28 runs. O'Neill, aged 21, on his Test debut, injected the first real class into the match. Davidson and Meckiff took ten wickets in the match and Benaud seven – the faster men both left-arm, the second-named having an action which some observers questioned. It was not until five years later, on this ground, that Meckiff was no-balled for throwing and retired instantly. During the series the bowling actions of Rorke, Slater and Burke also came under close scrutiny by some Pressmen and opponents. With Cowdrey out to a disputed catch, the 1958–59 rubber was not off to the most harmonious of beginnings.

789, above, left: *O'Neill, on debut, drives Bailey powerfully.* 790, right: *Kline takes a stroke from Cowdrey at square leg. The verdict of 'caught' did not satisfy everyone.* 791, below, left: *May is deceived by a Benaud googly and is lbw.* 792, right: *Benaud leaps to catch Richardson off his own bowling*

1958–59 SECOND TEST

Melbourne, December 31, January 1, 2, 3, 5

England *259 (P.B.H. May 113, T.E. Bailey 48, M.C. Cowdrey 44, A.K. Davidson 6 for 64) and 87 (I. Meckiff 6 for 38);* Australia *308 (R.N. Harvey 167, C.C. McDonald 47, J.B. Statham 7 for 57) and 42 for 2.* Australia won by 8 wickets.

A sensational six-ball spell by Davidson, in which he captured the wickets of Richardson, Watson and Graveney, had England three down for seven on the first morning. Then Bailey, opening, took the score to 92 with May, who was then joined by Cowdrey in a stand of 118. May, whose innings began on his 29th birthday, batted in all for 5¼ hours, and his century was the first in Australia by an England captain for 57 years. The innings fell away, and when Australia's Harvey (who batted 370 minutes without giving a chance) was joined in big stands by McDonald and O'Neill, England seemed to be slipping from the picture. But Statham's gallant effort, backed by Loader, kept the match poised . . . until Meckiff ran through England's second innings, aided by some deft catching and less than admirable batsmanship. This was England's lowest score in Australia for 55 years.

793, above, left: *Watson is bowled by Davidson in a sensational over.* 794, above, right: *Harvey steps out and drives Laker during his 167.* 795, left: *Bailey, having moved well across to Meckiff, is caught by Benaud at silly mid-on.* 796, right: *Burke, playing no stroke, is bowled by Statham*

1958–59
Sydney, January 9, 10, 12, 13, 14, 15

England 219 *(P.B.H. May 42, R. Swetman 41, R. Benaud 5 for 83) and 287 for 7 dec (M.C. Cowdrey 100*, P.B.H. May 92, R. Benaud 4 for 94);* Australia 357 *(N.C. O'Neill 77, A.K. Davidson 71, K.D. Mackay 57, L.E. Favell 54, C.C. McDonald 40, J.C. Laker 5 for 107, G.A.R. Lock 4 for 130) and 54 for 2.* Match drawn.

England, after a now-customary bad start, steadied with Graveney and May, then slipped, then recovered partially, Swetman, injured Evans's replacement, batting over 2½ hours. McDonald became set, in enviable contrast, and though Laker and Lock gave an idea of their greatness on an unresponsive pitch (though Lock throughout the series tended to bowl too flat and fast), O'Neill and Favell added 110 for the fourth wicket, and Mackay and Davidson a precious 115 for the seventh. England were tottering at 64 for 3 – still 74 behind – when Cowdrey joined May. The score was advanced to 246 before Burke got a ball through May's unsuspecting defence, during which time Benaud had gone on the defensive. Cowdrey's century took 362 minutes, the longest in these Tests until 1975.

797, above, left: *May and Cowdrey resume their fourth-wicket stand of 182.* 798, right: *O'Neill c Swetman b Laker 77 at Sydney.* 799, below, left: *May b Burke 92.* 800, right: *Mackay throws himself to catch Swetman (41) off Benaud*

1958–59 FOURTH TEST

Adelaide, January 30, 31, February 2, 3, 4, 5

Australia *476 (C.C. McDonald 170, J.W. Burke 66, N.C. O'Neill 56, R. Benaud 46, A.K. Davidson 43, R.N. Harvey 41, F.S. Trueman 4 for 90) and 36 for 0;* England *240 (M.C. Cowdrey 84, T.W. Graveney 41, R. Benaud 5 for 91) and 270 (P.B.H. May 59, T.W. Graveney 53*, P.E. Richardson 43, W. Watson 40, R. Benaud 4 for 82).* Australia won by 10 wickets.

Having won three tosses, batted and failed to make substantial first-innings totals, May this time put Australia in; but no wicket fell until 171, when Burke was caught. Australia were 200 for one by the first evening. Next day, still in fierce heat, England took wickets after lunch, when McDonald temporarily retired, Statham obtaining three good wickets. Umpire McInnes appeared to err on occasions, Mackay 'walking' after being given 'not out' to a catch by Evans, and when McDonald was given 'not out' as his runner raced for the crease *behind* the umpire, the batsman took matters into his own hands by swinging wildly and being bowled by Trueman for 170, made in 487 minutes, with 12 fours. Laker, unfit, was sorely missed. The blond giant, Rorke, dragging on his right boot several yards in delivery, broke through the centre of England's innings, and Benaud, having bowled May for 37, wrapped up the tail. Although Davidson had sprained an ankle, Australia enforced the follow-on, and Richardson (3¾ hours) and Watson began with 89. Thereafter wickets fell with regularity before Benaud, Lindwall and Rorke, and the match extended well into the sixth day only because of Graveney's disciplined innings of five hours. Australia thus had the Ashes back 5½ traumatic years after losing them.

801, above, left: *Bailey is hit on the head by a ball from Rorke. Burke has yet to show any concern.* 802, right: *The ball is on its way to Bailey, who runs out Harvey.* 803, below, left: *The lengthy 'drag' of gargantuan Australian fast bowler Rorke.* 804, right: *Favell hits the winning run and the Ashes are regained*

1958–59 FIFTH TEST

Melbourne, February 13, 14, 16, 17, 18

England *205 (P.E. Richardson 68, J.B. Mortimore 44*, R. Benaud 4 for 43) and 214 (T.W. Graveney 54, M.C. Cowdrey 46);* Australia *351 (C.C. McDonald 133, A.T.W. Grout 74, R. Benaud 64, F.S. Trueman 4 for 92, J.C. Laker 4 for 93) and 69 for 1 (C.C. McDonald 51*).* Australia won by 9 wickets.

Australia's fourth decisive victory of the series resulted from attacking fast bowling, probing leg-spin variations from Benaud (he finished the rubber with 31 wickets), and heavy scoring again from the tough, dependable McDonald. Australia's captain and the wicketkeeper, Grout, also took their side from an indeterminate 209 for 6 to 324 for 7. Bailey, opening for England, was twice dismissed by Lindwall without scoring, and Dexter – who had been flown out in December with Mortimore as replacements – was out first ball to Meckiff. O'Neill also went first ball, to Trueman. At 78 for 2 in the second innings, Cowdrey, having stroked a beautiful 46, was victim of a disputed run-out. In the first Test he had been considered to be unlucky to be given out 'caught' by Kline at square leg. McDonald, batting 339 minutes in the first innings and taking his aggregate for the series to 520 in the second, was Australia's batsman of the season.

805, above, left: *Trueman falls on his ear to secure a catch from Grout (74).* 806, right: *Bailey collects a 'pair' and becomes Lindwall's 217th wicket (which overtook Grimmett's Australian Test record).* 807, below, left: *McDonald hits the winning runs past Dexter.* 808, right: *Benaud and May, the captains, on the balcony at the end of the series*

1961 FIRST TEST

Edgbaston, June 8, 9, 10, 12, 13

England *195 (R. Subba Row 59, K.D. Mackay 4 for 57) and 401 for 4 (E.R. Dexter 180, R. Subba Row 112, K.F. Barrington 48*);* Australia *516 (R.N. Harvey 114, N.C. O'Neill 82, R.B. Simpson 76, K.D. Mackay 64, W.M. Lawry 57).* Match drawn.

England began the final day at 106 for one, still 215 behind; but Dexter and Subba Row (who was playing in his first Test against Australia) took their stand to 109, and after Cowdrey's dismissal at 239, Barrington stayed with Dexter while 161 further matchsaving runs were made. Dexter, showing unexpected powers of concentration, batted 344 minutes and hit 31 fours. Mackay, with deceptively innocuous-looking medium-pacers, stole four good England wickets on the first day, and Harvey and O'Neill mastered the bowling of Trueman, Statham, Illingworth and Allen in a stand of 146 in 117 minutes. Rain cut the third and fourth days' play, and in the 20 minutes he batted on the penultimate day Dexter looked anything but assured, being missed at one off Davidson – a costly chance. He was stumped eventually when trying for a six off Simpson.

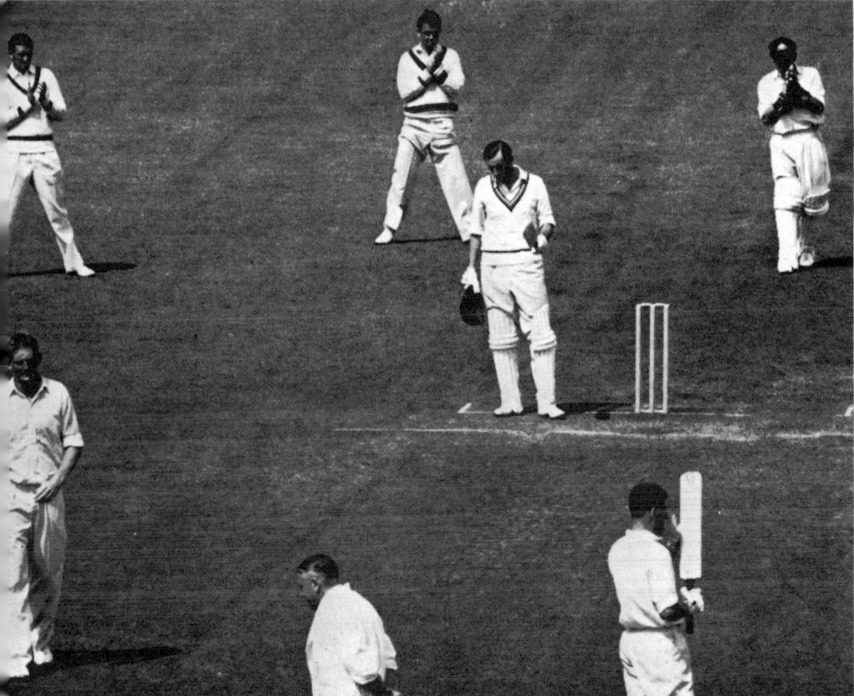

809, above, left: *England captain Cowdrey talks with chairman of selectors G.O. Allen during practice at Edgbaston.* 810, right: *M.J.K. Smith is caught by Lawry (out of picture) off Mackay.* 811, left: *Dexter acknowledges the applause. The bowler is Misson.* 812, below: *Mackay drives. England wicketkeeper Murray's eyebrow was injured by a ball that rebounded from a batsman's pad*

1961 SECOND TEST
Lord's, June 22, 23, 24, 26

England 206 *(R. Subba Row 48, A.K. Davidson 5 for 42) and* 202 *(K.F. Barrington 66, G. Pullar 42, G.D. McKenzie 5 for 37)*; Australia 340 *(W.M. Lawry 130, K.D. Mackay 54, P.J.P. Burge 46, F.S. Trueman 4 for 118) and 71 for 5.* Australia won by 5 wickets.

On a responsive pitch ideal for seam bowling (there was a 'ridge' at the Nursery end) Australia disposed of a strong England XI – with May returned – and were 42 for 2 by the first evening, having lost their own first two wickets for six runs. Harvey (leading Australia in Benaud's absence through injury) and O'Neill were gone by 88, but Burge then batted stoutly with the tall left-hander, Lawry, who was playing his second Test. They added 95, and Lawry went on to a courageous hundred, batting in all for 369 minutes. Mackay stretched the lead with stands of 53 for the ninth wicket with McKenzie and 49 for the tenth with Misson. The 20-year-old McKenzie, in his first Test, plunged the ball onto a still-lively pitch and, with Davidson and Misson, left his side to make only a handful of runs for victory. The handful soon seemed a mountain as Statham and Trueman swept four wickets away for 19, and Lock touched a misjudged hook by Burge as it fell to earth. Simpson went at 58, but Burge's galvanising strokeplay saw Australia to their eighth victory at Lord's.

813, above: *Lawry mis-hooks but survives.*
814, right: *O'Neill loses his off stump to Statham*

815, left: *Barrington lbw b Davidson 66*

816, below: *Burge ends the tension by pulling Statham over midwicket for the winning runs*

1961

THIRD TEST

Headingley, July 6, 7, 8

Australia *237 (R.N. Harvey 73, C.C. McDonald 54, F.S. Trueman 5 for 58) and 120 (R.N. Harvey 53, F.S. Trueman 6 for 30);* England *299 (M.C. Cowdrey 93, G. Pullar 53, A.K. Davidson 5 for 63) and 62 for 2.* England won by 8 wickets.

Two extraordinary breakthroughs by Trueman on an unpredictable pitch settled the match when, in each innings, Australia showed signs of increasing command. 183 for 2 at tea on the first day, Australia tumbled to 208 for 9 as Trueman with the new ball took 5 for 16 in six overs, aided by good catches by Cowdrey and Lock. England progressed well until Davidson, cutting his pace, and McKenzie ran through the middle and later order, Lock cracking a useful 30, many off Benaud, who was troubled throughout the series by a damaged shoulder. Australia reached 99 before the third wicket fell, and then Allen had Burge lbw for nought to make it 102 for 4. Trueman then proceeded to take five wickets without conceding a run, bowling off-cutters, with 40-year-old Les Jackson, in his first Test against Australia, operating from the other end. Trueman bowled Benaud for a duck for the second time, and took 6 for 4 all told in 45 balls. Australia's last eight wickets fell in 50 minutes. England made the necessary runs that evening.

817, above: *McDonald st Murray b Lock, first innings.* 818, right: *McDonald bowled by a prodigious breakback from Jackson, second innings*

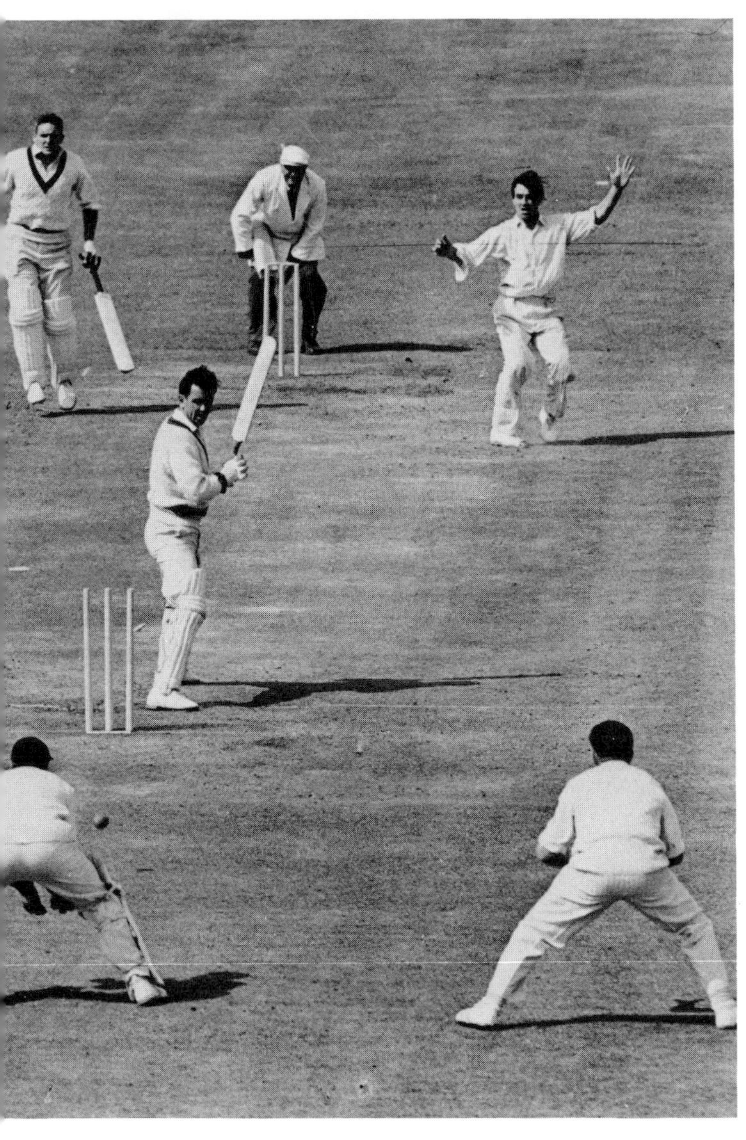

819, left: *Simpson is bowled by Trueman – the third of his five wickets for no runs.* 820, above: *Cowdrey scores off Simpson during his 93 at Leeds*

1961 FOURTH TEST

Old Trafford, July 27, 28, 29, 31, August 1

Australia *190 (W.M. Lawry 74, B.C. Booth 46, J.B. Statham 5 for 53) and 432 (W.M. Lawry 102, A.K. Davidson 77*, N.C. O'Neill 67, R.B. Simpson 51, D.A. Allen 4 for 58)*; England *367 (P.B.H. May 95, K.F. Barrington 78, G. Pullar 63, D.A. Allen 42, R.B. Simpson 4 for 23) and 201 (E.R. Dexter 76, R. Subba Row 49, R. Benaud 6 for 70).* Australia won by 54 runs.

On the final morning, when Allen spun out three Australians in 15 balls to make the score 334 for 9, England had the rest of the day to make 157 plus whatever the final wicket added. It added 98, Davidson taking 20 off an Allen over and persuading May to withdraw the off-spinner. McKenzie (32) gave the left-hand all-rounder staunch support, and eventually England needed 256 in 230 minutes if the series was to be left open. Pullar and Subba Row, both left-handers, began with 40, and Dexter than came in and played thrillingly for 76 in 84 minutes, apparently making certain of the match for England, who were 150 for one after 123 minutes. Having hit 14 fours and a huge six, Dexter then edged a ball that bounced and Grout took the catch. Benaud, the bowler, was coming from around the wicket, and pitching into the bowlers' rough. Second ball Peter May was bowled round his legs. Close then failed in his attempted crossbat assault, and just before tea Subba Row was yorked – another wicket to Benaud, who had 4 for 9 in 19 balls. After the interval he got Murray, Mackay trapped Barrington, and – back to over-the-wicket – Benaud had Allen brilliantly caught at slip by Simpson. The fieldsman, then daringly brought into the attack, had Trueman caught at short leg, and Davidson came back to bowl Statham, giving Australia a sensational victory with 20 minutes left. Much of the worthy cricket earlier has tended to be forgotten, but Lawry's two stout-hearted innings, Statham's use of the conditions, and May's fine 'comeback' innings all contributed to an exceptional cricket match.

821, top, left: *Lawry missed by Subba Row at slip.* 822, top, right: *Davidson hits Allen for a vital six.* 823, middle, left: *Dexter is caught by Grout – the start of the England collapse at Old Trafford.* 824, centre: *Close hits Benaud for six.* 825, right: *Subba Row b Benaud 49.* 826, below: *May b Benaud 0*

1961 FIFTH TEST

The Oval, August 17, 18, 19, 21, 22

England *256 (P.B.H. May 71, K.F. Barrington 53, A.K. Davidson 4 for 83) and 370 for 8 (R. Subba Row 137, K.F. Barrington 83, D.A. Allen 42*, J.T. Murray 40, K.D. Mackay 5 for 121);* Australia *494 (P.J.P. Burge 181, N.C. O'Neill 117, B.C. Booth 71, R.B. Simpson 40, D.A. Allen 4 for 133).* Match drawn.

In 104 overs on the first day England struggled to 210 for 8 after a poor start, when three wickets fell for 20. Gaunt finished with three good wickets, and only a three-hour stand of 80 by May and Barrington held the innings together. Australia began unsteadily, but O'Neill was in mighty form, and the even more strongly-built Burge added 123 with him. A delayed new ball enabled Booth to settle in, and with Burge hooking and sweeping powerfully the score advanced to 396 before Booth fell to Lock. Queenslander Burge batted chancelessly for almost seven hours, hitting 22 fours. There had been rain interruptions, and on the fourth day more time was lost, England finishing precariously at 155 for 4. Subba Row, batting with a runner because of a pulled muscle in this his final Test innings, added 172 with Barrington, and occupied the crease for 400 minutes for his 137 (having made a century in his first Test against Australia at Edgbaston). With Davidson injured, Australia hadn't the resources to come back at England in the remaining time. Benaud (51 overs) and Mackay (68 overs) bore the brunt of the second-innings work.

827, above, left: *Subba Row drives during his 137.* 828, right: *Pullar finely caught by Grout on the leg side off Mackay for 13.* 829, left: *Burge sweeps during his muscular 181.* 830, below: *O'Neill forces through the leg-trap*

1962–63 FIRST TEST

Brisbane, November 30, December 1, 3, 4, 5

Australia 404 (*B.C. Booth 112, K.D. Mackay 86*, R. Benaud 51, R.B. Simpson 50) and 362 for 4 dec (W.M. Lawry 98, R.B. Simpson 71, R.N. Harvey 57, N.C. O'Neill 56, P.J.P. Burge 47*)*; England 389 (*P.H. Parfitt 80, K.F. Barrington 78, E.R. Dexter 70, R. Benaud 6 for 115) and 278 for 6 (E.R. Dexter 99, G. Pullar 56, D.S. Sheppard 53).* Match drawn.

When Australia's sixth wicket went down for 194 a modest total seemed in prospect. The elegant Booth then added 103 with the dour Mackay, who then stayed with Benaud while 91 were put on for the eighth wicket. Booth's century lasted 217 minutes and contained not one brutal stroke. Dexter, leading England, had a fine double, batting briskly in each innings and being bowled by McKenzie for 99 when it seemed England had an outside chance on the final day. England's first innings was shored up by two four-hour innings, Parfitt's in his first Test against Australia, and Barrington's in demonstration of what a gritty and devoted player he had become. Lawry's 98 took him 260 minutes, and set up a declaration on the fourth evening that invited England to make 378 in six hours. Pullar and Sheppard started with 114, and Dexter's bold innings was the 14th half-century of the match.

831, above, left: *Opener Simpson glances Statham, and wicketkeeper Smith fields.* 832, right: *Parfitt lofts Benaud to be caught by Davidson at long-on for 80.* 833, below, left: *McKenzie wonderfully caught-and-bowled by Knight.* 834, right: *Dexter b McKenzie 99*

1962–63 SECOND TEST

Melbourne, December 29, 31, January 1, 2, 3

Australia *316 (W.M. Lawry 52, K.D. Mackay 49, A.K. Davidson 40, F.J. Titmus 4 for 43) and 248 (B.C. Booth 103, W.M. Lawry 57, F.S. Trueman 5 for 62);* England *331 (M.C. Cowdrey 113, E.R. Dexter 93, T.W. Graveney 41, A.K. Davidson 6 for 75) and 237 for 3 (D.S. Sheppard 113, M.C. Cowdrey 58*, E.R. Dexter 52).* England won by 7 wickets.

With the ball often beating the bat and occasional deliveries shooting through low, the scores would have been even more moderate but for the depth of Australia's batting and a splendid stand of 175 by Cowdrey and Dexter. Then, on the final day, Sheppard, who had failed to score in the first innings and dropped two catches, steered England to victory with a five-hour innings that included only five fours and as many as ten threes. The pitch was perhaps better than earlier, and Sheppard put on 124 with Dexter and 104 with Cowdrey before being run out with the scores level. Booth went in with Australia 69 for 4, and after Lawry (who took 275 minutes to reach 50) was out at 161, all responsibility devolved upon him. Booth batted 348 minutes, hitting only five fours, but ensuring that England were set a sizable target.

835, above, left: *Harvey run out for 10 by Trueman.* 836, right: *Dexter c Simpson b Benaud 93.* 837, below, left: *Sheppard straight-drives Benaud to reach his hundred.* 838, right: *The champagne comes out, poured by Benaud for victorious Dexter*

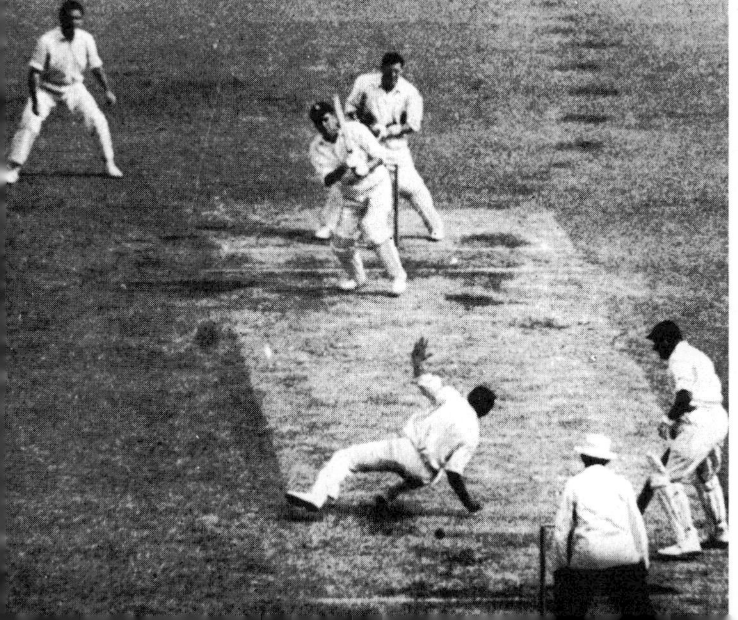

1962–63 THIRD TEST

Sydney, January 11, 12, 14, 15

England 279 *(M.C. Cowdrey 85, G. Pullar 53, R.B. Simpson 5 for 57, A.K. Davidson 4 for 54) and 104 (A.K. Davidson 5 for 25)*; Australia *319 (R.B. Simpson 91, B.K. Shepherd 71*, R.N. Harvey 64, F.J. Titmus 7 for 79) and 67 for 2.* Australia won by 8 wickets.

Simpson, without the accuracy of a Benaud, picked up five wickets with leg-breaks and googlies, and Davidson four with his lethal control of a new ball. Cowdrey batted 160 minutes, but Pullar existed for 3½ hours. Sheppard missed two catches during the stand of 160 between Simpson and Harvey, and with Murray off with a sprained shoulder in taking a diving catch to dismiss Lawry (Parfitt kept wicket in his place) England were in a sorry plight. Simpson batted four hours, but off-spinner Titmus brought his side back into the match with four wickets for five runs, using the breeze skilfully. Burly left-hander Shepherd hit Australia into a lead which was considered not quite enough to compensate for Australia's having to bat last, but this soon ceased to be relevant as Davidson broke open England's second innings with more fine swing bowling. McKenzie's speed, Benaud's vital dismissal of Cowdrey, and Simpson's glorious slip fielding shattered England, for whom Murray, with a painful shoulder, batted 100 minutes for three not out. Australia made the runs as rain fell; the scheduled fifth day was very wet.

839, above, left: *Murray, with an injured shoulder, drives McKenzie one-handed.* 840, right: *England 28 for 3, and the crowd on the Hill enjoying every moment.* 841, below, left: *Dexter beautifully caught by Simpson, and England hopes slump.* 842, right: *The Australian team dinner before the match*

1962–63 FOURTH TEST

Adelaide, January 25, 26, 28, 29, 30

Australia *393 (R.N. Harvey 154, N.C. O'Neill 100, A.K. Davidson 46) and 293 (B.C. Booth 77, R.B. Simpson 71, R. Benaud 48, F.S. Trueman 4 for 60);* England *331 (K.F. Barrington 63, E.R. Dexter 61, F.J. Titmus 59*, G.D. McKenzie 5 for 89) and 223 for 4 (K.F. Barrington 132*).* Match drawn.

Australia were 16 for 2 when Booth added 85 with Harvey, who was helped by dropped catches off successive balls from Illingworth and a missed slip catch at 26. O'Neill then entered and a transformation took place. In oppressive heat Harvey – whose century was the last of his six against England – added 194 with O'Neill in only 171 minutes, the strong, stylish O'Neill getting out as much from exhaustion as to Dexter's bowling. McKenzie led Australia's attack after Davidson pulled up with a torn hamstring in his fourth over, and gained lift from the pitch during his 33 overs. Titmus and Trueman (38) kept England within sight on the rain-shortened third day. Dexter then set about containing, and though Simpson and Booth added 133 for the third wicket, with Davidson absent, Benaud felt it necessary to bat until lunch on the last day. England's first two wickets fell for four, the fourth at 122, and Illingworth was called from a sick-bed; but Graveney saw it through with Barrington, who batted 227 minutes and reached his chanceless century with a six off Simpson. His first-innings 63 included four boundaries in four balls from Davidson – only one where it was intended – and the extra effort this provoked may have triggered the bowler's injury.

843, above: *Booth on-drives Titmus.* 844, top, right: *Statham is congratulated upon passing Bedser's all-Tests record of 236 wickets when he had Shepherd caught.* 845, bottom: *Trueman strikes Benaud for six*

846: Harvey (11) dropped by Cowdrey at slip off Illingworth at Adelaide

1962–63 FIFTH TEST
Sydney, February 15, 16, 18, 19, 20

England *321 (K.F. Barrington 101, E.R. Dexter 47) and 268 for 8 dec (K.F. Barrington 94, D.S. Sheppard 68, M.C. Cowdrey 53);* Australia *349 (P.J.P. Burge 103, N.C. O'Neill 73, R. Benaud 57, F.J. Titmus 5 for 103) and 152 for 4 (P.J.P. Burge 52*, W.M. Lawry 45*).* Match drawn.

With all to play for, neither side was prepared to take chances, and England's innings of 321, taking 9½ hours, set the pattern. Barrington managed only four fours in his 101 (but picked up 20 twos), and fell just short of a century in each innings. He occupied the crease for 9¾ hours in the match. Australia were 74 for 3 on the second evening, but O'Neill, using his feet to get to the off-spinners Titmus and Allen, added 109 with Burge, who batted 5½ hours before being lbw attempting a sweep. He was missed at 63. Illingworth and Sheppard opened with 40 in England's second innings, Cowdrey being indisposed, and Barrington anchored the innings, adding 97 with Sheppard and 94 with Cowdrey. At lunch on the last day Dexter declared, setting Australia 241 in four hours, but four wickets fell for 70 and Lawry (four hours) and Burge played out time to the echo of the crowd's dissatisfaction. For the first time a five-match series in Australia was drawn. Neil Harvey took six catches in the match, his last for Australia, and Alan Davidson took a wicket with his final ball in Tests.

847: *Barrington pulls a short one from Benaud in the first innings. The Surrey batsman had a sturdy double of 101 and 94, with only six boundaries*

848, above: *Graveney at short mid-on has caught O'Neill (out of picture) off Allen.* 849, below: *O'Neill plays an immaculate forward defensive.* 850, right: *Harvey (left) and Davidson lead Australia out in their final Test match, followed by their captain, Richie Benaud*

1964 FIRST TEST

Trent Bridge, June 4, 5, 6, 8, 9

England *216 for 8 dec (G. Boycott 48) and 193 for 9 dec (E.R. Dexter 68, G.D. McKenzie 5 for 53);* Australia *168 (R.B. Simpson 50) and 40 for 2.* Match drawn.

Rain ruined this opening contest of a frustrating series. It was the fourth morning before Dexter declared, the first day having been heavily curtailed, the second partially, and the third washed out. Boycott, in his first Test, batted cautiously, with Titmus his opening partner as John Edrich was injured before the start. Titmus was once stranded after colliding with the bowler, but Australia's wicketkeeper, Wally Grout, won much admiration by refusing to break the wicket. Bob Simpson, succeeding Benaud as Australia's captain, batting at No. 6, saved his side from a serious deficit, but Dexter, opening in place of Boycott (broken finger), thrashed 68 and a climax seemed imminent. Instead, England's run rate fell back against McKenzie, Corling and Hawke, and the closure did not come until Australia were faced with making 242 in 195 minutes. The only remaining excitement came as O'Neill hooked the first four balls of Trueman's second over to the boundary. Rain washed out play after 9.2 overs.

851, left: *Dexter drives Corling to the boundary, O'Neill following the swift passage of the ball.* 852, above: *Titmus is stranded after colliding with bowler Hawke, but Grout, the Australian wicketkeeper, nobly refrained from removing the bails*

853, above: *Booth, having just completed his stroke off Allen, is run out by Trueman from short leg.* 854, right: *Sharpe sweeps Veivers for four at Trent Bridge*

1964 SECOND TEST
Lord's, June 18, 19, 20, 22, 23

Australia *176 (T.R. Veivers 54, F.S. Trueman 5 for 48) and 168 for 4 (P.J.P. Burge 59);* England *246 (J.H. Edrich 120, G.E. Corling 4 for 60).* Match drawn.

Again, something like half the match was lost through rain. Play could not begin until the third day, and Dexter then put Australia in. The sixth wicket fell at 88, but left-hander Veivers held on for 2½ hours. Dexter chipped in with the wickets of O'Neill and Burge, and Parfitt took two superlative diving catches close to the wicket. Dexter opened again, but was yorked by McKenzie second ball for two. Edrich, however, a cousin of Bill Edrich, went to a commendable hundred on his debut against Australia, batting altogether for 6¼ hours and hitting two sixes and nine fours. It was the day after his 27th birthday. Stands with Parfitt, Sharpe (35) and Titmus hauled England into the lead, but on the last day Australia withstood a pace attack, Gifford and Titmus surprisingly not being called in until well into the morning. Redpath was 53 minutes on 36 before falling to Titmus. More rain after lunch caused an abandonment at 5.20 pm.

855: *O'Neill drives handsomely at Lord's*

856, above: *Parfitt's great diving catch at short leg to dismiss Redpath (30) at Lord's.* 857, left: *Lawry bowled leg stump by Trueman for four.* 858, below: *John Edrich comes in having made a century in his debut innings against Australia, the first of seven*

1964
Headingley, July 2, 3, 4, 6

England 268 *(J.M. Parks 68, E.R. Dexter 66, N.J.N. Hawke 5 for 75, G.D. McKenzie 4 for 74) and 229 (K.F. Barrington 85)*; Australia 389 *(P.J.P. Burge 160, W.M. Lawry 78, F.J. Titmus 4 for 69) and 111 for 3 (I.R. Redpath 58*).* Australia won by 7 wickets.

Wonderful fielding and accurate pace bowling restricted England to 268 on a good pitch, a bright innings from Dexter and valuable batting by wicketkeeper Parks saving England's face. The performance seemed adequate, nonetheless, when Australia were 178 for 7, Gifford having taken two wickets and Titmus three, bowling cleverly. Dexter then gave Trueman and Flavell the new ball. Peter Burge fed well on it, especially Trueman's persistent long-hops, and 42 runs were scored off seven overs. Burge's stand with Hawke realised 105, and the massive Queenslander had further support next morning from Grout, who added 89 with him, transforming the match. Burge batted 5¼ hours and hit – resoundingly – 24 fours. Parfitt's knuckle was broken in England's second innings, and though Edrich and Barrington resisted grimly and Dexter played untypically defensively, Australia pressed home their advantage. Flavell could not bowl, having damaged a tendon, and Titmus earned figures of 27-19-25-2 as Australia moved carefully to victory on the fourth evening.

859, above: *Burge pulls Flavell for four.* 860, below: *Grout pulls Trueman, whose short bowling was often hammered in this Test at Leeds*

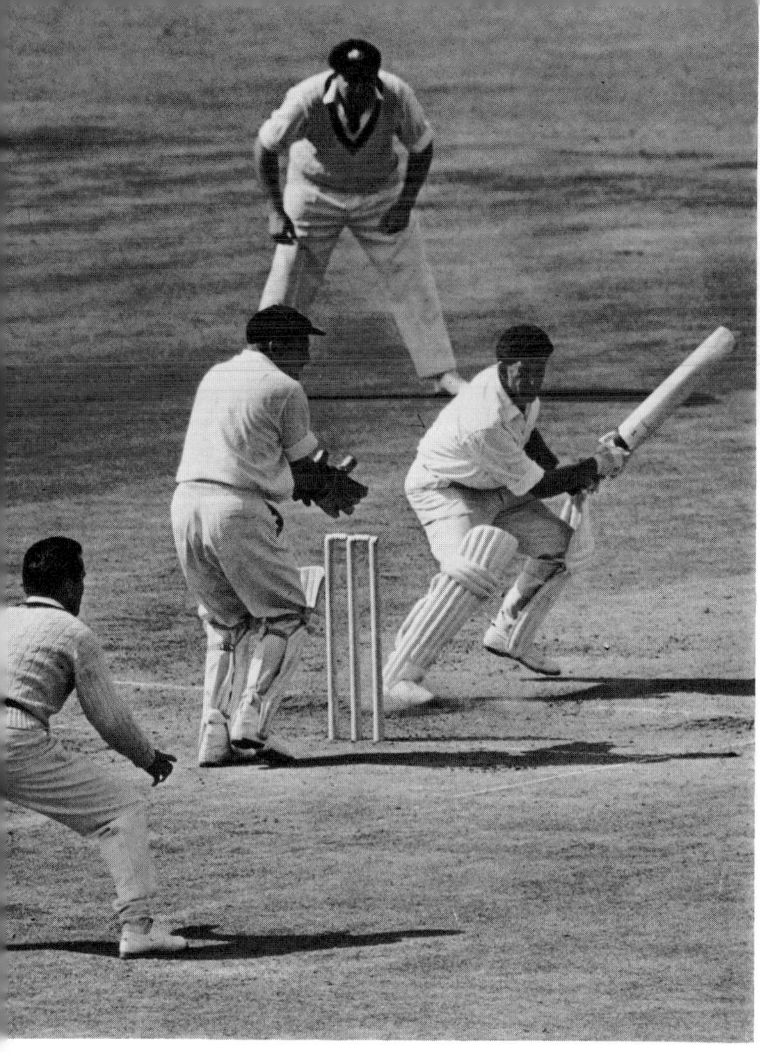

861, above, left: *Barrington cuts Veivers at Leeds.* 862, right: *A powerful back-foot stroke by Burge*

1964 — FOURTH TEST

Old Trafford, July 23, 24, 25, 27, 28

Australia *656 for 8 dec (R.B. Simpson 311, W.M. Lawry 106, B.C. Booth 98, N.C. O'Neill 47) and 4 for 0;* England *611 (K.F. Barrington 256, E.R. Dexter 174, J.M. Parks 60, G. Boycott 58, G.D. McKenzie 7 for 153).* Match drawn.

Winning the toss and with a perfect pitch awaiting, Simpson set about making the Ashes safe. His innings, the longest ever played against England (12 hours 42 minutes), was his first century in his 30 Tests, and contained 23 fours and a six. He was 109 at the end of the first day, when Australia were 253 for 2, and 265 at the end of the second (570 for 4). His opening stand of 201 with Lawry broke the 1909 record of Bardsley and Gregory, and he added 219 with Booth for the fifth wicket, hitting uninhibitedly on the third morning with no serious regard for the individual Test record. Rumsey, Price and Cartwright – of whom only Price had previously played Test cricket – took all seven wickets that fell to bowlers, Cartwright returning 77-32-118-2. Faced first with avoiding the follow-on, and later with only the prestige target of first-innings supremacy, England lost Edrich at 15 and Boycott at 126 before Dexter and Barrington settled down for a partnership that realised 246 in 325 minutes. The crowd at times expressed their impatience, but the normally restless Dexter set himself to the task, and Barrington, who batted all told for 685 minutes, with 26 fours, was not removed until just before tea on the final day. Both batsmen were dropped, McKenzie missing three chances, though he bowled gallantly for 60 overs. Off-spinner Veivers sent down 95.1 overs to take 3 for 155: only Ramadhin of West Indies has bowled more balls (588) in a Test innings.

863, top: *Simpson drives Mortimore for six during the later stages of his 311.* 864, centre: *Lawry hooks left-arm fast bowler Rumsey for six on the opening day.* 865, right: *Simpson out at last, hitting out at Price and being caught by wicketkeeper Parks*

866, left: *An out-of-character Dexter plays forward with restraint during England's Old Trafford marathon.*
867, right: *Barrington lbw b McKenzie 256*

1964 — FIFTH TEST

The Oval, August 13, 14, 15, 17, 18

England *182 (K.F. Barrington 47, N.J.N. Hawke 6 for 47) and 381 for 4 (G. Boycott 113, M.C. Cowdrey 93*, F.J. Titmus 56, K.F. Barrington 54*);* Australia *379 (W.M. Lawry 94, B.C. Booth 74, T.R. Veivers 67*, I.R. Redpath 45, F.S. Trueman 4 for 87).* Match drawn.

A rained-off final day deprived England of the outside chance of squaring the series and Cowdrey, restored to the side, of a century. Boycott reached his – his first in Tests – but the outstanding incident was Trueman's dismissal of Hawke, which made him the first bowler to take 300 wickets in Test matches. McKenzie finished the series with 29 in the five matches, equalling Grimmett's Australian record for a rubber in England. Batting was least easy on the first day, and distinctly the largest stand was 44 for the first wicket. One of the few moments to lighten the proceedings was when Dexter's bat split in half as he drove Hawke, who bowled cleverly at fast-medium pace. Australia's innings was sluggish, with Titmus and Cartwright returning very tight figures and Lawry spending 5¼ hours on his 94. Veivers later brought some vigour into the batting. 255 for 4, England were then steadied by a stand of 126 between Cowdrey and Barrington, rain having the final say in a mainly unsatisfying series.

868: *Fred Trueman takes his 300th Test wicket as Hawke is safely pouched by Cowdrey at slip*

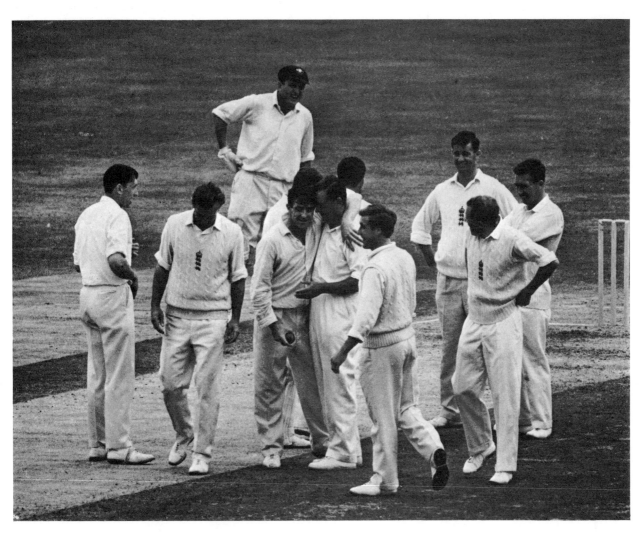

869, above: *Trueman, having taken his 300th Test wicket, hugs his accomplice, Cowdrey, and the England team share his pleasure.* 870, below, left: *Parfitt plays on to McKenzie for three and shows his chagrin.* 871, right: *Boycott comes in after making the first of his Test centuries*

1965–66 FIRST TEST

Brisbane, December 10, 11, 13, 14, 15

Australia *443 for 6 dec (W.M. Lawry 166, K.D. Walters 155, T.R. Veivers 56*)*; England *280 (F.J. Titmus 60, K.F. Barrington 53, J.M. Parks 52, G. Boycott 45, P.I. Philpott 5 for 90) and 186 for 3 (G. Boycott 63*).* Match drawn.

Rain permitted only 36 overs on the first day and washed out the second. Australia thus set out to raise a total sufficient to test England in the matter of a follow-on. This the tourists failed to avoid, but they saw out time without serious difficulty. Walters, not quite 20, batted 322 minutes in his first Test, showing deft footwork and a willing range of strokes. He added 187 with Lawry when Australia were 125 for 4, and then 119 with Veivers. Lawry who was to make nearly a thousand runs in Tests and other matches off M.J.K. Smith's side, batted here for seven hours. England began hesitantly but were lifted by Parks's bright innings and survived through Barrington's purposeful effort in the first innings and Boycott's in the second.

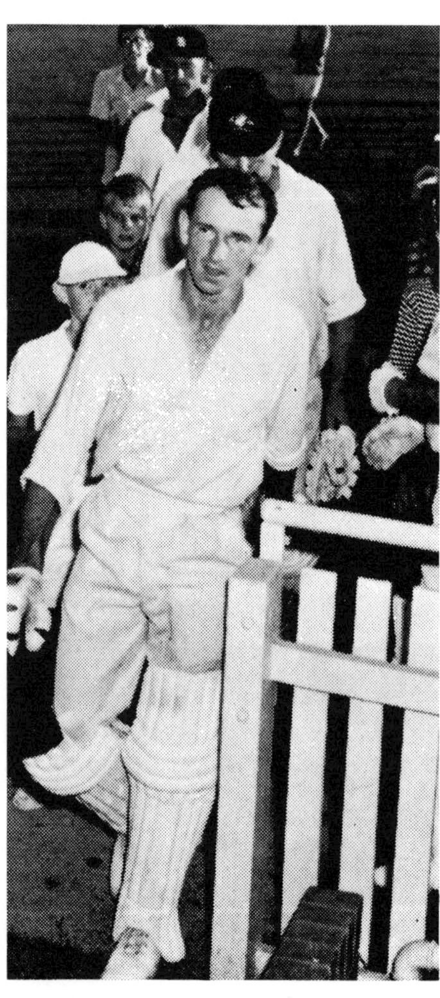

872, top, left: *Walters c Parks b Higgs 155.* 873, centre: *Walters returns after his stirring debut innings.* 874, right: *Edrich hooks Philpott for two during his 32.* 875, left: *Lawry is dropped by Barrington at slip off Titmus*

1965–66 SECOND TEST
Melbourne, December 30, 31, January 1, 3, 4

Australia *358 (R.M. Cowper 99, W.M. Lawry 88, R.B. Simpson 59, B.R. Knight 4 for 84) and 426 (P.J.P. Burge 120, K.D. Walters 115, W.M. Lawry 78, R.B. Simpson 67);* England *558 (J.H. Edrich 109, M.C. Cowdrey 104, J.M. Parks 71, K.F. Barrington 63, F.J. Titmus 56*, G. Boycott 51, R.W. Barber 48, M.J.K. Smith 41, G.D. McKenzie 5 for 134) and 5 for 0.* Match drawn.

Australia seemed doomed on the last day when their fourth wicket fell at 176, when they were still 24 runs behind. Then, having edged in front, they almost lost Burge, who left his crease to play Barber, missed, and gave Parks a stumping chance which he could not consummate. Burge and Walters were not separated until their stand was worth 198 and the match was saved. Simpson, who had missed the first Test because of a broken wrist, gave his side two good starts with Lawry (93 and 120), but apart from left-hander Cowper's 200-minute innings – ended by a slip catch off Jeff Jones – there was nothing of distinction about Australia's batting until the reprieved Burge and young Walters set about frustrating England. In contrast, England's first seven batsmen all made 41 or more, and there were five sizable stands, Edrich staying over five hours in spite of much discomfort against the spinners. Cowdrey's hundred was his third at Melbourne. The stumping miss apart, England might have grasped control earlier if the brisk opening of 98 given them by Boycott and Barber had been developed. Knight, flown out as a reinforcement to the MCC side, took his four wickets in a spell in which he conceded only 18 runs.

876, above: *Lawry c Cowdrey b Allen 88.* 877, below: *Edrich caught-and-bowled by Veivers for 109*

878, above: *Substitute wicketkeeper Barrington catches Simpson for 67.* 879, below: *Simpson and Lawry, Australia's reliable opening pair, about to start the first innings at Melbourne*

1965–66 THIRD TEST

Sydney, January 7, 8, 10, 11

England *488 (R.W. Barber 185, J.H. Edrich 103, G. Boycott 84, D.A. Allen 50*, N.J.N. Hawke 7 for 105);* Australia *221 (R.M. Cowper 60, G. Thomas 51, D.J. Brown 5 for 63) and 174 (F.J. Titmus 4 for 40, D.A. Allen 4 for 47).* England won by an innings and 93 runs.

A memorable five-hour innings by left-hander Barber set up an England victory which was made certain by Brown and Jones in a first-innings breakthrough and Titmus and Allen, the off-spinners, as the pitch became more and more helpful to the turning ball. Barber and Boycott (who was missed by Sincock at short leg when 12) opened with 93 before lunch and 234 in all (in four hours). Edrich then added 69 with Barber, but in the last session of the first day Hawke, with the new ball, took four quality wickets, and two more next morning. Edrich battled on, and reached his hundred with a four driven off leg-spinner Philpott. Allen and Jones put on 55 for the last wicket. Australia that evening were 113 for 4, and the stand of 81 between Thomas and Cowper was to be the largest of either Australian innings. Cowper stayed over four hours. Brown's taking of three wickets in an over made the follow-on fairly certain, and England's off-spinners, supported especially well by Smith, their captain, at short leg, had Australia floundering. Walters, batting for over two hours, was left 35 not out.

880, left: *Barber goes to 104 with a sweep off Cowper.* 881, above: *England captain Smith is caught behind off Hawke*

882, left: *Edrich hoists spinner Philpott to the boundary to bring up his century.* 883, right: *Burge about to be run out: Boycott throws to the far end. Lawry is the non-striker*

884, left: *Smith, ever alert at short leg to his spin bowlers, takes a rebound from Philpott's pad.* 885, right: *Boycott straight-drives McKenzie*

1965–66 FOURTH TEST

Adelaide, January 28, 29, 31, February 1

England 241 *(K.F. Barrington 60, J.M. Parks 49, G.D. McKenzie 6 for 48) and* 266 *(K.F. Barrington 102, F.J. Titmus 53, N.J.N. Hawke 5 for 54);* Australia 516 *(R.B. Simpson 225, W.M. Lawry 119, G. Thomas 52, K.R. Stackpole 43, I.J. Jones 6 for 118).* Australia won by an innings and 9 runs.

Having missed the first Test through a broken wrist and the third through chickenpox, Simpson returned as Australia's captain, and reminded everyone what his side had been lacking. For just over nine hours he withstood England's pace and spin attack, hitting 18 fours and a six, and setting a new Australian first-wicket record against England with Lawry – 244. This in itself gave Australia a first-innings lead. McKenzie, originally dropped in favour of Queensland's Allan, was recalled when Allan was injured, and bowled with zest on a lively pitch in humid conditions. Cowdrey's dismissal, not for the first time, was shrouded in controversy: he had mistaken a shout from the wicketkeeper for a call by his partner, and was run out. In the second innings England were destroyed by careless batting then over-cautious batting, and persistent and skilful bowling by Hawke. Barrington hit only four boundaries in a stay of 5½ hours, and Cowdrey (35) hit only two in over 2½ hours.

886, top, left: *Lawry almost falls in hooking Jones.* 887, centre: *Simpson is congratulated on his century by partner Lawry. The Australian captain went on to 225.* 888, below: *Nightwatchman Veivers c Parks b Jones – seagulls unmoved.* 889, above: *Barrington cheerfully responds to the slow handclapping at Adelaide*

1965–66
Melbourne, February 11, 12, 14, 15, 16

England *485 for 9 dec (K.F. Barrington 115, J.M. Parks 89, J.H. Edrich 85, M.C. Cowdrey 79, F.J. Titmus 42*, K.D. Walters 4 for 53) and 69 for 3;* Australia *543 for 8 dec (R.M. Cowper 307, W.M. Lawry 108, K.D. Walters 60).* Match drawn.

The deciding match was blighted by the loss of the fourth day because of rain, a refusal to take risks, and a tedious over rate, particularly when England, with Knight replacing slow bowler Allen, were in the field. After being 41 for 2, England were steadied by an even-time stand of 178 between Edrich and Barrington, the latter reaching his hundred off only 122 balls in 147 minutes. His century came with an on-driven six off Veivers. Walters dismissed them both, as well as Smith – caught behind by Grout, whose last Test this was. Grout died two years later, having had a heart complaint for some years. Cowdrey and Parks took England into higher reaches with 138 for the sixth wicket, but there was to be no overthrowing Australia once Simpson and Thomas had been dismissed cheaply. Lawry batted over six hours, taking his tenancy of the crease against England and MCC this season to over 41 hours. He and Cowper put on 212, and Walters then stayed with Cowper while 172 were added. The likelihood of a decision faded the longer Cowper batted. He reached 100 in 310 minutes, spent a further 225 minutes getting to 200, passed Bradman's record for Australia in Australia, and when Knight bowled him for 307 he had been in for 12 hours 7 minutes, hitting 20 fours.

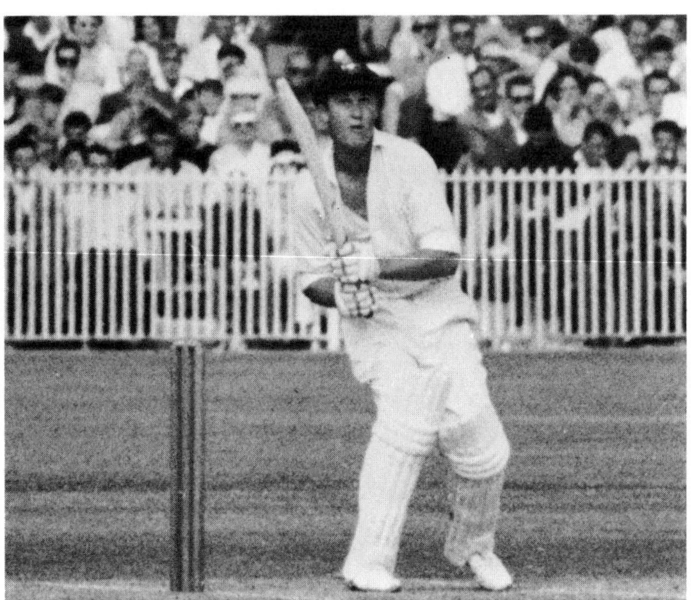

890, above, left: *Cowper hooks during his 307.* 891, right: *He acknowledges the applause that greeted his triple-century.* 892, below, left: *Cowper b Knight 307.* 893, right: *Barrington brings up his century with a six off Veivers*

894: *Wally Grout leads Australia out in his final Test appearance. Following are Hawke, Cowper, Thomas, Veivers, Stackpole, and McKenzie*

1968 FIRST TEST
Old Trafford, June 6, 7, 8, 10, 11

Australia *357 (A.P. Sheahan 88, W.M. Lawry 81, K.D. Walters 81, I.M. Chappell 73, J.A. Snow 4 for 97) and 220 (K.D. Walters 86, B.N. Jarman 41, P.I. Pocock 6 for 79);* England *165 (J.H. Edrich 49, R.M. Cowper 4 for 48) and 253 (B.L. D'Oliveira 87*, R.W. Barber 46).* Australia won by 159 runs.

On a sporting pitch, the youngest-ever Australian side to visit England – with a very wet spring behind them – used the conditions better than the home side, whose bowling resources were thin for this match. Australia were 319 for 4 at the end of the first day, Lawry and Walters mixing watchful defence with strong attacking strokes during their stand of 144. Sheahan and Chappell then took charge with 152 for the fifth wicket. After the run-out of Chappell the innings disintegrated. Hampered by drizzle and poor light, England stuttered to 165, saving the follow-on only with the last pair together. Boycott and Edrich made 86 – more than half the total – for the first wicket. Walters' masterly handling of the bowling – especially Pocock's off-spin – ensured that Australia's lead was beyond reasonable expectation as England began the fourth innings with 9¼ hours remaining. South African-born D'Oliveira, playing his strokes late and very powerfully at times, averted a débâcle and Barber showed promise before Hawke got him. Amiss, like his opponent McKenzie, was out twice without scoring. Only 52,037 attended the match.

895, left: *Graveney caught by McKenzie at short leg off Cowper for two.* 896, opposite page, left: *Cowper bowled by Snow for 0.* 897, centre: *Sheahan, who made 88, edges a ball over Graveney at slip.* 898, right: *Walters pulls Pocock in Australia's second innings*

1968 SECOND TEST

Lord's, June 20, 21, 22, 24, 25

England *351 for 7 dec (C. Milburn 83, K.F. Barrington 75, G. Boycott 49, M.C. Cowdrey 45);* Australia *78 (D.J. Brown 5 for 42) and 127 for 4 (I.R. Redpath 53).* Match drawn.

The 200th Test between the two countries coincided with some bad weather, and only half the scheduled 30 hours of play was possible. The first day's play was ended at lunchtime by a prodigious hailstorm when England were 53 for the loss of Edrich to an unplayable lifter from McKenzie. Boycott and Milburn played with conspicuous courage and skill, the latter, one of the heaviest men to play Test cricket, absorbing blow after blow on his legs and body. On the second day he tore into the bowling, adding a six off Cowper (into the grandstand under the Father Time weathervane) to his previous hooked six into the Mound Stand off McKenzie. He was finally caught on the boundary off 'mystery' spinner Gleeson. Cowdrey and Barrington added 97, but the flooding had left its mark, and many were the painful knocks received: Barrington had to retire for a time and Australia's wicketkeeper, Jarman, suffered a chipped finger. Little play was possible on the third day, and Cowdrey declared on the fourth morning, when it was felt Australia might have problems. So it transpired. Lawry, the captain, was wonderfully caught by Knott, and midst a succession of catches as Snow, Brown and Knight (3 for 16) moved the ball in the air and off the pitch were three by Cowdrey at slip – taking him past Hammond's Test record of 110 – and a thrilling full-length catch by Knight at gully to dismiss Walters, who top-scored with 26. Only Gleeson, of the rest, reached double-figures. Lawry and Redpath began with 66 in the follow-on, but play was restricted by the weather to under 2½ hours on the final day. Sheahan batted 50 minutes for 0 not out. Colin Cowdrey had tossed (successfully) with a gold sovereign presented him by Sir Robert Menzies.

899: *The England team meet the Duke of Edinburgh during the 200th Test match. The Duke is about to shake hands with wicketkeeper Knott, with MCC president Arthur Gilligan following*

THE TIMES

**OUND
TER
DAY**

**refuses
fere**

**ays is expected to
yesterday's decision
ocomotive Engineers
-rule from midnight**

**which ran yesterday
to suffer widespread
ion commuters, who
ay, face far greater
the decision by the**

**sport, said yesterday
he dispute. The rail-
eir own and could
nment.**

**n of the Railways
ef decision will com-
ust be worse tomor-
e that we shall find**

**'S A NOTE
RET**

ort Correspondent

said he could offer little
f an early end to the dispute
the railwaymen demanded
rease across the board.

hael Thomas writes:—One
why services were not
worse affected yesterday
mply that more than two-
of the men defied their
's instructions and worked
ne or on their rest days as
Only a handful worked
e in the sense that they
d out their duties in an
mal way.

British Railways Board
consider today whether to
nd the railwaymen's guaran-
eek agreement. This would
it possible to send home men
ithout work by the indus-
ction of others and save the
f their wages.

Henry Johnson, chairman of
ard, said last night that dis-
ary action could not be
against men for working to
r for declining to volunteer
ertime, but it could be taken
t any man who refused to
egitimate instructions.

proposals on train man-
an issue which reached
ock in the productivity nego-
s, were sent to both unions
day with an invitation from
Railways to discuss them
Affecting some 80,000
atemen and guards, they
cost £2m. a year to intro-
but this would be offset by
s. One proposal is that
s' milage bonuses should be
ed by a flat weekly allow-
Another attempts to break
adlock over the manning of
otives by men apart from
s.

n if talks take place on these
sals they are unlikely to
the main dispute, which is
the unions' demand for an
diate all-round increase with-
roductivity conditions.

thern Region cuts, page 2.

**ust act
sh says**

NT—Carlisle, June 24

ime Mr. Marsh was flying to
le.

r could the question be
d to Mr. Swingler, Minister
ate, Ministry of Transport.
as in Lancashire for the day,
ing in the Nelson and Colne
ction campaign.

hout the facts, several
mentarians on both sides of
ouse thought Mr. Marsh had
iorities wrong, for the ques-
dealt with what the Ministry
ing "to minimize inconven-
to public and industry".

Carmichael made a holding
nent decribing the day's
s, and did not allow himself
e drawn into controversy
the dispute.

s. Castle, Secretary of State
mployment and Productivity,
to 10 Downing Street last
to discuss the work-to-rule
Mr. Wilson, but Government
ers went out of their way to
asize that the discussion did
presage any possibility of
rnment intervention to bring
a settlement on terms that
ct with incomes policy. Mr.
n and Mrs. Castle are said
standing firm in their view
the Government's incomes
has been brought under
challenge and they have no
ion of surrendering to the
ure from the railway unions.

liamentary report, page 14.

HOW THE AUSTRALIANS WERE SKITTLED OUT AT LORD'S

England dismissed Australia for 78 in their first innings at Lord's yesterday. Good fast bowling supported by magnificent close-catching combined to put out the Australians for their lowest score in a Test match in this country since 1912. At the close of play Australia had scored 50-0 in their second innings. Report page 15.

W. M. Lawry, c. Knott, b. Brown 0

I. R. Redpath, c. Cowdrey, b. Brown 4

R. M. Cowper, c. Graveney, b. Snow 8

K. D. Walters, c. Knight, b. Brown 26

A. P. Sheahan, c. Knott, b. Knight 6

I. M. Chappell, Lb.w. b. Knight 7
G. D. McKenzie, b. Brown 5

J. W. Gleeson, c. Cowdrey, b. Brown 14

B. N. Jarman retired hurt 0

N. J. N. Hawke, c. Cowdrey, b. Knight 2
A. N. Connolly, not out 0
Extras 6
Total 78

**Gaullist
back w
ma**

From CHARLES H

The victory of the Gaullist par
in the first ballot of the Fren
parliamentary elections yesterd
could turn into a landslide in t
second vote next Sunday. Ev
on the most conservative estimat
the Gaullist majority in the ne
Assembly will be much more su
stantial than it was in the last.

The Government can even lo
forward to the possibility
having an absolute majority in
own right without having to re
on the qualified and critical su
port of M. Giscard d'Estain
Independent Republicans.

On the first vote the Gover
ment has recovered three-fifths
the seats it held in Parliame
with another 333 to be filled. Ve
few of its candidates have fail
to obtain the 10 per cent of vo
cast in the first ballot that th
need to remain in the second, a
a substantial number are very w
placed to win under mutual wit
drawal arrangements which w
be struck with Independent R
publican candidates.

A new development came t
night when M. Pompidou su
gested a similar arrangement
candidates of the centre—offeri
to withdraw the Gaullist candida
if the centrist had emerged in
better place in the first ballot whe
ever there was risk that a co
munist might win.

He went even further. He sa
that he was prepared to withdr

**Inquiry ove
bank chief's
salary**

BY OUR POLITICAL STAFF

Payment of a £4,279 increase
director's remuneration to M
Jocelyn Hambros, chairman
Hambros Bank is being inves
gated by the Department
Employment and Productivi
Mr. Walker, Parliamentary Sec
tary to the Ministry, said in t
Commons yesterday.

He told Mr. Allaun, Labo
M.P. for Salford East, that t
Prices and Incomes White Pap
made it clear that the princip
of the policy applied to directo
remuneration.

"The Government expect dir
tors to show the same sense
responsibility towards these prin
ples as is being asked of wa
and salary earners", he said. "
will be keeping the question
directors' remuneration und
close review, as details beco
increasingly available through t
operation of the Companies A
1967."

Mr. Allaun said in his questi
that the chairman of Hambros h
a rise of from £20,866 to £25,1
a year in the past 12 mont
besides share dividends.

Business News, page 21.

**Police alerted b
strike ship**

FROM OUR CORRESPONDENT

DOVER, JUNE 24

For five hours today memb
of the crew of the Israel s
Avocadocore (18.433 tons) argu
with officials as the vessel lay
anchor in the middle of the f
shrouded harbour at Dov
Police stood by on shore.

The ship, sailing to Brem
haven with a cargo of fruit w
diverted to Dover to land ei
members of the crew who w
refusing to take orders. But wh
the ship was preparing to lea
Dover the crew were still
board.

After immigration officers w
out by launch to board the shi
radio message asked Kent pol
to stand by. The message s
some of the seamen were arm
with knives and wire hawsers.
convoy of vehicles took police
the pierhead, but they were la
withdrawn.

**13 die in Swiss
rail crash**

FROM OUR CORRESPONDENT

GENEVA, JUNE 2

Thirteen people were killed a
119 injured, some seriously, wh
two trains collided head-on o
single-track stretch of the m
line from Lake Geneva to
Simplon tunnel today.

Picture, page 7.

**Woman's body
near camp**

FROM OUR CORRESPONDENT

GUILDFORD, JUNE 2

A murder hunt began toni
after the body of a woman in
early twenties had been fou
naked and mutilated on a tr
near the Women's Royal Ar
Corps depot at Guildford, Surr
She had been strangled and a
attacked with a blunt instrume

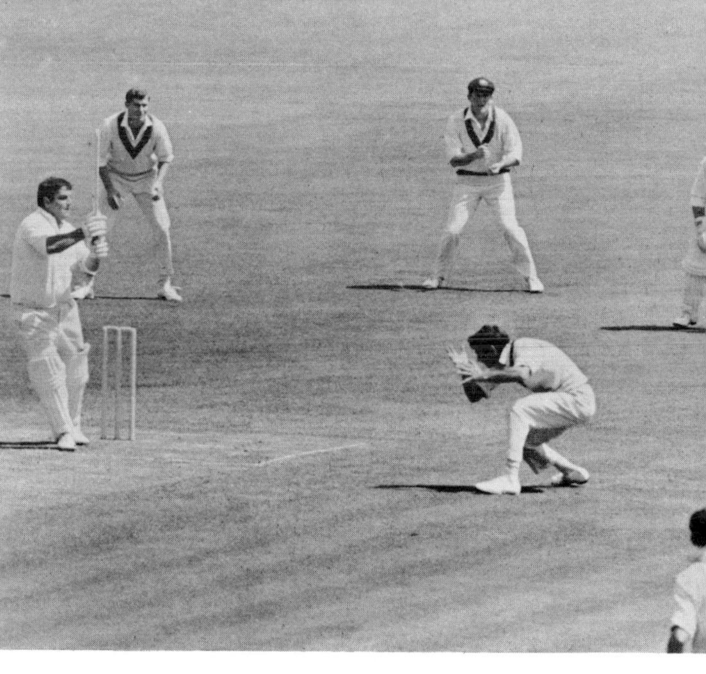

900, left: The Times *considered Australia's collapse for 78 worthy of front-page treatment.* 901, top: *Milburn hooks McKenzie fearlessly for four.* 902, above: *Lord's after the hailstorm; Sydney must have looked similar when the elements rebelled during the third Test of the 1884–85 series*

1968 THIRD TEST
Edgbaston, July 11, 12, 13, 15, 16

England 409 *(M.C. Cowdrey 104, T.W. Graveney 96, J.H. Edrich 88, E.W. Freeman 4 for 78) and 142 for 3 dec (J.H. Edrich 64);* Australia *222 (I.M. Chappell 71, R.M. Cowper 57, K.D. Walters 46) and 68 for 1.* Match drawn.

Further rain spoilt a contest in which England held the upper hand almost throughout. After a blank first day Boycott and Edrich began with 80, and then Cowdey, playing in his 100th Test, put on 108 with Edrich, reaching his celebratory century during a fourth-wicket stand of 93 with Graveney. Cowdrey, who also became only the second batsman (after Hammond) to make 7000 Test runs, badly pulled a leg muscle halfway to his landmark, and had Boycott as a runner. Graveney's 96, like his partner's innings, contained many fine strokes. Australia experienced a grim start, Brown bowling Redpath for nought and Snow breaking Lawry's finger; yet by the third evening they were 109 for one. After Cowper and Chappell were out, however, only Walters lasted long, and the score went from 213 for 4 to 222 all out, with Lawry unable to bat. England extended their lead at more than three runs an over (Graveney leading in Cowdrey's absence), and Australia were set 330 in 370 minutes. Heavy rain before lunch drove the players from the field, and there was no resumption.

903, below, left: *Redpath is bowled by Brown without scoring.* 904, bottom, left: *Australia's captain Lawry, out of action after a blow on the finger by Snow, catches up on his letter-writing.* 905, below, right: *Cowdrey, playing in his 100th Test, drives Gleeson to the boundary.* 906, bottom, right: *Cowdrey is congratulated by Graveney upon reaching his century*

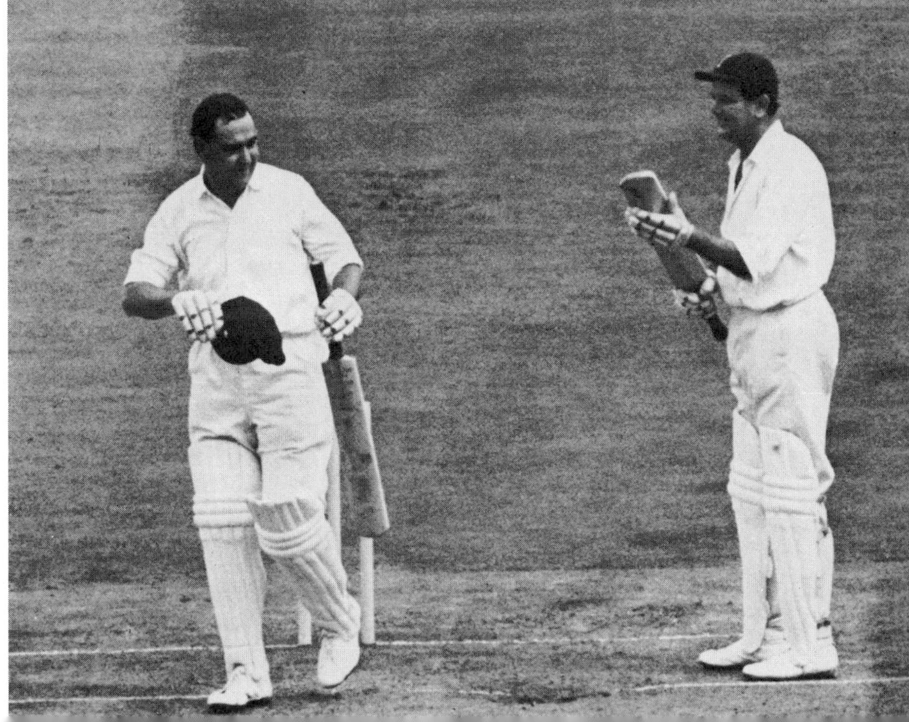

1968 FOURTH TEST

Headingley, July 25, 26, 27, 29, 30

Australia *315 (I.R. Redpath 92, I.M. Chappell 65, K.D. Walters 42, D.L. Underwood 4 for 41) and 312 (I.M. Chappell 81, K.D. Walters 56, I.R. Redpath 48, R. Illingworth 6 for 87)*; England *302 (R.M. Prideaux 64, J.H. Edrich 62, K.F. Barrington 49, D.L. Underwood 45*, A.N. Connolly 5 for 72) and 230 for 4 (J.H. Edrich 65, K.F. Barrington 46*, T.W. Graveney 41).* Match drawn.

Jarman and Graveney led their teams in the absence of the injured Lawry and Cowdrey, and for once there was hardly any weather interruption. Australia held the Ashes by virtue of this draw, and owed much to the young trio of batsmen, Redpath, Walters and Chappell, and the relentless attack of McKenzie and Connolly. For England, Prideaux, playing his only Test against Australia, aided Edrich in an impressive opening stand of 123, after which there was a falling away. It was left to Underwood, the last man, to put on 61 with Brown. Connolly at fast-medium moved the ball around disconcertingly. On the first day Cowper was 15 at lunch after two hours' batting. Walters and Chappell in the second innings were almost as resolute. England's eventual target was 326 at 66 an hour. The risk involved in chasing the bait was too high. Knott made three stumpings off Illingworth in the second innings, but Keith Fletcher's Test debut was unhappy: he missed three sharp slip chances and made nought and 23 not out.

907, top, left: *Prideaux swings a ball to leg only to be caught by Freeman for 64.* 908, left: *Fletcher caught by Jarman down the leg side off Connolly.* 909, above: *Ian Chappell cuts Underwood for four*

910: *Cowper, having made only five at Leeds, is stumped by Knott off Illingworth – a mode of dismissal somewhat rare in modern times*

1968 FIFTH TEST

The Oval, August 22, 23, 24, 26, 27

England *494 (J.H. Edrich 164, B.L. D'Oliveira 158, T.W. Graveney 63) and 181 (A.N. Connolly 4 for 65)*; Australia *324 (W.M. Lawry 135, I.R. Redpath 67, A.A. Mallett 43*) and 125 (R.J. Inverarity 56, D.L. Underwood 7 for 50).* England won by 226 runs.

When Australia were 65 for 5 just before lunch on the final day the match was England's. When a storm turned the field into a lake an abandonment seemed certain – yet again the elements had defied England. Then came a miraculous transformation. The ground staff, helped by volunteers from the crowd, spiked the lower outfield areas and mopped up countless gallons of water, and a resumption was possible at 4.45 pm. England then bowled to no avail for 40 minutes . . . until D'Oliveira bowled Jarman, and Underwood was put on at the pavilion end and used the drying surface to such effect that he took the wickets of Mallett, McKenzie and Gleeson, and – with time for only two more overs – Inverarity, who was on the verge of carrying his bat. Much good cricket had gone before: Edrich's 7¾-hour century (his aggregate for the series was 554), the recalled D'Oliveira's spirited 158, Lawry's stoic century, the only one for Australia in the series – begun on the second evening and ended with a disputed catch behind on the fourth morning – and Redpath's soundness, Mallett's dismissal of Cowdrey in his first over in Test cricket (and his 43 not out in over three hours), England's dash for quick second-innings runs. As Inverarity was given out lbw, each journalist had to rewrite his story.

911, below, left: *Milburn b Connolly 8.* 912, below, right: *Edrich on-drives Gleeson during his 164*

913, top, left: *The Oval outfield is flooded after the storm, but willing hands at the spikers and sacking transformed a seemingly hopeless scene.* 914, centre: *With only a few minutes remaining, Inverarity pads up to Underwood and is lbw. England, against the odds, have won.* 915, left: *23-year-old Underwood, having taken 7 for 50, gives the grateful crowd a wave.* 916, above: *D'Oliveira drives Ian Chappell on his way to 158*

1970–71 FIRST TEST

Brisbane, November 27, 28, 29, December 1, 2

Australia 433 *(K.R. Stackpole 207, K.D. Walters 112, I.M. Chappell 59, J.A. Snow 6 for 114) and 214 (W.M. Lawry 84, K. Shuttleworth 5 for 47);* England 464 *(J.H. Edrich 79, B.W. Luckhurst 74, A.P.E. Knott 73, B.L. D'Oliveira 57) and 39 for 1.* Match drawn.

Australia rode high at 372 for 2 on the second day, only to collapse against Snow and Underwood. Indeed, the last seven wickets fell for 15 runs. Stackpole, very strong in the cut and hook, hit 25 fours and a six, though he was lucky to survive a run-out appeal at 18, and gave two sharp chances. His robust batting was in marked contrast with that of Lawry, his opening partner, who in the second innings held his side together with 84 in 5½ hours. Chappell and Stackpole added 151, and Walters, sometimes brilliant, sometimes uncomfortable, put on 209 with the double-centurion. Luckhurst batted most convincingly for England, most of the others taking their time about their runs – time that might better have been used chasing victory after Shuttleworth with the new ball had hurried through Australia's tail on the last day.

917: *Stackpole receives the benefit of a close run-out call at 18 (bowler Shuttleworth in mid-air). The Australian opener went on to 207*

918: *Over the top – six runs for Stackpole off Illingworth*

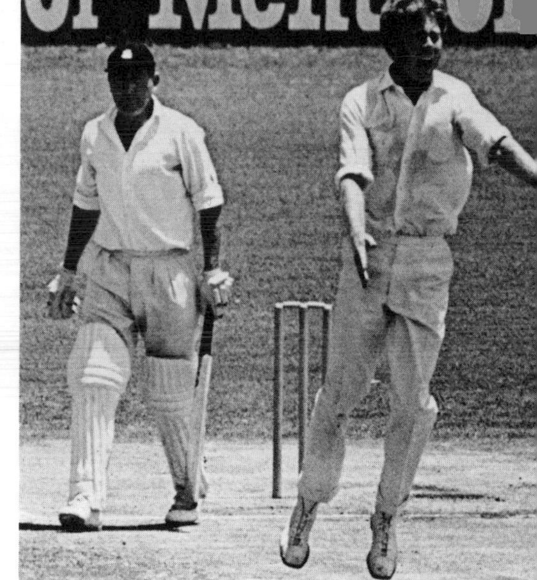

919, above, left: *Illingworth at short leg dives to pick up a catch from Redpath.* 920, right: *'Froggy' Thomson takes his only wicket of the match – Illingworth, caught by Marsh*

1970–71 — SECOND TEST

Perth, December 11, 12, 13, 15, 16

England 397 *(B.W. Luckhurst 131, G. Boycott 70, J.H. Edrich 47, M.C. Cowdrey 40, G.D. McKenzie 4 for 66) and 287 for 6 dec (J.H. Edrich 115*, G. Boycott 50);* Australia 440 *(I.R. Redpath 171, G.S. Chappell 108, I.M. Chappell 50, R.W. Marsh 44, J.A. Snow 4 for 143) and 100 for 3.* Match drawn.

Perth's first Test match, well-attended, was distinguished by a debut century from Greg Chappell, who saved his side with a stand of 219 with Redpath, who made his first hundred against England. Replying to England's 397, which was founded on an opening of 171 by Boycott and Luckhurst, Australia were 107 for 5 after Snow's early breakthrough. The 22-year-old Chappell then went in and settled against the pace bowlers, stepping up the attack after tea to such an extent that 74 runs came from 10 overs. His innings lasted little more than half the time taken by Redpath. England were unhappy against Gleeson, and on the final day were in some peril, until Illingworth and then Knott stayed with Edrich. A token declaration was made when safety had been reached, and Lawry saw out the 32 overs, making 38 not out, which included his 5000th Test run and his 2000th against England.

921: *Luckhurst bowled by McKenzie after his plucky 131*

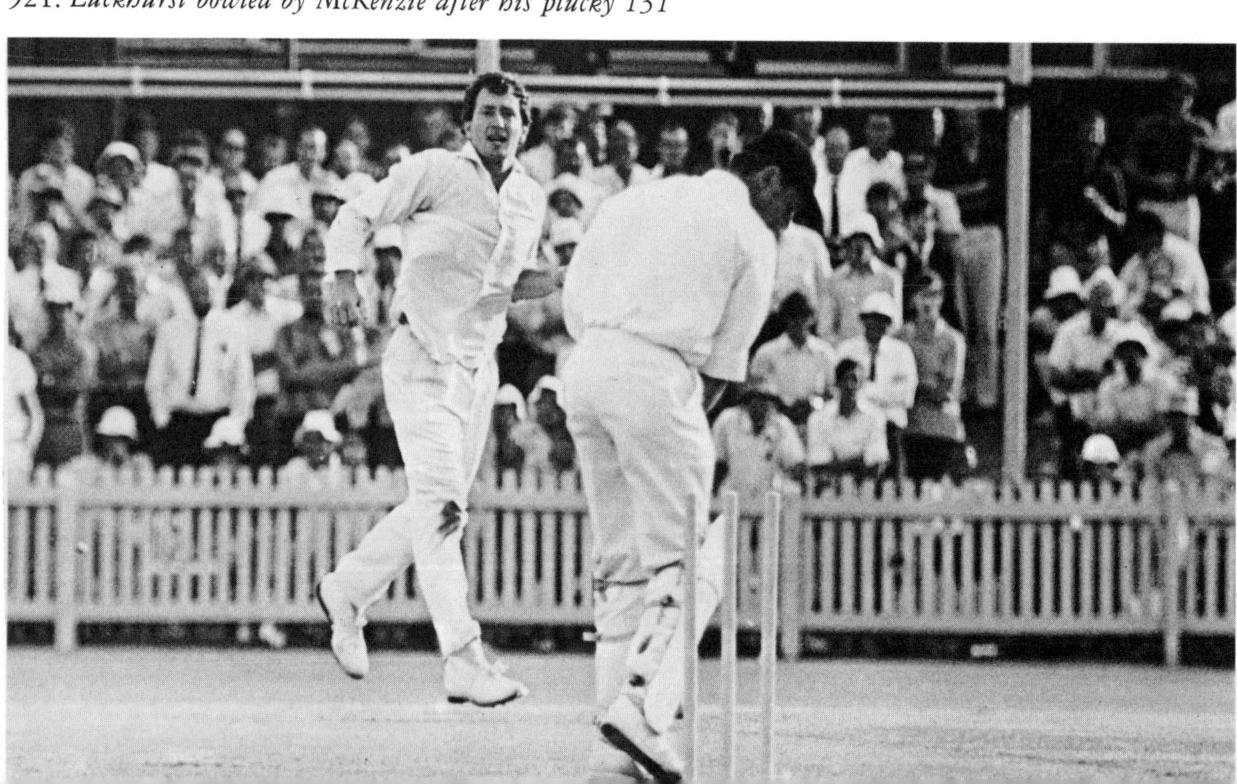

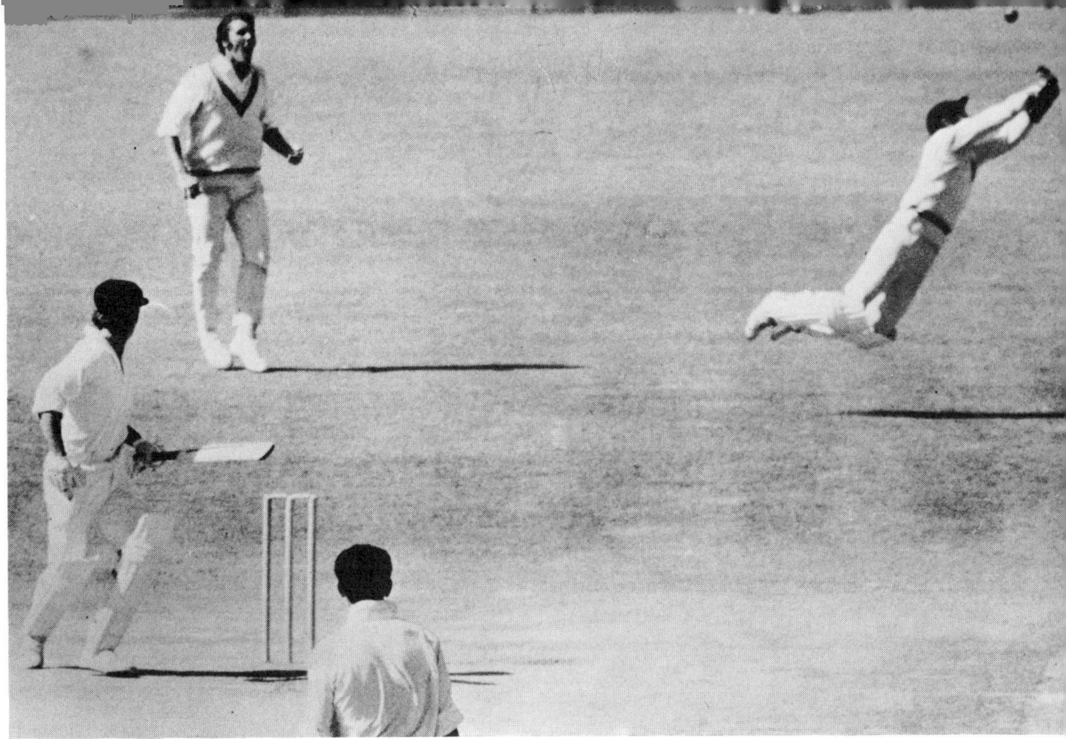

922 above: *Greg Chappell, Australia's fine discovery, during his debut century.* 923, top, right: *Knott leaps to a touch off Ian Chappell's glove, but fails to hold it.* 924, right: *A portion of Perth's population invades the pitch to let Greg Chappell know they appreciate his hundred*

1970–71 FOURTH TEST

Sydney, January 9, 10, 12, 13, 14

England *332 (G. Boycott 77, J.H. Edrich 55, A.A. Mallett 4 for 40, J.W. Gleeson 4 for 83) and 319 for 5 dec (G. Boycott 142*, B.L. D'Oliveira 56, R. Illingworth 53);* Australia *236 (I.R. Redpath 64, K.D. Walters 55, D.L. Underwood 4 for 66) and 116 (W.M. Lawry 60*, J.A. Snow 7 for 40).* England won by 299 runs.

The New Year's Test at Melbourne having been washed out without a ball bowled (though the captains did toss), it was decided to stage an extra Test and to play a one-day international in Melbourne. This match at Sydney, therefore, had three to follow it; and England seized the chance to go one-up with some high-class batting and Snow's fiery bowling on a pitch which had seemed more in favour of spin. Boycott and Luckhurst began the match with 116, and the consistent Edrich again played his part. Mallett then unbalanced England with a spell of 3 for 6, but the later batsmen recovered the initiative. Only Redpath and Walters, with a stand of 99, withstood the varied England attack for long, and when the touring side went in again 96 ahead, quick runs were needed. Boycott obliged with a technically admirable innings, adding 133 with D'Oliveira after three wickets had fallen for 48. Illingworth's bowlers were then left over nine hours to dispose of Australia – who survived less than half that time in the face of Snow's devastation. Lawry carried his bat; McKenzie had his nose smashed by a lifting ball; Australia's batsmen seemed not to know which way to turn against such hostility.

925, above, left: *Knott is stumped by Marsh, his opposite number.* 926 above, right: *Lever makes a magnificent catch in the gully to end Stackpole's innings.* 927, below, left: *Mallett, caught by Knott, gives Willis his first Test wicket.* 928, below, right: *McKenzie is hit in the face by a ball from Snow; he retired hurt with blood pouring from the wound*

1970–71 — FIFTH TEST
Melbourne, January 21, 22, 23, 25, 26

Australia *493 for 9 dec (I.M. Chappell 111, R.W. Marsh 92*, I.R. Redpath 72, W.M. Lawry 56, K.D. Walters 55) and 169 for 4 dec (W.M. Lawry 42)*; England *392 (B.L. D'Oliveira 117, B.W. Luckhurst 109, R. Illingworth 41) and 161 for 0 (G. Boycott 76*, J.H. Edrich 74*).* Match drawn.

England's deplorable fielding – Cowdrey in particular had a wretched match – forced them into second place throughout a match notable for unpleasant crowd behaviour. The field was overrun when Chappell reached his century, and several items were stolen in the mêlée. Catcalling was prevalent also. Chappell and Redpath scored fast in the last session of a hot first day, which ended at 260 for one, Lawry having retired with a damaged finger. Wicketkeeper Marsh, an aggressive left-hander, dominated the second day, hitting his way to the verge of a unique (for Australia) hundred when Lawry declared. England, 88 for 3 and in serious danger, were stabilised by Luckhurst – who batted for most of his innings with a broken little finger – and D'Oliveira, who also went on to a century, driving and cutting with great force. The first-innings disparity became less than expected, but Australia were slow to capitalise, and advanced at less then four an over. Nonetheless, they had four hours in which to dismiss England. Illingworth's attitude, in return, was to decline the invitation to make 271, and to the accompaniment of clanking beer-cans England's openers played out time.

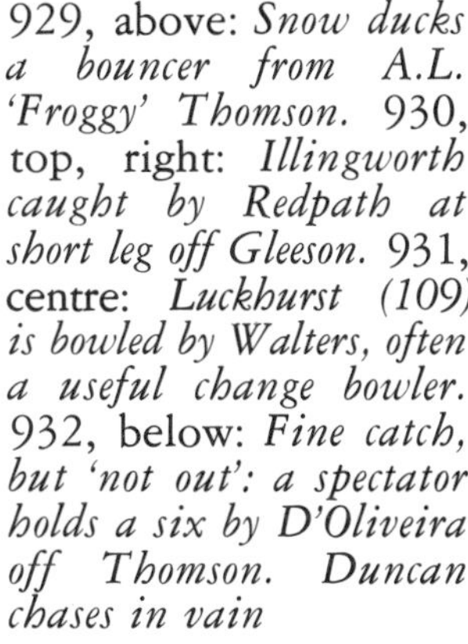

929, above: *Snow ducks a bouncer from A.L. 'Froggy' Thomson.* 930, top, right: *Illingworth caught by Redpath at short leg off Gleeson.* 931, centre: *Luckhurst (109) is bowled by Walters, often a useful change bowler.* 932, below: *Fine catch, but 'not out': a spectator holds a six by D'Oliveira off Thomson. Duncan chases in vain*

1970–71 SIXTH TEST

Adelaide, January 29, 30, February 1, 2, 3

England 470 *(J.H. Edrich 130, K.W.R. Fletcher 80, G. Boycott 58, J.H. Hampshire 55, B.L. D'Oliveira 47, D.K. Lillee 5 for 84) and 233 for 4 dec (G. Boycott 119*, R. Illingworth 48*, J.H. Edrich 40);* Australia 235 *(K.R. Stackpole 87, P. Lever 4 for 49) and 328 for 3 (K.R. Stackpole 136, I.M. Chappell 104).* Match drawn.

England, with century opening stands by Boycott and Edrich in both innings, controlled this match, and though there was much debate upon Illingworth's decision not to enforce the follow-on, he was probably right, since the pitch was benevolent and his fast bowlers were engaged in four Tests in five weeks. Boycott brought much criticism down on his head from near and far by throwing his bat to the ground in annoyance after being given run-out, but the momentum of the innings was maintained with a stand of 169 between the patient Edrich and Fletcher, whose first notable Test innings this was. Solid middle batting saw England to a near-impregnable total, Lillee, in his first Test, keeping up his pace well and taking five wickets. Stackpole, with 87 out of 117, was the soul of a disappointing Australian innings, Snow, Lever, Underwood, Willis and Illingworth going about their job determinedly. Boycott was in sprightly form as England set about extending their lead, and Australia were finally left with 500 minutes and a target of 469. They began the last day at 104 for the loss of Lawry. Stackpole and Chappell put on 202 for the second wicket, the former batting almost seven hours, Chappell 5½, and at last Australia had batted for a day and a half without being dismissed.

933, above: *Stackpole b Underwood 87.* 934, centre: *Boycott, having been run out, is prompted to leave the field by Australian fieldsmen close enough to detect his reluctance.* 935, below: *Walters caught behind off Lever*

1970–71
Sydney, February 12, 13, 14, 16, 17

England *184 (R. Illingworth 42) and 302 (B.W. Luckhurst 59, J.H. Edrich 57, B.L. D'Oliveira 47);* Australia *264 (G.S. Chappell 65, I.R. Redpath 59, K.D. Walters 42) and 160 (K.R. Stackpole 67).* England won by 62 runs.

Ray Illingworth, in leading his side to a 2-0 victory, became the first to captain England in recapture of the Ashes in Australia since D.R. Jardine 38 years earlier. His opposing captain this time was Ian Chappell, Lawry having been dropped. The 27-year-old South Australian, grandson of V.Y. Richardson, put England in to bat, and had them out by 5.18 pm, spinners Jenner and O'Keeffe taking three wickets each. The second day was eventful. Redpath and Walters halted a collapse, but in the last session Snow cut Jenner's head with a lifting ball, was warned by umpire Rowan, and then had his shirt grabbed by an inebriated spectator on the long-leg fence. Beer-cans rained onto the ground, Illingworth sat down, as did others in his team, and soon the England captain was leading his men off the field. The umpires warned him that he would forfeit the match if he did not return, and, peace restored, Australia were ahead that evening with three wickets left. The final lead of 80 was cleared in the first-wicket stand of Edrich and Luckhurst, the Kent right-hander this time proving an able replacement for the injured Boycott. The first nine batsmen all reached double-figures, and gradually Australia were set a stiffish target. Snow bowled Eastwood, Lawry's replacement, with no run yet scored, but then broke his right forefinger running for a big hit to the long-leg pickets. This placed extra onus on Underwood and Illingworth, who carried England's hopes on the fifth-day pitch. The last day began with Australia 123 for 5 – 100 needed, Greg Chappell and Marsh in. Illingworth got the vital wicket, that of Chappell, by drifting one past his bat and having him stumped. With surprising ease the rest were accounted for, and England's 38-year-old captain was chaired by his players from the field.

936, below, left: *Jenner collapses after being struck by a lifting ball from Snow. The incident brought a warning to the bowler from umpire Rowan.* 937, below, right: *Snow's shirt is grabbed by a spectator on the Paddington Hill – another irritating moment in an inflammatory afternoon*

938, above: *The victorious MCC side of 1970–71 record* The Ashes Song *as a permanent if unmelodic souvenir of an historic win.* 939, centre: *England's triumph coincided with a British postal strike, and a London delivery service chose what purported to be the final ball of the series as the motif on their first-day cover.* 940, below: *England did it without two key players, Snow and Boycott, seen nursing their injuries after the match*

1972 FIRST TEST
Old Trafford, June 8, 9, 10, 12, 13

England *249 (A.W. Greig 57, J.H. Edrich 49) and 234 (A.W. Greig 62, G. Boycott 47, D.K. Lillee 6 for 66)*; Australia *142 (K.R. Stackpole 53, J.A. Snow 4 for 41, G.G. Arnold 4 for 62) and 252 (R.W. Marsh 91, K.R. Stackpole 67, A.W. Greig 4 for 53, J.A. Snow 4 for 87)*. England won by 89 runs.

A poorly-attended match, marred by long periods of cold and damp weather, offered encouragement to bowlers throughout, and Snow and Arnold used the conditions best of all. Swinging and cutting the ball, they continually pressed the Australians. The fielding of both sides was not at its best, and Arnold once saw three catches go down in one of his overs. Tony Greig, South African-born, and at 6ft 7½ins the tallest cricketer to play in these Tests, had a superb Test debut, batting boldly in both innings, holding two catches, and taking five wickets. Stackpole chanced his luck in the first innings and batted 3½ hours in the second, but in contrast Ian Chappell, the captain, was out twice cheaply as he hooked. Marsh, who took five catches behind the wicket in England's second innings, thrashed 91 in a late gesture of defiance, putting Gifford four times into the crowd, but they were English conditions, and the competent home side always seemed to have a command – however tenuous – of the match. Illingworth, 40 on the opening day, had taken the chance when it offered . . . and was to be glad of it as Chappell's young side found itself as the series progressed.

941, above, left: *Stackpole, having been missed off the previous ball, watches Snow put him down at slip off Arnold.* 942, above, right: *M.J.K. Smith caught behind off Lillee, England second innings.* 943, right: *Marsh lashes Greig through the covers as he races to 91 in a lost cause*

1972 SECOND TEST

Lord's, June 22, 23, 24, 26

England 272 (*A.W. Greig 54, A.P.E. Knott 43, R.A.L. Massie 8 for 84) and 116 (R.A.L. Massie 8 for 53)*; Australia 308 (*G.S. Chappell 131, I.M. Chappell 56, R.W. Marsh 50, J.A. Snow 5 for 57) and 81 for 2 (K.R. Stackpole 57*)*. Australia won by 8 wickets.

Bob Massie, a 25-year-old Western Australian (the state had four men in the Test XI for the first time), put his name on this match with an astonishing exhibition of swing bowling – mostly from around the wicket – to return analyses of 32.5-7-84-8 and 27.2-9-53-8. These are easily the best figures in a Test debut, and for Australia in any Test. He curved the ball suddenly and late, either way and to a length, and no England player could work out a reliable method of combating him. The other four wickets went to Lillee, who bowled fast and accurately. The biggest stand of England's first innings was 96 by Greig (making his third half-century in as many Test innings) and Knott. Australia began disastrously, but the Chappells steadied the innings, the upright Greg going on to a beautiful fighting century, batting in all for 6¼ hours. Marsh hit a strong 50 to gain a lead for Australia, only Snow drawing prolonged respect from the batsmen. By Saturday evening Massie had shattered England again. At 86 for 9 they were a mere 50 ahead. Massie took his 16th wicket on Monday morning, and the runs were obtained with a minimum of fuss, Stackpole hitting out in no-nonsense fashion. One-all the series stood, and if Massie had been fit for the first Test, the tourists might well have been two-up.

944, left: *The members at Lord's rise to Greg Chappell at the end of his century innings.* 945, above: *Boycott, bemused and bowled, becomes one of Massie's 16 victims in the match*

946, left: *Smith, with no answer to the violent swing of the ball, is bowled by Massie.* 947, above: *The effect of victory: Marsh, Massie, manager Steele, Lillee, Mallett, Edwards, and Hammond (seated) react to Australia's series-levelling win*

1972 — THIRD TEST

Trent Bridge, July 13, 14, 15, 17, 18

Australia *315 (K.R. Stackpole 114, D.J. Colley 54, R.W. Marsh 41, J.A. Snow 5 for 92) and 324 for 4 dec (R. Edwards 170*, G.S. Chappell 72, I.M. Chappell 50)*; England *189 (D.K. Lillee 4 for 35, R.A.L. Massie 4 for 43) and 290 for 4 (B.W. Luckhurst 96, B.L. D'Oliveira 50*, P.H. Parfitt 46).* Match drawn.

Illingworth put Australia in, assured that the pitch would become easier the longer the match went on. The ploy might have worked, but for feeble outcricket. Parfitt held four fine slip catches, but missed Stackpole when 46. The burly opener was in for 5½ hours, steering his side to a sound position. Marsh and Colley gave a boost to the tail, but had Snow had better support Australia could have been in trouble. Instead, England struggled. They took 6½ hours to make 189 – though only 88.3 overs were bowled. Luckhurst was two hours reaching double-figures. Marsh held five catches behind the stumps, and was often stretched by Lillee's bouncers and widish deliveries. Once more Massie swung the ball disconcertingly. In place of the injured Francis, Edwards opened with Stackpole, and grasped his opportunity well. He added 124 with Ian Chappell and 146 with Greg, and had been in for 5½ hours when the innings was closed. England needed 451 – a somewhat academic calculation – and had 9½ hours left. Luckhurst, in making England's highest score of the entire series, provided the base for survival, putting on 117 with Parfitt, and after a ripple of tension as three wickets fell, D'Oliveira and Greig played out time.

948: *Lillee bowling during the D'Oliveira-Greig stand on the final day that assured England of a draw*

949, left: *Greg Chappell b Snow 72 at Trent Bridge.* 950, above: *Edwards swings at a ball from Illingworth, taken by Knott*

1972 FOURTH TEST

Headingley, July 27, 28, 29

Australia *146 (K.R. Stackpole 52, D.L. Underwood 4 for 37) and 136 (A.P. Sheahan 41*, D.L. Underwood 6 for 45);* England *263 (R. Illingworth 57, J.A. Snow 48, J.H. Edrich 45, A.A. Mallett 5 for 114) and 21 for 1.* England won by 9 wickets.

The sub-standard nature of the Leeds pitch – put down to devastation of the turf by fusarium disease when heavy rain compelled lengthy protection under covers – allowed the spinners to achieve turn even before lunch on the opening day. Australia were 79 for one at lunch, but on the bare, drying wicket they tumbled to 146 all out, Underwood using the ideal conditions to take 4 for 37 off 31 overs and Illingworth taking two wickets and two catches in the field. Edrich and Luckhurst made 43 that evening, but by lunch on the second day England were struggling at 112 for 6, Mallett, pushing through his off-breaks, having taken five quality wickets, and Inverarity, not usually a front-line bowler, mesmerising the batsmen with slow left-arm. The innings was saved by Illingworth and Snow, who made 104 for the eighth wicket, the captain batting in all for 4½ hours. Australia were given little chance against Underwood and Illingworth in their second innings: and so it transpired. After Edwards had followed his big score at Nottingham with a 'pair', and Arnold had got Ian Chappell caught behind for nought, Underwood tore through the middle in a spell of 5 for 18. The ball turned quickly and often lifted. Only Sheahan, playing straight, faced his task without the air of a condemned man. At 5.03 pm England had retained the Ashes; but some bitter discussions ensued.

951, above: *Ian Chappell caught-and-bowled by Illingworth.* 952, top, right: *Sheahan brilliantly caught by Illingworth off Underwood.* 953, centre: *Mallett dives and just misses a caught-and-bowled chance from Edrich.* 954, below: *Stackpole, already halfway through a run, receives the bad news: he is lbw to Underwood for 28 in the second innings*

1972 FIFTH TEST

The Oval, August 10, 11, 12, 14, 15, 16

England 284 (*A.P.E. Knott 92, P.H. Parfitt 51, J.H. Hampshire 42, D.K. Lillee 5 for 58) and 356 (B. Wood 90, A.P.E. Knott 63, B.L. D'Oliveira 43, D.K. Lillee 5 for 123);* Australia 399 (*I.M. Chappell 118, G.S. Chappell 113, R. Edwards 79, D.L. Underwood 4 for 90) and 242 for 5 (K.R. Stackpole 79, A.P. Sheahan 44*, R.W. Marsh 43*).* Australia won by 5 wickets.

A fine match concluded halfway through the sixth day in a result which gave much satisfaction to the Australians – and suspense and entertainment to everyone in its achievement. England were humbled on the first day by Lillee, varying his pace and using the bouncer to effect, and Mallett, now a nagging off-spinner. Knott, batting inventively and bravely, then led Arnold in a stand of 81. Australia's innings was built upon a third-wicket stand of 201 by the Chappells – the first instance of centuries by brothers in a Test match. Ian bustled, was watchful, and quick to pounce on wayward deliveries; Greg was cool and stylish and just as unemotional. They took their side within sight of the England total, and Edwards, solidly, steered Australia to a useful lead on an interrupted third day. Underwood prevented a greater deficit. Wood, in his first Test, batted fearlessly and correctly until Massie had him lbw, but it took another nimble innings from Knott to set up a sizable target for Australia. He was last out – Lillee's 31st wicket of the series: a record for Australia in England. The fast bowler sent down 56.4 overs in the match, to take 10 for 181. Set 242, Australia were 116 for one on the fifth evening, by which time Illingworth had been put out of the match with a sprained ankle. With D'Oliveira also unable to bowl and Snow with a damaged arm from a Lillee bouncer, England, now led by Edrich, made little impression. After Ian Chappell and Stackpole had added 116 for the second wicket, three wickets fell quickly, but Sheahan and Marsh in their contrasting manners gathered 71 in an unfinished stand that gave Australia – for the first time without a New South Wales player – a victory to square the series.

955, top, left: *Parfitt loses his middle stump to a quick one from Lillee.* 956, bottom: *Hampshire succumbs to a high slip catch by Ian Chappell.* 957, top, right: *D'Oliveira is victim of a smart catch by Greg Chappell.* 958, bottom: *Ian Chappell edges Illingworth through the vacant slips area to reach his century*

959, left: *Wood (90) stands up and drives Mallett for four.* 960, right: *Sheahan and Marsh hurry off after an Australian victory which marked the emergence of a strong, young side, led positively by Ian Chappell*

1974–75 FIRST TEST

Brisbane, November 29, 30, December 1, 3, 4

Australia *309 (I.M. Chappell 90, G.S. Chappell 58, M.H.N. Walker 41*, R.G.D. Willis 4 for 56) and 288 for 5 dec (G.S. Chappell 71, K.D. Walters 62*, R. Edwards 53, R.W. Marsh 46*);* England *265 (A.W. Greig 110, J.H. Edrich 48, M.H.N. Walker 4 for 73) and 166 (J.R. Thomson 6 for 46).* Australia won by 166 runs.

Australia's new fast bowler Jeff Thomson – a strong, athletic slinger of the ball – and his opening partner Dennis Lillee, who had come back after a serious back injury, established a mastery over England which was to last until towards the end of the series, when both sustained injuries. The opening Test, on a dubious pitch hastily prepared after storms, was won as much by their bowling, backed by Walker's medium-pace, as anything else. Ian Chappell saw to it that the first Australian innings rose to some height, and his brother was watchful in both innings. England's misfortunes were compounded by Amiss's broken thumb and Edrich's broken hand – both caused by very fast balls. Greig's was the exceptional innings of the match. Willis and Lever may have been hostile at times, but the tall England batsman had to contend with the raw, sometimes wild, and lifting speed of Thomson and the deft variations of the only slightly less fast Lillee. Greig drove them and sliced them over slips with great arrogance. His century was only the second ever for England at the Woolloongabba ground. Ten for none at the start of the last day, England could not cope with Thomson until he began to tire. Using the yorker to effect, and with the support of an umbrella field that was to serve Australia exceedingly well during the series, he took 6 for 46, and Australia, one-up, seemed to be well on the way to regaining the Ashes.

961: *'Ashes to ashes, dust to dust – if Thomson don't get ya, Lillee must . . . .' Rigby's famous cartoon in the Sydney* Sunday Telegraph *which summed up the 1974–75 series*

962, left: *Greig reaches a bold century and shows his pleasure.* 963, centre: *Second-innings comedown: b Thomson 2.* 964, right: *Thomson, having taken 6 for 46, comes in to face the backslapping and the worship*

1974–75 SECOND TEST

Perth, December 13, 14, 15, 17

England *208 (A.P.E. Knott 51, D. Lloyd 49) and 293 (F.J. Titmus 61, C.M. Old 43, M.C. Cowdrey 41, J.R. Thomson 5 for 93);* Australia *481 (R. Edwards 115, K.D. Walters 103, G.S. Chappell 62, I.R. Redpath 41, R.W. Marsh 41) and 23 for 1.* Australia won by 9 wickets.

On the fast Perth pitch Australia's superiority was revealed in fast bowling, batting and fielding (17 out of 18 catches offered were held – a record seven of them by Greg Chappell). Thomson, with seven wickets in the match, created further difficulties for England by inflicting agonising blows on Luckhurst's hand and Lloyd's abdomen. Cowdrey had been flown out as a reinforcement, and found himself going out to bat only four days after arrival. He, Knott and Titmus (playing his first Test for seven years, and 42 years old, like Cowdrey) were the only England batsmen to get into the line of the bowling with consistency. Australia, having put England in, then batted solidly down the order, Edwards, strong off the back foot, adding 170 with Walters, who reached his century – and a hundred between tea and the close of the second day – by hooking a short ball from Willis, the last of the day, for six. The innings restored Walters' reputation. The pattern of the match reaffirmed that Mike Denness's side were outclassed.

965: *David Lloyd wishes he were somewhere else after taking a quick one from Thomson in the groin on the fast Perth pitch*

966, left: *Veteran Colin Cowdrey, flown out as a reinforcement, resisted bravely, then was bowled by Thomson.* 967, right: *Walters pulls Willis for six to reach his century – and a hundred between tea and close of play at Perth*

1974–75 THIRD TEST
Melbourne, December 26, 27, 28, 30, 31

England *242 (A.P.E. Knott 52, J.H. Edrich 49, J.R. Thomson 4 for 72) and 244 (D.L. Amiss 90, A.W. Greig 60, D. Lloyd 44, A.A. Mallett 4 for 60, J.R. Thomson 4 for 71);* Australia *241 (I.R. Redpath 55, R.W. Marsh 44, R.G.D. Willis 5 for 61) and 238 for 8 (G.S. Chappell 61, R.W. Marsh 40, A.W. Greig 4 for 56).* Match drawn.

With 55 runs needed in the final hour, and four wickets in hand, Australia dithered, Marsh and Walker making only seven runs off seven overs from Titmus and Underwood. England took the new ball, and a brief batting assault took place; then Underwood bowled the penultimate over, 14 still needed. It was a model maiden. Greig bowled the last, dismissing Lillee, and the draw was played out, Australia eight runs and England two wickets short of victory. Chappell had put England in again, before 77,165 spectators on Boxing Day. Edrich and Cowdrey made 76 for the third wicket, but there was no other prolonged resistance until Knott went in. Willis, bowling shortish spells, was fast and lively, and his effort was doubly important since he lacked the support of Hendrick, who bowled 2.6 overs only before pulling a hamstring. Amiss, having batted splendidly, was caught off Mallett two runs short of R.B. Simpson's record aggregate of 1381 runs in Tests in a calendar year. He gave England a start of 115 with Lloyd, but the middle of the innings fell away in familiar fashion, only an extrovert innings by Greig, supported by Willis, seeing to it that Australia needed to make marginally the highest total of the match to win. In the event neither side was disposed to commit itself boldly enough for victory. Thomson now had 24 wickets in three Tests.

968, below, left: *Redpath c Knott b Greig 55.* 969, right: *Amiss drives during his 90, which left him two runs short of Simpson's calendar-year aggregate of 1381 in all Tests (passed by Viv Richards in 1976)*

970, above: *Titmus sunk by an agonising blow on the knee from Thomson.* 971, centre: *Typifying the glorious catching of the Australians, Greg Chappell ensnares Cowdrey at Melbourne.* 972, above: *Marsh is told the direction of the dressing-room by Greig, who has just dismissed him in Australia's second innings. Verbal exchanges were a feature of the series*

1974–75 — FOURTH TEST

Sydney, January 4, 5, 6, 8, 9

Australia *405 (G.S. Chappell 84, R.B. McCosker 80, I.M. Chappell 53, G.G. Arnold 5 for 86, A.W. Greig 4 for 104) and 289 for 4 dec (G.S. Chappell 144, I.R. Redpath 105);* England *295 (A.P.E. Knott 82, J.H. Edrich 50, J.R. Thomson 4 for 74) and 228 (A.W. Greig 54, A.A. Mallett 4 for 21).* Australia won by 171 runs.

Australia regained the Ashes, four years after losing them on the same ground, with a decisive victory achieved with 5.3 overs in hand. Denness dropped himself for this match, Edrich taking over the captaincy, and the veteran left-hander had two ribs cracked first ball from Lillee on the last day, which forced him into the casualty ward. He returned, and held fast for 33 not out, showing that but for the accident England might reasonably have expected to play out time. McCosker had a distinguished first Test innings, opening for the first time in big cricket, and once more the Chappells contributed valuably. Lillee, Thomson and Walker again did an effective job, only Edrich, who batted 3¾ hours, and Knott, driving spiritedly, offering any real fight. Lloyd brilliantly caught Ian Chappell at leg slip as Australia's second innings got under way, but Greg Chappell and Redpath then partook of a stand of 220. The bowling was tight – especially that of Arnold – but Chappell's hundred had an inevitability about it. Redpath's took two hours longer. England were thus set 400 in 8½ hours. A thunderstorm cut 95 minutes away that evening, but having progressed to 68 without loss on the last day, England began to lose wickets to the fast bowlers and then to Mallett's off-spin. Fletcher was once hit on the head, the ball flying to cover, and Greig was stumped at the peak of the crisis. A calamitous afternoon for England; a day of unbounded joy for Australia. The attendance of 178,027 was a Sydney match record.

973, below, left: *Fletcher hit on his St George and Dragon badge by a ball from Thomson which bounced off to cover point.* 974, right: *Edrich helped off after taking his first ball, from Lillee, in the ribs; two were cracked*

975, left: *Greg Chappell hits Willis for four during his 144.* 976, right, top: *The Ashes are won, with Arnold's dismissal, and Marsh rushes to shake his captain's hand.* 977, below: *The Sydney Hill with 1975 decor. During this Test 864,000 empty beer-cans had to be cleared away*

1974–75 FIFTH TEST

Adelaide, January 25, 26, 27, 29, 30

Australia *304 (T.J. Jenner 74, K.D. Walters 55, M.H.N. Walker 41, D.L. Underwood 7 for 113) and 272 for 5 dec (K.D. Walters 71*, R.W. Marsh 55, I.R. Redpath 52, I.M. Chappell 41, D.L. Underwood 4 for 102);* England *172 (M.H. Denness 51, K.W.R. Fletcher 40, D.K. Lillee 4 for 49) and 241 (A.P.E. Knott 106*, K.W.R. Fletcher 63, D.K. Lillee 4 for 69).* Australia won by 163 runs.

After the first day was lost through rain, Australia found themselves put in to bat by Denness, who soon had Underwood bowling on a drying pitch. Australia advanced to 52, then the left-arm spinner struck. Soon after lunch Australia were 84 for 5 – all to Underwood. It was felt by many that Titmus should have been used at the other end, but Denness's policy was to contain, and the off-spinner had only one over before lunch and seven in the innings. Walters and Jenner extricated their side by aggressive means, and as the pitch eased, Australia forgot their woes with a total of 304. England, Denness and Fletcher apart, then batted dismally. Lillee bowled at a great pace, and Thomson took three top wickets, taking his aggregate for the series to 33, a final figure since a shoulder injury when he played tennis on the rest day kept him from the rest of the series. Australia, with Willis laid low by knee damage, remorselessly enlarged their lead, Walters and Marsh accelerating to a 112-run stand before the closure, and once more England faced a target that was clearly beyond them. Amiss, Arnold and Underwood all completed 'pairs', but Knott, with the last man in with him, reached only the second century in these Test matches by a wicketkeeper.

978, left: *Greig, intimidatingly close at point, catches Redpath off Underwood.* 979, right: *Knott pulls during his century*

980, left: *Ian Chappell miscues a ball from Underwood on the first morning; the ball fell into Knott's gloves.* 981, right: *Lloyd wonderfully caught down the leg side by Marsh off Lillee at Adelaide*

1974–75 SIXTH TEST

Melbourne, February 8, 9, 10, 12, 13

Australia *152 (I.M. Chappell 65, P. Lever 6 for 38) and 373 (G.S. Chappell 102, I.R. Redpath 83, R.B. McCosker 76, I.M. Chappell 50, A.W. Greig 4 for 88);* England *529 (M.H. Denness 188, K.W.R. Fletcher 146, A.W. Greig 89, J.H. Edrich 70, M.H.N. Walker 8 for 143).* England won by an innings and 4 runs.

With Thomson out of the side and Lillee retiring with a foot injury after six overs (having inflicted a third consecutive 'duck' on Amiss), England seized the opportunity to come to terms with comparatively ordinary bowling after Peter Lever had routed Australia on a humid morning, a damp patch serving as a psychological if not physical hazard (though Greg Chappell was hit in the jaw by a Lever flyer). The Lancastrian kept the ball well up, in contrast to his last Test, at Brisbane, when he took 0 for 111. He took four key wickets for five runs in one spell. Only a dogged innings by Ian Chappell spared Australia total humiliation. After having made only one century stand in the series to date, England now enjoyed three in a row: 149 by Edrich and Denness for the third wicket, 192 by Denness and Fletcher for the fourth, and 148 – taking the total to 507 – by Fletcher and Greig. Denness, missed three times, batted 8½ hours for the highest score by an England captain in Australia (passing A.E. Stoddart's 173 made 80 years before), both he and Fletcher repaying Australia's subsidiary bowlers for much torment endured during the series. Max Walker picked up five quick wickets as the tail subsided, and finished with the reward of 42.2-7-143-8, deservedly fine figures after a manful performance. Thirteen hours remained when Australia, on a good pitch, set out to resist England. Redpath batted six hours (32 in the whole series), Greg Chappell four, but the tourists kept at their task, and Greig, Arnold and Lever saw them home by 2.15 pm.

982, left: *Greg Chappell hit in the jaw by a flyer from Lever.* 983, below: *Denness's leg glance eludes Marsh and he has his century.* 984, right: *Denness c and b Walker 188 – the highest by an England captain in a Test in Australia*

1975 FIRST TEST
Edgbaston, July 10, 11, 12, 14

Australia *359 (R.W. Marsh 61, R.B. McCosker 59, R. Edwards 56, I.M. Chappell 52, J.R. Thomson 49)*; England *101 (D.K. Lillee 5 for 15, M.H.N. Walker 5 for 48) and 173 (K.W.R. Fletcher 51, J.R. Thomson 5 for 38)*. Australia won by an innings and 85 runs.

Denness, after consulting his senior players, gambled against an ominous weather forecast by putting Australia in – and lost comprehensively. Turner and McCosker took Australia to 77 without loss at lunch, and from 243 for 5 that evening the tourists progressed to 359, Marsh and Thomson hitting hard and Edwards, often playing and missing, batted four hours to ensure Australia's sound position. Fatefully, after one over of England's innings a thunderstorm drenched the ground, and after 100 minutes were lost, a new regulation added an hour to the day's play. By the close England were 83 for 7. Lillee, with his controlled ferocity, and Walker, unorthodox of action, used the favourable bowling conditions much better than some of their predecessors over the years, and England were following on half an hour into the Saturday. This time Thomson, who had been wildly erratic in the first innings, found his rhythm, length and direction. After two further rain delays, England were in ruins at 93 for 5 that evening. Further fine catching, a second 'duck' for Gooch on his Test debut, and a paralysing blow on Amiss's arm bestowed gloom upon the England camp. By mid-afternoon on the fourth day England had suffered their first defeat at Edgbaston, and Australia's dominance of the 1974–75 series was re-established.

985, above: *Fletcher at slip misses Edwards.* 986, below: *Denness c G.S. Chappell b Walker 3 during England's disastrous second day at Edgbaston*

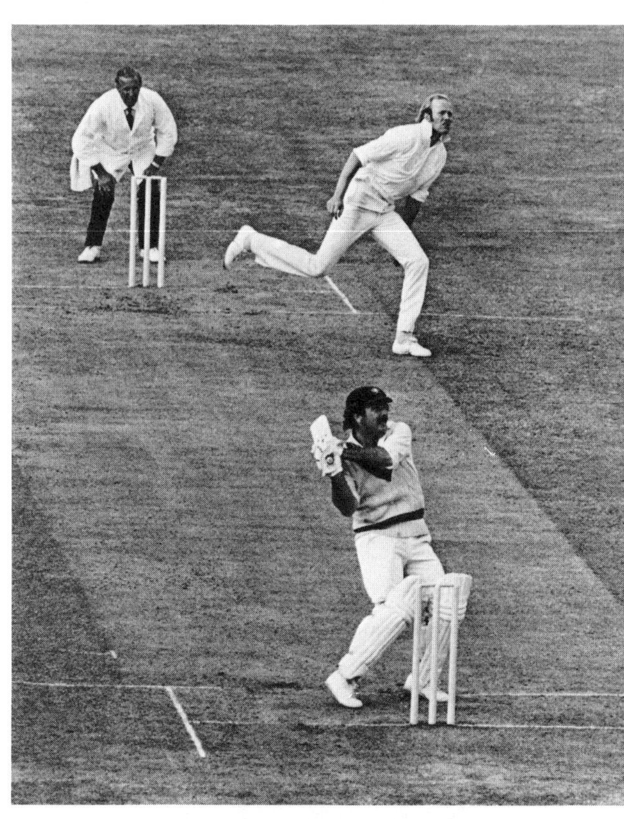

987, above: *Marsh gets all his weight into a hook for six off Greig.* 988, below: *The mighty pace trio of Lillee, Walker and Thomson relax after demolishing England in the first Test of the 1975 series*

1975 SECOND TEST
Lord's, July 31, August 1, 2, 4, 5

England *315 (A.W. Greig 96, A.P.E. Knott 69, D.S. Steele 50, D.K. Lillee 4 for 84) and 436 for 7 dec (J.H. Edrich 175, B. Wood 52, D.S. Steele 45, A.W. Greig 41)*; Australia *268 (R. Edwards 99, D.K. Lillee 73*, J.A. Snow 4 for 66) and 329 for 3 (I.M. Chappell 86, R.B. McCosker 79, G.S. Chappell 73*, R. Edwards 52*)*. Match drawn.

Spirit returned to the England XI when, after another horrendous start (49 for 4: Lillee 4 for 33), Greig, the new captain – Denness having been dropped – and Steele, prematurely grey, bespectacled, and in his first Test at 33, put on 96 for the fifth wicket to initiate a batting recovery later backed up by an inspired bowling performance. Snow matched Lillee in relentless, varied attack; but just as the doughty Steele, cavalier Greig and nimble Knott saved England's innings, so Edwards, with Thomson's help, lifted Australia from the emergency of 81 for 7, and Lillee, at No.10, clubbed three sixes and eight fours in 2¼ hours, dominating a final stand of 69 to reduce the leeway to 47. Ross Edwards, so often Australia's 'make-or-break' batsman, hit 15 fours in his 99, and fell eventually to Woolmer, lbw. First Wood then Steele stayed with Edrich while England carefully built up a sizable lead on the third day, the rugged Surrey left-hander going to his seventh – and highest – century against Australia. Greig's declaration set Australia 484 in 500 minutes, and they were 97 for one as the final day began. England's hoped-for thunderstorm arrived – but before play began. The covered pitch consequently was unharmed, and with an hour lost, Australia sedately played out time. England now needed to win both remaining matches to regain the Ashes.

989, left: *Steele, who brought character and pugnacity to England's batting, gets a ball away past Turner during his first Test innings.* 990, right: *Gooch congratulates his partner Edrich upon reaching 150*

991, centre: *Her Majesty the Queen exchanges cordialities with Max Walker.* 992, below, left: *Edrich drives during his marathon 175; Marsh waits in vain.* 993, right: *Edwards pulls Underwood, but is destined to miss his century by one run, falling lbw to Woolmer. Wood is at short third man*

1975

Headingley, August 14, 15, 16, 18, 19

England *288 (D.S. Steele 73, J.H. Edrich 62, A.W. Greig 51, G.J. Gilmour 6 for 85) and 291 (D.S. Steele 92, A.W. Greig 49)*; Australia *135 (P.H. Edmonds 5 for 28) and 220 for 3 (R.B. McCosker 95*, I.M. Chappell 62)*. Match drawn.

With the match interestingly poised after the fourth day – Australia needing a further 225 runs with seven wickets in hand – there was general dismay at the discovery that vandals had gouged the pitch and poured crude oil over it. They wished to draw attention to the alleged wrongful imprisonment for armed robbery of one George Davis. The match was therefore abandoned as a draw, the only comfort being that rain, which descended at noon, would have prevented victory by either side. Steele, top-scorer in both England innings, added 112 with the equally consistent Edrich for the second wicket, but, the eager Greig apart, there was little resistance to Australia's pace quartet. Gilmour, left-arm fast-medium, swung the ball late, and took nine wickets in his debut match against England. Another debutant, however, was to make an even more conspicuous mark: Phil Edmonds, tall, Zambian-born, left-arm spinner, took 5 for 17 in his first 12 overs, without maintaining faultless accuracy. He got rid of the Chappells, Edwards, Walters and Walker as Australia slid from 78 for 2 to 107 for 8. England built slowly on their lead until the fourth morning, when a concerted effort to score fast paid off. Marsh, opening the innings in this match, helped McCosker put 55 up for the first wicket, and Ian Chappell hit 50 in boundaries during the next stand, an even-time 116. Though he and his brother were out by the close, McCosker was very steady and Walters was untroubled. But a compelling final day was not to be.

994, above: *Edwards, playing no stroke, is lbw to Edmonds.* 995, right: *Greig is run out for 51 in England's first innings*

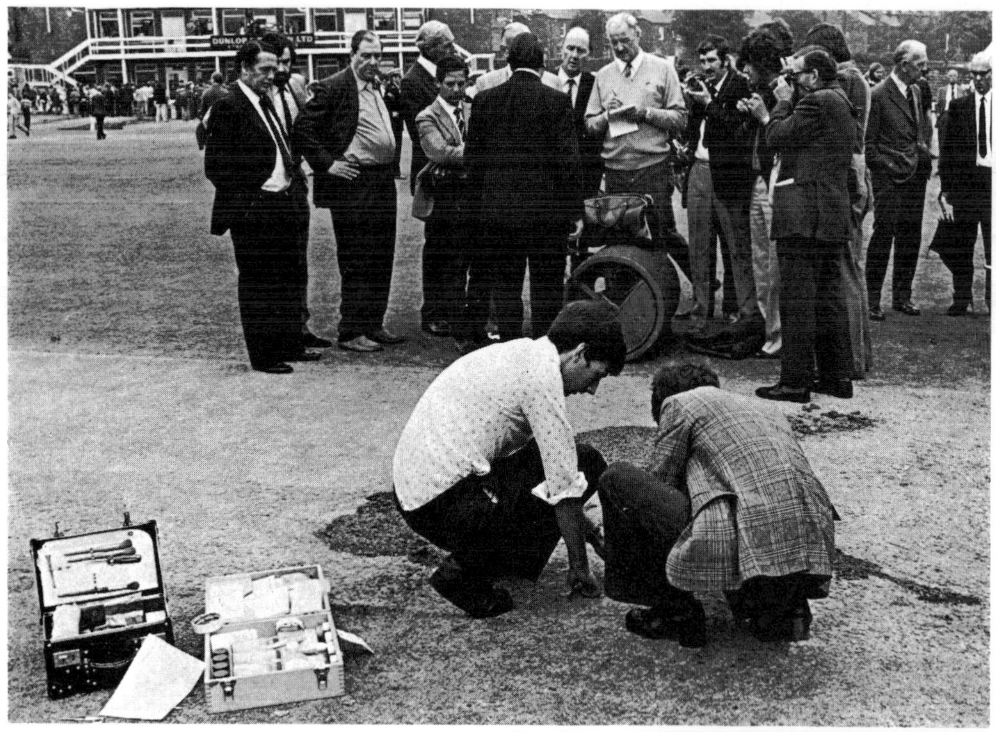

996, above: *Forensic investigators examine the damage inflicted on the Headingley pitch by vandals during the night, while Yorkshire's secretary interprets an unprecedented situation for the benefit of journalists and broadcasters.* 997, right: *How the nation's television-watchers learned of the outrage*

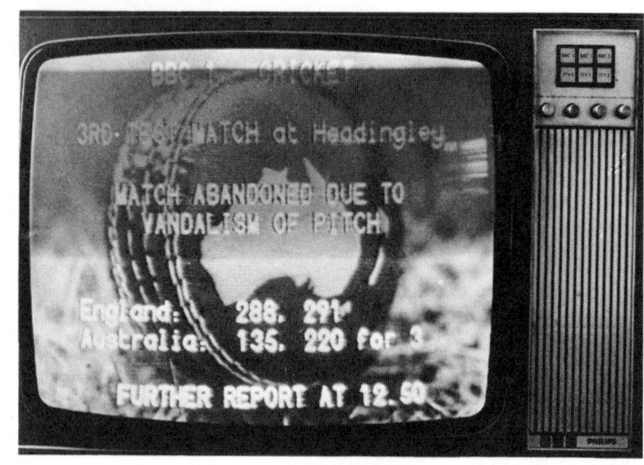

1975 FOURTH TEST

The Oval, August 28, 29, 30, September 1, 2, 3

Australia *532 for 9 dec (I.M. Chappell 192, R.B. McCosker 127, K.D. Walters 65, R. Edwards 44) and 40 for 2;* England *191 (J.R. Thomson 4 for 50, M.H.N. Walker 4 for 63) and 538 (R.A. Woolmer 149, J.H. Edrich 96, G.R.J. Roope 77, D.S. Steele 66, A.P.E. Knott 64, K.D. Walters 4 for 34, D.K. Lillee 4 for 91).* Match drawn.

After winning the toss, Australia made almost certain of holding their series lead by finishing the first day at 280 for one. Chappell and McCosker's stand realised 277, the ninth-highest for any wicket in England-Australia Tests. Greg Chappell's unaccountable run of failures continued with a first-ball dismissal by Old. Ian Chappell, who announced his retirement from the captaincy during this match after having led Australia 30 times, batted 442 minutes. Walters' score was his highest in a Test in England since his first, in 1968. There was a sinister change in the weather on the third day, and in poor light and intermittent drizzle England laboured to 169 for 8. Following on 341 behind, they 'set up camp' in better conditions second time round, and with Edrich and Wood grinding out 77 for the first wicket in almost three hours it was soon apparent that only concentration lapses or inspired bowling could bring about a result. Patience in abundance from the batsmen matched by growing frustration in the field saw the match creep through the fifth day – with Woolmer and Roope centre-stage for most of it – and through the sixth. Woolmer's drive to the boundary off Mallett on the final morning brought him his century in 396 minutes – slowest to date in these Tests. His innings stretched across 495 minutes altogether, and ensured – though not until some time into the last day – that England would be safe. This was the longest cricket match ever played in England, and a further indictment of over-prepared pitches.

998, left: *Picture of a happy man: Rick McCosker acknowledges the reception given him upon reaching his first Test century.*
999, below: *Ian Chappell, captaining Australia for the 30th and final time, sweeps during his masterly innings of 192*

1000, bottom: *Bob Woolmer, who had seldom batted as high as No. 5 for his county, Kent, reaches his hundred with a drive off the back foot. Wicketkeeper Rod Marsh was behind the stumps while 1425 balls (including wides and no-balls) were sent down during the innings*

1976–77 CENTENARY TEST

Melbourne, March 12, 13, 14, 16, 17

Australia *138 (G.S. Chappell 40) and 419 for 9 dec (R.W. Marsh 110*, I.C. Davis 68, K.D. Walters 66, D.W. Hookes 56, C.M. Old 4 for 104);* England 95 *(D.K. Lillee 6 for 26, M.H.N. Walker 4 for 54) and 417 (D.W. Randall 174, D.L. Amiss 64, J.M. Brearley 43, A.P.E. Knott 42, A.W. Greig 41, D.K. Lillee 5 for 139).* Australia won by 45 runs.

The hundredth birthday of England v Australia Test cricket was celebrated in grand style when, with heavy sponsorship and through immaculate organisation by the authorities in Melbourne, all willing and able surviving participants of the Tests played in Australia gathered in the city where Test cricket began and partook of a festival of reunion and reminiscence such as cricket had never known. Oldest of the veterans present was Jack Ryder, 87, who died less than a month later, and with England's 'Tiger' Smith, Frank Woolley and Andrew Sandham unable to travel, Percy Fender, at 84, was the senior touring player. George Geary and Herbert Sutcliffe were also too infirm to make the journey. The much-publicised presence of this galaxy of almost 200 former Test cricketers might have reduced the specially-arranged Test match (the Ashes were not at stake) to a mere exhibition, and indeed, after two days, with Australia 104 for 3 batting a second time, there were doubts that the match would last beyond three days. An exhibition match was mooted to fill the vacant time and to welcome Her Majesty the Queen on the fifth day. However, the pitch and the players' nerves settled down, and the match was carried through to a thrilling last day. Tony Greig called correctly when Greg Chappell tossed the gold coin, and Australia were put in to bat. Their destruction for 138 at the hands of the four bowlers used, John Lever and Willis two wickets each, Old and Underwood three, was made certain by some wild strokeplay and brilliant English catching, with Chappell (who became Underwood's 250th Test wicket) alone applying himself with a four-hour innings devoid of boundaries. McCosker was bowled off his jaw by Willis, the resultant fracture rendering him an unlikely starter in the second innings. On the second day Lillee and Walker demolished England before a crowd again in excess of 60,000. The day was made even more memorable by two wicketkeeping records, Marsh passing Grout's all-Tests Australian total at 187 and Knott, that evening, passing Lilley's England record of 84 Australian wickets. By the third evening the home side were 430 ahead with two wickets left. Hookes,

1001, left: *Dennis Lillee, having destroyed England's first innings, saved his side in the second by bowling tirelessly for 34.4 overs, taking 5 for 139.* 1002, below: *Few batsmen have made such a spectacular entrance to Test cricket as Derek Randall. Here his courageous 174 is terminated by a catch by Cosier off O'Keeffe*

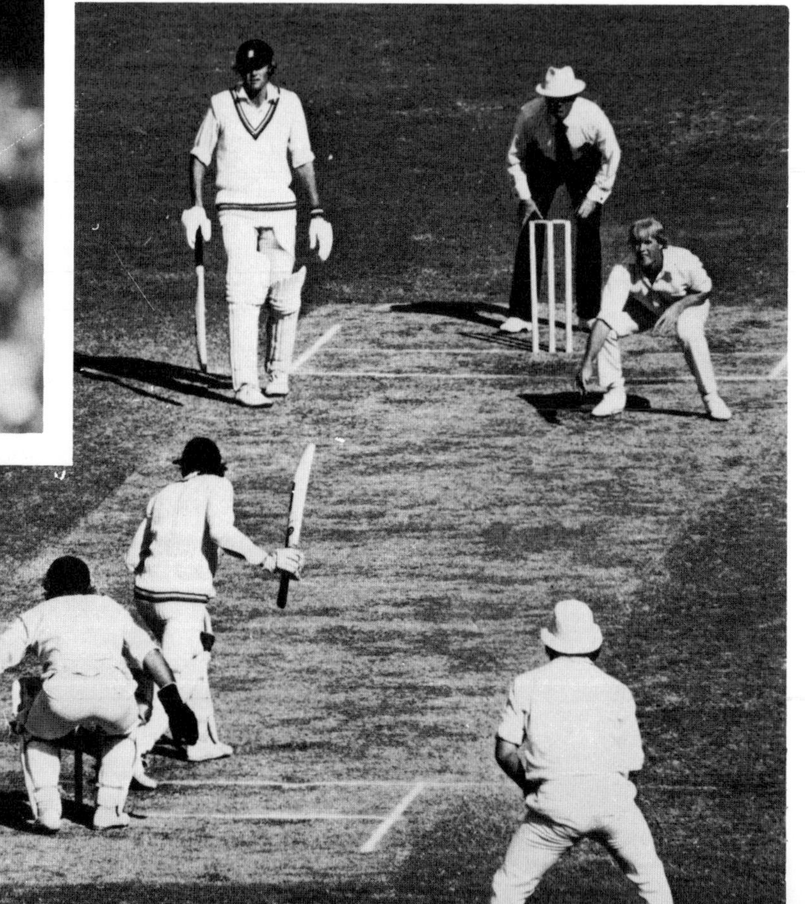

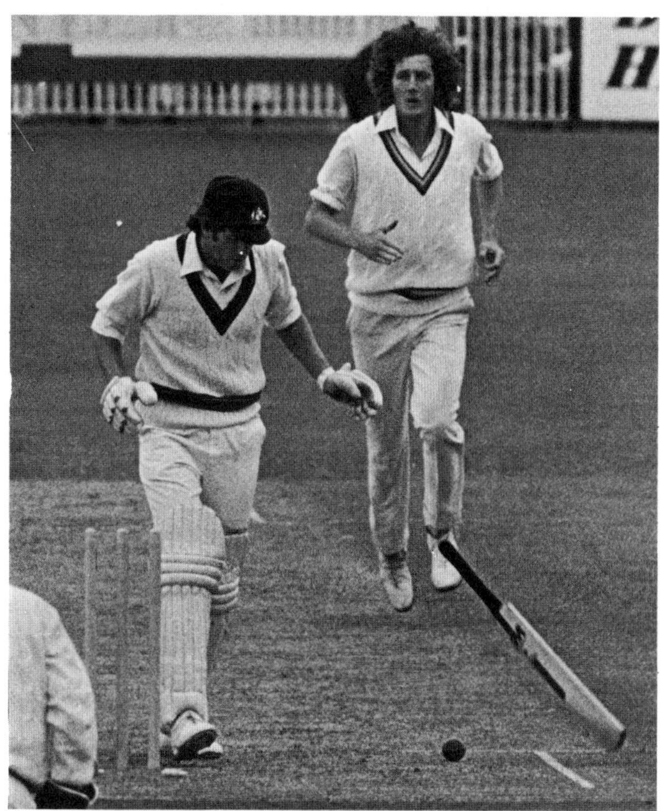

Heroes of past battles enjoy the Melbourne Centenary reunion – 1003, above, left: *Clarrie Grimmett, Ben Barnett, Fred Trueman.* 1004, above, centre: *Percy Fender with grandson.* 1005, left: *Denis Compton and Sir Donald Bradman.* 1006, above: *In one dreadful moment McCosker has his jaw splintered and his wicket wrecked by Willis*

on Test debut, had stroked five fours in an over from Greig, and Marsh (with a photograph of Blackham in his pocket) was within five runs of the first century by an Australian wicketkeeper against England. Cheered to the echo, the bandaged McCosker came in at number 10 and was to make an important 25. When Chappell declared an hour before lunch on the fourth day England needed 463 in just on 11 hours, and by stumps they were some way towards their 'hopeless' target at 191 for 2, Randall 87, Amiss 34. The final day saw a gradual growth of tension. The third-wicket stand reached 166 before Amiss fell, Randall by this time having reached his hundred in his maiden Test – soon after which he was felled by a lifter from Lillee, only to spring back upright with a grin and a rub of the head. A sensational England victory seemed in prospect as Lillee, off a shorter run, bowled heroically on and Chappell bowled with crucial economy. The fifth to eighth wickets fell during the 300s, the first being Randall's, after he had been recalled by Marsh when he was given out for a catch behind at 161. His 174, second only to R.E. Foster's 287 as a debut score, made in 448 minutes with 21 fours, was full of cavalier hooks, cuts and drives, and won him the Man of the Match award. With his departure, the end was predictable, but not before Greig and Knott had batted defiantly. When Lillee trapped Knott lbw, England had achieved the highest fourth-innings score in these matches and Australia had won by 45 runs, exactly the margin in the first Test match 100 years all but two days previously. Never can such euphoria have drenched an England-Australia Test occasion. And never can delight have turned so swiftly to concern as, within weeks, it transpired that even while this classic was being played secret moves had been afoot to set up a commercial 'circus' involving almost the entire Australian team, several key members of the England team, and dozens of players from other countries. This 'revolution', backed by Australian media baron Kerry Packer and partially aimed at putting more money into the players' pockets, was to disrupt, disquiet and, in some quarters, disgust the world of international cricket during the two years leading up to a settlement between the established authorities and World Series Cricket (as it became known) two years later.

The Centenary teams: Australia – G.S. Chappell (captain), I.C. Davis, R.B. McCosker, G.J. Cosier, D.W. Hookes, K.D. Walters, R.W. Marsh, G.J. Gilmour, K.J. O'Keeffe, D.K. Lillee, M.H.N. Walker, R.J. Bright (12th man). England – A.W. Greig (captain), R.A. Woolmer, J.M. Brearley, D.W. Randall, D.L. Amiss, K.W.R. Fletcher, A.P.E. Knott, C.M. Old, J.K. Lever, D.L. Underwood, R.G.D. Willis, G.D. Barlow (12th man). Umpires – T.F. Brooks and M.G. O'Connell. Total attendance 247,873; takings $262,086.

1977 FIRST TEST

Lord's, June 16, 17, 18, 20, 21

England *216 (R.A. Woolmer 79, D.W. Randall 53, J.R. Thomson 4 for 41) and 305 (R.A. Woolmer 120, A.W. Greig 91, J.M. Brearley 49, J.R. Thomson 4 for 86);* Australia *296 (C.S. Serjeant 81, G.S. Chappell 66, K.D. Walters 53, R.G.D. Willis 7 for 78) and 114 for 6 (D.W. Hookes 50).* Match drawn.

The Jubilee Test match – so named in honour of the Queen's 25 years on the throne – was overshadowed in part by the exposure, five weeks earlier, of the formation of the rebel organisation, World Series Cricket. However, the Australian touring team, divided in spirit though it may have been, remained intact, and England continued to regard all their players as open to selection, though Greig was stripped of the captaincy, which was given to Brearley. England owed everything to Woolmer, sound and safe, and Randall, eager to take on the bowling. They put on 98 for the third wicket; but the pace and movement of Thomson, Pascoe and Walker (Lillee did not tour) were too much for the home side. Play was severely curtailed by bad light on the second day, but the innings was built up on the Saturday by disciplined batting from Chappell, who waited three hours for a boundary, and Serjeant, who made his first Test run after 40 minutes. Serjeant added 84 with his captain and 103 with Walters, but Willis swept the tail away to complete his best Test figures. Amiss failed again, but Brearley and Woolmer wiped off the deficit with a stand of 132, and Greig's initiative and Woolmer's solidity and immaculately straight bat saw a further 92 for the third wicket. From there the Australian pace bowlers inflicted a collapse, the last eight wickets falling for 81, four of them on 286. Woolmer's five-hour vigil might still not have been enough. Needing 226 at roughly five an over, Australia tried for victory. But wickets fell in the effort, and a Willis bouncer to Marsh prompted the umpires to 'offer the light' to the batsmen, who accepted. The total attendance of 101,050 paid £220,384, a record for a cricket match in Britain.

1007, right: *Greig caught by O'Keeffe nine runs short of his century.* 1008, below, left: *Woolmer, who made a towering contribution to England's cause in this and the next Test, prepares to deal with a ball from Pascoe, who, in his first Test, was pronounced a 'thrower' by former England captain Ted Dexter.* 1009, below, right: *Pain for Craig Serjeant, whose dedicated batting in his maiden Test evoked much admiration. The alert fielder is substitute Ealham*

1977
Old Trafford, July 7, 8, 9, 11, 12

Australia *297 (K.D. Walters 88, G.S. Chappell 44) and 218 (G.S. Chappell 112, D.L. Underwood 6 for 66);* England *437 (R.A. Woolmer 137, D.W. Randall 79, A.W. Greig 76) and 82 for 1 (J.M. Brearley 44).* England won by 9 wickets.

A fine all-round team performance by England gave them the lead in the series. Australia's 297, owing much to Chappell, Walters (who made his highest Test score in England), and Marsh (36), seemed worthwhile, but Woolmer, who made a century in his third consecutive home Test against Australia, Randall and Greig pushed England's first-innings lead to 140, and Underwood was at his penetrative best on a responsive wicket on the fourth day. Woolmer batted for 6½ hours and succumbed through exhaustion, having stroked 22 fours, and his stand of 160 with Greig beat the previous best at Old Trafford for England's fourth wicket, by Sutcliffe and Hendren in 1934. Australia's second innings provided the contrast of ill-judged batting from most of the specialists and a showpiece century – his sixth against England – by Chappell, who played freely and with a mastery which placed him a class apart. Brearley and Amiss took England to the brink of victory early on the final day, despite a fiery spell from Thomson, and the celebrations were greater for the knowledge that this was England's first home Test victory against any country for 14 matches.

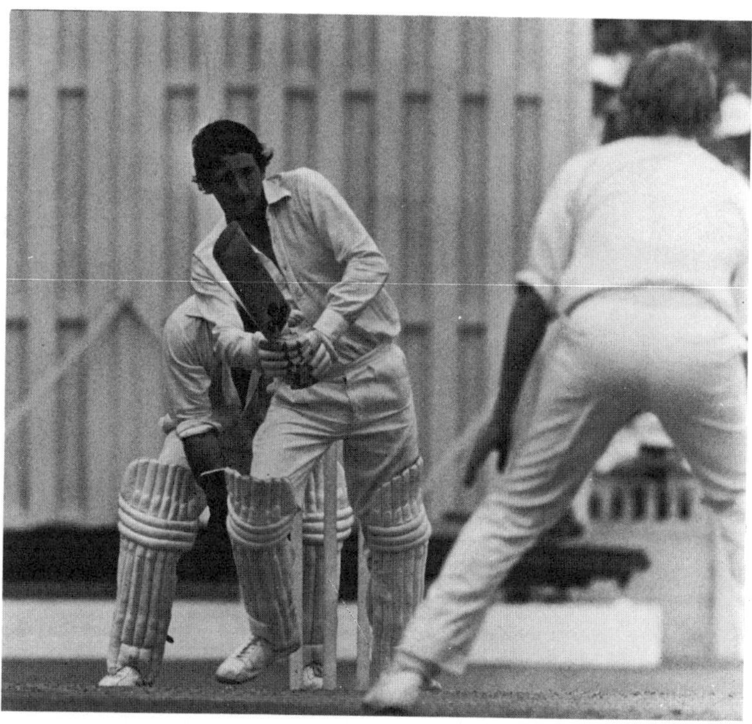

1010, left: *Four to Chappell during his splendid century.* 1011, above: *Randall, back in successful vein, moves across his stumps to play O'Keeffe.* 1012, below: *Walters carves Greig for four*

1977 THIRD TEST

Trent Bridge, July 28, 29, 30, August 1, 2

Australia *243 (R.B. McCosker 51, K.J. O'Keeffe 48*, I.T. Botham 5 for 74) and 309 (R.B. McCosker 107, D.W. Hookes 42, R.G.D. Willis 5 for 88);* England *364 (A.P.E. Knott 135, G. Boycott 107, L.S. Pascoe 4 for 80) and 189 for 3 (J.M. Brearley 81, G. Boycott 80*).* England won by 7 wickets.

England's first victory over Australia at Trent Bridge since 1930 was memorable for the comeback after three years of self-imposed exile by Boycott, the Jessopian batting of Knott, and the Test debut of Botham. McCosker – returning to form – and Davis made 79 for the first wicket, but England probed their way down the order, bowling tightly and catching superlatively, especially Hendrick in the slips cordon. Less tense after lunch, Botham went on to take 5 for 48. By the second evening England were only a run behind with five wickets in hand, Boycott, having run out the local hero Randall and having been missed when 20 (after three hours at the crease), being 88 not out, Knott 87 not out. McCosker's fatal mistake was probably the turning point of the series. From 82 for 5, Boycott and Knott took England to 297, their partnership of 215 equalling the 1938 record by Hutton and Hardstaff. Boycott's seven-hour innings and Knott's, which lasted just on five hours and seemed to inspire his partner out of his semi-paralysed state, gave Chappell's inexperienced side much to ponder. Australia fought for over eight hours in their second innings, with McCosker occupying the crease for six hours. He reached his century with a hooked six off Willis, but Hookes's three-hour innings, O'Keeffe's two-hour 21 not out, and Robinson's knees-and-elbows resistance of 34 in 95 minutes were still not enough. Marsh made two ducks in his 50th Test match. Although the weather reports suggested that the final afternoon might be shortened, Brearley and Boycott took England to 92 without loss at lunch at less than two per over during the morning. But by the time their stand was broken at 154 the win was assured, though Walker then took three wickets in six balls. Boycott had emphasised his return to Test cricket by batting altogether for more than 12 hours.

1013: *Harold Larwood, on holiday from Australia, enjoys talking over old times with Bill Voce during the Nottingham Test*

1014, above: *Knott reaches his century with a single to third man. Minutes later Boycott also reached three figures.* 1015, left: *A much-talked-about run-out – Randall is sacrificed after a poor call by Boycott, who had tapped the ball just wide of the bowler, Thomson*

1977
Headingley, August 11, 12, 13, 15

England 436 *(G. Boycott 191, A.P.E. Knott 57, A.W. Greig 43, L.S. Pascoe 4 for 91, J.R. Thomson 4 for 113)*; Australia 103 *(I.T. Botham 5 for 21, M. Hendrick 4 for 41)* and 248 *(R.W. Marsh 63, M. Hendrick 4 for 54)*. England won by an innings and 85 runs.

England confidently regained the Ashes so traumatically lost at Sydney in January 1975, and chalked up their third victory over Australia in a home series for the first time since 1886. And again Boycott was the central figure. First in and last out, he batted for over 10 hours and became the first batsman to register his 100th first-class century in a Test match. To add to the excitement, the feat was achieved before his own Yorkshire crowd. The gates were shut before the start of play on the first two days, and after Brearley's dismissal in the opening over, although ball beat bat quite frequently, it was to be England's day at 252 for 4, Boycott 110 not out. Runs had to be earned on the second day, but a staid sixth-wicket stand of 123 between the Trent Bridge heroes Boycott and Knott took England to total security, Boycott batting more and more slowly (30 between lunch and tea). His 191 passed F.S. Jackson's 144 not out as the highest for England v Australia at Leeds. Australia's innings was soon in ruins, five wickets falling for 67 by the end of the second day. Hendrick made the early break-through with two wickets and a catch, and McCosker was smartly run out by Randall after backing up too far. Botham completed the demolition on the third day and by the end Australia were 120 for 4 in the follow-on. Play started late on the fourth day, after rain, and when Chappell's three-hour vigil for 36 ended, the rest was foreseeable. Willis, in delivering Thomson of a 'pair', took his 100th Test wicket, and Marsh lashed out defiantly until he was caught at cover by Randall, who did a cartwheel. The Ashes had been recaptured by the home side at The Oval in 1926, the year of the Queen's birth, again in 1953, the year of her Coronation, and now, for the first time ever at Headingley, in the year of her Jubilee.

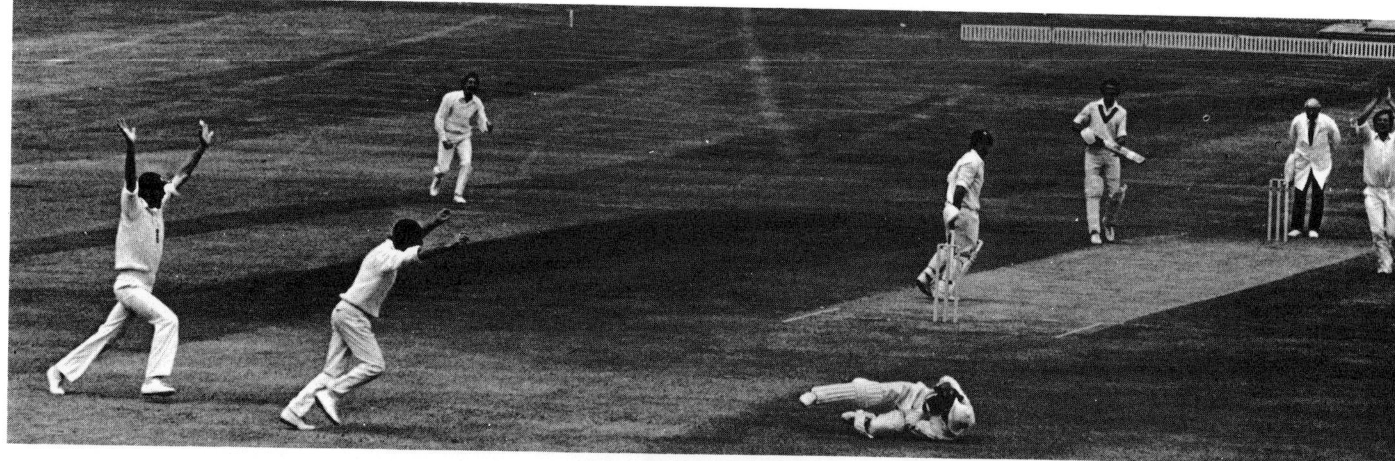

1016, above: *Australia's first-innings rot spreads as Knott swoops to catch Marsh off the all-conquering Botham.* 1017, below: *Ashes victory for England in Jubilee year, and all is joy on the Headingley players' balcony.* 1018, right: *Boycott's 100th century, and the crowd throws a party*

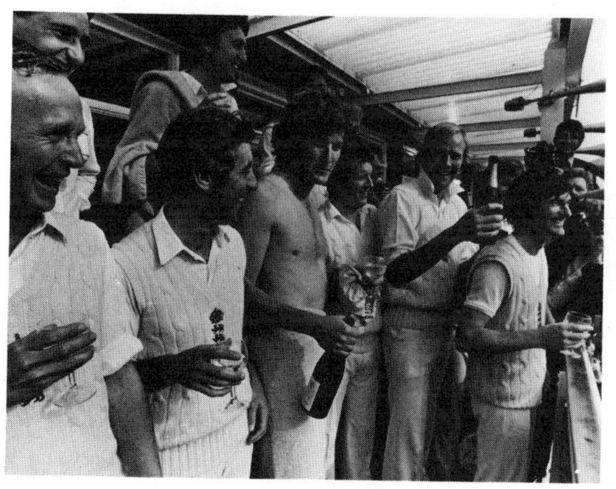

1977 FIFTH TEST

The Oval, August 25, 26, 27, 29, 30

England *214 (M.F. Malone 5 for 63, J.R. Thomson 4 for 87) and 57 for 2;* Australia *385 (D.W. Hookes 85, M.H.N. Walker 78*, R.W. Marsh 57, M.F. Malone 46).* Match drawn.

At last some of Chappell's Australians lived up to promise; but the loss of the first day after days of rain left too little time for an outright result. England, put in, were 181 for 9 at the end of a laboured first day, Brearley and Boycott having begun with 86 in two hours. Fast-medium swing bowler Malone, in his maiden Test, bowled 43 of the 45 overs delivered from the Vauxhall end without conceding a boundary. It was a special day for Thomson, who made Roope his 100th Test wicket. The last-wicket stand of 40, completed next day by Hendrick and Willis, was the second-highest of the innings, but further frustration lay in store as a heavy rainstorm approached and did its worst, cutting 4¾ hours from Saturday's play. McCosker, dropped at two, batted for over three hours for 32, and as the pitch dried Hookes settled and showed some fine off-side strokes. Marsh joined him at 104 for 5 and helped add 80. Australia's academic honours, however, were assured by Walker and Malone, who surprised with a ninth-wicket stand of 100. Both dropped early, they offered the kind of brave resistance so desperately needed in the preceding Tests. Willis's 27 wickets in the series was a record for a pace bowler against Australia in England. Left 175 minutes to bat, with a deficit of 171, England lost two early wickets and Boycott made his 5000th Test run before play was called off in gloomy conditions and in an air of anticlimax. Distraction, bred by the split in the game's international promotion, had hovered over the series and now expressed itself in both sadness that so many top-class cricketers were about to become 'outlaws' and apprehension for the game's future.

1019, below: *Mick Malone, whose stamina at both batting and bowling creases gave him an unusually fine Test debut.* 1020, right: *Roope becomes Thomson's 100th Test wicket.* 1021, right, bottom: *Greg Chappell falls prey to Underwood for the 11th time in Tests. Chappell's announcement of retirement was rescinded two years later, to Australia's immense relief*

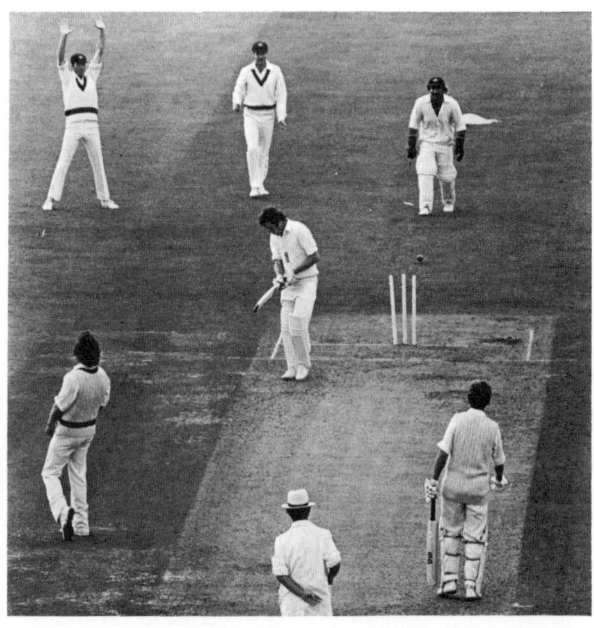

1978–79 FIRST TEST

Brisbane, December 1, 2, 3, 5, 6

Australia *116 (R.G.D. Willis 4 for 44) and 339 (K.J. Hughes 129, G.N. Yallop 102);* England *286 (D.W. Randall 75, I.T. Botham 49, D.I. Gower 44, R.M. Hogg 6 for 74, A.G. Hurst 4 for 93) and 170 for 3 (D.W. Randall 74*, D.I. Gower 48*).* England won by 7 wickets.

Australian fears that the Test team, depleted drastically by the exodus of World Series players, would be no match for England (who had lost Knott, Underwood, Woolmer, Greig and Amiss) were borne out horrifically in the humid opening session when new captain Yallop won the toss and unwisely batted. Australia were 26 for 6 before Maclean (33 not out), Yardley (17) and Hogg (36) dragged the score into three figures. England's seam bowlers having done an admirable job, aided by some unsophisticated batting, the batsmen then struggled in turn against the probing fast pair Hurst and Hogg. The substantial first-innings lead was acquired thanks chiefly to Randall and to the patience of night-watchman Taylor, whose 20 took almost three hours; the stand of 95 for the sixth wicket by Gower and Botham grasped control for England. When three second-innings wickets were lost for 49, Australia – and the series, which faced strong competition from the World Series programme – seemed doomed. Then came the sturdy resistance of Yallop and Hughes. They added 170 in 266 minutes, Yallop's century marking a unique feat in that it was by a player not only playing in his first England-Australia Test, but captaining his side. Hughes battled on and reached his century in the slowest time ever for Australia in all Tests: 369 minutes. It was a memorable example of self-control in one who prefers to attack. The tail gave slight resistance however, and England's target late on the fourth day was 170. The third wicket fell at 74, but Randall – Man of the Match for the second time in his two Tests in Australia – and Gower, who completed an attractive double in his first Australian Test, saw England through in a thought-provoking match fifty years after the first ever at Brisbane.

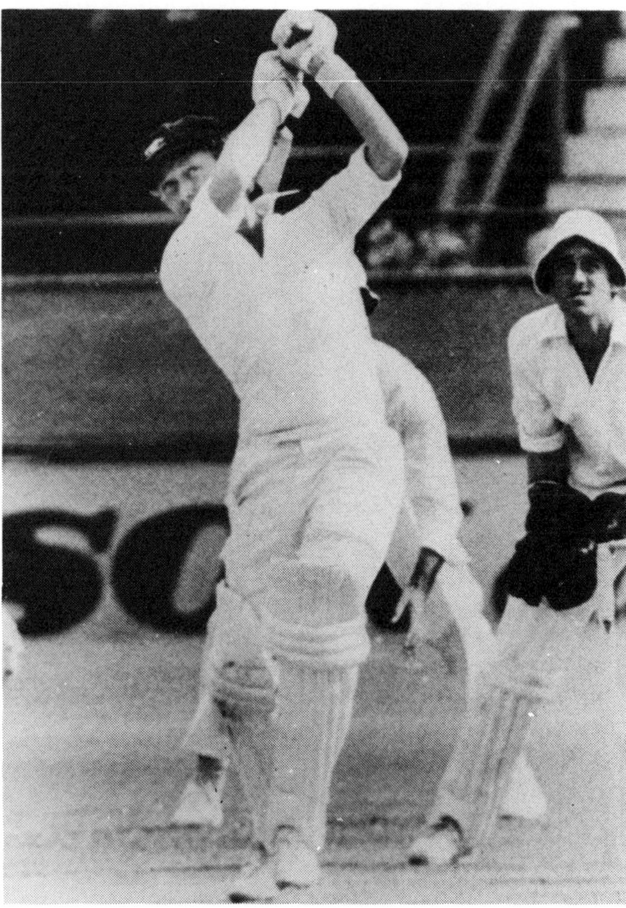

1022, above, left: *Randall swings with typical gusto.* 1023, left: *Yallop evades a bouncer from Willis. His discretion and ability to choose the right ball to hit brought him a century.* 1024, above: *Hughes enlivens his record slow century with a six-hit off Miller*

1978–79 SECOND TEST

Perth, December 15, 16, 17, 19, 20

England *309 (D.I. Gower 102, G. Boycott 77, G. Miller 40, R.M. Hogg 5 for 65) and 208 (D.W. Randall 45, G.A. Gooch 43, R.M. Hogg 5 for 57);* Australia *190 (P.M. Toohey 81*, R.G.D. Willis 5 for 44) and 161 (G.M. Wood 64, G.J. Cosier 47, J.K. Lever 4 for 28).* England won by 166 runs.

Yallop this time put England in, and seemed justified with the score 41 for 3 soon after lunch, Hogg again having made a breakthrough (taken off with figures of 2 for 0 because of breathing problems in the heat). The rescue operation was mounted by Boycott, whose 77 lasted all of 7½ hours, and Gower, who at 21 became the youngest England centurymaker against Australia since Compton in 1938. By the end of the first day the score was 190 for 3, Boycott 63, Gower 101, and their stand was eventually broken when it was worth 158. The Australian pace bowlers again stuck at their job, but the batting in its turn was abysmal, only Toohey resisting the fire of Willis. His unbeaten 81 lasted 4½ hours and his driving and hooking showed the Englishmen that comparisons with Walters at his best were not exaggerated. His eighth-wicket partner was with him before the follow-on was avoided. Another admirable five-wicket return by Hogg and three wickets by off-spinner Yardley restricted England to 208 in six hours after an opening stand of 58, and Australia were left to make 328 for victory. Losing Darling, a great-nephew of the Australian captain at the turn of the century, they were spared further agonies on the fourth evening by the first-ever rain interruption to a Perth Test, but on the final day the state of collapse which was now almost customary came to pass. Apart from a free-hitting innings by Cosier, the only real resistance came from the left-handed Wood, who batted almost four hours. Willis, Hendrick, left-arm Lever, and off-spinner Miller all played a part in placing England two-up with four to play.

1025, left: *Gower progresses elegantly towards his century, with Darling a helpless spectator at cover.* 1026, below, left: *Australia's batting discovery Toohey failed to reach 20 in seven of his 10 innings in the series, but at Perth he showed what he was worth at his best.* 1027, below: *England captain Brearley goes first ball, caught by Maclean; Hughes and Cosier (capless) are at slip*

1978–79 THIRD TEST

Melbourne, December 29, 30, January 1, 2, 3

Australia *258 (G.M. Wood 100, G.N. Yallop 41) and 167 (K.J. Hughes 48);* England *143 (R.M. Hogg 5 for 30) and 179 (D.I. Gower 49, G.A. Gooch 40, R.M. Hogg 5 for 36).* Australia won by 103 runs.

The victory that gave all Australia new hope was inspired by Graeme Wood, who reached a painstaking hundred after batting throughout the first day, and Rodney Hogg, whose amazing striking rate in his maiden Test series had by now made his the name on everyone's lips. Bowling at a brisk pace and to an accurate off-stump line, he cut the ball back sharply, and here at Melbourne found a pitch much to his liking. Wood and Darling made 65 for the first wicket, easily Australia's best throughout the series, before Darling was suicidally run out – a mode of dismissal that became a recurring nightmare for the home side in these Tests. A breezy innings by Yallop and a gritty maiden Test innings of 29 by Border helped the score along, but some brilliant England catching saw to it that no partnership took longlasting root. England were destroyed by Hogg's opening burst, when he removed Boycott and Brearley for a single apiece, and then by Dymock's persistence and a comeback spell by Hogg. England fought, none harder than Miller, whose seven runs took 125 minutes, but a deficit of 115 looked ominous. Only 122 runs were scored on the second day, for the loss of 14 wickets. An hour before lunch on the third day Australia went in again, and Wood and Darling put on 55 this time. But wickets fell steadily to the accuracy and movement of Botham and off-spinners Miller and Emburey. The last eight wickets fell for 66 runs. England thus needed 283 to win in 11½ hours, but the loss of two early wickets dispelled any reasonable expectation, and the bowlers, spearheaded again by Hogg, worked their way through the order. On a pitch of uneven bounce, Boycott (38) survived for 3¼ hours and Gower was in for almost three hours. Early on the fifth day Australia moved to convincing victory and the series remained alive.

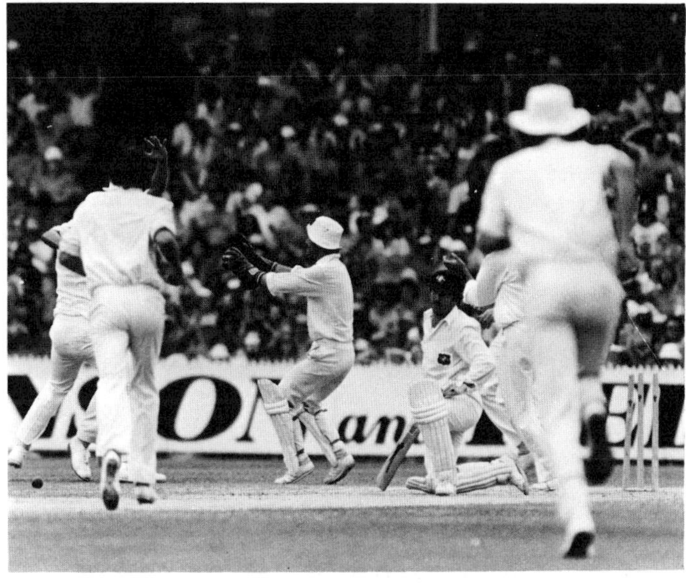

1028, left: *Endlessly among the England wickets, Rod Hogg celebrates two in Melbourne – Brearley and Boycott.* 1029, above: *A bewildered Border slowly comes to realise that he has been run out by a flick from short leg by Hendrick.* 1030, below: *An Australian opener was run out in each of the six Tests. Here Darling has himself to blame*

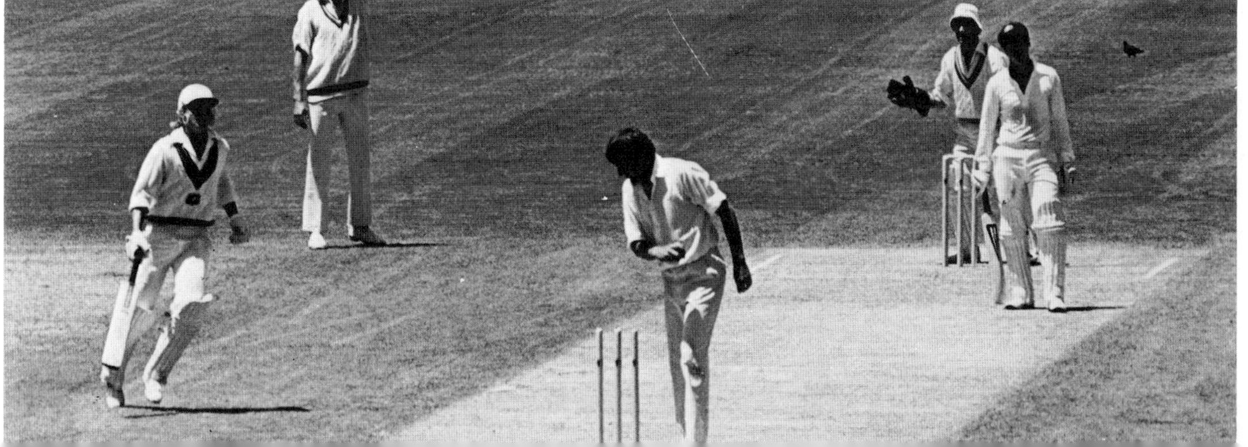

1978–79 FOURTH TEST
Sydney, January 6, 7, 8, 10, 11

England *152 (I.T. Botham 59, A.G. Hurst 5 for 28) and 346 (D.W. Randall 150, J.M. Brearley 53, J.D. Higgs 5 for 148, R.M. Hogg 4 for 67);* Australia *294 (W.M. Darling 91, A.R. Border 60*, K.J. Hughes 48, G.N. Yallop 44) and 111 (A.R. Border 45*, J.E. Emburey 4 for 46).* England won by 93 runs.

A great tactical victory in the face of illness, inordinate heat, and a large first-innings deficit ensured England's retention of the Ashes and earned Mike Brearley the honour of being the first captain to win successive series against Australia at home and away since Hutton in '53 and '54–55. It seemed the series would soon be level at two-all after Hurst's demolition of England and Australia's opportunist advantage on first innings. The tourists' humiliation would have been deep but for the initiative of Botham (59). On a sporting wicket, Higgs's leg-spin was gripping even on the first day, and Hurst gained sharp lift. Yet it was superb catching by Australia as much as anything else which humbled England; and then bold strokeplay, especially to leg, by Darling, backed by Hughes after Wood's dismissal without scoring, which set up a reasonable score for Australia as the pitch became subdued. With Willis and Hendrick sick, Botham and Emburey bore the brunt of the bowling, and runs were never given away. Australia's lead, however, was extended at a vital time by Border, who cut and pulled sweetly during a four-hour innings. When England lost Boycott first ball to Hogg, still 142 in arrears, the odds on their winning would have been astronomical. But Brearley and Randall (who was perilously close to lbw when 3) resisted for 3½ hours to put on 111, and when the captain left, Gooch stayed with the extraordinarily self-controlled Randall for a further 2¼ hours while 58 were added. Next, on the fourth morning, came Gower, who shared a stand of 68. Botham dedicated himself to the extent of a mere six singles in 97 minutes. Past his hundred and battling against exhaustion, Randall was now missed a couple of times; but he ground on, trying to see out the fourth day. He just failed, Hogg ending his epic by having him lbw after ten hours, all but 11 minutes, at the crease. His century, in 411 minutes, was the slowest in these Tests. England now led by 150. Miller, Taylor and Emburey added slow but crucial runs, and by lunch Australia, needing 205 in 4½ hours and trying perhaps unsuccessfully to put their immense frustration behind them, were 15 without loss. This was the first England-Australia series to feature protective helmets in regular usage both at the crease and in the field, and Darling now crashed a pull shot hard towards Botham, close to the wicket, chipping his helmet and dazing him for minutes. Soon Darling was out, and the rest of the innings became a shambles as Emburey and Miller spun their spell and Brearley balanced his field between attack and economy. Border's doughty effort was almost overlooked in the gloom that swept over Australian cricket.

1031, left: *Keeping the lovely art of leg-spin alive – Jim Higgs, who bowled 77.6 eight-ball overs in the match and took 8 for 190.*
1032, above: *Towards the end of his marathon innings Derek Randall sees out an interval in play, fatigue and strain etched on his usually grinning countenance*

1978–79 FIFTH TEST

Adelaide, January 27, 28, 29, 31, February 1

England *169 (I.T. Botham 74, R.M. Hogg 4 for 26) and 360 (R.W. Taylor 97, G. Miller 64, G. Boycott 49, J.E. Emburey 42, A.G. Hurst 4 for 97)*; Australia *164 (I.T. Botham 4 for 42) and 160 (K.J. Hughes 46)*. England won by 205 runs.

As in the previous Test, Australia threw away – or had wrested from them – a position of distinct advantage. Yallop put England in and his fast bowlers, Hogg and Hurst, reduced England to 27 for 5 before Botham's swashbuckling 74 effected some recovery, assisted by Miller (31). Hogg finished the innings with 37 wickets in the series, thus passing Thomson's 33 as a fast-bowling series record and Mailey's 36 for any Australian bowler in a series against England. All in attendance were stunned when the fifth ball of Australia's innings, bowled by Willis, struck Darling over the heart, causing him to collapse. Emburey administered the 'chest thump' and a physiotherapist snatched the chewing gum from his mouth and freed his tongue. After observation in hospital, Darling was able to resume his place in the match. Wickets now tumbled, however, and Australia were 24 for 4 before Yardley helped Wood see it through to the close of another day in which 14 wickets had fallen. Wood's 3½-hour 35 was top score as England, infused with determination by Botham's example, cut Australia down to an even smaller total than their own. When England themselves had slid to 132 for 6 (Boycott 49 in 4½ hours) second time round, it seemed a thriller was developing. Then Miller and wicketkeeper Taylor, both from Derbyshire, made a fighting stand worth 135, passing the record Hobbs-Hendren England seventh-wicket record for Adelaide (1925). Taylor's 97 equalled his highest first-class score and was the best for a number 8 for England against Australia. He batted six hours before being caught off a fine leg-side edge by his opposite number, Wright, who held six catches in his maiden Test. Emburey played an important innings, and the disconsolate Australians were faced with a victory target of 366, having fielded out to an England second innings lasting 700 or so minutes for the second Test in succession. The fourth innings lasted a mere 67 overs, only Hughes and Yallop (36) ever settling. England's all-round superiority in all departments was boldly underlined.

1033, above, left: *Wicketkeeper Kevin Wright's hopes of a rebound are dashed – Border misses Emburey.* 1034, above, right: *No catch – and no interruption to Taylor's valiant vigil as Yardley dives in vain.* 1035, left: *Rick Darling lies gasping after the blow over the heart from a ball by Willis*

1978–79 SIXTH TEST

Sydney, February 10, 11, 12, 14

Australia *198 (G.N. Yallop 121, I.T. Botham 4 for 57) and 143 (B. Yardley 61*, G. Miller 5 for 44, J.E. Emburey 4 for 52)*; England *308 (G.A. Gooch 74, D.I. Gower 65, J.M. Brearley 46, J.D. Higgs 4 for 69) and 35 for 1*. England won by 9 wickets.

England completed their biggest ever (5–1) series victory over Australia with fair ease on the fourth day, though the finest performance of the match came from Yallop, who ended the series as he had begun it – with a century. This one, however, was a demonstration of judicious attacking batsmanship, a statement of personal quality well apart from the areas of stigma which had spread around Australia's wretched team performance. Coming in at 19 for 2, Yallop made 100 out of 150 in four hours. England were determined not to relax in this final encounter, and several batsmen sold their wickets dearly. Gooch played his first characteristic innings of the series, hitting hard in a 2½-hour 74, and Hogg took his series aggregate to 41 wickets, easily the best for Australia v England, bettered only by Laker's 46 wickets for the other side, and a record for a maiden Test series. When Australia batted again, 110 behind, they gave another ignominious performance against off-spin, only Wood (29), Yallop (17) and the unorthodox Yardley staying for any length of time. The curling flight of Miller and Emburey seemed totally unfamiliar and alien to most of the batsmen, and an unsavoury series record was set by their ninth failure to total 200. The cry almost universally across Australia now was in favour of unifying the game and sending the best eleven cricketers into the field. The public view seemed to be that politics and power-clashes had to be forgotten, and players such as the Chappells, Lillee, Thomson, Hookes and Marsh should be restored to the Test team without delay so that the indignities of the '78–79 season could be buried. England, for their part, were well content with a heavy victory which some pundits felt distorted the true disparity between the sides.

1036, above, left: *Boycott was openly sceptical about the validity of Hilditch's catch at slip, but the appeal was upheld.* 1037, above: *Gooch came into his own in the final Test, his 74 including this six off Yardley.* 1038, left: *Graham Yallop during his scintillating century that did something to atone for captaincy which was never to please everybody*

1979–80 FIRST TEST
Perth, December 14, 15, 16, 18, 19

Australia *244 (K.J. Hughes 99, R.W. Marsh 42, I.T. Botham 6 for 78) and 337 (A.R. Border 115, J.M. Wiener 58, G.S. Chappell 43, I.T. Botham 5 for 98);* England *228 (J.M. Brearley 64, D.K. Lillee 4 for 73) and 215 (G. Boycott 99*, G. Dymock 6 for 34).* Australia won by 138 runs.

With agreement being reached in May 1979 between the Australian Cricket Board and the World Series organisation, cricket needed to restore not only credibility but financial balance after the two years of 'war'. Thus a three-way series of one-day matches involving Australia, England and West Indies was scheduled and three Tests each against England and West Indies were to be played by Australia. The six-ball over was restored after 46 years of eight-ball overs in Australia, a move likely to have been prompted by the needs of the commercial television company who had won exclusive rights to screen the matches. Brearley put Australia in, but after early successes his bowlers met resistance, chiefly from Hughes, whose maturity was now apparent. England's start was even more alarming, Lillee getting rid of Randall and Boycott for ducks, having earlier made headlines of a different nature by batting for a time with a bat made of aluminium. He took issue with the umpires and Brearley when an objection was raised, and the match was held up for 10 minutes before Lillee hurled the metal bat away. England were kept in contention by Brearley's 4¼-hour 64 (he was Lillee's 100th wicket in 19 Tests against England) and a defiant 38 not out in 3½ hours by Dilley, in his first Test at 20. Wiener and Laird started with 91 in Australia's second innings, and the home side's advance was carried by Border, who was badly cut near the eye when past his century as he missed a hook at a bouncer. Botham, bowling tirelessly and imaginatively, took a match haul of 11 wickets. Needing 354 for victory, England were never seriously in with a chance. Boycott emulated Abel and Hutton in carrying his bat through an innings in Australia – and for the unique score of 99 not out – but Dymock's swing won the day. Australia could have considered themselves well on the way to recapturing the Ashes – except that the authorities at Lord's, regarding the series as makeshift, had declared that the little urn was to be suspended until the 1981 series.

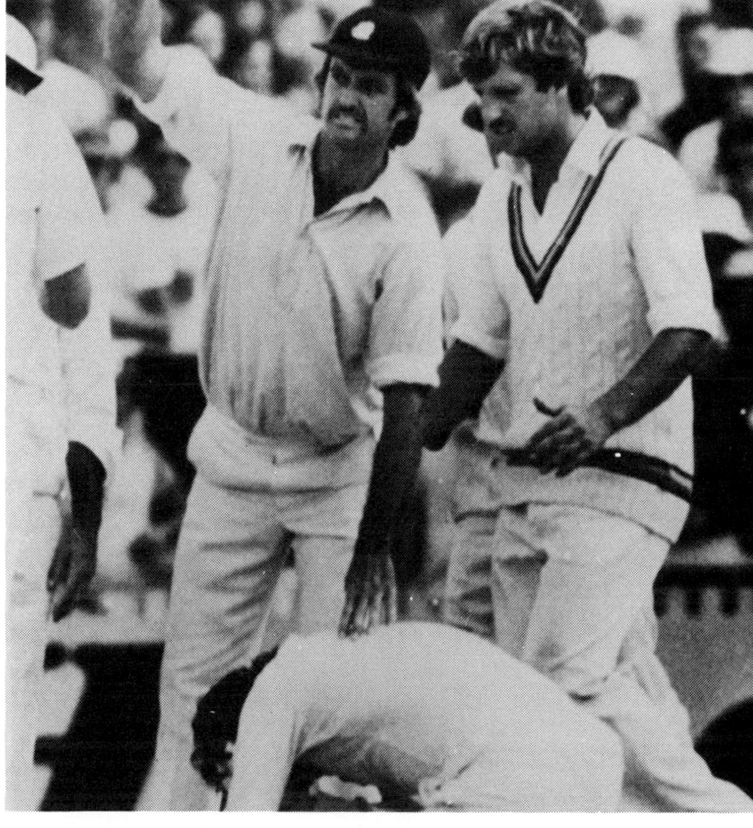

1039, above, left: *Geoff Boycott launches into a cover-drive during his unique score of 99 not out. The helmeted short leg fielder is Laird.* 1040, left: *Geoff Dymock, anything but a 'glamour' bowler, celebrates his Perth success with his captain, Greg Chappell.* 1041, above: *Allan Border, already with his first century against England, goes down after a blow from a rising ball. Willey and Botham try to assist him*

1979–80 SECOND TEST

Sydney, January 4, 5, 6, 8

England *123 (D.K. Lillee 4 for 40, G. Dymock 4 for 42) and 237 (D.I. Gower 98*, D.L. Underwood 43);* Australia *145 (I.M. Chappell 42, I.T. Botham 4 for 29) and 219 for 4 (G.S. Chappell 98*, K.J. Hughes 47, R.B. McCosker 41).* Australia won by 6 wickets.

Australia won the short series late on the fourth day, captain Greg Chappell, whose skill and determination saw his side through, stating afterwards that as far as the players were concerned the Ashes had been won. If an eager appeal for a catch at the wicket against Chappell had been upheld during the tense final innings Australia would have been 100 for 4. His stand with Hughes, however, amounted to 105, overcoming the threat posed chiefly by Underwood and Botham. The start of the match was delayed by rain, and it was widely felt that the toss would decide the match. Nevertheless, England, after seeing the first day out at 90 for 7, stayed in the game by holding the first-innings deficit to 22. Yet three good wickets were lost on the second evening, and it took a resolute innings by nightwatchman Underwood and a carefree and somewhat lucky 98 not out by Gower to raise Australia's target above 200. In the conditions, 216 was no easy requirement, especially with Underwood near his best. But McCosker's grittiness and Hughes's skill in support of their captain ensured that the luck with the toss of the coin at the outset was capitalised upon, even if the match was little more than a jamboree for fast-medium bowlers.

1042, above, left: *One of a number of torrid moments for Gower as Lillee bounces one clear over his helmet. Gower was to end up stranded two short of his century.* 1043, left: *Botham takes a bat-pad catch from Ian Chappell and Underwood, in his 30th Test against Australia, has his 100th wicket.* 1044, above: *Greg Chappell, playing to the on side with unique grace, takes his side further away from nervy indecision and closer to series victory*

1979–80
Melbourne, February 1, 2, 3, 5, 6

England *306 (G.A. Gooch 99, J.M. Brearley 60*, G. Boycott 44, D.K. Lillee 6 for 60) and 273 (I.T. Botham 119*, G.A. Gooch 51, D.K. Lillee 5 for 78, L.S. Pascoe 4 for 80)*; Australia *477 (G.S. Chappell 114, I.M. Chappell 75, B.M. Laird 74, A.R. Border 63, J.K. Lever 4 for 111) and 103 for 2 (G.S. Chappell 40*)*. Australia won by 8 wickets.

Australia made a clean sweep of the three-match rubber by dint of perseverance and discipline under pressure more usually associated with their traditional rivals. Having lost to West Indies by 408 runs that same week, Australia might have been reduced by low morale. Indeed, with England 170 for 1 on the first day there were signs that the tables would be turned. Then came the breakthrough. Four wickets went down for seven runs, and that England rose to 306 owed much to Brearley, the captain, who batted four hours. Gooch, in the final over before tea, missed his maiden Test century by inches when Hughes hit the bowler's stumps from mid-on as the batsman tried to scramble a single. Later that evening Lillee chalked up a further triumph by taking his 200th Test wicket. Australia applied themselves to the job in hand, spreading their innings of 477 over 180 overs. Laird, tough and patient, and Ian Chappell, sweeping vigorously at anything Underwood pitched to leg, added 127 for the second wicket; Border and Greg Chappell (hampered by a leg injury and throat infection) made sure of the advantage by putting on 126 for the fifth, the latter being 99 not out overnight. Lever and Underwood each bowled 53 overs, and Botham 40. Failure of the middle-order batsmen again ruined England's prospects, and at 157 for 6 on the fourth evening, with the ball keeping lower by the hour, admission prices were halved for the final day. However, Australia were held up by an overdue batting success by the hard-hitting Botham, who drove mightily during his 3¾-hour innings and was aided by Lever (12) in a stand of 89. Australia, with the Chappell brothers at the wicket, got home just into the final hour. The first day of this match was designated the Sir Robert Menzies Memorial Day in honour of the late Prime Minister's keen involvement in England-Australia cricket.

1045, below: *Graham Gooch's tragedy – a push to mid-on, an impulsive attempt at a single, and a direct hit by fieldsman Hughes sees the Essex batsman run out for 99.* 1046, right: *Laird, a latecomer to the Australian XI at 29, finds a gap in the field during his determined innings of 74.* 1047, below, right: *Congratulations for Dennis Lillee from his former Test captain Ian Chappell after the fast bowler had claimed his 200th wicket in all Tests. Also in the foreground is England's captain, Brearley, who went on to make an unbeaten 60*

1980 CENTENARY TEST

Lord's, August 28, 29, 30, September 1, 2

Australia *385 for 5 dec (K.J. Hughes 117, G.M. Wood 112, A.R. Border 56*, G.S. Chappell 47) and 189 for 4 dec (K.J. Hughes 84, G.S. Chappell 59)*; England *205 (G. Boycott 62, D.I. Gower 45, L.S. Pascoe 5 for 59, D.K. Lillee 4 for 43) and 244 for 3 (G. Boycott 128*, M.W. Gatting 51*)*. Match drawn.

A hundred years of Test cricket on English soil was commemorated with a special Test match and an airlift of over sixty former Australian players (as well as ACB officials and Larwood, Loader, Lock and Tyson, England players now resident in Australia). The oldest home player at the celebrations was Andrew Sandham, 90, and the senior Australians were Hendry, 85, and Ponsford, 79. Sir Donald Bradman was unable to attend. The match was staged at Lord's in deference to its facilities, although The Oval was not forgotten in that an Old England v Old Australia match was played there on the eve of the Centenary Test, Simpson's agile team beating Cowdrey's by seven wickets. Bad weather (eight hours were lost), illness in the veterans' ranks, and ugly scenes in the Long Room on the Saturday – the umpires and captains were jostled by some members who were frustrated at the long delay caused by poor covering of the square – prevented the Centenary occasion (sponsored by Cornhill Insurance) from taking on the gala atmosphere of its Melbourne counterpart 3½ years earlier; but the batting of Hughes (Man of the Match) in both innings will be remembered for its vigour and audacity, and Wood's determined century after Australia had taken first innings was a fine exhibition of composure. The start was delayed after overnight rain, and at the end of the first day Australia were well set with 227 for 2 on a firm pitch, Wood 100 not out off 89 overs. Only 75 minutes' play was possible on the second day, and irritation was widespread on the third when the start was delayed until 3.45, the umpires eventually filing out with a police escort. Hughes then completed his magnificent century, Border made a bold half-century, Chappell declared, and heavy rain fell after two balls from Lillee. Play on the last two days was extended by an hour, and a result seemed likely after all when England were bowled out inside 64 overs – Boycott and a free-stroking Gower making 96 for the third wicket and Pascoe having a fiery spell of 5 for 10 – and Australia were 287 ahead with eight wickets in hand by the fourth evening. But in the face of a target of 370 in 350 minutes, England were content to see it through, Boycott batting for 5¼ hours for his sixth century against Australia, and the match dying to a chorus of slow handclaps. Old, with 6 for 138 off 55 overs, was England's best bowler.

The Centenary teams: England – I.T. Botham (captain), G.A. Gooch, G. Boycott, C.W.J. Athey, D.I. Gower, M.W. Gatting, P. Willey, D.L. Bairstow, J.E. Emburey, C.M. Old, M. Hendrick, R.D. Jackman (12th man). Australia – G.S. Chappell (captain), G.M. Wood, B.M. Laird, K.J. Hughes, G.N. Yallop, A.R. Border, R.W. Marsh, R.J. Bright, D.K. Lillee, L.S. Pascoe, A.A. Mallett, J.R. Thomson (12th man). Umpires – H.D. Bird and D.J. Constant. Total paying attendance 73,409; takings £313,783.

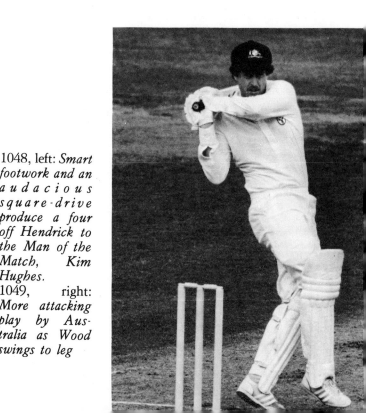

1048, left: *Smart footwork and an audacious square-drive produce a four off Hendrick to the Man of the Match, Kim Hughes.*
1049, right: *More attacking play by Australia as Wood swings to leg*

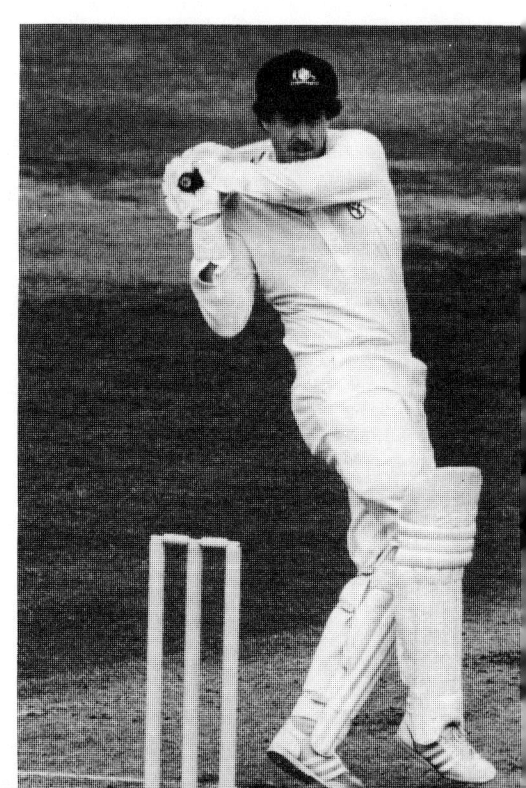

50, above: *Over 100 former Ashes campaigners joined the current teams and* *cials for a commemorative photograph during the rain-ruined Centenary Test* *Lord's. Some very distinguished faces – veterans of England–Australia Tests* *m as long ago as 1921 – appear in the front row: Bill O'Reilly, Len Darling,* *d a'Beckett, Bill Ponsford, Andrew Sandham, Ray Steele (ACB), Peter May,* *eg Chappell, Billy Griffith (MCC president), Ian Botham, Bob Parish (ACB* *irman), George Mann (TCCB chairman), 'Stork' Hendry, 'Gubby' Allen,* *b Wyatt, Percy Fender*

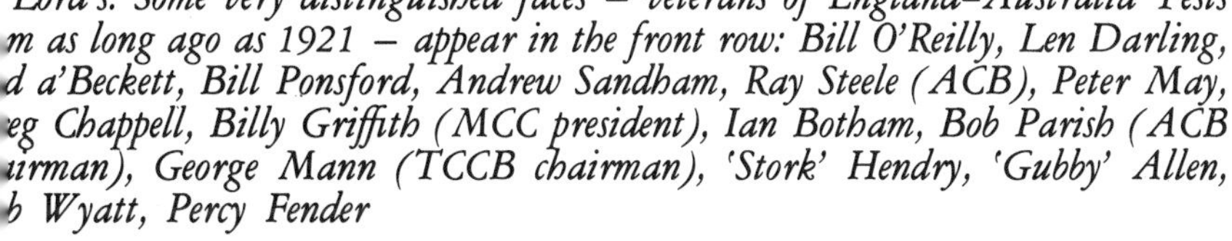

51, above: *Boycott, hemmed in by Laird and Border, inches towards his* *tury.* 1052, right: *Gower charms a four off the aggressive Pascoe*

1981 FIRST TEST

Trent Bridge, June 18, 19, 20, 21

England *185 (M.W. Gatting 52, T.M. Alderman 4 for 68) and 125 (D.K. Lillee 5 for 46, T.M. Alderman 5 for 62)*; Australia *179 (A.R. Border 63) and 132 for 6 (G.R. Dilley 4 for 24)*. Australia won by 4 wickets.

With Greg Chappell unavailable to tour and Thomson not chosen, Australia, led by Kim Hughes, began this series of sensations with an unexpected victory which was based as much as anything else upon missed catches. Put in, England made hard work of the seam bowling of Lillee, Hogg and debutant Alderman on an untypical Nottingham pitch and under heavy skies. Alderman, 25, from Western Australia, bowled half the first 48 overs of the match, showing fine stamina as well as control, while Gatting impressed with his determination. England fought back, Willis, having recovered from a third knee operation, taking his 200th Test wicket; but numerous catches went down, the most crucial being Downton's off Border at 10. On a weather-interrupted second day, Botham waited until the 55th over before bringing himself on, and though Australia's captain stated that his side would have made about 80 if the catches had stuck, they got to within six of England's first innings. The pitch never did settle down. English wickets toppled steadily, some to marvellous catches, such as Yallop's at gully to dismiss Gooch. Marsh took his 100th England wicket when he held Woolmer for his second duck of the match, and substitute Kent clung to a flashing Gower cut. Left to score an awkward 132, Australia met with some brisk Dilley overs before Trevor Chappell, the third of the brotherhood, in his maiden Test, saw Australia home on England's first Sunday of Test cricket. It was a sign of the times that not one over of spin was seen throughout.

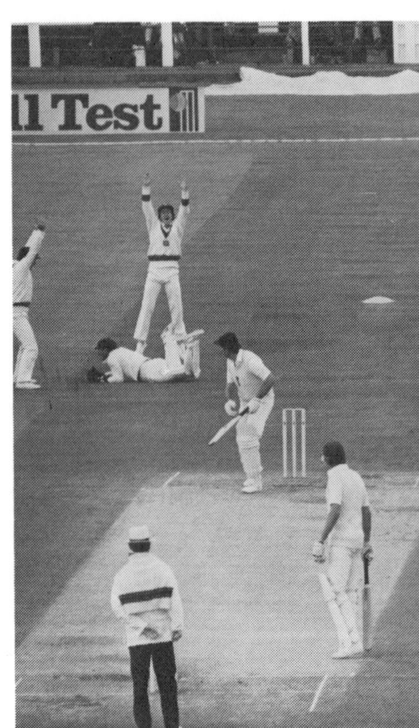

1054, right: *Australian keeper Rod Marsh snares his 100th England victim, a record. For batsman Bob Woolmer it was his second nought of the match.* 1055, below: *Bat beats ball – Australia's skipper, Hughes, drives past diving bowler Hendrick. Hughes was out lbw seven times in his 12 innings during the series*

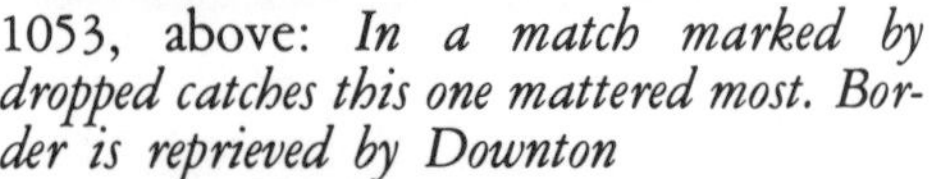

1053, above: *In a match marked by dropped catches this one mattered most. Border is reprieved by Downton*

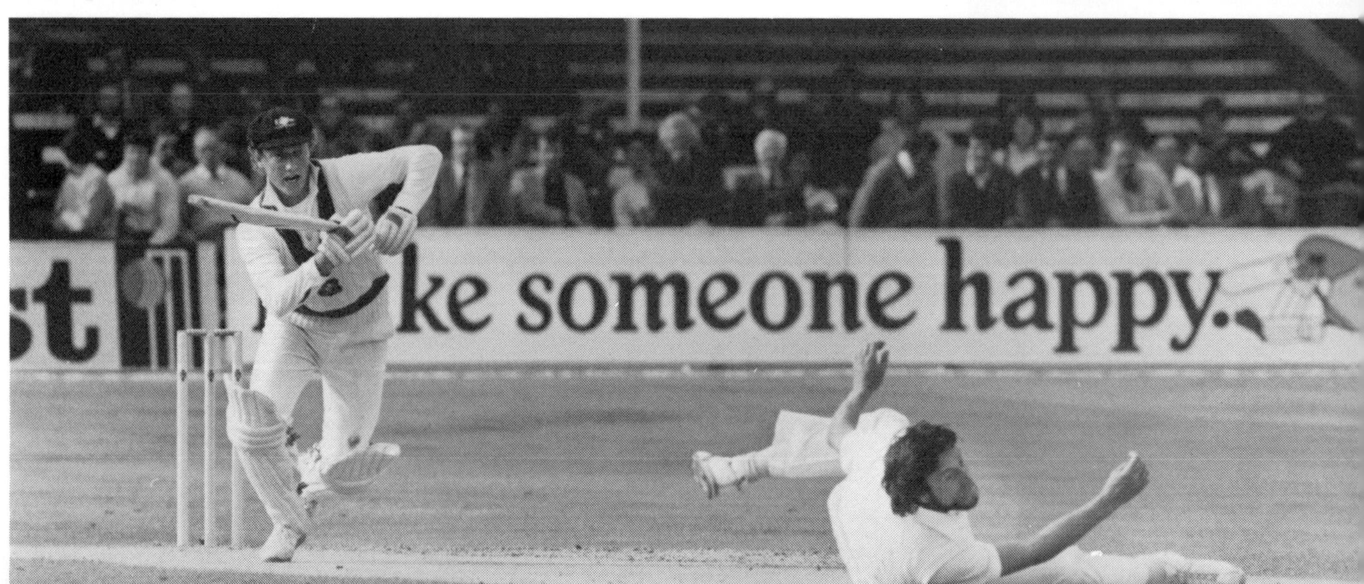

1981
Lord's, July 2, 3, 4, 6, 7

SECOND TEST

England *311 (P. Willey 82, M.W. Gatting 59, G.A. Gooch 44, G.F. Lawson 7 for 81) and 265 for 8 dec (D.I. Gower 89, G. Boycott 60);* Australia *345 (A.R. Border 64, R.W. Marsh 47, G.M. Wood 44, K.J. Hughes 42, D.K. Lillee 40*) and 90 for 4 (G.M. Wood 62*).* Match drawn.

Geoff Boycott's 100th Test match was spoilt by another dubious pitch – this time subject to variable bounce – and some negative batting. The over rate, too, despite the inclusion of spinners Bright and Emburey, was poor. Again Hughes sent England in, and Gooch began boldly; but Lawson, on his way to the best Australian figures at Lord's apart from Massie's in 1972, bowled with devilish effect, and only Willey, full of resolution, and Gatting, hooking and driving well, dragged England to a reasonable total. Emburey batted almost three hours for 31. Time was lost on the Friday, aggravated by the umpires' error in not recalling the players during the extra hour when the light improved. The TCCB later issued an apology; some frustrated spectators hurled seat-cushions onto the field. Border, first with Hughes then Marsh, rescued Australia from 81 for 4, Emburey being called into the attack later than seemed advisable. With only 16 wickets having fallen in the first three days, a draw was already likely, and after tailend resistance (and an Ashes record of 55 extras, Willis 28 no-balls), Australia found themselves with a lead of 34. Boycott now embarked on an innings lasting 279 minutes, and though Gower stroked willingly, and was one of four batsmen to hit a six, Australia were faced with no difficult task on a now-easy pitch if they were to save the match after the declaration. All was swiftly overshadowed by the announcement by Botham (who had just completed a 'pair') that he did not wish to stay as captain on a match basis. The selectors had been about to appoint someone new in any case.

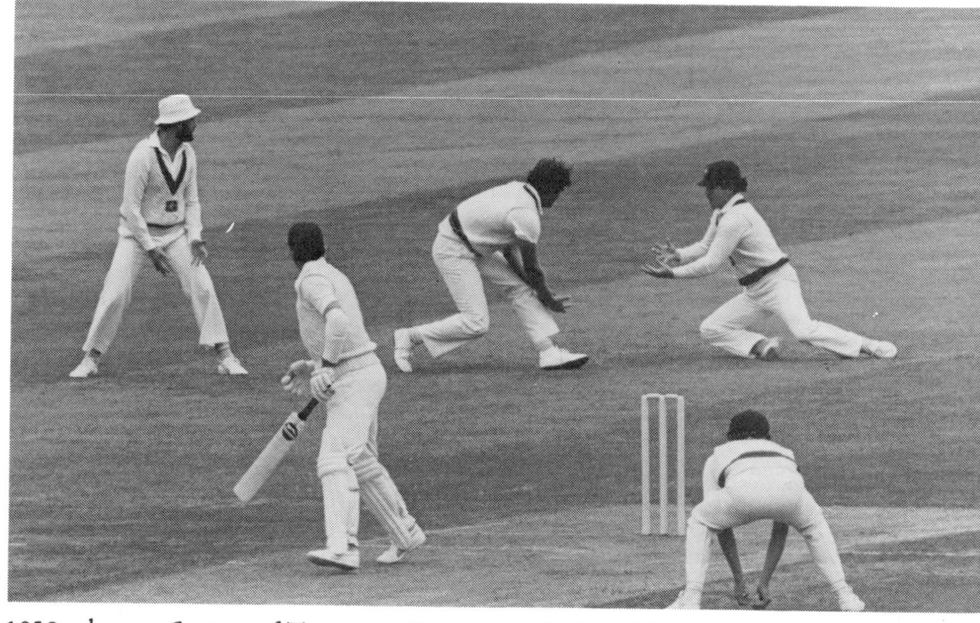

056, above: *Geoff Lawson (7 for 81) n vigorous action.* 1057, below: *Howzat? Not out! Trevor Chappell urvives*

1058, above: *Century-of-Tests man Boycott caught by Alderman (capless) on the rebound* 1059, below, right: *Gooch hooks and is caught for 44, his best score of the series*

1981 THIRD TEST

Headingley, July 16, 17, 18, 20, 21

Australia *401 for 9 dec (J. Dyson 102, K.J. Hughes 89, G.N. Yallop 58, I T. Botham 6 for 95) and 111 (R.G.D. Willis 8 for 43)*; England *174 (I.T. Botham 50, D.K. Lillee 4 for 49) and 356 (I.T. Botham 149, G.R. Dilley 56, G. Boycott 46, T.M. Alderman 6 for 135).* England won by 18 runs.

At around 3 p.m. on the fourth day, with England 135 for 7 in the follow-on and still 92 behind, odds of 500–1 were offered against the home team. Not quite 24 hours later, Ian Botham and Bob Willis had swung the match round in such storming fashion that it was hours, even days, before everybody had digested what had happened. Only once before, at Sydney in 1894, had a side won a Test after having followed on. Then, rain helped. Here, it was a thrilling, smashing innings by Botham which developed from 'nothing to lose' to 'everything to gain', followed by a frightening downwind spell by 32-year-old fast bowler Willis, whose 8 for 43 ensured that he was not playing his final Test after all. The wisdom bred by hindsight suggests that Alderman was left on too long during England's hectic assault, when Bright might have induced more risk; yet Alderman throughout the series always seemed to be taking wickets. Australia's daunting first-innings total owed much to the Woodfull-like Dyson, whose hard-earned maiden Test century was to be veiled by later events. Hughes played freely before falling to Botham, who had told his new captain, Mike Brearley, to leave him on and he would take five wickets. When England fell apart to the three-prong pace attack it served to emphasise how poorly their own bowlers had utilised a sporty wicket. They were back in again that evening and Gooch was soon out for the second time on a day in which Marsh passed Knott's Test record of 263 dismissals. On the fourth day England plunged into deeper trouble, and when the pugnacious Willey uppercut Lillee to third man and was caught, the Australian fast bowler passed Trumble's Ashes record of 141 wickets. Soon Boycott's 3½ hours of grim tenancy ended, and Taylor was seventh out. The graph had reached its low point. Now, in 80 riotous minutes, Dilley belted away, adding 117 with Botham. That put England 25 ahead. Defeat still seemed inevitable. Yet Old managed to stay nearly an hour, making 29, while Botham took complete command, finding

1060, left: *Botham and mastermind captain Brearley* *Leeds.* 1061, below, left: *Dilley strikes out. He made a vi* 56. 1062, below: *John Dyson forges toward an admira* *century which was due soon to be overshadowed*

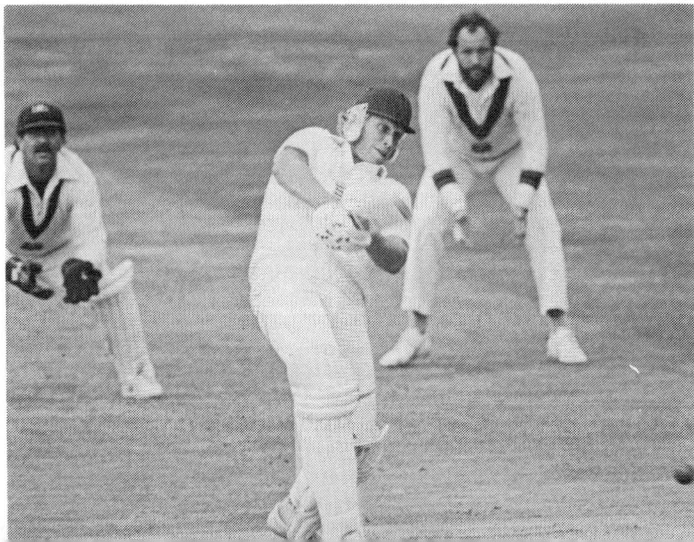

1063, left: *The magnificent Botham drives.* 1064, below: *and hooks.* 1065, right: *Old gets Border, another big turning point.* 1066, right, centre: *Marsh hooks Willis fatally.* 1067, right, bottom: *Bright is castled, and a great Test match ends*

the boundary even with mis-hits. The deposed captain drove like Hammond and hooked like O'Neill. The Australians were stunned, and left but to hope. Botham's hundred came in 157 minutes off only 87 balls, his second 50 taking only 40 minutes. The first Australian spin of the match came in the 129th over of the innings when Bright was tried, and when Lawson bowled Old, England's lead was 92 – not much, but threatening now that a tide of exhilaration went with it. By the close England were 351 for 9, Botham (145) having made 106 in the final session, with Willis playing a vital role. Five more runs came on the final morning, and Australia were left to gird themselves to make 130 for victory. Thirteen came quickly. Then Wood went, and Willis was switched to the Kirkstall end. Hair streaming, knees pumping, he hurled everything at the batsmen, and in a dramatic few minutes before lunch he had Chappell, Hughes and Yallop caught, two of them brilliantly. Old shot one through Border for a crucial wicket; Dyson was caught behind, hooking; Dilley held a Marsh hook on the line: 74 for 7. Willis beat Lawson with speed: 75 for 8; and then Lillee and Bright took 35 off four overs. Perhaps it had all been a vain English dream after all? Then Lillee popped a ball from Willis towards mid-on; Gatting dived forward and held the catch: 110 for 9. To cap it all, Old twice missed Alderman at third slip off Botham. A Willis yorker settled it. Bright was helpless. England were triumphant by 18 runs. Cricket brushed all else from the headlines. Botham edged out Willis for the Man of the Match award, and joined Jack Gregory as the only men to score a century and take five or more wickets in an innings in an Ashes Test.

1981 FOURTH TEST

Edgbaston, July 30, 31, August 1, 2

England *189 (J.M. Brearley 48, T.M. Alderman 5 for 42) and 219 (R.J. Bright 5 for 68)*; Australia *258 (K.J. Hughes 47, M.F. Kent 46, J.E. Emburey 4 for 43) and 121 (A.R. Border 40, I.T. Botham 5 for 11)*. England won by 29 runs.

The 'Miracle of Headingley' left greedy optimists expecting more and realists certain that this kind of drama was non-repetitive. Yet Edgbaston served up more excitement as nervous batting restricted the totals and the unstoppable Botham pulled another match out of the fire, guided by the shrewd Brearley, his 'father figure'. The Australians, left 1-2 down at the end, were depressed and shocked. England batted carelessly for their 189 after winning their first toss, Brearley's 48 in 166 minutes eventually becoming match top-score. Not for 46 years had a completed Test contained no half-century. Again, Alderman's movement through air and off pitch was demanding. Australia gained a handy lead through Wood's three-hour 38, Hughes's game knock, and Kent's handsome first Test effort. Willis's 28 no-balls were also a weighty contribution. England made morbid progress on the third day, the batsmen's trust low after recent events and in their idealistic desire for perfect pitches. The tension on both sides was apparent in the Australian innings, when verbal exchanges were frequent. England needed 90 minutes to wipe off the remaining 20-run deficit. Seventeen maiden overs were bowled in the morning session. Bowling into the rough, Bright seemed to have clinched the match during the afternoon when he dismissed Boycott, Gooch, Willey and Gatting, and at 167 for 8 England were only 98 ahead. Now came the important resistance. Emburey (37 not out) and Taylor (8) added 50 in 73 minutes. Needing 151, Australia lost Wood that night, and by lunch on the fourth day, adopting the gentle approach, they were 62 for 3: 89 wanted. Then Emburey broke through. Difficult deliveries had both left-handers caught; but again, a fine contribution was drowned in later sensations. Botham came on and dealt with Marsh, Bright, Lillee, Kent and Alderman – five wickets for one run in 28 balls; England, after hours of deafening crowd support, were winners by 29 runs. It was not so much the Lion and the Kangaroo: all along, it seemed, the cat had been playing with the mouse.

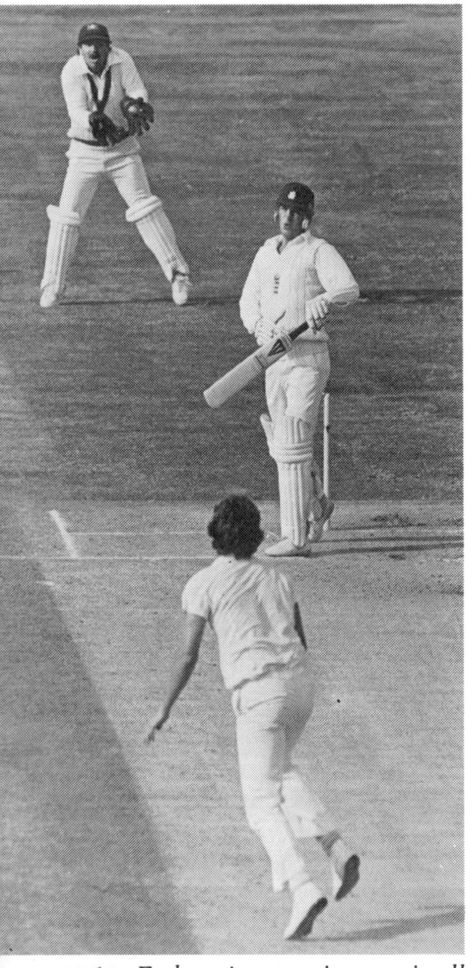

1068: *Emburey's expression says it all as Alderman buzzes one past*

1069: *Willis gave Yallop a torrid time, but he had his shining hour next Test*

1070: *Gatting turns Lillee. He played som useful innings during the '81 series*

1981 FIFTH TEST

Old Trafford, August 13, 14, 15, 16, 17

England *231 (C.J. Tavaré 69, P.J.W. Allott 52*, D.K. Lillee 4 for 55, T.M. Alderman 4 for 88) and 404 (I.T. Botham 118, C.J. Tavaré 78, A.P.E. Knott 59, J.E. Emburey 57, T.M. Alderman 5 for 109);* Australia *130 (M.F. Kent 52, R.G.D. Willis 4 for 63) and 402 (A.R. Border 123*, G.N. Yallop 114, R.W. Marsh 47, K.J. Hughes 43).* England won by 103 runs.

And yet another nailbiter, though the characteristics were different. Australia's batting was again dismal – until the second innings, when it seemed for some hours that another fantasy was to materialise. Needing 506 for victory, the tourists earned admiration by reaching 198 for 3, with the English bowlers starting to look ordinary on a beautiful pitch. Yallop had made an extraordinarily bright century, and Border was solid as Ayers Rock. But Kent quickly followed Yallop, and though Marsh and Lillee stayed a time, Border was left high and dry, batting seven hours in all and having made the slowest Test century ever for Australia (373 minutes) – this with a broken finger. The showpiece innings came from Botham. In at 104 for 5 in the second innings, when England were only 205 ahead, with six sixes (an Ashes record) and 14 fours, he made 118 in 123 minutes, treating Lillee's bouncers with disdain and reaching his century off only 86 balls this time. Another Ashes record was set when Botham (19) and his staunch ally Tavaré (3) took 22 off a Lillee over, and altogether 57 runs came off five overs with the new ball. Tavaré, following his 287 minutes at the crease in the first innings, hung around for seven hours in the second, unglamorous sheetanchor performances which deserved medals. His long tenancy was unique for an Ashes Test debutant. Later, Knott, England's third wicketkeeper of the series, and Emburey made half-centuries which seemed to have made England safe. Mike Whitney, a left-arm fast bowler from Sydney, with only six first-class matches behind him, was recruited from Gloucestershire when Hogg and Lawson were unfit. Another debutant, Allott, made his first fifty in big cricket, and that, with Tavaré's first masterpiece of patience, made England's total respectable. Australia then crumbled for 130 in 30.2 overs, their shortest innings since 1902, when Rhodes and Hirst felled them for 36 at Edgbaston in 23 overs. Willis began the crash with his 100th Australian wicket, taking three in that over; and later, after Gower at gully had somehow grasped a slash from Border, Knott made his 100th Australian dismissal, ending Kent's brave innings. On the third day England advanced turgidly: 10 in the first hour, 19 in the next. Tavaré's 50 took 306 minutes, the slowest ever in English first-class cricket. Then came Botham. Australia's final defiance was carried by Border, who took the contest into the final session. Even then, Botham had a hand in things. His catch to remove Lillee, who was becoming a nuisance, was a glorious leaping feat. It was a match for catches. Dyson's at third man to dismiss Knott was almost unbelievable. So England regained, or retained, the Ashes, while Australia's rusted pride was restored after 14 days of the most pulsating combat in Ashes history. And Boycott gloried in a further record: he passed Hammond's record England aggregate of 7624 runs.

1071, left: *Chris Tavaré, batting at Manchester in his first Ashes Test. He stayed at the crease longer than many a batsman with careers extending to a dozen Tests and more.* 1072, below, left: *Botham's power shows in a drive against Whitney.* 1073, right: *Down but never out – Allan Border mildly disturbed by a Botham bouncer. He resisted for seven hours*

1981 SIXTH TEST

The Oval, August 27, 28, 29, 31, September 1

Australia *352 (A.R. Border 106*, G.M. Wood 66, M.F. Kent 54, I.T. Botham 6 for 125, R.G.D. Willis 4 for 91) and 344 for 9 dec (D.M. Wellham 103, A.R. Border 84, R.W. Marsh 52, M. Hendrick 4 for 82, I.T. Botham 4 for 128)*; England *314 (G. Boycott 137, M.W. Gatting 53, D.K. Lillee 7 for 89) and 261 for 7 (A.P.E. Knott 70*, M.W. Gatting 56, J.M. Brearley 51, D.K. Lillee 4 for 70).* Match drawn.

In the last of the gripping 1981 Tests normality was restored. There were tensions, particularly on the last day, when England had to fight; but the highlights concerned individuals. The oldest player, Boycott, made his 21st Test century, his seventh against Australia, and the youngest, Dirk Wellham, his first, in his first Test. Botham crowned his own efforts with his 200th Test wicket, and Border made another courageous not-out century, followed by 84, taking his sequence to 15 hours before he lost his wicket. In the first ever 'sixth Test' in England, Brearley surprised by sending Australia in. Wood and Kent made 120, the first century opening for Australia for over four years, and the score rose to 260 for 4. A final 352 spelt recovery by England, who then suffered a similar slide, going from 246 for 2 to 314 all out. Boycott reached a record 61st Test half-century, and Lillee, in his famous headband, obtained his best Test figures, 7 for 89, earned by persistent menace. He was noticeably recovered from his illness earlier in the tour. Alderman, on his way to a new Australian series record of 42 wickets, inflicted a duck on debutant Paul Parker, while Lillee finished the series with 39 wickets, and 290 in all Tests. Boycott, batting better as he went on, eventually fell to a snap catch by Yallop at gully. The fourth day found England short on bowling: Willis, having passed Rhodes's record of 109 wickets for England v Australia, was off with a strain, and Botham and Hendrick carried injuries. Still Australia were made to fight. This time Border had Wellham with him. The bespectacled younger man was dropped at 18 but stayed cool, laying into hooks and drives of pleasing freshness. They added 101, and in the gloom of the evening Wellham, now down to Lillee as his partner, was on 99 for 25 minutes, and was missed by Boycott, before posting his hundred, the first by an Australian in England while on Test debut since Harry Graham in 1893. Australia were thus safe. Could they now steal victory? With all day to make 383, England lost Boycott for 0, and were 144 for 6 at 2.30 p.m. Brearley and Knott then sealed matters with a dedicated stand of 93, and though Emburey was dropped by Border in the 18th of the final 20 overs, real tension had long evaporated – which was a mercy. This series, it was roundly agreed, had been altogether too hard on the blood pressure.

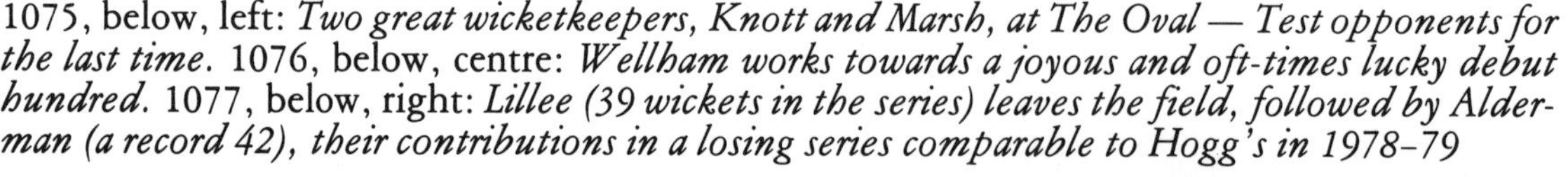

1075, below, left: *Two great wicketkeepers, Knott and Marsh, at The Oval — Test opponents for the last time.* 1076, below, centre: *Wellham works towards a joyous and oft-times lucky debut hundred.* 1077, below, right: *Lillee (39 wickets in the series) leaves the field, followed by Alderman (a record 42), their contributions in a losing series comparable to Hogg's in 1978–79*

1074, above: *Martin Kent, a fresh talent*

1982–83 FIRST TEST

Perth, November 12, 13, 14, 16, 17

England *411 (C.J. Tavaré 89, D.W. Randall 78, D.I. Gower 72, A.J. Lamb 46, B. Yardley 5 for 107) and 358 (D.W. Randall 115, A.J. Lamb 56, D.R. Pringle 47*, G.F. Lawson 5 for 108);* Australia *424 for 9 dec (G.S. Chappell 117, K.J. Hughes 62, D.W. Hookes 56, J. Dyson 52, G.F. Lawson 50, G. Miller 4 for 70) and 73 for 2.* Match drawn.

An alarming incident on the second day, when a player was seriously injured during an invasion of the playing area by spectators, created an unwanted kind of tension as the Ashes Centenary series got under way. England, put in, slowly amassed a comfortable total, thanks to an attractive 72 by Gower off 98 balls, a statuesque 89 by Tavaré in 466 minutes (he froze on 66 for 90 minutes), and a typically mixed innings by Randall. Botham's dismissal, given caught behind, came from a delayed and curious decision, one of many that clouded the series. But all else was overshadowed when a pack of youths ran on to 'celebrate' England's 400, two waving Union Jacks. One flicked Australian fast bowler Alderman on the head, and as the player chased him and tackled him, he damaged his own shoulder so badly that he had to withdraw from the match and played no more cricket that summer. Chappell led his men from the field until order was restored. Australia moved faster than England in overhauling their 411. Chappell, after some early luck, moved imperiously to his eighth Ashes century, and added 141 with Hughes in two hours for the fourth wicket. Botham, who had reached the unique Test double of 3000 runs and 250 wickets, bowled stoically into the breeze for several hours; but Miller could not match Yardley's sharpness of spin. Dyson, Hookes and Lawson all contributed half-centuries of varying class. By the end of the fourth day England were far from safe, having lost five for 163. Tavaré, the anchorman, took 64 minutes to open his score, but perished for 9. The chunky, South African-born Lamb completed a good Ashes debut double, but all hopes rested with Randall (45 not out) on the last morning. Mixing classic shots with manoeuvres all of his own invention, Randall moved to his third hundred in Australia, and stout efforts by Taylor and the tall Pringle saw England out of danger. Cowans, Jamaican-born and the 500th man to play for England, partially atoned for some erratic bowling with a timely career top-score of 36. A match full of incident also saw Yardley's 100th Test wicket and glorious catches by Dyson and Lamb. England captain Willis shared most of the bowling with Botham and took five wickets; but Lillee, now 33, was understandably no longer as sharp as before, even though his stamina and courage were unquestioned. Since early in 1982 England were without 15 major players – including Boycott, Gooch and Emburey – who had been banned for three years following their disapproved tour of South Africa.

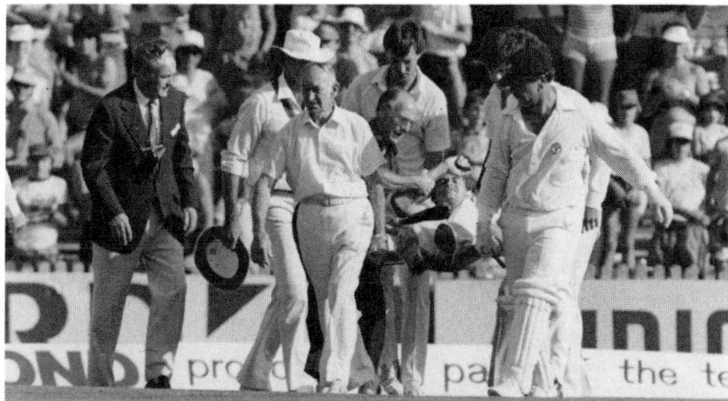

1078, left: *Test match tragedy: Alderman carried from the field.* 1079, below, left: *Chief runmaker Randall counterattacks Lillee.* 1080, below: *Hot time for the obdurate Tavaré (bowler Lawson)*

1982–83 SECOND TEST

Brisbane, November 26, 27, 28, 30, December 1

England *219 (A.J. Lamb 72, I.T. Botham 40, G.F. Lawson 6 for 47) and 309 (G. Fowler 83, G. Miller 60, J.R. Thomson 5 for 73, G.F. Lawson 5 for 87)*; Australia *341 (K.C. Wessels 162, G.S. Chappell 53, B. Yardley 53, R.G.D. Willis 5 for 66) and 190 for 3 (D.W. Hookes 66*, K.C. Wessels 46).* Australia won by 7 wickets.

Again put in, England wilted before the pace of the lanky Lawson and new man Rackemann, Lamb's brave 72 and Botham's bold 40 averting total humiliation. Australia then built up from a shaky start, South African-born Wessels batting for almost eight hours and becoming the 14th batsman to score a debut century for Australia in Ashes cricket. Tucked up awkwardly on his leg stump, the left-hander prospered off anything short or outside the off, and finished with 208 runs, a record for Australia in a maiden Test, surpassing Jackson's 164 and 36 at Adelaide in 1929. Wessels was one of five Queensland players, a record (12th man Ritchie and umpire Johnson were also Queenslanders). Willis, lacking faith in Cowans, did most of the work in harness with Botham, Hemmings and Miller, and at 171 for 6, Australia were under threat, having to bat last. But Yardley helped Wessels add 100, and when Wessels was last man out the lead was, after all, a reassuring 122. England's batsmen then had to withstand a torrid bouncer attack, much of it in poor light, and mixed in with numerous no-balls (Australia bowled 62 in the match, England 22). Fowler, in his first Ashes Test, often played and missed, and was hit, but fought gamely on for six hours. With Rackemann leaving the field injured, Australia were faced with the prospect of the match being turned round. But Thomson recaptured some of his 1974-75 firepower and cut away the top and middle of the innings. Miller hung on grimly, but while Yardley tied up one end securely, Lawson finished off the innings, becoming the first to take 11 wickets in a Brisbane Ashes Test. Had England raised the target by 50 runs, Australia might have been stretched. As it was, after losing three wickets for 23 runs – including Chappell, the tormentor of Cowans, who finally had him caught off a hook – Hughes and Hookes (who savagely punished Botham's short stuff) carried Australia to victory. Marsh, whose six catches in England's second innings, and nine in the match, were Ashes records, became the first wicketkeeper to hold 300 Test catches, while Border and Randall both reached 1000 runs in Ashes Tests. For only the second time in Ashes Tests, England lost all their wickets to catches (first innings), and 19 in the match (a world Test record).

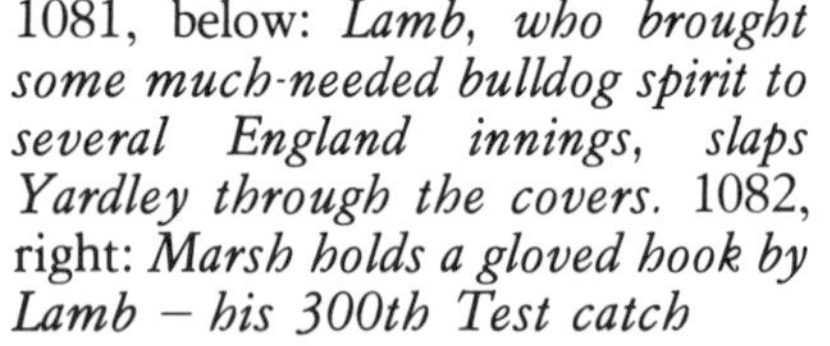

1081, below: *Lamb, who brought some much-needed bulldog spirit to several England innings, slaps Yardley through the covers.* 1082, right: *Marsh holds a gloved hook by Lamb – his 300th Test catch*

1083, below: *Thomson, often bowling with the speed and lift of eight years earlier, launches one to Gower*

1084, left: *Fowler hung on gamely despite some close shaves*

1085, right: *Kepler Wessels, born in Bloemfontein, makes some history with a Test debut innings of 162 – first in, last out – in 7¾ hours*

1982–83 THIRD TEST

Adelaide, December 10, 11, 12, 14, 15

Australia *438 (G.S. Chappell 115, K.J. Hughes 88, K.C. Wessels 44, J. Dyson 44, I.T. Botham 4 for 112) and 83 for 2;* England *216 (A.J. Lamb 82, D.I. Gower 60, G.F. Lawson 4 for 56) and 304 (D.I. Gower 114, I.T. Botham 58, G.F. Lawson 5 for 66).* Australia won by 8 wickets.

Australia went two-up not only because Willis gave them first use of a fair pitch but through inadequate English batting against brisk and often short-pitched bowling, Hogg completing a three-prong attack with Lawson and Thomson, Lillee, Alderman and Rackemann all being ruled out by injury. England bowled well enough to contain Australia to under three runs an over, Hemmings (1 for 96 off 48 overs) bowling particularly tightly. But Chappell was in brilliant form, scoring his 22nd Test century, his first at Adelaide. His four-hour display contained strokes of all varieties, and this time Hughes was content to play second fiddle. Before Chappell fell to an amazing catch at gully by Gower, he had joined Hill and Bradman as the only scorers of 2500 runs against England. Hughes twice hooked Botham for six, and Pringle played into Australia's hands with 27 no-balls. Botham's diving catch at fine leg to dismiss Hookes was a highlight, but Australia soon gained control by demolishing England's first innings for 216 and putting them in again. While the cavalier Lamb and Gower were adding 119, England held on. But the rest was like matchwood. Crease-occupation was important for England in the follow-on, but only Gower, with a delightful century which included a scoreless hour after he reached three figures, and Botham, with what proved to be his highest score in the series, lasted longer than the gutsy Fowler (37 in 139 minutes). The heat was intense, but Australia's bowlers stuck to their task heroically, with the umpires allowing great latitude with the short-pitched ball. Australia's eventual target proved to be no trouble.

1086, left: *Hughes punishes Botham.* 1087, below: *Lawson disturbs the seagulls as well as England's batting*

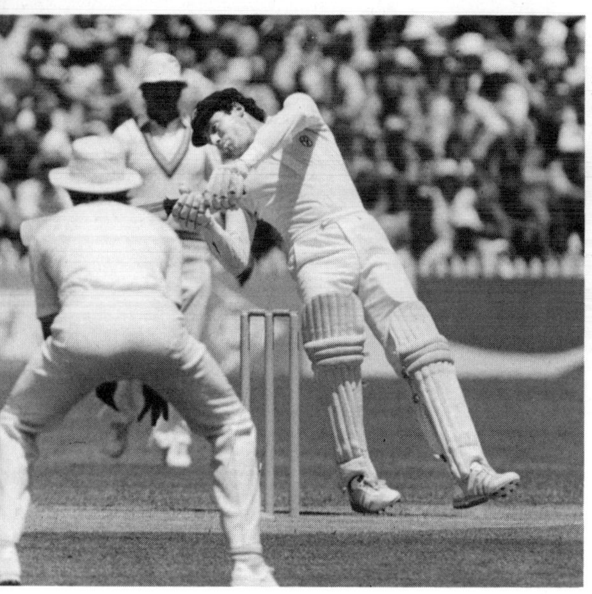

Adelaide century-makers: 1088, left: *Chappell, like a toy soldier, keels over as a Willis bouncer whistles by.* 1089, right: *Gower, cool and elegant, keeps England's faint hopes alive*

1982–83 FOURTH TEST

Melbourne, December 26, 27, 28, 29, 30

England *284 (C.J. Tavaré 89, A.J. Lamb 83, R.M. Hogg 4 for 69, B. Yardley 4 for 89) and 294 (G. Fowler 65, I.T. Botham 46, D.R. Pringle 42, G.F. Lawson 4 for 66);* Australia *287 (K.J. Hughes 66, D.W. Hookes 53, R.W. Marsh 53, K.C. Wessels 47) and 288 (D.W. Hookes 68, A.R. Border 62*, K.J. Hughes 48, N.G. Cowans 6 for 77).* England won by 3 runs.

The series was injected with fresh lifeblood with a painfully thrilling contest which marked the 250th Test match between the two countries. (It was also Melbourne's 75th Test in all). Only once before in any Test had the runs margin at the end been so slender, and that was at Old Trafford in 1902, when Tate was bowled, last man, with England four runs from victory. Yet this latterday match was even more exciting and closely-fought. All four innings were in the tight range of 284 to 294, and the climax was protracted as Border and Thomson (21) added 37 for the last wicket towards the end of the fourth day, and another 33 next morning, when over 15,000 came (free) to witness what might have been only one ball. Willis was criticised for easing the pressure on Border in order to get at Thomson, and panic began to show in the field. Then, no ordinary finish being scripted for this breathtaking match, Thomson edged Botham to Tavaré – who made a mess of the catch. Miller moved behind him, though, and held it safely, and the Englishmen sprinted from the field like excited schoolboys. Yet again the captain winning the toss put his opponents in, and before a Boxing Day crowd of 64,051 England (again losing all 10 wickets to catches) overcame a bad start by racing to 217 for 3 before Yardley and Hogg wiped out the remainder. Lamb again played aggressively and well, but the surprise was Tavaré, who hit 15 fours in his four-hour 89. Hughes (66 in 4¼ hours) batted more like the characteristic Tavaré as Australia worked their way to a lead of three runs, Chappell falling first ball, hooking Cowans. In their second innings England were half out for 129, Gower receiving a bad decision, and Hogg removing Tavaré for O. Fowler's 65 ended soon after he had driven a ball from Thomson onto his foot, breaking a bone. There had been a delay while Chappell reluctantly agreed to the choice of Gower as Fowler's runner. Though Australia's fast bowlers shared all the wickets, England's later batsmen held on, Pringle making 42, Taylor 37. Australia's target of 292 seemed remote on a pitch of uneven bounce, and three were out for 71, including Chappell (2) again to Cowans, who was now bowling fast and with confidence with the new ball. Hughes and Hookes then added 100, the Englishmen, Botham in particular, sometimes showing their dismay at the refusal of their appeals. Miller had Hughes caught by Taylor, and the dangerous Hookes was caught mis-pulling Cowans, who finished the day with six of the nine wickets plus a catch. Rain interrupted the evening play, but Thomson survived, with Border regaining his lost touch with every over. The final day's play lasted 85 minutes, with almost as many thrills. Special direct television was laid on to England, and almost everyone in Australia stayed tuned to TV or radio. The decisive ball brought Botham his 100 wickets against Australia, and gave him the fastest 1000/100 double (22 Tests). He joined Giffen, Noble and Rhodes in this elite list. Chappell passed Simpson's Australian record of 110 catches, and Marsh's 27th dismissal of the series took him to yet another record.

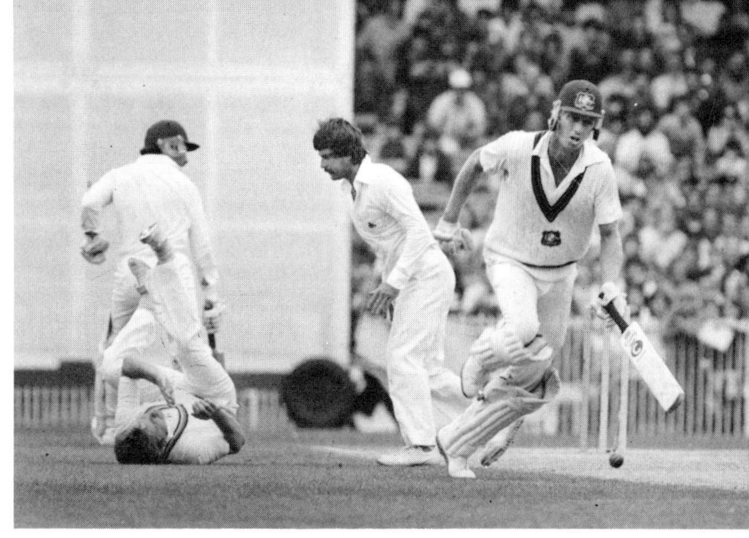

1090, above: *Fowler c Chappell b Hogg, one of several marvellous catches taken in the series by the Australian captain*. 1091, above, right: *Lamb and substitute fielder Gould collide, and Thomson and Border escape during the pulsating final-wicket stand of 70*. 1092, below: *the catch that ended it*

1093, above: *Skipper Willis finds he has a matchwinner in Cowans, the 21-year-old Middlesex paceman*

1094, above: *Botham is no stranger to exuberance, but even Willis lets go at the end*

1095 above: *The new electronic TV/scoreboard at the MCG added a dimension to the proceedings*. 1096, left: *Swashbuckler Hookes presented dangers to England in both innings*. 1097, right: *Cowans hurls his considerable frame into action. His 6 for 77 won him the Man of the Match award*

1982–83

Sydney, January 2, 3, 4, 6, 7

Australia *314 (A.R. Border 89, J. Dyson 79, I.T. Botham 4 for 75) and 382 (K.J. Hughes 137, A.R. Border 83, K.C. Wessels 53, R.W. Marsh 41)*; England *237 (D.I. Gower 70, D.W. Randall 70, J.R. Thomson 5 for 50) and 314 for 7 (E.E. Hemmings 95, D.W. Randall 44, B. Yardley 4 for 139).* Match drawn.

Australia recovered the Ashes by shutting England out in the final Test of a series in which, overall, they had outplayed – certainly outbowled – the visitors. An unsatisfactory aspect of their success, however, was that the umpiring seldom inspired confidence, and this left many English people erroneously believing that the better side lost the rubber. This decisive Test began with a controversy. Dyson, still to face a ball, seemed clearly run out by a throw from Willis, but was given the benefit of what the umpire saw as some doubt. Television revealed Dyson to be out by some distance. He batted efficiently and responsibly for five hours in all, the first day being shortened by rain. Border survived a hesitant start to bolster the innings vitally, but 314 looked good when Cook, Tavaré and Lamb were out, the last two bowled by Lawson cutters for O. The fiery Lawson finished the series with 34 wickets at 20.21, and was voted Man of the Series. Gower and Randall (recovering from a nasty blow in the mouth while batting in Tasmania) added 122 before the former fell to a great left-handed catch by Chappell four minutes past the scheduled lunch break. Randall played with glorious freedom, reaching 50 off 65 balls. Thomson then brought about a collapse with some express overs, and by stumps on the third day Australia, 90 for 3, were 167 ahead. By the end of the fourth, England needed a near-hopeless 452, having lost Cook. Australia's security was owed chiefly to Hughes, whose 137 came in 379 minutes of fierce concentration while containing 12 fours and three sixes. Off-spinners Hemmings and Miller were rendered ineffective as Hughes (in his 100th Test innings) and Border (in his 50th Test) used their feet well and capitalised on bad length. The last day saw England ward off any threat of defeat, with nightwatchman Hemmings the unlikely hero, his 95 coming in 3¾ hours. Hughes, with his eighth Test century, was made Man of the Match, and an anonymous donor presented the Australians with a silver urn containing a burnt bail – the 'new Ashes', or 'Urnie'.

THE AUSTRALIA

UMBER 5718 MONDAY JANUARY 3 1983

'In or out' riddle opens Ashes decider

By PHIL WILKINS

Match Report – Page 16

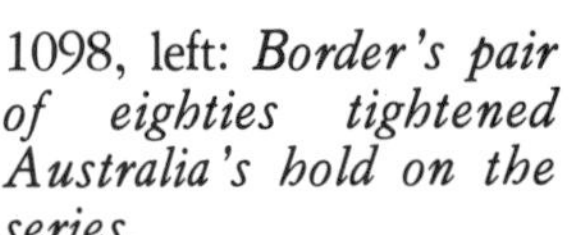

1098, left: *Border's pair of eighties tightened Australia's hold on the series*

1099, above: *Hughes and Chappell with the 'new Ashes'.* 1100, top, right: *The vital reprieve for Dyson received front-page treatment.* 1101, right: *His 95 having secured England's safety, nightwatchman Hemmings reflects on the lost hundred*

1985
Headingley, June 13, 14, 15, 17, 18

Australia *331 (A.M.J. Hilditch 119, G.M. Ritchie 46) and 324 (W.B. Phillips 91, A.M.J. Hilditch 80, K.C. Wessels 64, J.E. Emburey 5 for 82, I.T. Botham 4 for 107)*; England *533 (R.T. Robinson 175, I.T. Botham 60, P.R. Downton 54, M.W. Gatting 53, C.J. McDermott 4 for 134) and 123 for 5*. England won by 5 wickets.

England, strengthened by the return of Gooch and Emburey after their three-year ban for touring South Africa, got away to a convincing start in their quest to recapture the Ashes. Tim Robinson of Notts made the second-highest score (after R.E.Foster's 287) in a maiden England-Australia Test, hitting 27 fours in a calm innings lasting almost seven hours against an attack of four seam bowlers: youngsters McDermott and O'Donnell and older warriors Thomson and Lawson. Gatting gave Robinson support in a third-wicket stand of 136, and contributions right down the order, none more spectacular than Botham's 60 pounded off 51 balls, ensured a first-innings lead of 202 and England's highest total ever against Australia at Leeds, Downton and Cowans having put on 49 for the 10th wicket. Thomson conceded more runs (166) than any other Australian fast bowler in a Test innings. The tourists had had cause to be satisfied with their 331, built around Hilditch's untypically swift 119 off 182 balls (17 fours, two sixes) but despite a long second-wicket stand of 139 between Hilditch (80 this time) and Wessels, Australia lost six wickets in wiping off the arrears. That England had any sort of target was due to Phillips' elegant contribution of 91. The left-hander, also in his first Ashes Test, had to contend with balls which flew and others which shot through low, and it seemed he might deny England. But Botham forced a mis-hit pull, and England needed 123 in 200 minutes, with the weather uncertain. Lawson and O'Donnell bowled lion-heartedly and had England 83 for 4, 110 for 5. Eventually Lamb hooked high, and fieldsman Lawson found himself engulfed by spectators prematurely storming the field. England thus won, but the invasion would have been even more alarming had they been nine wickets down at the time. The overall run rate, 3.9 runs per over, the fruits of wayward bowling and a continuation of unreliable Australian catching, had produced a highly entertaining match, while Botham's three wickets in four balls in the first innings and blitzing half-century (10 fours and a six) remained an ominous reminder to the Australians of his influence on the 1981 series. The crowd-pleasing giant was now in second place behind Willis (128), and above Rhodes in England's list of wicket-takers against Australia.

1102, left: *Robinson prepares to celebrate his achievement of having made the second-best score ever in a maiden England-Australia Test. England built their highest total in an Ashes Test at Leeds on it.* 1103, below: *Andrew Hilditch contributed a splendid double to Australia's sinking cause, but the hook, here used well against Botham, was to let him down in the series*

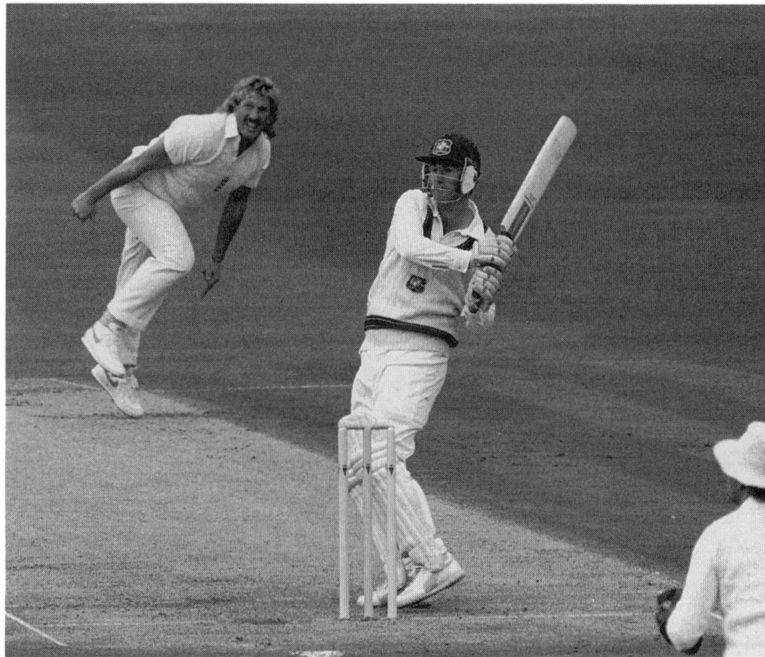

Brute force and elegance in the Headingley Test: 1104, left: Botham cracks Border into the football stand, and England go into the lead. 1105, right: A smooth drive by Phillips, who narrowly missed a debut hundred

1985 SECOND TEST

Lord's, June 27, 28, 29, July 1, 2

England *290 (D.I. Gower 86, A.J. Lamb 47, C.J. McDermott 6 for 70) and 261 (I.T. Botham 85, M.W. Gatting 75*, R.G. Holland 5 for 68);* Australia *425 (A.R. Border 196, G.M. Ritchie 94, S.P. O'Donnell 48, I.T. Botham 5 for 109) and 127 for 6 (A.R. Border 41*). Australia won by 4 wickets.*

Australia, again with only four main bowlers, pulled off their 10th Lord's victory and levelled at 1–1 in the series principally through Border's 7½-hour 196, the highest by an Australian captain on this ground (previously Woodfull, 155, 1930). Border had put England in, seen them manage 290 largely through Gower's lazily artistic 86, and then steered Australia from a parlous 101 for 4 towards an eventual lead of 135. His stand for the fifth wicket with Ritchie amounted to 216 in 4½ hours, and it turned the match. O'Donnell's brisk and challenging 48 ensured a retention of the initiative. Border fell to Botham (five wickets in a Test innings for the 25th time, and bowling fast and aggressively) four short of his double-century, having judged length scrupulously well and used his feet positively to the spinners. He reached 5000 Test runs in the shortest time to date (6 years 186 days). At 87 he had flicked a ball to Gatting at short leg and survived when the fielder inadvertently tossed the ball away in his eagerness to celebrate what would have been a superb catch. Otherwise, Border was in complete command. So were Australia by the third evening, when England had lost openers Gooch and Robinson and sent in two nightwatchmen. They both went early on Monday morning, and two more key wickets soon fell: 98 for 6. Then Gatting and Botham added 131 in 35 overs, Botham hitting with characteristic might. His duel with the 38-year-old, greying legspinner Holland was absorbing, and not until Botham had reached 85 off 117 balls did he fatally misjudge the flight, lofting a catch to Border near the cover boundary. Holland had Downton caught at slip next ball. Gatting was stranded on 75 as England left Australia 127 for victory, with time no problem. Botham soon blasted out Hilditch (caught again off a hook shot) and Wood, and Allott got an offcutter through Ritchie's defence, Australia finishing the fourth day an uncertain 46 for 3. Next morning Gower flicked the ball back from silly point to run out Wessels as he followed through from his defensive stroke, and Edmonds bowled Boon out of the rough. That made it 65 for 5. Phillips then supported his captain almost to the end, a half-chance off O'Donnell's bat being the closest England came to snatching sensational victory. Shaky umpiring and too-numerous withdrawals for imperfect light earlier in the match had not prevented it from becoming memorable in so many ways for the cricket played.

1106: *With Gower and wicketkeeper Downton helpless onlookers, the sprawling Gatting fails to complete a catch from Australian captain Border. Then 87, he went on to a worthy record 196*

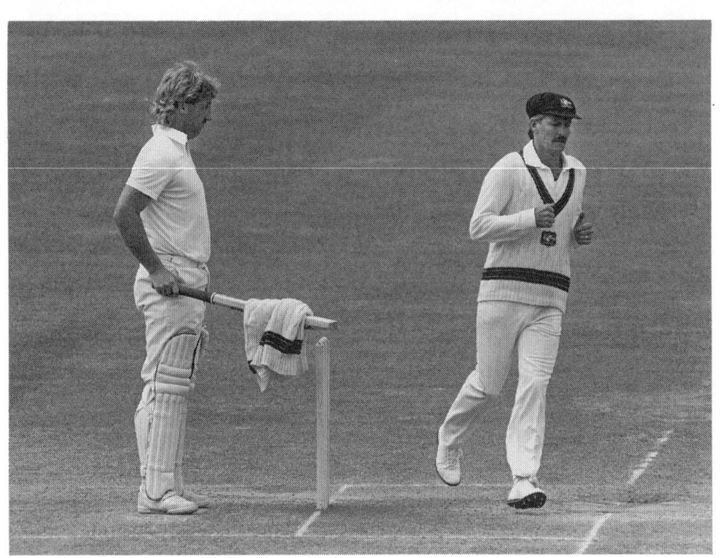

1107, above: *Quick thinking by Gower, bareheaded at silly mid-off, and the obdurate Wessels is run out. But Australia still scraped home for their 10th victory at Lord's.* 1108, left: *Between overs, Botham provides an informal sweater-care service for the opposition. His hard-hit 85 did much to keep England in the match, following his five-wicket haul, but Holland, here trotting past him, held Australia's advantage with a cool and lengthy spell of leg-spin*

1985 — THIRD TEST

Trent Bridge, July 11, 12, 13, 15, 16

England *456 (D.I. Gower 166, M.W. Gatting 74, G.A. Gooch 70, G.F. Lawson 5 for 103) and 196 for 2 (R.T. Robinson 77*, G.A. Gooch 48);* Australia *539 (G.M. Wood 172, G.M. Ritchie 146, A.M.J. Hilditch 47, S.P. O'Donnell 46). Match drawn.*

A high-scoring draw embodied three large and fascinating centuries and much toil for the bowlers on a 'flat' pitch — plus a dramatic confrontation between Botham and an umpire. Gower's stature grew still further with a high-class 166 after Gooch had made his first fifty in England against Australia (10 years after his debut). The Gower-Gatting stand took the score from 171 for 2 to 358 for 3. Gatting's freakish run-out, when bowler Holland tipped Gower's straight-drive into the stumps, then precipitated a steady fall of wickets wherein the last eight went down for 98. Still, a tall total had been established against an Australian side reckoned to be more fallible than many sent to England over the years. Lawson, never in perfect health on this tour, took five wickets in an innings against England for the sixth time, but McDermott could manage no better than 2 for 147 in 35 overs, while the two other bowlers, O'Donnell and Holland, took 2 for 194 between them. Australia's reply began solidly with 87 from Wood and Hilditch, and on the third day, when the gates were closed again, the score advanced to 366 for 5. England's woes began with Allott's sickness; then Sidebottom broke down; then Botham, denied wickets by a dropped catch, an umpire's divergent view of an lbw appeal, and a no-ball call, was then warned by umpire Whitehead for running down the pitch, and vented his fury in such a way that he was later reprimanded by the TCCB. Through all this, Graeme Wood batted on and on, resurrecting his status at this level and going on to an eventual 10-hour epic of 172, the second-longest innings for Australia in England after Simpson's 1964 triple-century and the second-highest for Australia on this ground after McCabe's 232. Wood eked out 51, 36 and 27 runs in the three sessions of this third day. Ritchie, almost caught-and-bowled first ball by Emburey, went on to an attractive 146, putting on 161 with Wood for the sixth wicket, and Australia's 539 was their highest at Trent Bridge, and best against England since 1965–66 (54 Tests). Edmonds (66 overs) and Emburey (55) carried the bulk of England's workload. Gooch and then Robinson ensured that there would be no catastrophic subsidence in the time remaining, which was reduced by rain. In five days a mere 22 wickets had fallen.

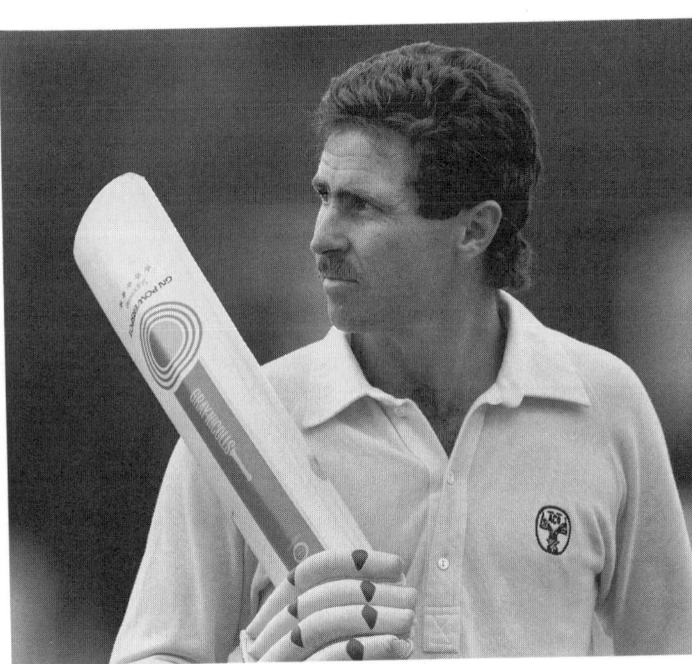

The three centurions of Trent Bridge: 1109, above: *David Gower, whose 166 secured England.* 1110, top right: *Graeme Wood comes in after the second-longest innings ever for Australia in England.* 1111, right: *Greg Ritchie, who went close at Lord's and made sure at Nottingham*

1985 FOURTH TEST

Old Trafford, August 1, 2, 3, 5, 6

Australia *257 (D.C. Boon 61, A.M.J. Hilditch 49, S.P. O'Donnell 45, P.H. Edmonds 4 for 40, I.T. Botham 4 for 79) and 340 for 5 (A.R. Border 146*, K.C. Wessels 50, A.M.J. Hilditch 40, J.E. Emburey 4 for 99)*; England *482 for 9 dec (M.W. Gatting 160, G.A. Gooch 74, A.J. Lamb 67, D.I. Gower 47, C.J. McDermott 8 for 141). Match drawn.*

The suspense of the series was sustained by another drawn encounter, Manchester's rain much reducing the playing time. Put in by Gower, Australia struggled to 257, Boon making his highest Test score to date, batting at No. 3. Disaster struck — or was self-inflicted — in the 39th over, when Border, having been tied down, lashed wildly at Edmonds and was stumped, and Ritchie was fooled into propping the ball back to the bowler three balls later. O'Donnell came forth with another valuable 40-odd, but this was a poor total on a lacklustre pitch, and by the second evening England were 233 for 3, Gooch and Gower (passing 5000 Test runs) having posted 121 for the second wicket. On a blustery, overcast day, Gatting and Lamb took up the challenge, continuing on the third day, when rain held up the start until 2 pm. The fourth-wicket stand was worth 156 when a throw by Matthews ran out Lamb. Gatting, sure of himself in all respects, reached his first Test century in a home Test (in the 40th innings), and Downton stayed with him while 91 important runs were added for the sixth wicket. The hefty Gatting then became McDermott's sixth wicket. The tall Queensland fast bowler was putting in a stamina performance worthy of Tom Richardson, and had taken all eight wickets to fall to a bowler when the innings was closed on the fourth morning. At 20 years 113 days, McDermott became the youngest to take eight wickets in an innings in Anglo-Australian Tests, and his tally for the series was already 24. Hopes that Lillee would soon be replaced seemed on the verge of satisfaction. Australia, lacking Wood (injured) in this match, began their second innings shakily, and were 138 for 4, still 87 behind, with eight scheduled hours of play left. The final day was Allan Border's. No stranger to backs-to-the-wall situations, he batted right through a day constantly interrupted by the weather, concentrating furiously. Starting on 49 (147 of his 186 balls had produced no runs), he stretched his right leg out or dropped the ball over the crease. Early on the fifth day he inside-edged, and Downton's reflex jerk almost resulted in a catch held. Otherwise, Border was impregnable. Ritchie helped him add 75, and Phillips then took 54 balls to open his score. The unbeaten stand of 127 shut England out completely and gave Australia renewed hopes of retaining the Ashes.

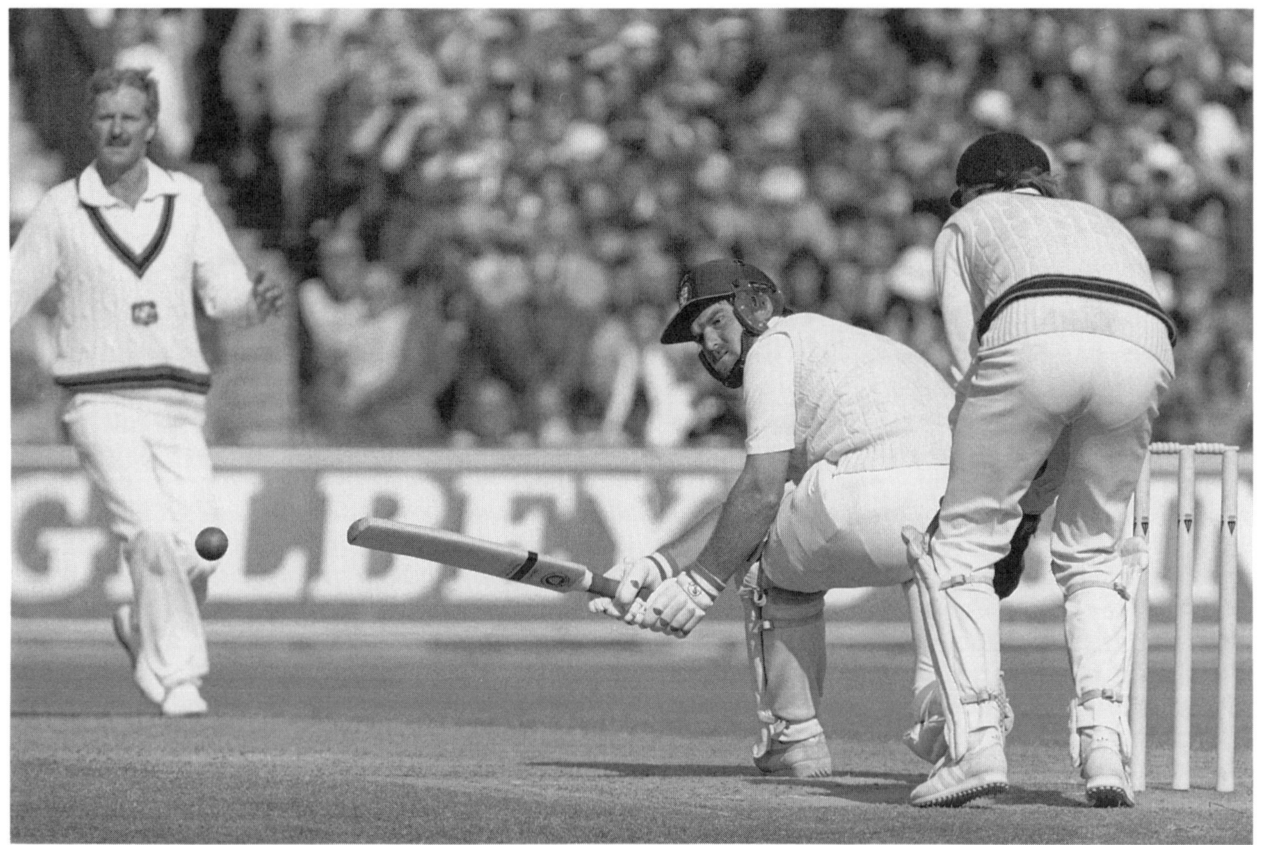

1112: *Mike Gatting sweeps Holland — a favourite shot — on his way to 160, his first Test century at home and his first against Australia*

1113, left: *Queenslander McDermott, 20, here pictured in the Lord's Test, when he took 6 for 70, excelled himself further at Manchester with 8 for 141 in 36 overs.* 1114, above: *Border had a rush of blood at Old Trafford and was stumped for 8. But in the second innings he proved unshiftable*

1985 FIFTH TEST

Edgbaston, August 15, 16, 17, 19, 20

Australia *335 (K.C. Wessels 83, G.F. Lawson 53, A.R. Border 45, R.M. Ellison 6 for 77) and 142 (W.B. Phillips 59, R.M. Ellison 4 for 27);* England *595 for 5 dec (D.I. Gower 215, R.T. Robinson 148, M.W. Gatting 100*, A.J. Lamb 46). England won by an innings and 118 runs.*

A disputed catch on the tense last day broke the deadlock and let England through to a one-match lead in the series with one match to play. With a little over an hour of the match remaining, Australia were 113 for 5, still 147 adrift in terms of an innings defeat, when Wayne Phillips, a pillar of resistance, carved Edmonds towards Lamb at silly point. The ball bounced up for Gower to hold it, and umpires Constant and Shepherd, after consultation, gave Phillips out. The television replay threw little light on the incident. Demoralised, Australia then faded away, and England took their first innings victory over them in 27 matches. Having bowled Australia out the first time for 335 — Gower became the first England captain to put them in in consecutive Tests — with the ungainly Wessels at his obstinate best and Ellison's swing bowling proving effective in the conditions, England then piled up 595 and declared when only half out, the highest by either side in the seven Birmingham Tests. The foundation was a second-wicket alliance of 331 between Robinson and Gower in 5¾ hours, the second-highest for any wicket by England in these matches after the Hutton-Leyland 382 of 1938. As Australia wilted, Gower played serenely and handsomely, Robinson calmly, both lofting into spaces and exploiting a full range of ground shots. Seldom in the history of England v Australia have two batsmen shown such prolonged dominance. The Australians bowled 28 no-balls and Holland surprisingly withheld his googly. On the fourth morning Robinson touched Lawson into his stumps, but there then began a stand of 94 between Gower and Gatting, and after the captain (7½ hours at the crease) had been caught at point for his highest score (only the second double-century for England against Australia since Hutton's 364, and the second-highest by an England captain in these matches after Hammond's 240), Lamb stayed with Gatting while 109 more were added swiftly. Botham came in at 572 for 4 and wafted his first and third balls (from McDermott) for six. Gatting reached another century and the closure came, England 260 ahead. Their scoring rate had been a dazzling 74 runs per 100 balls. In all five Tests to date England's first six in the batting order had been the same — a unique occurrence — and not since the Oval Test of 1938 had they registered three centuries in an innings against Australia. They now strove to finish the job, and that evening saw a dramatic collapse when the first five Australian wickets went down for 36, Ellison, on his way to 10 wickets in his first Ashes Test, taking 4 for 1 in 15 balls, the invaluable wicket of Border among them. The rain returned on the final day, and play was not resumed until 2.30 pm, with 48 overs to be bowled. Four overs were lost immediately when drizzle descended. Then Phillips and Ritchie seemed to be holding out . . . until the 'catch'. It was a fine English victory: Australia had still been in at 335 for 8 on the second evening. Among the many milestones, Thomson took his 100th England wicket (and 200th in all Tests); Botham passed Willis's record 128 wickets against Australia; Border passed 500 runs in a series in England for the second time: and Gower passed Compton's record 562 for a home series against Australia.

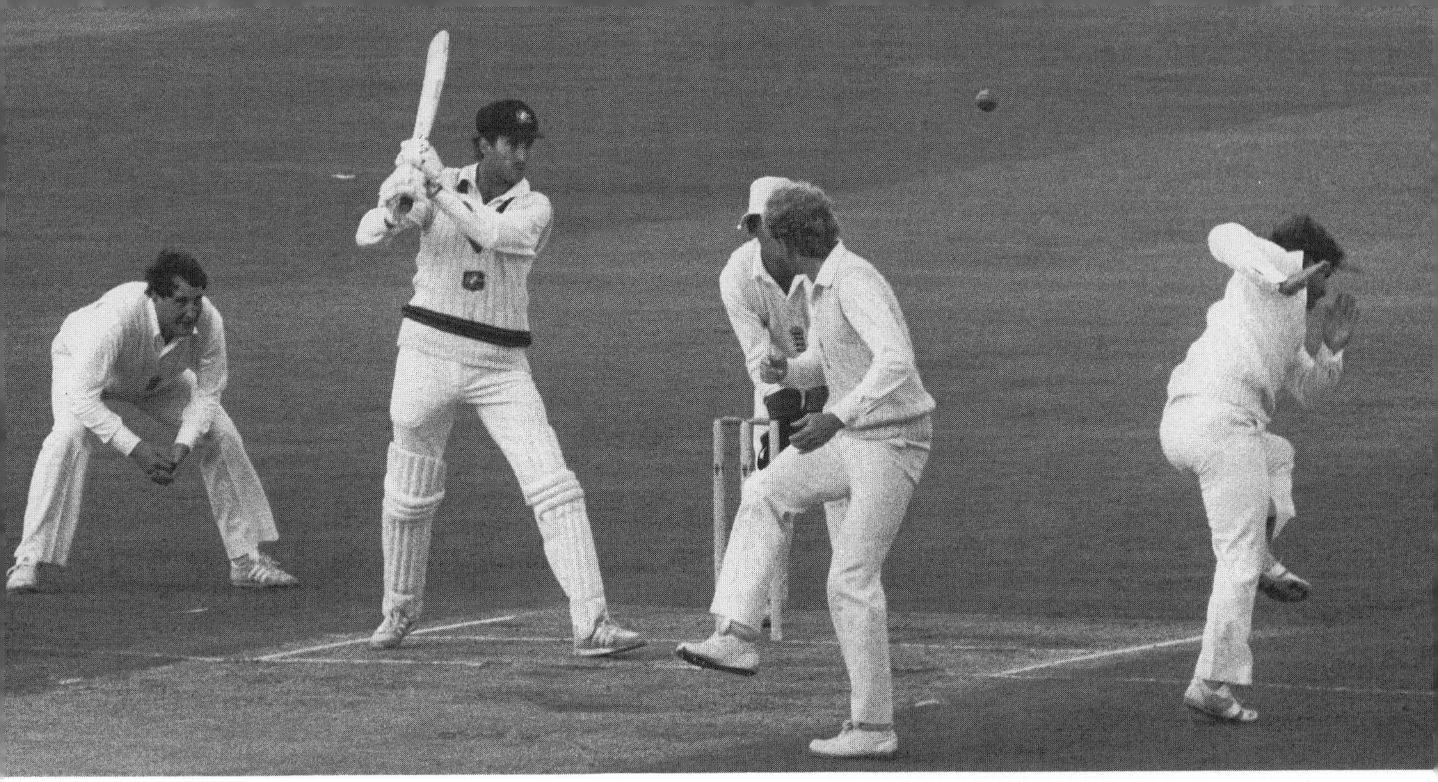

1115, above: *Phillips cuts low to Lamb, whose fair-haired 'dancing partner' Gower is about to catch the rebound. This contentious wicket decided the Test and swung the series.* 1116, below: *Ellison flows into his work. His swing bowling brought him 10 wickets at Edgbaston.* 1117, right: *Gower reaches his double-century, a congratulatory pat coming from fellow centurion Robinson. Bowler Thomson seems less impressed*

1985 — SIXTH TEST

The Oval, August 29, 30, 31, September 2

England *464 (G.A. Gooch 196, D.I. Gower 157, G.F. Lawson 4 for 101, C.J. McDermott 4 for 108);* Australia *241 (G.M. Ritchie 64*) and 129 (A.R. Border 58, R.M. Ellison 5 for 46). England won by an innings and 94 runs.*

Australia, in the face of an orgy of English runmaking, broke down spinelessly when it was their turn to bat, and failed to retain the Ashes. Winning the toss for the fourth time, England survived some early near-misses and were 100 for 1 at lunch, 200 for 1 at tea, and 376 for 3 off 90 overs at the end of the opening day. Gooch made his highest Test score, and his first century against Australia at the 40th attempt while Gower reached his third century of the series off only 123 balls and passed 2000 runs against Australia. Their second-wicket stand was a massive 351 in 337 minutes, and thus, within a fortnight, the second- and third-highest stands by England in 108 years of combat with Australia had been recorded. Thomson and Holland had been dropped, probably unwisely for this harder, bouncier pitch, and Gilbert and Bennett now supported McDermott and Lawson. But they were all powerless as the Gooch-Gower assault enchanted a sunlit capacity crowd. It made for an odd scorecard for the last nine wickets were scooped up for 93, and apart from the 50 extras, the next-highest score after Gooch and Gower was Downton's 16. Far from making 600, England finished with 464, and the match was still little more than a quarter complete. But by stumps Australia were severely wounded, 145 for 6 against England's varied attack. Ritchie resisted next day, showing a determination missing in most of his team-mates, but the rest were prised out, Botham holding a breath-taking slip catch. With the follow-on virtually went the handing-over of the Ashes to England, though some felt England should have played safe by batting again. Hilditch was caught at cover (for once not succumbing via the hook shot) after rain had held up play for three hours, and wickets fell steadily. Border hung on into the fourth day, gritting it out for over 2½ hours, but with his dismissal the trapdoor was finally sprung, and down went the body of Australian cricket. He had made 597 runs in the series, which combined with Gower's 732 to make a record for a pair of captains in Ashes cricket. England now had three successive home Ashes series victories for the first time since the 1890s, a welcome happening for success-starved English spectators, 373,000 of whom watched the six Tests, creating a record £2½-million profit.

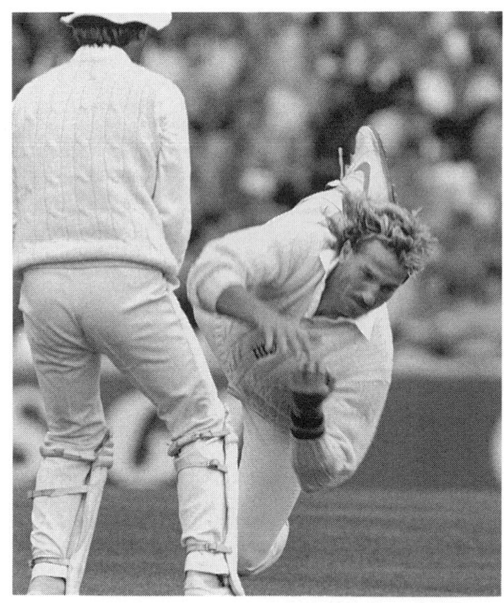

1118: *Botham was again a symbol of a rampant England: this blinding catch at The Oval got McDermott*

1119, above: *Gooch, steady in strokeplay as in facial expression, marches towards 196.* 1120, left: *Gower, his partner in a stand of 351 in better than even time, hammers more runs towards his huge series total of 732.* 1121, right: *Soon the popular England captain was showing a replica of the Ashes to the Oval crowd, backed by his ace allrounder Botham*

1986–87 FIRST TEST

Brisbane, November 14, 15, 16, 18, 19

England *456 (I.T. Botham 138, C.W.J. Athey 76, M.W. Gatting 61, D.I. Gower 51, A.J. Lamb 40, P.A.J. DeFreitas 40) and 77 for 3;* Australia *248 (G.R. Marsh 56, G.R.J. Matthews 56*, G.M. Ritchie 41, G.R. Dilley 5 for 68) and 282 (G.R. Marsh 110, G.M. Ritchie 45, J.E. Emburey 5 for 80). England won by 7 wickets.*

Australia's most dreaded opponent, Ian Botham, set England onto the road to first-up victory with a 174-ball innings of 138, with 13 fours and four sixes, one of them over third man. In one over from fast bowler Merv Hughes he hit 22 runs, a record for Ashes Tests by one batsman, and any thoughts that Australia had had about fielding a new, matchwinning team (only Border and Ritchie survived from the 1985 Oval Test) were scattered just like Border's defensive field setting. Athey had played a crucial, highly disciplined anchorman innings, and new captain Gatting made an important 61, supported by a half-century by Gower, whom he had deposed five months earlier. Australia's inexperienced new-ball bowlers Reid (at 6ft 8ins the tallest man to play for Australia), Hughes and Chris Matthews (Lawson surprisingly was omitted) were held at bay and then put under pressure themselves. Botham treated them all as if they were third-graders. DeFreitas, only 20, hit a useful 40 on debut, and England's 456 eventually proved enough to make Australia follow on for the first time at Brisbane. Marsh, Ritchie and Matthews resisted at length, and five others batted for the best part of an hour or more, but Dilley, at a fair speed, took five wickets in a Test innings for the first time, finishing the innings with the new ball when Australia were nine runs from saving the follow-on. On the fourth day Geoff Marsh became the 15th Australian to score a century in his maiden Test against England, batting into the fifth day, over 6½ hours in all, a study in concentration, though no artistic sight. Of the rest, Ritchie was the only one to pass 28. England had to fight a little harder to get their opponents out a second time, Emburey bowling 42.5 overs and taking his 100th wicket in all Tests. England, who had been put in, knocked off the winning runs just after lunch on the final day. Border, deeply disturbed by his side's poor performance, missed the presentation ceremony, when Botham received the Man of the Match prize.

1122, below: *Bill Athey allows himself a rare aggressive stroke during his studious 76, which gave England a platform.* 1123, right: *The man the Australians had come to dread during the 1980s, Ian Botham, gives the ball another thunderous whack during his explosive century*

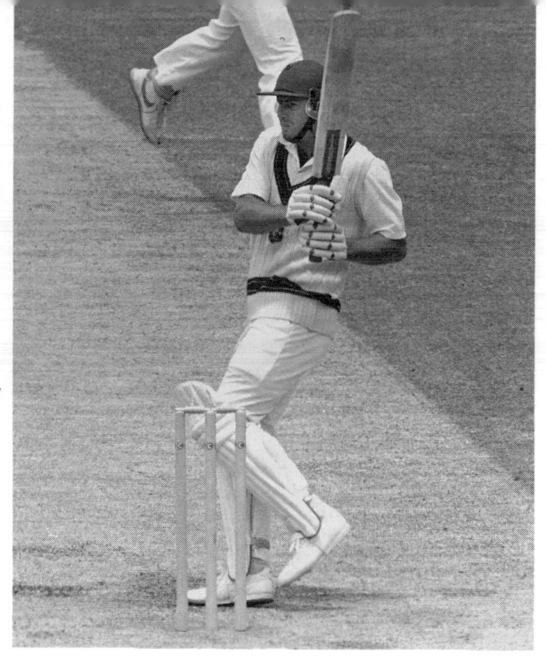

1124, left: *Graham Dilley's wholehearted effort broke down Australia's first innings at Brisbane.* 1125, right: *Geoff Marsh, pictured at Perth, scored an Ashes debut hundred at Brisbane and showed patience in the best Test match tradition*

1986–87 SECOND TEST

Perth, November 28, 29, 30, December 2, 3

England *592 for 8 dec (B.C. Broad 162, D.I. Gower 136, C.J. Richards 133, C.W.J. Athey 96, B.A. Reid 4 for 115) and 199 for 8 dec (M.W. Gatting 70, D.I. Gower 48, S.R. Waugh 5 for 69);* Australia *401 (A.R. Border 125, S.R. Waugh 71, G.R.J. Matthews 45, G.R. Dilley 4 for 79) and 197 for 4 (D.M. Jones 69, G.R. Marsh 49). Match drawn.*

Batting first on a dry pitch, England ran up an ominously high total — second in Australia only to their 636 at Sydney in 1928–29 — to which Australia responded well enough, in the longer term, to avoid defeat. England were able to indulge in a rare second declaration, and Australia were challenged to make 391 on the final day. England had begun with their fifth double-century opening stand since 1911–12 — 223 in 286 minutes, their highest for any wicket at Perth — with Athey being yorked by Reid when four from his century. Left-hander Broad extended his maiden Test century to 162 in 7¼ hours (25 fours), having seen a mini-collapse after Athey's departure. Spilt catches still cost Australia dearly. Gower and wicketkeeper Richards then came together in a remarkable stand of 207 (the highest for England's sixth wicket in Australia), raising the score to 546. It was only Richards' second Test, and he outscored his experienced partner much of the time. Gower's sixth century against Australia was actually achieved 11 minutes before the scoreboard registered it. Characteristically, it was a delight to behold. Waugh, batting at No. 3, made a valuable 71 in under 2½ hours for Australia in reply, but Border, yet again, was the main obstacle to an English takeover. His 20th century — the 200th for Australia against England — came in his 150th Test innings, and he became the 11th Australian to score 2000 runs against England. His 125 took 6¼ hours, and the No. 11 was with him as the follow-on was averted. Dilley again beset the Australians with problems of bounce and swing. As the cracks widened, England strove to extend their lead at a pace, but Waugh in particular bowled a tight line, forcing Gatting to delay his closure. Thanks chiefly to Marsh and Jones, who put on 126 for the second wicket, Australia swam to safety, after Boon had edged Dilley's first ball of the day to Botham, giving him his 100th catch in Tests. Botham later tore a chest muscle and had to cease bowling.

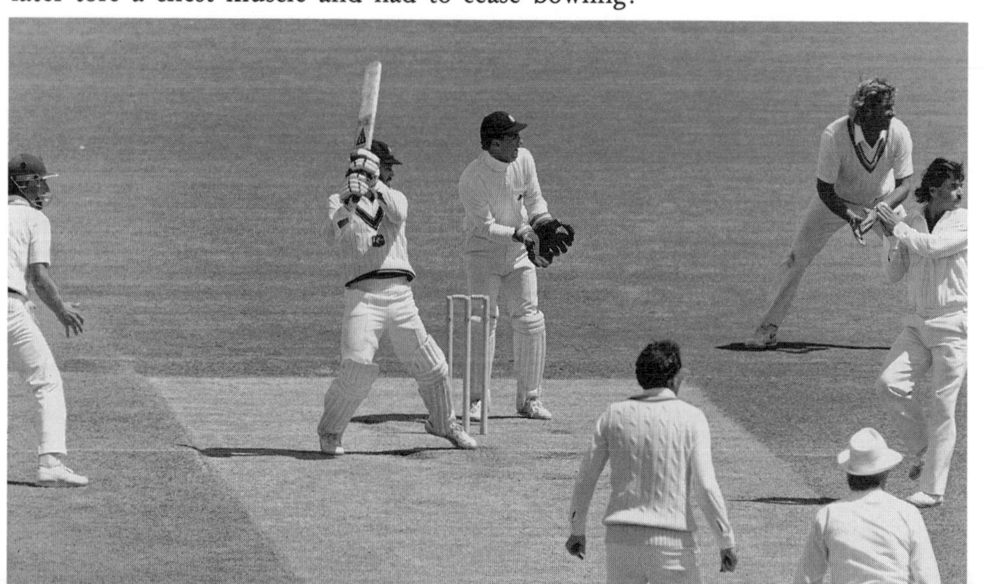

1126: *Allan Border, here cutting Emburey, played yet another saving captain's innings at Perth, producing his 20th century in all Tests, the 200th for Australia in 110 years of combat against England*

1127: *Young Australian newcomer Steve Waugh uses the crease in dealing with Botham at Perth*

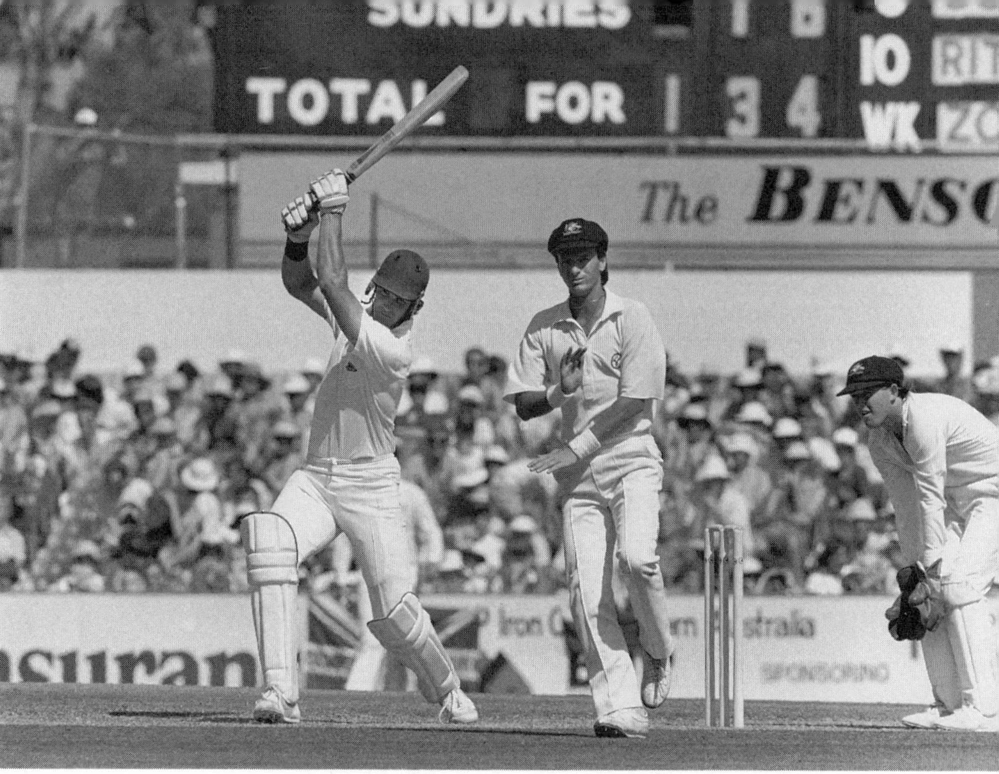

1128, above: *Chris Broad placed his name indelibly into the Ashes chronicle with 162 at Perth, with 25 fours included. There was more to follow as the series advanced.* 1129, right: *There were also two further centuries for England in this match: by Gower (in helmet) and, more surprisingly, by wicketkeeper Jack Richards. They put on 207 for the sixth wicket to ensure a massive total*

1986–87 THIRD TEST
Adelaide, December 12, 13, 14, 15, 16

Australia *514 for 5 dec (D.C. Boon 103, D.M. Jones 93, S.R. Waugh 79*, G.R.J. Matthews 73*, A.R. Border 70, G.R. Marsh 43) and 201 for 3 dec (A.R. Border 100*, G.M. Ritchie 46*, G.R. Marsh 41)*; England *455 (B.C. Broad 116, M.W. Gatting 100, C.W.J. Athey 55, J.E. Emburey 49, B.A. Reid 4 for 64, P.R. Sleep 4 for 132) and 39 for 2. Match drawn.*

Without the injured Botham, England risked going in with only four bowlers, all of whom 'made centuries' in Australia's long innings. The home side had a cautious first day (207 for 2), with the rotund Boon breaking through against England at last with a pleasant century in 4½ hours. Dean Jones came close to a century too, while Border, Waugh and Matthews made seventies, the last two making an unbroken 146, beating Kelleway and Pellew's 1920–21 Adelaide sixth-wicket record against England.

England's response was rock-steady: 112 for the first wicket by Broad and Athey, 161 for the second by Broad and Gatting, whose century was the 100th for England in Tests in Australia. Broad, again playing powerfully off his body either side of the wicket, batted for just over five hours (two hours longer than Gatting) for his second century in consecutive Tests. With Sleep (47 overs) getting through most work, Australia failed to effect a later collapse, and with the follow-on avoided, England seemed safe. Border, who then eased out his seventh century against England, later confessed that he wished he had let Australia's first innings run longer. On the last day, when both sides seemed content with a draw and rain cut play short, Australia's wicketkeeper Dyer suffered a broken nose when a ball from Sleep clipped Broad's pad-flap.

1130, left: *David Boon, from Tasmania, broke through a dismal sequence with a century at Adelaide, batting comfortably in the opening berth.*
1131, right: *Dean Jones clips the ball masterfully. He made 93 in good style that promised better things for Australia in due course*

1132: *Gatting sees England close to security with a century in support of Broad's*

1133: *Border, a bundle of concentration and pugnacity, approaches another hundred*

1986–87 FOURTH TEST
Melbourne, December 26, 27, 28

Australia *141 (D.M. Jones 59, I.T. Botham 5 for 41, G.C. Small 5 for 48) and 194 (G.R. Marsh 60, S.R. Waugh 49); England 349 (B.C. Broad 112, A.J. Lamb 43, M.W. Gatting 40, B.A. Reid 4 for 78, C.J. McDermott 4 for 83). England won by an innings and 14 runs.*

England held the Ashes with a punishing innings victory, their first in Australia in three days since 1901–02, Gatting becoming only the third England captain (after J.W.H.T. Douglas and D.I. Gower) to win after sending Australia in to bat. Condemned both for the composition of the side (only four specialist batsmen) and their attitude (ambitious for victory, almost to the point of negligence in their need to win both remaining Tests), Australia were floored by Small, in his first Ashes Test, and Botham, reduced to medium-pace, who took five wickets apiece. By the end of the first day, before a big crowd, England were already 95 for 1 in reply. Dilley was unfit, and Small and DeFreitas thus made a West Indian-born opening attack for England. Some superlative catches were held, and wicketkeeper Richards equalled the record five against Australia by Parks and Taylor. With McDermott restored to the side to share the new ball with Hughes, Australia had a belligerent cutting-edge. But again England had a sound and sensible start from Broad and Athey. Their 58 was followed by a partnership of 105 between Broad and Gatting, Broad as businesslike as ever, and reaching his third century in three Tests. Only the illustrious Hobbs, Sutcliffe and Hammond had done anything similarly outstanding for England in Ashes Tests in Australia. Broad batted 5½ hours this time, and had become as fixed an adversary at the crease as Marsh had been against England earlier in the season. Australia missed some catching and run-out chances on the second day, when the crowd was less than half that on the opening day, but England still realised fewer than had been expected. From 163 for 1 and 273 for 5, they made no more than 349, McDermott and Reid plugging away optimistically. Still, it was an English lead of 208 that faced Australia on the third morning, and by 4.30pm it was all over. Only Marsh (3½ hours before being run out), Border and Waugh batted for any length of time, and Australia, capitulating for 194, went down by an innings, as they had done twice in the climax of the 1985 rubber. The faster men took 22 of the 28 wickets to fall to bowlers in the match, but the hard-working Edmonds and Emburey were rewarded in the later stages, sharing five wickets. Gatting and his jubilant team had pulled off a proud series victory — and without Gooch, who had been unavailable for the tour. English pleasure was enhanced still further by success in two limited-overs tournaments in Australia.

1134, left: *Broad, making his third century in as many Tests, joined an elite list.* 1135, top: *England's two Melbourne destroyers, Botham and Small (bowler), collaborate in the dismissal of Greg Matthews.* 1136, above: *Bruce Reid, 6 ft 8 ins, whose 20 wickets in the series were twice the total of any other Australian's*

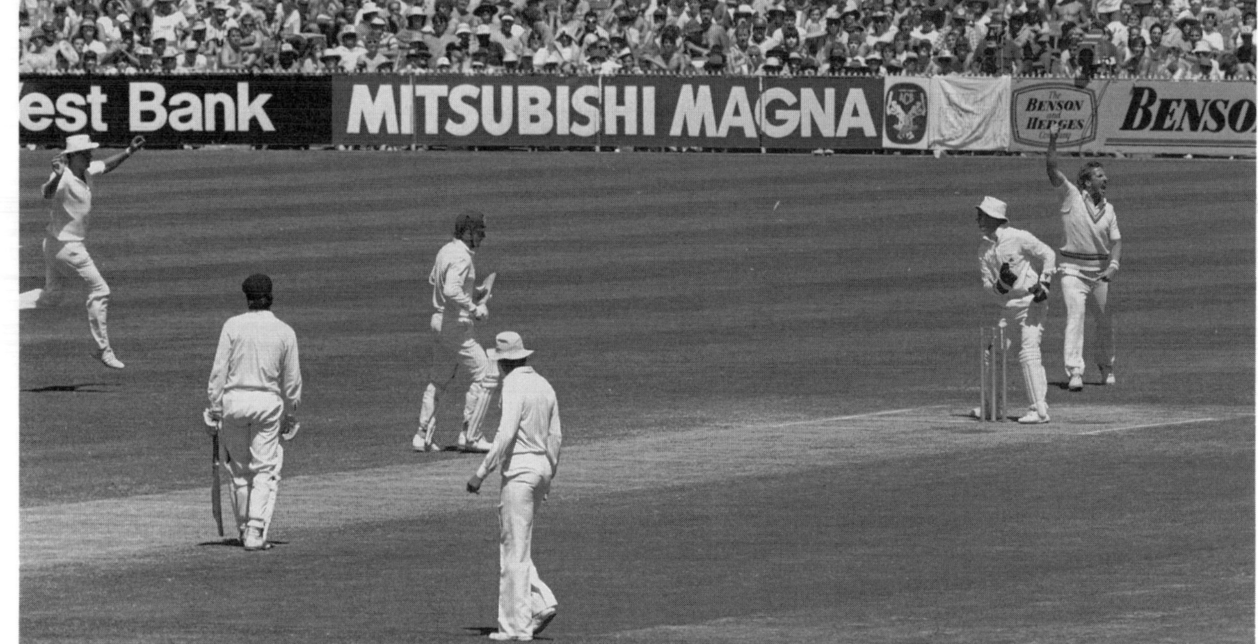

1137: *Australian hearts sink deeper as their match top-scorer, Marsh, is run out by yards by Edmonds' throw to Richards. Humiliating three-day defeat is imminent*

1986–87 FIFTH TEST

Sydney, January 10, 11, 12, 14, 15

Australia *343 (D.M. Jones 184*, G.C. Small 5 for 75) and 251 (S.R. Waugh 73, A.R. Border 49, P.L. Taylor 42, J.E. Emburey 7 for 78)*; England *275 (D.I. Gower 72, J.E. Emburey 69, C.J. Richards 46, P.L. Taylor 6 for 78) and 264 (M.W. Gatting 96, P.R. Sleep 5 for 72). Australia won by 55 runs.*

An entertaining match brought Australia their first victory in 15 Tests overall, a record run for that country. The spirit of cricket was best illustrated not only in the wider use of spin bowling by both sides but in England's positive approach on the final day, when the temptation to play for safety was always present. The romantic selection of little-known Peter Taylor, 30, an offspinner with six first-class matches behind him, promised the contest an extra fascination. Jones's nine-hour, unbeaten 184 guaranteed it. He was lucky to begin with, surviving an insistent appeal at 5 when Richards held an apparent leg-glance off Small, and Emburey missed him at slip when 8. Ritchie came back to replace Boon as opener, but soon went, and no batsman came within 150 runs of Jones's eventual epic performance. Border was next with 34. Jones, tall, confident and proudly Victorian, mixed exciting strokeplay with stubborn caution. The total might have been ordinary had not tailender Hughes batted for an unlikely couple of hours for 16 while 67 were added. Jones faced 420 balls, only 12 of which went for four and one for six. Hughes and Reid had soon lopped the top off England's first innings (17 for 3), but Gower put a handsomer face on things with a lovely 72, once stroking four fours off a Reid over. Newcomer Taylor floated down his off-spin variations, and claimed the scalps of Lamb, Botham, Gower, Edmonds, Emburey and Small. Richards and Emburey supplied good, hard-earned runs, but a deficit of 68 hung on their shoulders as England attempted to shift Australia cheaply second time round. They had them 115 for 5 on the fourth day, and, after a crucial stumping miss when Waugh was only 15, 145 for 7 (213 ahead). Taylor then joined Waugh and shut England out with a 2¼-hour stand of 98. Australia eventually set England 320 off a possible 108 overs. Broad was dismissed that evening. At 91 Border broke through with Gower's wicket, and without addition Athey was bowled sweeping at Sleep. Lamb failed again, and Botham was caught first ball off Taylor, making England 102 for 5. Richards (38) then stayed with Gatting, and the prospect of an either-way finish stirred back to life. Gatting, missed by Zoehrer behind the stumps, was 96 when drinks were taken as the final 20 overs began, England, five down, 90 from victory. He then popped a catch back to Waugh, the stand of 131 being the best for England's sixth wicket at Sydney, beating Ranji and Hirst's 124 in 1897–98. Richards' 3½-hour vigil was ended by a Sleep googly. The next ball accounted for Edmonds, hit on the back leg by a sharply-turning legspinner. Reid found Small's edge, and Australia had just over two overs to get the last wicket. Sleep was kept on — and bowled Emburey with his last ball, which kept low: Australia by 55 runs with six balls to spare. Sleep, like Emburey, had returned his best figures in eight years of Test cricket, while Jones's 184, which gave initial structure to the match, was the highest for Australia against England on this ground for 40 years, when Bradman and Barnes made 234 apiece.

1138, top left: *Division of the souvenirs (Merv Hughes seems to be about to spear Waugh or Ritchie) after Australia's droughtbreaking victory at Sydney. Taylor (centre) had a fine debut.* 1139, above: *Sleep, who took five wickets in England's second innings, becomes one of Emburey's seven (a personal best in Tests).* 1140, left: *Jones strikes out confidently in an unbeaten innings of 184 which laid the foundation for ultimate victory*

1987–88 BICENTENNIAL TEST

Sydney, January 29, 30, 31, February 1, 2

England *425 (B.C. Broad 139. B.N. French 47, R.T. Robinson 43, M.D. Moxon 40, P.L. Taylor 4 for 84)*; Australia *214 (D.M. Jones 56, P.R. Sleep 41) and 328 for 2 (D.C. Boon 184*, G.R. Marsh 56, A.R. Border 48*). Match drawn.*

With the nation's Bicentennial festivities well under way, Australia found only frustration on the first day of the special Test match scheduled as part of the celebration of 200 years of white settlement in the former British colony. Three catches went down before lunch, and England had laid a careful platform of 221 for 2 by the close. Only five England and six Australian players survived from the Test played here 12 months earlier. One was Chris Broad, who continued to pace his extraordinary pathway of prosperity on Australian pitches, making another century — his fourth in five Tests — not the best of them, but invaluable in that Gower, Lamb and Botham were absent from this three-part tour by England. Provocations had led to ugly reactions recently on the field in Pakistan, notably by Gatting, and if a peppery outlook was veiled for most of this celebratory match, the captain was in grim mood in spending 1¾ hours over his 13. Broad, however, so completely forgot the nature of the occasion as to commit the ugliest of outbursts when a short ball from Waugh bounced from his person into the stumps when he had scored 139 in 7¼ hours. He swung his bat into the wrecked wicket in a fit of pique, was booed from the field, and fined £500 by the England manager. More catches were missed, and after 10 hours England were 365 for 7. Wicketkeeper French batted for two hours for a useful 47 before Dyer, as at Adelaide 13 months earlier, had his nose lacerated while standing up at the stumps. England's 425 came at 2.46 per over. Australia then lost seven wickets before tea on the third day, including Border's, when he hooked a catch and was roundly condemned by a frustrated populace. England dropped catches too, but Jones, after nearly three hours, was held, as was Waugh (by a full-length effort from French). Relief came with a southerly which brought black clouds and an early finish. Brilliant catches next morning by Athey and Foster finished Australia off, 211 behind, and they followed on. Now the traditional and celebrated Australian truculence reasserted itself. Boon and Marsh had 101 on the board when Dilley's short-pitched bowling in poor light forced an early finish. Under blue skies, the match was saved, with comfort, Boon the Tasmanian being there at the end after a resistance lasting 492 minutes. He had failed in seven of his eight innings in the previous Ashes series, but now stood triumphant. His first-wicket stand with Marsh of 162 was Australia's best ever at Sydney against England, and he took the match award, which spared the judges any moral judgment on Broad. Bradman, O'Reilly, Lindwall, Harvey, Bedser, Morris, May, Benaud and Greg Chappell were among the 'living legends' in a vintage car motorcade during a luncheon interval, and a total of 103,831 spectators sampled the intermittent festive spirit of the match, knowing it would be absent when the two old enemies next faced each other from the armed trenches of a full Ashes series.

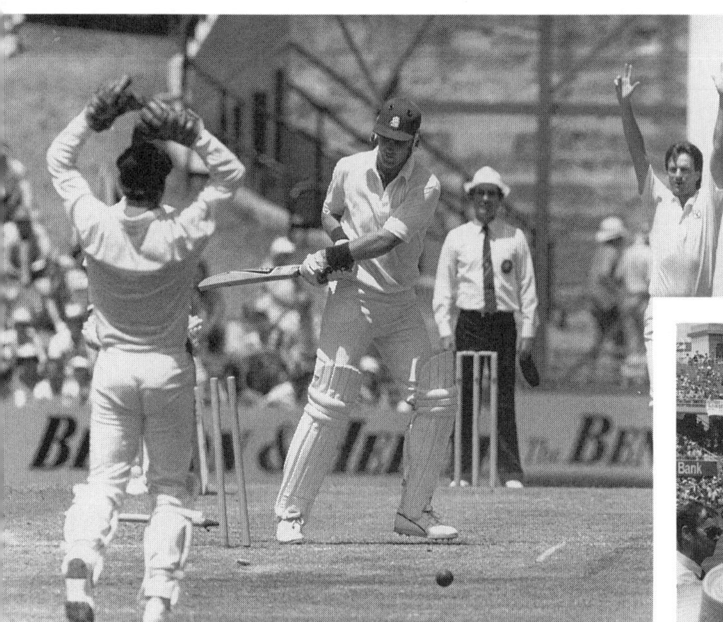

1141, left: *Broad, having recorded a remarkable fourth century in five Tests in Australia, plays on after 7¼ hours' batting. His ill-tempered swipe at the stumps in his disappointment cheapened the occasion and saddened a gathering which included many stars of England-Australia cricket*

1142, above: *The Don returns to the pavilion. This time, Sir Donald Bradman, 79, had led a vintage motorcade of celebrated players around the Sydney Cricket Ground as a further feature of the Bicentennial festivities.*
1143, left: *Boon steps out for another productive shot in his showpiece 184 not out which salvaged Australia's pride*

1989
Headingley, June 8, 9, 10, 12, 13

Australia *601 for 7 dec (S.R. Waugh 177*, M.A. Taylor 136, D.M. Jones 79, M.G. Hughes 71, A.R. Border 66) and 230 for 3 dec (M.A. Taylor 60, A.R. Border 60*, D.C. Boon 43, D.M. Jones 40*);* England *430 (A.J. Lamb 125, K.J. Barnett 80, R.A. Smith 66, T.M. Alderman 5 for 107) and 191 (G.A. Gooch 68, T.M. Alderman 5 for 44).* Australia won by 210 runs.

Starting as underdogs, Australia went a long way on the opening day towards establishing command in the series. The pitch was good, the England bowling poor, and the batting, led first by Taylor then Waugh, saw to it that Australia's Leeds 'jinx' was overturned. Taylor became the 16th Australian to make a century on debut against England, and batted 6½ hours. His stand with Border raised 117, and with Jones 99. Waugh, who batted with great style and confidence for his first Test century, then added 138 for the fifth wicket with Jones. Waugh, compared at times with McCabe, batted for just over five hours and hit 24 fours, and his 147 with Hughes (an Australian seventh-wicket record in England) dealt English morale another unexpected blow. DeFreitas, Foster, Newport and Pringle, away from their responsive county wickets, posed few problems for the Australians and all conceded over 100 runs. England replied well enough to avoid a follow-on, Lamb, who was to be grievously missed through injury for the rest of the series, making his first century against Australia, one which was richer in boundaries (76.80 per cent) than any of the 393 previous centuries in England–Australia Tests, surpassing Botham's 149 not out here eight years before. Lamb and Barnett put on 114 for the third wicket, the latter's 80 coming from only 118 balls, and Smith later gave substance to the innings, batting for 189 minutes. Merv Hughes stirred the crowd with his bristling aggression and melodramatic behaviour. With nine hours left, Australia briskly built on their lead of 171. In 10 overs on the final morning Border and Jones clocked up a hectic 72 runs before the declaration, which left England 402 to win in a possible 83 overs. Australia's victory came with almost two hours to spare. Again, Alderman bowled accurately and with enough variety to confuse the hesitant, shuffling batsmen. With five wickets in each innings, the West Australian had taken up from where he left off on the 1981 tour. Gower's decision to put Australia in on a grey day, with suspicion surrounding the pitch, was inevitably criticised with hindsight, Australia's 601 being the highest by either side on this ground (and Russell made it the highest in a Test in England free of byes). Truly depressing was the absence on both sides of a fulltime spin bowler, the first-ever instance. England were left hoping that a return by the injured Botham and Gatting would reverse their fortunes.

1144, below, left: *Mark Taylor sinks to safety as DeFreitas tries to deny him his Ashes debut hundred.* 1145, below, centre: *Steve Waugh, batting with sound sense and technique, approaches his maiden Test century.* 1146, below, right: *Allan Lamb's commanding century kept England in the match. He was sorely missed for the rest of the series*

1989 SECOND TEST

Lord's, June 22, 23, 24, 26, 27

England *286 (R.C. Russell 64*, G.A. Gooch 60, D.I. Gower 57, M.G. Hughes 4 for 71) and 359 (D.I. Gower 106, R.A. Smith 96, T.M. Alderman 6 for 128);* Australia *528 (S.R. Waugh 152*, D.C. Boon 94, G.F. Lawson 74, M.A Taylor 62, J.E. Emburey 4 for 88) and 119 for 4 (D.C. Boon 58*).* Australia won by 6 wickets.

Leg-spinner Hohns came in for Campbell, completing an Australian XI which would remain unchanged for the next five Tests. England began, in contrast, a merrygoround of team alterations, Gatting, Dilley, Emburey and Paul Jarvis (who was to finish with 2 for 290 in his two Tests) taking the places of Lamb (injured), Pringle, Newport and DeFreitas. Gower resisted any temptation to put Australia in under the cloud cover, and England were bowled out inside a day for 286 after having tried to snatch the initiative. Gooch was introspective, but the captain's 57 came off only 62 balls and Smith's 32 from 36, with 124 runs coming in the second session. Gatting was caught at short leg first ball, off Hughes, but wicketkeeper Russell's 160-minute resistance gave the innings respectability. Australia, over almost the whole of the second and third days, ran up their second-highest score at Lord's, Taylor and Boon putting on 145 for the second wicket and Waugh taking over from the middle of the innings and compiling another big hundred. His driving was magnificent and his ice-cool approach gave England's toiling bowlers not the slightest expectation that he would concede to them either weakness or mistake. He batted for five hours, and his stand of 130 with Lawson, who made a Test top score of 74, was an Australian record in England for the ninth wicket. By Saturday night England were 58 for 3, and effectively beaten. Gooch (0) had become Alderman's 100th Test wicket, and Gower was so exasperated at the situation that he stormed out of the evening Press conference. On the Monday, leaving his depression in the dressing-room, he made a charming century, his 106 taking 4½ hours and made up of all things elegant and unruffled. Robin Smith came within a boundary of his first Test century in characteristic style: watchful aggression, muscular pulls and cuts, with Hughes again whistling a steady flow of bouncers at him. A brief storm during lunch on the final day worried Australia, who needed 118. The loss of four wickets for 67 was also an unnerving scoreline. But Waugh marched in to join Boon, and the pair saw Australia home, Waugh's winning boundary taking his series aggregate to 350 without dismissal, an Australian record. Border thus became the first Australian captain to win twice at Lord's, and one of the few happy Englishmen was 18-year-old MCC groundstaff player Robin Sims, who, substituting, had clung to a catch from Border at long leg to make Australia 61 for 3. Another happy man was the TCCB's chief accountant, for this match produced the first £1 million gate in England.

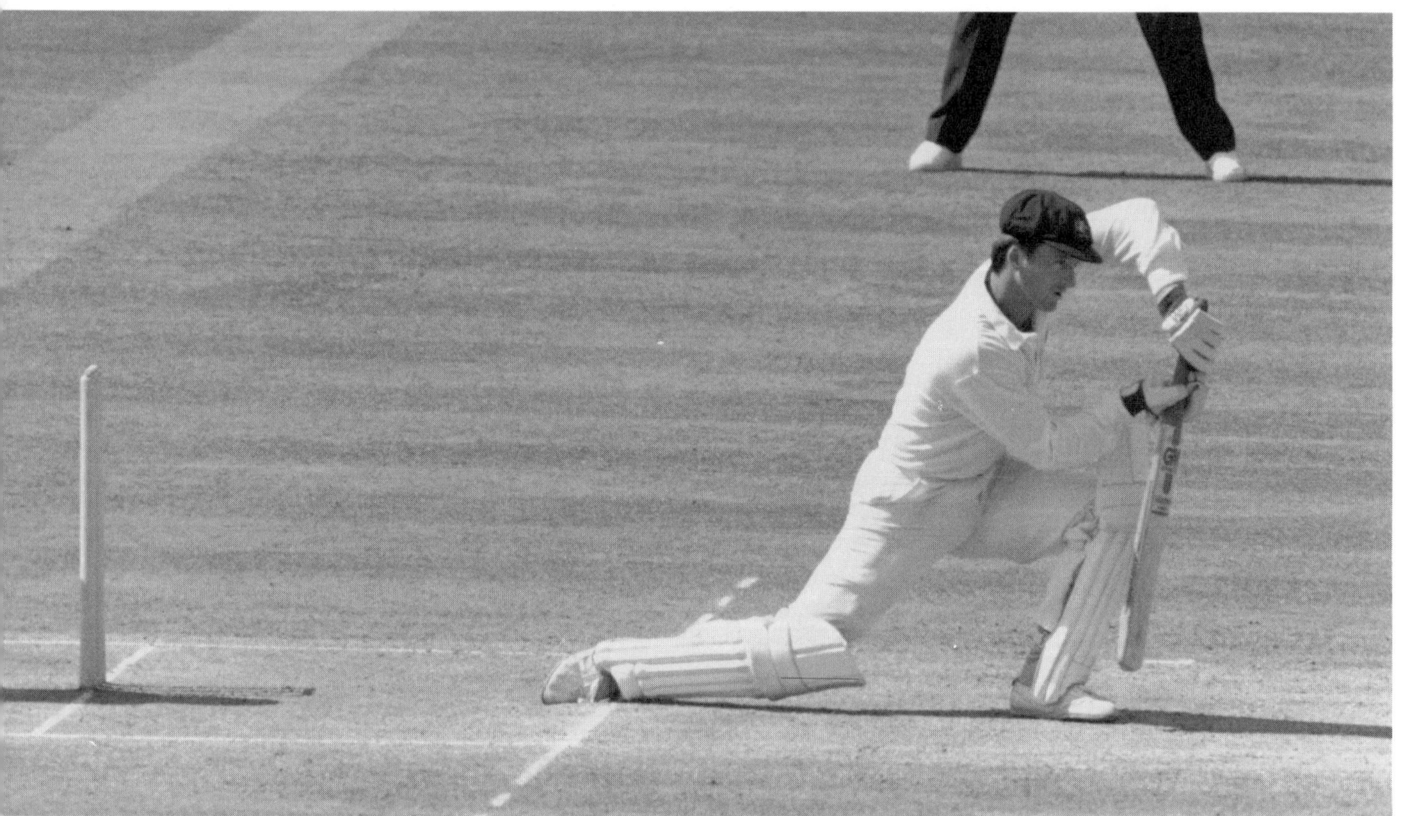

1147, above: *A picture of concentration and precision, Waugh continues his lengthy unbroken occupation of the crease, extending his unbeaten sequence to 350 runs as he hit the winning runs*

1148, above: *Lawson came in with Australia 381 for 8 and left at 511 for 9.* 1149, right: *Robin Smith falls four short of a century, one of Alderman's nine wickets in the match, following his five in each innings of the opening Test of the series*

1150, left: *Another Lord's victory for Australia is in the book and Boon, one of the batting heroes, has done well with souvenirs. David Gower, who made an attractive half-century and century, faces the troubled future, while Gooch wonders where his next run is coming from*

1989 — THIRD TEST

Edgbaston, July 6, 7, 8, 10, 11

Australia *424 (D.M. Jones 157, M.A. Taylor 43, S.R. Waugh 43, G.R. Marsh 42, T.V. Hohns 40, A.R.C. Fraser 4 for 63) and 158 for 2 (M.A. Taylor 51, G.R. Marsh 42)*; England *242 (I.T. Botham 46, R.C. Russell, 42, T.S. Curtis 41).* Match drawn.

The return of Botham, who had undergone major spinal surgery the year before, brought England renewed hope, but they were outplayed again and probably saved by rain and bad light, which cut over 10 hours from the match. Injuries and muddled selection now took England's list of participants in the series to 19 in three matches, Tavare among them, back in England colours after five years. Botham passed Underwood's record for England of 8000 balls bowled against Australia, but was a much subdued version of the bowler of old, concentrating on accuracy. Marsh and Taylor gave Australia a start of 88, but it took a fourth-wicket stand of 96 between Boon and Jones to halt a slide. Jones's straight-drive, clipping the bowler's hand, ran out his partner, but Waugh came in to take his unbroken run aggregate to 393 in 13 hours in the series before being dismissed at last, to give Fraser his maiden Test wicket. This was on the second day, which started at 4.30 pm, a violent storm having flooded the ground the evening before. Jones, strong in strokeplay and determined in defence, batted for 5½ hours for his 157, the highest score ever for Australia at Edgbaston (where he had scored 248 against Warwickshire five weeks earlier, marking his recovery from a fractured cheekbone). He was supported by Hohns in a stand of 92 for the eighth wicket, and after a much-shortened third day the fourth saw Australia's innings ending at last, their position safe. England then crumbled on the slow, bounceless pitch, most of their techniques proving faulty. Curtis held on for two hours for his 41, and Botham and Russell both stayed for 2½ hours, but only after some excitement—Fraser being foolishly run out—on the fifth morning did England scrape clear of the follow-on, last pair Dilley (11 in 85 minutes) and Jarvis (22) making the 10 necessary, and 17 more. With a possible 71 overs remaining, Australia were content to take batting practice. In the first innings, Border (8) had joined Sobers, Boycott and Gavaskar with his 8000th Test run. Dean Jones was a clear choice as Man of the Match.

1151, above: *Allan Border is bowled behind his legs by John Emburey for 8 and Australia are 105 for 3 at Edgbaston. The Australian captain at least had joined the elite by passing 8000 Test runs.* 1152, right: *Dean Jones masterminded the recovery, amassing an always-interesting 157, Australia's highest ever at Birmingham*

1989 — FOURTH TEST

Old Trafford, July 27, 28, 29, 31, August 1

England *260 (R.A. Smith 143, G.F. Lawson 6 for 72) and 264 (R.C. Russell 128*, J.E. Emburey 64, T.M. Alderman 5 for 66);* Australia *447 (S.R. Waugh 92, M.A. Taylor 85, A.R. Border 80, D.M. Jones 69, G.R. Marsh 47) and 81 for 1.* Australia won by 9 wickets.

Australia won back the Ashes with another resounding victory, coincidentally their 100th against England and 200th in all Tests. If the result was upstaged in British newspapers by the revelation of a planned 'rebel' English tour of South Africa, in Australia the excitement was unconfined for television viewers who had spent nights in their armchairs. Not since 1934 had the Ashes been regained in England. Smith saved his side from humiliation on the opening day, crouching in defence, powerful in attack, similar in many ways to O'Neill of 30 years before. Curtis had existed for 2¼ hours for 22 and Gower's 35 took 1½ hours, but Smith's best support came from Foster at No. 9. He made 39 and their stand amounted to 74. Botham's dismissal came as a shock. Jumping out at Hohns, he was bowled for a duck. Lawson bowled briskly to a steady line and earned his six wickets. At one stage England had posted only two runs in 66 minutes, and their plight can only be imagined had Smith's gully chance to Marsh when on 5 been held. The South African-born batsman batted just on six hours and hit 15 fours. Marsh and Taylor opened with 135, but at 154 for 3 the match was balanced. Then Border, with his highest score of the series, and Jones put on 120. Nick Cook bowled a leg-stump line or wider, and Botham, with figures of 5–2–15–1, bowled hardly at all in the first 80 overs. Waugh came in to torment England again, occupying the crease for 3½ hours and averaging 485 in the series before pulling Fraser to be caught high at square leg. Early on the fourth day Australia's innings came to an end with their lead 187, and just after lunch England were 59 for 6. Curtis fell to another Boon bat-pad catch; Lawson beat Robinson with pace; Smith touched one down the leg side; Gooch edged a good awayswinger; Botham played around a ball from Alderman; Gower cut throat-high to gully. It was a spectacular cavalcade of ways to get out. Russell and Emburey then doubled the score before rain curtailed the day. On the last day they dug in, and as their resistance developed, an Australian victory began to look less certain. The dogged Emburey hit Hohns for four just before lunch to wipe away the prospect of an innings defeat, and it took the new ball, in Alderman's skilled hand, to end the seventh-wicket stand at 142, an Ashes record at Old Trafford (beating that of Hayward and Lilley, 1899). Russell batted on, a model of concentration and judgment, showing up those higher in the batting order. He reached his maiden first-class century, and batted for nearly six hours in all, Foster and Fraser having stood by him for 40 minutes each. Australia thus needed 78 to win the Ashes, and had 80 minutes plus 20 overs on hand. Marsh (31) and Taylor (37 not out, reaching 501 runs for the series) compiled 62 for the first wicket in 95 minutes, and to David Boon fell the honour of sweeping Cook for the winning boundary that signified the completion of a rebirth of Australian cricket and buried England's deeper into the mire.

1153, below: *Much was expected of Ian Botham, and he knew it, but within minutes of his arrival at the crease at Old Trafford he leapt out at legspinner Hohns, missed, and heard the fatal click.* 1154, right: *Smith's unusual power was much in evidence as he carried England on his shoulders and made his first Test century*

1155, top, left: *England's wicketkeeper Jack Russell held out for almost six hours at Old Trafford for a sensible and heroic maiden hundred.* 1156, above: *The post-mortem—England's cricket chairman Ted Dexter, captain David Gower and manager Micky Stewart face the Press with dignity.* 1157, left: *The Australians were repeatedly congratulating each other as success came after success in the 1989 rubber. Here Lawson takes a pummelling for getting rid of Gower at Old Trafford—with Hughes (right) never far from the action*

1989 FIFTH TEST

Trent Bridge, August 10, 11, 12, 14

Australia *602 for 6 dec (M.A. Taylor 219, G.R. Marsh 138, D.C. Boon 73, A.R. Border 65*);* England *255 (R.A. Smith 101, T.M. Alderman 5 for 69) and 167 (M.A. Atherton 47).* Australia won by an innings and 180 runs.

Australia confirmed—if confirmation were still needed—their superiority over Gower's England side with a record-shattering victory at Nottingham. The margin was the biggest ever inflicted by Australia in England. The opening stand of 329 between Marsh and Taylor (both making their highest Test scores) was a new record for either side, the highest in any Test in England, and the fifth-highest in Test history. On the first day they scored 301 (Taylor 141, Marsh 125), the first instance of no wicket falling on a full day in a Test in England, and when the first wicket fell (Marsh c Botham b Cook) it was to the 744th ball of the innings. Marsh batted for seven hours, Taylor (stumped for the third time in the series, his aggregate now 720) for 9¼, making Australia's first double-century against England since Stackpole's in 1970. The total at the end of the second day was 560 for 5, Taylor and Boon having had a stand of 101 (the score stood at 502 for 2 before Boon was stumped), and a bizarre feature of the innings, which became Australia's highest ever at Trent Bridge, was Waugh's duck. Sixty-one extras were included, a new Ashes record. England had omitted the three South Africa signings, and Gooch asked to be rested, to regain his form. The bespectacled Devon

Malcolm, Jamaica-born, bowled fast but erratically, and without luck, to finish with 1 for 166 off 44 overs, and Fraser, Hemmings and Cook (giving the ball more air) did not bowl badly. Once Taylor and Marsh had posted the fifth consecutive first-wicket score of 50, a record for Australia against England, the pattern seemed inescapable. To such an extent was English luck poor, in keeping with its batsmanship, that when Botham missed a fast chance from Boon, his finger was horribly dislocated, preventing him from batting in his normal position—or at all in the second innnings. When England finally got in, during the third day, the pitch was behaving unpredictably, and Alderman probed defects in the surface and in his opponents' sheepish techniques with fiendish skill. The third wicket fell at 14, the fourth at 37, before Russell gave Smith some support. Hemmings and Fraser batted obdurately, but again it was Smith, almost alone, who saved England from complete ignominy. With some explosive shots and gritty defence, he reached his second century in successive matches in three hours, having removed Boon's helmet with one of his tremendous pull-shots. England followed on 347 behind and evaporated for 167, Atherton, on debut, making 47 in almost three hours of calm assessment. Hughes took three wickets, Alderman, Lawson and Hohns two each, and the victory was achieved with a day to spare. The only other Australian team to win four Tests in a series in England was Bradman's of 1948.

1158, left: *Geoff Marsh and Mark Taylor kept Australia's No. 3 batsman David Boon padded up in the pavilion through the whole of the first day of the Nottingham Test. The first Australian wicket fell next day to the 744th ball of the innings.* 1159, above: *Smith's patience and power were again in evidence in another century for England; Healy is the wicketkeeper.* 1160, left: *The bogeyman strikes again: Alderman delivers England debutant Mike Atherton of a first-innings duck. The 21-year-old Lancastrian held his ground for nearly three hours in the second innings*

1989 SIXTH TEST

The Oval, August 24, 25, 26, 28, 29

Australia *468 (D.M. Jones 122, A.R. Border 76, M.A. Taylor 71, D.C. Boon 46, I.A. Healy 44, D.R. Pringle 4 for 70) and 219 for 4 dec (A.R. Border 51*, D.M. Jones 50, M.A. Taylor 48);* England *285 (D.I. Gower 79, G.C. Small 59, T.M. Alderman 5 for 66) and 143 for 5 (R.A. Smith 77*).* Match drawn.

The uneven series closed with a draw which might have been a win had Border not batted on until lunch on the final day, setting England an out-of-sight 403 off 67 overs. Once more Australia zoomed past 400 in their first innings—for the eighth time running, a new world Test record—on a hot and hazy first day which turned to cloudiness and humidity on the second. Taylor passed 50 for the seventh time in the series, and by the end of the match had taken his aggregate in the six Tests to 839 (at 83.90), third behind Bradman (974 in 1930) and Hammond (905 in 1928–29), having batted for 38 hours overall. From 149 for 3, Border and Jones added 196, Jones reaching his century off 119 balls and 1000 against England in only his 20th innings. England's customary hardships began with Gooch's dismissal third ball for 0, his fifth lbw in eight Test innings, but a smooth 79 from Gower rebuilt the innings into the fourth morning. When he tickled Alderman to Healy, the follow-on loomed, but Small made a priceless 59 and Cook (31 in two hours) stayed while 73 were added for the ninth wicket. England now tried to contain Australia, who scored 87 for 1 that evening off 35 overs, Igglesden having trapped Marsh lbw for 4. On the final morning a further 132 runs were scrambled, Waugh passing 500 for the series, as Taylor and Jones had done, three past that aggregate being unique in an Ashes series, and Waugh preserved a series average of over 100 (126.50), a great rarity. At 67 for 4, England were in a wobble yet again, but Smith once more rose above the chaos and Capel (17) stayed with him to 138, and soon the light was too poor for play to continue, an irony for this longest and hottest of summers. England, having used 29 players in the series, had now won only one of their last 25 Tests, and entered a period of desperate self-examination. Australia, whose strategy was masterminded by coach Bob Simpson, had a number of heroes to cherish, Terry Alderman prominent among them. For the sixth time in the series he had taken five or more wickets in an innings, an Ashes record, and he was also the first bowler to take 40 wickets in a series on more than one occasion. His 41 this time included 19 lbws. A telling team statistic was Australia's 3877 runs in the six Tests, the most ever in an Ashes series, passing England's 3757 in the five Tests of 1928–29. Border and his men had done much to revive Australian spirits, both in cricket and on a wider scale. The team's wildly-acclaimed tickertape parade through Sydney was entirely justified.

1161, left: *Gladstone Small took all that Hughes and the rest could hurl at him while he made 59 and saved England from following on.* 1162, below: *Australian skipper Allan Border made two more fortifying half-centuries in the Oval Test, and finished the series with an average of 73.67—and the Ashes safely in the bag.* 1163, right: *David Gower, England's captain, hammers one of his 11 boundaries in his 79, but total disillusionment was soon to follow with his sacking*

1990-91
Brisbane, November 23, 24, 25

England *194 (D.I. Gower 61, B.A. Reid 4 for 53) and 114 (T.M. Alderman 6 for 47);* Australia *152 and 157 for 0 (G.R. Marsh 72*, M.A. Taylor 67*).* Australia won by 10 wickets.

Led by Lamb, with captain Gooch unable to play because of a heavily-stitched infected finger, England went tentatively into the opening Test and were overthrown with even greater ease than in 1989. The pitch was green-tinged, and under cloud cover Australia bowled the visitors out for 194 on the first day, England's lack of experience showing starkly with some poor shot-selection. Border had put England in here four years before, and lost. Now, he overcame any inhibition, and Reid and Hughes did their job well. At 117 for 2, England had seemed well-launched. But Gower's happy-go-lucky 61 was to be easily top score in an innings wherein Reid, his spine now surgically rebuilt, took four key wickets. Alderman finally took only his second England wicket ever in Australia, having bagged 83 in two series in England. The pitch quickened but remained responsive on Day 2, which saw Australia unexpectedly disposed of for 152, Fraser, Small and Lewis taking three wickets each, Matthews top-scoring with 35 in 127 minutes. Border scored only 9 in his 200th Test innings, and the 100 was grafted off 41 overs. England, with a lead of 42, managed to lose three wickets that evening, Larkins first ball, Gower (27, eventual top score) having passed Boycott's 2945 to become second in aggregate against Australia to Hobbs. Border was inconsolable after dropping Lamb, but the stand-in skipper soon went next morning to Alderman, who, under further heavy cloud cover, proceeded to his best Test figures. For the 11th time he took five or more wickets in an innings against England, equalling the record of Turner, Grimmett and Lillee. Nightwatchman Russell batted longest: 116 minutes for 15. Australia now sought 157 for victory, under sunny skies, and achieved it without loss, three minutes before the scheduled close of the third day, Taylor and Marsh batting confidently and shaming so much of the confused batsmanship which had gone before. Their unbroken stand was a new Brisbane first-wicket record. England's 114 was their lowest all-out total at Brisbane, and had turned a commanding position into reverse. Not since 1938 had Australia beaten them in three days.

1164, right: *England lose the key wicket of Robin Smith, bowled by Reid on the first day.* 1165, below: *The trusty opening pair, Taylor and Marsh, seal another fine partnership on the third evening.* 1166, below right: *Australian captain Allan Border adds to England's calamitous fortunes with a flying catch to send Chris Lewis on his way*

1990-91 SECOND TEST

Melbourne, December 26, 27, 28, 29, 30

England *352 (D.I. Gower 100, A.J. Stewart 79, W. Larkins 64, B.A. Reid 6 for 97) and 150 (G.A. Gooch 58, W. Larkins 54, B.A. Reid 7 for 51);* Australia *306 (A.R. Border 62, M.A. Taylor 61, D.M. Jones 44, A.R.C. Fraser 6 for 82) and 197 for 2 (D.C. Boon 94*, G.R. Marsh 79*).* Australia won by 8 wickets.

Australia's 500th Test match ended in triumph even though England again had a first-innings lead. As at Brisbane, a humiliating second-innings collapse then let Australia back in, and the biggest stand of the match, an unbeaten 187 between Marsh and Boon (both of whom passed 1000 runs against England), put Australia two-up in the series. Border, leading Australia in a record 20th Test against England (Bradman 19), lost the toss to Gooch, who was now almost fully fit, though Lamb was out with a leg injury. On a slow pitch, off which 20 catches were to be held behind the wicket, Gower (17th Test century), Larkins and Stewart all batted most creditably, the left-hander's 100 coming from 170 balls. Healy held five catches. Australia replied almost in kind, Taylor and Border both batting for around four hours, with Jones lifting the tempo with a 57-ball 44. Russell held six catches, a new record for England against Australia, while Fraser did a controlled Bedser-like job with a career-best 6 for 82. At 103 for 1, England had extended their lead to 149. But nine wickets then toppled for 47 (6 for 3 after tea), Reid bowling a testing left-arm-over at or just outside off stump while the Englishmen pushed and prodded. Gower's duck, caught at silly point off Matthews, sealed a record sequence of 119 Test innings without such failure, and when Reid was not cutting his opponents down, they appeared simply to be standing awaiting execution: Stewart's 8 lasted 70 minutes, Russell's 1, 46 minutes. The 6ft 8ins Western Australian finished with 13 wickets, joining the elite company of Spofforth, Noble and Mailey, with only Massie (16) and Spofforth (14) above them on the Australia v England table. Australia lost Taylor and Healy for 10 on the fourth evening, but Marsh and Boon applied themselves dourly and supportively for over five hours to make the day, and the match, entirely Australia's. In the second session Marsh chipped only 36 runs and Boon 19. The latter had been in over four hours before finding the boundary, and when Tufnell, on Test debut, had a caught-behind appeal rejected he put on an objectionable display of petulance. Not since 1891-92 had Australia won the first two Tests of a series after first-innings deficits.

1167, facing page, left: *Wayne Larkins, driving Matthews, showed why England selected him by making two gritty half-centuries.* 1168, facing page, right: *Bruce Reid gave England a nightmarish time by bowling relentlessly at the off stump, with a little movement, to pick up 13 wickets and help Australia to a 2-0 lead.* 1169, right: *Alderman, his best Test bowling figures behind him in the Brisbane Test, is bowled by Fraser for a duck. The anachronistically rural MCG background was caused by demolition of the Southern Stand prior to erection of a larger edifice*

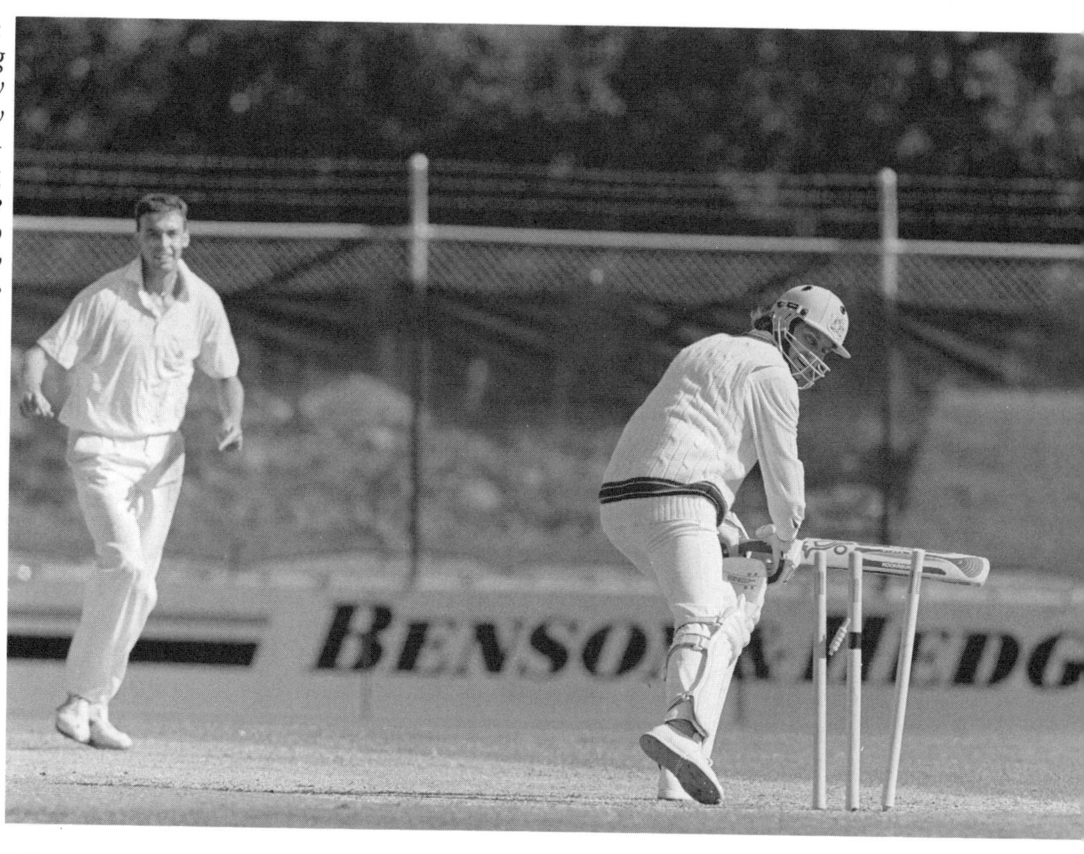

1990-91

Sydney, January 4, 5, 6, 7, 8

THIRD TEST

Australia *518 (G.R.J. Matthews 128, D.C. Boon 97, A.R. Border 78, D.M. Jones 60, S.R. Waugh 48, D.E. Malcolm 4 for 128) and 205 (I.A. Healy 69, P.C.R. Tufnell 5 for 61)*; England *469 for 8 dec (D.I. Gower 123, M.A. Atherton 105, A.J. Stewart 91, G.A. Gooch 59) and 113 for 4 (G.A. Gooch 54).* Match drawn.

Australia retained title to the little Ashes urn, though they were greatly relieved at the end to settle for a draw. At last batsmen of both sides came into their own; at last England found the reserves of strength to compete seriously for five days. Australia seemed quite safe with 518 first up, England, lacking the injured Fraser, going in with only Malcolm and Small to bowl fast and Tufnell and Hemmings to spin. Boon, having hit three fours off a Gooch over, perished attempting a fourth when 97, and Border, with his 50th score between 50 and 99 in Tests, laid the platform upon which Jones (his only fifty of the series) and Waugh built briskly and Matthews animatedly in his maiden Ashes century, a mixture of vigilance and opportunism. Using some borrowed gear, he was at the crease for four hours and hit 17 fours and a five. His ninth-wicket stand of 55 with Alderman frustrated England almost beyond endurance. Gooch and Atherton gave England a start of 95, but the captain, Larkins and Smith were all out by the third evening, Atherton slowly moving towards a century which, reached next day, was the slowest in first-class cricket at Sydney and in any England v Australia Test, displacing Randall's 411-minute devotion at the SCG 12 years earlier. Atherton's took 424 minutes, with only eight fours. Gower had begun the fourth day by cracking eight fours in little more than half-an-hour, and with Atherton, still short of his century, shown on television to have been run out by 15ins, the excitement factor was sustained in the finest tradition. Gower's ninth century equalled Hammond's tally and left only Hobbs (12) ahead for England against Australia. With Stewart, Gower added 99 for the fifth wicket, cheered lustily by flag-waving English supporters on what remained of the Hill. Marsh's brilliant gully catch disposed of Gower, and Stewart seemed rather unlucky to be adjudged lbw when only nine short of a century. Suddenly, Gooch declared, 49 behind. That evening England plucked out Marsh and Taylor, and after morning rain, the fifth day began on time, with Australia bewilderingly on the back foot. Had nightwatchman Healy fallen to an airborne catch attempt by Gower at 12, and had Rackemann been dislodged early by pace bowling, which he quite famously disliked, Australia would have lost. Instead, midst the wreckage of the innings, Healy fought on for almost three hours, and Rackemann created a record by taking 72 minutes to open his score. Malcolm, not fully fit, bowled him for 9 as soon as he was called up. Tufnell almost performed the hat-trick when he had Border (sweeping to square leg) and Jones (caught-and-bowled) nearly followed by Waugh, whose parry reached Gower's fingertips.

The two prodding, padding Queenslanders, Healy and Rackemann, ensured that England's target was just too much at 255 off 28 overs. Still, Gooch and Gower (who passed 8000 Test runs) raced to 81 off 11 overs with brazen attack, including the reverse-sweep, and Border's frown was fixed and deep. Gooch reached a 40-ball half-century, but the sacrifice of four wickets saw a reversion to caution as Australia's fielders came in from the outfield to crowd the bat. Further milestones in this memorable match were Gooch's 6000 Test runs, Border's 3000 against England, and Taylor's 1000 against England in only his 17th innings.

1170, top: *For four hours Greg Matthews occupied the stage at Sydney, stroking and fidgeting his way to an invaluable 128.* 1171, left: *Mike Atherton, the young Lancashire opener, raises his bat upon reaching the slowest century in the 272 Anglo-Australian Test matches played to date. He reached three figures in 7 hours 4 minutes, and the first to congratulate him was David Gower, who scored an enchanting century as well, adding 139 with Atherton and 99 with Stewart*

1172, above: *Rackemann edges short of Gooch during his matchsaving innings of 9 on the last day. He waited 72 minutes for his first run, passing Murdoch's record (70 minutes, Sydney 1882–83, fourth Test)*

1173, above: *Dean Jones caught by bowler Phil Tufnell first ball, and Australian nerves jangle.* 1174, below: *Almost a Tufnell hat-trick as Gower can no more than touch Steve Waugh's first-ball parry.* 1175, left: *Five-wicket hero Tufnell applauded off by Gooch, Atherton and Gower*

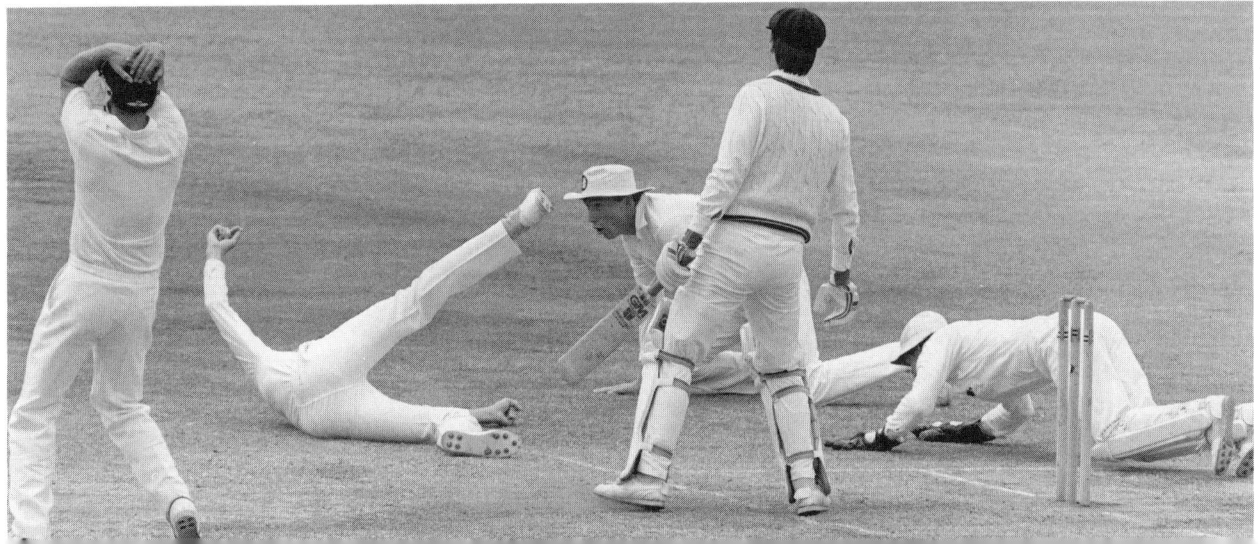

1990-91 FOURTH TEST

Adelaide, January 25, 26, 27, 28, 29

Australia *386 (M. E. Waugh 138, G. R. J. Matthews 65, D. C. Boon 49, C. J. McDermott 42*, P. A. J. DeFreitas 4 for 56) and 314 for 6 dec (D. C. Boon 121, A. R. Border 83*);* England *229 (G. A. Gooch 87, R. A. Smith 53, P. A. J. DeFreitas 45, C. J. McDermott 5 for 97, B. A. Reid 4 for 53) and 335 for 5 (G. A. Gooch 117, M. A. Atherton 87, A. J. Lamb 53).* Match drawn.

A bland pitch was the stage for some stirring cricket, outstanding being Mark Waugh's debut century, fashioned stylishly from a crisis of 104 for 4 on the first day. Selected in place of his brother Steve (the first twins to play Test cricket), Waugh displayed craftsmanship refined in county cricket with Essex and, even more patently, a grace of movement granted only to the rare likes of Archie Jackson. Matthews (65 in 5¼ hours) backed him in a rescuing stand of 171 (a sixth-wicket Australian record against England at Adelaide), Waugh's century coming off 126 balls, with 15 fours. McDermott, reinstated after two years, made his highest Test score and raised Australia to the security of 386. Fraser had to retire with hip and ankle problems and Tufnell with a throat infection. Stewart kept wicket, Russell having been dropped. McDermott and Reid now disposed of England for 229, the last eight wickets tumbling for 92. McDermott inflicted ducks on Atherton and Lamb before Gooch and Smith (with his first fifty of the series) added 126. DeFreitas, a tour reinforcement before the second Test, made 45 from 56 balls. No dismissal was more disappointing for England than Gower's. He was caught in an obvious trap at fine leg on the stroke of lunch. Wicketkeeper Healy again took five catches. Australia, 157 ahead, lost Marsh, Taylor (run out for the second time in the match), Jones and Waugh for 68 that evening, but Boon, scoring a patient, chanceless third century against England, and Border led their side towards a safe lead: 471 when Border declared. Three of his bowlers were not fully fit, and when Gooch (first Test century in Australia) and Atherton opened with 203 (beating Hayward and MacLaren's 1901-02 England record at Adelaide) in almost even time, Australia felt some concern. Lamb contributed a run-a-ball 53, but the loss of three wickets for 10 caused England to call off the attempt to stay in the series.

1176, left: *Cool and elegant Mark Waugh, joining brother Steve (who was dropped to make way for him) as the first twins to play Test cricket, moves easefully and confidently towards his hundred on debut. From the first ball he looked the part, the century seeming almost an inevitability*

1177, below: *England captain, Graham Gooch, needing to win at Adelaide, bats as boldly as at Sydney, but with just as disappointing an outcome. His robust century was his first in Tests in Australia.* 1178, right: *David Boon, Australia's most valuable batsman of the series, gives his customary low-key acknowledgement to the applause which greeted his century*

1990-91 *Perth, February 1, 2, 3, 5*

FIFTH TEST

England *244 (A. J. Lamb 91, R. A. Smith 58, C. J. McDermott 8 for 97) and 182 (R. A. Smith 43, P. J. Newport 40*, M. G. Hughes 4 for 37)*; Australia *307 (D. C. Boon 64, G. R. J. Matthews 60*, I. A. Healy 42) and 120 for 1 (G. R. Marsh 63*)*. Australia won by 9 wickets.

Allan Border, leading Australia for a record 23rd time in Ashes Tests (A. C. MacLaren 22), paid tribute to England's bowlers as Australia took the series 3–0 with a four-day triumph on the fast WACA pitch. Graham Gooch, his opposite number, was scathing in his criticism of his team's 'nightmare' performance in which the same mistakes had been made time and again. He considered it also the worst fielding side he had seen. Further condemnation followed when it was calculated that England's over rate (14.1 per hour, against Australia's 14.5) was probably the slowest in Ashes history. Although their *bête noire* Reid (27 wickets at 16 in four Tests) was rested with callused feet, England failed now to withstand McDermott's withering fire. Though sometimes off-target, he pounded the batsmen remorselessly enough to take career-best figures (the best in Ashes Tests at Perth) and hasten another collapse from 191 for 2 to 244 all out. Lamb (91 off 122 balls) hit his highest Test score in Australia and added 141 with Smith at a fast rate, aided by a smooth outfield. Gower, equalling Cowdrey's 114 Test appearances for England, was left stranded at 28 not out. Australia were made to fight for their runs, but contributions down the order led to a 63-run advantage. England then produced a trademark collapse, this time seven wickets for 69 from 75 for 2. Atherton had stood fast for just over 2½ hours for 25, and only a bright, unbeaten 40 in an hour by reinforcement Newport (for Fraser) took the match into the fourth day. McDermott, Alderman and Hughes shared the bowling and the rewards, Alderman becoming, in only his 17th Test against England, the 10th to take 100 wickets. Hughes bagged his 100th in all Tests, and Healy took his series dismissals to 24, all catches. Australia attained the modest target with ease, Boon raising his series aggregate to 530 (75.71), having batted for over 26 hours in all. Matthews' valuable batting contribution amounted to 353 runs at 70.60. Australia—especially Taylor and Jones—had not played as well as in 1989, and yet the final margin was just as emphatic. Left-handers Border and Gower each finished in second place in the England v Australia batting aggregate tables: the Australian with 3115 (41 matches) to Bradman's 5028 (37), the Englishman with 3269 (42) to Hobbs's 3636 (41).

1179, above: *Terry Alderman (back to camera) has DeFreitas caught by wicketkeeper Healy and becomes only the 10th Australian bowler to take 100 England wickets. Only 17 of them were taken in Australia.* 1180, left: *The picture of aggression, Craig McDermott leaves Alec Stewart in no doubt that Healy has caught him. The big Queenslander's first-innings 8 for 97 were the best figures to date in an Ashes Test at the WACA ground.* 1181, below: *Allan Lamb at last showed an Australian crowd his full worth with a vigorous 91, which included this six off Matthews. Taylor is at slip*

1993
Old Trafford, June 3, 4, 5, 6, 7

Australia *289 (M.A. Taylor 124, M.J. Slater 58, P.M. Such 6 for 67) and 432 for 5 dec (I.A. Healy 102*, D.C. Boon 93, S.R. Waugh 78*, M.E. Waugh 64);* England *210 (G.A. Gooch 65, S.K. Warne 4 for 51, M.G. Hughes 4 for 59) and 332 (G.A. Gooch 133, C.C. Lewis 43, S.K. Warne 4 for 86, M.G. Hughes 4 for 92).* Australia won by 179 runs.

Australia's emphatic opening victory sent an ominous warning through English cricket, specifically via Shane Warne's first delivery—the 'ball of the century' or 'ball from Hell'—which spun across Gatting to clip the off stump. No bowler in Ashes history had hit the stumps with his maiden ball. Gooch had put Australia in after recent rain, but Taylor and Slater (Test debut) posted 128 for the first wicket. Wickets fell steadily thereafter, Such finding response for his offspin. His analysis was the best by an England debutant against Australia since 1890, when Martin took six wickets in each innings. Gooch and Atherton started with 71, but wickets fell cheaply, Warne dismissing Robin Smith six balls after Gatting, and Hughes bowling with the same menace as in 1989. Hick was second-top scorer with 34, though his slip fielding was fallible in this match. By the third evening Australia had a firm grip, 231 for 3 second time round, the pitch having dried, the lead now 310. Tufnell had bowled Mark Waugh out of the rough, but Such was destined not to add to his eight wickets. New Zealand-born Caddick made Border his first wicket, and Boon holed out seven short of a century. Steve Waugh and Healy, taking runs with impunity, then added 180 before the declaration left England 8½ hours to survive, Healy going on to his maiden first-class century and becoming only the second wicketkeeper, after Marsh, to score an Australian Test century against England. For a time it seemed England would escape. McDermott bowled testingly but without reward throughout the match, and after losing Atherton to Warne, Gooch resisted with all the shrewdness at his disposal. Gatting, though, was yorked by the last ball of the day, from Hughes. Survival still seemed likely halfway through the fifth day, but Gooch's admirable 133 closed when he instinctively punched the ball away as he saw it rebound towards the stumps, and umpire Bird gave him out 'handled the ball', the first such instance in Ashes history. With 58 balls to spare, Australia went on to seal victory, Warne's catch at leg-slip to dismiss Caddick being almost as memorable as that monstrous legbreak to Gatting.

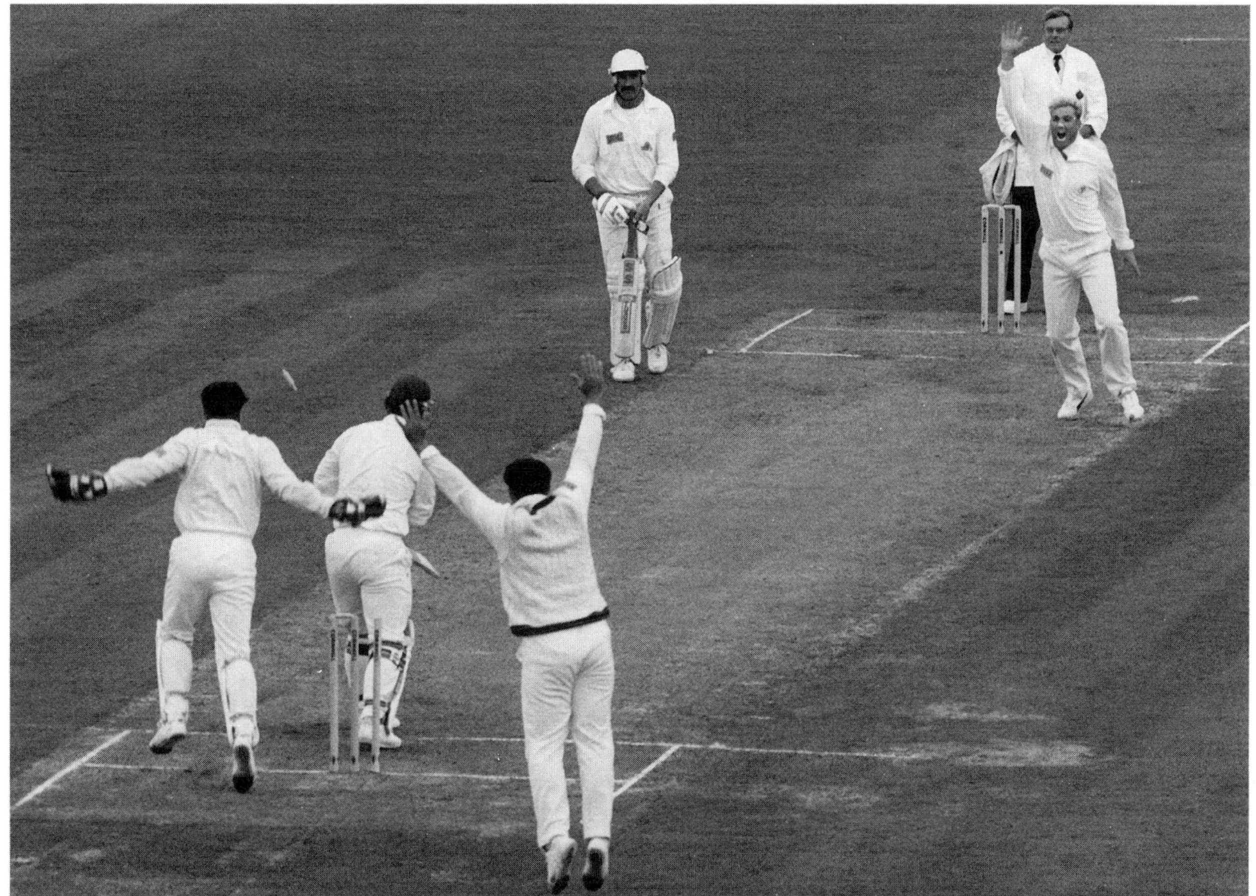

1182: *Gatting b. Warne 4—the first time a bowler's first ball in an Ashes Test has hit the stumps*

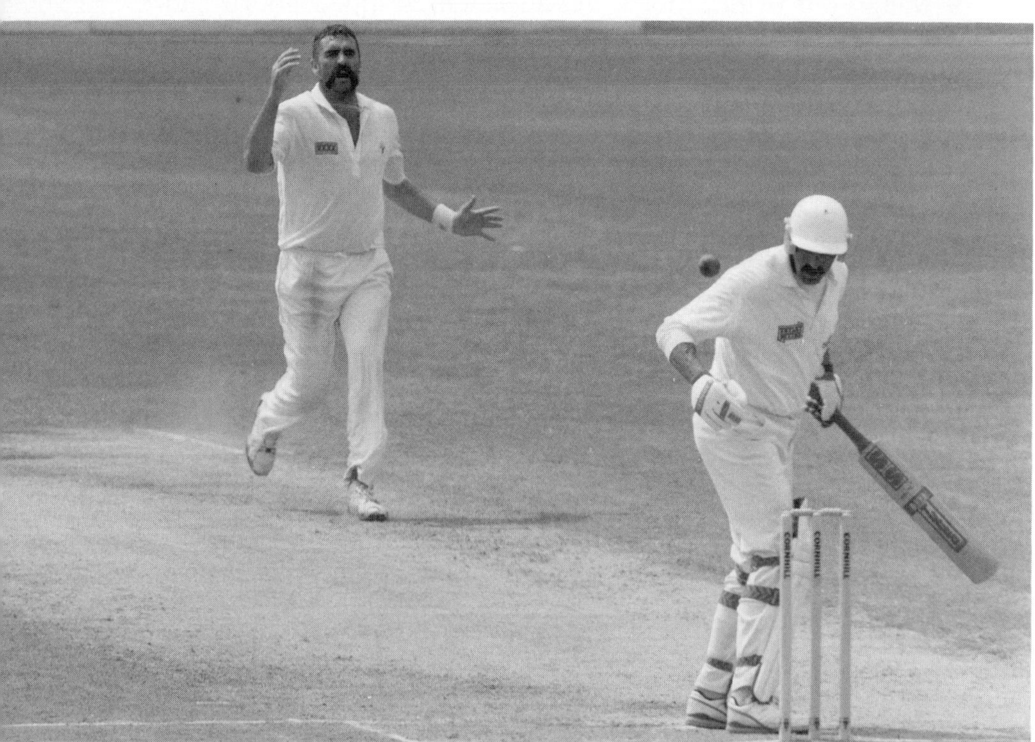

1183, top, left: *Offspinner Peter Such traps Australian captain Mark Taylor lbw, his seventh wicket of the match, and England are still in the game.*
1184, above: *Ian Healy reaches his first century in first-class cricket, having helped to secure Australia's position in the second innings.*
1185, left: *In the 275th Test match between England and Australia, the first 'handled the ball' dismissal occurs: Graham Gooch (133 in 5¹/₄ hours) punching away a rebound off Merv Hughes's bowling*

1993 SECOND TEST

Lord's, June 17, 18, 19, 20, 21

Australia *632 for 4 dec (D.C. Boon 164*, M.J. Slater 152, M.A. Taylor 111, M.E. Waugh 99, A.R. Border 77)*; England *205 (M.A. Atherton 80, M.G. Hughes 4 for 52, S.K. Warne 4 for 57)* and *365 (M.A. Atherton 99, G.A. Hick 64, A.J. Stewart 62, M.W. Gatting 59, T.B.A. May 4 for 81, S.K. Warne 4 for 102)*. Australia won by an innings and 62 runs.

Australia's most decisive victory ever (only four wickets lost) over England deepened the home nation's gloom, for it was also the 15th Test in succession in which England had failed to beat Australia, a new record. There were others: Taylor (passing 1000 Test runs in England) and Slater opened with 260, the highest stand by either side for any wicket in a Lord's Test; and if Mark Waugh had scored one more run, it would have seen the first four in the order making centuries for the first time in Test history. Only once (1930) had Australia made a higher total at Lord's, and Boon at last reached a Test hundred in England. He added 175 with Mark Waugh for the third wicket and 139 for the fourth with Border, who finished with a Test average at Lord's of 100. England's innocuous bowling made grim reading, the recalled Foster (0 for 94) being one of five wicketless bowlers. England were soon in trouble again, Atherton alone weathering the bombardment of Hughes and the spin of Warne and May for any length of time. Smith became the first batsman to be given out (stumped) in an English Test after referral to the video-replay third umpire. Following on, England offered stouter resistance, Gooch and Atherton making 71, which rose to 175 before Atherton's nightmarish run-out for 99. Sent back on the third run, he slipped as Hughes's throw was gathered by Healy, who dived at the stumps to complete the execution. Gatting, Hick and Stewart all made half-centuries, but there was an inevitability about Australia's march to victory. For the 13th time running in Tests, Smith was out to spin bowling. Some dubious umpiring decisions hastened the end, and Australia now had 10 wins at Lord's this century to England's one. And this latest triumph came—embarrassingly for England—from a 10-man team, McDermott having collapsed on the second evening. He returned to Australia after surgery for a twisted bowel.

1186, above: *To his horror, Mark Waugh is bowled by Tufnell for 99.* 1187, above, right: *Robin Smith is beaten by Tim May and, a minute later, learns of his dismissal, stumped.* 1188, below: *Mike Atherton run out for 99.* 1189, right: *Michael Slater with his Man of the Match champagne, and fellow centurian David Boon*

1993 — THIRD TEST

Trent Bridge, July 1, 2, 3, 5, 6

England *321 (R.A. Smith 86, N. Hussain 71, M.G. Hughes 5 for 92) and 422 for 6 dec (G.A. Gooch 120, G.P. Thorpe 114*, R.A. Smith 50, N. Hussain 47*);* Australia *373 (D.C. Boon 101, M.E. Waugh 70, M.J. Slater 40, M.J. McCague 4 for 121) and 202 for 6 (B.P. Julian 56*, S.R. Waugh 47*).* Match drawn.

England's resurgence at Nottingham might have been crowned with victory had not Steve Waugh and Brendon Julian steadied Australia on the final afternoon with a doughty stand of 87 in just over two hours which secured the draw. England blooded four new players: Lathwell (20 and a two-hour 33), Thorpe, Ilott and McCague (Ulster-born but raised in Australia). Smith's bold 86 came from only 113 balls, and Hussain, in for 4¼ hours, aided by another long, defensive innings by Caddick, ensured that a reasonable total was reached. Hughes took his first five-wicket haul against England. Again, Boon and Mark Waugh shared a century stand, the latter's 70 coming from only 68 balls, and though McCague bowled fast and was well supported, Boon moved to his fifth hundred against England. Australia went to a 52-run lead, and England, in their second innings, slipped to 159 for 5 before young Thorpe joined Gooch. Warne spun the ball feet, sometimes past his wicketkeeper, but the resistance continued, Gooch (who went into the match with more Test runs and wickets than the rest of his team combined) reaching his 19th century in his 104th Test, passing 8000 runs, and becoming the 10th England batsman to make 2000 against Australia. His driving and pulling were notable for their power and certainty. Warne then had him caught at slip, and Hussain joined Thorpe in a refreshingly strokeful stand of 113 before the declaration on the fifth day, Thorpe having reached his hundred on debut with a hooked four. Australia, challenged to make 371 off at least 77 overs, soon found themselves 115 for 6 (Caddick three wickets), but Waugh and Julian (who reached his fifty with a six) hung on against bowling and fielding that seemed resigned to a draw. Border moved into third place in these Tests behind Bradman and Hobbs with 3280 runs.

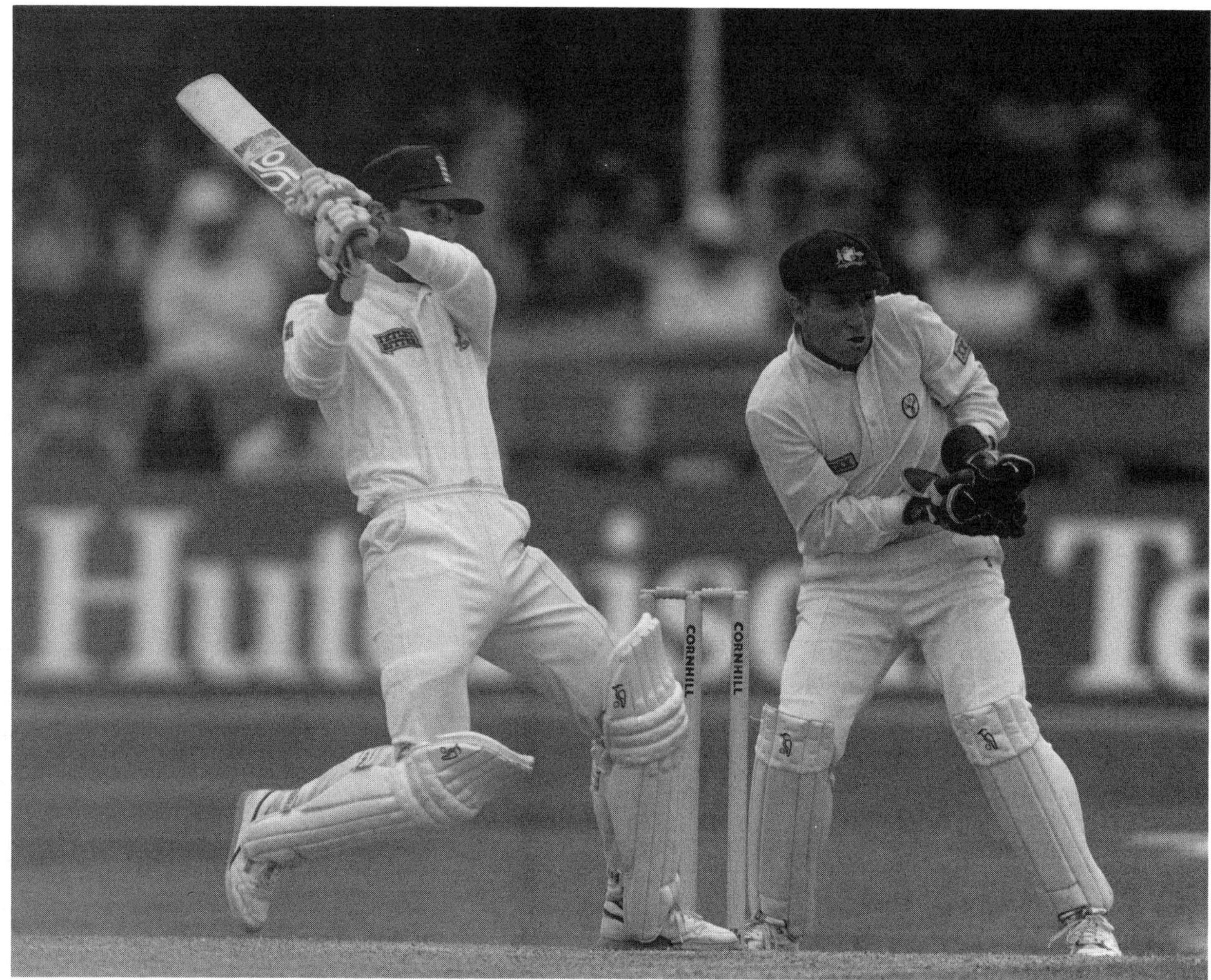

1190: *Graham Thorpe, 23-year-old Surrey left-hander, on his way to becoming the 16th batsman to score a century on his maiden Test appearance against Australia*

1191, above: *Graham Gooch slams more runs towards his 19th Test hundred (fourth against Australia).* 1192, above: *The England captain with the seven new faces for the Trent Bridge Test: Hussain, McCague, Thorpe, Bicknell, Gooch, Igglesden, Lathwell, Ilott (Bicknell and Igglesden did not make the final XI). England used 24 players during the six-match Test series*

1993 — FOURTH TEST
Headingley, July 22, 23, 24, 25, 26

Australia *653 for 4 dec (A.R. Border 200*, S.R. Waugh 157*, D.C. Boon 107, M.J. Slater 67, M.E. Waugh 52);* England *200 (G.A. Gooch 59, M.A. Atherton 55, P.R. Reiffel 5 for 65)* and *305 (A.J. Stewart 78, M.A. Atherton 63, T.B.A. May 4 for 65).* Australia won by an innings and 148 runs.

Resuming top gear, Australia retained the Ashes at Leeds with a victory even heavier than the one at Lord's, again losing only four wickets in the entire match. Their 653 for 4 was the highest total in any match at Headingley, surpassing Somerset's 630 in 1901, and the gate-takings reached £1-million for the first time there. Taylor and Slater began with 86, Australia's highest first-wicket

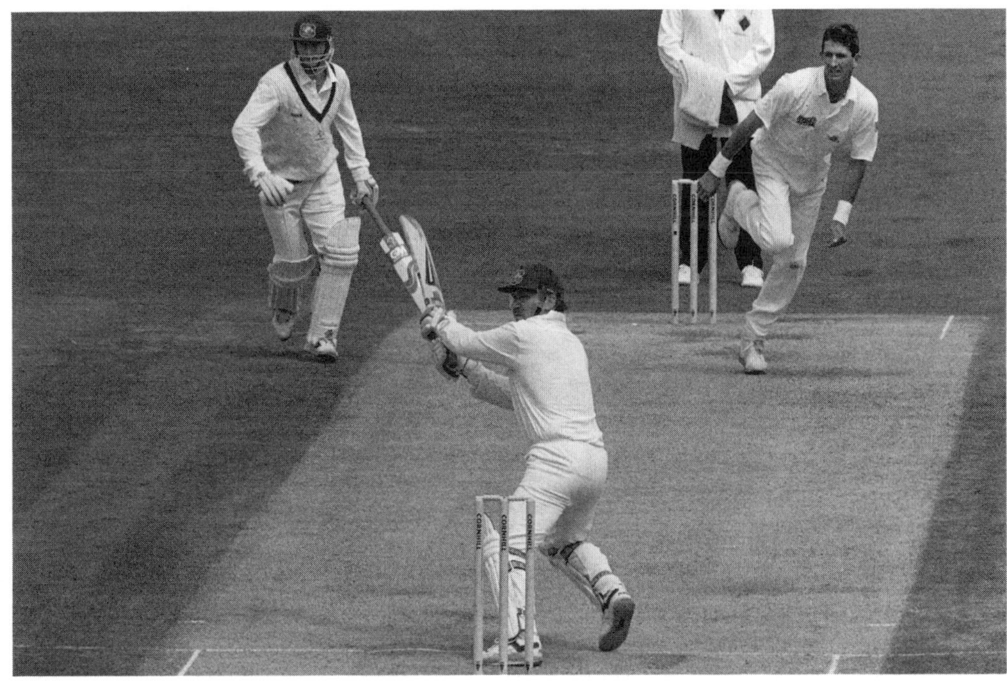

1193: *Allan Border steers a ball from Caddick to bring up his double-century, only the third by an Australian captain in a Test in England (following W.L. Murdoch and R.B. Simpson). It was Border's fourteenth century as captain*

stand at Headingley, and England's inexperienced four-prong pace attack of McCague, Ilott, Caddick and Bicknell toiled in vain as Boon added 106 with Mark Waugh and 105 with Border. The Tasmanian's 50th first-class century was his third in successive Ashes Tests—the first such instance since Bradman in 1938—and saw him past 1000 Test runs in England. At 321 for 4, England were still just in it, but nearly seven hours later, when Border declared, only Australia could win. Border and Steve Waugh had put on 332 without being separated, the second-highest fifth-wicket stand in all Test history. Border's 200 was his 26th Test century, his first double-century against England, and the 100th Test century by an Australian in England. He was in for almost 10 hours. England's woes multiplied. McCague was sidelined with a stress fracture of the spine, and the crowd booed the team off on the second evening. Of England's limp response of 200, 108 came in a fourth-wicket stand between Atherton and Gooch. Warne took only one tailend wicket in this match, but May was always probing. However, it was Reiffel, the Victorian seamer, who broke up England's first innings, taking five wickets on Ashes debut with accurate inward movement. Batting again, England took the match into the fifth day, when rain interfered. Atherton again batted grittily and Gooch, already having decided to resign the captaincy, adopted a carefree approach before, like Atherton, being stumped off May. Stewart, too, batted as if he could stand no more of this Australian domination, and hit Hughes for fours off four consecutive balls. Soon he was brilliantly caught at gully by Mark Waugh, and just before the end Hughes secured his 200th Test wicket.

1194, above: *A lifting ball goes safely over the helmet of David Boon, who made 107 at Headingley, which was his third century in consecutive Tests.* 1195, left: *Paul Reiffel, on his way to eight wickets in the match, sees Nasser Hussain chop the ball into his wicket when 15*

1993
Edgbaston, August 5, 6, 7, 8, 9

England *276 (M.A. Atherton 72, J.E. Emburey 55*, A.J. Stewart 45, P.R. Reiffel 6 for 71) and 251 (G.P. Thorpe 60, G.A. Gooch 48, S.K. Warne 5 for 82, T.B.A. May 5 for 89);* Australia *408 (M.E. Waugh 137, I.A. Healy 80, S.R. Waugh 59) and 120 for 2 (M.E. Waugh 62*).* Australia won by 8 wickets.

Atherton, the youngest man to captain England at home against Australia, won his first toss and played another long, steady innings, but most of his batsmen let him down, failing chiefly against Reiffel, who again moved the ball about and recorded the best figures ever for Australia at Birmingham. From 160 for 6 there was a rally led by the pragmatic Emburey, now 40, who batted in the match for six hours, making 37 in the second innings in 200 minutes. Australia's reply, for once, was uncertain, Such, Emburey and a run-out reducing them to 80 for 4. Steve Waugh then should have been stumped by Stewart off Such second ball, but survived to put on 153 with his twin, the highest stand by any country for the fifth wicket here. Mark Waugh's characteristically stylish hundred was Australia's 10th of the series, equalling the Ashes record (Australia 1920–21 and 1946–47). Six wickets had fallen before Australia moved into a lead that became substantial as Healy and Hughes added 107 at a run a minute. England were 89 for 1 by the close, still 43 behind, and on the Sunday five wickets toppled before lunch, effectively settling the match. Warne, back on song, took three of them, bowling Gooch behind his legs with a huge legbreak, and May took two. Warne's two lbws seemed dubious. No wicket fell in the second session, Thorpe, who batted for four hours, and Emburey setting up a barricade, weathering the bounce of the wicketless, frustrated Hughes. They inflated the score by 104, but at 229 May took two wickets and Warne one. The eventual target for Australia was 120, with grey skies and rain about on the final day. There was a tremor of excitement when both openers fell to spin, but Boon and Mark Waugh yet again constructed a century stand, their fifth in the five Tests of the series, thought to be unique. Border's 250th Test innings had brought him only three runs, but he had yet more satisfaction in having led Australia into the lead (38 to 37) in Tests played in England for the first time ever. England's depression was complicated by the resignation of Ted Dexter as chairman of selectors.

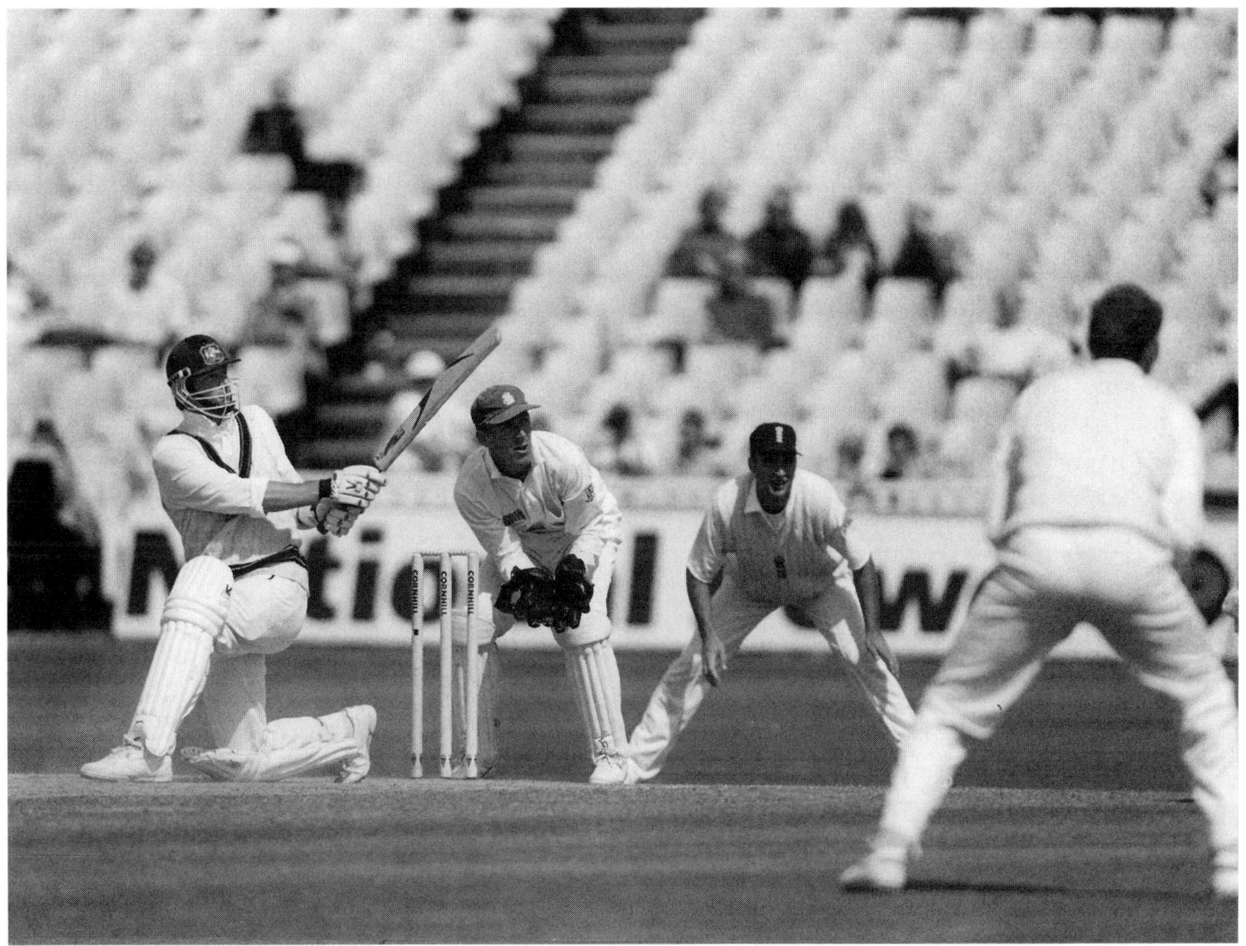

1196: *Mark Waugh, having steered Australia to a good first-innings lead with a four-hour 137, sweeps Such for six on the way to an unbeaten 62 that ensured Australia did not falter in pursuit of victory*

1197, left: *Another massive Warne legbreak, this one turning in behind the batsman's legs, bowls Gooch at Edgbaston.* 1198, above: *Matthew Maynard is caught behind by Healy off May, and England's second-innings slide continues*

1993 SIXTH TEST

The Oval, August 19, 20, 21, 22, 23

England *380 (G.A. Hick 80, A.J. Stewart 76, G.A. Gooch 56, M.A. Atherton 50) and 313 (G.A. Gooch 79, M.R. Ramprakash 64, M.A. Atherton 42);* Australia *303 (I.A. Healy 83*, M.A. Taylor 70, A.R. Border 48, A.R.C. Fraser 5 for 87) and 229 (P.R. Reiffel 42, M.E. Waugh 40, S.L. Watkin 4 for 65).* England won by 161 runs.

Ashes Test cricket regained some credibility with England's first win since December 1986. This was their 19th Test against Australia since then, and there were five changes in the team, Ramprakash coming in when Thorpe's thumb was broken in the nets just before the start. England thus used 24 players in the series, Australia 13. Gooch, Atherton, Hick and Stewart hastened England to 353 for 7 on the first day, 59 boundaries being hit, and Fraser (28 in 140 minutes) helped them to 380. Against expectation, Australia fell short of this, and would have been well short but for another sterling effort by Healy. Malcolm bowled with real pace, and Fraser, back after a career-threatening hip injury, was fast and accurate. Healy and the tail could still not deny England their first lead on first innings for nine Tests against Australia, a lead they quickly swelled, Gooch and Atherton taking 50 off eight overs before lunch on the third day. The older man passed Gower's England runs record of 8231 and finally fell to a model Warne legbreak at 79, having made a weighty 673 runs in the six Tests. Before that, Atherton was out with a series aggregate of 553, the highest in Test history by a batsman who had not made a century in the series. After a mid-innings slide, England recovered through Stewart and Ramprakash, who made his first Test fifty, alert to all that magician Warne and the puffing, limping, never-say-die Hughes could offer. Hughes finished the series with a worthy 31 wickets, Warne with 34 (off 440 overs). Healy's 26 wicketkeeping dismissals created a new record for any Test series in England. Needing 391 for their fifth victory of the series, Australia lost time to rain on the fourth evening and faced a target of 390 on the full final day on a pitch still firm. When Slater was given out caught off his forearm and Boon was lbw to Watkin's next ball and the Welshman then bowled Taylor, Australia were 30 for 3. Malcolm crashed through with three wickets; for once Healy did not last, Maynard running a long way back from slip to catch him, Mark Waugh just having hooked a catch to a fieldsman he had not noticed. Reiffel and Warne soldiered away for a time, then the tail crumbled, giving England a comforting victory that kept the candle of hope alive.

1199, above: *Mark Ramprakash sweeps. His maiden Test half-century was crucial to England's second-innings build-up which led to long-awaited victory.* 1200, right: *The bounce in the Oval pitch is seriously evident as England's young captain, Mike Atherton, parries a missile approaching his face. His 553 runs in the series, second to Gooch's 673, contained no century*

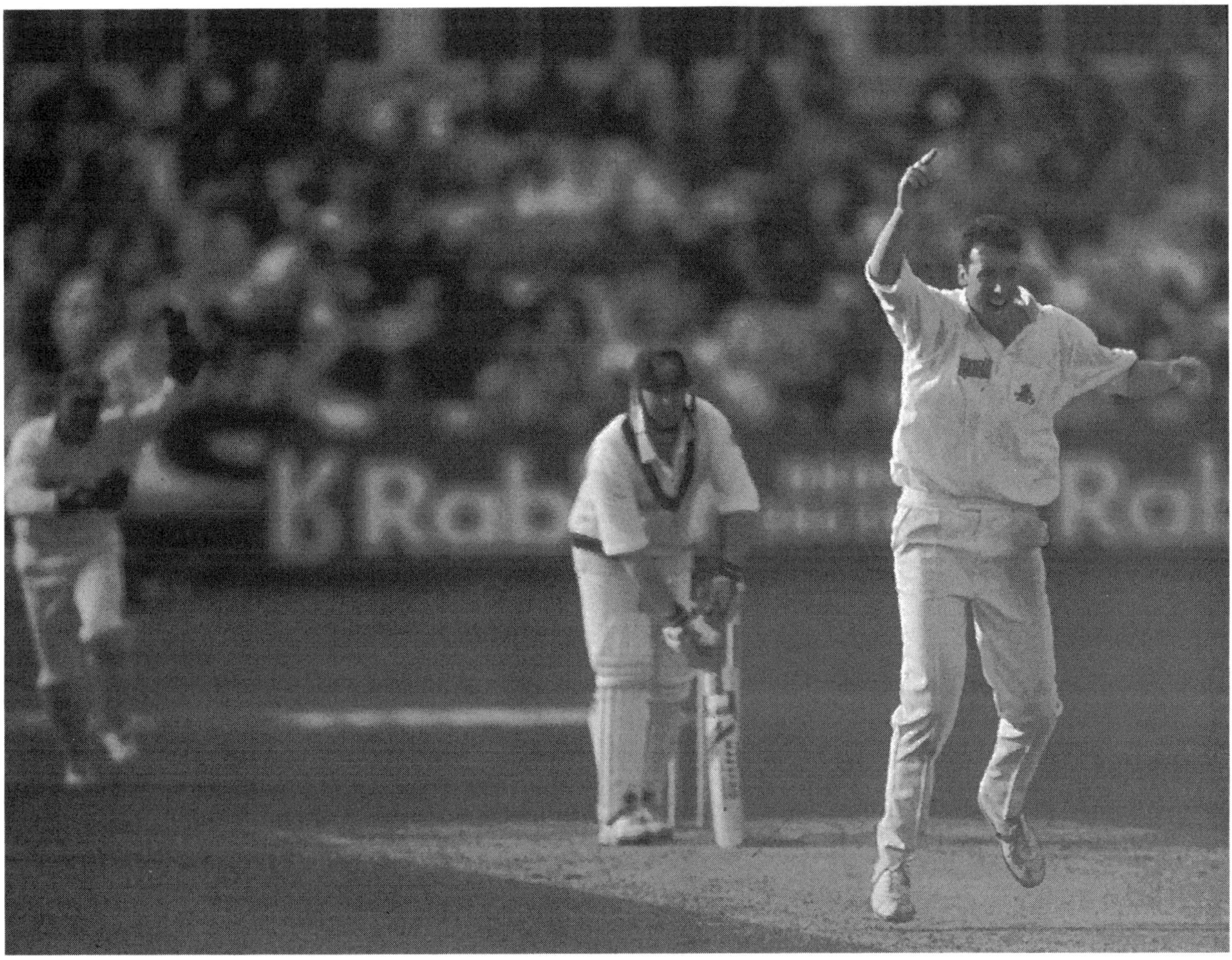

1201: *Angus Fraser, back after career-threatening injury, traps Warne lbw, his eighth wicket, to seal victory*

1994-95 FIRST TEST

Brisbane, November 25, 26, 27, 28, 29

Australia *426 (M.J. Slater 176, M.E. Waugh 140, M.A. Taylor 59, D. Gough 4 for 107) and 248 for 8 dec (M.A. Taylor 58, M.J. Slater 45, I.A. Healy 45*, P.C.R. Tufnell 4 for 79);* England *167 (M.A. Atherton 54, C.J. McDermott 6 for 53) and 323 (G.A. Hick 80, G.P. Thorpe 67, G.A. Gooch 56, S.K. Warne 8 for 71).* Australia won by 184 runs.

Australia struck early, 100 years on from 'the first great Ashes series', deflating English hopes that this time there would be nothing between the two sides. Warne made huge inroads again, and seemed now to have every bowling record at his mercy. The 25-year-old Victorian legspinner beat Keith Miller's best figures for a Brisbane Test, spinning in all directions and imprisoning the batsmen from the leg-side rough on the final day to finish with 11 for 110. Taylor and Slater had begun positively with 99 before the captain was run out, and Slater's audacity and the charm of Mark Waugh's strokeplay reaped 182 runs for the third wicket in only 2½ hours. Slater scored 100 runs in boundaries. Next day, Waugh went to his 50th first-class century while McCague struggled with direction. Gough finally got Waugh and finished with four wickets, but the total of 426 looked big that evening with England 133 for 6 in reply, Atherton 49 not out. McDermott, fired up by suggestions that his best days were behind him, stormed in and bowled fast and straight, with shrewd use of the bouncer. Gough hit him for two sixes, but the big Queenslander finished with an impressive 6 for 53. Surprisingly, Taylor did not enforce the follow-on, and England were glad to regain the feel of taking wickets as Australia lost eight for 92 after another sizable opening stand (109) by Taylor and Slater. Tufnell's left-arm spin posed the largest problems, though England realised that this was almost certainly only a pointer to Warne's effectiveness in the fourth innings. Set to score 508, England looked good for survival at 211 for 2 on the fourth evening. But Hick and Thorpe, having scored only 54 off 31 overs in the final session, took their stand to 160, and though Gough resisted, Warne came on after the new ball and delivered the decisive overs. The batsmen tried to keep him at bay with pad-play, but he was irresistible, wrapping it up with three wickets in four balls. During this well-attended match, Boon reached 2000 runs against England and Healy had a record-equalling nine catches in the match. England, rueing the absence of strike bowler Devon Malcolm with chickenpox, had dreaded such an early reversal. This was the first Ashes Test played under the newly-devised ICC system whereby one of the umpires came from a 'neutral' country—in this instance South Africa (C.J. Mitchley).

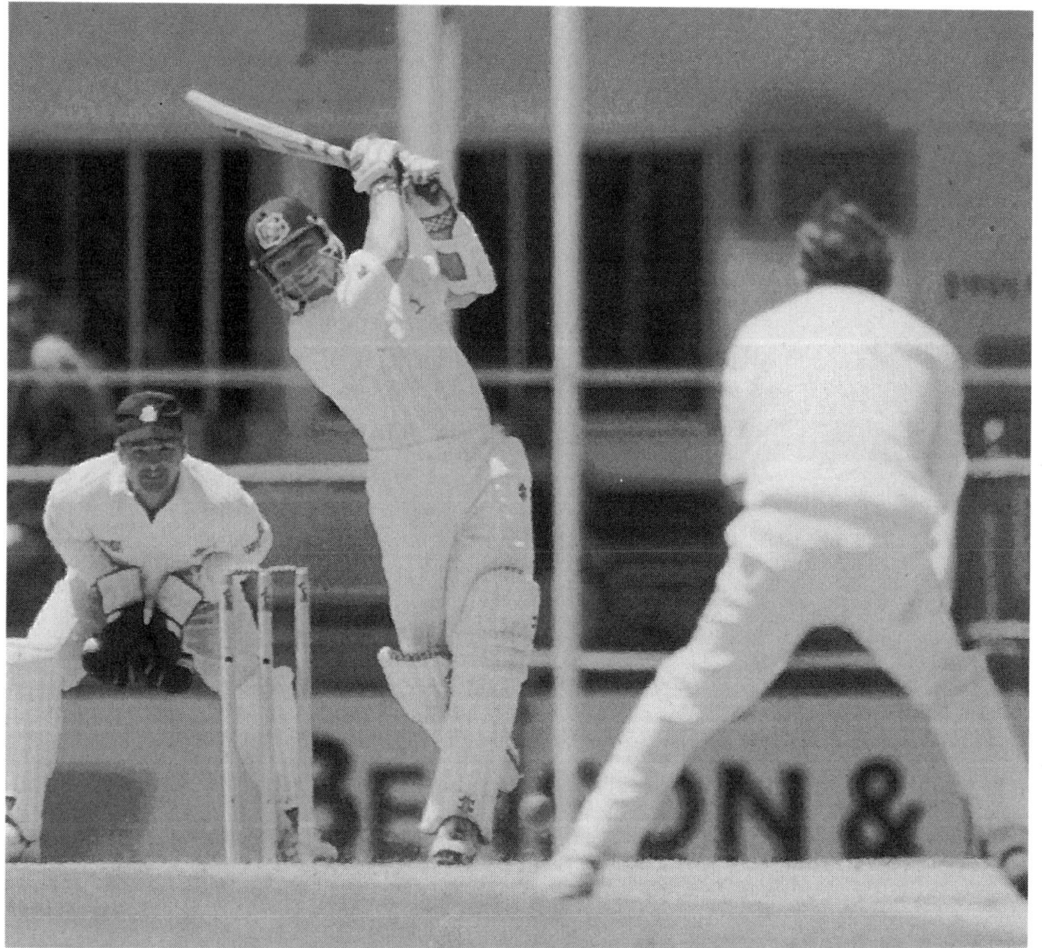

1202: *Michael Slater launched Australia's defence of the Ashes by hitting the first ball of the match for four, and reached the boundary twenty-four more times in his dashing 5½-hour innings of 176*

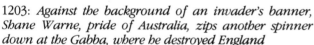

1203: *Against the background of an invader's banner, Shane Warne, pride of Australia, zips another spinner down at the Gabba, where he destroyed England*

1204: *Warne dismissed England opener Alec Stewart (33) with a memorable 'flipper' in the second innings at Brisbane. Shaping to pull the short delivery, the batsman saw too late that it was about to scuttle through. There were times in this match when it seemed that the blond Victorian legspinner could not be repelled, so persistent was he with his range of wristy deliveries, sometimes bowled into the rough patches from around the wicket*

1994-95 SECOND TEST
Melbourne, December 24, 26, 27, 28, 29

Australia *279 (S.R. Waugh 94*, M.E. Waugh 71, D.C. Boon 41, D. Gough 4 for 60) and 320 for 7 dec (D.C. Boon 131, M.J. Slater 44);* England *212 (G.P. Thorpe 51, M.A. Atherton 44, S.K. Warne 6 for 64) and 92 (C.J. McDermott 5 for 42).* Australia won by 295 runs.

It began to seem that this England team was one of the unluckiest. Four major questionable umpiring decisions went against them, and Stewart's index-finger was broken by McDermott. Put in on a moist pitch which suited England's three pace bowlers, Australia had struggled to 220 for 7 on the first day, saved from total humiliation by the Waugh twins. After Christmas Day, only 207 runs accrued on the second day, Steve Waugh dragging his side closer to 300 and England reaching 148 for 4, having been 119 for 1. Thorpe again mixed aggression with caution but was the victim of a pad-bat decision. Australia swept the last six wickets away next day for only 64, Gooch pushing a return catch to McDermott first ball. Stewart, resuming at 151 for 6 after injections to his fractured finger, became Warne's 50th England wicket (150th in all), and Australia's lead was finally as big as 67—extended to 237 by the close as Tufnell (1 for 37 in 23 overs) probed and Gough showed boundless enthusiasm. Before the fourth day's play there was a pause for remembrance of Peter May, who had just died. Boon went to his 20th Test century (7th v England), adding 112 with Bevan (35) as England endeavoured to keep things tight, and at the tea-time declaration the target was 388 in four sessions. Fleming made a twin breakthrough and by nightfall England were beleaguered again, 79 for 4, with good weather forecast. The last six wickets crashed for 13, with

 Warne performing the first Ashes hat-trick (DeFreitas, Gough, Malcolm) since Trumble, also at the MCG, 91 years earlier. Boon's diving short-leg catch secured the honour. Warne's chance of taking four in four was lost when McDermott forced Tufnell to give Healy his fifth catch of the innings, sealing victory by a weighty margin and taking the fast bowler's tally to 254 Test wickets, second to Lillee (355) for Australia. Melbourne's 50th Australia–England Test attracted almost 145,000 paying spectators, but ended with columns of derision from critics and former players in the wake of England's seeming capitulation.

1205, above: *David Boon, with a slick catch off Malcolm, seals the first Ashes hat-trick in almost a century, with bowler Warne descending his way to express his gratitude.*
1206, right: *Boon passes leaping fieldsman Atherton during his Melbourne century, his 20th in Tests, and fourth against England in the last seven Tests*

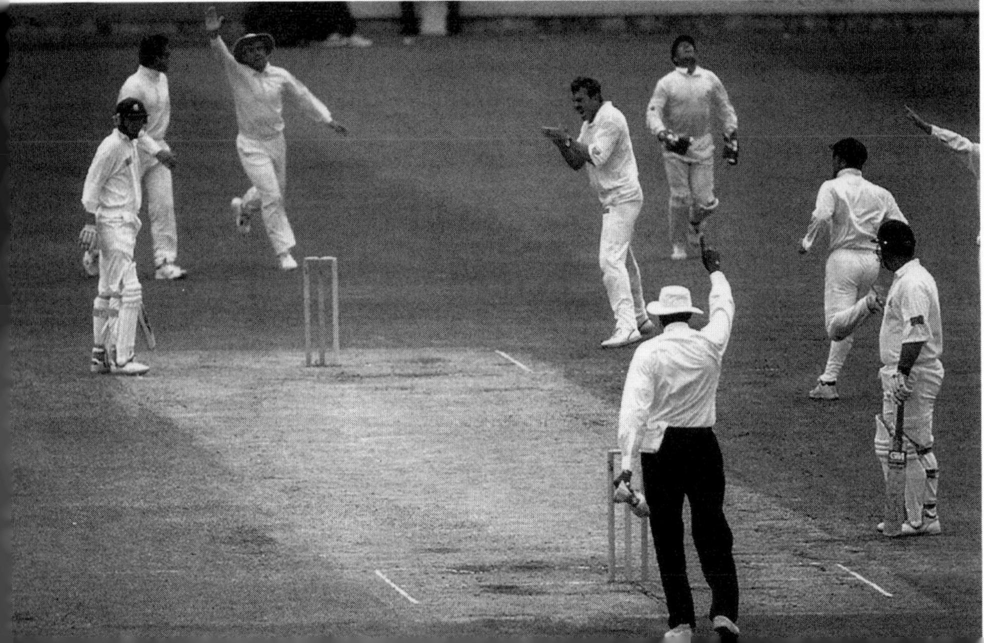

1207, left: *England's poor luck with umpiring continues as Atherton, joint top scorer with 25 in the shambolic second innings of 92, is given out by umpire Bucknor, caught by Healy off McDermott. Ball seemed nowhere near bat*

1994-95
Sydney, January 1, 2, 3, 4, 5

England *309 (M.A. Atherton 88, J.P. Crawley 72, D. Gough 51, C.L. McDermott 5 for 101) and 255 for 2 dec (G.A. Hick 98*, M.A. Atherton 67, G.P. Thorpe 47*);* Australia *116 (M.A. Taylor 49, D. Gough 6 for 49) and 344 for 7 (M.A. Taylor 113, M.J. Slater 103, A.R.C. Fraser 5 for 73).* Match drawn.

This was a worthy 50th Australia-England Test at the SCG, with an 8½-hour final day that ranked with the most dramatic in Ashes history. The draw meant that Australia retained the Ashes in this first post-Allan Border series, but relief outweighed jubilation after England's great surge and the controversy that stopped them short. There were shocks at the start, England losing Gooch, Hick and Thorpe with only 20 up. Atherton, escorted by fellow Lancastrian Crawley, put on 174 in a five-hour saving stand reminiscent of that by May and Cowdrey 40 years earlier. McDermott, who was off with illness for 1¼ hours, then bowled captain Atherton with the new ball, and four wickets went down for 3, Gatting going for a duck and wicketkeeper Rhodes run out in mad confusion. Cheered on by the 'Barmy Army' of travelling British supporters, Gough tore into the bowling next morning and reached 50 off 54 balls, and then Malcolm (29) heaved Warne for two sixes before becoming the demon spinner's only wicket of the match (after he had taken 20 in the first two Tests). Fraser aided England's revival with a 27 that spanned more than two hours. As Australia began their reply, rain washed out the day, and they were uncertain in their approach next morning, when Malcolm (who took his 100th Test wicket), Fraser and especially Gough harried all the batsmen. The third wicket fell at 18, the eighth at 65, and the follow-on seemed certain. Taylor, who was 62 minutes in finding his first run, was ninth out, the immediate danger having passed. England's last chance went with a spooned shot from McDermott wide of 41-year-old Gooch, though Taylor, having survived a close lbw call, was missed by Malcolm from a high return catch at 87 for 8. The pair saved the day with a stand of 51. Harold Larwood, now 90, telephoned congratulations to Darren Gough in the dressing-room. There was more rain loss, but more solid batting from Atherton and positive play by Thorpe in support of Hick built a huge lead, with Hick finally stunned by the declaration when he was two away from a century after 4¼ hours. Needing 449 off a possible 128 overs, Australia raced to 208 after lunch on the final day before Slater fell. He and Taylor made centuries, though Taylor seemed to have been run-out 160 minutes before his eventual dismissal, umpire Hair declining to refer the incident to the third umpire. Then Australia slid to 292 for 7 as Fraser, called up from Sydney grade cricket, manfully exploited a helpful pitch, Atherton gradually restoring the pressure. Malcolm was still cruelly unlucky, and Tufnell was tight without being an Underwood. When May joined Warne, 18.1 overs remained, and they fought grimly. England now, with the light poor, had to employ only slow bowling. The pair survived the 77 minutes as English frustration mounted, the umpires erroneously ushering the players from the field early, the 'final' 15 overs having been bowled some minutes inside the hour. They returned, but there was no breakthrough. At least the former predictability of this series had evaporated.

1208: *With Englishmen desperately surrounding the bat, Phil Tufnell appeals yet again to Umpire Hair, who remains impassive. May and Warne held on for an hour and a quarter in the gloom, and the Ashes were made safe for Australia*

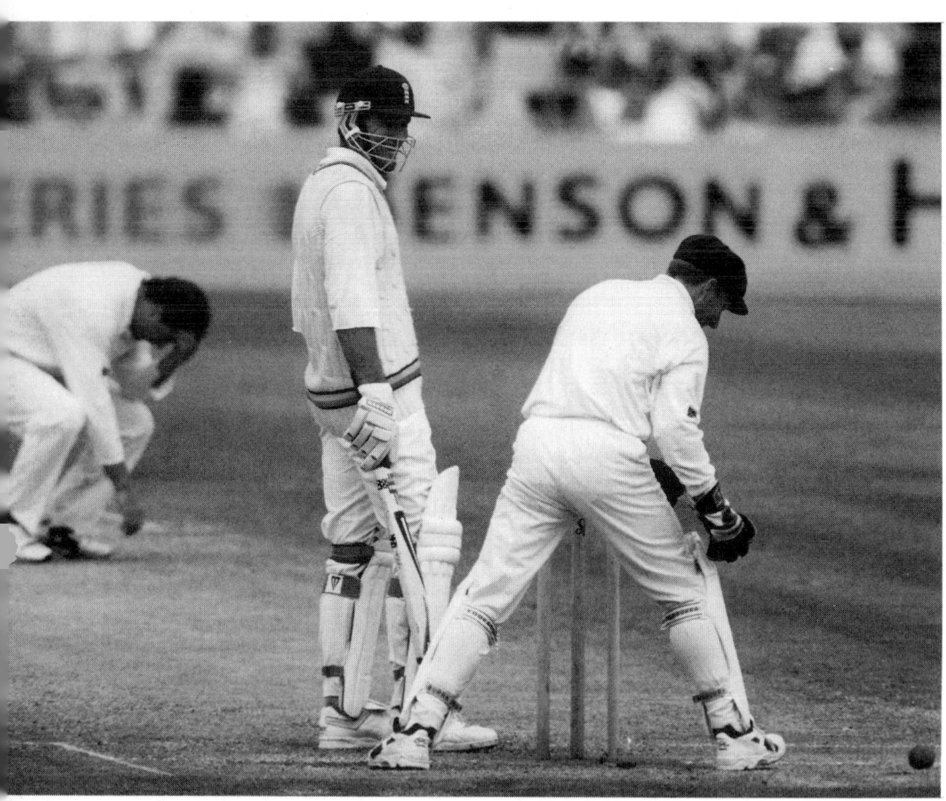

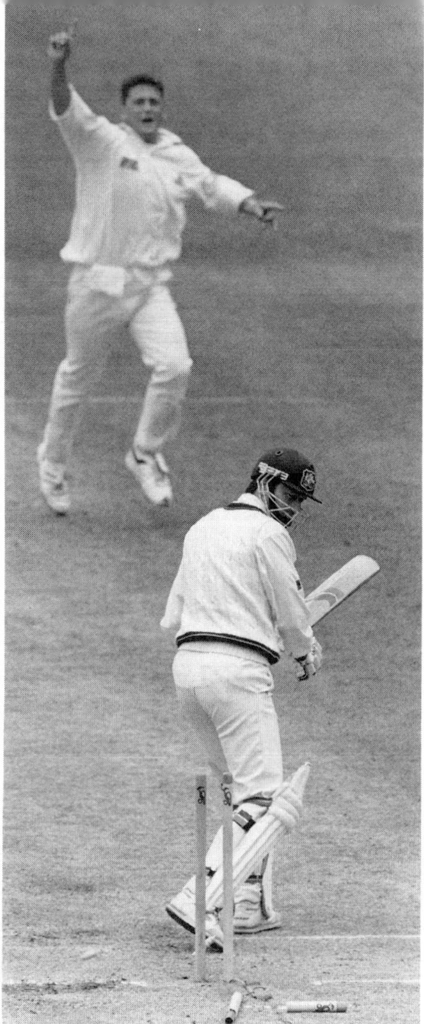

1209, above: *Just as Sutcliffe had done on the same ground, Sydney, 62 years previously, Graeme Hick plays a ball down onto the stumps without disturbing the bails. He was not amused at Atherton's declaration when he was 98.* 1210, right: *Darren Gough, England's new hope, bowls Steve Waugh*

1994-95 FOURTH TEST
Adelaide, January 26, 27, 28, 29, 30

England *353 (M.W. Gatting 117, M.A. Atherton 80, G.A. Gooch 47) and 328 (P.A.J. DeFreitas 88, G.P. Thorpe 83, J.P. Crawley 71, M.E. Waugh 5 for 40);* Australia *419 (G.S. Blewett 102*, M.A. Taylor 90, I.A. Healy 74, M.J. Slater 67) and 156 (I.A. Healy 51*, C.C. Lewis 4 for 24, D.E. Malcolm 4 for 39).* England won by 106 runs.

England's potential was realised at last, even though they were without three key men through injury: Hick and Gough (both repatriated, as was White) and Stewart. (McCague, earlier, and Udal also were forced to return home.) England's first victory in Australia since December 1986 was founded on a solid first-innings total, Gooch and Atherton starting with 93, and Gatting (411 minutes) reasserting himself with 117, his first Test century for 7½ years. It was the 200th by an England batsman against Australia. Thanks to newcomer Greg Blewett, 23, the home side took a 66-run lead. Slater and Taylor began with 128, but the only other large stand was 164 for the sixth wicket between Blewett—who became the 18th Australian batsman to make a century on debut against England—and Healy, the runs coming at a brisk rate. Blewett, 91 overnight, lost Healy first thing on the fourth day. Then, with eight down and McDermott not yet back at the ground after treatment for a stomach upset, Blewett had to rely on debutant McIntyre (who made a 'pair') to stay long enough for his hundred to arrive. It seemed a familiar story when England lost two wickets before wiping off the arrears, Gatting making a duck. Thorpe (83 off only 117 balls) took the initiative and Crawley too responded to the crisis. At 181 for 6, DeFreitas joined Crawley and sent Australia reeling with 88 off 95 balls, including 22 off a McDermott over (440446), equalling the record in these Tests (Botham off Hughes, Brisbane, 1986-87). Mark Waugh secured his first five-wicket Test haul. Against all expectation, Australia were faced with a target as high as 263, with 67 overs available. They were soon in trouble at 23 for 4, Malcolm having blasted out Taylor, Slater and Steve Waugh (first ball) for 5 in 11 balls. Lewis, recruited from Melbourne club cricket, moved the ball about, and Tufnell was lucky when Mark Waugh chipped him to short-leg Gatting's boot from where it bounced up for a catch. It was 83 for 8 when Lewis dismissed McDermott, gesturing frantically and earning a sizable fine. Healy and Fleming now resisted for almost two hours, adding an incidental 69 as

English anxiety grew. Lewis had Fleming lbw, and with 35 balls left Malcolm trapped McIntyre. Gooch, who reached 1000 runs in Tests in Australia and moved to 8859 overall, third behind Border and Gavaskar, announced his impending Test retirement, a move soon followed by Gatting. Rhodes's seven catches equalled the record in a match by an England wicketkeeper against Australia (J.T. Murray and R.W. Taylor).

1211, above, left: *Mike Gatting making a last-gasp Test hundred at Adelaide.* 1212, above, right: *Greg Blewett approaches his debut century.* 1213, left: *John Crawley's second important batting contribution of the series contained some crisp shots.* 1214, right: *After a painful blow, Phil DeFreitas exploded with the bat—88 off 95 balls*

1994-95 — FIFTH TEST
Perth, February 3, 4, 5, 6, 7

Australia *402 (M.J. Slater 124, S.R. Waugh 99*, M.E. Waugh 88) and 345 for 8 dec (G.S. Blewett 115, S.R. Waugh 80, M.A. Taylor 52, M.J. Slater 45);* England *295 (G.P. Thorpe 123, M.R. Ramprakash 72, C.C. Lewis 40) and 123 (M.R. Ramprakash 42, C.J. McDermott 6 for 38).* Australia won by 329 runs.

In the 150th Australia-England Test to be played in Australia, the home country renewed its mastery over the visitors, though England's failure was substantially self-induced. They dropped nine or 10 catches during the match. On a fast, bouncy pitch, Australia's 402 was first set up by Slater and Mark Waugh in a stand of 183, and Steve Waugh—only the second batsman in Test history to finish 99 not out (G. Boycott, also at Perth, 1979-80)—was the grim overseer of the later stages. He was stranded one short of his century when his brother, running for the injured McDermott, failed to make his ground. England began calamitously, losing four for 77 to McGrath and Mark Waugh. Thorpe (five hours) and Ramprakash (four hours) then batted nimbly through a stand of 158, revealing a heartening fresh face for English batting. Angel then wiped away the tail, and Australia were soon building a giant lead. Five wickets fell for 123, but Steve Waugh, shrugging away his occasional difficulties, then put on 203 with Blewett, who scored another pleasant century in his second Test. England's catching failures piled up, as did their theoretical target (453). They collapsed for 123, their lowest at the WACA. At 27 for 6 utter humiliation beckoned, but Ramprakash again battled valiantly, and Rhodes (39 not out) reached double figures for only the second time in the series. McDermott, almost fully fit again, took his series tally to 32 wickets (unexpectedly five ahead of Warne), and Healy finished with 25 dismissals. Gatting made only 0 and 8, while Crawley bagged a pair. Slater's fourth century against England helped him to an aggregate of 623 for the series, bettered only by Bradman (twice) in five-Test series against England in Australia, and he passed 1000 runs against England in his 11th Test. Australia were more effective throughout the 11-week campaign by virtue of the consistent penetration of McDermott and Warne, but better luck with injuries and umpiring would have brought England very much closer to parity.

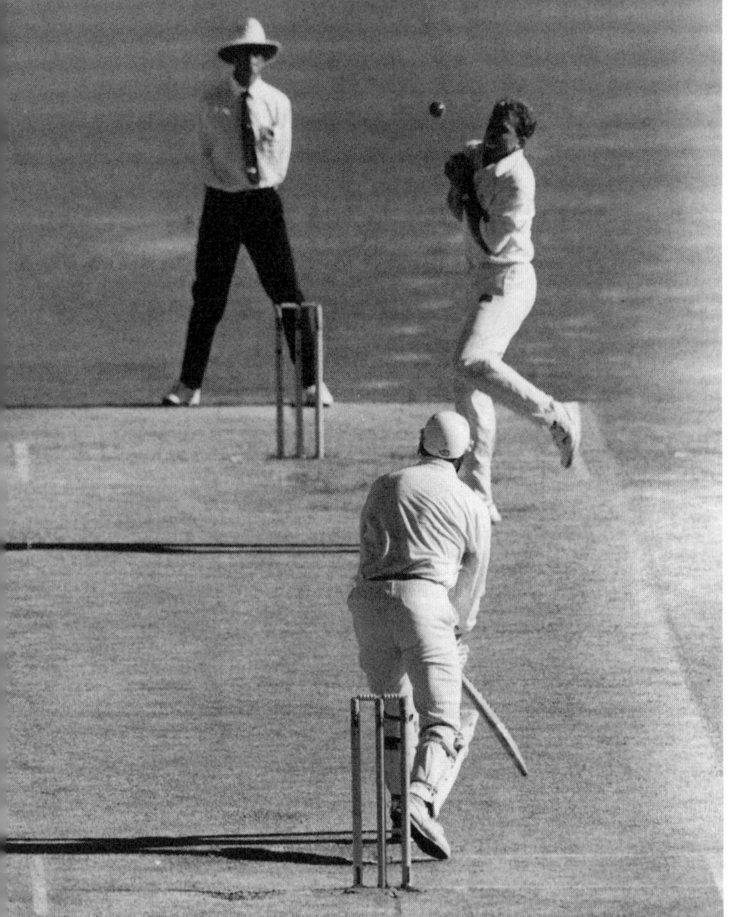

1215, above, left: *Telepathy failure as Mark Waugh, acting as a runner, fails to make it to safety, leaving twin brother Steve (far end) 99 not out.* 1216, above: *Thorpe (123) capitalises off McGrath's short delivery.* 1217, left: *Gooch's last ball in Test cricket—a juggled return catch to McDermott.* 1218, below: *Thoughtful final presentation line-up: Bob Simpson (coach), Mark Taylor (captain), Mike Atherton (captain), Keith Fletcher (coach)*

1997
Edgbaston, June 5, 6, 7, 8

Australia *118 (S.K. Warne 47, A.R. Caddick 5 for 50) and 477 (M.A. Taylor 129, G.S. Blewett 125, M.T.G. Elliott 66)*; England *478 for 9 dec (N. Hussain 207, G.P. Thorpe 138, M.A. Ealham 53*, M.S. Kasprowicz 4 for 113) and 119 for 1 (M.A. Atherton 57*, A.J. Stewart 40*)*. England won by 9 wickets.

At last England's pre-series hopes were upheld with victory in an opening encounter. The Australians were under-prepared, and the pitch was juicy and not altogether to be trusted. By lunch, the visitors were reeling at 54 for 8 at the hands of Gough, Malcolm and Caddick, the arena trembling with the roar of a patriotic crowd. Warne (eight fours) led a bold rearguard, but by the close England were already 82 ahead with three down, Hussain (80) and Thorpe (83) having rallied their side with an unbroken stand of 150 which they extended to 288 next day, beating the Hammond-Paynter record 222 for England's fourth wicket at Lord's in 1938. Both made highest Test scores, Thorpe batting almost five hours, Hussain (England's seventh double-centurion against Australia) for 7¼. They scored 135 before lunch on the rain-shortened second day, which ended at 449 for 6, Gillespie now sidelined with a hamstring injury and Warne frustrated with 1 for 110 on this slow surface. Ealham's half-century took England to the declaration—Healy having taken six catches—and then Australia dug in as world champions were expected to do. Elliott and Taylor started with 133, and Blewett saw his captain to his century before making one of his own. Taylor's was a brave answer to all the critics who had been questioning his selection—it was his first time past 50 in 22 Test innings—and he reached 2000 runs in Tests against England. Blewett's innings was historic in that he became the first ever to score a century in each of his first three Ashes Tests. Against the background fear of further rain, England worked their way through the Australian order on the Sunday after further resistance from Taylor and Blewett, who took their stand to 194. Blewett's driving was as confident and elegant as Hussain's had been. Wickets then tumbled, Croft and Gough taking three each, as did Ealham in wrapping up the tail. It left England needing 118 in 24 overs plus a day, and after the loss of debutant Butcher, Atherton and Stewart galloped to victory in 21.3 overs, the captain becoming the 12th England batsman to reach 5000 Test runs. Only the third victory in the last 25 Tests against Australia, the result bathed England in euphoria and reinforced visions of a regaining of the Ashes after four losing series.

1219, below: *First blood of the series: Matthew Elliott scuttled by Darren Gough*. 1220, right: *The men who built England's winning total with their record stand of 288: Hussain and Thorpe*

1221: *Centurions in Australia's losing cause at Edgbaston: Greg Blewett, with helmet off, going where none had gone before by scoring a century in his third Ashes Test, having reached three figures in his first and second, and Mark Taylor, who made a long-awaited hundred after a campaign to oust him as captain*

1997 SECOND TEST
Lord's, June 19, 20, 21, 22, 23

England *77 (G.D. McGrath 8 for 38) and 266 for 4 dec (M.A. Butcher 87, M.A. Atherton 77);* Australia *213 for 7 dec (M.T.G. Elliott 112, G.S. Blewett 45, A.R. Caddick 4 for 71).* Match drawn.

Bad weather ensured that England retained their hard-won advantage from the first Test. The draw also meant that the home side were left with only that solitary victory in 1934 among the 24 Ashes Tests at Lord's during the 20th Century (Australia won 10). No play was possible on the first day, and only 21 overs could be bowled on the second, during which England floundered to 38 for 3, McGrath, moving the ball about in favourable conditions, taking all three, including Atherton (1), who was captaining England for the 42nd time, passing Peter May's record. It could have been worse, but Healy made it clear to the umpires that he was uncertain about a low catch off Thorpe's first ball. The MCC secretary's stern plea before play that the traditional atmosphere and sportsmanship be upheld (Atherton had approved of the robust and noisy support at Edgbaston) seemed unwarranted. There was to be no recovery. McGrath, supported by the skilful Reiffel, a reinforcement to the touring team, scythed through England, whose 77 was their lowest total against Australia at Lord's apart from the 53 and 62 they mustered against Turner and Ferris on an even damper surface in 1888. McGrath's 8 for 38 had been bettered by an Australian bowler in Ashes Tests only by Mailey (9 for 121, Melbourne, 1920–21) and Laver (8 for 31, Old Trafford, 1909), and there was apprehension in the England camp at what the tall NSW bowler might do in the second innings now that he had discovered a fuller 'English' length. Australia were 131 for 2 that evening, Elliott unbeaten on 55 after several breaks for showers, a simple let-off by Malcolm at long leg, and two

other misses by Butcher. More showers sprayed Lord's next day, when 82 runs were plundered from the 17.4 overs, 57 of them by Elliott, who attacked almost every ball, pulling and hooking many. His maiden Test century came from 171 balls and included 20 fours, emulating fellow left-handers Darling and Morris in most boundaries in a hundred for Australia in Ashes Tests. Taylor declared overnight, leaving England, 136 behind, facing a tense last day. The pitch—condemned by Geoff Boycott as 'unfit for Test cricket'—was now benign, and with Taylor dropping Butcher at slip when 2, frustration now dogged Australia. Atherton and Butcher put on 162 for the first wicket in almost four hours, and after the captain's heel broke his wicket as he played back to Kasprowicz, interest shifted to Butcher's prospects. But when he was 13 short of a century in his second Test, he fell to a ball from Warne which spun out of the footmarks. There was to be no collapse this time.

1222, facing page, bottom: *Glenn McGrath's unforgettable passage of glory: he leaves the field with record bowling figures for an Australian at Lord's.* 1223, left: *Elliott pounds a short ball from Caddick during a century that contained 20 fours.* 1224, above: *Another new name in the Ashes register, Mark Butcher, passes Blewett at short leg. The Surrey left-hander fell 13 short of a century*

1997 THIRD TEST

Old Trafford, July 3, 4, 5, 6, 7

Australia *235 (S.R. Waugh 108, M.T.G. Elliott 40, D.W. Headley 4 for 72) and 395 for 8 dec (S.R. Waugh 116, M.E. Waugh 55, S.K. Warne 53, I.A. Healy 47, P.R. Reiffel 45*, D.W. Headley 4 for 104);* England *162 (M.A. Butcher 51, S.K. Warne 6 for 48) and 200 (J.P. Crawley 83, G.D. McGrath 4 for 46).* Australia won by 268 runs.

Steve Waugh (twin centuries), McGrath (seven wickets) and Warne (nine) put Australia resoundingly back on course to hold the Ashes after their disconcerting start to the series. Not that the first day pointed in that direction. Taylor bravely chose to bat, only to see his side half out for 113. Headley, grandson of the legendary West Indies batsman George, bowled fast and accurately on his Test debut, especially to Australia's three left-handers, who each fell to him twice. The innings was saved by Steve Waugh, who followed his Lord's duck with a century of supreme concentration and pugnacity. Until Reiffel (31) at No.9, only Elliott settled in—he was given out caught off his shirt-sleeve—and at times it seemed like Waugh alone against all that England could hurl at the Australians. By the close of the second day, the visitors held the whiphand. England were 161 for 8 in reply, and it was clear that Warne was back to his best. Taking his first 'five-for' for 16 Tests, the legspinner went into third place in Australia's all-time bowling list, and secured his 250th Test wicket in the second innings when he bowled Stewart. His use of the rough and his variety and control were masterly. Butcher, Stewart and Ealham fought patiently in England's first innings, but a deficit of 73 looked ominous. And when Australia finished the third day at 262 for 6, the host nation was overwhelmed by a familiar gloom. A sour note was struck over Hussain's ground-level catch to dismiss Blewett for 19, but with Mark Waugh returning to some kind of form, and his twin, nursing a bruised hand, already on the way to his second century of the match with 82, Australia slept well. Batting for over six hours this time, Steve Waugh became the first for 50 years to score two centuries in an Ashes Test, and the first right-hander for Australia. Totally watchful, he countered erratic bounce with carefully-chosen strokes, occupying the crease for 380 minutes on top of the four hours in the first innings. Taylor delayed his declaration until the lead was 468, Healy, Warne (second Test fifty), Reiffel and even Gillespie adding to England's demoralisation. With almost five sessions to survive, England were all but done by the end of the fourth day, the top five men out for 130, Gillespie having whipped out three. Crawley went on to an impressive 83, but the series was levelled by 12.30pm next day, England having squandered the best of conditions for both bowling and batting. Stewart's eight catches set a new mark for England in an Ashes Test, his six in the first innings equalling Russell's record (Melbourne, 1990–91).

1225, right: *Bevan disappoints, caught by record-breaking wicketkeeper Alec Stewart off debutant Headley, one of his eight wickets in the match.* 1226, below: *John Crawley dabs at Warne and Healy claims the catch. The Englishman made his side's top score in the second innings.* 1227, below right: *Again Steve Waugh makes batting history by reaching his second hundred of the match*

Headingley, July 24, 25, 26, 27, 28

England *172 (M.A. Atherton 41, J.N. Gillespie 7 for 37) and 268 (N. Hussain 105, J.P. Crawley 72, P.R. Reiffel 5 for 49)*; Australia *501 for 9 dec (M.T.G. Elliott 199, R.T. Ponting 127, P.R. Reiffel 54*, D. Gough 5 for 149)*. Australia won by an innings and 61 runs.

Australia further re-established their superiority with an emphatic victory, their third in a row on Yorkshire's ground, following the two previous totals there over 600. England, put in, had two false starts broken by rain, then two hours in evening sunshine on the opening day, hanging on for 106 for 3 on a lively pitch controversially chosen in preference to the one originally prepared. Next day, stern-faced young Gillespie swept them away with accurate, waspish fast bowling from the Kirkstall Lane end, his figures of 7 for 37 bettering the best on this ground by an Australian, left-arm spinner Macartney's 7 for 58 in 1909. The last seven wickets clattered for 34, Gillespie also catching top-scorer Atherton at long leg, ending the captain's 3¾-hour vigil. The first four Australian wickets were shared by Gough and Headley with only 50 on the board (Steve Waugh's 4 giving him a Leeds Test average of 338), but Elliott and Ponting batted for the second half of the day after 11 wickets had toppled in the first half. The pitch had eased, and yet the Australian recovery owed everything to a missed catch by Thorpe, above his head at first slip, when Elliott was 29. The bowler was left-armer Mike Smith, on debut, and he later dropped Elliott at long leg, Atherton also having put him down when he was 63. Elliott applied himself diligently, batting in all for 7½ hours and hitting 23 fours and three sixes (two pulled off Headley, one driven off Croft). Regularly compared with fellow Victorian runmaker of the 1960s, Bill Lawry, Elliott now became the first batsman to make 199 in an Ashes Test. His stand with Ponting was 208 overnight, and extended to 268 on the abbreviated third day, when the confident, compact Tasmanian, restored to the side, secured his first Test century. By the close of that third day, Elliott was 164 and Australia were already 201 ahead. The declaration came after a sensible half-century by Reiffel at No.9, and with extras rising to 54, including a shameful 35 no-balls. Gough's 36-over effort brought the best reward. England's prayers for more rain were deservedly unanswered, and but for two batsmen their batting was again painful to behold, with Reiffel this time seizing best figures with another steady performance. Hussain knuckled down for over four hours for his fifth century in his last 14 Tests, putting on 133 with Crawley, the first ever for the fifth wicket against Australia at Headingley, and providing a vision of what might have been had the other batsmen lived up to their best. England had been bowled out twice in a total of barely 150 overs, and the excitement of the opening days of this series had now been completely buried. This was the 50th Test match the Waugh twins had played together.

1228: *Thorpe, trying to pull Gillespie, edges into his stumps.* 1229: *Ponting in command during his first Test century*

1230: *One of the most telling of spilt catches: Matthew Elliott is spared by Graham Thorpe off Mike Smith. The Australian had made only 29 at the time, but went on to a poignant distinction in becoming the first to score 199 in an Ashes Test. Australia's huge victory here at Leeds seemed to leave England with minimal hope*

1997 FIFTH TEST

Trent Bridge, August 7, 8, 9, 10

Australia *427 (M.A. Taylor 76, S.R. Waugh 75, M.T.G. Elliott 69, M.E. Waugh 68, G.S. Blewett 50, D.W. Headley 4 for 87) and 336 (I.A. Healy 63, G.S. Blewett 60, M.A. Taylor 45, R.T. Ponting 45);* England *313 (A.J. Stewart 87, G.P. Thorpe 53, A.J. Hollioake 45, G.D. McGrath 4 for 71, S.K. Warne 4 for 86) and 186 (G.P. Thorpe 82*).* Australia won by 264 runs.

Australia proved to be just as unbeatable on a good pitch when the Ashes were at stake as on an unreliable one. Winning the toss for the fifth time, Taylor made a watchful 76 (taking him past 6000 Test runs) and saw his other top four batsmen reach half-centuries. Towards the end of a sunlit first day, in which Australia made 302 for 3, there occurred the unique sight of twins (the Waughs) batting against brothers (Adam and Ben Hollioake, both on debut), all having been born in Australia. Ben had played only 10 County Championship matches, and at 19 years 269 days was England's youngest player after Close and Compton. Several tight lbw decisions went against England, but the home side performed proudly on the second day, removing the last seven wickets for 125, Headley, Malcolm and Caddick (Gough had missed selection through injury) bowling with purpose. When England replied with 106 before Warne had Atherton (27) caught at the wicket it seemed an even contest. But Stewart's bright 87 (107 balls) ended with a diving rebound catch by Healy, also off Warne, and they moved gingerly to 188 for 4 by the close. Healy's next catch, off Crawley's bat, was his 101st against England and 301st in all Tests. Thorpe and Adam Hollioake extended their stand to 102, then both fell. The younger Hollioake made a breezy 28, but McGrath dispatched the tail, and Australia's advantage was 114, to which they added 167 on the Saturday for the loss of their first four—Elliott to an amazing diving outfield catch by Crawley. Ponting, determinedly, and Healy (reaching 1000 runs against England), with his usual mixture of cheek and unorthodoxy, stretched the lead while Taylor smiled and chewed gum on the balcony. When they were all out, they left England a derisory victory target of 451 for the series to be kept alive. By that fourth evening, Taylor was able to claim the extra half-hour, and finish the job. McGrath, Gillespie and Warne took three wickets each, and apart from Crawley (33) only Thorpe batted for longer than an hour. The Surrey left-hander's unbeaten 82 included his 1000th run against Australia. Once again, there could be no question as to the superior side in this Ashes campaign, and Australia's decisive victory brought them yet another record, for never before had one country beaten the other in five successive major Ashes series.

[12]31: *Stewart's brisk 87 ends with an acrobatic catch by Healy, his 100th against [E]ngland and 300th in all Tests.* 1232, right: *Thorpe was left high and dry with a [?]3-ball 82.* 1233, below: *During a freakish period of play brothers bowled to [b]rothers. Adam Hollioake nearly gets Mark Waugh*

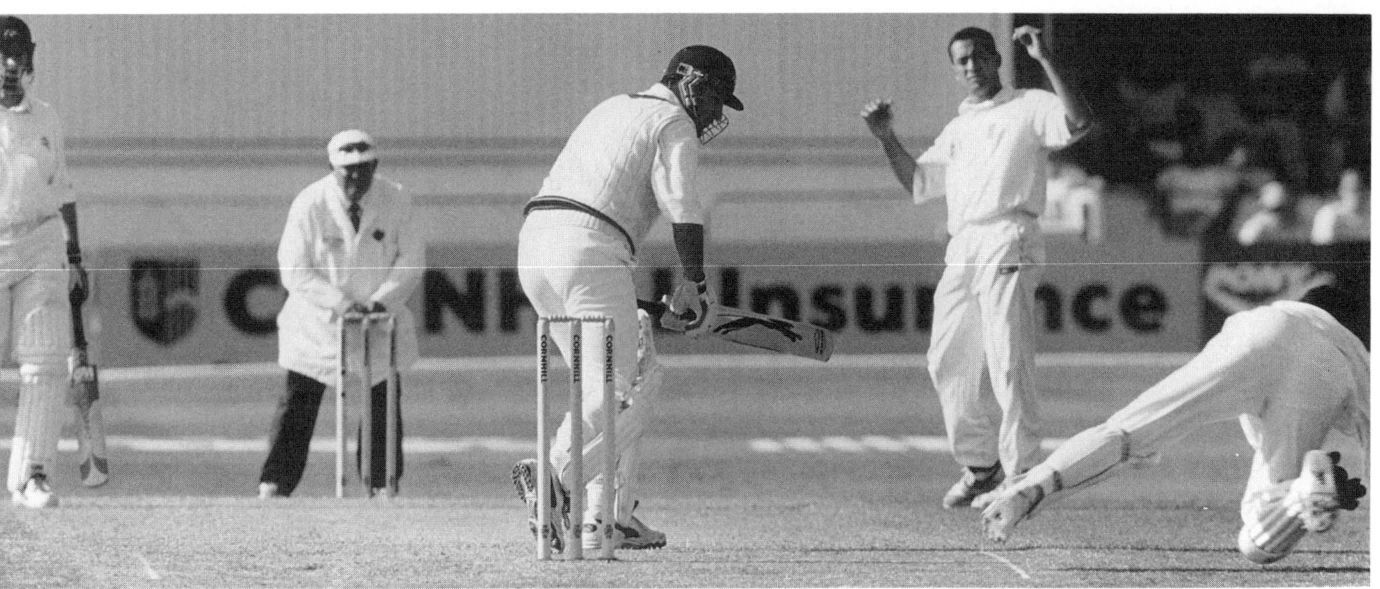

1997 SIXTH TEST

The Oval, August 21, 22, 23

England *180 (G.D. McGrath 7 for 76) and 163 (G.P. Thorpe 62, M.R. Ramprakash 48, M.S. Kasprowicz 7 for 36);* Australia *220 (G.S. Blewett 47, R.T. Ponting 40, P.C.R. Tufnell 7 for 66) and 104 (A.R. Caddick 5 for 42, P.C.R. Tufnell 4 for 27).* England won by 19 runs.

Even if Australia yet again succumbed once the main business of winning the series had been achieved, and could point to the loss of Reiffel (flown home on compassionate grounds) and Gillespie (spinal stress fracture), this match was a thriller of classic proportions. After three days of derring-do and blunder, a victory target of 124 proved beyond the tourists, giving England a 2–3 deficit, so much better than 1–4. It seemed the same old story when England were bowled out, principally by McGrath, for 180. Taylor had failed to win a record sixth toss, but wickets tumbled steadily, Atherton falling for the seventh time to McGrath in his last 10 dismissals in the series, and only Stewart and Hussain reaching 30. Adam Hollioake, one of four Surrey players in the side, was bowled for 0 without offering a shot at Warne. By stumps, Australia were 77 for 2, Tufnell having dismissed both openers in his first match of the series, after having been left out of the final XI in all five previous Tests. Even on the opening day, he was turning the ball a considerable distance, and getting bounce. Preferred to Croft, the offspinner who had managed only eight wickets in the five Tests, the Middlesex left-arm spinner now teased his way to seven wickets, restricting Australia's lead to 40. Blewett fought hard, and was unlucky to be given out caught (in both innings) when it seemed certain he had not touched the ball, and Healy was caught by opposing wicketkeeper Stewart when the ball lodged between his thighs. There were also some unimpressive lbw decisions. Warne's 30 at No.9 put Australia's nose in front, and England lost three key wickets before the arrears were cleared, the third day beginning with them 12 in front, seven wickets left. Few would have predicted that 17 wickets would fall that day. Much was owed to Thorpe and the recalled Ramprakash, who made 79 for the fifth wicket, but the final four wickets fell for three runs, Kasprowicz wiping out the tail to become the third bowler in this match to bag seven wickets in an innings, a unique Test occurrence. Warne had been expected to embarrass England again, but was hindered by a groin strain. Australia's target was now an uncomplicated-looking 124, their main concern Tufnell once again. He took four wickets, but Caddick took five, including a juggled return from Healy, giving him eight in the match and 24 at 26.42 in the series. Tufnell, though, always had a stranglehold on his adversaries, not least Mark Waugh, in both innings, for 19 and 1, leaving him with a dismal average of 20.90 for the series. The fifth wicket fell at 54, the seventh at 92, the ninth at 99. When McGrath (36 wickets in the series, to Warne's 24) popped a catch to Thorpe at mid-off from another snaking Tufnell delivery, the frenzy was as if England had won the Ashes rather than a consolation prize. Elliott topped the aggregates with 556 runs at 55.60, while Thorpe, the only scorer of a half-century in this match, headed England's table with 453 runs at 50.33.

1234, left: *A poor series for Mark Waugh draws closer to the end as Butcher snaps him up off Tufnell, who feasted on 11 wickets in his comeback Test.* 1235, below, left: *Comeback too for Mark Ramprakash, whose neat, confident 48 was crucial to England's turnaround in this final Test.* 1236, below: *Australia, set only 124, slide nearer to sensational defeat as Caddick completes a juggled return catch from Healy*

1998–99 FIRST TEST
Brisbane, November 20, 21, 22, 23, 24

Australia *485 (I.A. Healy 134, S.R. Waugh 112, D.W. Fleming 71*, M.A. Taylor 46, A.D. Mullally 5 for 105) and 237 for 3 dec (M.J. Slater 113, J.L. Langer 74);* England *375 (M.A. Butcher 116, G.P. Thorpe 77, M.R. Ramprakash 69*, N. Hussain 59, G.D. McGrath 6 for 85) and 179 for 6 (N. Hussain 47, M.A. Butcher 40).* Match drawn.

This Ashes series was launched rousingly with both national anthems being sung as the players lined up on the Gabba turf, and although Taylor marked his 100th Test with a typically defiant 46, Australia were placed none too promisingly when half out for 178 against England's pace line-up of Gough, Cork, Fraser and left-armer Mullally. Waugh and Healy then secured control with a stand of 187, helped by sloppy fielding and catching, Waugh's 16th century spanning 5½ hours of relentless concentration, Healy frustrating England for five hours. Fleming unexpectedly put together his highest score, and once more Australia were in control. All the same, England managed a reasonable response after losing Atherton for 0. Butcher, with hardly a tour run to his name and a recent bloody blow to the face fresh in memory, constructed a fine hundred and was backed up by an aggressive Hussain and watchful Thorpe, skipper Stewart failing in both innings. Ramprakash fought for almost four hours, but McGrath blew the tail away, giving Australia a handy lead. England's last six wickets and Australia's push for a solid target took the fourth day to 7½ hours, thanks to the elasticated rules governing over rates and weather interruptions. Excited at returning to the colours after nearly three years in the wilderness, Slater smashed his fifth century against England (as in 1994–95, he would make three in the series), and added 162 with the steady Langer after Cork bowled Taylor for 0. From 26 without loss that evening, England progressed to 96 for 1 just after lunch, and a draw seemed assured. Then Mark Waugh plucked out Stewart and Thorpe, and MacGill, playing instead of the injured Warne, began to penetrate. A brilliant wrong'un bowled Hussain, and Ramprakash, deceived through the air, was stumped. Then the light deteriorated, and a ferocious storm, a Brisbane special, flooded the ground, establishing one thing: England were not going to be 'greenwashed' in this series.

1237: *The Brisbane special that denied the opening Test match of 1998–99 a tense finish. The lightning flashes and darkening sky gave way to a heavy storm that left England free to fight another day, outgunned though they still appeared to be*

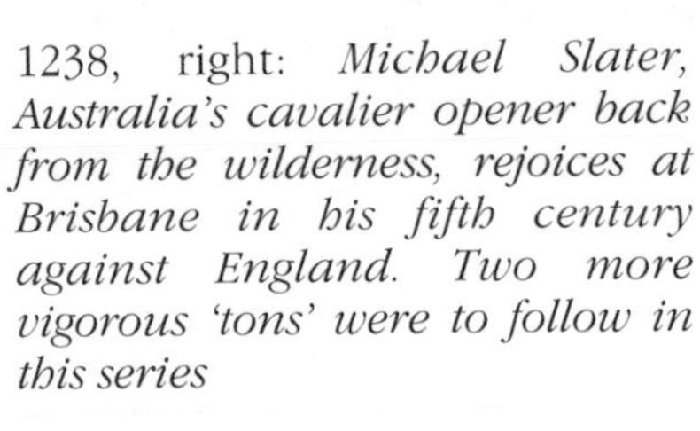

1238, right: *Michael Slater, Australia's cavalier opener back from the wilderness, rejoices at Brisbane in his fifth century against England. Two more vigorous 'tons' were to follow in this series*

1239, above: *Ian Healy's Gabba century gave Australia control as he and his captain doubled the score.* 1240, right: *With more stitches (10) to a facial wound than runs (9) on the tour, Mark Butcher works his way to a precious hundred for England*

1998–99 SECOND TEST

Perth, November 28, 29, 30

England *112 (D.W. Fleming 5 for 46) and 191 (G.A. Hick 68, M.R. Ramprakash 47*, J.N. Gillespie 5 for 88, D.W. Fleming 4 for 45);* Australia *240 (M.A. Taylor 61, A.J. Tudor 4 for 89) and 64 for 3.* Australia won by 7 wickets.

It was over inside three days, but on a fast bowler's surface the ball flew and there was much dramatic cricket. Taylor sent England in and bowled them out in three hours (39 overs), Fleming, McGrath and Gillespie carrying out their hit-men duties to perfection: Butcher 0, Atherton 1, Hussain 6, before Stewart (38 off 29 balls) and Ramprakash clawed out 43 runs, the latter's shirt blood-spattered after a ball from McGrath cut his chin. The wound needed six stitches. Crawley was out for 4, Hick (replacing the injured Thorpe) 0, and the decision to drop MacGill now seemed justified. England's fast men, particularly Gough and new-boy Tudor, also kept the pressure on the batsmen, though the catching again proved faulty. After an opening stand of 81 Australian wickets fell steadily, the last six toppling for 31. The lead, though, was already substantial, and when England subsided for 191 after another ghastly beginning – Butcher, Hussain and Stewart all out to Fleming with two runs between them – Hick batted boldly, once smiting Gillespie for 6, 4 and 6 at the start of an over. His 68 came off 73 balls, but Gillespie stormed through the order, leaving Ramprakash stranded, with Australia needing a mere 64. A scoreline of 36 for 3 was interesting, but the Waugh twins saw their side home. With only one further victory needed in the remaining three Tests, Australia's retention of the Ashes was already almost unbackable.

1241: *Damien Fleming crippled both England innings in Perth to help Australia go one ahead with three to play. Butcher (0 and 1) was his first victim in each innings*

1242, left: *Australia's captain Mark Taylor skilfully steered his side to a substantial first-innings lead in Perth before his fast bowlers ran through England a second time.* 1243, above: *Graeme Hick was the only England batsman to make a half-century on the bouncy WACA pitch. Here he punishes a short ball from Gillespie*

1998-99 THIRD TEST

Adelaide, December 11, 12, 13, 14, 15

Australia *391 (J.L. Langer 179*, M.A .Taylor 59, S.R. Waugh 59, D.W. Headley 4 for 97) and 278 for 5 dec (M.J. Slater 103, J.L. Langer 52, M.E. Waugh 51*)*; England *227 (N. Hussain 89*, M.R. Ramprakash 61, M.A. Atherton 41, S.C.G. MacGill 4 for 53) and 237 (A.J. Stewart 63*, M.R. Ramprakash 57, N. Hussain 41, G.D. McGrath 4 for 50)*. Australia won by 205 runs.

Taylor did Australia great service simply by winning the toss. So too did little Langer, who endured for over eight hours, displaying supreme determination and the kind of patriotic fervour that has fired this team for some years. Century stands with his captain and Steve Waugh set up a solid total that would have been substantially less had England's toll of catching errors not risen by three to reach a shameful 14 (half of them off Gough's wholehearted bowling) thus far in the series. In their reply only three batsmen reached double figures as MacGill spun and dipped and McGrath, Fleming and Miller took two wickets each. A fourth-wicket resistance of 103 by Hussain and Ramprakash preceded a crash of seven wickets for 40, and the deficit was an ominous 164. An explosive century from Slater headed Australia's second-innings charge, with fifties from Langer and the ridiculed Mark Waugh, the recent revelation of whose dealings with an Indian bookmaker had brought abuse from the crowd. Langer was missed twice before substitute Ben Hollioake caught him off the studious, persevering Such. Seeking 443 for the unlikeliest victory in Test history, England lost three and nightwatchman Headley that evening, and were strangled next day by the unremitting attack, pace and spin. It surprised nobody when the last six wickets went for 74 (5 for 16 to the new ball) after Ramprakash had made another soulful contribution. Stewart, in the runs at last, was left stranded. The Ashes remained in Australia's keeping after a mere 13 days' play.

1244, top, left: *Nasser Hussain cuts crisply at Adelaide where he and Ramprakash were England's leading rungetters in another losing cause.* 1245, above: *Australia's substantial first innings was built around Justin Langer's unbeaten 179.* 1246, left: *Michael Slater, on his way to his sixth century against England, blazes away with the characteristic vigour that caused his trousers to split*

1998–99 FOURTH TEST

Melbourne, December 26, 27, 28, 29

England *270 (A.J. Stewart 107, M.R. Ramprakash 63, S.C.G. MacGill 4 for 61) and 244 (G.A. Hick 60, A.J. Stewart 52, N. Hussain 50);* Australia *340 (S.R. Waugh 122*, J.L. Langer 44, S.C.G. MacGill 43, D. Gough 5 for 96) and 162 (M.E. Waugh 43, D.W. Headley 6 for 60).* England won by 12 runs.

This Melbourne classic started unpromisingly: nearly 60,000 people in the ground on Boxing Day, toss won by Taylor and England to bat, then not a ball bowled because of rain–a very costly washout with refunds having to be paid out. The next three days however, each extended at both ends to make up for lost playing time, were packed with thrills. On a cold, grey morning McGrath disposed of Atherton and Butcher for ducks, but Stewart, returning to the opener's position (Hegg kept wicket), fought his way to his first century in eight years of combat against Australia. With well-timed drives and hooks and the occasional edge, he faced 160 balls and had a stand of 119 with Ramprakash that gave the innings some body. The last seven wickets went for only 70, but towards the close Gough's speed accounted for both Australian openers. Half out for 151 by lunch next day, the home side (Lehmann taking Ponting's place and Gillespie out injured) were rescued by Steve Waugh. His gritty seventh century against England (during which he passed Bradman's overall Test aggregate of 6996) was supported by Healy (36) and the hard-swinging No.10, MacGill, who once played and missed every ball of a Gough over. The Waugh-MacGill stand of 88 took Australia to a decent lead, and when Atherton completed a pair and two further wickets fell before the arrears had been cleared it looked ominous yet again for England. But half-centuries were carved out by Stewart, Hussain and Hick, and a last-wicket resistance of 23 by Fraser and Mullally not only raised Australia's target to 175 but cost McGrath a suspended fine, so frustrated did he become. Two wickets were lost in reaching 100, and the outcome seemed certain. Then Ramprakash held a sizzling catch at square leg from Langer's bat off Mullally, and Headley surged in to take 4 for 4 and spread panic. Steve Waugh, who finished 30 not out, chipped out 21 further runs with Nicholson, but Headley had the newcomer caught behind soon after Stewart's request to draw stumps at 7.22 pm had been turned down. The session was already approaching four hours, but Waugh claimed the extra half-hour while his eye was in and England fought fatigue. But Gough dealt with MacGill and McGrath as soon as Waugh exposed them, and England stole a sublime victory in the gloaming after the longest day's play in Test history (483 minutes). Players, spectators and televiewers alike were left exhausted.

1247: *Alec Stewart, having recorded an Ashes century at long last (and one of only two by England during this series), is bowled by Stuart MacGill. The legspinner took seven wickets in this Melbourne Test, but was to be an even greater influence in the next one, on the spin-friendly SCG pitch*

1248, above: *Dean Headley, fighting fatigue, gives his all in the final hour of the memorable marathon final day at Melbourne. Here Fleming is his fifth wicket and Australia are 140 for 7.* 1249, right: *Darren Gough takes off in his euphoria at having McGrath lbw to seal England's 12-run win*

1998–99 FIFTH TEST

Sydney, January 2, 3, 4, 5

Australia *322 (M.E. Waugh 121, S.R. Waugh 96, D.W. Headley 4 for 62) and 184 (M.J. Slater 123, P.M. Such 5 for 81, D.W. Headley 4 for 40);* England *220 (J.P. Crawley 44, N. Hussain 42, S.C.G. MacGill 5 for 57) and 188 (N. Hussain 53, A.J. Stewart 42, S.C.G. MacGill 7 for 50).* Australia won by 98 runs.

But for a reprieve given to Slater by the off-field umpire after a run-out appeal when he was 35, England might well have stolen this Test match. Most fieldsmen and viewers felt he was out, but he carried on to smash 123, his third hundred of the series, and save Australia's second innings. Mark Waugh (24), shortly after pocketing his 100th Test catch, was the only other batsman to reach double figures. England's target therefore swelled to 287, far too many. Australia took a grip on the match with their first-innings advantage of 102. Winning all five tosses (emulating Noble and Hassett) and taking his success with the coin to 11 out of his last 12 Ashes Tests, Taylor acquired first innings on a pitch that would welcome spin more each day. He finished his own final Ashes series with more failures (2 and 2), but the Waugh brothers masterminded a sound total with an attractive fourth-wicket stand of 190 in front of the biggest SCG crowd (42,124) for 23 years. England gave them several let-offs but made sure the tail was no trouble. The last five wickets tumbled for three runs, and those who left the ground early will forever regret missing Gough's hat-trick (Healy, MacGill, Miller), the first for England against Australia since 1899. Missing Atherton (back strain), England were confronted chiefly by spin: MacGill, Miller, and Warne, who returned after months of recuperation after a shoulder operation and struck fourth ball. It was clear, though, that MacGill was England's biggest problem, and his range of legspin variations reaped him five wickets in the first innings and seven in the second, his 12 for 107 being the best Test figures ever at Sydney apart from Turner's 111 years earlier. The first of McGrath's three wickets in the match was his 200th in Tests. Headley again bowled well in Australia's second innings, and offspinner Such took the last five wickets, including McGrath for the 37th duck of the series, equalling the record. England's fourth-innings approach was positive–witness both openers, Butcher and Stewart, stumped–but after Taylor held a record 157th catch (Ramprakash) and Hussain's stout effort ended with a return catch to MacGill, the tourists slipped away and Australia were presented with the new crystal blow-up replica of the Ashes as the first full century of Anglo-Australian cricket closed.

1250, left: *The closing minutes of the first day's play at Sydney were enlivened by Gough as he found the perfect delivery to Colin Miller to collect England's first Ashes hat-trick since J.T.Hearne's 99 years previously.* 1251, above: *Slater trots past the broken wicket, unsure of whether he was run out or not. By general consensus he seemed out, but the video umpire was uncertain, and the batsman stayed on to make a further 88 crucial runs*

1252, above: *Gough is leg-before to MacGill, and England are almost all out, with a first-innings deficit, as was the case in all five Tests. MacGill went on to a 12-wicket triumph, completely overshadowing Shane Warne.* 1253, right: *Mark Taylor and his successor Steve Waugh carefully handle the large crystal model of the Ashes urn commissioned by MCC, who own the delicate little 1882 original*

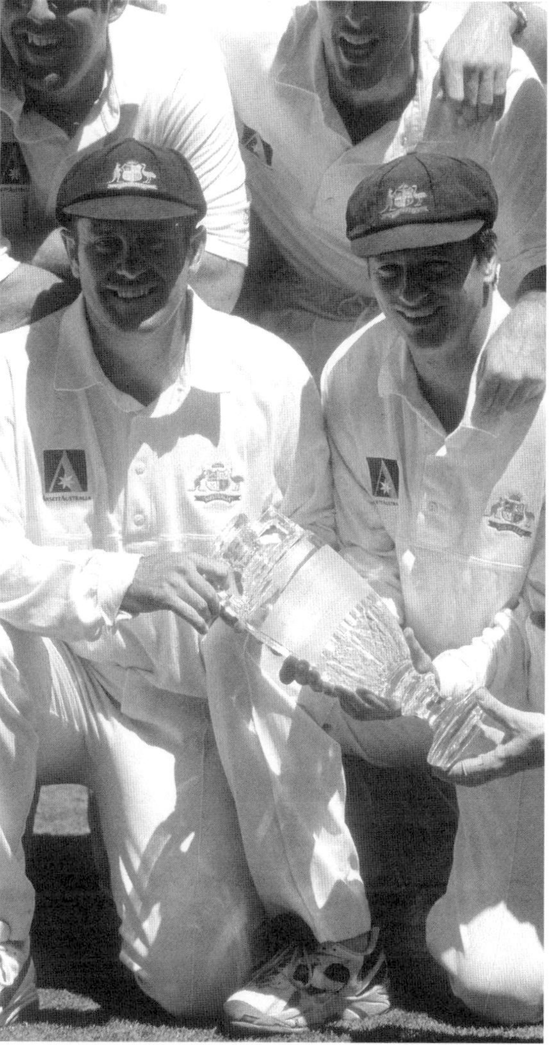

2001 FIRST TEST

Edgbaston, July 5, 6, 7, 8

England *294 (A.J.Stewart 65, M.A. Atherton 57, S.K. Warne 5 for 71) and 164 (M.E. Trescothick 76, M.A. Butcher 41);* Australia *576 (A.C. Gilchrist 152, S.R. Waugh 105, D.R. Martyn 105, M.J. Slater 77, M.A. Butcher 4 for 42).* Australia won by an innings and 118 runs.

Ashes Test cricket entered the 21st Century with a severely compressed series: five Tests in 54 days. And hopes of a closely-fought contest once more soon collapsed. England's team-building and recent successes elsewhere came to nothing as injury deprived them of Thorpe and Giles (each for 4 Tests), captain Hussain (2), and Vaughan (all 5). When some poor cricket (especially the catching) followed, there was no stopping the mighty machine that was Australia under Steve Waugh's stewardship. England's freakish first innings was mainly constructed from century stands for the second wicket (Atherton and Butcher) and the 10th (Stewart and Caddick), with Warne's spin tearing away the lower order. Slater and Hayden then smashed 98 for Australia's first wicket, beyond which the bowlers were toyed with as captain Waugh passed 9000 Test runs in making his century and Martyn and Gilchrist registered hundreds in their maiden Ashes Tests. As catches were spilt like slippery crockery, Gilchrist scythed onward, his brutal display contrasting with Martyn's sleek and correct approach. Martyn was 99 at tea, but soon secured his mark in history. The stand was worth 160. When last man McGrath entered, Gilchrist was 93 after Butcher's swing bowling had potted four wickets. The final stand amounted to 63 of which the No.11 scored 1. Gilchrist smote Butcher for 22 in one over (equalling the Ashes record), having flicked Caddick high over the keeper to reach his century (the 250th for Australia v England), and finishing with a breathtaking 152 off 143 balls, five of which were hacked for six, equalling Loxton's Ashes record (for Australia). Reaching 99 before they lost their second wicket, a demoralised England fell away to an innings defeat. Ashes debutant Trescothick alone–after Butcher–displayed determination and aggression and the necessary technique. Gillespie inflicted telling damage in breaking Hussain's left hand, and another decisive Australian victory was in the bag in little more than three days.

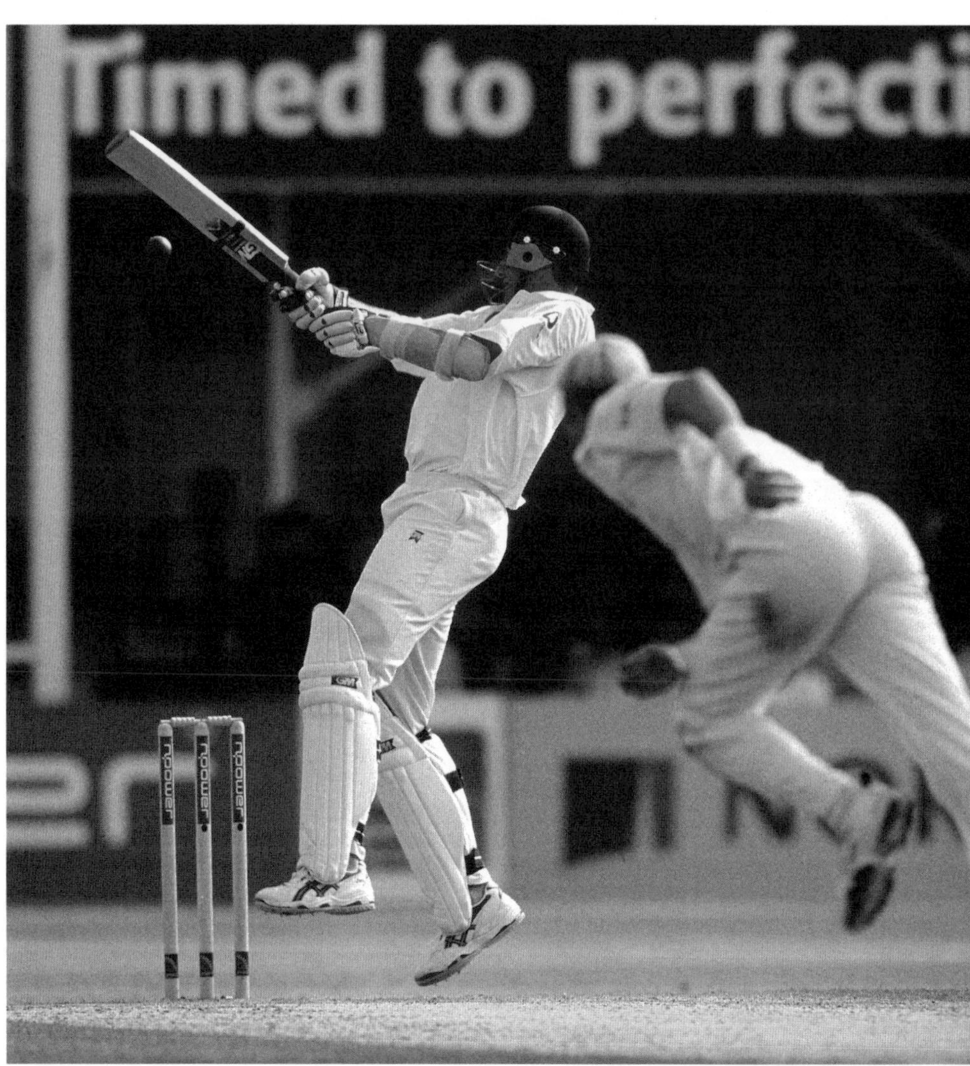

1254: *The opening Test of 2001 embraced some bizarre episodes in terms of batting aggression. Here Andrew Caddick, England's No.11, lashes out at Australia's fastest bowler, Brett Lee, during a 10th-wicket stand of 103 with Alec Stewart*

1255, above, left: *Damien Martyn's polished performance at Edgbaston was rewarded with a century in his maiden Ashes Test match.* 1256, above, right: *Soon Martyn was joined in the list by Adam Gilchrist, whose 152 was memorable for its power-packed shots. Mark Waugh and Ricky Ponting, team-mates who also played in this Test, had also scored centuries on Ashes debut—a novel situation*

2001 — SECOND TEST

Lord's, July 19, 20, 21, 22

England *187 (G.D. McGrath 5 for 54) and 227 (M.A. Butcher 83, M.R. Ramprakash 40, J.N. Gillespie 5 for 53);* Australia *401 (M.E. Waugh 108, A.C. Gilchrist 90, D.R. Martyn 52, S.R. Waugh 45, A.R. Caddick 5 for 101) and 14 for 2.* Australia won by 8 wickets.

Once again Australia were at their efficient best for a Lord's Test, and their superiority was emphatically underlined. Following Hussain's Edgbaston injury Atherton resumed as captain, Stewart and Butcher having declined. With the return of Thorpe and Ramprakash, England had five Surrey batsmen in the middle order. It made no difference. Australia won the toss for the 13th time in the last 14 Ashes Tests and bowled hard at England on a rain-interrupted first day (121 for 3). McGrath launched some cruel deliveries next day, and Australia faced an anaemic total of 187. The reply wobbled at first, but after Gough had spilt a sharp return catch from Steve Waugh, the seemingly inevitable large total took shape. The Waugh brothers composed another century stand, Mark relishing the wayward leg-stump line of the squad of seamers. Catches fell like chestnuts–Gough suffering repeatedly–as Australia took control, and Gilchrist, one of the main beneficiaries, again hammered almost everything within reach. Eight

England wickets were captured before the first-innings deficit of 214 was erased. Butcher and Ramprakash raised visions of hope with a stand of 96, but McGrath was unstoppable and Gillespie for once returned deservedly fine figures. Lee's modest analysis disguised the fact that he had pushed England substantially further into the ground by breaking Thorpe's right hand. England's best batsman was out of the series. A late additional plaudit came Australia's way when Mark Waugh pouched his 158th catch, a world Test record.

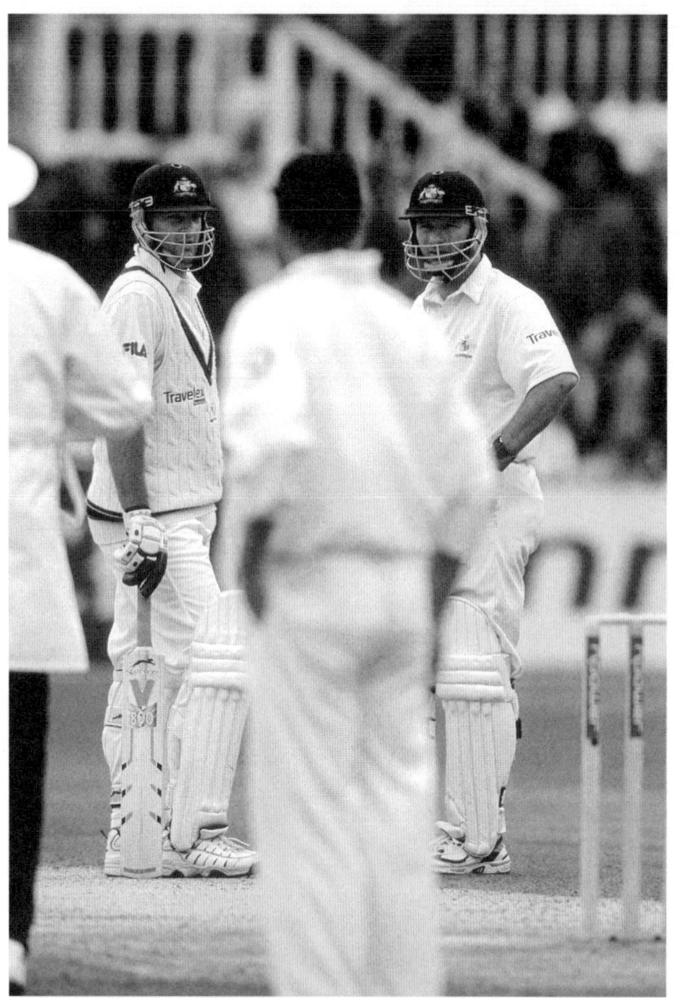

1257, left: *Staring match between Test match warriors. Mike Atherton, returning as England's captain, looks towards Mark and Steve Waugh, whose batting has blighted most of his career in Ashes cricket since his debut in 1989. The Australian twins, settled in another century stand, stare defiantly—perhaps pityingly—back.*
1258, below: *As with most dropped catches, things would have been so different if . . . This one, from Steve Waugh to bowler Gough when he was only 14, was the most difficult of England's spillages. If it had been held, the tourists would have been 136 for 4*

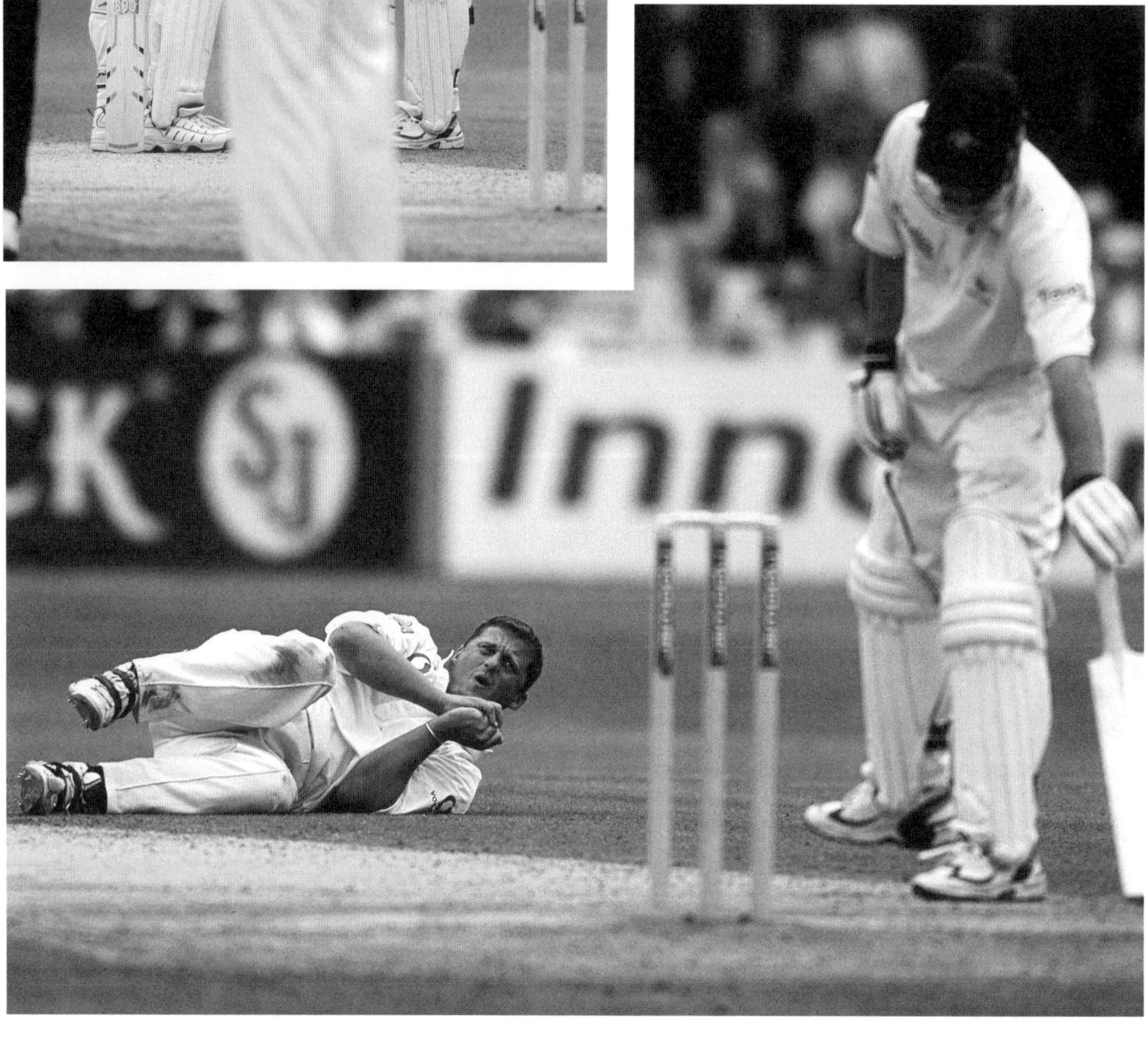

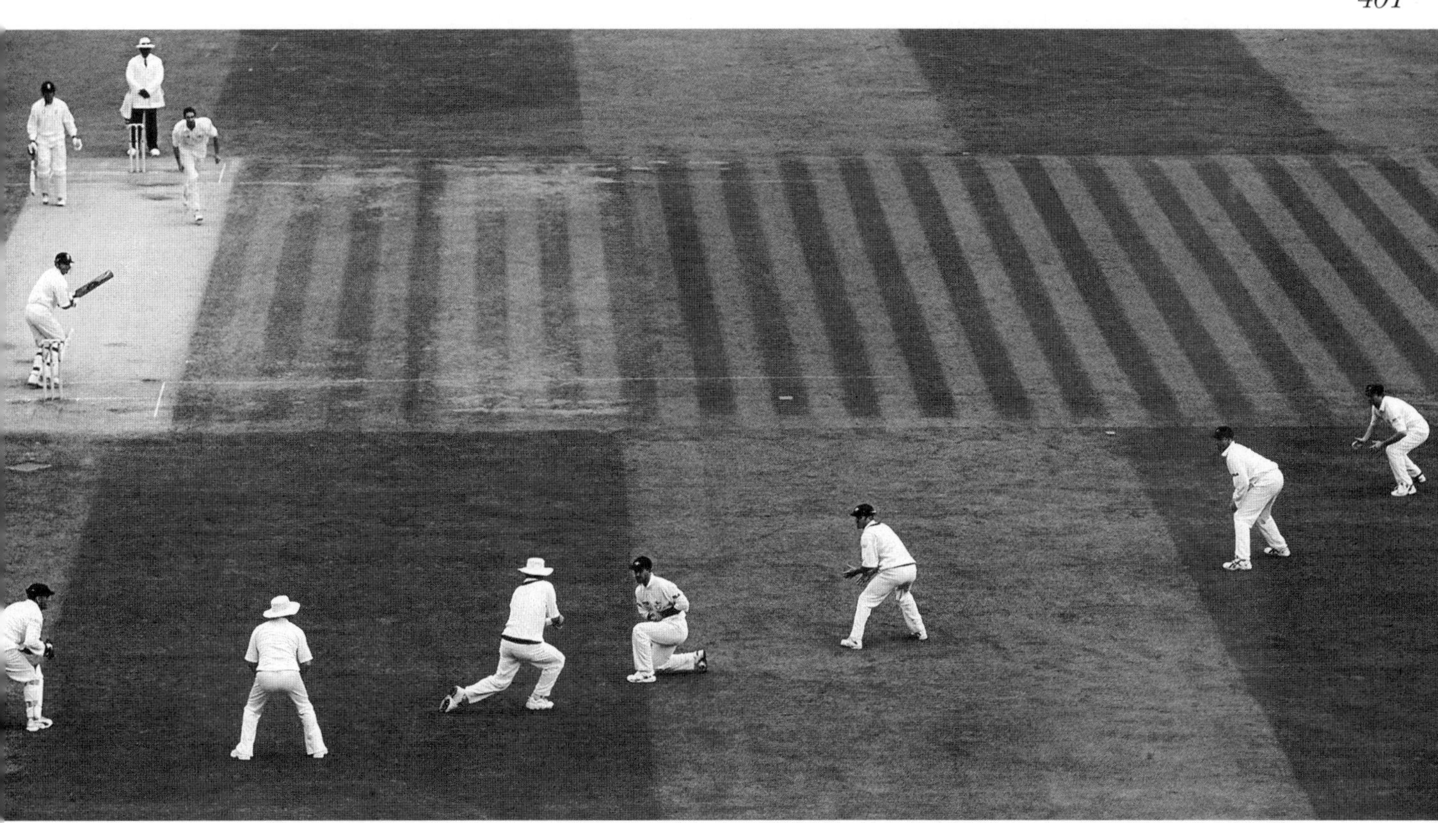

1259: *Where no man has gone before: as another anaemic England batting effort draws to a close at Lord's, Gough edges Jason Gillespie to slip where Mark Waugh holds his 158th Test catch, a new record. No fieldsman in the history of England-Australia cricket can have had softer, surer hands than the younger of the Waugh twins*

2001 THIRD TEST

Trent Bridge, August 2, 3, 4

England *185 (M.E. Trescothick 69, A.J. Stewart 46, G.D. McGrath 5 for 49) and 162 (M.A. Atherton 51, S.K. Warne 6 for 33)*; Australia *190 (A.C. Gilchrist 54, A.J. Tudor 5 for 44) and 158 for 3 (M.L. Hayden 42, M.E. Waugh 42*)*. Australia won by 7 wickets.

A mere 30 days after the first ball of the series, Australia wrapped up the Ashes once more. It had taken no more than 11 days' play, some of them incomplete. And yet England twice held the key to victory here. The close-of-play score on the first evening had an old-fashioned–perhaps 1880s–touch about it: England 185, Australia 105 for 7. Atherton's 20th Test duck (all but the umpire were aware that the ball flicked only his armguard) headed a sorry scorecard. Apart from Trescothick's mature and resolute 69 and Stewart's 46, nobody reached 15. Warne became the 11th Australian to take 100 England wickets (England 7 bowlers in return). There was then an unfamiliar tumble of Australian wickets after Hayden and Slater had led off with 48. Gough, Tudor (five wickets for the first time) and Caddick in turn now exploited the pitch's receptiveness, and seven wickets were swept away for 57. Gillespie (27 not out) helped Gilchrist add 66 for the ninth wicket, putting Australia's nose in front, and once more riding his luck, Gilchrist shaped the match. Then Atherton and Trescothick gave England a solid start, before the latter was unluckily caught via Hayden's ankle (it was actually a no-ball from Warne) just before rain drove the players off. England were next faced with Warne's spin torture and Lee's speed and bounce, and it was no great surprise when another collapse ensued. Ramprakash was stumped for 26, and only Ward (13) of the remainder reached double-figures. Warne's 6 for 33 was his best Test analysis for five years, since before his finger and shoulder operations. Australia needed only 158 to win, and English fans were aghast when Langer survived a fairly central lbw appeal second ball, but runs were quarried and the chins of the home side began to drop. Steve Waugh's latest hour of glory was spoilt by a torn muscle as he ran his opening single, and he was wheeled off the ground and taken to hospital. But victory duly came, and for an unprecedented seventh time in succession Australia had won the Ashes.

1260, above, left: *Marcus Trescothick delivered some overdue brightness to success-starved England fans. The Somerset left-hander pounded a defiant 69 to kick off the short-lived Trent Bridge Test.* 1261, above, right: *Cricket's long-overdue new gesture: Glenn McGrath acknowledges the applause for his fifth wicket in England's first innings at Trent Bridge. Why should only batsmen communicate their pleasure to the audience?*

1262, left: *Alex Tudor, back in England colours after two years, celebrates Matthew Hayden's dismissal as he heads for five wickets at Trent Bridge.* 1263, above: *Australia are poised to retain the Ashes when the party is spoiled by a calf injury to skipper Waugh. Physio Errol Alcott gives a preliminary opinion*

2001 FOURTH TEST

Headingley, August 16, 17, 18, 19, 20

Australia *447 (R.T. Ponting 144, D.R. Martyn 118, M.E. Waugh 72, D. Gough 5 for 103) and 176 for 4 dec (R.T. Ponting 72);* England *309 (A.J. Stewart 76*, M.A. Butcher 47, N. Hussain 46, M.R. Ramprakash 40, G.D. McGrath 7 for 76) and 315 for 4 (M.A. Butcher 173*, N. Hussain 55).* England won by 6 wickets.

Mark Butcher's innings of a lifetime crowned the 300th England v Australia Test match and brought long-awaited jubilation to English cricket. Had the weather not cut into the time-scale of the match on the fourth day Australia's stand-in captain Gilchrist would have set a stiffer target. But even 315 seemed well beyond England's capabilities, especially when two early wickets fell and McGrath and Gillespie on the final morning looked like taking a wicket almost every ball. Then Hussain hooked Gillespie for six and the ball had to be replaced. Thereafter England took control. Butcher's strokeplay off either foot was spectacular, and after his stand of 181 with Hussain he was backed by Ramprakash at a time when it might have seemed to English supporters that it had all been too good to be true. It was bad luck for Ponting that his splendid batting double should have been overshadowed, as it was also for Martyn, who made another smooth century and was last out. Ponting's 144 (20 fours, 3 sixes) came from only 154 balls sent down by England's all-pace attack on a dry pitch. All of England's top seven got a start, but only Stewart, blazing away at No.7, passed 50. They fell so far short on first innings as McGrath bagged another handsome return that Australia's ambitions for a 'greenwash' seemed to be heading for fulfilment,. Their advantage was being inflated when weather disrupted Sunday's play and caused Gilchrist to rearrange the target downwards. And so, against all probability, England clattered their way to victory in 73.2 overs, with 20 to spare. Butcher's 173 spanned 5½ hours (227 balls) and he hit 23 fours and one six (over backward point off Gillespie). It was the second-largest successful run-chase by England in Ashes history after Melbourne 1928-29 (third Test).

1264, right: *Australia were in control almost from the start of the Headingley Test, thanks chiefly to Ricky Ponting. The 26-year-old Tasmanian stroked an attractive century, as he had done at this same Leeds ground four years earlier on his Ashes Test debut. Here he treats Caddick to yet another crackling hook stroke*

1265, left: *Backing Ponting's century at Headingley was another fine hundred by the Western Australian, Damien Martyn, whose clean strokeplay once again caught the eye*

1266, above: *The innings of the match—and of his lifetime—came from Surrey left-hander Mark Butcher, whose bold play harvested a victory for England against heavy odds*

1267, right: *England veteran Alec Stewart entered when England were half out and still 74 short of avoiding the follow-on. With a complete lack of inhibition he cracked 76 not out to help set up one of the most amazing conclusions*

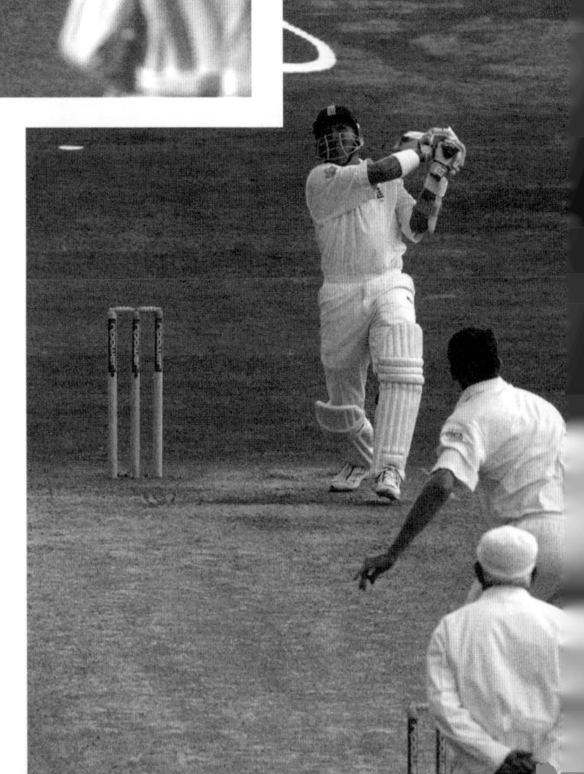

2001

The Oval, August 23, 24, 25, 26, 27

FIFTH TEST

Australia *641 for 4 dec (S.R. Waugh 157*, M.E. Waugh 120, J.L. Langer 102*, M.L. Hayden 68, D.R. Martyn 64*, R.T. Ponting 62)*; England *432 (M.R. Ramprakash 133, M.E. Trescothick 55, U. Afzaal 54, N. Hussain 52, S.K. Warne 7 for 165) and 184 (G.D. McGrath 5 for 43, S.K. Warne 4 for 64).* Australia won by an innings and 25 runs.

With only two days between Tests, English euphoria was shortlived. Winning another toss, Steve Waugh, not fully recovered from the leg injury but utterly determined to play, made the major contribution to Australia's massive total and finished the series with an average of 107. Opener Langer replaced Slater and shed the frustration of having been sidelined by carefully creating a century that ended when he was struck a stunning blow on the helmet by Caddick. His opening stand with Hayden was worth 158. The rest of the batsmen feasted, accelerating on the second day, the Waugh brothers putting on 197 together—four short of the Chappell brothers' stand here in 1972—Mark registering his 20th Test century, Steve hobbling to his 27th. Thereafter the result depended on the follow-on, and with three half-centuries and Ramprakash's fine maiden Ashes hundred England were heading for salvation. Then Warne's 400th Test wicket (Stewart, dubiously caught behind, and fined for showing dissent) exposed the tail, and England narrowly missed their target. Gilchrist completed his 100th wicketkeeping dismissal in only his 22nd Test, a new record. Warne's stoic 44.2 overs brought rich reward, and he now spun through a further 28 positive overs as England's second innings subsided tamely. The first of McGrath's five wickets was Atherton's yet again, the former captain walking off to retirement after 12 years of Test cricket during which he was never part of an Ashes-winning side. McGrath took 32 wickets (16.94) in the series, Warne 31 (18.71). Top score now grotesquely came from Gough (39 not out at No.10), and Australia's victory was the 20th in their past 23 Tests. Against England their supremacy since the start of the 1989 series was equally obvious: Australia have triumphed in 24 Ashes Tests, England in only six.

1268: *Having worked his way to a rehabilitating century after having been excluded from the first four Tests, Justin Langer took a blow on the helmet that left him reeling. But he and Hayden had laid a sturdy foundation for Australia's sixth-highest total in England*

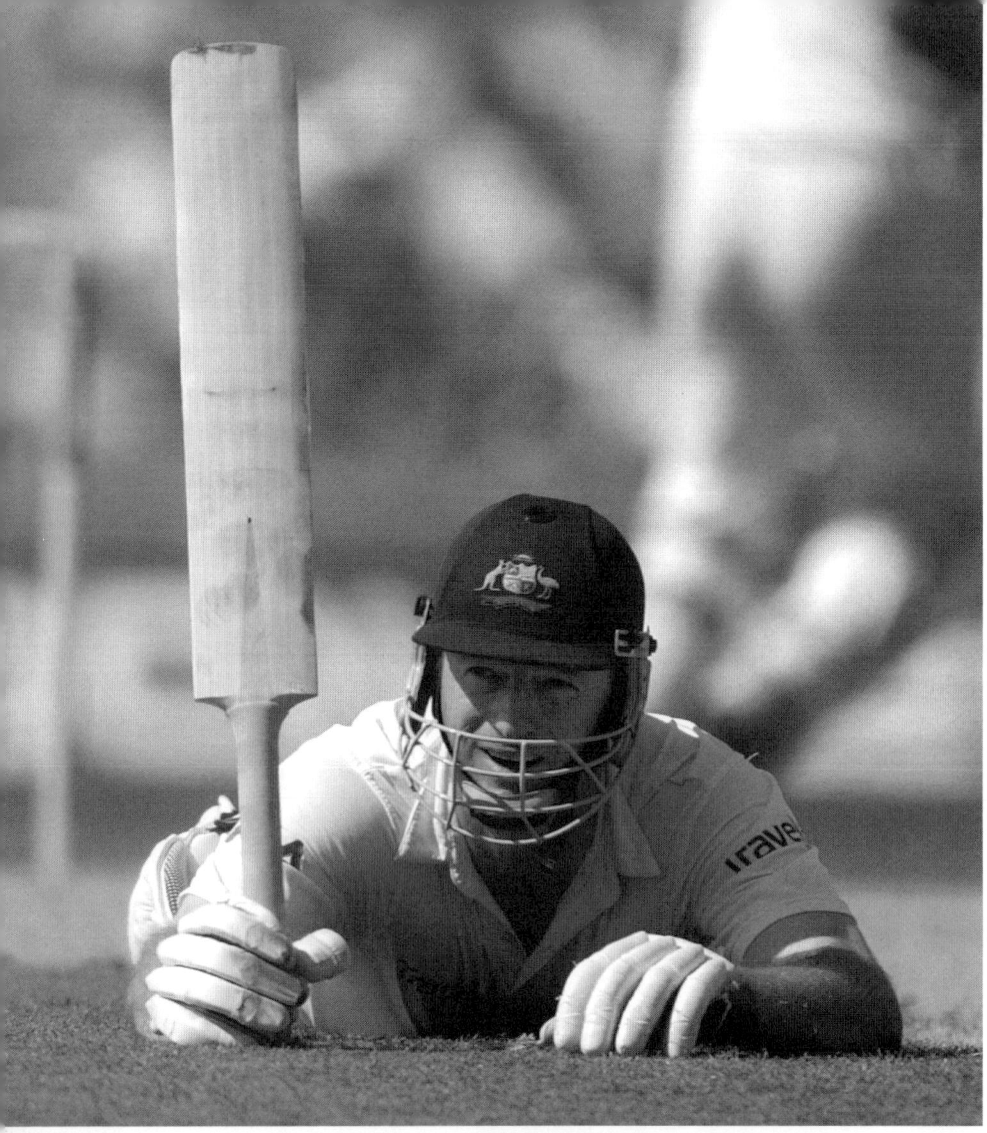

1269, left: *Steve Waugh, handicapped by the leg injury sustained in the third Test, slides in to complete his century at The Oval, his ninth against England. None of the previous 255 hundreds scored for Australia in these Tests can have been celebrated in quite the same horizontal manner.* 1270, bottom, left: *Mark Ramprakash dispersed the haunting memories of so much earlier frustration with a superb innings of 133 that so nearly averted the follow-on for England.* 1271, bottom, right: *The conspicuous figure of Shane Warne in yet another gesture of celebration: he has just become the first spin bowler to take 400 wickets in Test cricket. His tally in Ashes Tests (118 in 23 Tests) by the end of the 2001 series placed him fifth behind Lillee (167), Botham (148), Trumble (141) and Willis (128)*

2002-03
Brisbane, November 7, 8, 9, 10

Australia *492 (M.L.Hayden 197, R.T.Ponting 123, S.K.Warne 57, A.F.Giles 4 for 101) and 296 for 5 dec (M.L.Hayden 103, D.R.Martyn 64, A.C.Gilchrist 60*);* England *325 (M.E.Trescothick 72, J.P.Crawley 69*, M.A.Butcher 54, N.Hussain 51, G.D.McGrath 4 for 87) and 79 (M.A.Butcher 40, G.D.McGrath 4 for 36).* Australia won by 384 runs.

English hopes of pushing Australia hard this time were again swiftly dashed. With key players Thorpe and Gough absent, and faced with a monstrous tour casualty list, the tourists came to attract pity and derision in equal parts. An apprehensive Nasser Hussain gifted Australia first use of a sound Gabba pitch, and the runs flowed. Hayden displayed awesome power and his blitzing stand of 272 with Ponting was a new second-wicket record for Australia in Ashes Tests at home (G.S.Chappell/Redpath, Sydney 1974-75). Dropped three times after reaching his century, the Queensland giant next morning spliced a hook at his 298th ball, and England regained some ground, though they were now a man short after Simon Jones's grievous knee injury from a fall in the outfield. Their reply was spirited (170 for one at one stage), but Butcher became McGrath's 100th wicket in Ashes Tests (at only 20.10, the best after C.T.B.Turner), and the deficit was an ominous 167. Hayden's second century was faster and placed him on an elite list. Martyn played shots, and Gilchrist, belting a six to get off a 'pair', registered a 51-ball fifty. England needed to survive 137 overs. It was all over in 28.2. A poor lbw decision against Vaughan, the ridiculous run-out of Crawley (0), and some smart catching ended the affair on the fourth evening. It was Australia's third-highest runs victory over England and the visitors' lowest score in Australia for 99 years.

1272, above: *Losing battle: England left-handers Marcus Trescothick and Mark Butcher survive to the interval, but the strain of the uphill battle at the Gabba shows*

1273, right: *Muscular Matt Hayden blazes away on his home territory. Only Warren Bardsley, Arthur Morris and Steve Waugh had previously scored twin centuries for Australia in Test matches against England*

1274, above: *The senseless run-out of John Crawley in the opening Test of the 2002–03 series was indicative of England's lamentable state of mind.* 1275, below: *Hayden and Ponting, who made 426 runs between them in this Brisbane Test, show how it's done*

2002-03 — SECOND TEST

Adelaide, November 21, 22, 23, 24

England *342 (M.P.Vaughan 177, N.Hussain 47, J.N.Gillespie 4 for 78, S.K.Warne 4 for 93) and 159 (A.J.Stewart 57, M.P.Vaughan 41, G.D.McGrath 4 for 41);* Australia *552 for 9 dec (R.T.Ponting 154, D.R.Martyn 95, A.C.Gilchrist 54, J.L.Langer 48, A.J.Bichel 48, M.L.Hayden 46, C.White 4 for 106).* Australia won by an innings and 51 runs.

Vaughan, his knee strapped, played a classical innings, driving majestically and pulling enterprisingly, but there was little support from an England line-up with three changes enforced by injuries. The opener's 205-minute hundred preceded a painful blow to the shoulder from Gillespie, but he held on, adding 140 with Hussain, Australia flooring six catches in the day before Vaughan's dismissal in the final over. England then plunged into shambles. Langer and Hayden posted another century opening stand, but the dominant hand came from the finely-tuned Ponting and the polished Martyn, who added 242 in five hours, the latter eventually falling on 95 to Harmison's short-pitched blast. Gilchrist and Bichel took Australia past 500, White standing out in a lacklustre attack led by Caddick and Hoggard. An oddity was Lehmann's dismissal by his brother-in-law, Craig White. Bichel, McGrath and Warne tore through demoralised England's second innings, with only Vaughan and Stewart seeming worthy to share the same field as their opponents. McGrath's diving boundary catch to end Vaughan's innings stretched credibility. Afterwards came enough rain to suggest that with more backbone England might just have salvaged this match.

1276, above: *Shane Warne, with an ever-alert field, applies unrelenting pressure on England at Adelaide.* 1277, right: *Damien Martyn on his way to a 95 that blended with Ponting's 154 in a partnership of 242, steering the match Australia's way.* 1278, below: *Michael Vaughan punches a ball back past Gillespie during his masterly century, the first of three registered by him in the series to alleviate England's recurring difficulties*

2002-03

Perth, November 29, 30, December 1

England *185 (R.W.T.Key 47) and 223 (A.J.Stewart 66*, N.Hussain 61);* Australia *456 (D.R.Martyn 71, R.T.Ponting 68, S.R.Waugh 53, D.S.Lehmann 42, B.Lee 41, C.White 5 for 127).* Australia won by an innings and 48 runs.

Australia won their eighth Ashes series in succession with a hostile exhibition of purposeful cricket on a typical WACA surface. Although the spoils were evenly spread, Brett Lee's speed and bounce induced apprehension in onlookers let alone opposing batsmen. The lifter which floored Tudor, England's No.9, left a pool of blood by the pitch. After openers Trescothick and Vaughan had made 47, the former was caught behind again, and the familiar slide began, only newcomer Key holding steady. He hit Warne for six before falling to part-timer Martyn. In reply Australia batted with assurance right down the order as White stood out in the toiling England attack, with Waugh notching his first fifty of the series. Replacement new-ball bowler Silverwood withdrew with a damaged ankle after bowling only four overs. Humiliation beckoned again with England 34 for 4 in their second innings, still 237 behind, and Gillespie bowling a hat-trick ball to Hussain: Warne at slip spilt the catch. A cosmetic recovery took place, but after Tudor's facial injury the hyper-efficient Australians quickly wrapped up the match. As in 2001, it had taken the holders a mere 11 days to retain the Ashes.

1279, left: *Marcus Trescothick, England's calm left-hand opening batsman, was caught by wicketkeeper Gilchrist off Lee in both innings at Perth. In nine of 10 innings in this series he fell to a fast bowler, and his series average of 26 was a disappointment to his supporters*

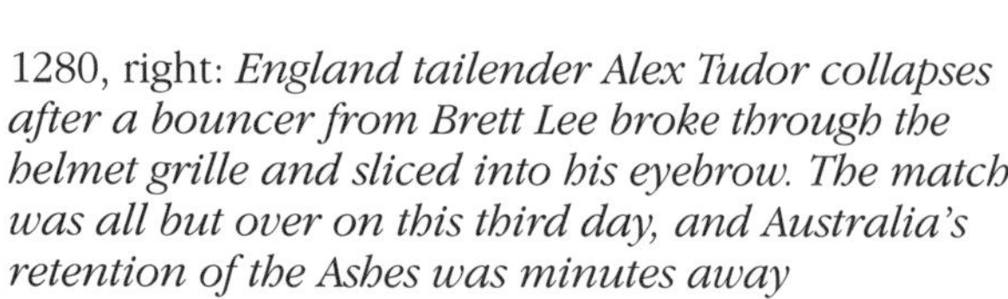

1280, right: *England tailender Alex Tudor collapses after a bouncer from Brett Lee broke through the helmet grille and sliced into his eyebrow. The match was all but over on this third day, and Australia's retention of the Ashes was minutes away*

1281, above: *Carrying on from captains Border and Taylor, Steve Waugh extends Australia's hold on the urn for the eighth series running, displaying a replica of the urn at the sunlit WACA*

2002-03 — FOURTH TEST

Melbourne, December 26, 27, 28, 29, 30

Australia *551 for 6 dec (J.L.Langer 250, M.L.Hayden 102, S.R.Waugh 77, M.L.Love 62*) and 107 for 5;* England *270 (C.White 85*, J.N.Gillespie 4 for 25) and 387 (M.P.Vaughan 145, R.W.T.Key 52, S.C.G.MacGill 5 for 152).* Australia won by 5 wickets.

It could at least be said that the fourth encounter went to the fifth day, though from the opening day (Australia 356 for 3) the familiar pattern prevailed. Langer's monumental 578-minute innings stretched deep into the second day, while England's four major bowlers, Caddick, Harmison, White and Dawson, all conceded over 100 runs. Langer's opening stand with Hayden this time was worth 195, easily surpassing Australia's MCG record in Ashes Tests (Trumper and Noble, 1907-08, before the present members' stand – now about to be demolished – was built), and he posted his hundred with a six. Only Bradman (four times), Simpson, Cowper and Ponsford had made higher scores for Australia in an Ashes Test than Langer, who had further century partnerships with his captain, whose fifty came off 48 balls, and then with the mature debutant Love, who had recently made two double-centuries against the tourists. England's response (without the injured Stewart: Foster kept wicket) was again feeble, apart from the defiance of White, the only player in the match with any Victorian connection, Warne being absent, having damaged his shoulder in the one-day series. In the follow-on, however, Vaughan produced another high-class exhibition, being especially severe on MacGill, and passing Amiss's England record Test aggregate for a year. Vaughan's worthiest support came from Key's maiden Test fifty. Needing merely 107, Australia were made to fight, losing wickets at 8, 58, 58, 83 and 90. Waugh survived a thin edge to which there was no appeal and a 'catch' to cover off a no-ball, and soon Australia were 4-0 up and eyeing a 'greenwash' of the series.

1282, left: *Justin Langer becomes the fifth Australian to reach 250 in an Ashes Test at home.* 1283, above: *Craig White bowled and batted with great heart in the Melbourne Test, as in the previous three.* 1284, below, left: *Stuart MacGill, probing as ever, pleads for another wicket at the MCG.* 1285, below: *For the second time in the series Michael Vaughan acknowledges the applause for a cultured century*

2002-03 — FIFTH TEST

Sydney, January 2, 3, 4, 5, 6

England *362 (M.A.Butcher 124, N.Hussain 75, A.J.Stewart 71) and 452 for 9 dec (M.P.Vaughan 183, N.Hussain 72);* Australia *363 (A.C.Gilchrist 133, S.R.Waugh 102, M.J.Hoggard 4 for 92) and 226 (A.J.Bichel 49, B.Lee 46, A.R.Caddick 7 for 94).* England won by 225 runs.

Above and beyond any reflections on England's long-delayed victory, Australians – Sydneysiders in particular – will remember this Test for Steve Waugh's century, which seemed to have saved his career just when hatchets were being sharpened. Shorn of the services of McGrath and Warne, Australia still aimed to emulate their 1920-21 team in winning all five Tests. But spilt catches assisted England to a solid total, built around their best-ever third-wicket stand at Sydney, Butcher/Hussain 166 passing Hammond/Leyland (1936-37); to be bettered again in the second innings by the Vaughan/Hussain 189.

An important 71 came from Stewart and an unusual contribution from Crawley (35 in 3½ hours) in the face of Lee's hostility. When Caddick and then Harmison sliced into Australia's innings, onlookers leaned forward. But Waugh batted aggressively, passing 10,000 Test runs, and Gilchrist joined him in a third-session assault that delivered Australia 170 runs. The final ball of the day brought Waugh his century, his 29th in all Tests, and the SCG can never have known such uproar. Next day Gilchrist too reached his hundred (94 balls), and Australia stole a first-innings lead for the 20th consecutive time in these Tests. Trescothick became Lee's 100th Test wicket, but with unreserved strokeplay Vaughan and Hussain manoeuvred England to a position of strength on a dusting pitch. Vaughan's third century of the series sealed his contemporary rating as the world's best batsman and advanced his series aggregate to 633, and late on the fourth day Hussain declared 451 ahead. Langer and Hayden quickly fell to bad lbw decisions, but on a helpful surface Caddick came into his own, finishing with 10 wickets in a Test for the only time. To the cheering and beery singing of the visiting fans on the old Hill area, England thus applied a silver lining to a series characterised by English physical and mental frailty, poor umpiring, and awesome cricket by Australia.

1286, left: *Mark Butcher, 16 months after his momentous hundred at Headingley, reaches an equally important century at Sydney.* 1287, right: *In his final Ashes Test match Steve Waugh registers an emotional hundred, his tenth against England, second only to Bradman's 19.* 1288, below, left: *Another hundred for Vaughan, his third, with partner Hussain contributing two invaluable seventies.* 1289, below, right: *Andy Caddick in pose of thanksgiving as wickets came his way at last*

2005 FIRST TEST

Lord's, July 21, 22, 23, 24

Australia *190 (J.L.Langer 40, S.J.Harmison 5 for 43) and 384 (M.J.Clarke 91, S.M.Katich 67, D.R.Martyn 65, R.T.Ponting 42);* England *155 (K.P.Pietersen 57, G.D.McGrath 5 for 53) and 180 (K.P.Pietersen 64*, M.E.Trescothick 44, G.D.McGrath 4 for 29, S.K.Warne 4 for 64).* Australia won by 239 runs.

A hostile first-morning showing by Harmison, who struck Langer, Hayden and Ponting (cutting the captain's face), with purposeful back-up by Hoggard, Flintoff and Jones and shrewd field placings by Vaughan, earned England an early initiative. Flintoff struck with his fourth ball, Jones with his first. But belief that this was England's year was soon vaporised by McGrath. Starting with his 500th Test wicket (Trescothick, the only England survivor from the 2001 Lord's Test), he used the slope and a responsive patch of turf to take 5 for 2, including Flintoff, bowled for a duck on Ashes debut. Pietersen, in his maiden Test match, kept his team in the contest with a half-century full of outrageous shots (including sixes into the pavilion off McGrath and the Grandstand off Warne) until Martyn's diving catch by the rope; wicketkeeper Geraint Jones was second-top-scorer with 30. The outcome remained unpredictable until Martyn and young Clarke built a fourth-wicket stand of 155 delightful runs in Australia's second innings, made possible by the most costly of England's seven misses, Pietersen's drop at cover when Clarke was 21. Australia were 314 ahead after two days with three wickets left, and Katich hauled them to an impregnable position on the Saturday. Seeking an improbable 420, Trescothick and Strauss responded stoutly with 80 for the first wicket, but embarrassment followed, only one of the remaining nine batsmen scoring more than 8. Vaughan (seven runs in the match) was again bowled. Warne, Lee and McGrath were overwhelming, except unto Pietersen again, whose commanding, unorthodox method brought him another half-century, with a memorable six off Lee into the Tavern Stand. After a rain hold-up, Australia charged to victory, with England's last five batsmen scoring not a run on that fourth day. Amazingly, as with Hutton's team after the Brisbane thrashing of 1954, England, adept at bouncing back after recent Test losses, claimed to have seen enough in this match to strengthen their conviction that they had the beating of Australia this time. Bookmakers and the man in the street understandably refused to buy into this.

1290, below: *England's expectations are high as the aggressive Harmison finishes off Australia's innings for 190 at Lord's. But Glenn McGrath, in a purple patch, soon had his team back in the reckoning*

, above: *After the first-innings failure at Lord's the Australians counter-attacked decisively, Glenn McGrath leading the charge a devastating spell of 5 for 2, starting with Trescothick, who became McGrath's 500th Test wicket (and 118th England wicket).* 2, above, right: *With refreshing bravado Kevin Pietersen burst onto the Test scene, his two bold half-centures including hits into rowd off McGrath, Warne and Lee.* 1293, below: *'Freddie' Flintoff had a sobering debut in Ashes Test cricket, being bowled th ball for a duck by McGrath and managing only three runs in England's equally sad second innings*

2005 SECOND TEST

Edgbaston, August 4, 5, 6, 7

England *407 (M.E.Trescothick 90, K.P.Pietersen 71, A.Flintoff 68, A.J.Strauss 48, S.K.Warne 4 for 116) and 182 (A.Flintoff 73, S.K.Warne 6 for 46, B.Lee 4 for 82);* Australia *308 (J.L.Langer 82, R.T.Ponting 61, A.C.Gilchrist 49*, M.J.Clarke 40) and 279 (B.Lee 43*, S.K.Warne 42).* England won by 2 runs.

Had a freakish tornado a week earlier tracked a kilometre from its course it would have been impossible to have staged what became the most exciting Test match ever between these countries. When, 75 minutes before the start, McGrath trod on a ball and suffered torn ankle ligaments, Ponting's decision to insert England surprised everyone. The lunch score was 132 (Trescothick 77) for the loss of Strauss, who had hit Warne hard before being bowled by a huge turner after the Hobbs/Fry first-wicket record here (105) against Australia in 1909 had been bettered. Australia fought back, though the run rate held at a dazzling 5 per over. Pietersen and Flintoff crashed on to their century stand in 66 minutes, and the sixes flew, with Warne, taunted by spectators after recent scandal stories in the red-top press, revealing his exasperation. With 54 fours and 10 sixes, England (407) scored their most runs against Australia on any day since June 10, 1938. Australia then fell 99 short, Ponting batting aggressively, Langer the sheet-anchor, Gilchrist getting as close to a fifty as he ever would in this series. Others got a start

1294, left: *Shane Warne, who worked his way through 252.5 overs in the series, tossed one of his special fizzers down at Andrew Strauss to break England's opening stand on the first day of the most thrilling of all Ashes Test matches to date*

1295, right: *Justin Langer creams the ball through the covers at Edgbaston. He headed Australia's batting averages for the series*

1296, above: *'Freddie' Flintoff lashes Australia's bowling at Edgbaston, where he hit an Ashes record number (9) of sixes in the match*

1297, above: *Ian Bell, whose only solid contributions were to come in the next Ashes Test, falls to Kasprowicz, who was to find heartache awaiting at the end of this Test.* 1298, below: *Steve Harmison's relief is mixed with disbelief as the match is won. Geraint Jones, who took the catch, is jubilant, while England captain Michael Vaughan is about to lose his composure*

but failed to go on. But the wily Warne led a resurgence in England's second innings, spinning six out (another haunting metre-wide deviator accounting for Strauss), with Lee's pace prising out two key early wickets. The match would have been turned around completely but for Flintoff's booming 73 (86 balls: four sixes – one high into the pavilion off Lee – to add to his five sixes in the first innings, a record match tally in Ashes Tests). Four down for 31 became 131 for 9, only 230 ahead, when Simon Jones put on a crucially significant 51 with Flintoff. Needing 282 to go two up, Australia seemed doomed that third evening when England's bowlers reaped multiple rewards, including Ponting for 0 and Gilchrist for 1. Clarke (30) was still there, his side perched on 175 for 7, when Harmison seemed to have clinched the match by yorking him with a slower ball. Next morning, with only Warne, Lee and Kasprowicz to do the job, Australia still needed 107. Their determination impressed deeply. England's slide from easy expectation to edginess and then unconcealed panic in this bizarre session of play was cricket at its most fascinating. Escorted by recurrent luck, Warne and Lee stole runs where they could, and gaps opened up in the field. They added 45 before Warne accidentally kicked his wicket over with 62 still needed. By drinks, 77 runs had come in 63 minutes. Vaughan continued to switch bowlers and juggle his field. Millions of fans in both countries sat trembling by television sets and radios. Forty extras in the innings were a pointer to the tension felt by the bowlers. Simon Jones's diving miss off Kasprowicz at third man seemed decisive. A five from a wild no-ball from Flintoff left only nine runs to be found. Cover-drives cracked by Lee would have brought victory but for interceptions, and wicketkeeper Jones just managed to arrest a high bouncer from Flintoff which would have seen Australia home. Then Kasprowicz gloved a vicious ball from Harmison and the keeper threw himself forward for the catch. Victory was England's by two runs and the series was level.

2005

Old Trafford, August 11, 12, 13, 14, 15

England *444 (M.P.Vaughan 166, M.E.Trescothick 63, I.R.Bell 59, A.Flintoff 46, G.O.Jones 42, S.K.Warne 4 for 99, B.Lee 4 for 100) and 280 for 6 dec (A.J.Strauss 106, I.R.Bell 65, M.E.Trescothick 41, G.D.McGrath 5 for 115);* Australia *302 (S.K.Warne 90, S.P.Jones 6 for 53) and 371 for 9 (R.T.Ponting 156, A.Flintoff 4 for 71).* Match drawn.

Another classic followed. With a muted McGrath restored to the side (0 for 86 his worst-ever Test analysis), Vaughan recaptured his form of the previous tour of Australia, leading England to a substantial total on a good pitch after McGrath had him missed on 41 by Gilchrist and then bowled him next ball – with a no-ball. A new England second-wicket record on this ground (137) ended with Warne's 600th Test wicket (Trescothick), but Bell now played his first telling innings against Australia (205 minutes), with Vaughan still in command, notably through the off side, notching his fourth bulky hundred in eight Tests against Australia. More chances went begging during another century stand. Gillespie seemed lost, but the high-speed Lee kept Australia in contention, and Warne not only dealt with the lower order but rescued Australia from total humiliation when they batted. His three-hour 90 at No.7 retrieved a shaky scoreline of 133 for 5 as Giles spun out three top wickets and Simon Jones baffled the batsmen with sharp reverse swing. The follow-on was saved during the little play possible after rain on the Saturday, with Clarke batting at No.8 because of a back strain. England, 142 ahead, now went for quick runs, led by Strauss, whose century contained some bold hits after Lee had cut his ear with a bouncer. Bell again looked the part, and the declaration challenged Australia to make 423 in 50 minutes and a day. Thousands were locked out of the ground on the final morning, and a long, tense chapter climaxed with Australia's last batsmen, Lee and McGrath, surviving 24 balls to force a draw. At 182 for 5 (Martyn lbw although thin-edging) the visitors had seemed doomed. But chances were missed, valid appeals denied, and Clarke (39) helped his skipper almost double the score. Warne stayed in for 99 minutes, and when Ponting's determined captain's innings ended after 6½ hours of devout resistance, the last pair clung on for 17 minutes – often with seven men in the slips cordon – to smother an England victory chance which had seemed certain. The only consolation for Vaughan and his crew was the sound of ecstatic relief from the Australian dressing-room after their narrow escape.

1299, below: *Shane Warne's astronomical Test tally rises to 600 as Trescothick is flukily caught via Gilchrist's chest.*
1300, right: *Simon Jones, forty years after his father Jeff played against Australia, speeds and swings his way to an admirable 6 for 53*

1301, above: *Andrew Strauss, England's prolific yet undemonstrative opener, secured his side's advantage in the second innings at Old Trafford with a positive century.* 1302, right: *Australia owed so much to captain Ricky Ponting for escaping with a draw. He had to withstand some fiery bowling from Harmison, Flintoff and Jones but occupied the crease for 6½ hours. He thought his dismissal had rendered it all in vain, but Lee and McGrath survived the last four overs*

2005 FOURTH TEST

Trent Bridge, August 25, 26, 27, 28

England *477 (A.Flintoff 102, G.O.Jones 85, M.E.Trescothick 65, M.P.Vaughan 58, K.P.Pietersen 45, S.K.Warne 4 for 102) and 129 for 7 (S.K.Warne 4 for 31);* Australia *218 (B.Lee 47, S.M.Katich 45, S.P.Jones 5 for 44) and 387 (J.L.Langer 61, S.M.Katich 59, M.J.Clarke 56, R.T.Ponting 48, S.K.Warne 45).* England won by 3 wickets.

The 150th of these Test matches to be staged in England uniquely produced a third consecutive touch-and-go nail-biter. Another 400-plus first innings by the home side was launched with 105 by Trescothick and Strauss, but the substantial total also owed much to the 177 put on by Flintoff and wicketkeeper Jones for the sixth wicket, after Gilchrist had chalked up his 300th dismissal behind the stumps. This was England's seventh century stand of the series to Australia's one, and it was Flintoff's first hundred against Australia. Newcomer Tait (replacing McGrath: inflamed elbow) took three wickets, and skipper Ponting dismissed his opposite number, but Australia wasted several chances. Two wayward lbw decisions helped reduce the visitors to 99 for 5, and although a Hoggard over cost 22 and Lee's pyrotechnics (he hit Harmison into the street) put a little gloss on the innings, Australia had to follow on for the first time in 191 Tests. Days later people were still talking about Strauss's flying left-hand catch to hold an edge from Gilchrist. Batting again, Australia did better, though nobody played a giant innings. A turning point was the run-out of Ponting by substitute Gary Pratt at cover. The captain was livid, having long believed that England were manipulating the substitute regulation. But with Simon Jones injured (and out of the series) Pratt's presence was legitimate. Ponting's outburst, directed at the opposition and their chief coach, cost him 75% of his match fee. Katich and Clarke consolidated, Jones fumbling a stumping chance offered by the latter off Giles, and on the fourth day it was 76 minutes before the first four was hit. The stand was worth 100 when Clarke fell, soon followed by Gilchrist. Katich was victim of a poor lbw decision and lost half his fee for his human show of exasperation. Errors by Jones and Pietersen, and Warne's robust 45, contributed to some sort of fourth-innings target, but when 27 came off the new ball in the chase for the 129 needed to go 2-1 up, England were smiling. Then Warne took centrestage with brisk spin and brio. He instantly trapped Trescothick and, next over, found Vaughan's edge. At 57 Strauss was caught at leg slip, and Bell holed out off Lee. Panic coursed through England's ranks. Some desperate strokeplay by Pietersen and Flintoff took the total to 103, when three more

1303, above: *Strauss launches himself into space to bring off a sensational catch at Trent Bridge, Adam Gilchrist the disbelieving batsman. He failed to reach fifty in this series, a major factor in England's success.* 1304, below, left: *Flintoff's bold century, his first against Australia, set up a commanding position, his stand of 177 with wicketkeeper Jones being England's highest of the series*

1305, above: *Ricky Ponting was not amused at being run out by a substitute named Pratt.* 1306, right: *Giles and Hoggard leave the sunlit field after the Nottingham thriller, having nervously got England to their modest target*

wickets fell quickly, a fired-up Lee proving as dangerous as crafty Warne. Flintoff was bowled by an off-cutting flash of a ball, and when G.O.Jones tried to break the spell with a drive off Warne, he lofted a catch: 116 for 7, 13 still needed. Giles and Hoggard tried to fortify each other. With two nations frozen by tension, Hoggard cracked a full-toss from Lee to the rope. Soon Giles was prodding Warne for a two to midwicket, and the match was won – to hysterical scenes on the ground and far beyond. Later, both teams will have reflected on the plethora of no-balls debited to them (30 each), as in the knife-edge Edgbaston Test (E23, A28). If England were now to turn dreams into reality, all they had to do was avoid defeat at The Oval.

2005 FIFTH TEST
The Oval, September 8, 9, 10, 11, 12

England *373 (A.J.Strauss 129, A.Flintoff 72, M.E.Trescothick 43, S.K.Warne 6 for 122) and 335 (K.P.Pietersen 158, A.F.Giles 59, M.P.Vaughan 45, S.K.Warne 6 for 124);* Australia *367 (M.L. Hayden 138, J.L. Langer 105, A. Flintoff 5 for 78, M.J. Hoggard 4 for 97) and 4 for 0.* Match drawn.

Many England fans were blatantly praying for rain to assist a draw, but the sun shone sufficiently over this historic Ashes Test for some memorable cricket to be played. England had to make their first team change of the series when reverse-swing bowler Jones's ankle injury proved serious. Collingwood replaced him, and McGrath returned for Australia, who lost the toss and saw England get away to a flying start of 82 before Warne dismissed the first five in the order – though not before Strauss had made his second century of the series, batting for almost six hours. His stand of 143 with Flintoff was the core of the innings. Under grey skies Australia looked like dwarfing England's 373 as Langer and Hayden laid a strong foundation. Hayden (highest score in the series to date 36) played determinedly. In contrast, Langer reached a 63-ball fifty, lofting Giles for two sixes, and surviving a slip chance. He was 75 when the hundred came up, but the batsmen's tactical acceptance of a bad-light offer from the umpires caused bemusement. On a murky third day the opening stand advanced, while umpiring errors contin-

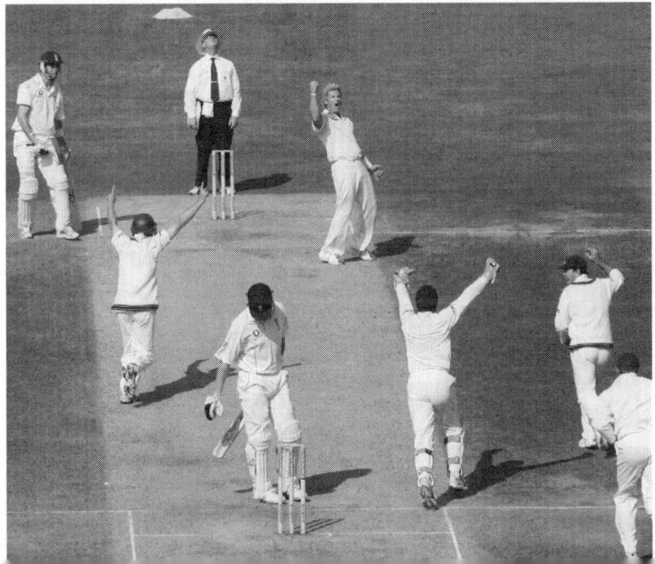

1307, above, left: *Another vital contribution to England's cause by Strauss came on the opening day of the tense Oval Test. He acknowledges the applause for his most important century to date.* 1308, above: *No more famous dropped catch than this has ever occurred in Ashes history: Pietersen (18) is put down by Warne as Lee starts to celebrate.* 1309, left: *It seemed to matter less when Flintoff (8) hit a return catch to Warne and England were wobbling on 126 for 5 in their second innings*

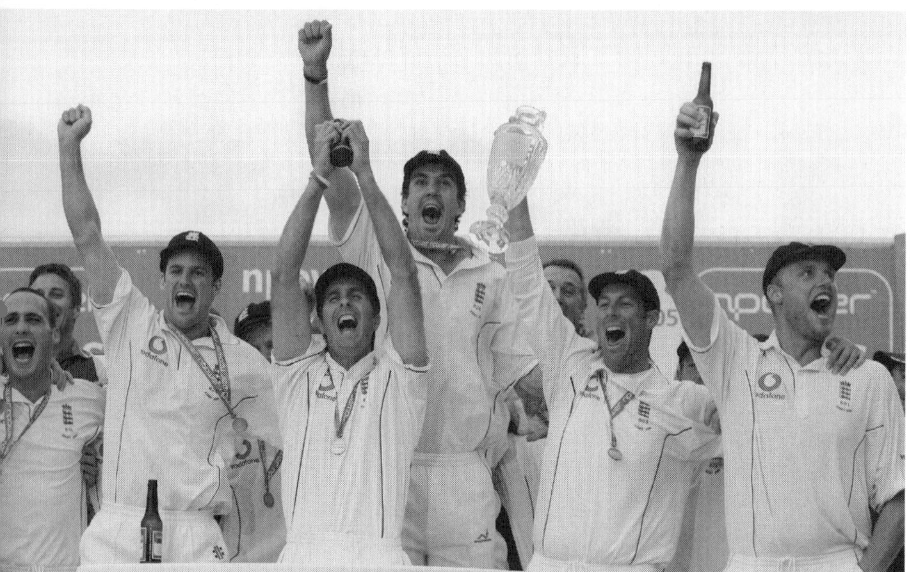

1310, above, left: *A legend is born: Kevin Pietersen, a man of unique gifts and unusual personality, comes in after his dramatic match-saving 158 at The Oval.* 1311, above: *Frustration for Australian opener Justin Langer as drizzle and poor light keep the players off the field, though the position for Ponting's team had long been beyond hope.* 1312, left: *After 16 years the Ashes are England's again*

ued to generate irritation. After a rain hold-up Hayden reached a 191-minute fifty, and Langer posted his century and 7000 Test runs before playing on to Harmison, the stand of 185 having broken Australia's Oval first-wicket record (Bardsley/Gregory, 1909). Midst further rain interruptions came Hayden's career-saving century. But then an amazing transformation came with the loss of nine wickets for 103 runs as Flintoff and Hoggard gave their all on the sometimes overcast fourth day. By late afternoon, when the light deteriorated again, England were unexpectedly 40 ahead with nine wickets still in hand. It was to be an unnervingly intense final day of a possible 98 overs. Trescothick passed 1000 runs against Australia without having made a century, but Vaughan and Bell (a 'pair') edged successive balls from McGrath, and Pietersen might have given him a hat-trick had not the umpire detected a shoulder blow without bat contact. Still scoreless, Pietersen edged Warne against the keeper's glove, and on 15 he saw Warne himself spill a slip catch off a Lee rocket which would have settled the match. It was cruel luck for Warne, whose 40 wickets set an Australian record for a five-Test Ashes rubber and stretched his supreme tally in Ashes Tests to 172 (above Lillee). Pietersen weathered some ferocious bowling from Lee, and hit Warne for two sixes in an over (adding more that afternoon off Lee and Warne to set a rare Ashes record of seven, and breaking two bats during this extraordinary innings). At lunch England had been in a wobble at 127 for 5, and Australia saw only too temptingly their opportunity to save the Ashes at the last gasp. Collingwood's 72-minute innings of 10 was worth so much more, but even at his dismissal England, six down, led by only 192 with 56 overs remaining. Jones then went, and Giles joined the defiant, audacious Pietersen, who cracked Tait for four to secure his first Test century (124 balls). A backs-to-the-wall strategy was not for him in the face of this overwhelming 'what if?' situation. The timely and conclusive Pietersen-Giles stand of 109 supplanted the 1886 eighth-wicket record at The Oval against Australia (90 by W.W.Read and Briggs), and Warne, 12 wickets off 76 overs in the match, was now exhausted. Australia needed 342, but only 18 overs at most remained. Poor light permitted only a few Harmison bouncers – a striking reminder of how the series had begun – and in a low-key gesture some time later the Ashes changed hands with the formal drawing of stumps. After 16 years of massive Australian ascendancy, England had the little urn back There was a tumultuous celebration in Trafalgar Square; all 12 players and immediate support staff were later decorated by the Queen; and the ecstatic celebrations and re-runs continued for weeks.

2006-07

Brisbane, November 23, 24, 25, 26, 27, 2006

Australia *602 for 9 dec (R.T.Ponting 196, M.E.K.Hussey 86, J.L.Langer 82, M.J.Clarke 56, B.Lee 43*, A.Flintoff 4 for 99) and 202 for 1 dec (J.L.Langer 100*, R.T.Ponting 60*);* England *157 (I.R.Bell 50, G.D.McGrath 6 for 50) and 370 (P.D.Collingwood 96, K.P.Pietersen 92, A.N.Cook 43, S.R.Clark 4 for 72, S.K.Warne 4 for 124).* Australia won by 277 runs.

Although an ageing side, Australia were widely favoured to recover the Ashes. England were missing Vaughan and Simon Jones through injury, Trescothick had just suffered a breakdown, and for the first time since 1877 England's first seven batsmen were new to Test cricket on Australian soil. Harmison's opening ball portentously went straight to Flintoff, his captain, at second slip, and by the close Australia, watched by a record Gabba crowd of 39,288, were 346 for 3. Langer's 82 came from only 98 balls, and Ponting was in fine touch in registering his 32nd Test hundred. Hussey seemed set for an Ashes debut century until Flintoff bowled him, and the declaration left the visitors with an overwhelming task. Keen to show he was no back number, McGrath took six wickets as England were mown down 445 in arrears. Bell batted determinedly for almost four hours, but it was overall a limp England performance. Ponting chose to bat again. Never before in an Ashes Test had the follow-on been shunned after such a huge first-innings advantage, but Australia now crushed their adversaries' spirit, stretching the lead to 647 before the declaration early on the fourth day. Langer's fifth hundred against England came in just over three hours, and the bowlers were left nursing some painful match figures: Harmison 1 for 177, Anderson 1 for 195, Hoggard 2 for 141. Pride was partially restored by Collingwood and Pietersen, whose aggressive stand of 153 (surpassing the Brisbane fourth-wicket record 99 by Barnett and Leyland in 1936-37) frustrated Australia – and Warne in particular during his marathon spell – after Strauss had again fallen to the hook shot. Collingwood was stumped going for his century, and first thing next morning Pietersen went, which precipitated the end of a match that brought Australia much satisfaction and strengthened their belief that revenge for 2005 was close at hand. Not least pleasing were the successful Ashes debuts of Stuart Clark (seven wickets) and the dedicated left-hander Hussey.

1313: *Captain Ponting, aglow with 128 runs to his name, and Ashes debutant Hussey (54) come in after the first day's play, Australia a commanding 346 for 3 at the Gabba*

1314: *McGrath soon showed that he was not a spent force by taking six wickets in England's limp first innings. Warne at slip has just caught newcomer Cook for 11*

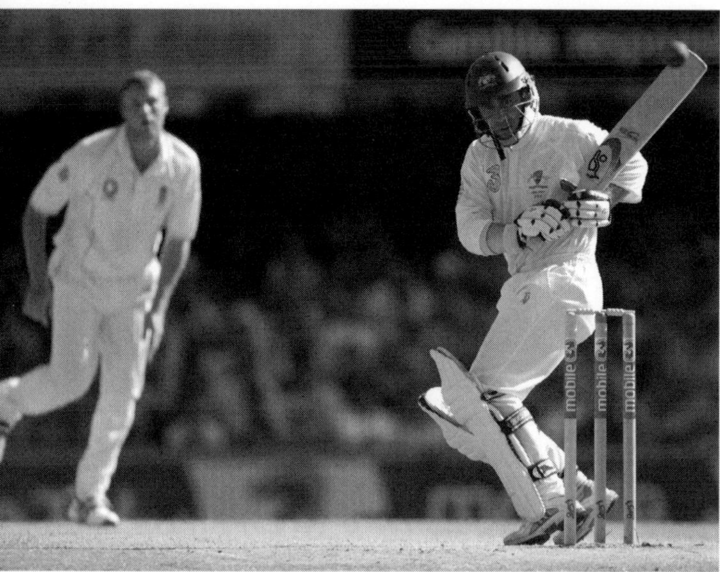

1315, left: *A determined Langer returned a century in Australia's second innings to secure his place in the side once more. It came from 146 balls, following his 98-ball 82 in the first innings*

1316, right: *Only when Pietersen (92) and Collingwood (96) came together in the second innings of the opening Test in Brisbane did England show any prolonged defiance and determination. Here Collingwood uppercuts a fast one from Lee*

2006-07 — SECOND TEST

Adelaide, December 1, 2, 3, 4, 5, 2006

England *551 for 6 dec (P.D.Collingwood 206, K.P.Pietersen 158, I.R.Bell 60) and 129 (S.K.Warne 4 for 49);* Australia *513 (R.T.Ponting 142, M.J.Clarke 124, M.E.K.Hussey 91, A.C.Gilchrist 64, S.K.Warne 43, M.J.Hoggard 7 for 109) and 168 for 4 (M.E.K.Hussey 61*, R.T.Ponting 49).* Australia won by 6 wickets.

This topsyturvy Ashes match began with caution on England's part as they grafted to 266 for 3 on the first day on a slow pitch, building this to a challenging 551 before a declaration which some still perceived as premature. Collingwood scored 98 on the opening day, first in the company of the watchful Bell and then with Pietersen, who was 60 by the close. Collingwood advanced to England's first Test double-century in Australia since Hammond's 70 years ago, batting with great determination for almost nine hours. Pietersen replicated his famous 158 at The Oval, and together they added 310, a new England record against Australia for the fourth wicket overall (Hussain/Thorpe 288, Edgbaston 1997) and for any England wicket at Adelaide (Hammond/Jardine 262 in 1928-29). A frustrated McGrath failed to take a wicket (0 for 107) and Warne's 53 overs of toil, many directed wide of leg stump, brought him only 1 for 167. The series seemed to be turning when Australia lost three wickets for 65, but on 35 Ponting was missed at deep square leg by Giles, and thereafter Australia climbed back. The captain went on to another century, his Australian record 33rd, and seventh against England, putting on 192 with the rock-like Hussey, and then the disciplined Clarke proceeded elegantly to a maiden Ashes hundred at the same steady pace as his captain, putting on 98 with Gilchrist, and then 118 with Warne, lifting his side close to parity. Hoggard's heroic effort brought him rich reward: figures of 42-6-109-7. The final day began with England 97 ahead and nine wickets in hand, but their palsied efforts in the pre-lunch session produced a mere 30 runs while four wickets went down, triggered by a poor umpiring decision against Strauss (34). Bell was run out as the ferocious Australian pressure, orchestrated by Warne, unnerved the opposition. Key batsman Pietersen was bowled behind his legs sweeping at Warne, who toiled through 85 overs in the match, and as wickets continued to topple, Collingwood alone hung on. His unbeaten 22 spanned 193 minutes. Australia were left 36 overs after tea in which to score 168 for victory, and with first Ponting and then Hussey taking control, by 6.43pm the target was reached fairly comfortably. Never in Test history had a declared score as high as this been followed by defeat. Onlookers and players alike were left dazed by such an unlikely victory, snatched by dint of sheer superiority of will.

1317, left: *Paul Collingwood cracks a short ball during his 8½–hour innings of 206 in the amazing Adelaide Test. The Durham man's partnership with Kevin Pietersen was a new fourth-wicket record for England against Australia.* 1318, below, left: *Ashley Giles at deep square leg has just put down a difficult catch from Ponting, who was now about to add 107 runs to his score. It was a decisive incident.* 1319, below right: *Matthew Hoggard's skill and perseverance were rewarded at the Adelaide Oval with seven wickets in Australia's innings of 513. Here he celebrates no. 6.* 1320, bottom: *England's somewhat unexpected crash in the second innings continues as Pietersen is bowled by Shane Warne for 2. Out of nowhere Australia suddenly had a vision of victory*

2006-07 THIRD TEST

Perth, December 14, 15, 16, 17, 18, 2006

Australia *244 (M.E.K.Hussey 74*, M.S.Panesar 5 for 92, S.J.Harmison 4 for 48) and 527 for 5 dec (M.J.Clarke 135*, M.E.K.Hussey 103, A.C.Gilchrist 102*, M.L.Hayden 92, R.T.Ponting 75);* England *215 (K.P.Pietersen 70, A.J.Strauss 42) and 350 (A.N.Cook 116, I.R.Bell 87, K.P.Pietersen 60*, A.Flintoff 51, S.K.Warne 4 for 115).* Australia won by 206 runs.

Further capacity crowds rolled up to the WACA, although local hero Martyn was not playing, having surprised everyone by announcing his retirement and vanishing. Symonds replaced him. England at last brought in left-arm spinner Panesar for Giles. Ponting won the toss, but wickets toppled all day, only Hussey scoring more than 37 as Harmison showed some fire and Panesar spun out five men, starting with Langer, whom he bowled with his seventh ball. Later Symonds hit 17 off one of his overs, but fell to him next over, to be followed by Gilchrist (0): 172 for 6. Hussey's 273-minute defiance put a respectable face on the innings, and when England began to lose wickets – two through faulty umpiring – Australia's grip was renewed. Lee, McGrath and Clark shared seven wickets and Symonds picked up two, leaving the tourists 29 behind, a deficit which would have been much greater but for another stout contribution by Pietersen. The biggest stand was 40 by Harmison and Panesar for the tenth wicket. On a settled surface Australia now constructed a formidable advantage – but only after the shock of Langer's dismissal, bowled by Hoggard first ball of the innings. Patient innings by Hayden and Ponting preceded centuries by three others, Hussey's and Clarke's polished and skilful (their stand worth 151), Gilchrist's absolutely explosive. On this scorchingly hot third day balls missed bats' edges and nicks eluded catchers' hands while a sense of inevitability was established. Yet nothing quite prepared anyone for Gilchrist's onslaught. His fifty (40 balls) was posted during an over by Panesar off which he smashed 24 runs (.26646), an Ashes record. On and on Gilchrist went, belting everything within reach, until he had his hundred off only 57 balls, another Ashes record. It had taken him only 98 minutes. With the declaration, England had just over two days to make 557. Strauss was wrongly adjudged lbw second ball, but young Cook and Bell raised their team's spirits with a long partnership of 170, Bell lofting two sixes off Warne. Cook, 22 on Christmas Day, became the youngest England centurion in an Ashes Test since Gower here in 1978-79, and this was already his fourth Test century. But his dismissal by McGrath late on the fourth day restored the inevitable direction of the match, although Pietersen and Flintoff struck some defiant blows before the end. Fifteen playing days into the series and only 462 days after losing the Ashes, Australia had the urn back per medium of three resounding victories. It so happened that the precious little symbol was currently on display locally as part of its celebratory nationwide tour.

1321, below, left: *Ian Bell worked hard in England's cause throughout the 2006–07 series. At the WACA he made 0 and 87.* 1322, below, right: *Mike Hussey moves towards a coveted century*

1323, above: *A maiden Ashes century at Adelaide by Michael Clarke was followed by another equally handsome hundred in this decisive Perth Test*

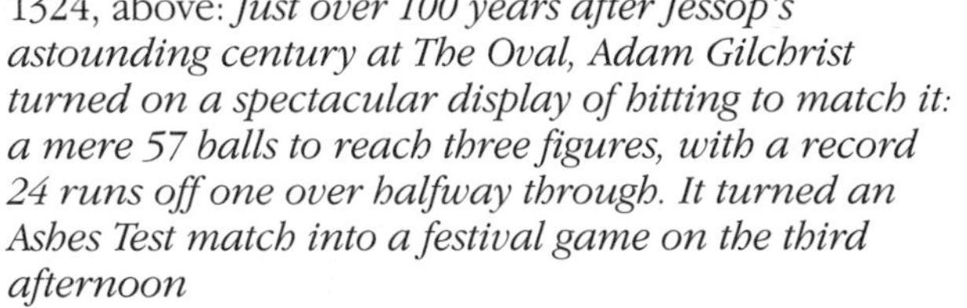

1324, above: *Just over 100 years after Jessop's astounding century at The Oval, Adam Gilchrist turned on a spectacular display of hitting to match it: a mere 57 balls to reach three figures, with a record 24 runs off one over halfway through. It turned an Ashes Test match into a festival game on the third afternoon*

1325, above: *Alastair Cook's patient innings of 116 ended under floodlights at the WACA ground. In all, the young left-hander batted for 6½ hours*

1326, above: *M.S. Panesar b. Warne 1. England all out for 350, and the Ashes are back in the hands of Australia only 462 days after they had been relinquished at The Oval. This was the shortest period of custody of the little urn ever*

2006-07 FOURTH TEST

Melbourne, December 26, 27, 28, 2006

England *159 (A.J.Strauss 50, S.K.Warne 5 for 39) and 161 (B.Lee 4 for 47);* Australia *419 (A.Symonds 156, M.L.Hayden 153, S.K.Warne 40*, S.I.Mahmood 4 for 100).* Australia won by an innings and 99 runs.

The preamble to Melbourne's 100th Test match was headlined by the announcements that Shane Warne and then Glenn McGrath, who had taken over 1200 Test wickets between them, would be retiring from Test cricket at the end of the series. Within a week Justin Langer was making a similar statement. Flintoff chose to bat on a slightly damp pitch on a moist morning, with the floodlights on for much of the time. The innings was held together by Strauss, who batted for 205 minutes for his 50 before being bowled by Warne, bringing the spinner what was widely trumpeted as his 700th Test wicket (this included six against a World XI at Sydney in a match questionably given Test status by the ICC). Lee, McGrath and Clark pressed hard, but it was Warne who came away with the main spoils. Spared on 3 from a stumping chance, Pietersen fell to the spinner for 21 after again being left with only the tail. England's last eight wickets fell for 58. On the second day a classic match seemed in prospect as Australia in reply found themselves 84 for 5 at the hands of the pace quartet. Instead, a patient Hayden and bold Symonds took the initiative, riding a fair measure of luck including the refusal of a seemingly plumb lbw appeal against Symonds by Panesar. Hayden reached a 278-minute century, and Symonds soon afterwards hoisted Collingwood for six to reach his hundred. It was the first time two Queensland players had scored centuries in an Ashes Test. The mayhem ended after a stand of 279, leaving England deflated. Symonds, with the second-highest score by a No.7 batsman in a Test (behind Bradman's 270 here in 1936-37), was out on the third morning. Wicketkeeper Read, on Ashes debut, neatly held six catches in the innings. Under a persistently grey sky England were now overwhelmed yet again by Lee, McGrath, Clark and Warne, managing no more than 161 and losing by an innings. Over the three days 244,351 people went through the MCG turnstiles. But the early finish caused $2.3-million taken for the fourth day to be refunded.

1327: *Andrew Strauss, having reached 50 for the only time in the series, is bowled by Shane Warne on Boxing Day, giving the spinner his 700th wicket in Test cricket – although six of those wickets had come his way in a World XI match which purists refused to regard as a genuine Test match*

1328, above: *Andrew Symonds had a rollicking good time while making a century in only his second Ashes Test. Coming in with Australia perilously placed at 84 for 5, he batted for 5½ hours and hit 15 fours and a six (to reach his hundred). He then leapt into the arms of his Queensland mate, Matt Hayden. Their partnership was the sixth-highest for the sixth wicket in any Test match, and effectively settled the match for Australia out of a critical situation.* 1329, right: *Despair is written into Andrew Flintoff's features as he leaves the field after yet another failure at the MCG. The probing seam bowler Stuart Clark got him in both innings*

2006-07 — FIFTH TEST

Sydney, January 2, 3, 4, 5, 2007

England *291 (A.Flintoff 89, I.R.Bell 71, K.P.Pietersen 41) and 147;* Australia *393 (S.K.Warne 71, A.C.Gilchrist 62, A.Symonds 48, R.T.Ponting 45) and 46 for 0.* Australia won by 10 wickets.

Australia needed less than four days to wrap up their second 5-0 whitewash over England, the first since 1920-21. England, without their leading bowler (13 wickets at 37) Hoggard (side strain), batted on a good, lively pitch, and seemed to be heading for a sizable total when Bell, making his fourth half-century of the series, and Pietersen, batting higher in the order and hitting only one four, added 108. Langer, emotional about his final Test appearance, involuntarily aided the visitors' cause by grassing three catches. McGrath, Lee and Clark each took three wickets, while Flintoff's bold 146-ball effort carried his side close to 300. But the tail again contributed next to nothing. In contrast, Australia's numbers 8-10 scored 111 runs, Warne making a robust 71 off 65 balls to acquire the initiative, with Clark a useful 35 after Hussey (37) and the hard-hitting Symonds and Gilchrist had built a foundation. Again Read completed six dismissals behind the stumps, giving him 12 in two Ashes innings. Anderson (three good wickets for 98 and the run-out of Ponting) got some reward at last, but by the third evening the match was all but over. Strauss, after being felled by a 150 kph ball from Lee, made 24, Bell 28, Pietersen 29, and the rest very few. When Warne had Flintoff (7) stumped it was his 195th and final England wicket. On the fourth morning Gilchrist made his 26th dismissal of the series behind the stumps – and ninth of the match – when Pietersen edged McGrath, who was to finish later with a wicket with his final ball. Again the faster bowlers gleaned most of the rewards (eight wickets), and after Hayden and Langer had hit off the runs required there was prolonged celebration on the field. Langer, McGrath and Warne were given rousing farewells by the crowd, and Ponting was left to reflect proudly that his side had now won 12 consecutive Test matches. The Englishmen walked across to the Randwick end and appeared to be bowing to their fans by way of apology.

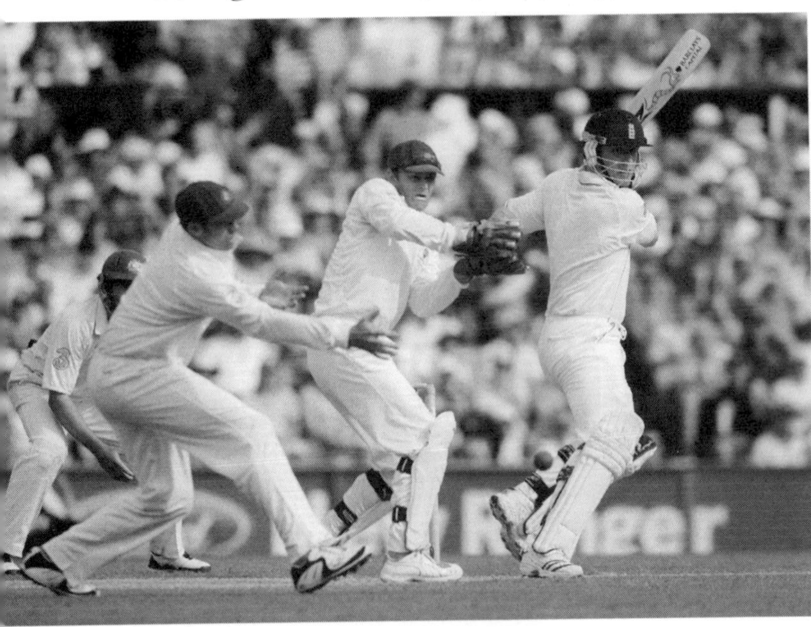

1330: *Flintoff was more like the 2005 model as he worked his way to 89 in the Sydney Test, top score for either side in this final contest. It was widely believed that the burden of captaincy had interfered with his game. He scored only 254 runs in the series and took only 11 wickets*

1331, above: *Shane Warne makes a decorous bow to his adoring crowd after he had Flintoff stumped on the third evening. It was his 195th and last England wicket, easily an Ashes record.*
1332, below: *The jubilant Australians have retrieved their honour only 16 months after losing the Ashes. The quiet hero was Stuart Clark (next to Lee on left of picture, partly obscured). He topped the bowling for either side with 26 wickets at 17.04*

1333: *never again to be seen on a Test match field, Australian heroes Justin Langer, Glenn McGrath and Shane Warne made the display of the crystal Ashes replica a memorable family occasion on the SCG outfield*

In Affectionate Remembrance
OF
ENGLISH CRICKET,
WHICH DIED AT THE OVAL
ON
29th AUGUST, 1882,
Deeply lamented by a large circle of sorrowing friends and acquaintances.

R. I. P.

N.B.—The body will be cremated and the ashes taken to Australia.

The 1882 Australians sent shockwaves through Englar the 'Ashes' announcement in the Sporting Times. *Th G. J. Bonnor, F. R. Spofforth, J. M. Blackham, W. L. I H. H. Massie, P. S. McDonnell, T. P. Horan.*